بسم الله الرحمن الرحيم

اللهم صل على محمد وآل محمد

كنت كنزا مخفيا فاحببت ان اعرف
فخلقت الخلق لكي اعرف

"I was a Hidden Treasure and I loved to be recognized; so I created the creatures that I might be recognized."

True Servitude And The Reality Of Knowledge

An Insightful Commentary On The Narration of Unwan al-Basri

Ayatullah Muhammad Baqir Tahriri

Translated By Kazim Bhojani

Edited By Muhammad Mahdi Kassamali

ISBN 10 1-953192-00-9

ISBN 13 978-1-953192-00-4

Published and distributed by Hidden Treasure Publications

Contents

Transliteration Table

The method of transliteration of Islamic terminology from the Arabic language has been carried out according to the standard transliteration table mentioned below:

ء	ʾ	ض	ḍ
ا	a	ط	ṭ
ب	b	ظ	ẓ
ت	t	ع	ʿ
ث	th	غ	gh
ج	j	ف	f
ح	ḥ	ق	q
خ	kh	ک	k
د	d	ل	l
ذ	dh	م	m

ر	r	ن	n
ز	z	و	w
س	s	ي	y
ش	sh	ه	h
ص	ṣ		

Long Vowels		Short Vowels	
ا	ā	—َ	a
و	ū	—ُ	u
ي	ī	—ِ	i

Translator's Dedication

O Allah shower Your abundant mercy on Muḥammad and his infallible progeny.

O Allah, if this little contribution is accepted by Your Exalted Self, then send Your abundant mercy on Muḥammad and his infallible progeny, and bestow its reward on my noble parents, my paternal and maternal grandparents, my deceased relatives, and all the martyrs of Islam, especially the martyrs of Karbala.

O Allah shower Your abundant mercy on Muḥammad and his infallible progeny.

The Proximity of Lady Maʿsūmah (peace be upon her)
The Islamic Seminary of the Holy City of Qum

About the Author

Āyatullāh Muḥammad Bāqir Taḥrīrī was born in Tehran in the year 1955 to a family of religious scholars. His mother was a respectable lady from a middle class, religious family with a strong love for the Ahlul-Bayt (a). His father was the late Āyatullāh Maḥmūd Taḥrīrī, who was a well-known scholar and mystic.

Ayatullah Mahmud Tahriri (His Father)

From a young age his father busied himself acquiring knowledge of the Qur'ān and the Ahl al-Bayt (peace be upon them) along with practicing and preaching this knowledge. While still young, he associated with spiritual personalities such as Shaykh Rajab 'Alī Khayyaṭ and later began his studies in the Islamic seminaries of Tehran. There he became acquainted with great scholars such as Āyatullāh Shāh Ābādī and Sayyid Riḍā Darbandī. Afterwards, he enrolled in the Islamic seminary of Qom and studied under great scholars such as Ayatullāh Shahābuddīn Mar'ashī Najafī, Ayatullāh Muḥammad Riḍā Gulpaygāni, Imam Rūhullāh Khumaynī, and Ayatullāh Ḥusayn Burūjardī.

In addition to this Āyatullah Maḥmūd was in touch with and benefited spiritually from Ayatullah Bahjat as well as some of the students of the well-known mystic Mīrzā Jawād Malikī Tabrīzi such as Sayyid Ḥusayn Qummi and Shaykh 'Abbās Tehrāni. However, his primary teacher in matters of mysticism and spirituality was 'Allāmah Muḥammad Ḥusayn Tabātabā'ī. At the same time, he established a spiritual bond with the great mystic, Shaykh Jawād Anṣāri Hamadānī.

From the age of 30, Āyatullah Maḥmūd led congregational prayers and held many sermons, preaching and enlightening the youth. He passed away in the mosque before leading the prayers in the year 1990.

Early Life in Tehran

Āyatullāh Muḥammad Bāqir Taḥrīrī entered elementary school at the age of six and spent two years in high school while also attending religious gatherings and benefiting from his father's spiritual presence. It was his father who inspired him to acquire religious knowledge. He entered the Islamic seminary of Mullā Muḥammad Jaʿfar in Tehran in the year 1969, which at the time was under the management of Ayatullah Mujtahidī. Here he studied the majority of the book Sharḥ al-Lumʿah along with other introductory studies under Āyatullāh Mujtahidī and other teachers.

In addition to benefiting from the spiritual presence of Āyatullāh Mujtahidī, he also benefited spiritually from Shaykh Jawad Karbalāʾī and the gatherings of Sayyid Hāshim Tehrānī.

Arrival in Qom

Because of the lack of scholars in Tehran and also in order to benefit spiritually, Āyatullāh Taḥrīrī sought permission from his mentor Āyatullāh Mujtahidī to move to the city of Qom. In 1973 he did so, first living in the Ḥujjatiyyah school and then later Āyatullāh Marʿashī Najafī's school. When he first entered Qom, on his father's advice, he went to the holy shrine of Sayyidah Maʿṣūmah (peace be upon her) and requested from her both a home and a mentor to guide and teach him. God Almighty fulfilled both of these requests for him.

In the year 1977 Āyatullāh married a respectable and devoted lady from a religious family, who has stood by him through all stages of life and supported him throughout his endeavors. Together they have two daughters and two sons.

Teachers

Some of Āyatullāh Taḥrīrī's teachers in the holy city of Qom and books that he has studied with them include:

- Shaykh Bākūʾī: A large part of the book Maʿālim

- Āyatullāh Dūzdūzāni: Qawānīn al-Usūl
- Āyatullāh Ustādi: Parts from the Sharh al-Lumah
- Āyatullāh 'Alawī Gorgāni: Parts from the Sharh al-Lumah
- Āyatullāh Sayyid Abū al-Faḍl Mūsawī Tabrīzī: Parts from the Sharh al-Lumah
- Āyatullāh Salawātī: Makāsib al-Muharramah
- Āyatullāh Sitūde: Kitāb al-Bayʿ, Makāsib and Matājir
- Āyatullāh Sayyid Rasūl Mūsawī: A large part of Rasā'il
- Āyatullāh Dhihnī: Parts of Rasā'il
- Āyatullāh Fāḍil Lanakrānī: Kifāyah al-Usul, Volume One
- Āyatullāh Husayn Mazāhirī Isfahānī: Kifāyah al-Usul, Volume Two
- Āyatullāh Ibrāhīm Amīnī: A part of Bidāyah al-Hikmah and Ishārāt
- Āyatullāh Muhammad Gīlānī: Manẓumah of Mulla Hādi Sabzwārī
- Āyatullāh Girāmī: Mantiq Manẓūmah
- Āyatullāh Misbāh Yazdī: Nihāyah al-Hikmah and some subject-wise tafsīr
- Āyatullāh Jawādi Āmulī: Parts from five volumes of al-Asfār al-Arba'ah
- Āyatullāh Hasanzāde Āmulī: Parts from two volumes of al-Asfār al-Arba'ah. Parts of the Ilāhiyāt and Ṭabī'iyāt of the Shifā as well as parts of the Tamhīd al-Qawā'id, Fusus al-Hikm and Misbāh al-Uns (textbooks in 'Irfān).
- Āyatullāh Sayyid Muhammad Rūhānī: Approximately two years dars al-khārij in Usūl
- Āyatullāh Tabrīzī: 10 years dars al-khārij in Fiqh and 7 years dars al-khārij in Usūl
- Āyatullāh al-Uẓamā Bahjat: Approximately 17 years of dars al-khārij in Fiqh

Teachers in Akhlaq (Ethics) and Spirituality

Āyatullāh Taḥrīrī attended Āyatullāh Bahjat's congregational prayers and *rozeh* (mourning gatherings) from the beginning of his time in

Qom. In addition to this, he maintained a spiritual bond with Āyatullāh Bahjat until the end of his life.

In the early days of his coming to Qom, Āyatullāh Tahrīrī also developed a bond with Āyatullāh Saʿādat Parvar. He used to attend private sessions with Āyatullāh Saʿādat Parvar, and it was through him that Āyatullāh Tahrīrī became acquainted with the great mufassir (exegete) of the Qurʾān, ʿAllāmah Tabātabāʾī. Āyatullāh Tahrīrī joined the Thursday and Friday question-answer sessions with ʿAllāmah which lasted almost until the end of ʿAllāmah's life. More importantly he was mentored spiritually by these two great teachers, ʿAllamah Tabātabāʾī and Āyatullāh Saʿādat Parvar until the end of their lives.

In addition to all of the above, he also benefited spiritually from his esteemed father.

Academic and Educational Activities

From the early days of his time in the Islamic seminaries, Āyatullāh Taḥrīrī began to teach. Aside from the courses he taught in the introductory levels, some of the other courses he has taught include:

- Chapters from Sharh al-Lumʿah and Makāsib al-Muharramah (books in Fiqh)
- Chapters from ar-Rasāʾil and Kifāyah al-Usūl (books in Usūl al-Fiqh)
- A full dars al-khārij course on Usūl al-Fiqh
- Courses in philosophy such as the Manz⊠ūmah, Bidāyah al-Hikmah, Hikmah al-Ishārāt, and two courses on Asfār al-Arbaʿah
- About 15 years of Tafsir al-Mizan, repeatedly teaching it from the beginning until Surah Māʾidah
- Islamic theology and ethics at the University of Tehran for four years
- Islamic theology, ethics and philosophy at the IRGC college of mentor training
- Islamic theology and ethics to the IRGC land and navy forces
- Head of the Beliefs group at the IRGC Research Centre of Qom for about five years

Tabligh (Missionary) Activities:

Towards the end of the second stage of his seminary studies, Āyatullāh Taḥrīrī began to go for *tablīgh*. This was in the year 1977. From then onwards he would regularly engage in *tablīgh* activities.

After the death of his father in 1990, Āyatullāh Taḥrīrī continued his father's Friday morning gatherings in Tehran. This continues till today. His father Āyatullah Maḥmūd Taḥrīrī was giving a commentary on the famous narration of the *ʿaql* and *jahl* (the intellect and ignorance) when he passed away. Āyatullāh Taḥrīrī first continued this, then moved on to discuss commentaries on Ziyārah al-Jāmiʿah al-Kabīrah, the letter of Imām ʿAlī (peace be upon him) to Mālik al-Ashtar, the Noble Prophet's (peace and blessings be upon him and his family) instructions to Abū Dharr, and now he is currently discussing the Duʿā of Imam al-Husayn (peace be upon him) on the day of ʿArafah.

He is also conducting another session on Fridays in Tehran that has been running for more than 15 years. In this gathering, topics such as the Munājat ash-Shaʿbāniyyah, Duʿā Kumayl, Letter 31 of Nahj al-Balāghah (Imām ʿAli's instructions to Imam al-Ḥasan, peace be upon them), Munājāt Khamsah ʿAshar, and the Sermon of Sayyidah Zahrā (peace be upon her) have been discussed.

In addition, he holds *akhlāq* (ethical) classes in Qom during the week in which ethical and spiritual topics are covered. For example, commentaries on the *ḥadīth* of ʿUnwān al-Baṣri and Duʿā al-Iftitāḥ are discussed during these classes. One example of these is a regular class that has been running in Imam Khomeni University in Qom since the year 1988. In this class various books, letters and supplications have been discussed. Initially the book Miʿrāj-i Saʿādah of Mullā Mahdī Narāqi was discussed, then Letter 31 of Nahj al-Balāgha, the Noble Prophet's (peace and blessings be upon him and his family) instructions to Abū Dharr, Imam Sajjād's (peace be upon him) Risālah al-Ḥuqūq and lastly Duʿā Makārim al-Akhlāq.

He is also currently teaching the book 40 Ḥadīth by Imam Khomeini at The Supreme Assembly of Islamic Philosophy in Qom.

Apart from having the responsibility of leading the congregational prayers at Imam Khomeini University in Qom for the last 15 years, one of his continuous works is to counsel people in ethical and spiritual matters. Despite his busy schedule, large numbers of students in Tehran and Qom regularly meet him for this purpose. After leading congregational prayers or conducting public classes, he humbly allocates time to meet with students, patiently listening to them one-by-one and guiding them in accordance with the true spirituality of the Ahl al-Bayt (peace be upon them).

Notable Works

1. Viewpoints of Scholars on Wilāyah al-Faqīh
2. The Viewpoints of Shaykh al-Mufīd in Kalām (Dogmatic Beliefs)
3. Islamic ʿIrfān (Mysticism): Its Nature, Necessity and Goals
4. Sīmāy-i Mukhbitīn - A Commentary on Ziyārah Amīnullāh
5. Jilvehāy-i Lāhūtī - A Commentary on Ziyārah Jāmiʿah al-Kabīrah (three volumes)
6. Najvāy-i ʿĀrifāni - A Commentary on the Munājāt ash-Shaʿbāniyyah
7. Bandigīyi Haqīqī va Haqīqati ʿIlm (True Servitude and True Knowledge) - A Commentary on the ḥadīth of ʿUnwān al-Baṣrī
8. ʿUrūj-i ʿAql - A Commentary on the ḥadīth of the armies of the ʿaql (intellect) and the jahl (ignorance)
9. Bāzgasht Bi Sūy-i Ū - A Commentary on the Munājāt at-Tāʾibīn
10. Dard-i Dil Bā Khudāwand - A Commentary on the Munājāt ash-Shākīn
11. Risalat al-Huquq - A Commentrary on the treatise of rights by Imam Zayn al-Abidin (a)

INTRODUCTION

Allah (the Provider of abundance and the Sublime) made man to be the complete mirror of His beauty and majesty from amongst all the creation. In this light, He enthroned him on the station of *khilāfah* [i] on Earth and said:

إِنِّي جَاعِلٌ فِي الْأَرْضِ خَلِيفَةً

Indeed, I am going to set a khalīfah on the Earth. (2:30)

Due to this station, man was able to bear the burden of the Divine Trust which the heavens and the Earth were unable to bear:

إِنَّا عَرَضْنَا الْأَمَانَةَ عَلَى السَّمَاوَاتِ وَالْأَرْضِ وَالْجِبَالِ فَأَبَيْنَ أَن يَحْمِلْنَهَا وَأَشْفَقْنَ مِنْهَا وَحَمَلَهَا الْإِنسَانُ إِنَّهُ كَانَ ظَلُومًا جَهُولًا

Indeed, We presented the trust [the wilāyah or the burden of man's responsibility] to the heavens and the Earth and the mountains, but they refused to bear it, and were apprehensive of it; but man undertook it . . . (33:72)

Allah also placed a special capacity of gaining knowledge in the nature of man, for him to actualize this station of *khilāfah*, to manifest attributes of Divine beauty and majesty, and to realize the Divine Trust

i. Khilāfah means to represent someone else, either in their absence, after their death, due to their incapability or as a means of honouring the representative. It is in this final meaning that the awliyā of Allah (His close servants), are considered His khulafā (plural of khalīfah, meaning representatives) on the Earth.

and *wilāyah*[i] in him:

وَعَلَّمَ آدَمَ الْأَسْمَاءَ كُلَّهَا

And He [Allah] taught Adam [the meanings of] the Names, all of them... (2:31)

Also, He equipped him with the necessary tools for understanding[ii] the realities (through the intellect), for witnessing[iii] them, and for choosing the right path (through his free will and strength):

وَاللَّهُ أَخْرَجَكُم مِّن بُطُونِ أُمَّهَاتِكُمْ لَا تَعْلَمُونَ شَيْئًا وَجَعَلَ لَكُمُ السَّمْعَ وَالْأَبْصَارَ وَالْأَفْئِدَةَ لَعَلَّكُمْ تَشْكُرُونَ

Allah has brought you forth from the bellies of your mothers while you did not know anything. He made for you hearing, eyesight, and hearts so that you may give thanks. (16:78)

Also, through His messengers Allah introduced to man the clear and straight path towards Him. He warned him and cautioned him against traversing the wrong path, and choosing deviation and misguidance, saying:

أَلَمْ أَعْهَدْ إِلَيْكُمْ يَا بَنِي آدَمَ أَن لَّا تَعْبُدُوا الشَّيْطَانَ إِنَّهُ لَكُمْ عَدُوٌّ مُّبِينٌ وَأَنِ اعْبُدُونِي هَٰذَا صِرَاطٌ مُّسْتَقِيمٌ

Did I not exhort you, O children of Adam, saying, "Do not worship Satan. He is indeed your manifest enemy. Worship Me. That is a straight path." (36:61)

وَلَقَدْ بَعَثْنَا فِي كُلِّ أُمَّةٍ رَّسُولًا أَنِ اعْبُدُوا اللَّهَ وَاجْتَنِبُوا الطَّاغُوتَ

---

i. Wilāyah and walāyah are nouns derived from the trilateral root verb waliya, indicating a type of closeness and intimacy. From this root meaning stems related meanings such as guardianship, assistance, and friendship.

ii. Understanding means acquiring *al-ʿilm al-ḥuṣūlī* (conceptual knowledge) in which man knows a reality through mental concepts and ideas.

iii. Witnessing means reaching *al-ʿilm al-ḥuḍūrī* (presential knowledge) in which man directly witnesses the reality of a matter without the mediation of mental concepts.

> Certainly, We raised an apostle in every nation [to preach:] "Worship Allah and shun fake deities." (16:36)

Therefore, every man is taking efforts and toiling to reach this lofty goal—from the beginning of his creation until death. This is termed "the innate perfection-seeking disposition". It is possible however, that this inclination to seek perfection gets directed in the wrong direction and man desires a limited and unworthy object in place of the Unlimited and Infinite Perfection. However, there have always been free men, who like the Prophet Abraham (peace be upon him) did not submit to the wretched and limited objects of this material world, and when they encountered these objects they called out to all, saying, "I do not like those who set." (i) They sought their perfection in reaching the infinite knowledge, unlimited power and indestructible eternal life of Allah the Exalted, the Creator of all beings, and they tirelessly and passionately tread the straight path of uniting with Him.

دست از طلب ندارم تا کام دل برآید
یا جان رسد به جانان یا جان ز تن درآید

I'll not stop seeking my desire until my desire is attained,
Either the soul will reach the Beloved, or the soul will leave the body. (ii)

ʿUnwān al-Baṣrī was an old man who after reaching the age of nearly a hundred years found the true path of spiritual guidance that he sought, at the hands of Imam Jaʿfar al-Ṣādiq (peace be upon him). He humbled himself in the Imam's presence and underwent an inner transformation because of the Imam's constructive instructions. He abandoned the superficial knowledge and conclusions of his own, and like a novice student, learned the fundamentals of the journey towards Allah in the *Jaʿfarī* school of thought. (Without us knowing whether he continued this path or not?) The constructive instructions of Imam al-Ṣādiq (peace be upon him) opened new avenues for him and for all the wayfarers and those who aspire to the Truth. It recalled for them

---

i. لَا أُحِبُّ الْآفِلِينَ

ii. Shīrāzī, Dīwān-i Ḥāfiẓ (Taṣḥīḥ-i Qudsī), ghazal 192, couplet 1

the fundamental principles and laws of the journey towards Allah. This narration is amongst the best recommendations in this field, because of how it considers the fundamental aspects of the journey towards perfection and provides a precise and systematic path that is suitable for all believers.

These instructions from Imam al-Ṣādiq (peace be upon him) to ʿUnwān al-Baṣrī are of such great importance that great *wāṣil*[i] *ʿurafā*[ii] such as Āyatullāh Sayyid ʿAlī Qāḍī (may Allah be pleased with him) would instruct their students, disciples and those who sought the path of spiritual wayfaring, to write out the tradition of ʿUnwān al-Baṣrī. Thereafter, he instructed them to always keep it with them, and read it once or twice a week, making sure that they act according to the instructions mentioned therein.[iii]

Apart from its rich content, this narration also contains deep points that can be understood from the constructive behaviour and instructions of Imam al-Ṣādiq (peace be upon him) to ʿUnwān al-Baṣrī. Paying attention to these points is necessary for those who desire the abode of the Beloved.

This book has been structured according to the words of Imam al-Ṣādiq (peace be upon him) to ʿUnwān al-Baṣrī. In the book, answers to the ideological and practical requirements for the journey towards true perfection have been discussed. It has been written with a practical approach in mind. Bringing up purely theoretical discussions has been avoided and special attention has been paid to the following topics: the lofty goal of creation and the way to reach this goal, the general prerequisites and conditions of wayfaring towards true perfection, the obstacles along the path, and the effects of wayfaring towards this

---

i. Wāṣil (plural: wāṣilūn) literally means to be connected and here refers to one who has reached the station of Divine Proximity and has united with his Lord.

ii. ʿUrafā is the plural of ʿārif, literally meaning one who has cognizance, is aware, knows. However, it is used in Islamic sciences as a term for one whom God has made to reach a level whereby he witnesses the Divine Essence, Names and Attributes. This station appears for him by means of unveiling and experiencing, not simply knowledge and cognizance.

iii. Hāshamiyān, Daryā-yi ʿIrfān, 88

goal. These topics will be elaborated over a few chapters so that it can serve as a guiding light for those who are determined to undertake wayfaring towards the Lord.

The discussions present in this book elucidate the ideological concepts and practical issues related to spiritual education and training. In the view of its author these discussions are at a secondary level.[i] They depict the goal of servitude along with the fundamental and overall course of action necessary to attain it; it is possible to benefit from these discussions without being in contact with a spiritual teacher.

In the end, I would like to thank all those who played a role in preparing this work (from typing the audio recordings, type-setting, referencing, and editing to printing and publishing). May Allah appreciate their efforts by the station of Muḥammad and his pure family—may the blessings of Allah be upon all of them.

Muḥammad Bāqir Taḥrīrī

---

i. The author, Āyatullāh Muhammad Bāqir Tahrīrī (may his blessings remain), has released several works pertaining to the subject of spiritual education and training. Amongst these works are a commentary on Risālah al-Huqūq of Imam al-Sajjād (peace be upon him), this commentary on the narration of ʿUnwān al-Baṣrī, as well as a commentary on al-Munājāt al-Shaʿbāniyyah of Amīr al-Mu'minīn (peace be upon him). These three works respectively constitute a first, second, and third level of studying this subject.

The Narration of Unwan al-Basri

عَنْ عُنْوَانَ الْبَصْرِيِّ وَ كَانَ شَيْخاً كَبِيراً قَدْ أَتَى عَلَيْهِ أَرْبَعٌ وَ تِسْعُونَ سَنَةً قَالَ: كُنْتُ أَخْتَلِفُ إِلَى مَالِكِ بْنِ أَنَسٍ سِنِينَ

[It is narrated] from ʿUnwān al-Baṣrī while he was a very old man who had reached the age of ninety-four years. He says, "For many years I would [regularly] visit Mālik ibn Anas.

فَلَمَّا قَدِمَ جَعْفَرٌ الصَّادِقُ ع الْمَدِينَةَ اخْتَلَفْتُ إِلَيْهِ وَ أَحْبَبْتُ أَنْ آخُذَ عَنْهُ كَمَا أَخَذْتُ عَنْ مَالِكٍ

Then when Jaʿfar al-Ṣādiq (peace be upon him) arrived in Madinah I started visiting him and wished to benefit from his knowledge in the same manner that I had benefitted from Mālik.

فَقَالَ لِي يَوْماً إِنِّي رَجُلٌ مَطْلُوبٌ وَ مَعَ ذَلِكَ لِي أَوْرَادٌ فِي كُلِّ سَاعَةٍ مِنْ آنَاءِ اللَّيْلِ وَ النَّهَارِ فَلَا تَشْغَلْنِي عَنْ وِرْدِي وَ خُذْ عَنْ مَالِكٍ وَ اخْتَلِفْ إِلَيْهِ كَمَا كُنْتَ تَخْتَلِفُ إِلَيْهِ

One day he said to me, 'I am a man under surveillance [from the government]. Besides, I have recitations for every hour of the day and night [that I must recite]. Therefore, do not prevent me from my recitations and acquire [knowledge] from Mālik and visit him like you have visited him [in the past].'

فَاغْتَمَمْتُ مِنْ ذَلِكَ وَ خَرَجْتُ مِنْ عِنْدِهِ وَ قُلْتُ فِي نَفْسِي لَوْ تَفَرَّسَ فِيَّ خَيْراً لَمَا زَجَرَنِي عَنِ الِاخْتِلَافِ إِلَيْهِ وَ الْأَخْذِ عَنْهُ فَدَخَلْتُ مَسْجِدَ الرَّسُولِ ص وَ سَلَّمْتُ عَلَيْهِ ثُمَّ رَجَعْتُ مِنَ الْغَدِ إِلَى الرَّوْضَةِ وَ صَلَّيْتُ فِيهَا رَكْعَتَيْنِ وَ

قُلْتُ أَسْأَلُكَ يَا اللَّهُ يَا اللَّهُ أَنْ تَعْطِفَ عَلَيَّ قَلْبَ جَعْفَرٍ وَ تَرْزُقَنِي مِنْ عِلْمِهِ مَا أَهْتَدِي بِهِ إِلَى صِرَاطِكَ الْمُسْتَقِيمِ

I was grieved by these words. I left his presence and said to myself, 'If he had seen any goodness in me, he would not have stopped me from visiting him and acquiring [knowledge] from him.' Then I entered the Mosque of the Messenger (peace and blessings be upon him and his family), greeted the Messenger of Allah (peace and blessings be upon him and his family) [and left the place]. I returned to the holy sanctuary the next day, prayed two units of prayers in it and said, 'O Allah! O Allah! I ask you to soften heart of Ja'far towards me and provide for me from his knowledge [a share] through which I am guided to your Straight Path.'

وَ رَجَعْتُ إِلَى دَارِي مُغْتَمّاً وَ لَمْ أَخْتَلِفْ إِلَى مَالِكِ بْنِ أَنَسٍ لِمَا أُشْرِبَ قَلْبِي مِنْ حُبِّ جَعْفَرٍ فَمَا خَرَجْتُ مِنْ دَارِي إِلَّا إِلَى الصَّلَاةِ الْمَكْتُوبَةِ حَتَّى عِيلَ صَبْرِي

I returned to my home in the state of grief and stopped visiting Mālik ibn Anas, for my heart had been imbued with the love of Ja'far. I did not leave my house except for the prescribed [obligatory] prayers until I ran out of patience.

فَلَمَّا ضَاقَ صَدْرِي تَنَعَّلْتُ وَ تَرَدَّيْتُ وَ قَصَدْتُ جَعْفَراً وَ كَانَ بَعْدَ مَا صَلَّيْتُ الْعَصْرَ

When my heart became constricted, I wore my slippers and cloak, and started walking towards the house of Ja'far. This was after I had prayed the *'aṣr* prayers.

فَلَمَّا حَضَرْتُ بَابَ دَارِهِ اسْتَأْذَنْتُ عَلَيْهِ فَخَرَجَ خَادِمٌ لَهُ فَقَالَ مَا حَاجَتُكَ فَقُلْتُ السَّلَامُ عَلَى الشَّرِيفِ فَقَالَ هُوَ قَائِمٌ فِي مُصَلَّاهُ فَجَلَسْتُ بِحِذَاءِ بَابِهِ

When I reached his door, I sought permission to enter. One of his servants came out and said, 'What do you want?' I said, 'I want to greet the noble personality.' He said, 'He is busy praying in his place of prayers.' So, I sat [waiting] at the door.

فَمَا لَبِثْتُ إِلَّا يَسِيراً إِذْ خَرَجَ خَادِمٌ فَقَالَ ادْخُلْ عَلَى بَرَكَةِ اللَّهِ فَدَخَلْتُ وَ سَلَّمْتُ عَلَيْهِ فَرَدَّ السَّلَامَ وَ قَالَ اجْلِسْ غَفَرَ اللَّهُ لَكَ

After a short while, the servant came out and said, 'Enter with Allah's blessing.' I entered and greeted him. He replied to my greeting and said, 'Sit down! May Allah forgive you.'

فَجَلَسْتُ فَأَطْرَقَ مَلِيّاً ثُمَّ رَفَعَ رَأْسَهُ وَ قَالَ أَبُو مَنْ قُلْتُ أَبُو عَبْدِ اللَّهِ قَالَ ثَبَّتَ اللَّهُ كُنْيَتَكَ وَ وَفَّقَكَ يَا أَبَا عَبْدِ اللَّهِ مَا مَسْأَلَتُكَ فَقُلْتُ فِي نَفْسِي لَوْ لَمْ يَكُنْ لِي مِنْ زِيَارَتِهِ وَ التَّسْلِيمِ غَيْرُ هَذَا الدُّعَاءِ لَكَانَ كَثِيراً

I sat down. He paused for a while [looking down], then he raised his head and said, 'What is your *kunyah* (i)?' I replied, 'I am Abū 'Abd Allah.' He said, 'May Allah preserve your *kunyah* and make you successful, O Abū 'Abd Allah. What is your request?' [At this point] I said to myself, 'If I did not gain anything from visiting and greeting him except this prayer of his for me, it would still be a great thing.'

ثُمَّ رَفَعَ رَأْسَهُ ثُمَّ قَالَ مَا مَسْأَلَتُكَ فَقُلْتُ سَأَلْتُ اللَّهَ أَنْ يَعْطِفَ قَلْبَكَ عَلَيَّ وَ يَرْزُقَنِي مِنْ عِلْمِكَ وَ أَرْجُو أَنَّ اللَّهَ تَعَالَى أَجَابَنِي فِي الشَّرِيفِ مَا سَأَلْتُهُ

He raised his head and asked, 'What is your request?' I said, 'I asked Allah to soften your heart towards me and provide for me from your knowledge, and I hope Allah has answered what I asked for concerning your noble personality.'

فَقَالَ يَا أَبَا عَبْدِ اللَّهِ لَيْسَ الْعِلْمُ بِالتَّعَلُّمِ إِنَّمَا هُوَ نُورٌ يَقَعُ فِي قَلْبِ مَنْ يُرِيدُ اللَّهُ تَبَارَكَ وَ تَعَالَى أَنْ يَهْدِيَهُ فَإِنْ أَرَدْتَ الْعِلْمَ فَاطْلُبْ أَوَّلًا فِي نَفْسِكَ حَقِيقَةَ الْعُبُودِيَّةِ وَ اطْلُبِ الْعِلْمَ بِاسْتِعْمَالِهِ وَ اسْتَفْهِمِ اللَّهَ يُفْهِمْكَ

---

i. The word *kunyah* refers to the teknonymy of an individual. It is a respectful way of addressing them by using the name of their eldest child.

At this point, he said, 'O Abū 'Abd Allah! Knowledge is not [obtained] through learning. Rather it is a light which Allah casts into the heart of whomever He wishes to guide. If you desire knowledge, then first seek the reality of servitude in your soul. Seek knowledge by applying it in actions. Ask Allah to grant you understanding and He will grant it to you.'

قُلْتُ يَا شَرِيفُ فَقَالَ قُلْ يَا أَبَا عَبْدِ اللَّهِ قُلْتُ يَا أَبَا عَبْدِ اللَّهِ مَا حَقِيقَةُ الْعُبُودِيَّةِ

I said, 'O noble personality!' He said, 'Call me Abū 'Abd Allah'. I said, 'O Abū 'Abd Allah! What is the reality of servitude?'

قَالَ ثَلَاثَةُ أَشْيَاءَ أَنْ لَا يَرَى الْعَبْدُ لِنَفْسِهِ فِيمَا خَوَّلَهُ اللَّهُ مِلْكاً لِأَنَّ الْعَبِيدَ لَا يَكُونُ لَهُمْ مِلْكٌ يَرَوْنَ الْمَالَ مَالَ اللَّهِ يَضَعُونَهُ حَيْثُ أَمَرَهُمُ اللَّهُ بِهِ وَ لَا يُدَبِّرُ الْعَبْدُ لِنَفْسِهِ تَدْبِيراً وَ جُمْلَةُ اشْتِغَالِهِ فِيمَا أَمَرَهُ تَعَالَى بِهِ وَ نَهَاهُ عَنْهُ

He said, 'It is three things: [Firstly] that the servant does not see for himself ownership over that which Allah has bestowed on him. That is because the slaves do not own anything. In their eyes, their wealth is Allah's wealth; they place it wherever Allah has commanded them. [Secondly] that the servant does not direct and plan his own affairs. [Thirdly] that he completely preoccupies himself with what Allah the Exalted has commanded him to do and what He has prohibited him from.

فَإِذَا لَمْ يَرَ الْعَبْدُ لِنَفْسِهِ فِيمَا خَوَّلَهُ اللَّهُ تَعَالَى مِلْكاً هَانَ عَلَيْهِ الْإِنْفَاقُ فِيمَا أَمَرَهُ اللَّهُ تَعَالَى أَنْ يُنْفِقَ فِيهِ

So, when a servant does not see for himself ownership over that which Allah has bestowed him, spending in that which Allah has commanded him to spend, becomes easy for him;

وَ إِذَا فَوَّضَ الْعَبْدُ تَدْبِيرَ نَفْسِهِ عَلَى مُدَبِّرِهِ هَانَ عَلَيْهِ مَصَائِبُ الدُّنْيَا

and when the servant entrusts the direction of his affairs to its Director, the afflictions of this world become easy for him;

وَ إِذَا اشْتَغَلَ الْعَبْدُ بِمَا أَمَرَهُ اللَّهُ تَعَالَى وَ نَهَاهُ لَا يَتَفَرَّغُ مِنْهُمَا إِلَى الْمِرَاءِ وَ الْمُبَاهَاةِ مَعَ النَّاسِ

and when the servant busies himself with [observing] Allah's commands and His prohibitions, he does not get free time for disputes with the people and for boasting.

فَإِذَا أَكْرَمَ اللَّهُ الْعَبْدَ بِهَذِهِ الثَّلَاثَةِ هَانَ عَلَيْهِ الدُّنْيَا وَ إِبْلِيسُ وَ الْخَلْقُ وَ لَا يَطْلُبُ الدُّنْيَا تَكَاثُراً وَ تَفَاخُراً وَ لَا يَطْلُبُ مَا عِنْدَ النَّاسِ عِزّاً وَ عُلُوّاً وَ لَا يَدَعُ أَيَّامَهُ بَاطِلًا فَهَذَا أَوَّلُ دَرَجَةِ التُّقَى قَالَ اللَّهُ تَبَارَكَ وَ تَعَالَى تِلْكَ الدَّارُ الْآخِرَةُ نَجْعَلُهَا لِلَّذِينَ لَا يُرِيدُونَ عُلُوًّا فِي الْأَرْضِ وَ لَا فَسَاداً وَ الْعَاقِبَةُ لِلْمُتَّقِينَ

When Allah honours a servant with these three, the world, Satan and the people becomes easy and meek for him [to deal with]. He does not pursue the world for rivalry and vainglory, he does not seek what people possess due to his dignity and status,[i] and he does not squander his days in vain [things]. This is the first rank of *taqwā*.[ii] Allah the Exalted says, 'This is the abode of the Hereafter, which We shall grant to those who do not desire to domineer in the Earth nor to cause corruption, and the outcome will be in favour of those with *taqwā*.'[iii]

قُلْتُ يَا أَبَا عَبْدِ اللَّهِ أَوْصِنِي

I said, 'O Abū 'Abd Allah! Admonish me.'

---

i. The Arabic words of this blessed narration 'izzan wa 'ulūwan (seeking dignity and status) may be understood to be the state of the base individual who the honoured servant is far from. This understanding (that the base individual seeks false dignity and status in this world), would be in line with the sentence before and after. However, the Arabic may also be understood in the manner translated, that it is the honoured servant who seeks true dignity and status, and thus does not pursue that which others possess.

ii. The word taqwā is a noun that comes from the root verb waqiya meaning to protect something against that which may damage it. However, in the sharī'ah the word refers to protecting one's self from committing sins.

iii. تِلْكَ الدَّارُ الْآخِرَةُ نَجْعَلُهَا لِلَّذِينَ لَا يُرِيدُونَ عُلُوًّا فِي الْأَرْضِ وَلَا فَسَادًا ۚ وَالْعَاقِبَةُ لِلْمُتَّقِينَ

قَالَ أُوصِيكَ بِتِسْعَةِ أَشْيَاءَ فَإِنَّهَا وَصِيَّتِي لِمُرِيدِي الطَّرِيقِ إِلَى اللَّهِ تَعَالَى وَ اللَّهَ أَسْأَلُ أَنْ يُوَفِّقَكَ لِاسْتِعْمَالِهِ ثَلَاثَةٌ مِنْهَا فِي رِيَاضَةِ النَّفْسِ وَ ثَلَاثَةٌ مِنْهَا فِي الْحِلْمِ وَ ثَلَاثَةٌ مِنْهَا فِي الْعِلْمِ فَاحْفَظْهَا وَ إِيَّاكَ وَ التَّهَاوُنَ بِهَا

He said, 'I enjoin you towards nine things. For indeed, it is my admonition to [all] those who desire the path towards Allah and I ask Allah to grant you success in acting upon them. Three of them pertain to controlling the soul, three others are about forbearance and [the last] three are in relation to knowledge. So, memorize them and beware of being neglectful of them.

قَالَ عُنْوَانُ فَفَرَّغْتُ قَلْبِي لَهُ

'Unwān said, 'I emptied my heart for him [to listen to him attentively].'

فَقَالَ أَمَّا اللَّوَاتِي فِي الرِّيَاضَةِ فَإِيَّاكَ أَنْ تَأْكُلَ مَا لَا تَشْتَهِيهِ فَإِنَّهُ يُورِثُ الْحَمَاقَةَ وَ الْبَلَهَ وَ لَا تَأْكُلْ إِلَّا عِنْدَ الْجُوعِ وَ إِذَا أَكَلْتَ فَكُلْ حَلَالًا وَ سَمِّ اللَّهَ وَ اذْكُرْ حَدِيثَ الرَّسُولِ ص مَا مَلَأَ آدَمِيٌّ وِعَاءً شَرّاً مِنْ بَطْنِهِ فَإِنْ كَانَ وَ لَا بُدَّ فَثُلُثٌ لِطَعَامِهِ وَ ثُلُثٌ لِشَرَابِهِ وَ ثُلُثٌ لِنَفَسِهِ

He said, 'As for the affairs which pertain to controlling the soul: do not eat that for which you have no appetite, because it leads to stupidity and foolishness. Do not eat except when you are hungry. When you eat, eat that which is *ḥalāl* (permissible) and take Allah's name [over it]. Remember the words of the Messenger of Allah (peace and blessings be upon him and his family), "A human being has not filled any container worse than his stomach. When one must partake of food, he should allot one-third for food, one-third for water and one-third for breathing."

وَ أَمَّا اللَّوَاتِي فِي الْحِلْمِ فَمَنْ قَالَ لَكَ إِنْ قُلْتَ وَاحِدَةً سَمِعْتَ عَشْراً فَقُلْ إِنْ قُلْتَ عَشْراً لَمْ تَسْمَعْ وَاحِدَةً وَ مَنْ شَتَمَكَ فَقُلْ لَهُ إِنْ كُنْتَ صَادِقاً فِيمَا

تَقُولُ فَأَسْأَلُ اللَّهَ أَنْ يَغْفِرَ لِي وَ إِنْ كُنْتَ كَاذِباً فِيمَا تَقُولُ فَاللَّهَ أَسْأَلُ أَنْ يَغْفِرَ لَكَ وَ مَنْ وَعَدَكَ بِالْخَنَا فَعِدْهُ بِالنَّصِيحَةِ وَ الرِّعَاءِ

And as for the things in relation to forbearance: When someone says to you, "If you say a word [against me,] you will hear ten [against you]," say to him, "If you say ten things [against me], you will not even hear one." Also, if anyone slanders you, say to him, "If what you have said is true, then may Allah forgive me, but if you are lying, then I ask Allah to forgive you." Likewise, if anyone threatens you with something unpleasant, then [in return] promise him good-will and that you will observe [his rights].

وَ أَمَّا اللَّوَاتِي فِي الْعِلْمِ فَاسْأَلِ الْعُلَمَاءَ مَا جَهِلْتَ وَ إِيَّاكَ أَنْ تَسْأَلَهُمْ تَعَنُّتاً وَ تَجْرِبَةً وَ إِيَّاكَ أَنْ تَعْمَلَ بِرَأْيِكَ شَيْئاً وَ خُذْ بِالاحْتِيَاطِ فِي جَمِيعِ مَا تَجِدُ إِلَيْهِ سَبِيلًا وَ اهْرُبْ مِنَ الْفُتْيَا هَرَبَكَ مِنَ الْأَسَدِ وَ لَا تَجْعَلْ رَقَبَتَكَ لِلنَّاسِ جِسْراً

And as for the things [which must be observed] with regards to knowledge: Ask the scholars what you do not know, do not ask them to render them powerless or to test them. Abstain from acting according to your own opinion [without relying on any religious or intellectual justification], and act with *iḥtiyāṭ* (precaution) in all the affairs for which you find a way [to do so]. Flee from giving *fatāwā* (legal opinion) like you flee from a lion, and do not make your neck a bridge for the people.

قُمْ عَنِّي يَا أَبَا عَبْدِ اللَّهِ فَقَدْ نَصَحْتُ لَكَ وَ لَا تُفْسِدْ عَلَيَّ وِرْدِي فَإِنِّي امْرُؤٌ ضَنِينٌ بِنَفْسِي وَ السَّلَامُ عَلَى مَنِ اتَّبَعَ الْهُدَى.

[Now] rise from near me, O Abū 'Abd Allah! Indeed, I have advised you. Therefore, do not ruin my recitations [by taking up my time], for I am a man who is strict with respect to myself [and my time]. And may peace be upon him who follows the guidance.'" (i)

---

i. Majlisī, Biḥār al-Anwār, 1:224, narration 17

Chapter One

Prerequisites of Wayfaring towards Allah

The Prerequisites and Conditions for Spiritual Training

Wayfaring towards Allah the Exalted and reaching the station of Divine Proximity—which is the ultimate goal of man's creation—has a particular method and course. The highest level of proximity and the loftiest method was traversed by the Noblest Messenger (peace and blessings be upon him and his family) and his Ahl al-Bayt (peace be upon them), and they have taught this method to us. In addition, wayfaring towards Allah has certain prerequisites, some of which are beyond man's freewill. Others must be procured with consciousness and voluntary effort. These prerequisites must be possessed by the wayfarer from the beginning of the journey until the end. However, the state of these prerequisites changes and they are perfected as the wayfarer progresses through the stations of the spiritual journey. In this chapter, we will discuss these prerequisites.

Any course that is chosen to reach a certain goal, requires a background that naturally must exist, so that it can serve as a prerequisite to create the suitable conditions required. Inevitably, these suitable conditions are also needed. Man must procure them by means of his knowledge and awareness of the goal, such that traversing this course becomes possible for him. In addition to this, there are hindrances along the path of wayfaring such that if the wayfarer is heedless or unaware of them, his journey will be unsuccessful.

The spiritual journey towards true perfection and Allah the Exalted's proximity also has specific prerequisites, conditions and obstacles. These will be discussed—to the extent possible and to the extent of our understanding—from the tradition of ʿUnwān al-Baṣrī as well as from the Qurʾān and the Sunnah. (i)

Awakening and Benefitting from Divine Breaths of Mercy

Allah the Exalted created man, like all other beings, such that in his innate nature he is aware of the qudsī realm (ii) and His Absolute Perfection.

> فَأَقِمْ وَجْهَكَ لِلدِّينِ حَنِيفًا ۚ فِطْرَتَ اللَّهِ الَّتِي فَطَرَ النَّاسَ عَلَيْهَا ۚ لَا تَبْدِيلَ لِخَلْقِ اللَّهِ ۚ ذَٰلِكَ الدِّينُ الْقَيِّمُ وَلَٰكِنَّ أَكْثَرَ النَّاسِ لَا يَعْلَمُونَ
>
> So, set your heart as a person of pure faith on this religion, the original nature endowed by Allah according to which He originated mankind. There is no altering Allah's creation; that is the upright religion, (30:30)

However, association with the entities of this material world plunges man into the sleep of oblivion and makes him heedless of the fervour and zeal found in paying attention towards the *qudsī* realm. It is from this realm that the crux and reality of man stems. It is only the prophets and the *awliyāʾ* (close servants) of Allah (peace be upon them) that are an exception to this, as they have not forgotten their eternal covenant whilst living in this material world and have remained steadfast on the pledge of servitude to Allah the Exalted.

Despite this, Allah (the Provider of abundance and the Sublime)

---

i. The word *sunnah* refers to the speech and conduct of the Prophet (peace and blessings be upon him and his family) as well as the Imams (peace be upon them).

ii. The word *quds* means purity and being far from defect or fault. In the radiant Supplication of Kumayl, Amīr al-Muʾminīn (peace be upon him) asks Allah saying, "*bi haqqika wa bi qudsika*" (by the station of Your right, and Your *quds*). In the same sense, the *qudsī* realm here is a term referring to an immaterial realm where the purity of Allah is witnessed.

due to His infinite mercy, has given everybody different means of awakening from heedlessness. These means are either present inside man's own existence (by bringing about deficiencies, limitations and weaknesses), or in the outside world (through encountering adversities and failures). As a result, any man who has reached the slightest cognition of his own self and the world outside, turns his attention towards the *qudsī* realm and the realm of infinite *rubūbiyyah* [i] and humbles himself in front of it:

وَمَا أَرْسَلْنَا فِي قَرْيَةٍ مِّن نَّبِيٍّ إِلَّا أَخَذْنَا أَهْلَهَا بِالْبَأْسَاءِ وَالضَّرَّاءِ لَعَلَّهُمْ يَضَّرَّعُونَ

> We did not send a prophet to any town without visiting its people with stress and distress so that they might entreat [for Allah's forgiveness] (7:94)

How many an individual, after awakening from the sleep of oblivion—due to events and calamities in their life—turned to the Beloved, turning their back on the temporary abode of this world?!

Some others, due to their untainted Divine disposition and by taking heed of the radiant invitation of the prophets and the awliyā' of Allah (peace be upon them), had the curtains of heedlessness removed from their Divine disposition. Consequently, by seeking help from the Imams (peace be upon them) and with the help of a spiritual teacher and mentor, they busied themselves with training their souls.

For others with ready hearts, Allah the Granter of Favours—out of His Mercy—gives special warnings and invites towards Himself in a unique manner. This is indicated in what Allah revealed to the Prophet David (peace be upon him):

إِنَّ لِلَّهِ فِي أَيَّامِ دَهْرِكُمْ نَفَحَاتٍ أَلَا فَتَرَصَّدُوا لَهَا

> Certainly, in the days of your lifetime, there are [Divine]

---

i. Rubūbiyyah is a noun that indicates the position that the rabb holds. If rabb is translated as Lord, then rubūbiyyah would be Lordship. However, the word stems from the verb rabba رَبَّ meaning to nurture or train something until it reaches its perfection. Thus, Trainer or Nurturer may be a more appropriate translation of rabb.

> breezes from Allah. So, behold! Wait for them [and benefit from them!] (i)

The more man places himself in the course of these breezes of Divine Mercy and benefits from them, the more Allah's attention is attracted towards him, and the curtains of veils are removed, until he witnesses the realities of the creation.

Therefore, after this blessing of awakening from negligence is granted by Allah, it is necessary that man join this caravan of spiritual wayfarers while the opportunity of this short life remains. It is incumbent on him to turn his face away from the false and perishing attractions of this world. In this regard, Imam ʿAlī (peace be upon him) says:

وَ الْفُرْصَةُ تَمُرُّ مَرَّ السَّحَابِ فَانْتَهِزُوا فُرَصَ الْخَيْرِ

> Opportunities drift like passing of clouds. So, catch hold of the good opportunities. (ii)

الْفُرْصَةُ سَرِيعَةُ الْفَوْتِ وَ بَطِيئَةُ الْعَوْدِ

Opportunities escape quickly and return late. (iii)

إِضَاعَةُ الْفُرْصَةِ غُصَّة

The wasting of opportunities is a [source of] remorse. (iv)

کاروان رفت و تو در خواب و بیابان در پیش

کی روی؟ ز که پرسی؟ چه کنی؟ چون باشی؟

The caravan has gone whilst you are asleep, and in front the desert lies,
When shall you go? From who shall you ask the path? What will you do? How will you be? (v)

نوبهار است در آن کوش که خوشدل باشی

---

i. Majlisī, Biḥār al-Anwār, 77:168

ii. al-Raḍī, Nahj al-Balāghah, saying 21

iii. al-Āmudī, Ghurar al-Ḥikam, narration 2019

iv. al-Raḍī, Nahj al-Balāghah, saying 118

v. Shirāzī, Divān-i Hāfiz (Tashīh-i Qudsī), ghazal 527, couplet 5

که بسی گل بدمد باز و تو در گل باشی

It's a fresh spring, so try then to be happy of heart,
Because many roses will blossom whilst you remain under dust. (i)

The cause of these breaths of Divine Mercy in man's life can be the occurrence of different incidents and events. What is important is to derive the maximum benefit from these events which have the potential to bring about a transformation. This transformation sometimes appears in the form of a type of awareness and remorse for one's apathetic course of action in the past. At other times, it manifests itself in the form of a desire and longing for the spiritual stations and perfections that one must traverse.

How many *ʿurafā* and *wāṣilūn*, at the beginning of their journey of ascension, made correct use of these Divine opportunities!

Al-Fuḍayl bin ʿIyyāḍ, one of the renowned *ʿurafā*, was a thief and a highway robber before an inner transformation occurred in him and he repented sincerely. One night a caravan was passing by him, and a man in the caravan was reciting the Qurʾān. Al-Fuḍayl heard him recite this verse,

أَلَمْ يَأْنِ لِلَّذِينَ آمَنُوا أَن تَخْشَعَ قُلُوبُهُمْ لِذِكْرِ اللَّهِ

Is it not time yet for those who have faith, that their hearts should be humbled for Allah's remembrance? (57:16)

This verse pierced the heart of al-Fuḍayl like an arrow. He immediately answered to this verse and said to himself, "Yes, the time has come." After this an amazing transformation occurred in his soul and he started compensating for his past mistakes. (ii)

منم غریب دیار و تویی غریب نواز

دمی به حال غریب دیارِ خود پرداز

I am the stranger of Your land. O One who caresses the stranger!

i. Shirāzī, Divān-i Hāfiz (Tashīh-i Qudsī), ghazal 590, couplet 1

ii. ʿAṭṭār, Tadhkirat al-Awliyāʾ, 90

For but a moment, pay attention to this stranger of Your land.

درون سینه، دلم چون کبوتران بطپید
چه آتشی است که بر جان ما نهادی باز

Inside my bosom my heart beats like pigeons,
What fire is this, that again you have lit in my heart? (i)

There have always been people who possessed the appropriate ground for receiving spiritual training and who had not tainted their *fiṭrah* (innate disposition) with the veils of this material world. When the Imams (peace be upon them) would encounter such people, they would awaken them from the sleep of oblivion and forgetfulness and would show them the path of Allah's servitude.

One day Imam Mūsā ibn Jaʿfar (peace be upon him) was passing by a house when he heard the sounds of *ḥarām* music and singing coming from within. He asked the maid who had come out from the house at that time, "Is the owner of this house a free man or a slave?" She replied, "He is a free man." The Imam (peace be upon him) said, "You have uttered the truth. Had he been a slave he would have feared his Master." When the maid returned, her master Bishr al-Ḥāfī was sitting at a table with wine. He asked her, "Why did you return late?" She described her conversation with Imam Mūsā ibn Jaʿfar (peace be upon him) and mentioned what the Imam said. Bishr ran outside barefoot and hurriedly reached the presence of the Imam. With tears in his eyes, he expressed his remorse and by means of the Imam (peace be upon him) he repented.

A spiritual transformation engulfed Bishr because of the Imam's indirect speech, to the extent that he became one of the mystics! (ii)

Similarly, ʿUnwān al-Baṣrī's soul and existence underwent a transformation due to his interaction with Imam al-Ṣādiq (peace be upon him) and the Imam's constructive instructions. ʿUnwān abandoned all his previous knowledge, and like a novice student, humbled himself

---

i. Shirāzī, Divān-i Hāfiz (Tashīh-i Qudsī), ghazal 310, couplet 2 and 8.

ii. Qummī, Muntahā al-Āmāal, 2:348

before Imam al-Ṣādiq's (peace be upon him) system of spiritual training—with which he learned the basics of spiritual wayfaring.

Preparing Oneself for Acquiring Knowledge and Divine Teachings

After a servant is warned and awakened through one of the ways mentioned, he realizes that he should start his journey towards acquiring both knowledge and spiritual perfection. At this point, he should know that one of the etiquettes of knowing and acting upon true Divine Teachings is to not have any deviant views with regards to them, or at the very least to be ready to remove such views. A second such etiquette is to instil the readiness within himself to receive and benefit from Divine Teachings. This readiness has different levels.

The first level necessary for gaining religious knowledge and Divine Teachings (regardless of whether they are theoretical or practical teachings) is to not have any aversion or negative outlook towards them. It is possible that at the beginning the spiritual wayfarer may not yet have a positive outlook towards these lofty realities and teachings, but it is necessary that he believe they do exist, and that man can understand and witness them. In this first stage, the obstacles that stop man from entering this domain are narrow-mindedness, denying these lofty realities, or even having conviction that one cannot reach and witness them. How can one who does not have any grasp over these realities—neither theoretically nor practically—have such conviction!

Imam ʿAlī (peace be upon him) says about such people:

وَ إِنَّ الْجَاهِلَ مَنْ عَدَّ نَفْسَهُ بِمَا جَهِلَ مِنْ مَعْرِفَةِ الْعِلْمِ عَالِماً وَ بِرَأْيِهِ مُكْتَفِياً فَمَا يَزَالُ لِلْعُلَمَاءِ مُبَاعِداً وَ عَلَيْهِمْ زَارِياً وَ لِمَنْ خَالَفَهُ مُخَطِّئاً وَ لِمَا لَمْ يَعْرِفْ مِنَ الْأُمُورِ مُضَلِّلاً فَإِذَا وَرَدَ عَلَيْهِ مِنَ الْأُمُورِ مَا لَمْ يَعْرِفْهُ أَنْكَرَهُ وَ كَذَّبَ بِهِ وَ قَالَ بِجَهَالَتِهِ مَا أَعْرِفُ هَذَا وَ مَا أَرَاهُ كَانَ وَ مَا أَظُنُّ أَنْ يَكُونَ وَ أَنَّى كَانَ وَ ذَلِكَ لِثِقَتِهِ بِرَأْيِهِ وَ قِلَّةِ مَعْرِفَتِهِ بِجَهَالَتِهِ فَمَا يَنْفَكُّ بِمَا يَرَى مِمَّا يَلْتَبِسُ

عَلَيْهِ رَأْيَهُ مِمَّا لَا يَعْرِفُ لِلْجَهْلِ مُسْتَفِيداً وَ لِلْحَقِّ مُنْكِراً وَ فِي الْجَهَالَةِ مُتَحَيِّراً وَ عَنْ طَلَبِ الْعِلْمِ مُسْتَكْبِرا

> Verily, an ignorant man considers himself knowledgeable about the sciences [and teachings] which he does not know, and he considers his own opinion sufficient. So, he is always away from the scholars and harms them. He rejects anyone who opposes him and misguides others in matters which he is ignorant about. If things that he does not have any knowledge about are presented to him, he denies and rejects them, saying, "I don't know this. I don't believe that such a thing exists, nor do I think that it will come into existence. How is it possible that such a thing be real?!" This state of his is due to his confidence in his own opinion and his lack of knowledge about his own ignorance. Therefore due to this mistake of his, his ignorance continuously increases, he continuously denies the truth, remains confused in the state of ignorance, and does not seek knowledge out of arrogance.[i]

This attitude usually results in verbal or practical denial of the Divine Realities and Teachings. It becomes the cause of man's downfall and distance from these lofty religious teachings and realities. Amīr al-Muʾminīn ʿAlī (peace be upon him) says:

الجاهل ميّت و إن كان حيّا

> An ignorant man is dead, even though he is [physically] alive.[ii]

How many a great sage and scholar during history, has been accused of blasphemy and forced into isolation because of this ignorant opposition and rejection of lofty religious teachings!

گر اهلْ نه‌ای، ز اهل حق خُرده مگیر

ای مُرده! چو خود زنده‌دلان، مُرده مگیر

---

i. al-Ḥarrānī, Tuḥaf al-ʿUqūl, 73

ii. al-Āmudī, Ghurar al-Hikam, narration 1125

If you be unworthy yourself, do not find fault with the men of Truth,
Do not suppose the enlivened hearts to be dead like you, O one bereft of true life!

برخیز از این خواب گران، ای مهجور
بیدار دلان خواب گران برده مگیر

Rise from this deep slumber O godforsaken,
Do not suppose those with awakened hearts to be victims of deep slumber. (i)

The great mystic, Imam Khumaynī (may Allah be pleased with him), was also not safe from the harm of this group. With grief, he recounts this painful period and says:

> Learning a foreign language was considered heresy. Philosophy and ʿirfān (ii) was considered a sin and polytheism. In Madrasah-yi Faydīyyah (iii), my son Mustafā who was then a child, drank water in a vessel and this vessel was washed [to remove ritual impurity]. This was because I taught philosophy. (iv)

Similarly, ʿUnwān al-Baṣrī had been a student of Mālik ibn Anas for years and he had benefitted from his knowledge. He believed in the authenticity and truth of the knowledge acquired from sources other than the Ahl al-Bayt (peace be upon them). At the same time, he also

i. Khumaynī, Dīvān-i Imam Khumaynī, 216

ii. The word ʿirfān comes from the same root word as ʿārif. Linguistically the former is a verbal noun that means to know and have cognizance, while the latter is a noun for the doer, that is the one who knows and has cognizance. However, as a term, ʿirfān is the name of one of the Islamic sciences that consists of two distinct parts. Theoretical ʿirfān attempts to explain the reality of existence, a goal like that of Islamic philosophy. Practical *ʿirfān* on the other hand focuses on the actions one must carry out to go closer to Allah and is thus like the science of *akhlāq*.

iii. Madrasah-yi Fayzīyyah is one of the famous schools of the Islamic seminary located in Qom, Iran. Founded during the reign of the Safavid empire, this school is adjacent to the holy shrine of Lady Fātimah al- Maʿsūmah (peace be upon her)

iv. Khumaynī, Sahifah-yi Nūr, 21:91

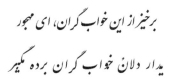

desired to benefit from the knowledge of Imam al-Ṣādiq (peace be upon him), as he himself says:

كُنْتُ أَخْتَلِفُ إِلَى مَالِكِ بْنِ أَنَسٍ سِنِينَ فَلَمَّا قَدِمَ جَعْفَرٌ الصَّادِقُ ع الْمَدِينَةَ اخْتَلَفْتُ إِلَيْهِ وَ أَحْبَبْتُ أَنْ آخُذَ عَنْهُ كَمَا أَخَذْتُ عَنْ مَالِكٍ

> For many years I would [regularly] visit Mālik ibn Anas. When Jaʿfar as-Sādiq (peace be upon him) arrived in Madinah I started visiting him and wished to benefit from his knowledge in the same manner that I had benefitted from the knowledge of Mālik.

However, with this belief and conviction he would not be able to benefit from the lofty teachings of Imam Jaʿfar al-Ṣādiq (peace be upon him). Holding fast to and clenching the rope of the Ahl al-Bayt (peace be upon them) necessitates rejection and separation from every falsehood and *ṭāghūt*[i]:

فَمَن يَكْفُرْ بِالطَّاغُوتِ وَيُؤْمِن بِاللَّهِ فَقَدِ اسْتَمْسَكَ بِالْعُرْوَةِ الْوُثْقَىٰ لَا انفِصَامَ لَهَا

> So, one who disavows the tāghūt and has faith in Allah has held fast to the firmest handle for which there is no breaking; (2:256)

Similarly, the Noble Prophet of Islam (peace and blessings be upon him and his family) says in this regard:

مَنْ أَحَبَّ أَنْ يَرْكَبَ سَفِينَةَ النَّجَاةِ وَ يَسْتَمْسِكَ بِالْعُرْوَةِ الْوُثْقى وَ يَعْتَصِمَ بِحَبْلِ اللَّهِ الْمَتِينِ فَلْيُوَالِ عَلِيّاً بَعْدِي وَ لْيُعَادِ عَدُوَّهُ وَ لْيَأْتَمَّ بِالْأَئِمَّةِ الْهُدَاةِ مِنْ وُلْدِهِ

> One who desires to board the Ark of Salvation, hold fast to

---

i. *Ṭāghūt* is a word used both in the plural and the singular meanings and refers to one who transgresses the limit or any object of worship other than Allah, the Exalted.

the firmest handle and cling to Allah's cord, then he should follow 'Alī (peace be upon him) after me, he should take his enemies to be his own enemies and he should follow the Imams of Guidance (peace be upon them) from his progeny. [(i)]

For this reason, Imam al-Ṣādiq (peace be upon him) gave 'Unwān al-Baṣrī a calculated and constructive response, saying:

إِنِّي رَجُلٌ مَطْلُوبٌ وَ مَعَ ذَلِكَ لِي أَوْرَادٌ فِي كُلِّ سَاعَةٍ مِنْ آنَاءِ اللَّيْلِ وَ النَّهَارِ فَلَا تَشْغَلْنِي عَنْ وِرْدِي وَ خُذْ عَنْ مَالِكٍ وَ اخْتَلِفْ إِلَيْهِ كَمَا كُنْتَ تَخْتَلِفُ إِلَيْهِ

I am a man under surveillance [from the government]. Besides, I have recitations for every hour of my day and night. Therefore, do not prevent me from my prayers and acquire [knowledge] from Mālik and visit him like you have visited him [in the past].

These words are from an Imam whose first and foremost duty from Allah the Exalted is to guide, show the path, assist and save the seekers of Divine Realities and knowledge! However, the motive behind Imam's response was to create a spiritual refinement in 'Unwān al-Baṣrī, make him disinclined towards the path of other than the Ahl al-Bayt (peace be upon them), and create in him the readiness to receive the insightful teachings of the Ahl al-Bayt (peace be upon them). As a result, 'Unwān al-Baṣrī says after this response:

وَ رَجَعْتُ إِلَى دَارِي مُغْتَمّاً وَ لَمْ أَخْتَلِفْ إِلَى مَالِكِ بْنِ أَنَسٍ لِمَا أُشْرِبَ قَلْبِي مِنْ حُبِّ جَعْفَرٍ

I returned home in a state of sorrow and grief. I stopped visiting Mālik ibn Anas as my heart was filled with love for Ja'far.

Therefore, the tongue of the heart of every seeker of perfection

---

i. al-Huwayzī, Tafsīr Nūr al-Thaqalayn, 1:263

should utter these words:

قبله و محراب من ابروی دلدار است و بس

این دل شوریده را با این چه و با آن چه کار؟

My Qibla and my prayer niche, are the eyebrow of the Beloved,
What does this frenzied heart have to do with this and with that?! (i)

It was only after this inner awakening and transformation, that Imam al-Ṣādiq (peace be upon him) accepted him in his noble presence and allowed him to benefit from his Divine teachings.Correctly Understanding the Goal and the Path to Reach it

All the created beings in this world have been placed upon a path of movement towards perfection, a journey of ascent towards Absolution Perfection, Allah the Exalted. This path is the path of existential humility and submission to Him. As explained in the Noble Qur'an:

إِنْ كُلُّ مَنْ فِي السَّمَاوَاتِ وَ الْأَرْضِ إِلاَّ آتِي الرَّحْمٰنِ عَبْداً

There is none in the heavens and the Earth, but he comes to the Beneficent as a servant. (19:93)

The difference between man's journey towards perfection as compared to the rest of creation is that man's movement towards perfection becomes valuable and worthy when it is accompanied by an awareness and understanding of his Lord, the nature of his own being, and the manner of the connection between him and his Lord. It is only this expression of humility and submission that can take man to high stations of servitude. Therefore Allah—by sending His messengers—has specifically instructed man to traverse this distinct path and said:

وَ لَقَدْ بَعَثْنَا فِي كُلِّ أُمَّةٍ رَسُولاً أَنِ اعْبُدُوا اللَّهَ وَ اجْتَنِبُوا الطَّاغُوتَ

Certainly, We raised an apostle in every nation [to preach]: "Worship Allah and shun the [deceitful] tāghūt." (16:36)

وَ مَا أَرْسَلْنَا مِنْ رَسُولٍ إِلاَّ لِيُطَاعَ بِإِذْنِ اللَّهِ

i. Shirāzī, Divān-i Hāfiz (Tashīh-i Qudsī), ghazal 302, couplet 4

> We did not send any apostle but to be obeyed by Allah's leave. (4:64)

In a similar manner, He addresses man and broadly divides him into two groups:

> يَا أَيُّهَا الْإِنْسَانُ إِنَّكَ كَادِحٌ إِلَى رَبِّكَ كَدْحاً فَمُلاَقِيهِ فَأَمَّا مَنْ أُوتِيَ كِتَابَهُ بِيَمِينِهِ فَسَوْفَ يُحَاسَبُ حِسَاباً يَسِيراً وَ يَنْقَلِبُ إِلَى أَهْلِهِ مَسْرُوراً وَ أَمَّا مَنْ أُوتِيَ كِتَابَهُ وَرَاءَ ظَهْرِهِ فَسَوْفَ يَدْعُو ثُبُوراً وَ يَصْلَى سَعِيراً
>
> O man! You are labouring toward your Lord laboriously, and you will encounter Him. Then, as for him who is given his record [of deeds] in his right hand, he will receive an easy reckoning, and he will return to his folks joyfully. But as for him who is given his record from behind his back, he will soon pray for [his own] annihilation and enter the Blaze. (84:6-12)

With regards to those in the second group, their journey will not be spiritual or Divine—rather it is an animalistic striving. In fact, it is even worse than an animalistic striving because in this case man has not recognized the nature of his being, revered it, or made correct use of his faculties of perception or the Divine favours:

> وَ لَقَدْ ذَرَأْنَا لِجَهَنَّمَ كَثِيراً مِنَ الْجِنِّ وَ الْإِنْسِ لَهُمْ قُلُوبٌ لاَ يَفْقَهُونَ بِهَا وَ لَهُمْ أَعْيُنٌ لاَ يُبْصِرُونَ بِهَا وَ لَهُمْ آذَانٌ لاَ يَسْمَعُونَ بِهَا أُولٰئِكَ كَالْأَنْعَامِ بَلْ هُمْ أَضَلُّ أُولٰئِكَ هُمُ الْغَافِلُونَ
>
> Certainly, We have winnowed out for hell many of the jinn and humans: [because] they have hearts with which they do not understand [the truth], they have eyes with which they do not see [the truth], they have ears with which they do not hear [the truth]. They are like cattle; indeed, they are more astray. It is they who are the heedless." (7:179)

Imam ʿAlī (peace be upon him) also compares a man who worships

Allah without the backing of Divine Teachings, to an animal tied to a millstone that continuously revolves around itself and never reaches its destination:

الْمُتَعَبِّدُ عَلَى غَيْرِ فِقْهٍ كَحِمَارِ الطَّاحُونَةِ يَدُورُ وَ لَا يَبْرَح

> A devoted worshipper who has not understood [what worship is] is like the donkey of the grinding mill that revolves [around itself] and does reach [the destination].[i]

Therefore, the first duty of the wayfarer is to obtain adequate knowledge and an understanding of man's goal and destination (which is Divine Proximity) and to realize that this proximity is not physical, rather it is an existential proximity to Allah. Its reality can only be actualized by undertaking a specific journey and attaining consciousness. The Noble Qur'ān also says in this regard:

وَ مَا خَلَقْتُ الْجِنَّ وَ الْإِنْسَ إِلاَّ لِيَعْبُدُونِ

> I did not create the jinn and the humans except that they may worship Me. (51:56)

وَ مَا أُمِرُوا إِلاَّ لِيَعْبُدُوا اللَّهَ مُخْلِصِينَ لَهُ الدِّينَ حُنَفَاءَ

> They were not commanded except to worship Allah, dedicating their faith to Him as men of pure faith, (98:5)

Worship accompanied with sincerity in faith requires correct knowledge of the religion and its teachings. Therefore, Allah describes reaching this knowledge and cognition as the purpose behind the creation of all beings:

اللَّهُ الَّذِي خَلَقَ سَبْعَ سَمَاوَاتٍ وَ مِنَ الْأَرْضِ مِثْلَهُنَّ يَتَنَزَّلُ الْأَمْرُ بَيْنَهُنَّ لِتَعْلَمُوا أَنَّ اللَّهَ عَلَى كُلِّ شَيْءٍ قَدِيرٌ وَ أَنَّ اللَّهَ قَدْ أَحَاطَ بِكُلِّ شَيْءٍ عِلْماً

> It is Allah who has created seven heavens, and of the Earth [a number] like them. The command [of Allah] gradually

---

i. Majlisī, Biḥār al-Anwār, 1:208

> descends through them, that you may know that Allah has power over all things, and that Allah comprehends all things in knowledge. (65:12)

It is with this correct knowledge that the curtain of ambiguity is lifted from many of the other false goals and the wayfarer understands that he should not undertake this journey with the goal of gaining the ability to perform supernatural and extraordinary actions (miracles and other such things). He understands that he should not short-change himself by selling the capital of his existence in exchange for extraordinary feats and miracles. He becomes attentive to the fact that conceptual and intellectual knowledge of Allah is just a precursor for reaching Allah the Exalted. In itself it is not the primary goal or aim. He also realizes that deviated and non-Divine paths do nothing other than stop him from reaching the True Goal and Destination. As a result, different branches of learning never become a veil that stops such a man from the right path. Rather, he is always seeking correct knowledge of the goal, so that with an accurate understanding of the way and the path of reaching the lofty goal of creation, he can discern the correct path from the deviated paths. Without this recognition, his journey and movement will not yield any result except remoteness and distance from the destination. In the words of Imam al-Ṣādiq (peace be upon him):

> الْعَامِلُ عَلَى غَيْرِ بَصِيرَةٍ كَالسَّائِرِ عَلَى غَيْرِ الطَّرِيقِ وَ لَا يَزِيدُهُ سُرْعَةُ السَّيْرِ مِنَ الطَّرِيقِ إِلَّا بُعْداً.
>
> One who strives without knowledge and insight, is like a traveller on the wrong path. The speediness of his journey does not increase him except in his remoteness from the path.[i]

At the beginning of his contact with Imam al-Sādiq (peace be upon him), 'Unwān al-Basrī did not possess the necessary incentive and understanding to receive the lofty teachings of the Imam. He was

i. Majlisī, Biḥār al-Anwār, 1:206

entangled in a state of confusion, as he himself says:

كُنْتُ أَخْتَلِفُ إِلَى مَالِكِ بْنِ أَنَسٍ سِنِينَ فَلَمَّا قَدِمَ جَعْفَرٌ الصَّادِقُ ع الْمَدِينَةَ اخْتَلَفْتُ إِلَيْهِ وَ أَحْبَبْتُ أَنْ آخُذَ عَنْهُ كَمَا أَخَذْتُ عَنْ مَالِكٍ

> For many years I would [regularly] visit Mālik ibn Anas. When Jaʿfar al-Sādiq (peace be upon him) arrived in Madinah I started visiting him and wished to benefit from his knowledge in the same manner that I had benefitted from the knowledge of Mālik.

Such an outlook towards the teachings of Ahl al-Bayt (peace be upon them) cannot help man on the path of spirituality and perfection. Placing the knowledge and teachings of the Ahl al-Bayt (peace be upon them) next to the knowledge of others does not create the suitable spiritual readiness in man so that he can benefit from Divine Teachings. The Imams (peace be upon them) have repeatedly spoken about this.[i] For example, Imam al-Bāqir (peace be upon him), while addressing two people who had come to visit him, says:

شَرِّقَا وَ غَرِّبَا لَنْ تَجِدَا عِلْماً صَحِيحاً إِلَّا شَيْئاً يَخْرُجُ مِنْ عِنْدِنَا أَهْلَ الْبَيْتِ

> Travel to the east and to the west, by no means will you find correct knowledge except that which has emerged from us the Ahl al-Bayt (peace be upon them).[ii]

In another narration he says:

أَمَا إِنَّهُ لَيْسَ عِنْدَ أَحَدٍ مِنَ النَّاسِ حَقٌّ وَ لَا صَوَابٌ إِلَّا شَيْءٌ أَخَذُوهُ مِنَّا أَهْلَ الْبَيْتِ

> Behold! Certainly not a single person from the people possesses any truth and correct knowledge, except that which

---

i. Refer to Majlisī, Biḥār al-Anwār, volume 1

ii. Majlisī, Biḥār al-Anwār, 2:92

> they have taken it from us the Ahl al-Bayt (peace be upon them).(i)

Amīr al-Mu'minīn 'Alī (peace be upon him) also used to invite the people to the origin and source of Divine Teachings present with him, by using these words:

> لَـو اقْتَبَسْـتُمُ الْعِلْـمَ مِـنْ مَعْدِنِـهِ وَ شَـرِبْتُمُ الْمَـاءَ بِعُذُوبَتِـهِ وَ ادَّخَرْتُـمُ الْخَيْـرَ مِـنْ مَوْضِعِـهِ وَ أَخَذْتُـمْ مِـنَ الطَّرِيـقِ وَاضِحَـهُ وَ سَـلَكْتُمْ مِـنَ الْحَـقِّ نَهْجَـهُ لَنَهَجَـتْ بِكُـمُ السُّـبُلُ وَ بَـدَتْ لَكُـمُ الْأَعْـلَام
>
> If you had drawn knowledge from its reserve, drunk agreeable water, accumulated goodness from its [correct] place, adopted the clear path, and taken the true way, you would have traversed the paths [of guidance], and the signs [of truth] would have become apparent for you.(ii)

Similarly, we read in *Ziyārah al-Jāmi'ah* about the Ahl al-Bayt (peace be upon them):

> آتَاكُمُ اللّهُ مَا لَمْ يُؤْتِ أَحَداً مِنَ الْعَالَمِين
>
> Allah has granted you that which he did not grant anyone from the worlds.(iii)

Therefore, every path other than the path of the Ahl al-Bayt (peace be upon them) is nothing but deviation and the wayfarer must disown and reject it. This rejection should be expressed in his beliefs, words and actions:

> بَرِئْـتُ إِلَى اللَّهِ عَزَّ وَ جَلَّ مِنْ أَعْدَائِكُـمْ ... وَ الشَّـاكِّينَ فِيكُـمْ وَ الْمُنْحَرِفِيـنَ عَنْكُـمْ وَ مِـنْ كُلِّ وَلِيجَـةٍ دُونَكُـمْ وَ كُلِّ مُطَـاعٍ سِـوَاكُـمْ وَ مِـنَ الْأَئِمَّـةِ الَّذِيـنَ يَدْعُـونَ إِلَى النَّـار
>
> I reject and express my aversion to your enemies, seeking

---

i. Majlisī, Biḥār al-Anwār, 2:94

ii. al-Kulaynī, al-Kāfī, 8:32

iii. Majlisī, Biḥār al-Anwār, 102:103

> refuge in Allah . . . and [I express my aversion to] those who harbour doubts about you, deviate from you, from every confidant other than you, and from every obeyed-one other than you, and from the leaders who invite towards the fire.[i]

Benefitting from Encountering the Awliyā'

Sometimes man becomes aware of his goal and the path to reach it, but his mind and soul is preoccupied and enamoured with other things. In this situation, his inclination and desire for perfection turns into an artificial attraction, or his mind stays preoccupied with other vain affairs and he starts believing in them. In both cases, when such a person encounters the awliyā' of Allah and spiritual mentors, he is faced with rejection from them. This rejection is intended to cause a transformation in his mind and soul, such that he becomes prepared to undertake the journey towards True Perfection. In this same manner, Imam al-Sādiq's (peace be upon him) response to 'Unwān Basrī was such that it impelled him to acquire an increased understanding and motivation for receiving the Divine Teachings. The Imam directed him to Mālik ibn Anas and said, "Acquire knowledge from Mālik and visit him as you did in the past."

This, even though the Divine duty of an Imam is to guide and aid men, such that anyone who refers to him, the Imam must make him aware and show him the path! But this kind of response to 'Unwān al-Baṣrī was aimed at creating a readiness in him, so that his heart would become detached from other paths, and love of the true path and the true leader would manifest in his existence. Consequently, the words of the Imam ignited a fire in his existence, left him dispassionate about other paths, and more than ever, made him enamoured of receiving the lofty Divine knowledge of the Ahl al-Bayt (peace be upon them). So much so that after this response, grief overtook him, and he said to himself, "If the Imam had seen any goodness in me he would have never prevented me from visiting him and acquiring knowledge from him."

With this state, he learnt of his own shortcoming and understood

---

i. Ibid.

that this shortcoming must be remedied at the hands of a perfect man. This is one of the aims behind such a response from the *awliyā'* of Allah. For as long as man does not recognize his own shortcoming, he does not refer to those who are qualified to remedy it and thereby acquire perfection. 'Unwān did not consider this response as a shortcoming on the part of the Imam, rather he considered it as a defect in himself. After *tawassul* (i) to the revered Prophet of Islam (peace and blessings be upon him and his family), he prayed to Allah saying, "O Allah, O Allah! I ask you to make Ja'far's heart considerate towards me and make me benefit from his knowledge, so that I may be guided to the right path."

گرم نه پیرمغان در به روی بگشاید

کدام در بزنم؟ چاره از کجا جویم؟

If the Pīr of the Magians (ii) doesn't open the Winehouse's (iii) door to us,
On what door shall I knock? From whence do I seek the remedy? (iv)

After this incident and after imploring Allah the Self-Sufficient, he no longer went to visit Mālik ibn Anas, as his heart was brimming with love for Imam al-Ṣādiq (peace be upon him).

Therefore, the other aim behind this kind of response is to cause a transformation in man, so that his attachment to the false and deviated ways is cut off, and instead he becomes an ardent lover who is attached to the true path and its leader—thus following and persisting along

---

i. The noun tawassul means to seek closeness (to Allah) by using a wasīlah (a channel, a means). Wasīlah stems from the trilateral root wasala وَسَلَ and indicates a sense of longing and desire.

ii. The Magians are the clerics of the Zoroastrian faith. The term "Pīr of the Magians" here apparently refers to the Perfect Man, or the teacher of those on the path of spiritual wayfaring.

iii. Wine in the poetry of the 'urafā is commonly explained as love of Allah. However, a more beneficial explanation that has been provided by some 'urafā is that it refers to murāqabah (having vigilance over one's actions and ensuring that no sins are committed). This in turn leads to a profound attention and love of Allah. The Winehouse here refers to the place where this love (or murāqabah) is handed out.

iv. Shirāzī, Divān-i Ḥāfiẓ (Taṣḥīḥ-i Qudsī), ghazal 422, couplet 3

this path.

Steadfastness on the Path of Perfection

One of the most important and effective elements for man on the path towards perfection, is to remain steadfast in working towards creating the suitable conditions for the spiritual journey and countering the obstacles and difficulties along the path.

The Noble Qur'ān has not considered belief and conviction in the rubūbiyyah of Allah the Exalted, as being sufficient for reaching lofty spiritual ranks and stations. Rather, it has described steadfastness and perseverance on this conviction—while carrying out worldly activities and in the face of difficulties and inadequacies—as one of the qualities of the wāsilūn and those who are successful:

إِنَّ الَّذِينَ قَالُوا رَبُّنَا اللَّهُ ثُمَّ اسْتَقَامُوا تَتَنَزَّلُ عَلَيْهِمُ الْمَلاَئِكَةُ أَلاَّ تَخَافُوا وَ لاَ تَحْزَنُوا

> Indeed, those who say, "Our Lord is Allah!" and then remain steadfast, the angels descend upon them, [saying,] "Do not fear, nor be grieved!" (41:30(

In another verse, steadfastness on the true path and al-sirāt al-mustaqīm (the straight path) is considered a necessary condition for benefitting from the bounties of spiritual life, from Allah's wilāyah and that of His awliyā':

وَ أَنْ لَوِ اسْتَقَامُوا عَلَى الطَّرِيقَةِ لَأَسْقَيْنَاهُمْ مَاءً غَدَقاً

> If they [mankind] are steadfast on the path, We shall provide them with abundant water.[i] (72:16)

This is because in the first stage, Satan wants man to disbelieve in God and the truth:

---

i. Water in this noble verse has been understood to be a metaphor for rizq (sustenance). 'Allāmah Tabātabā'ī says, "From the context it can be understood that His words 'We shall provide them with abundant water' is an example intending by it an increase in sustenance". See Tafsīr al-Mīzān, 20:46.

كَمَثَلِ الشَّيْطَانِ إِذْ قَالَ لِلْإِنْسَانِ اكْفُرْ

. . . like Satan when he tells man to disbelieve. (59:16)

And if he fails in this temptation, he then seeks to prevent man from the path of faith by means of the false glitter of this world,[i] or by tempting man to follow different paths that are in opposition to the truth. The result is that Satan wants man to either not obey the truth from the very beginning or not remain steadfast on the path of obedience to the truth. Allah says in this regard:

يَا أَيُّهَا النَّاسُ كُلُوا مِمَّا فِي الْأَرْضِ حَلاَلاً طَيِّباً وَ لاَ تَتَّبِعُوا خُطُوَاتِ الشَّيْطَانِ إِنَّهُ لَكُمْ عَدُوٌّ مُبِينٌ

O mankind! Eat of what is lawful and pure in the Earth, and do not follow in Satan's steps. Indeed, he is your manifest enemy. (2:168)

Benefit from material objects is derived quickly. On the contrary, developing a connection with the Unseen World and performing meritorious actions requires struggle and unrelenting efforts, it requires that man oppose and limit his base desires and worldly inclinations. As a result, Satan uses the glitters of worldly objects to make man loose hope and despair in undertaking the journey towards true perfection.

Therefore, despair and loosing hope is one of the banes and calamities that constantly threatens the wayfarer. By constantly displaying and magnifying the failures and defeats of the past, Satan tries to slacken the determination and will of those who seek to rectify their souls and journey towards the alley of the Beloved. One of the negative effects of this state of despair is laziness and apathy which stops the wayfarer from acting. For us to be saved from this state and to acquire the state of steadfastness, it is necessary to pay careful attention to this saying of Imam ʿAlī (peace be upon him):

---

i. (27:24) and (47:25)

الْمُؤْمِنُ يَرْغَبُ فِيمَا يَبْقَى وَ يَزْهَدُ فِيمَا يَفْنَى
... بَعِيدٌ كَسَلُهُ دَائِمٌ نَشَاطُه

> A believer is eager and inclined towards that which lasts and is detached [in his heart] from that which perishes . . . he is away from indolence [and laziness] and is constantly active [and energetic].[i]

This is because he has faith in the true Divine Perfection; he considers attention to, and attaining other than Him, as an imperfection for himself. Whenever his advancement is slowed, and he faces obstacles, this realization encourages him to remove the obstacles of the path and to not just continue but to accelerate his movement towards Allah. He continuously renews his determination and persists in performing righteous deeds and refraining from disobedience. In this manner he continues his journey:

ضادّوا التّواني بالعزم

Counter laziness with determination [and firm resolution].[ii]

Therefore, it is necessary to ward off laziness at any cost. Based on the statement of Imam al-Bāqir (peace be upon him), laziness harms man's worldly life and the Hereafter, and if a person is lazy regarding his worldly affairs then he will be even lazier with respect to his Hereafter.[iii]

The Necessity of Planning One's Affairs

In order that man's actions reach the desired outcome—in addition to being free from laziness and indolence—they must be performed with planning, prudence, firmness and foresight. Until his actions are not performed with these qualities, steadfastness and continuity of action cannot be acquired. The *awliyā'* of the religion (peace be upon them) have also demanded from us that we follow this method, just

---

i. Majlisī, Bihār al-Anwār, 78:26, narration 92

ii. al-Āmudī, Ghurar al-Hikam, narration 5927

iii. al-Kulaynī, al-Kāfī, 5:85, narration 4

as Amīr al-Muʾminīn ʿAlī (peace be upon him) says:

التَّدْبِيرُ قَبْلَ الْعَمَلِ يُؤْمِنُكَ مِنَ النَّدَمِ

Planning [and prudence] before action makes you secure from remorse. (i)

أَعْقَلُ النَّاسِ أَنْظَرُهُمْ فِي الْعَوَاقِبِ

The most intelligent of the people is one who is the most precise in judging the consequences [of actions and events]. (ii)

لَا خَيْرَ فِي عَزْمٍ بِلَا حَزْمٍ

There is no goodness in that determination and resolve which is not accompanied by firm action. (iii)

He has also said:

الْحَزْمُ النَّظَرُ فِي الْعَوَاقِبِ وَ مُشَاوَرَةُ ذَوِي الْعُقُول

Firm and solid action is [a result of] examining the consequences [of the action] and consulting with people of intellect [and wisdom]. (iv)

الطُّمَأْنِينَةُ قَبْلَ الْخِبْرَةِ خِلَافُ [ضِدُّ] الْحَزْمِ

Trust [in an action or a person] before examining it, is contrary to solid action and farsightedness. (v)

Therefore, a person undertaking the journey towards perfection must do so by being attentive towards these constructive and effective instructions of the *awliyāʾ* of the religion (peace be upon them).

ʿUnwān al-Basrī—despite struggling with the naturally occurring pains and difficulties of old age—did not lose hope after the initial response of the Imam and did not forsake the true path that had become clear for him. Rather, he remained steadfast against the satanic

i. al-Ṣadūq, ʿUyūn akhbār al-Riḍā (peace be upon him), 2:54, narration 204

ii. al-Āmudī, Ghurar al-Ḥikam, narration 3367

iii. Ibid., narration 10682

iv. Ibid., narration 1915

v. Ibid., narration 1514

temptations and let-downs. With prudent action and by taking the right course (that is by beseeching Allah in the presence of the Messenger of Allah—peace and blessings be upon him and his family—and praying to Allah that the Imam's heart becomes considerate towards him), he persisted in his demand until he reached his goal (which was to benefit from the company of Imam al-Sādiq—peace be upon him).

از ثبات خودم این نکته خوش آمد، که به جور

بر سر کوی تو، از پای طلب ننشستم

From my steadfastness, happily came this subtle knowledge,
that by force,I never ceased to seek Your alley. [i]

Al-Shahīd al-Awwal[1] during the days of his imprisonment, would unceasingly raise his hands in prayers and would beseech Allah for deliverance and guidance.

One night while in prison, he wrote this phrase on a piece of paper,

رَبِّي ظُلِمْتُ فَانتَصِر

O my Lord, I am oppressed. Assist and help me!

Then he hid this piece of paper under his pillow, and when a part of the night had passed, he woke up and was astonished to see that behind this piece of paper it was written:

إن كُنْتَ عَبْدِي فَاصْطَبِر

If you are My servant, then be patient and steadfast. [ii]

Severing Worldly Attachments and Bonds

The first and the most significant obstacle on the path of wayfaring is the attachments and ties of the heart. These cause a man to be captivated and imprisoned in the realm of this world. Until a person does not take the courageous step to sever his attachments to the natural world, he is not considered 'a *muhājir* (one who migrates) towards

---

i. Shirāzī, Divān-i Ḥāfiẓ (Taṣḥīḥ-i Qudsī), ghazal 412, couplet 7

ii. Mukāshifāt-i Awliyā-yi Ilāhī, 79

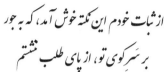

Allah' and this noble verse is not applicable to him:

> وَ مَنْ يُهَاجِرْ فِي سَبِيلِ اللَّهِ يَجِدْ فِي الْأَرْضِ مُرَاغَماً كَثِيراً وَ سَعَةً وَ مَنْ يَخْرُجْ مِنْ بَيْتِهِ مُهَاجِراً إِلَى اللَّهِ وَ رَسُولِهِ ثُمَّ يُدْرِكْهُ الْمَوْتُ فَقَدْ وَقَعَ أَجْرُهُ عَلَى اللَّهِ
>
> Whoever migrates in the way of Allah will find many havens and plenitude in the Earth. And whoever leaves his home [with the intention of] migrating toward Allah and His Apostle, and is then overtaken by death, his reward shall certainly fall on Allah (4:100)

To achieve success on the path of acquiring intellectual and spiritual perfections, one must limit his material attachments and must take steps in the direction of achieving Allah's pleasure, just as Imam al-Ṣādiq (peace be upon him) says:

> جُعِلَ الْخَيْرُ كُلُّهُ فِي بَيْتٍ وَ جُعِلَ مِفْتَاحُهُ الزُّهْدَ فِي الدُّنْيَا
>
> Goodness in its entirety has been placed in a house and *zuhd* (abstinence) from the world has been made the key [of this house].[i]

The Messenger of Allah (peace and blessings be upon him and his family) describes the necessary and minimum limit of *zuhd* in the following words:

> الزُّهْدُ فِي الدُّنْيَا قَصْرُ الْأَمَلِ وَ شُكْرُ كُلِّ نِعْمَةٍ وَ الْوَرَعُ عَنْ كُلِّ مَا حَرَّمَ اللَّهِ
>
> *Zuhd* from the world is to curtail hopes, to be grateful of every favour, and to abstain from things forbidden by Allah.[ii]

Similarly, he describes the highest level of *zuhd* from the world such that man should be striving to attain it, in the following words:

---

i. Majlisī, Biḥār al-Anwār, 73:49, narration 20

ii. al-Ḥarrānī, Tuḥaf al-ʿUqūl, 58

لَيْسَ الزُّهْدُ فِي الدُّنْيَا ... بِتَحْرِيمِ الْحَلَالِ بَلِ الزُّهْدُ فِي الدُّنْيَا أَنْ لَا تَكُونَ بِمَا فِي يَدِكَ أَوْثَقَ مِنْكَ بِمَا فِي يَدِ اللَّهِ عَزَّ وَ جَلَ

Zuhd from this world does not mean . . . to make lawful things forbidden [on oneself], rather it is that one should have more confidence in what is with Allah than in what is with himself. (i)

This means that a person must strive to administer his worldly life; to achieve his soul's perfection he must learn the related disciplines of knowledge—among them being the religious sciences and the science of *tawḥīd* (monotheism)—but at the same time his reliance on these acquired matters should not be more than his reliance on that which is with Allah and is granted to him by Allah. Therefore, the wayfarer must turn his back on all the attachments, even attachments of the heart to the Divine and *tawḥīdī* Sciences. Man can reach such a high station in severing the heart's attachments that in words of Imam ʿAlī (peace be upon him), he does not desire that his *zuhd* becomes known to others. (ii)

The sign of *zuhd* is that:

إِذَا هَرَبَ الزَّاهِدُ مِنَ النَّاسِ فَاطْلُبْه ... إِذَا طَلَبَ الزَّاهِدُ النَّاسَ فَاهْرُبْ مِنْه

When a *zāhid* [one who is detached from the world] runs away from people then seek him, and when he goes after people [to show off] then distance yourself from him. (iii)

تو کز سرای طبیعت نمی روی بیرون

کجا به کوی حقیقت گذر توانی کرد

You who does not step out from the natural and sensual abode,

---

i. Majlisī, Biḥār al-Anwār, 77:172, narration 8

ii. al-Raḍī, Nahj al-Balāghah, saying 28

iii. al-Āmudī, Ghurar al-Ḥikam, narration 4078

How then can you make your way to the alley of the Truth? [i]

For this very reason, the Divine Trainers always advise the wayfarers of the path to cut off the attachments to this world and to disregard one's perfections and knowledge on the path of spirituality. This is because *ḥuṣūlī* (conceptual) knowledge is a preliminary step towards attaining the true *ḥuḍūrī* (presential) knowledge; *ḥuṣūlī* knowledge cannot be the goal and the purpose.[ii] Therefore, not being attached to this knowledge is very different from remaining ignorant and staying away from this knowledge.

Imam Khumaynī (may Allah be pleased with him) says in this regard:

> If spiritual refinement is not given importance, then even the knowledge of tawhīd is of no use. Knowledge is the greatest veil. The more knowledge is accumulated in a person's brain and heart—even if it is the knowledge of tawhīd which is loftiest of all knowledge—if that person is not spiritually refined then it leads him away from Allah.[iii]

با مدعی مگویید اسرار عشق و مستی

تا بی خبر بمیرد در درد خودپرستی

Don't tell the imposter the secrets of love and intoxication,
So that he dies, ignorant and in the suffering of self-adoration.

تا فضل و علم بینی، بی معرفت نشینی

یک نکته‌ات بگویم: خود را مبین که رستی

As long as you see [your own] merit and knowledge, of Divine Wisdom you are bereft,
I'll say one thing to you: Do not see yourself and you will be free!

عاشق شو ار نه روزی کار جهان سر آید

---

i. Shirāzī, Divān-i Ḥāfiẓ (Taṣḥīḥ-i Qudsī), ghazal 132, couplet 7

ii. A more detailed description of these two terms is provided in the second chapter.

iii. Tibyān, 337

ناخوانده نقش مقصود از کارگاه هستی

Become a lover! Or else one day the world's work will end,
While the desired inscription from the workshop of Creation [the orld], would remain unread. [(i)] [(ii)]

When the Imams (peace be upon them) interacted with people, they responded to them in a manner that their audience would not become proud or deceived by their apparent knowledge. The Imams (peace be upon them) turned people's attention towards the true knowledge and genuine Divine Teachings. Those like Hishām Ibn Ḥakam[(2)]—who possessed a soft and tender spirit and a disposition that was ready to accept the truth—humbly submitted themselves to the knowledge of the Ahl al-Bayt (peace be upon them) and drew benefit from it.

Some others like Ibn Abī al-ʿAwjāʾ[(3)]—who had drowned in the veils of this material world—could not benefit from the ocean of the Imam's mercy and died in the state of faithlessness and materialism.

ʿUnwān al-Baṣrī—being over ninety years of age and having crossed various ranks of education under different scholars—initially possessed the distinction of being a scholar. However, with this kind of attachment to his own knowledge he could not truly benefit from the Jaʿfarī teachings. For this reason, Imam al-Ṣādiq (peace be upon him) with his constructive behaviour compelled him to rethink and deliberate on his state, in a manner that he lost trust in all his previous knowledge. He said to himself, "If the Imam had seen any goodness in me he would have never prevented me from visiting him and acquiring knowledge from him." This was a new beginning for him to benefit from the reality of the knowledge of Imam al-Ṣādiq (peace be upon him) and for him to become free from inner obstacles:

به سرّ جام جم آن که نظر توانی کرد

---

i. In this couplet, Ḥāfiẓ (may Allah be pleased with him) is saying that if one does not become a lover of the Almighty during the limited opportunity bestowed to them, then they would not have not read and witnessed the true purpose that He intended them to see in this world.

ii. Shirāzī, Divān-i Ḥāfiẓ (Taṣḥīḥ-i Qudsī), ghazal 538, couplet 1, 3, and 5

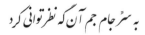

که خاک میکده کحل بصر توانی کرد

A glance at the mysteries of Jamshīd's cup [i] you can only make,
When the dust of the Winehouse is the kohl of your eyes.

گدایی درِ میخانه طرفه اکسیریست

گر این عمل بکنی، خاک زر توانی کرد

Begging at the door of the Winehouse is a wonderful elixir,
If you perform this act, you can make dust into gold.

ولی تو تا لب معشوق و جام می خواهی

طمع مدار که کار دگر توانی کرد

As long as you desire to have the Beauty's lip and the cup of wine,
Don't think that it's possible to have another employment. [ii]

Ḥājj Shaykh Hādī Tihrānī, known as 'Ḥājj Muqaddas', was one of the prominent speakers of Tehran. In terms of the effectiveness of his speech and his reciting of the tragedy of Karbala, very few reciters were as good as him. Hence, he often delivered several speeches in a single day and thus had a shortage of time. He was also from the devotees of the spiritually-refined scholar Marḥūm Āghā Shaykh Murtaḍā Zāhid,[(4)] and attended the gatherings of *akhlāq* (ethics) conducted by that great man. One day, a gathering was organized in the house of Āqā Shaykh Murtaḍā Zāhid. While Shaykh Murtaḍā was reading some narrations of the Ahl al-Bayt (peace be upon them) for the audience, Ḥājj Muqaddas suddenly stood up to leave. Shaykh Murtaḍā Zāhid stopped reading the book, and turning to him as he was about to leave, said, "Where are you going?" Ḥājj Muqaddas replied, "Āqā, I have some work, I must leave." (Apparently, he wanted to go to deliver a speech.) Ḥājj Shaykh

i. The mythological cup of the Persian King Jamshīd was such that the seven heavens of the world could be observed by looking into it. It has been used here to refer to the realm of the *malakūt*, that only one who has reached a lofty spiritual station can look at.

ii. Shirāzī, Divān-i Ḥāfiẓ (Taṣḥīḥ-i Qudsī), ghazal 132, couplet 1, 2, 10

in response said, "Sit for a few minutes and then go!"

Ḥājj Muqaddas again replied saying, "No Āqā, I have work, I must go."

Āqā Shaykh Murtadā in a humorous and witty tone, and with a meaningful smile, calmly said, "You are always saying 'I have work', 'I have work.' Muqaddas, may you become unengaged and free!"

Ḥājj Muqaddas left the session that day to attend to his work, but from that day onwards strange and unusual problems start arising for him. A short while later he became free! Many of his speeches were cancelled due to different reasons, and no one invited him anymore for reciting lectures or narrating the tragedy of Karbala. Whereas earlier he was always short on time due to his commitments, now he had become totally free. As a result, he started thinking about the matter, seeking to find its cause. Finally, he recalled the words of Shaykh Murtaḍā Zāhid when he had said, "You are always saying 'I have work', 'I have work.' Muqaddas, may you become unengaged and free!"

As Hājj Muqaddas himself described, this state continued for two months until he became aware of its cause, visited the Shaykh and offered his apology.

In this manner, Shaykh Murtadā Zāhid detached his spiritual disciple from attention and attachment to affairs other than the Hereafter, even though they may be beneficial things like delivering religious sermons. [i]

Making Positive Use of Failures and Difficulties

Every difficulty and calamity that afflicts man in this world has two different aspects to it. Firstly, the aspect of hardship, strain and unpleasantness that a person must face. Secondly, the aspect of how this calamity relates to Allah. For it is Allah the Wise who has desired to test his faithful servant in the ups and downs of these failures and afflictions; it is He who has sought to reward him with the reward of the patient and the virtuous and elevate him in his spiritual station. Such elevation is the result of steadfastness, success in this examination, and performing one's duty in the face of calamity. The Noble Qur'ān

i. Sayfullāhī, Aqā Shaykh Murtaḍā Zāhid

explains this lofty reality in this manner:

مَا أَصَابَ مِن مُّصِيبَةٍ فِي الْأَرْضِ وَلَا فِي أَنفُسِكُمْ إِلَّا فِي كِتَابٍ مِّن قَبْلِ أَن نَّبْرَأَهَا ۚ إِنَّ ذَٰلِكَ عَلَى اللَّهِ يَسِيرٌ ﴿٢٢﴾ لِّكَيْلَا تَأْسَوْا عَلَىٰ مَا فَاتَكُمْ وَلَا تَفْرَحُوا بِمَا آتَاكُمْ

No affliction visits the land or yourselves, but it is in a Book before We bring it about – that is indeed easy for Allah – so that you may not grieve for what escapes you, nor boast for what comes your way. (57:22-23)

Most people only see the dimension of hardship, strain and unpleasantness in affliction—they complain about the difficulties and unpleasant events. However, true believers pay attention to the other dimension of these calamities and see its connection with Allah. In this manner they are directed and guided towards their Beloved. For this reason, Allah the Exalted says in another verse:

مَا أَصَابَ مِنْ مُصِيبَةٍ إِلاَّ بِإِذْنِ اللَّهِ وَ مَنْ يُؤْمِنْ بِاللَّهِ يَهْدِ قَلْبَهُ

No affliction visits [anyone] except by Allah's leave. And whoever has faith in Allah, He guides his heart . . . (64:11)

At times, afflictions that visit man are apparently unrelated to his voluntary actions and choice. In this case, he must know that there is some wisdom behind it. Allah the Wise has desired to test him through this event and see how much patience he has, and whether he acts according to his duty or not. For example, being confronted by the enemies of religion, diseases and other calamities are afflictions that man's own actions may not have caused. As Imam al-Ṣādiq (peace be upon him) says:

الصَّبْرُ رَأْسُ الْإِيمَان

Patience is the foundation of the faith.(i)

Similarly, Amīr al-Mu'minīn ʿAlī (peace be upon him) says:

بِالصَّبْرِ تُدْرَكُ مَعَالِي الْأُمُور

i. al-Kulaynī, al-Kāfī, 2:87, narration 1

With patience are lofty affairs reached.[i]

Also, the Messenger of Allah (peace and blessings be upon him and his family) when faced with afflictions would say:

الْحَمْدُ لِلَّهِ عَلَى كُلِ حَال

Praise be to Allah in every state.[ii]

Similarly, he says:

بِالصَّبْرِ يُتَوَقَّعُ الْفَرَجُ وَ مَنْ يُدْمِنْ قَرْعَ الْبَابِ يَلِج

With patience relief can be expected. If one persistently knocks on a door, [eventually] it will open.[iii]

Imam al-Ṣādiq (peace be upon him) also says:

الْحَمْدُ لِلَّهِ الَّذِي لَمْ يَجْعَلْ مُصِيبَتِي فِي دِينِي وَ الْحَمْدُ لِلَّهِ الَّذِي لَوْ شَاءَ أَنْ تَكُونَ مُصِيبَتِي أَعْظَمَ مِمَّا كَانَتْ لَكَانَت

All praise is for Allah who did not make my affliction to be in my religion; and all praise is for Allah who if He would have desired my affliction to be greater than this, it would have been so.[iv]

Therefore, sometimes being afflicted with difficulties—such as constriction and narrowness of the soul on the path towards Allah—is a test for man to ensure his firmness and perseverance on this path. In this phase, one must lend his ear to Imam ʿAlī's (peace be upon him) advice:

مَنْ صَبَرَ عَلَى اللَّهِ وَصَلَ إِلَيْه

One who has patience on [the separation or chastisement of] Allah, will reach Him.[v]

گر رنج، پیشت آید و گر راحت ای حکیم

i. al-Āmudī, Ghurar al-Ḥikam, narration 4276

ii. al-Kulaynī, al-Kāfī, 2:97, narration 19

iii. Majlisī, Biḥār al-Anwār, 71:96, narration 61

iv. Ibid., 78:268, narration 183

v. Ibid., 71:95, narration 60

نسبت مکن به غیر، که این‌ها خدا کند

ما را، که درد عشق و بلای خمار هست

یا وصل دوست، یا می صافی دوا کند

Wise man! If sorrow comes your way or if it is ease,
Attribute it to none other, for it is God who does these.
For us is love's pain and the affliction of the Winemaker,[i]
Either connection to the Beloved, or pure wine is our remedy.[ii]

Therefore, not only do the *ʿurafā* and the ardent lovers of the Beloved not flee from tests and tribulations, rather they welcome them. This is because they see these tests as a channel that leads to their encounter and union with the Beloved, just as Allah revealed to Prophet Moses (peace be upon him):

إِذَا رَأَيْتَ الْفَقْرَ مُقْبِلًا فَقُلْ مَرْحَباً بِشِعَارِ الصَّالِحِين

When you see poverty coming your way then say, 'Welcome!
O distinguishing mark of the Righteous.'[iii]

بی‌وفا نگار من، می‌کند به کار من

خنده‌های زیر لب، عشوه‌های پنهانی

ما سیه گلیمان را جز بلا نمی‌شاید

بر دل بهائی نه هر بلا که بتوانی

My disloyal Beloved responds to my acts [my expressions of love],
With a silent giggle and hidden flirting.
Us who are clothed in black robes [of unworthiness] deserve naught
but affliction,

---

i. The affliction of the Winemaker refers to the pain of separation from the Beloved, from not being able to witness Him.

ii. Shirāzī, Divān-i Ḥāfiẓ (Taṣḥīḥ-i Qudsī), ghazal 228, couplet 4 and 5

iii. al-Kulaynī, al-Kāfī, 2:263, narration 12

Place every affliction that You can on the heart of Bahā'ī![5] [i]

Undoubtedly, amid their struggle with these afflictions, such astute people search for the hidden ailments of their soul. In this manner they discover their weak points on the path of spiritual struggle, and subsequently engage in rectifying them. From every failure they reach their desired goal, and in every bitter incident they taste the sweet nectar of perfection. This is because, in every failure and affliction they address themselves and say:

وَمَا أَصَابَكَ مِن سَيِّئَةٍ فَمِن نَّفْسِكَ

And whatever ill befalls you is from yourself. (4:79)

They always bear this important reality in their mind:

مَا مِنْ نَكْبَةٍ تُصِيبُ الْعَبْدَ إِلَّا بِذَنْب

There is no misfortune or calamity that befalls a servant except that it is due to his sin. [ii]

هرچه هست از قامت ناساز بی اندام ماست
ورنه تشریف تو بر بالای کس کوتاه نیست

All that is here [from our faults] is due to our unfitting form,
Otherwise, the garment of Your honour is not too short for anyone [iii]

Marḥūm Ḥājj Shaykh Rajab 'Alī Khayyāṭ (Nikūgūyān)[6] was one of the enlightened individuals who had made vigilance and protection of his heart to be the most important pursuit in his daily routine. As a result, the spark of Divine Mercy had enlightened his heart. The great teacher of *akhlāq*, Marḥūm Ḥājj Shaykh Maḥmūd Taḥrīrī[7] narrates:

> Once Shaykh Rajab 'Alī Khayyāt was crossing a street, when an animal which was tied to a carriage passed from near him. Suddenly the animal came close and kicked in the direction of Shaykh. Shaykh Rajab 'Alī at once sat down

i. Shaykh Bahā'ī

ii. al-Kulaynī, al-Kāfī, 2:269, narration 4

iii. Shirāzī, Divān-i Ḥāfiẓ (Taṣḥīḥ-i Qudsī), ghazal 35, couplet 8

> by the roadside and started pondering over what mistake did he commit. Why did this animal that is Allah's creation, turn against him like this?! After much deliberation and thought, he found the cause and sought forgiveness, then he continued along his way.
> Shaykh Rajab ʿAlī drew the attention of others to such points when they were confronted with difficulties. One day a person who had received a blow to his head that had injured him, came to the Shaykh to know the cause of this mishap. After some consideration the Shaykh said, "You have bothered a young boy at your workplace and if you do not make him happy, then this story [this calamity] will continue." This man confirmed the words of the Shaykh that he had bothered a young boy at the factory. The Shaykh said, "Calamities do not befall you unduly and without a cause." (i)

Undoubtedly, most of the afflictions that visit a person are due to his mistakes and problems in his actions or in his *akhlāq*. These befall him to train and educate him. To dispel these afflictions, man must carry out the appropriate remedy for each affliction, thus ensuring that any evil effects in the Hereafter are wiped out. There are many Islamic narrations that indicate this reality. Amīr al-Muʾminīn ʿAlī (peace be upon him) says:

مَا مِنَ الشِّيعَةِ عَبْدٌ يُقَارِفُ أَمْراً نَهَيْنَاهُ عَنْهُ فَيَمُوتَ حَتَّى يُبْتَلَى بِبَلِيَّةٍ تُمَحَّصُ بِهَا ذُنُوبُهُ إِمَّا فِي مَالٍ وَ إِمَّا فِي وَلَدٍ وَ إِمَّا فِي نَفْسِهِ حَتَّى يَلْقَى اللَّهَ عَزَّ وَ جَلَ وَ مَا لَهُ ذَنْبٌ وَ إِنَّهُ لَيَبْقَى عَلَيْهِ الشَّيْءُ مِنْ ذُنُوبِهِ فَيُشَدَّدُ بِهِ عَلَيْهِ عِنْدَ مَوْتِهِ

> There is no Shia who commits an act prohibited by us and then dies, except that he will first be afflicted with a calamity in his wealth or his children or his own self, so that because of this affliction his sins are shed, and he meets Allah the Invincible and the Majestic with no sin upon him. Sometimes some sins remain, but at the time of his death he is

---

i. Rayshahrī, Tandīs-i Ikhlāṣ, 66

> dealt with severely [so that these remaining sins are also wiped out].(i)

The Messenger of Allah (peace and blessings be upon him and his family) also says:

> مَا أَصَابَ الْمُؤْمِنَ مِنْ نَصَبٍ وَ لَا وَصَبٍ وَ لَا حُزْنٍ حَتَّى الْهَمِّ يُهِمُّهُ إِلَّا كَفَّرَ اللَّهُ بِهِ عَنْهُ مِنْ سَيِّئَاتِه
>
> There is no suffering or illness or grief that reaches a believer—even a worry which preoccupies his mind—except that Allah pardons his sins because of this [affliction].(ii)

Such an outlook and such observations are necessary and inevitable for the wayfarer of the path of spirituality, and a person obtains this outlook because of reflecting on the events and happenings of this world.

Pondering Over Events That Occur in the World

Keeping in mind the previous discussion, and by paying close attention to the events and incidents of this world, it can be understood how many small and insignificant events occur around us that are full of useful and constructive points! These points have the potential to open the knots of our spiritual problems, they can even turn into man's guide, as Amīr al-Mu'minīn ʿAlī (peace be upon him) says:

> مَنِ اعْتَبَرَ أَبْصَرَ وَ مَنْ أَبْصَرَ فَهِمَ وَ مَنْ فَهِمَ عَلِم
>
> Whoever takes instruction [from things around him] perceives, whoever perceives gains understanding, and whoever gains understanding obtains knowledge.(iii)

Of course, a superficial outlook towards these events causes a person to move past them without paying attention to their cause. As a result, he suffers from their undesirable consequences without taking a lesson from it or gaining any desirable benefit from it:

---

i. al-Ṣadūq, al-Khiṣāl, 635, narration 10

ii. al-Ḥarrānī, Tuḥaf al-ʿUqūl, 38

iii. al-Raḍī, Nahj al-Balāghah, saying 208

مَا أَكْثَرَ الْعِبَرَ وَ أَقَلَّ الِاعْتِبَار

How plenty are the admonitions, but how few are the taking of lessons [from these admonitions].[i]

Therefore, according to the Qur'ānic viewpoint, one should view all the events that occur around him as a sign and an indicator that seeks to guide man towards Allah (the Provider of abundance and the Sublime):

سَنُرِيهِمْ آيَاتِنَا فِي الْآفَاقِ وَ فِي أَنْفُسِهِمْ حَتَّى يَتَبَيَّنَ لَهُمْ أَنَّهُ الْحَقُّ

Soon We shall show them Our signs in the horizons and in their own souls until it becomes clear to them that He is the Truth. (41:53)

Reaching this state is not possible until man becomes habituated to reflecting and thinking about the signs and events that occur around him—until he does not carelessly pass by them.

Imam al-Ḥusayn (peace be upon him) says in this regard:

التَّفَكُّرُ حَيَاةُ قَلْبِ الْبَصِير

Reflecting is the life of a clear-sighted and insightful heart.[ii]

Similarly, Imam 'Alī (peace be upon him) says:

مَنْ تَفَكَّرَ أَبْصَر

One who reflects perceives.[iii]

لَا عِلْمَ كَالتَّفَكُّرِ

There is no knowledge like reflection.[iv]

This very factor was the turning point that lead to the guidance of 'Unwān al-Baṣrī. He correctly analysed his disappointment and

i. Ibid., saying 297

ii. Majlisī, Biḥār al-Anwār, 78:115, narration 11

iii. al-Raḍī, Nahj al-Balāghah, saying 31

iv. Ibid., saying 113

failure in his initial encounter with Imam al-Ṣādiq (peace be upon him). Instead of acting emotionally and becoming upset due to the Imam's response, he turned to thinking and pondering about his own self, and said:

> لَوْ تَفَرَّسَ فِيَّ خَيْراً لَمَا زَجَرَنِي عَنِ الاِخْتِلَافِ إِلَيْهِ وَ الْأَخْذِ عَنْهُ
>
> If he had seen any goodness in me, he would not have stopped me from visiting him and acquiring [knowledge] from him.

This matter—at the outset—is very burdensome for the *nafs al-ammārah* (the aspect of man's soul that commands towards evil), because the wayfarer at the beginning of his journey is constantly seeking praise and extolment from others—he flees from others' criticism. But the constructive instructions of the *awliyā'* of religion (peace be upon them) say that man's criticism must start from within his own self, so that this state of criticizing one's self is kindled within him. This state is materialized by careful and realistic self-examination of one's deeds and actions, such that if he has performed a good deed then he resolves to continue it, and if he has committed an evil action, he becomes aware and ashamed of his mistake, makes an earnest intention to not commit it again and seeks forgiveness. Observing these practical points awakens a state in a person such that he accepts the criticism of others and gradually, the malady of self-centeredness present in him is rectified.

The great *'ārif* Imam Khumaynī (may Allah be pleased with him) in a letter addressed to his son, advises him in the following manner:

> O my son!... We must pay attention that the source of our liking the praise and admiration [of others] and our dislike for [their] criticisms and rumours, is love of the self which is the biggest trap of the accursed Satan. We wish that others should praise us even if it is by displaying imaginary meritorious deeds and good qualities as if they are a hundred times better [than they are]... We get dejected due to the fault-finding [of others] not because it is an unjust deed, and we become happy at praise and admiration not because it is just and fair. Rather, [we get upset] because it is my

> shortcoming and it is not my praise. It is this selfishness that is dominant over us, here, there and everywhere ... Maybe and [rather] certainly these fault findings and spreading of rumours [about us] are beneficial for curing the defects of the soul, like a painful surgery that returns a sick person to sound health.[i]

Determination and Tawakkul[ii] on the Path towards Perfection

Correctly discerning the factors that are effective in spiritual wayfaring and the journey towards perfection, and employing them in a proper and timely way, plays a fundamental role in reaching the lofty spiritual goals.

Undoubtedly, some of these factors prepare the ground for the wayfarer to receive spiritual blessings. Having a firm determination and a strong will is one such factor. When man discovers his imperfection and his distance from the lofty goal and realizes the path to reach this goal, if he wishes to achieve success and reach the destination, he must immediately endeavour to remedy this state and create favourable conditions for reaching perfection. In this path he must possess an earnest determination such that whenever he faces failure he does not stop his efforts and his journey.

The Noble Qur'ān, after describing the fact that man will be certainly tested through various affairs, says:

وَ إِنْ تَصْبِرُوا وَ تَتَّقُوا فَإِنَّ ذٰلِكَ مِنْ عَزْمِ الْأُمُورِ

> But if you are patient and God-wary, that is indeed the steadiest of courses. (3:186)

---

i. Khumaynī, Nuqtah-yi ʿAṭf: ʿIrfānī Poems of Imam Khumaynī (may Allah have mercy on him), 29

ii. The original meaning of the noun *tawakkul* is to display weakness and inability. However, in the Islamic context to have *tawakkul* on the Almighty means to exclusively depend on Him and not have any hope or trust in other than Him. Subtleties of this concept will be explained by the author (may his blessings remain) in the forthcoming pages.

In another verse, determination is mentioned prior to tawakkul.[i] Likewise, Imam al-Sajjād (peace be upon him) says addressing Allah:

وَ قَدْ عَلِمْتُ أَنَّ أَفْضَلَ زَادِ الرَّاحِلِ إِلَيْكَ عَزْمُ إِرَادَةٍ يَخْتَارُكَ بِهَا وَ قَدْ نَاجَاكَ بِعَزْمِ الْإِرَادَةِ قَلْبِي

> And I know with certainty that the best provision for a person who has departed towards you, is firmness of determination. Through this he chooses You [over others]. And my heart has whispered to You with a firm determination.[ii]

Other factors effective in spiritual wayfaring perform the function of clearing obstacles and eliminating worldly attachments that appear on the path of wayfaring. For example, remembering death and the Hereafter liberates man from his attachments to the material world. Amīr al-Mu'minīn ʿAlī (peace be upon him) considered the remembrance of death to be the destroyer of false wishes and desires, saying:

مَنْ رَاقَبَ أَجَلَهُ قَصَّرَ أَمَلَه

> One who is heedful of death, his longings are curtailed.[iii]

ذِكْرُ الْآخِرَةِ دَوَاءٌ وَ شِفَاءٌ

> Remembrance of the Hereafter is a remedy and cure [for the ailments of man's soul and the heart].[iv]

More important than all these is a factor that connects man to the source of Divine Grace and Mercy, and in reality, is itself a cause of man's spiritual development. Through this factor, man's soul—which now with its determination, will and remembrance of death is ready to acquire perfection—attains spiritual blessings and realities. Tawakkul is this element that links man to the Source of all the creation, Allah the Exalted. On the other hand, tawassul is the direct connection of

---

i. (3:159)

ii. Ibn Ṭāwūs, Iqbāl al-Aʿmāl, 678

iii. al-Āmudī, Ghurar al-Ḥikam, narration 5175

iv. Ibid., narration 7944

the wayfarer's heart to the intermediaries of Divine Grace. No ʿārif and wayfarer is free from needing these two factors, and any kind of discrepancy and flaw in these two, disrupts the descending of Divine Grace onto the heart of the wayfarer.

Therefore, it is necessary that the position of these two factors is clarified with regards to other factors. Undoubtedly, while one is attentive to the importance and necessity of tawakkul and tawassul, attention must also be paid to other factors that prepare the ground for benefitting from these two.

Extremes in Tawakkul and Striving

The more a factor plays a decisive and fundamental role in man's ascent to the peaks of spiritual perfection, the more it should be subjected to careful and special consideration—thereby the wayfarer can derive correct and complete benefit from it. If the wayfarer is heedless of the banes and potential threats to this factor, then this same factor can hinder his progress and perfection.

For example, an incorrect understanding of *tawakkul* and going to either extreme (laxity or excessiveness) regarding it, has led to the deviation of many wayfarers of the path. Those who do not take any efforts, and by solely depending on trust in Allah await the emanation of Divine Grace, are grossly mistaken. That is because the Noble Qurʾān says:

وَ الَّذِينَ جَاهَدُوا فِينَا لَنَهْدِيَنَّهُمْ سُبُلَنَا

> As for those who strive in Us, We shall surely guide them in Our ways, (29:69)

گرچه وصالش نه به کوشش دهند

آن قدر ای دل! که توانی بکوش

Although union with Him is not the result of efforts,
Yet, O heart! Strive to the extent you can. [i]

i. Shirāzī, Divān-i Ḥāfiẓ (Taṣḥīḥ-i Qudsī), ghazal 843, couplet 5

In the affairs of this worldly life, this reality holds true:

جَاءَ رَجُلٌ إِلَى رَسُولِ اللَّهِ فَقَالَ يَا رَسُولَ اللَّهِ أُرْسِلُ نَاقَتِي وَ أَتَوَكَّلُ أَوْ أَعْقِلُهَا وَ أَتَوَكَّلُ قَالَ اعْقِلْهَا وَ تَوَكَّلْ.

A person said to the Messenger of Allah (peace and blessings be upon him and his family), "O Messenger of Allah! Should I tie my camel and then place trust in Allah or should I set it free and then put trust in Allah?" Messenger of Allah replied, "Tie it and then place your trust in Allah." (i)

Similarly, Imam al-Sādiq (peace be upon him) says:

إِنَّ قَوْماً مِنْ أَصْحَابِ رَسُولِ اللَّهِ ص لَمَّا نَزَلَتْ وَ مَنْ يَتَّقِ اللَّهَ يَجْعَلْ لَهُ مَخْرَجاً وَ يَرْزُقْهُ مِنْ حَيْثُ لا يَحْتَسِبُ أَغْلَقُوا الْأَبْوَابَ وَ أَقْبَلُوا عَلَى الْعِبَادَةِ وَ قَالُوا قَدْ كُفِينَا فَبَلَغَ ذَلِكَ النَّبِيَّ ص فَأَرْسَلَ إِلَيْهِمْ فَقَالَ مَا حَمَلَكُمْ عَلَى مَا صَنَعْتُمْ قَالُوا يَا رَسُولَ اللَّهِ تُكُفِّلَ لَنَا بِأَرْزَاقِنَا فَأَقْبَلْنَا عَلَى الْعِبَادَةِ فَقَالَ إِنَّهُ مَنْ فَعَلَ ذَلِكَ لَمْ يُسْتَجَبْ لَهُ عَلَيْكُمْ بِالطَّلَب

When this verse, "And whoever puts his trust in Allah, He will suffice him" (ii) was revealed, a group of companions of the Messenger of Allah (peace and blessings be upon him and his family) confined themselves in their houses and busied themselves in worship and said, "We have been taken care of [by Allah]!" This news reached the Messenger of Allah (peace and blessings be upon him and his family). He sent a group towards them and said to them, "What has led you to act in this manner?!" They replied, "O Messenger of Allah! Our sustenance has been guaranteed so we have turned to worship." He replied, "Someone who acts in this manner, [his prayer] is not heard. It is upon you to seek

---

i. Rayshahrī, Mīzān al-Ḥikmah, 10:685

ii. (65:3)

[your sustenance]." (i)

Similarly, those who only depend on their efforts without attention to this factor of *tawakkul*, are striving in vain. Amīr al-Mu'minīn 'Alī (peace be upon him) says:

إِيَّاكَ وَ الثِّقَةَ بِنَفْسِكَ فَإِنَّ ذَلِكَ مِنْ أَكْبَرِ مَصَايِدِ الشَّيْطَان

Beware of relying on your own self. For certainly it is one of the biggest traps of Satan. (ii)

به جدّ و جهد چو کاری نمی رود از پیش

به کردگار رها کرده، به مصالح خویش

If [even] by striving and struggling, the work does not progress,
Hand over [the affairs] to the Creator, that is better for your interests. (iii)

The correct path is that a person recognizes the position of each of these effective factors that play a role on the path of spiritual wayfaring, and then appropriately benefits from each of them to the degree of their effectiveness. The Noblest Messenger (peace and blessings be upon him and his family) once asked the angel Gabriel about *tawakkul* and he replied:

الْعِلْمُ بِأَنَّ الْمَخْلُوقَ لَا يَضُرُّ وَ لَا يَنْفَعُ وَ لَا يُعْطِي وَ لَا يَمْنَعُ وَ اسْتِعْمَالُ الْيَأْسِ مِنَ الْخَلْقِ فَإِذَا كَانَ الْعَبْدُ كَذَلِكَ لَمْ يَعْمَلْ لِأَحَدٍ سِوَى اللَّهِ وَ لَمْ يَرْجُ وَ لَمْ يَخَفْ سِوَى اللَّهِ وَ لَمْ يَطْمَعْ فِي أَحَدٍ سِوَى اللَّهِ فَهَذَا هُوَ التَّوَكُّل

[It is] knowing that the created beings neither cause harm nor benefit, they neither grant nor forbid; [it is] expressing a lack of hope in the people. So, when a servant becomes such, he does not work for [anyone] other than Allah, and

---

i. al-Kulaynī, al-Kāfī, 5:84, narration 5

ii. al-Āmudī, Ghurar al-Ḥikam, narration 2678

iii. Shirāzī, Divān-i Ḥāfiẓ (Taṣḥīḥ-i Qudsī), ghazal 332, couplet 1

he neither hopes nor fears [anyone] other than Allah, and he aspires for none other than Allah. This is [the reality of] trust in Allah.[i]

It means that, even though a person performs all his apparent activities and engages in social relationships, still his heart is attentive and has faith in the Eternal and Sufficient Divine Source. He seeks the real outcome from Him, and thus, he does not perform any action for other than Him.

Tawakkul in the Conduct of the *Awliyā'* of Allah

The important position of *tawakkul*—along with efforts, striving and *jihād*[ii] on the path of Allah—is clearly seen in the conduct of the *awliyā'* of religion (peace be upon them) and the eminent *'urafā*. How many individuals were at the zenith of *jihād* and struggle against their self but would still not see their own efforts and would not rely on them! Rather, they would place their hope in Allah the Exalted's All-Embracing Mercy. This very quality caused the doors of spirituality to open for them. This is the secret behind the unceasing worships of the Imams (peace be upon them) on one hand, and their expression of helplessness, need and humility in front of Allah on the other. For example, Imam Zayn al-'Ābidīn (peace be upon him) says to Allah:

اللَّهُمَّ إِنِّي أُصْبِحُ وَ أُمْسِي مُسْتَقِلّاً لِعَمَلِي، مُعْتَرِفاً بِذَنْبِي، مُقِرّاً بِخَطَايَاي ... وَ إِيَّاكَ أَسْتَعِينُ، وَ بِكَ أُومِنُ، وَ عَلَيْكَ أَتَوَكَّلُ، وَ عَلَى جُودِكَ وَ كَرَمِكَ أَتَّكِل

O Allah! I spend my day and my night considering my actions little, confessing my sins, admitting my mistakes . . . from You alone I seek help, in You alone I have faith, in You alone I put trust, and only on Your generosity and

i. al-Ṣadūq, Ma'ānī al-Akhbār, 261, narration 1

ii. The word *jihād* as well as *mujāhadah* are two gerunds (verbal nouns) of the verb *jāhada*. Linguistically, they mean to exert the utmost effort, strive, endeavour, etc. As an Islamic term, they refer to exerting efforts in resisting the enemy—both external enemies and internal (Satan and the soul).

munificence do I rely. (i)

The great *ʿārif* and *mufassir* (exegete) of the Noble Qurʾān, ʿAllāmah Muḥammad Ḥusayn Ṭabāṭabāʾī (may Allah be pleased with him) was like this. Despite his striving and *murāqabah,* (ii) he would always consider the cause of his success to be the hidden favours of Allah which strengthened him and protected him from the very beginning of his spiritual development. He has beautifully explained this reality in a poem, saying:

من به سرچشمه خورشید نه خود بردم راه

ذره ای بودم و مهر تو مرا بالا برد

To the source of the radiant Sun, I did not lead myself,
I was nothing but a speck that out of Your mercy, You raised.

من خسی بی سروپایم که به سیل افتادم

او که می رفت مرا هم به دل دریا برد

Unworthy, insignificant, and feeble was I until the flood overcame me,
He who moved [in the flood] also carried me to the heart of the river.

همه یاران به سر راه تو بودیم ولی

غم روی تو مرا دید و ز من یغما برد

We were all devotees of Your path, however,
The sorrow of Your face saw me and pillaged me. (iii)

همه دل باخته بودیم و پریشان که غمت

i. Zayn al-ʿĀbidīn (peace be upon him), al-Ṣaḥīfah al-Sajjādiyyah, supplication 52

ii. *Murāqabah* literally means to attentively watch and supervise something. Here it refers to a state of self-vigilance whereby the wayfarer ensures he does not neglect any of his duties.

iii. In the same manner that sorrow engulfs a grief-stricken individual, the love of the Almighty overwhelms the *ʿārif* and becomes his sole concern. In the same manner that a band of thieves plunder and pillage, leaving behind nothing, similarly His love leaves behind no other attachments when it descends upon a heart.

همه راپشت سر انداخت مرا تنها برد

We were all enraptured by You and anxious, when Your sorrow,
Left everyone else behind and took me alone. [(i)]

The great *ʿārif* and the revered teacher, Shaykh ʿAlī Saʿādatparwar (may Allah be pleased with him)—himself a product of the spiritual training of ʿAllāmah Ṭabāṭabāʾī (may Allah be pleased with him)—at the peak of his spiritual struggle and *murāqabah*, describes his state in the following words:

> From the beginning of the formation of my embryo in my mother's womb, and thereafter in this world, [many] incidents have occurred in my life such that I have always seen the hidden hand of the Beloved, training and protecting me.

گر نگهدار من آن است که من می دانم
شیشه را در بغل سنگ نگه می دارد

If my protector is the One whom I know,
Then he can keep glass safe despite being surrounded by stone [(ii)]

After recalling the factors of his success in the spiritual journey, he says:

> All that was mentioned until now and was read by the readers, was not so that I introduce myself as someone who has reached perfection and who was a student of ʿAllāmah Tabātabāʾī (may Allah be pleased with him). Although, "The soul indeed prompts [men] to evil, except inasmuch as my Lord has mercy." [(iii)] However, the purpose [behind mentioning these things] was to show how the Divine Hand trained me from my childhood until the demise of the late teacher [ʿAllāmah Tabātabāʾī], and so that it serves as an eye-opener for those to come. [(iv)]

---

i. ʿAllāmah Ṭabāṭabāʾī

ii. Sabū-yi ʿIshq, 17

iii. (12:53)

iv. Sabū-yi ʿIshq, 44

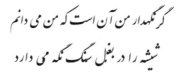

These great *'urafā* who have reached the alley of the Beloved, at the height of their spiritual struggle and *murāqabah*, considered Allah's Grace and His Divine hand to be the sole cause of their success—they would only rely on this cause. By no means would such *tawakkul* cause any inadequacy in their efforts and struggle.

Similarly, 'Unwān al-Baṣrī, after his initial encounter with Imam al-Ṣādiq (peace be upon him), visited the Prophet's Mosque, offered two units of prayer, and supplicated to Allah:

أَسْأَلُكَ يَا اللَّهُ يَا اللَّهُ أَنْ تَعْطِفَ عَلَيَّ قَلْبَ جَعْفَرٍ وَ تَرْزُقَنِي مِنْ عِلْمِهِ مَا أَهْتَدِي بِهِ إِلَى صِرَاطِكَ الْمُسْتَقِيمِ

> O Allah! O Allah! I ask you to soften heart of Ja'far towards me and provide for me from his knowledge [a share] through which I am guided to your Straight Path.

Then after a few days, he visited the Imam again and this time the Imam accepted him in his presence, advising and guiding him.

The Necessity of Tawassul in Reaching Perfection

Entities of this world, due to their existential limitations, have been created in a manner that they are dependent on each other. Due to this reason, Allah creates and administers them through intermediaries. Although at times Allah attributes this administration to Himself:

يُدَبِّرُ الْأَمْرَ

[Allah] directs the affairs [of the World] (10:3)

At other times He ascribes it to the intermediaries:

فَالْمُدَبِّرَاتِ أَمْرًا

By those who direct the affairs [of creatures] (79:5)

All other affairs of the World are also the same. Therefore, it is not wrong and detestable to attribute these affairs to the intermediaries of Divine Grace. In fact, these intermediaries are themselves aware of this attribution, like the Prophet Jesus (peace be upon him) who says:

أَنِّي أَخْلُقُ لَكُم مِّنَ الطِّينِ كَهَيْئَةِ الطَّيْرِ فَأَنفُخُ فِيهِ فَيَكُونُ طَيْرًا
بِإِذْنِ اللَّهِ وَأُبْرِئُ الْأَكْمَهَ وَالْأَبْرَصَ وَأُحْيِي الْمَوْتَىٰ بِإِذْنِ اللَّهِ

I will create for you the form of a bird out of clay, then I will breathe into it, and it will become a bird by Allah's leave. I heal the blind and the leper and I revive the dead by Allah's leave. (3:49)

In addition to this, asking the intermediaries for our needs is also mentioned in the Noble Qurʾān, as can be seen when Prophet Joseph (peace be upon him) said to his brothers:

اذْهَبُوا بِقَمِيصِي هَٰذَا فَأَلْقُوهُ عَلَىٰ وَجْهِ أَبِي يَأْتِ بَصِيرًا وَأْتُونِي
بِأَهْلِكُمْ أَجْمَعِينَ

Take this shirt of mine and cast it upon my father's face; he will regain his sight and bring me all your folks. (12:93)

Or when sons of Prophet Jacob (peace be upon him) said to him:

يَا أَبَانَا اسْتَغْفِرْ لَنَا ذُنُوبَنَا

Father! Plead [with Allah] for forgiveness of our sins! (12:97)

Prophet Jacob (peace be upon him) also said in reply:

سَوْفَ أَسْتَغْفِرُ لَكُمْ رَبِّي

I shall plead with my Lord to forgive you; (12:98)

Therefore, *tawassul* is to establish a connection with the intermediaries of the abundant Divine Mercy; it is to ask for the manifestation of the names of beauty and majesty of Allah in this world through their means. Because the Imams (peace be upon them) are the complete manifestations of all the beautiful names of Allah, every Divine perfection that man seeks, must be sought through them. Every wayfarer must request the manifestation of those names in his heart by their means. For this reason, we read in the *Ziyārah al-Jāmiʿah*, addressing the Imams (peace be upon them):

> مَنْ أَرَادَ اللَّهَ بَدَأَ بِكُمْ ... وَ مَنْ وَحَّدَهُ قَبِلَ عَنْكُمْ وَ مَنْ قَصَدَهُ تَوَجَّهَ بِكُم
>
> One who desired Allah, started with you; . . . one who brought faith in His Oneness, accepted it from you; one who intended Him, became attentive [of Him] through you.(i)

Wilāyah of the Ahl al-Bayt (peace be upon them) has different manifestations and many different aspects on the path of man's spiritual perfection—understanding it in brief is necessary and essential at the beginning of the journey.

The First Manifestation of Wilāyah in Wayfaring

The first manifestation of *wilāyah* is through *tawassul* to the *awliyā'* (guardians) of religion and the infallible Imams (peace be upon them). *Tawassul* to the Ahl al-Bayt (peace be upon them) is amonZg the factors that no wayfarer is needless of, from the beginning of the journey up until its end. This is because the Imams (peace be upon them) are the intermediaries of Divine Grace; every material and spiritual goodness and benefit in this world that reaches the servants of Allah and all entities, reaches through them. As has been said in the *Ziyārah al-Jāmi'ah*:

> فَازَ الْفَائِزُونَ بِوَلَايَتِكُمْ بِكُمْ يُسْلَكُ إِلَى الرِّضْوَانِ وَ عَلَى مَنْ جَحَدَ وَلَايَتَكُمْ غَضَبُ الرَّحْمَن
>
> The successful ones have succeeded through your *wilāyah*, through you it is possible to traverse and reach Divine Pleasure, and upon the one who rejects your *wilāyah* is the wrath of the Merciful.(ii)

'Allāmah Ṭabāṭabā'ī (may Allah be pleased with him) says regarding the role of *tawassul* on the path of spiritual wayfaring:

> Most of those who succeeded in freeing the mind from thoughts—those who managed to clear and purify their

---

i. Majlisī, Biḥār al-Anwār, 102:129-131

ii. Ibid.

> mind, cleanse it from thoughts, and eventually reach the level where the Divine Teachings dawned and disclosed themselves for them—achieved this in one of two states: First is the state of recitation of the Noble Qur'ān and paying attention to its reciter as to who in reality is the reciter of the Qur'ān? In this state it was revealed to them that the reciter of the Qur'ān is Allah, the Almighty. Second is through tawassul to Abū ʿAbd Allah al-Husayn (peace be upon him), because his existence is a great Divine Favour for removing veils and obstacles from the path of spiritual wayfaring.(i)

This same point has also narrated from the great man of God, Marḥūm Qāḍī (may Allah be pleased with him). He has said:

> The flow of Divine Grace and goodness is through the Master of the Martyrs (peace be upon him) and which in turn flows through the Qamar (shining full moon) of the Banū Hāshim, Abū al-Fadl al-ʿAbbās (peace be upon him).(ii)

ای دل! غلامِ شاه جهان باش و شاه باش

پیوسته در حمایتِ لطفِ إله باش

O heart! Be the servant of the King of the World(iii) and [then you will] be a king,
You will continuously be in the protection of the Grace of God.

از خارجی، هزار به یک جو نمی خرند

گو: کوه تا به کوه، منافق سپاه باش

From the khārijī [one outside of the wilāyah] one-thousand actions are not bought for a single grain of barley,
Say [it is so], even if he has an army of hypocrites from mountain to

---

i. Ṭabāṭabā'ī, Risālah Lubb al-Albāb, 158

ii. Āmūlī, Duwwumīn Yādnāmih-yi ʿAllāmah Ṭabāṭabā'ī (may Allah's mercy be on him), 296

iii. A reference to the eighth noble Imam, Imam ʿAlī ibn Mūsa al-Riḍā (peace be upon him) as is clear from the remainder of the poem, not included here by the author (may his blessings remain).

mountain.

آن را که دوستی علی نیست، کافر است

گو زاهدِ زمانه و گو شیخِ راه باش

He who has not the friendship of ʿAlī is a disbeliever,
Say [it is so], even if he is the [most famous] ascetic of his time or a Shaykh of the path.

امروز زنده ام، به ولای تو یا علیّ!

فردا به روح پاک امامان، گواه باش

Today I am alive by your wilāyah O ʿAlī!
Tomorrow bear witness [for me] in front of the spirits of the pure Imams. (i)

It is also narrated from Marḥūm Qāḍī (may Allah be pleased with him):

> Reaching the station of *tawḥīd*, correct wayfaring towards Allah, and *ʿirfān* of the essence of the One God, is impossible without the *wilāyah* of the Shīʿah Imams and the true Caliphs, ʿAlī ibn Abī Ṭālib and his progeny from the pure Lady Fāṭimah (peace be upon them). (ii)

For this same reason, Āyatullāh Sayyid ʿAlī Qādī would consider the Qurʾān and the sacred progeny (peace be upon them) to be the source of all his spiritual stations and perfections. He would say:

> If I have reached any spiritual station it is due to two things: One is the Noble Qurʾān, and the other is *ziyārah* of the Master of Martyrs (peace be upon him). (iii)

از رهگذرِ خاکِ سرِ کوی شما بود

هر نافه که در دستِ نسیمِ سحر افتاد

---

i. Shirāzī, Divān-i Ḥāfiẓ (Taṣḥīḥ-i Qudsī), ghazal 328, couplet 1, 2, 4, and 5

ii. Tihrānī, Rūḥ-i Mujarrad, 320

iii. Hāshimīyān, Daryā-yi ʿIrfān, 98

It was due to the dust of Your alley,
That every fragrant musk which fell into hand of the early-morning breeze, came. [(i)]

The Second Manifestation of *Wilāyah* in Wayfaring

The wayfarer on the path towards true spirituality must know that the Imams (peace be upon them) are not only the intermediaries of spiritual grace from Allah the Immaculate. In addition to this, the effect and results of the wayfarer's beliefs, moral attributes and inward qualities are achieved through the *wilāyah* of the Ahl al-Bayt (peace be upon them). This is the case regarding all his actions that have effects both in the next world and on his soul. Every reward that affects man's soul has its effect based on the hidden and esoteric dimension of the Imam's *imāmah* (leadership). This is one of the most important points that the wayfarer must pay attention to.

ʿAllāmah Ṭabāṭabāʾī (may Allah be pleased with him) says in this regard:

> Just as the Imam is the leader and guide of the people in their outward actions, he also holds the position of leadership and *imāmah* with regards to the inward, spiritual dimension. He is the leader of the caravan of humanity that undertakes this inward and esoteric journey to Allah. [(ii)]

After explaining this reality, he goes on to say:

> A person who is entrusted by Allah with the leadership of a nation, in the same manner that he is their leader and the guide at the level of their outward actions, similarly he is their leader in the spiritual life. It is through his leadership that the reality of their actions moves forward. [(iii)]

It is this reality that is intended when the Imams (peace be upon them) are referred to as being the *ṣirāṭ* (the path). This is because the wayfarer not only journeys with the help of the Imam (peace be upon

---

i. Shirāzī, Divān-i Ḥāfiẓ (Taṣḥīḥ-i Qudsī), ghazal 142, couplet 5

ii. Ṭabāṭabāʾī, Shīʿah dar Islām, 122

iii. Ibid., 124.

him) but rather he journeys with the Imam and in the context of the Imam's *wilāyah*. We read in the *Ziyārah al-Jāmiʿah*:

أَنْتُمُ الصِّرَاطُ الْأَقْوَمُ وَ شُهَدَاءُ دَارِ الْفَنَاءِ وَ شُفَعَاءُ دَارِ الْبَقَاءِ وَ الرَّحْمَةُ الْمَوْصُولَةُ وَ الْآيَةُ الْمَخْزُونَةُ ... إِلَى اللَّهِ تَدْعُونَ وَ عَلَيْهِ تَدُلُّونَ وَ بِهِ تُؤْمِنُونَ وَ لَهُ تُسَلِّمُونَ وَ بِأَمْرِهِ تَعْمَلُونَ وَ إِلَى سَبِيلِهِ تُرْشِدُونَ

You are the upright path [to Allah], and witnesses of the temporary abode, and the intercessors in the lasting abode, and the perpetual mercy, the reserved sign [of Allah], . . . towards Allah you invite, to Him you guide, in Him you believe, to Him you submit, by His command you act, and to His path you show the way.[i]

In the words of Khwāja-yi Shirāz[8]:

من به سر منزل عنقا، نه به خود بردم راه

قطع این مرحله با مرغ سلیمان کردم

By myself I did not find the path to the home of the ʿanqā, [ii]
Traversing this journey, I did along with the bird of Solomon [iii] [iv]

---

i. Majlisī, Biḥār al-Anwār, 102:129

ii. The *ʿanqā* is a mystical bird in Persian literature, like the phoenix in Greek mythology. The bird lives on top of Mount Qāf, and its inaccessible home is used in such poetry to refer to a lofty spiritual station. In another poem Ḥāfiẓ says:

عنقا شکار کس نشود دام بازچین

The ʿanqā is not the prey of anyone, gather your hunting net!

iii. The bird of Solomon is the hoopoe, also mentioned in the Noble Qurʿān. Here it is used to refer to the perfect man, or the spiritual teacher, one who can lead the other birds to the *ʿanqā*.

iv. Shirāzī, Divān-i Ḥāfiẓ (Taṣḥīḥ-i Qudsī), ghazal 421, couplet 2

The Third Manifestation of *Wilāyah* in Wayfaring

Seeking help from the infallible Imams (peace be upon them) is not only necessary and essential while traversing the stages and stations of the spiritual journey, but even after reaching the intended destination and the heart's witnessing of *tawḥīd*, it is still needed. At that stage the reality of the *wilāyah* of the Imams (peace be upon them) and their station of light becomes apparent for the *'ārif*, as Amīr al-Mu'minīn 'Alī (peace be upon him) says:

> مَعْرِفَتِي بِالنُّورَانِيَّةِ مَعْرِفَةُ اللَّهِ عَزَّ وَ جَلَ وَ مَعْرِفَةُ اللَّهِ عَزَّ وَ جَلَّ مَعْرِفَتِي بِالنُّورَانِيَّةِ وَ هُوَ الدِّينُ الْخَالِص
>
> My recognition of the light is [in fact] the recognition of Allah the Invincible and the Majestic, and the recognition of Allah the Invincible and the Majestic is [in fact] my recognition of the station of light, and this is the pure religion.(i)

It is due to this that Marḥūm Qāḍī (may Allah be pleased with him) believed that it is impossible that an *'ārif* has not recognized the reality of *wilāyah*. It is narrated from him:

> It is impossible that a person reaches the station of *tawḥīd* and *'irfān*, and acquires *tawḥīdī* stations and perfections, while the matter of *wilāyah* is not uncovered for him.

He believed that:

> The renowned personalities whose names have been recorded in the books of *'irfān* and have been considered *wāṣil* and *fānī* [one who has annihilated himself in the Divine], but were not people of *wilāyah* and were from the Sunnis, either they were not *wāṣil* and they falsely claimed to have reached this reality, or they had witnessed the reality of *wilāyah* but due to some reason they were in state of *taqiyyah*(ii) and would not divulge their beliefs. Examples

---

i. Majlisī, Biḥār al-Anwār, 26:1, narration 1

ii. *Taqiyyah* is a noun derived from the root verb *waqaya*. Linguistically it means to exercise restraint and caution. As an Islamic term, it refers to dissimulating and hiding one's beliefs to protect oneself.

of such personalities are Shaykh Sulaymān Qandūzī Ḥanafī the writer of 'Yanābī' al-Mawaddah', Sayyid 'Alī Hamadānī the writer of 'Mawaddat al-Qurbā' and Mawlā Muḥammad Rūmī Balkhī the writer of 'Mathnawī'. (i)

Types of Tawassul to the Awliyā' of Religion (peace be upon them)

By observing the conduct of the folk of gnosis (*ahl al-ma'rifah*), we come to understand that there are three overall types of *tawassul* one can perform to the holy station of the Infallibles (peace be upon them). Through these three, the *'urafā* would show their reverence to the Ahl al-Bayt (peace be upon them) and would cause the ocean of their mercy to pour down upon them.

1. Outward Tawassul

This type of *tawassul* is carried out in the form of religious rituals. Examples of its manifestation are: organizing weekly mourning sessions (*'azādārī*), participating in gatherings of joy and mourning for the Ahl al-Bayt (peace be upon them), and mentioning their virtues and their teachings and the oppression meted out to them by their enemies. *Ziyārah* of the noble shrines of the Ahl al-Bayt (peace be upon them) while in the state of humility, is also an example of this type of *tawassul*.

Imam al-Ṣādiq (peace be upon him) says in this regard:

نَفَسُ الْمَهْمُومِ لَنَا الْمُغْتَمِّ لِظُلْمِنَا تَسْبِيحٌ وَ هَمُّهُ لِأَمْرِنَا عِبَادَة

> The breath of a person aggrieved for us, anguished at the oppression done to us, is [Allah's] glorification, and his concern for our affair is worship. (ii)

مَنْ قَالَ فِينَا بَيْتَ شِعْرٍ بَنَى اللَّهُ تَعَالَى لَهُ بَيْتاً فِي الْجَنَّة

> One who reads one verse of poetry about us, Allah the Exalted builds a house for him in the Garden. (iii)

---

i. Tihrānī, Tawḥīd-i 'Aynī wa 'Amalī, 40 (slightly summarised)

ii. al-Kulaynī, al-Kāfī, 2; 226, narration 16

iii. al-Ṣadūq, 'Uyūn Akhbār al-Riḍā (peace be upon him), 1:7, narration 1

It is written in the biography of the great *ʿārif* and philosopher Mullā Ṣadrā:(9)

> One of the regular activities of Mullā Ṣadrā was to undertake difficult journeys to the Ḥajj (Makkah) and the land of *Ḥijāz*, the *ziyārah* of the sacred graves of Amīr al-Muʾminīn (peace be upon him), the third Imam, Imam al-Ḥusayn (peace be upon him), and the other martyrs of Karbala in Iraq. In this manner, seven times he journeyed to perform *ziyārah* and the Ḥajj. It was during his last such journey that he passed away in Iraq because of an illness and was buried there. [i]

Similarly, it is mentioned in the biography of the pious scholar Shaykh Murtaḍā Zāhid:

> He had an intense devotion for the Ahl al-Bayt (peace be upon them) and would consider reciting in the mourning ceremonies for Imam al-Ḥusayn (peace be upon him) to be an honour. One day, after performing *tawassul* to the Master of Martyrs (peace be upon him), in a dream he saw himself amidst the grief-stricken tents of Imam al-Ḥusayn (peace be upon him) in Karbala. In this state, these words were being imparted to him and he also started to repeat them:
>
> هَذَا عَزَاكَ يَا حُسَيْن، رُوْحِي فِدَاكَ يَا حُسَيْن
>
> This is your mourning O Husayn! May my soul be sacrificed for you O Husayn!
>
> While these words were communicated to him, a strange agony and grief overcame him. From then onwards, whenever he would read this lamentation on the day of *ʿĀshūrāʾ* or *Tāsūʿā* [ii] the people would wail and cry in loud voices. [iii]

Reciting the *Ziyārah ʿĀshūrā*, *Ziyārah al-Jāmiʿah*, and other similar *ziyārāt* is also one act of *tawassul* which can connect a man with the pure and infallible Ahl al-Bayt (peace be upon them).

---

i. Ṣadrā, al-Maẓāhir al-Ilāhiyyah (Introduction), 266

ii. The 9th of the month of Muharram.

iii. Sayfullāhī, Aqā Shaykh Murtaḍā Zāhid, 189

Āyatullāh al-ʿUẓmā Bahjat (may Allah be pleased with him) narrates:

> Everyday Shaykh Anṣārī (may Allah be pleased with him)[(10)] would recite the *Ziyārah ʿĀshūrā* with the hundred salutations and hundred curses in the *ḥaram* (shrine) of Amīr al-Muʾminīn (peace be upon him), in half an hour. Undoubtedly, he was able to recite very quickly because in normal circumstances it is not possible to complete the *Ziyārah ʿĀshūrā* with the hundred curses and salutations in half an hour. Combining all the worship, religious deeds and devotions [that he would perform], along with all the reading, teaching and writing that he would [also] perform, was [like] a contradiction and an extraordinary act. The religious devotions that he would perform regularly were the *nawāfil* (the daily supererogatory prayers), the prayer of *Jaʿfar al-Ṭayyār*, *Ziyārah al-Jāmiʿah*, *Ziyārah ʿĀshūrā* and one *juzʾ* of the Noble Qurʾān.[(i)] [(ii)]

The great *ʿārif*, Marḥūm Qāḍī (may Allah be pleased with him) recommends this point in his will and testament:

> As for some other advice . . . do not be careless of the *mustaḥabb* (supererogatory) actions of conducting mourning ceremonies and the *ziyārah* of the Master of Martyrs (peace be upon him). A weekly mourning ceremony for Imam al-Ḥusayn (peace be upon him), even if only two or three people are present, is a means of unlocking and removing difficulties. Even if we—from the beginning of our life up until its end—offer our condolences, perform the *ziyārah* and other acts of devotion in the service of that noble personality, we can never pay back his right on us. If it is not possible to hold such weekly gatherings, then do not forsake

---

i. These acts of worship were part of the daily routine of this great scholar (may Allah be pleased with him). Undoubtedly, such a routine is not feasible for most people and would lead to negative consequences. However, what is important is that—after taking the advice of pious and trustworthy experts—we must be working towards such a station, continuously improving and slowly increasing the amount of worship we perform.

ii. Rukhshād, Dar Maḥḍar-i Ayatullāh Bahjat, 1:254 (slightly summarised)

them in the first ten days of Muharram. [i]

The important point to note about this type of *tawassul* is that firstly one must refrain from going to the extremes (excessiveness or laxity) and should plan them in such a manner that it does not negatively affect man's other duties and obligations.

It is mentioned in the accounts of Imam Khumaynī (may Allah be pleased with him) that during his fifteen-year stay in Najaf, he would never forsake the *ziyārah* of Amīr al-Mu'minīn (peace be upon him). But despite being at the peak of this wholehearted devotion to the Imams (peace be upon them), he once said to the Iraqi Chief of Intelligence Sadoun Shakir, "I am not one of those *sayyids* whom *ziyārah* would make him forgetful of his duty." [ii]

Also, in the long-term, excessive loud weeping incurs negative physical effects on the wayfarer's body and the nerves such that attention must be paid to this issue.

The great *'ārif*, Marḥūm Shaykh Maḥmūd Taḥrīrī—who himself was amongst the constant weepers and his weeping for the calamities of the Ahl al-Bayt (peace be upon them) is still remembered by his friends—would always advise some of his sons that they should abstain from loud weeping so that they are saved from its physical and neural harms.

Without a doubt, endurance and continuity in showing humility to the Ahl al-Bayt (peace be upon them) as a form of *tawassul* is desirable and fruitful. Therefore, the wayfarer should assign time for *tawassul* in his schedule, such that he always maintains a connection with the Ahl al-Bayt (peace be upon them).

2) Practical Tawassul

This means to pay precise attention to and implement the instructions of the Imams (peace be upon them) in all aspects of life (be it devotional, domestic, economic, social, cultural or political). This is a point emphasized in many Islamic narrations, that one should not consider love of the Ahl al-Bayt (peace be upon them) alone, to be

i. Hāshamiyān, Daryā-yi 'Irfān, 1119

ii. Yād-i Yār, Islamic Republic of Iran Newspaper, 13th Khordād 1369, 9-10 sufficient. Imam al-Bāqir (peace be upon him) says:

وَ اللَّهِ مَا مَعَنَا مِنَ اللَّهِ بَرَاءَةٌ وَ لَا بَيْنَنَا وَ بَيْنَ اللَّهِ قَرَابَةٌ وَ لَا لَنَا عَلَى اللَّهِ حُجَّةٌ وَ لَا نَتَقَرَّبُ إِلَى اللَّهِ إِلَّا بِالطَّاعَةِ فَمَنْ كَانَ مِنْكُمْ مُطِيعاً لِلَّهِ تَنْفَعُهُ وَلَايَتُنَا وَ مَنْ كَانَ مِنْكُمْ عَاصِياً لِلَّهِ لَمْ تَنْفَعْهُ وَلَايَتُنَا وَيْحَكُمْ لَا تَغْتَرُّوا وَيْحَكُمْ لَا تَغْتَرُّوا

> By Allah! We do not possess any guarantee from Allah of freedom [from the Hellfire and difficulties], and there is no kinship between us and Allah and we have no *ḥujjah* [i] on Allah, and we do not seek His proximity except through obedience. So, if a person amongst you is obedient to Allah then our *wilāyah* will benefit him, and if a person amongst you is disobedient to Allah then our *wilāyah* has no benefit for him. Woe unto you! Do not be deceived! Woe unto you! Do not be deceived! [ii]

Therefore, this type of *tawassul* is the foundation of a relationship accompanied with humility, and an expression of devotion and love to the holy station of the Ahl al-Bayt (peace be upon them). Along with the first kind of *tawassul*, this second type prepares man's soul so that he can then enter the third level (which embodies a very profound reality).

3) Inward Tawassul

Attentiveness to the radiant station of the Ahl al-Bayt (peace be upon them) in all conditions and always is a lofty stage of *tawassul* to them.

This attentiveness, which manifests itself to the wayfarer at a specific stage of spiritual wayfaring, causes him to always witness himself in the presence of the Imam (peace be upon him). He sees all his affairs and the affairs of all other created beings to be in the Imam's control. This is because the Imams (peace be upon them) are the intermediaries of

---

i. The word *ḥujjah* is a noun that means a clear proof. The word stems from the verb *iḥtajja*, meaning to argue or protest something. Therefore, a *ḥujjah* is a proof that is used in an argument.

ii. al-ʿĀmilī, Waṣāʾil al-Shīʿah, 11:185, narration 4

Allah the Exalted's grace. Through the heart's comprehension of this reality, the wayfarer at this stage always sees himself to be in a state of humility, in the noble presence of the Imam (peace be upon him). In every need that he has (be it to do with the creation or not), he extends his needy hand towards these eminent personalities, so that they manifest for him their station of mediation and make him reach the perfection he is worthy of.

It is quoted from the great *ʿārif* and *wāṣil*, Ḥājj Shaykh Maḥmūd Taḥrīrī (may Allah be pleased with him) that he said, "At every moment I am in state of *tawassul* to the Ahl al-Bayt (peace be upon them)."

Also, the *wāṣil ʿārif*, Āyatullāh Bahjat (may Allah be pleased with him) has said in this regard:

> The Imam of the time (may Allah hasten his noble reappearance) is
>
> عَيْـنُ اللَّـهِ النَّاظِـرَةُ وَ أُذُنُـهُ السَّـامِعَةُ وَ لِسَـانُهُ النَّاطِـقُ فِـي خَلْقِـهِ وَ يَـدُهُ الْمَبْسُـوطَة
>
> *Allah's eye that watches, His ears that hears, His tongue that speaks; and His hands that are wide open.* [i]
>
> He is aware of our speech, our actions, our thoughts and our intentions. Despite this, it is as if we do not consider our Imams (peace be upon them), especially the Imam of the time (may Allah hasten his noble reappearance), to be present and watching. Rather, it is as if, like the Sunnis, we do not consider him alive and are totally heedless of him. [ii]

ʿUnwān al-Baṣrī was eager to benefit from the enlightened presence of Imam Jaʿfar al-Ṣādiq (peace be upon him) and after his initial encounter with Imam al-Ṣādiq (peace be upon him) he completely lost hope in all outward means that would allow him to benefit from the Imam. At this point, he turned to the two factors of *tawakkul* and *tawassul*. Thus,

---

i. This description of the Imam (peace be upon him) may be found in the following sources with slight variations in the wording: Majlisī, Biḥār al-Anwār, 26:240; al-Ṣadūq, al-Tawḥīd, 167; al-Ṣadūq, Maʿānī al-Akhbār, 16.

ii. Rukhshād, Dar Maḥḍar-i Ayatullah Bahjat, 1:22

by resorting to the Noblest Messenger (peace and blessings be upon him and his family) he prayed in this manner, "O Allah! O Allah! I ask you to soften heart of Jaʿfar towards me and provide for me from his knowledge [a share] through which I am guided to your straight path."

Having the Company of a Spiritual Teacher the Reasons for its Need

Allah (the Provider of abundance and the Sublime), administers the system of creation based on the rules of cause-and-effect. He has made the coming into existence of every phenomenon and entity dependent on the existence of its causes, its conditions and its necessary environment. Education and spiritual training—which is the purpose behind the sending of prophets (peace be upon them)—is not an exception to this principle of cause-and-effect:

هُوَ الَّذِي بَعَثَ فِي الْأُمِّيِّينَ رَسُولاً مِنْهُمْ يَتْلُو عَلَيْهِمْ آيَاتِهِ وَ يُزَكِّيهِمْ وَ يُعَلِّمُهُمُ الْكِتَابَ وَ الْحِكْمَةَ

> It is He who sent to the unlettered [people] an apostle from among themselves, to recite to them His signs, to purify them, and to teach them the Book and wisdom . . . (62:2)

For the latent human potential to bear fruit and manifest Allah's names of majesty and beauty in the mirror of man's existence, a suitable background and environment is required. This is necessary for the container of man's existence to acquire the ability to receive the Divine Grace from the Unseen Realm.

One of the factors that prepares the ground for the wayfarer, is the presence of pure-natured persons for whom the veils of darkness and light have been lifted from the face of their *fiṭrah*. Such people can guide others out of the darkness of the physical world and teach the wayfarer the manner of journeying in the *malakūtī*[i] realm. Imam

---

i. The word *malakūt*, is a noun derived from the word *mulk* meaning kingdom, dominance, or authority. The former however contains a higher level of intensity not present in the latter. The meaning in this context is a realm that the wayfarer enters after the reality of Allah's true dominance over the creation is witnessed.

al-Sajjād (peace be upon him) says:

هَلَكَ مَنْ لَيْسَ لَهُ حَكِيمٌ يُرْشِدُه

> Destroyed is one who does not have a wise [teacher] to guide him.(i)

Therefore, the teacher must be someone acquainted with the realties, the path to reach them, and the obstacles along the way; he must himself be spiritually developed, have traversed the path, and be aware of its obstacles so that he can save others from destruction. Certainly, such a person is someone other than the Imams (peace be upon them) because the Imams are themselves the leaders of such spiritually-developed individuals. This spiritual teacher must have reached wisdom and perfection by adhering to the enlightened teachings of the Imams (peace be upon them), so that he can then help others reach this wisdom and perfection.

به کوی عشق منه بی دلیلِ راه، قدم
که گم شد آن که در این ره به رهبری نرسید

Do not step in the Alley of Love without a guide,
For lost is the one who did not find a leader on this path (ii)

The great *'ārif*, Imam Khumaynī (may Allah be pleased with him) has said in this regard:

> Man must try to find a proficient [spiritual] doctor . . . In his *malakūtī* journey man must try to find a guide of the path, and when he finds the guide, then he should submit to him . . . We who are afflicted with sickness [of the heart] and are astray, need to obtain the prescription for the *malakūtī* journey and the diseases of our heart from the guides of the path of guidance, the healers of souls and doctors of spirits. We should act according to it [their prescription] without employing our own inadequate thoughts and weak opinions so that we can reach the destination, which is to

i. Majlisī, Biḥār al-Anwār, 78:159

ii. Shirāzī, Divān-i Ḥāfiẓ (Taṣḥīḥ-i Qudsī), ghazal 201, couplet 6

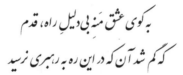

reach the secrets of *tawḥīd*.[(i)]

یارِ مردان خدا باش که در کشتی نوح
هست خاکی که به آبی نخرد طوفان را

Be the friend of the men of God, for in the Ark of Noah,
There is dust that not a drop of the flood has touched.[(ii)] [(iii)]

1. Referring to an Expert in Every Branch of Knowledge

To learn any branch of knowledge or discipline, one must refer to an expert in that field. In their day-to-day affairs, people naturally refer to experts and specialists in every area. For example, following the progress and development of science and the introduction of many branches and specializations, referring to a general practitioner and physician for a critical illness related to the heart or brain would be considered illogical.

The great teacher of *akhlāq*, Imam Khumaynī (may Allah be pleased with him) says about this:

> Why is it that the science of Jurisprudence (*Fiqh*) and the Principles of Jurisprudence (*Uṣūl al-Fiqh*) requires a teacher, studying and academic discussion, [in fact] for every science and industrial field a teacher and an expert is required, and no one becomes a specialist, a *faqīh* (jurist), a scholar just by himself? However, the fields of spiritual knowledge and *akhlāq*—which is the goal of the raising of the prophets and is amongst the most subtle and precise sciences—does not require teaching and learning?! They can be learnt without a teacher and through self-study?![(iv)]

Likewise, the complete teacher Marḥūm Āyat al-Ḥaqq, Shaykh ʿAlī

---

i. Khumaynī, Sharḥ-i Junūd-i ʿAql wa Jahl, 403

ii. That is, companionship with the men of God will protect you from the afflictions, just as how there was dust in Noah's ark that remained unscathed from the flood.

iii. Shirāzī, Divān-i Ḥāfiẓ (Taṣḥīḥ-i Qudsī), ghazal 10, couplet 5

iv. Khumaynī, Jihād-i Akbar, 23

Saʿādatparwar says:

> It is no secret for any person of sound intellect that it is not possible to learn any of the material sciences (required for the continuity of life) or the non-material sciences, without a teacher. Spiritual wayfaring and reaching the lofty stations of spirituality is higher than all other sciences and is more difficult than any other discipline. It is impossible to complete [this journey] without a teacher and guide. Therefore, before all else it is incumbent upon the seekers of this path to choose a guide possessing purity of character, who is well-acquainted with the principles of Islam, and who himself was trained under a teacher, so that by acting on his instructions he can traverse this dangerous and lofty Divine Path. (i)

2. Safety from the Perils of the Spiritual Journey

The more valuable and important a goal is, the more perils and dangers threaten those who seek that goal. To the degree that man comes closer to the lofty spiritual perfections, the precision and sensitivity of the path increases, and man's fall from this station will be more difficult and onerous.

If the teacher of the path and the guide of the way has himself traversed the path and reached perfection, he can take the wayfarer through the difficult and arduous passageways and can help him confront the calamities of the path.

حافظا! از دست مده صحبت آن کشتی نوح

ورنه طوفان حوادث، ببرد بنیادت

Ḥāfiẓ! Don't let that Ark of Noah slip from your hand,
Or else the deluge of calamities will destroy your foundation. *(ii)*

The story of Balʿam bin Bāʿūrāʾ serves as a good lesson for those who are in pursuit of acquiring spiritual perfection. He had traversed

---

i. Saʿādatparwar, Jamāl-i Āftāb, volume 3, preface

ii. Shirāzī, Divān-i Ḥāfiẓ (Taṣḥīḥ-i Qudsī), ghazal 72, couplet 7 stages of spiritual perfection and had even acquired the *ism al-aʿẓam* (the Supreme Name of Allah). But in a Divine test he gave precedence to his own ego over Allah's pleasure, and became abased, wretched, and was cast out from the Divine proximity:

> وَ اتْلُ عَلَيْهِمْ نَبَأَ الَّذِي آتَيْنَاهُ آيَاتِنَا فَانْسَلَخَ مِنْهَا فَأَتْبَعَهُ الشَّيْطَانُ فَكَانَ مِنَ الْغَاوِينَ وَ لَوْ شِئْنَا لَرَفَعْنَاهُ بِهَا وَ لٰكِنَّهُ أَخْلَدَ إِلَى الْأَرْضِ وَ اتَّبَعَ هَوَاهُ فَمَثَلُهُ كَمَثَلِ الْكَلْبِ إِنْ تَحْمِلْ عَلَيْهِ يَلْهَثْ أَوْ تَتْرُكْهُ يَلْهَثْ ذٰلِكَ مَثَلُ الْقَوْمِ الَّذِينَ كَذَّبُوا بِآيَاتِنَا فَاقْصُصِ الْقَصَصَ لَعَلَّهُمْ يَتَفَكَّرُونَ
>
> Relate to them an account of him to whom We gave Our signs, but he cast them off. Thereupon Satan pursued him, and he became one of the perverse. Had We wished, We would have surely raised him by their [the signs'] means, but he clung to the Earth and followed his [base] desires. So, his parable is that of a dog: if you make for it, it lolls out its tongue, and if you let it alone, it [still] lolls out its tongue. Such is the parable of the people who deny Our signs. So, recount these narratives [unto them], so that they may reflect. (7:76)

قطع این مرحله بی همرهی خضر مکن
ظلمات است، بترس از خطر گمراهی

Unless you have Khiḍr as a companion, don't travel this road,
For it is darkness: fear the danger of losing your way. (i)

The great *ʿārif*, Imam Khumaynī (may Allah be pleased with him) says the following about the danger of the ego meddling in the heart and the intention of the wayfarer, and the necessity of benefiting from a spiritual teacher:

> In this journey if even a small portion of the wayfarer's ego

i. Ibid., ghazal 572, couplet 7.

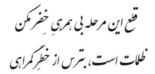

> remains, the Satan which is inside him appears with the attribute of Lordship ... And therefore, the people of wayfaring believe that it is indispensable for the wayfarer to have a [spiritual] teacher that leads him to the path of wayfaring.[i]

3. Benefitting from Appropriate Instructions

In the corpus of Islamic teachings, there are many programs and practical instructions for man's spiritual development and progress. But all of them are not on the same level. Some of them are for the public while some others are only suitable for those who have attained a certain degree of perfection.

Some of them are like food in that they must be continuously consumed by the soul, while others are like medicine that must be used only at specified times and with specific instructions. Naturally, if a program which is intended for medicinal use is used as food, then it will be lethal and destructive. One of the dangerous things for the wayfarer is the way he performs certain recitations and spiritual programs that need the instructions of a learned and experienced teacher to derive benefit from them. The great teacher of *akhlāq* and spiritual training, ʿAllāmah Ṭabāṭabāʾī (may Allah be pleased with him) was once asked:

> The scholars of *akhlāq* and the teachers of mysticism instruct their students to recite certain *adhkār*[ii] and prayers, as part of their spiritual training and purification on the path of wayfaring. Can others also perform the same *adhkār* without instructions from a spiritual teacher?

He replied:

> No, it's not possible. Because they teach these *adhkār* to them according to their situation and the conditions of their [spiritual] state. These same instructions for others are like a grenade in their hands! It can be dangerous for them.

---

i. Imam Khumaynī, Miṣbāḥ al-Hidāyah, 209

ii. *Adhkār* is the plural of *dhikr*. Lexically the word *dhikr* means to remember or remind. As an Islamic term it is used to refer to the words and phrases by which Almighty Allah is mentioned, praised, thanked, glorified, or besought for help.

He was then asked, "If these instructions are dangerous, then how can the teachers instruct them to their students? Does it not create any danger for them?" ʿAllāmah said in reply, "The concern of the teacher alongside the *dhikr*, averts its danger." (i)

4. Preventing Excessiveness and Laxity of the Wayfarer

Another peril that threatens the wayfarer is going to either extreme of excessiveness or laxity (*ifrāṭ or tafrīṭ*). This can afflict the wayfarer and prevent him from traversing the path. As Amīr al-Mu'minīn ʿAlī (peace be upon him) says:

لَا تَرَى الْجَاهِلَ إِلَّا مُفْرِطاً أَوْ مُفَرِّطا

> You will not see an ignorant person except [in the state of being] excessive or lax and neglectful. (ii)

Only a proficient teacher—who thoroughly understands the student's spiritual state—can guide and control him, thereby saving him from this danger. Studying Islamic narrations or books of *akhlāq* and wayfaring, without referring to a teacher and without proficient understanding of the principles of this journey of self-refinement, is not only unhelpful, but sometimes can lead to ideological, spiritual, psychological or physical abnormalities. At times this can be seen in pure-hearted youth who desire to undertake the spiritual journey. Sometimes when such individuals do not achieve results, they deny the path itself and are then incapable of traversing the path!

One of the scholars narrates:

> In the days of my youth, I started thinking about [taking steps for] self-refinement and because I was naïve I would often end up going to the extremes of excessiveness and laxity. One day I went to the house of my teacher Āyatullāh Shaykh ʿAbbās Ṭihrānī.(11) He saw that my face had turned dark because of the hardships I had subjected myself to. He said, "What are these things that you are doing?! This is against *sharīʿah*." I said, "But alas, the *nafs al-ammārah*

---

i. Rukshaād, Dar Maḥḍar-i ʿAllāmah Ṭabāṭabāʾī, 376

ii. al-Raḍī, Nahj al-Balāghah, saying 70

is such and such." He said, "The *nafs al-ammārah* will not be corrected through these actions. Once I went with my son to an orchard. When we entered there, a dog attacked us. I did everything [to ward off the dog], but I saw this is a ferocious dog and there is no way to escape. I called out to the owner of the orchard that, 'Come and get your dog.' The dog's owner came and made one gesture to the dog and the dog left. Ask Allah to free you from the evil of your soul!" In any case, I was destroying myself [with these actions] but with this instruction of my teacher, I was awakened and [thereafter] I took care of myself. (i)

5. Giving Hope to the Wayfarer

Despair and hopelessness is one of Satan's weapons through which he deprives many wayfarers from the path of perfection. Along the path of self-refinement man faces ups and downs, and sometimes the periods of stagnation and regress become long. As a result, a state of spiritual pressure, laziness and indolence afflicts the wayfarer and prevents him from movement. The spirit of despair appears in him and Satan also aggravates this state. At this moment there is a need to motivate and encourage him to continue the path and strengthen himself.

The teacher, with his Messiah-like breath, can breathe the spirit of hope into the wayfarer's being.

ای دل! ار سیل فنا، بنیادِ هستی بَر کَنَد

چون تو را نوح است کشتیبان، ز طوفان غم مخور

O Heart! If the flood of fate sweeps away life's foundation,
When in this torrent, Noah is your Captain, do not grieve! *(ii)*

'Allāmah Ṭabāṭabā'ī (may Allah be pleased with him) narrates:

During the time that I was studying in Najaf, one of the years our connection in Iraq with Iran, was cut off. This brought about poverty and a lack of the basic necessities of life. In

i. Nūrmuḥammadī, Du 'Ārif-i Sālik, 140

ii. Shirāzī, Divān-i Ḥāfiẓ (Taṣḥīḥ-i Qudsī), ghazal 305, couplet 9 addition to financial problems, the intense heat of the long summer had put us under more stress. One day—extremely tired of these unpleasant and uneasy circumstances, and with dark clouds of despair and grief that had troubled my mind and thoughts—I went to visit the teacher of *akhlāq*, Āyatullāh Sayyid ʿAlī Qāḍī (may Allah be pleased with him) and recounted to him my heart's sorrow. In a fascinating manner, he admonished and consoled me. The wondrous statements of my teacher became engraved in my heart in such a manner that all the sorrows were purged from my heart, and when I returned from the presence of this great teacher, it seemed my heart had become so light that I had no worry in life.[i]

پیر خرد پیشه و نورانی ام

برد ز دل رنگ پریشانی ام

گفت: که در زندگی آزاد باش

هان! گذران است جهان، شاد باش

My wise and radiant Pīr effaced the colour of distress from my heart,
He said: In life, be free. Look! This life is fleeting, so be happy.[ii]

6. Curing the Diseases of the Soul

Man's soul, just like his body, can be exposed to injuries and diseases. In this situation, it requires treatment and clinical attendance, as Imam ʿAlī (peace be upon him) says addressing his son:

أَلَا وَ إِنَّ مِنَ الْبَلَاءِ الْفَاقَةَ وَ أَشَدُّ مِنَ الْفَاقَةِ مَرَضُ الْبَدَنِ وَ أَشَدُّ مِنْ مَرَضِ الْبَدَنِ مَرَضُ الْقَلْبِ

Certainly, one of the calamities is poverty and destitution, and more severe than poverty and destitution are bodily illness, and more severe than bodily illnesses are disease of

i. Qāsimlū, Ṭabīb-i ʿAshiqān, 43

ii. ʿAllāmah Ṭabāṭabāʾī

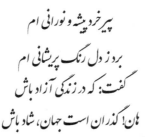

the heart.[i]

No one can claim that his soul is secure from diseases and ailments, except self-refined and trained men who have given a Divine colour to their inclinations and who have been connected to the source of Divine Grace. In the words of Amīr al-Muʾminīn ʿAlī (peace be upon him):

> الشَّرُّ كَامِنٌ فِي طَبِيعَةِ كُلِّ أَحَدٍ فَإِنْ غَلَبَهُ صَاحِبُهُ بَطَنَ وَ إِنْ لَمْ يَغْلِبْهُ ظَهَر
>
> Evil lurks in every person's nature. So, if it is overcome by that person then it remains hidden, and if the person does not overcome it then it becomes apparent.[ii]

It is evident that self-treatment, in the same way that it is dangerous for the treatment of bodily diseases, is many times more dangerous for the treatment of spiritual diseases. That is because it causes a man to lose all his spiritual assets. As Allah has said:

> قُلْ هَلْ نُنَبِّئُكُمْ بِالْأَخْسَرِينَ أَعْمَالاً الَّذِينَ ضَلَّ سَعْيُهُمْ فِي الْحَيَاةِ الدُّنْيَا وَ هُمْ يَحْسَبُونَ أَنَّهُمْ يُحْسِنُونَ صُنْعاً
>
> Say, "Shall we inform you who are the biggest losers in their works? Those whose efforts are misguided in the life of the world, while they suppose they are doing good." (18:4-5)

The Noble Qurʾān introduces these naïve, deluded labourers as the biggest losers. Allah the Immaculate has sent the prophets (peace be upon them) and the *awliyāʾ* towards mankind for the treatment of spiritual diseases. Amīr al-Muʾminīn (peace be upon him) describes the Noblest Messenger (peace and blessings be upon him and his family) in this manner:

---

i. al-Raḍī, Nahj al-Balāghah, saying 388

ii. al-Āmudī, Fihrist-i Mawḍūʿī-yi Ghurar al-Ḥikam, chapter on *sharr* (evil)

> طَبِيبٌ دَوَّارٌ بِطِبِّهِ قَدْ أَحْكَمَ مَرَاهِمَهُ وَ أَحْمَى مَوَاسِمَهُ يَضَعُ ذَلِكَ حَيْثُ الْحَاجَةُ إِلَيْهِ مِنْ قُلُوبٍ عُمْيٍ وَ آذَانٍ صُمٍّ وَ أَلْسِنَةٍ بُكْمٍ مُتَتَبِّعٌ بِدَوَائِهِ مَوَاضِعَ الْغَفْلَةِ وَ مَوَاطِنَ الْحَيْرَةِ
>
> [He is like] a roaming doctor who has made ready his ointments and heated his instruments. He uses them wherever the need arises for curing blind hearts, deaf ears, and dumb tongues. By means of his medicine, he seeks out the spots of heedlessness and places of perplexity.[i]

After the prophets (peace be upon them) and *awliyā'* (peace be upon them), it is the scholars of *akhlāq* and the educators of the souls who bear this responsibility of treating the souls of people. They treat every disease in a manner that is appropriate for its stage and condition, by relying on the Qur'ān and the Sunnah.

Keeping this point in mind, 'Unwān al-Baṣrī went back to the Imam after the initial rejection by Imam al-Ṣādiq (peace be upon him). After performing *tawassul* to the Messenger of Allah (peace and blessings be upon him and his family), and after prayer and supplication in the sacred proximity of his grave, he again visited the house of the Imam so that Imam's heart would become soft towards him. When he knocked on the door, the Imam (peace be upon him) allowed him in his house.

Gratitude Towards the Teacher

Those who are thirsty for the clear water of *ma'rifah* know very well that finding a spiritual teacher who can guide them to the destination of intellectual or practical perfection, is extremely valuable and important. Anyone who acquires this significant godsend should know that he has traversed a major portion of the journey and that this is a great blessing that Allah has apportioned for him. As Allah quotes from the words of Prophet Moses (peace be upon him) when he meets Khiḍr (peace be upon him)—someone whom Allah had conferred His Mercy upon, and had granted abundant knowledge:

---

i. al-Raḍī, Nahj al-Balāghah, sermon 108

قَالَ لَهُ مُوسَىٰ هَلْ أَتَّبِعُكَ عَلَىٰ أَن تُعَلِّمَنِ مِمَّا عُلِّمْتَ رُشْدًا

Moses said to him, "May I follow you for the purpose that you teach me some of the right knowledge you have been taught?" (18:66)

Therefore, when someone gains access to this great blessing (Divine Knowledge and Realities) through a knowledgeable and enlightened teacher, he should be grateful for it. He should pursue it with seriousness and should not object to it and complain about it. Rather, he should submit to the teacher and follow him. Also, he should not enter matters that are inappropriate for him, until he develops the readiness for it.

Imam ʿAlī (peace be upon him) says in this regard:

جَالِسْ أَهْلَ الْوَرَعِ وَ الْحِكْمَةِ وَ أَكْثِرْ مُنَاقَشَتَهُمْ فَإِنَّكَ إِنْ كُنْتَ جَاهِلًا عَلَّمُوكَ وَ إِن كُنْتَ عَالِماً ازْدَدْتَ عِلْماً

Associate with people of piety and wisdom and increase your discussion with them. For if you lack knowledge they will teach it to you, and if you are knowledgeable then your knowledge will increase. [(i)]

He also says:

جَالِسِ الْحُكَمَاءَ يَكْمُلْ عَقْلُكَ وَ تَشْرُفْ نَفْسُكَ وَ يَنْتَفِ عَنْكَ جَهْلُكَ

Associate with the wise! Your intellect will become complete, your soul will become noble, and your ignorance will be effaced. [(ii)]

The great *ʿārif* of the century, Āyatullāh Sayyid ʿAlī Qāḍī (may Allah be pleased with him) has said:

If one spends half of his life in search of a complete [spiritual]

---

i. al-Āmudī, Ghurar al-Ḥikam, narration 4783

ii. Ibid., narration 4787

> teacher, he has not suffered loss. It is for this reason that in the olden days, great scholars—despite having already studied extensively—would undertake journeys to reap the harvest of teachers who were scattered around different cities. Shaykh Anṣārī (may Allah be pleased with him) made various trips to the cities of Isfahan, Kashan, Shushtar, etc. The intellectual or spiritual reputation of any scholar would draw him to that scholar's abode.

Similarly, Marḥūm Mullā Ḥusaynqulī Hamadānī(12) underwent great pain and hardship in search of a spiritual teacher. Therefore, those who have the *tawfiq* (Divinely provided opportunity) to benefit from the presence of teachers—either teachers of intellectual or spiritual matters—should be thankful for this *tawfiq*. Even if they are only able to be in the presence of this teacher for a short duration, they must be thankful that they can benefit from his spiritual personality, his heavenly admonitions, and his prayers. 'Unwān al-Baṣrī was also overcome with joy when he was allowed to enter the presence of Imam al-Ṣādiq (peace be upon him) and in response to Imam's kindness and prayer for him, he said to himself:

لَوْ لَمْ يَكُنْ لِي مِنْ زِيَارَتِهِ وَ التَّسْلِيمِ غَيْرُ هَذَا الدُّعَاءِ لَكَانَ كَثِيراً

> If I did not gain anything from visiting and greeting him except this prayer of his for me, still it would be a great thing.

How many individuals had a transformation occur in them due to their encounter with a great personality! That one moment became a turning point in their intellectual and spiritual life:

It is narrated that a person named Qāsim lived in the city of Najaf. He was known for engaging in sin and debauchery. Despite possessing all these moral vices, he has a special attachment and love of Marḥūm Qāḍī (may Allah be pleased with him). He would always lie in wait for him so that when he arrived, he could greet him. Marḥūm Qāḍī (may Allah be pleased with him) would also—out of his concern for him—constantly advise him and say to him that he must recite his prayers and act according to the *sharī'ah*, but Qāsim paid no attention to these words. Many years passed by. Then one day Marḥūm Qāḍī (may Allah be pleased with him) said to him, "Tonight you must wake up for the Night Prayer (*Ṣalāt al-Layl*)." Qāsim replied, "O my Sayyid! Firstly, I am at the bar until late at night, therefore I cannot wake up in the middle of the night. Secondly, I do not pray at all and you are advising me to recite the Night Prayer." Marḥūm Qāḍī replied, "Do not worry! I will wake you up from the sleep at any time you want." Qāsim woke up from the sleep in the middle of the night in an unusual state. He went to the courtyard to perform *wuḍū'*. But as soon as his eyes fell upon the water, a marvellous inner transformation and change occurred in him and the same Qāsim who was famous for debauchery and sin, now became one of the spiritual personalities and ascetics of Najaf.[i]

To express his gratitude towards his teacher, the wayfarer should take this statement of Imam Zayn al-'Ābidīn (peace be upon him) as his role model:

وَ حَقُّ سَائِسِكَ بِالْعِلْمِ التَّعْظِيمُ لَهُ وَ التَّوْقِيرُ لِمَجْلِسِهِ وَ حُسْنُ الِاسْتِمَاعِ إِلَيْهِ وَ الْإِقْبَالُ عَلَيْهِ وَ أَنْ لَا تَرْفَعَ عَلَيْهِ صَوْتَكَ وَ لَا تُجِيبَ أَحَداً يَسْأَلُهُ عَنْ شَيْءٍ حَتَّى يَكُونَ هُوَ الَّذِي يُجِيبُ وَ لَا تُحَدِّثَ فِي مَجْلِسِهِ أَحَداً وَ لَا تَغْتَابَ عِنْدَهُ أَحَداً وَ أَنْ تَدْفَعَ عَنْهُ إِذَا ذُكِرَ عِنْدَكَ بِسُوءٍ وَ أَنْ تَسْتُرَ عُيُوبَهُ وَ تُظْهِرَ مَنَاقِبَهُ وَ لَا تُجَالِسَ لَهُ عَدُوّاً وَ لَا تُعَادِيَ لَهُ وَلِيّاً فَإِذَا فَعَلْتَ ذَلِكَ شَهِدَ لَكَ مَلَائِكَةُ اللَّهِ بِأَنَّكَ قَصَدْتَهُ وَ تَعَلَّمْتَ عِلْمَهُ لِلَّهِ جَلَّ اسْمُهُ لَا لِلنَّاسِ.

And it is the right of the one who teaches you knowledge that you: show reverence to him, respect his gathering, listen to him properly, turn to face him, and do not raise your voice over his voice. Also, do not answer if someone else asks him a question, until he himself answers it; do not speak with others in his gathering, do not backbite anyone in his presence, and defend him if someone speaks ill about him. You must: hide his defects and make apparent his virtues and good traits, not associate with his enemy and not harbour

i. Hāshimīyān, Daryā-yi 'Irfān, 76

> enmity towards his friend. If you act in this manner, then Allah's angels will testify that you [really] intended him and that you have acquired his knowledge for the sake of Allah—exalted be His name—and not for the sake of the people.[i]

Likewise, in another statement this great Imam (peace be upon him) says:

> أَنْ تُفَرِّغَ لَهُ عَقْلَكَ وَ تُحَضِّرَهُ فَهْمَكَ وَ تُزَكِّيَ لَهُ قَلْبَكَ وَ تُجَلِّيَ لَهُ بَصَرَكَ بِتَرْكِ اللَّذَّاتِ وَ نَقْصِ الشَّهَوَاتِ وَ أَنْ تَعْلَمَ أَنَّكَ فِيمَا أَلْقَى إِلَيْكَ رَسُولُهُ إِلَى مَنْ لَقِيَكَ مِنْ أَهْلِ الْجَهْلِ فَلَزِمَكَ حُسْنُ التَّأْدِيَةِ عَنْهُ إِلَيْهِمْ وَ لَا تَخُنْهُ فِي تَأْدِيَةِ رِسَالَتِهِ وَ الْقِيَامِ بِهَا عَنْهُ إِذَا تَقَلَّدْتَهَا
>
> [It is the right of your teacher that] you: disengage your intellect for him, bring your understanding at his disposal, purify your heart for him, and brighten your eyes for him by forsaking pleasures and curtailing selfish desires. And you should know that you are his messenger with regards to the knowledge he has granted you, [sent on his behalf] to the ignorant people whom you meet. Therefore, you should convey it to them in the best manner. Do not betray him in communicating his message and performing this duty when you have assumed it.[ii]

---

i. Majlisī, Biḥār al-Anwār, 2:42, narration 6

ii. al-Ḥarrānī, Tuḥaf al-ʿUqūl, 260, narration 15

Chapter Two

The Best Preliminary in the Journey towards Allah

Introduction

One of the preliminaries that occupies a special position in the journey towards Allah is the seeking of knowledge. Knowledge must be acquired so that this journey can take place in the correct manner. This is due to the key role knowledge plays in explaining the goal of creation, the way to reach this goal as well as the outcomes and consequences of traversing this journey. The more accurate and precise the acquisition of knowledge is, the better and easier the journey will be. After acting appropriately in accordance with correct knowledge, man reaches higher levels of knowledge regarding the source of existence and the goal of creation.

This chapter discusses the position of knowledge and its different types, as well as the characteristics of true scholars and the banes of knowledge.

The Role of Knowledge in Reaching the Desired Goal

After becoming familiar with the introductory matters needed to enter the Straight Path towards reaching the goal of creation, [i] man must strengthen his resolve and start out on the journey. At this point, he must have the correct outlook about the goal of creation, its implications, and the preliminaries required for reaching the goal

i. Such as those discussed in the first chapter of this book.

and implementing it. This correct outlook is needed to ensure that his wayfaring is correct, successful and yields the desired results. The preliminaries of this journey are discussed in the first sections of this book,[i] whereas in the later sections the main discussions (such as the goal of creation and the signs of reaching the goal and its effects) will be presented.

Given that knowledge has a profound influence on all the endeavours of a person and that it is one of the distinctive traits of man's existence, Imam al-Ṣādiq (peace be upon him) advised ʿUnwān al-Baṣrī to acquire knowledge. This knowledge when put into practice would allow him to comprehend the realities of this world and the reality of his own self.

This role of knowledge can be seen in how Allah—in the beginning of man's creation—granted him the capacity to know and comprehend His Names. Moreover, along with granting man his existence Allah also gave him the potential to develop that knowledge:

وَ عَلَّمَ آدَمَ الْأَسْمَاءَ كُلَّهَا

And He taught Adam the Names, all of them (2:31)

Also, He explained that the goal of creation and the management of all beings is to reach a special knowledge:

اللَّهُ الَّذِي خَلَقَ سَبْعَ سَمَاوَاتٍ وَ مِنَ الْأَرْضِ مِثْلَهُنَّ يَتَنَزَّلُ الْأَمْرُ بَيْنَهُنَّ لِتَعْلَمُوا أَنَّ اللَّهَ عَلَى كُلِّ شَيْءٍ قَدِيرٌ وَ أَنَّ اللَّهَ قَدْ أَحَاطَ بِكُلِّ شَيْءٍ عِلْماً

> It is Allah who has created seven heavens, and of the Earth [a number] like them. The command [of Allah] gradually descends through them, that you may know that Allah has power over all things, and that Allah comprehends all things in knowledge. (65:12)

Also, according to some Islamic narrations, the worship mentioned in the verse, "I did not create the jinn and the humans except that they may worship Me," (51:56) refers tognosis (*maʿrifah*) of Allah

---

i. That is, the first and second chapter.

the Exalted. For example, Imam al-Ḥusayn (peace be upon him) says:

إِنَّ اللهَ مَا خَلَقَ الْعِبَادَ إِلَّا لِيَعْرِفُوهُ فَإِذَا عَرَفُوهُ عَبَدُوهُ فَإِذَا عَبَدُوهُ اسْتَغْنَوْا بِعِبَادَتِهِ عَنْ عِبَادَةِ مَا سِوَاه

> Certainly, Allah did not create the servants except so that they know Him [attain His gnosis]. So, when they know him, they worship him and when they worship him, then through his worship they become free from the need to worship other than Him.[i]

As a result, knowledge must be of two types: one type is a preliminary to the journey of perfection, and the other type is itself the goal—this second type manifests itself in true servitude of the Almighty and is inseparable from this. Therefore, in the coming sections, the relationship between these preliminary discussions (about knowledge) and the main discussion (about the reality of servitude and reaching the true knowledge) will be examined. In the viewpoint of the Qurʾān and the Sunnah[ii], seeking knowledge has certain conditions and obstacles that must be adhered to for the knowledge to be applied. As a result, we have also indicated these conditions and obstacles in the forthcoming sections.

Section One
Knowledge and its Different Types in the Qurʾān and the Sunnah

Knowledge is awareness and perception of reality. Knowledge can be divided into various types based on the branch of knowledge, the tools used to acquire it, how it is obtained, and its uses. Each of these types has rules, preliminaries, and conditions that are specific to it and cannot be generalized to other types.

The sacred religion of Islam, keeping in view the essential merit of

---

i. Majlisī, Biḥār al-Anwār, 23:83, narration 22

ii. The word *sunnah* refers to the speech and conduct of the Prophet (peace and blessings be upon him and his family) as well as the Imams (peace be upon them).

knowledge, has made it compulsory on all Muslim men and women to acquire knowledge. The Messenger of Allah (peace and blessings be upon him and his family) says in this regard:

طَلَبُ الْعِلْمِ فَرِيضَةٌ عَلَى كُلِّ مُسْلِمٍ وَ مُسْلِمَةٍ

> Seeking knowledge is obligatory on every Muslim man and woman.[i]

The Noble Qur'ān, divides knowledge into two comprehensive types:

1. Presential Knowledge (al-'Ilm al-Hudūrī)

Presential knowledge is to become aware and to directly perceive the essence and reality of an entity without using any other object as a medium. Allah's knowledge of the created beings is of this type:

وَ اللَّهُ يَعْلَمُ مَا فِي السَّمَاوَاتِ وَ مَا فِي الْأَرْضِ وَ اللَّهُ بِكُلِّ شَيْءٍ عَلِيمٌ

> Allah knows whatever there is in the heavens and whatever there is in the Earth (49:16)

Man's knowledge of his own self, his inner states, and his actions is also of this type:

عَلِمَتْ نَفْسٌ مَا قَدَّمَتْ وَ أَخَّرَتْ

> Then a soul shall know what it has sent ahead and left behind. (82:5)

Different expressions such as *shuhūd* (witnessing), *liqā'* (encountering), *ru'yah* (seeing) and others, have been used in the Noble Qur'ān to denote this type of knowledge:

أَ وَ لَمْ يَكْفِ بِرَبِّكَ أَنَّهُ عَلَى كُلِّ شَيْءٍ شَهِيدٌ

> Is it not sufficient that your Lord is witness to all things? (41:53)

---

i. Karājakī, Kanz al-Fawā'id, 2:107

فَمَنْ كَانَ يَرْجُو لِقَاءَ رَبِّهِ فَلْيَعْمَلْ عَمَلاً
صَالِحاً وَ لاَ يُشْرِكْ بِعِبَادَةِ رَبِّهِ أَحَداً

So, whoever expects to encounter his Lord, let him act righteously, and not associate anyone with the worship of his Lord (18:110)

وَ لَقَدْ رَآهُ نَزْلَةً أُخْرَى عِنْدَ سِدْرَةِ الْمُنْتَهَى

Certainly, he saw it yet another time, by the Lote Tree of the Ultimate Boundary (53:13-14)

2. Conceptual knowledge (al-ʿIlm al-Husūlī)

Conceptual knowledge is the knowledge that is acquired through the medium of mental images and conceptions of things. The learning and teaching that is prevalent amongst men is based on this type of knowledge:

هُوَ الَّذِي بَعَثَ فِي الْأُمِّيِّينَ رَسُولاً مِنْهُمْ يَتْلُو عَلَيْهِمْ آيَاتِهِ وَ
يُزَكِّيهِمْ وَ يُعَلِّمُهُمُ الْكِتَابَ وَ الْحِكْمَةَ

It is He who sent to the unlettered [people] an apostle from among themselves, to recite to them His signs, to purify them, and to teach them the Book and wisdom (62:2)

This knowledge has requirements and conditions such as an appropriate background, mental capacity of the learner, educational environment, intellectual ability of the teacher, and so on.

The Difference Between Presential Knowledge and Conceptual Knowledge

The difference between these two types of knowledge is not in terms of intensity—that is they do not have the same reality and only differ in that one is intense and the other weak. Rather, they differ in their existential reality. As a result, each of them has characteristics and rules that are specific to themselves. Some of these differences are:

1) In presential knowledge—since the known object is present with the knowing person and perception is not accomplished with the help

of a mental concept—there is no room for any type of mistake or error. On the contrary, conceptual knowledge—due to how it is dependent on tools of acquiring knowledge like ears, eyes and touch, as well as mental concepts—is prone to mistake and error.

2) Presential knowledge is existentially prior in rank over conceptual knowledge and therefore enjoys a special distinction and nobility. This is because man—even before his conceptual knowledge about the external world acquired by using the sensory organs and the intellect—has presential knowledge about himself. In addition, presential knowledge is prior in rank because the knowledge of Allah the Exalted is of this type. The existence of the world originates and subsists due to Allah's Incomparable Being, such that His Essence is the same as His knowledge of Himself and all beings, even before their creation. As a result, His knowledge is presential knowledge.

It is true that man must first acquire appropriate conceptual knowledge before he can reach the higher levels of presential knowledge of the world's realities and make the presential knowledge of his own existence more conscious. Therefore, from this aspect conceptual knowledge is in fact prior to presential knowledge. Nonetheless, due to its nobleness and its other distinctive characteristics—as well as how it is the origin and the true goal of other types of knowledge and information—presential knowledge possesses an existential precedence, and it is termed as 'true knowledge'. On the other hand, because conceptual knowledge is a preliminary to presential knowledge it is called 'outward knowledge'.

3) One of the differences between these two types of knowledge is in the preliminaries they require and the manner that they are realized and obtained in man's existence.

Conceptual knowledge requires a mental learning capacity, environment, text book, teacher, etc. However, presential knowledge of the realities of the world does not require teaching and learning in this manner, rather because of practical preliminaries and actions, presential knowledge flows into man. However, these practical preliminaries do require conceptual knowledge regarding which actions must be performed and the manner of performing them correctly. Therefore, when 'Unwān al-Baṣrī sought to benefit from Imam al-Ṣādiq's (peace be upon him) knowledge and said to him, "May Allah provide me from your knowledge", the Imam replied saying, "Knowledge is not [obtained] through learning." He wanted to say that this knowledge which you are requesting is not acquired through learning and study.

It is worthy of attention that Imam's (peace be upon him) reply was in accordance with the request of ʿUnwān. He did not request general knowledge in order that the Imam guide him to the fundamentals of studying conceptual knowledge. Rather, he asked for benefitting from the knowledge of the Ahl al-Bayt (peace be upon them). Evidently, the knowledge of the Ahl al-Bayt (peace be upon them) is presential knowledge which is only realized in man's existence through true servitude and worship of Allah, and through the emanation of Divine guidance upon man. Therefore, the Imam drew his attention to the practical requirements of this path, servitude and Divine guidance, thereby reminding him of the difference between the knowledge of the Ahl al-Bayt (peace be upon them) and that of others. [i]

However, the Imams (peace be upon them) are also compelled to impart this true knowledge they possess to others in the form of appropriate words and suitable mental concepts. Therefore, their knowledge also takes on a dimension of conceptual knowledge, and to reach their true knowledge one must make use of their conventional knowledge—that is the different sciences in which the Ahl al-Bayt (peace be upon them) trained students. Hence, Imam al- Ṣādiq (peace be upon him) first says in, "If you are seeking that true knowledge, first desire the reality of servitude in your own self and seek knowledge to put it into practice," then later he indicates some of the manners of gaining conceptual knowledge. He also guides ʿUnwān al-Baṣrī to detach himself

i. From the perspective of Arabic grammar, the definite article 'al' in the word 'al-ʿilm' found in the reply of the Noble Imam (peace be upon him)—ليس العلم بالتعلّم—is not the 'al' of *istighrāq* or *jins* (two types of the article 'al' as discussed in Arabic syntax). If this were the case, the article would encompass all types of knowledge. Rather, the article 'al' refers to the word علمك mentioned in the request of ʿUnwān. It is therefore a response to ʿUnwān, showing him that the knowledge of the Ahl al-Bayt (peace be upon them) is presential knowledge that cannot be obtained by studying and education. (From the author).

from the knowledge of others and to learn from his own knowledge.

The discussion about the knowledge of the Imams (peace be upon them) in terms of its manifestation, its degrees and dimensions, all occupy a prominent and lofty place in Islamic traditions. This has been mentioned in the noble book of *Uṣūl al-Kāfi* and the first volume of the book *Baṣā'ir al-Darajāt*. This issue has also been discussed by the author in the book "Lahūtī Manifestations in the Exposition of the Ziyārah al-Jāmi'ah al-Kabīrah (*Jilvihā-yi Lahūtī dar Sharḥ-i Ziyāra-yi Jāmi'a-yi Kabīrah*)."

Conceptual knowledge,[i] if it is acquired through experimentation, experience and observations, is called 'experimental knowledge'. Sciences that are acquired not through experimentation and observations, but instead based on traditional sources like the Qur'ān and the Sunnah, are termed 'traditional sciences.' Examples of this are the science of *fiqh* (jurisprudence) and *akhlāq* (ethics). Lastly, if a science is founded on logical reasoning and deductive intellectual proofs, then it is called 'intellectual knowledge,' like philosophy, logic, and *kalām* (theology).

The Position of Knowledge in Islam

Islam has charged every man and woman with the obligation and duty of acquiring knowledge, especially religious knowledge. It has ordained great virtues and abundant rewards for gaining knowledge. Despite this, all sciences do not hold the same place and rank from the Islamic viewpoint, rather each science—based on various factors—has a specific value and credence.

For example, if the Muslim society—during a particular time—needs specialists in a certain field or science and enough people are not engaged in studying it, then studying that field or science is *wājib-i kifā'ī* (a shared religious obligation) on all the Muslims until this need is alleviated from the society. As the Messenger of Allah (peace and blessings be upon him and his family) says:

---

i. Here, we do not intend to enumerate all the different types of conceptual knowledge. Rather we mention those types of conceptual knowledge that are common in educational institutions. (From the author)

الْعِلْمُ عِلْمَانِ عِلْمُ الْأَدْيَانِ وَ عِلْمُ الْأَبْدَانِ

Knowledge is of two types: knowledge of religions and knowledge of bodies.[i]

The knowledge mentioned in the following narration undoubtedly refers to the science of medicine and the body, since the seat of this knowledge during that time was China:

اطْلُبُوا الْعِلْمَ وَ لَوْ بِالصِّينِ

Seek knowledge, even if it is in China.[ii]

From another viewpoint, it is possible to classify knowledge in terms of the preliminaries they require and their inherent nobleness. For example, Imam ʿAlī (peace be upon him) classifies knowledge into four types: fiqh for the religion, medicine for the body, Arabic syntax for the (protection) of the tongue (from making verbal mistakes) and astronomy for knowing time.[iii]

Of course, from the Islamic viewpoint, presential knowledge such as gnosis of Allah and the soul is considered the noblest of all knowledge and sciences. After this in nobility are those sciences that are a preliminary to acquiring the knowledge of God and the soul, such as the science of *fiqh*, *akhlāq*, philosophy and *kalām*.

Imam al-Ṣādiq (peace be upon him) says in this regard:

وَجَدْتُ عِلْمَ النَّاسِ كُلَّهُ فِي أَرْبَعٍ أَوَّلُهَا أَنْ تَعْرِفَ رَبَّكَ وَ الثَّانِي أَنْ تَعْرِفَ مَا صَنَعَ بِكَ وَ الثَّالِثُ أَنْ تَعْرِفَ مَا أَرَادَ مِنْكَ وَ الرَّابِعُ أَنْ تَعْرِفَ مَا يُخْرِجُكَ مِنْ دِينِكَ.

I found all the knowledge of mankind in four [things]: first is that you recognize your Lord, second is that you know what He has done to you [He has created you in this manner], third is that you know what He wants from you,

---

i. Majlisī, Bihār al-Anwār, 1:220, narration 52

ii. al-Hindī, Kanz al-ʿUmmāl, narration 28697

iii. Majlisī, Biḥār al-Anwār, 1:218, narration 42

and fourth is that you know what causes you to exit from your religion.[i]

At the same time, he says the following about the gnosis of Allah:

لَوْ يَعْلَمُ النَّاسُ مَا فِي فَضْلِ مَعْرِفَةِ اللَّهِ عَزَّ وَ جَلَّ مَا مَدُّوا أَعْيُنَهُمْ إِلَى مَا مَتَّعَ اللَّهُ بِهِ الْأَعْدَاءَ مِنْ زَهْرَةِ الْحَيَاةِ الدُّنْيَا وَ نَعِيمِهَا وَ كَانَتْ دُنْيَاهُمْ أَقَلَّ عِنْدَهُمْ مِمَّا يَطَئُونَهُ بِأَرْجُلِهِمْ وَ لَنُعِّمُوا بِمَعْرِفَةِ اللَّهِ جَلَّ وَ عَزَّ وَ تَلَذَّذُوا بِهَا تَلَذُّذَ مَنْ لَمْ يَزَلْ فِي رَوْضَاتِ الْجِنَانِ مَعَ أَوْلِيَاءِ اللَّهِ

If people knew what [great] virtue lies in the gnosis of Allah, the Mighty and Exalted, they would never extend their glance toward that which Allah has granted the enemies from the splendours and blessings of the worldly life. Their world would be more worthless to them than that which they trample under their feet and they would certainly benefit from Allah, the Mighty and Exalted's gnosis, and they would have enjoyed it like the enjoying of a person who does not cede to be in the Gardens of Paradise with the *awliyā'* of Allah.[ii]

For this reason, Imam ʿAlī (peace be upon him) says:

مَعْرِفَةُ اللَّهِ سُبْحَانَهُ أَعْلَى الْمَعَارِف

Allah's gnosis is the loftiest knowledge[iii]

ثَمَرَةُ الْعِلْمِ مَعْرِفَةُ اللَّه

The fruit [outcome] of knowledge is Allah's gnosis.[iv]

Therefore, gnosis of Allah the Exalted—that too His presential and witnessed gnosis—is the most superior of all knowledge, such that no

---

i. al-Kulaynī, al-Kāfī, 1:50, narration 11

ii. al-Kulaynī, al-Kāfī, 8:447, narration 347

iii. al-Āmudī, Ghurar al-Ḥikam, narration 9864

iv. Ibid., narration 4586

other knowledge can be compared to it. All other matters and sciences are preliminaries to it. In fact, the recommendation and command to learn other sciences is either so that man can make use of them in his worldly life, or because these sciences are a preliminary to reaching spiritual and true perfection. The Messenger of Allah (peace and blessings be upon him and his family) says regarding this:

خَيْرُ الْعِلْمِ مَا نَفَعَ

The best knowledge is that which gives benefit. (i)

For this reason, sciences that cause material and worldly harm to the individual or society, such as magic, sleight of hand, (ii) and so on, are prohibited by the Divine *sharīʿah*. Similarly, those things that cause deviation, spiritual, and ideological harm to a group of people are also prohibited—for example learning ideological doubts for the layman, or preserving, buying and selling books of this nature.

The Relationship between Outward Knowledge and the True Knowledge

Presential knowledge—due to its rank, nobleness and precedence—is called 'true knowledge,' while conceptual knowledge with all its types is termed as 'outward knowledge.' These two types of knowledge are essentially different and hence, the laws governing them, and their characteristics are also different. However, this difference does not mean that there is no relationship between them.

The relationship between true knowledge and outward knowledge must be sought in man's system of perception. It is through presential knowledge that man witnesses the realities of the world and of his

---

i. al-Ṣadūq, al-Amālī, 394, narration 1.

ii. Magic (*siḥr*) is an extraordinary action wherein the magician overpowers the senses of others and their imagination to make them sense and imagine things that have no reality. This is prohibited in the *sharīʿah* and is one of the major sins. Legerdemain or sleight of hand (*shaʿbadhah*) is an associated discussion in Islamic jurisprudence, referring to an entertainer who conjures tricks by carrying out ordinary, quick movements. While the common opinion in the past was that this is also prohibited, some contemporary *marājiʿ* have allowed it.

self—this is the goal of his creation. However, this is only acquired by performing a set of outward and inward actions; and these specific actions require prior conceptual perception and outward knowledge.

This type of conceptual knowledge is the product of sciences like *kalām*, philosophy, *fiqh* and *akhlāq*. These sciences explain the nature of the existential relationship between man and his Lord—in terms of how He is the Origin and the End of man's existence—and they determine the set of actions and practical instructions which man requires from the beginning of his wayfaring until the end. This knowledge can be acquired through one of the two ways: *ijtihād* or *taqlīd*. [i]

To reach the lofty aim of humanity, creating suitable conditions (learning the necessary sciences) and clearing the obstacles, is a necessary and inevitable step. Therefore, Imam al-Ṣādiq (peace be upon him) invited 'Unwān al-Baṣrī—who was seeking the true knowledge of the Ahl al-Bayt (peace be upon them)—towards true servitude and acquiring its preliminaries (gaining knowledge and seeking comprehension from Allah) and said to him:

فَإِنْ أَرَدْتَ الْعِلْمَ فَاطْلُبْ أَوَّلًا فِي نَفْسِكَ حَقِيقَةَ الْعُبُودِيَّةِ

> If you desire knowledge, then first seek reality of servitude in your soul.

Therefore, learning religious knowledge and teachings—even in a basic manner through *taqlīd*—is necessary to traverse the path of servitude.

Section Two
Effective Factors in the Growth of Knowledge

There exist factors that are effective in the growth of man's knowledge. Some of these are outward factors which are beneficial for all—these will be explained in this section. Other factors are effective in the growth of true knowledge; these are inward elements which

i. *Ijtihād* refers to the ability to derive religious laws and injunctions from their primary sources such as the Qur'ān and the Sunnah. *Taqlīd* means to follow an expert in the field of jurisprudence (a *mujtahid*) with regards to these laws and injunctions.

are especially beneficial for students of religious studies and will be discussed in the next section.

1) Putting Knowledge into Practice

Allah (the Provider of abundance and the Sublime) has preferred man over other beings by giving him a special comprehension and understanding. As a result, every action he performs originates in his perception of himself and his needs, as well as the world of existence and the environment around him. Actions that do not originate from such a perception are termed as actions performed in the state of heedlessness (*ghaflah*) or neglect (*sahw*).

That which is important is the type of perception based on which man performs his actions. Sometimes his actions are based on imaginations and illusions, other times hypothetical affairs and assumptions lead him to perform a certain action. In all these cases, his actions are considered ignorant—naturally the end result of such behaviour is deviation and destruction. Imam ʿAlī (peace be upon him) says in this regard:

الْعَامِلَ بِغَيْرِ عِلْمٍ كَالسَّائِرِ عَلَى غَيْرِ طَرِيقٍ فَلَا يَزِيدُهُ بُعْدُهُ عَنِ الطَّرِيقِ الْوَاضِحِ إِلَّا بُعْداً مِنْ حَاجَتِهِ وَ الْعَامِلُ بِالْعِلْمِ كَالسَّائِرِ عَلَى الطَّرِيقِ الْوَاضِحِ فَلْيَنْظُرْ نَاظِرٌ أَ سَائِرٌ هُوَ أَمْ رَاجِعٌ؟

> He who acts without knowledge is like one who treads without a path. The more he moves away from the clear path, the further he is from his destination. And he who acts with knowledge is like one who treads the clear path. Therefore, let every observer observe if he is advancing forward or turning backwards.[i]

Therefore, man's actions must be based on certainty, definite knowledge and conviction. He must not tread and act according to uncertain and doubtful knowledge.

It is extremely unfortunate that a great number of people, after

---

i. al-Radī, Nahj al-Balāghah, sermon 154

reaching certainty and conviction, do not act according to it. Despite having reached certainty they still rely on imagination and illusion, performing their actions ignorantly. This type of conduct is strongly reproached by the *awliyā'* of the religion (peace be upon them) and it is considered to be the same as ignorance. Imam ʿAlī (peace be upon him) says:

مَا عَلِمَ مَنْ لَمْ يَعْمَلْ بِعِلْمِه

> He has no knowledge—one who does not act according to his knowledge. (i)

The Noble Messenger of Islam (peace and blessings be upon him and his family) did not consider knowledge that does not lay the foundation for action, to be permanent and enduring. He says:

إِنَّ الْعِلْمَ يَهْتِفُ بِالْعَمَلِ فَإِنْ أَجَابَهُ وَ إِلَّا ارْتَحَلَ عَنْه

> Certainly, knowledge calls out towards action. So, if its call is answered [it stays], and if not then it departs. (ii)

But if man acts according to what he knows, unknown and obscure matters also become manifest for him. As Imam al-Ṣādiq (peace be upon him) explains, action and knowledge go together, and the result of such action is a higher level of knowledge. He says:

الْعِلْمُ مَقْرُونٌ بِالْعَمَلِ فَمَنْ عَلِمَ عَمِلَ وَ مَنْ عَمِلَ عَلِمَ

> Knowledge is accompanied by action. So, if a person knows, he acts. And when a person acts, he will become knowledgeable. (iii)

Therefore, one of the factors that increase man's knowledge and causes it to grow, is to act on the things that he knows. In words of Imam ʿAlī (peace be upon him):

مَا زَكَا الْعِلْمُ بِمِثْلِ الْعَمَلِ بِه

---

i. al-Āmudī, Fihrist-i Mawḍūʿī-yi Ghurar al-Ḥikam, the chapter on *ʿilm* (knowledge)

ii. Majlisī, Bihār al-Anwār, 2:33

iii. Ibid.

> Nothing causes knowledge to grow like acting upon it does. (i)

Of course, every knowledge necessitates a commensurate action with itself. Empirical sciences, beliefs, *akhlāq* and *fiqh*, each of these sciences lead to a specific action and this action becomes a cause of the growth and increase of that science in the existence of man. For this reason, Imam al-Ṣādiq (peace be upon him) said to ʿUnwān Baṣrī, whose intention was to gain knowledge:

اطْلُبِ الْعِلْمَ بِاسْتِعْمَالِهِ

Seek knowledge through its application.

The Noble Qurʾān also describes true knowledge to be the outcome of *taqwā*, saying:

إِنَّ الَّذِينَ اتَّقَوْا إِذَا مَسَّهُمْ طَائِفٌ مِنَ الشَّيْطَانِ تَذَكَّرُوا فَإِذَا هُمْ مُبْصِرُونَ

> When those who have *taqwā* are touched by an insinuation of Satan, they remember [Allah] and, behold, they perceive. (7:201)

Similarly, Imam al-Bāqir (peace be upon him) says:

مَنْ عَمِلَ بِمَا يَعْلَمُ عَلَّمَهُ اللّٰهُ مَا لَمْ يَعْلَمْ

> One who acts according to what he knows, Allah teaches him what he does not know. (ii)

Once someone had a request that he asked from Āyatullāh Shaykh ʿAbd al-Karīm Ḥāʾirī (may Allah be pleased with him), the founder of the Islamic seminary in Qom.(13) This request was contrary to what he had recognized to be his responsibility. When that person insisted a great deal, he said:

---

i. al-Āmudī, Fihrist-i Mawḍūʿī-yi Ghurar al-Ḥikam, the chapter on *ʿilm* (knowledge)

ii. Majlisī, Bihār al-Anwār, 75:189

> I am ready to go to a village, wear a *lung*[i] and do the work of a labourer, but I am not ready to act against my certainty and conviction.[ii]

Similarly, the great *ʿārif*, Āyatullāh Bahjat (may Allah be pleased with him) has said in an ethical admonition:

> Young and old, we [all] must know that the only path to felicity in this world and the Hereafter, is servitude to Allah the Exalted. And servitude lies in abandoning sins, [both sins] related to the faith and the actions. We should act upon what we know, and we should stop at and exercise precaution (*iḥtiyāṭ*) with regards to what we do not know, until we gain its knowledge. [If we act in this manner,] remorse and loss will never find its way into us. If this resolution is firm and deep-rooted in a servant, then Allah the Exalted is worthier [than to not] grant him *tawfiq* (success) and help him.[iii]

In another place, he says:

> Act upon what you know and exercise precaution in what you do not know until it becomes clear. And if it does not become clear then know that you have trampled upon some of your knowledge [you have not acted upon it].[iv]

The application of each piece of knowledge is different from the other. For example, if man establishes the existence of the Divine Origin and the resurrection using proofs and evidence, but this knowledge is only stored in his memory, then he has not applied it and put it to use. Putting them to use means that a person is constantly attentive to it at the level of his intellect, and this knowledge is constantly subject to analysis and examination, until it gradually becomes a belief and firmly penetrates the core of his existence. Such beliefs should not remain at the same level of understanding, rather man's faith about the

---

i. A lung is a piece of cloth that is wrapped around the waist such that it covers the lower half of a person's body.

ii. Rukhshād, Dar Mahdar-i Ayatullah Bahjat, 1:276

iii. Faryādgar-i Tawḥīd, 210

iv. Ibid., 223

Divine Origin, the resurrection, the unseen worlds, and so on, should be increasing day-by-day.

Knowledge of *akhlāq* is put into practice in two ways:

First is through admonishing and reminding oneself. Man's heart becomes afflicted with heedlessness, therefore reminding and admonishing oneself is a desirable and praiseworthy act. As Imam ʿAlī (peace be upon him) says addressing his son Imam al-Hasan (peace be upon him):

أَحْيِ قَلْبَكَ بِالْمَوْعِظَةِ

Bring your heart to life with admonition.[i]

In performing this act, man should not expect to learn something new, but he should remind his heart and soul of the knowledge that he already knows. For this reason, many of the great scholars who themselves were proficient in the Qurʾān and the Sunnah, would spend hours sitting in lessons and sessions of akhlāq, thereby enlivening their souls through such admonition and counsel.

Imam Khumaynī (may Allah be pleased with him) would at times attend the akhlāq lessons of Marhūm Āyatullāh Khandaq Ābādī, one of his own students. Also, he once sent a person to inform his learned son Sayyid Mustafā—himself a mujtahid—that he should also attend this session.

The great marjaʿ and faqīh, Shaykh Murtadā Ansārī (may Allah be pleased with him) would also attend the akhlāq lessons of his student Marhūm Sayyid ʿAlī Shustarī, thus benefitting from his presence.[ii]

Second is through acquiring moral virtues and abstaining from vices based on the methods and recommendations of the pure and infallible Ahl al-Bayt (peace be upon them) as well as the scholars of *akhlāq*.

Acting upon *fiqhī* laws and instructions means abiding by the five types of *sharʿī* rulings: *wājib* (obligatory), *mustaḥabb* (supererogatory), *ḥarām* (prohibited), *makrūh* (disapproved), and *mubāḥ* (permissible). These rulings must form the basis of man's daily routine and his actions.

---

i. al-Radī, Nahj al-Balāghah, letter 31

ii. Imām Khumaynī, Jihād-i Akbar, 30

Employing the preliminary sciences like Arabic syntax and morphology, logic, principles of *fiqh*, and so on, will also result in a correct understanding of the lofty teachings of the Qurʾān and the Sunnah.

Also, to put the empirical sciences into practice is to use them to raise our own and other people's understanding and outlook towards Allah (the Provider of abundance and the Sublime) and the world of existence. Resolving problems, development and increasing the standard of living of the Muslim society, is also one of the results of putting empirical sciences to use.

An individual who seeks to put his knowledge into practice always places a question mark over all the sciences he knows, and asks "What is it for?" In addition, he:

- Firstly, he learns the knowledge that gives practical results, and abstains from learning marginal, unimportant, and non-beneficial subjects.
- Secondly, he is never perplexed and confused, and knows in which direction he is moving, what he should be seeking, and what goal he should pursue through each of these sciences.
- Thirdly, he constantly puts his knowledge to use in his individual and social life and abstains from storing it in his mind.

2) Seeking Comprehension from Allah

From the Islamic viewpoint, learning (taʿallum) is a preliminary to knowing (ʿilm) and knowing must be a preliminary to comprehension (fahm). Hence, knowing is not the goal, rather it is a preliminary to comprehension. Comprehension is a state in which man deeply understands the concepts, truths and realities of existence, and their relationship with the Origin of all existence.[i] Comprehension is also that man understands the things that are required for him to reach this goal and the things that are necessary to refrain from, as well as what is the true purpose of religion, its teachings and its instructions. Sometimes man has knowledge but does not know how to apply this

---

i. al-Isfahānī, al-Mufradāt fī Gharīb al-Qurʾān, the root verb fahima (to comprehend)

knowledge to achieve genuine results.

For this reason, some people move toward hypocrisy [i] and by remaining on it become from the people of Hell. It is not the case that they did not have awareness and conceptual knowledge of the realities, rather as the Noble Qur'ān says, "they have hearts with which they do not understand." [ii]

In fact, it is possible that such individuals had even more knowledge than the common people who perceived the correct path and goal and acted according to it, thus reaching delightful results.

This deep understanding and comprehension is termed in the expressions of the Qur'ān and the Sunnah, as '*fiqh*' (to have *baṣīrah* or insight in religion). The Noble Qur'ān has invited people to this understanding when learning the religious sciences:

فَلَوْ لاَ نَفَرَ مِنْ كُلِّ فِرْقَةٍ مِنْهُمْ طَائِفَةٌ لِيَتَفَقَّهُوا فِي الدِّينِ وَ لِيُنْذِرُوا قَوْمَهُمْ إِذَا رَجَعُوا إِلَيْهِمْ لَعَلَّهُمْ يَحْذَرُونَ

> But why should not then a group from each of their sections go forth [so that another group stay back] to become learned [acquire *fiqh*] in religion, and to warn their people when they return to them, so that they may beware [of the Divine punishment]? (9.122)

The Noblest Messenger (peace and blessings be upon him and his family) says about the difference between knowledge and comprehension:

فَرُبَّ حَامِلِ فِقْهٍ غَيْرُ فَقِيه

> Many are those who transmit knowledge but have not themselves comprehended that knowledge. [iii]

How many illiterate men are there, whose comprehension of themselves and the world of creation, is much more than some of those who

---

i. (63:3-7)

ii. (7:179)

iii. Rayshahrī, Mīzān al-Hikmah, 6:507

have knowledge of academic terminologies! To gain this lofty existential rank that is comprehension, certain preliminaries and an appropriate background is required, for example studying, gaining knowledge and acting upon it. However, the actualization of this perfection in man's being requires Divine favour and attention. This is because comprehension is a non-material virtue and a spiritual perfection that must be conferred by Allah.

Thus, it is necessary that after readying the preliminaries of comprehension, one entreats and beseeches from the Divine, requesting Allah (the Absolutely Knowledgeable) for this understanding. For this reason, Imam al-Ṣādiq (peace be upon him) says to ʿUnwān al-Baṣrī after exhorting him to seek knowledge and put it into practice:

وَ اسْتَفْهِمِ اللَّهَ يُفْهِمْكَ

> Ask Allah to grant you comprehension and He will grant it to you.

Similarly, it has been said in the *Duʿā Abū Ḥamzā al-Thumāli*:

اللَّهُمَّ أَعْطِنِي بَصِيرَةً فِي دِينِكَ وَ فَهْماً
فِي حُكْمِكَ وَ فِقْهاً فِي عِلْمِكَ

> O Allah! Grant me insight in Your religion, comprehension of Your command, and a deep understanding of Your knowledge.[i]

In the beginning of his studies, ʿAllāmah Ṭabāṭabāʾī (may Allah be pleased with him) found it very difficult to understand his lessons. So much so that it once took him four years to complete a single book with a teacher! At the end of it, his teacher expressed his frustration and asked him not to waste his time anymore. This great man left the presence of his teacher broken-hearted and turned to the Almighty, asking Allah to grant him understanding. No one has narrated the details of this beautiful connection and intimate supplication. But after this incident, he would understand all the *suṭūh*[ii] level lessons before

---

i. Majlisī, Bihār al-Anwār, 98:92

ii. Studies in the Islamic seminary are divided into three levels: preliminary, inter-

attending the class, and—as he said himself—he would only attend the lessons of the teacher to clarify remaining doubts. (i)

This favour and insight which Allah the Exalted bestowed upon ʿAllāmah Ṭabāṭabāʾī in that period, resulted in him authoring of the great Qurʾānic Encyclopaedia (the exegesis of *al-Mīzān*) in which the most complex concepts and subtleties of the Qurʾān and the Sunnah are deciphered and explained.

Signs of a Faqīh (One Endowed with Deep Insight in Religion)

There are certain signs and indications of those who have torn the curtains of false illusions and have reached deep insight in religion. These signs have been indicated in some of the narrations:

لَا يَفْقَـهُ الْعَبْـدُ كُلَ الْفِقْـهِ حَتَّـى يَمْقُـتَ النَّـاسَ فِـي ذَاتِ اللَّـهِ، وَ حَتَّـى يَرَى لِلْقُـرْآنِ وُجُوهاً كَثِيرَةً، ثُـمَّ يُقْبِـلُ عَلَـى نَفْسِـهِ فَيَكُـونُ لَهَـا أَشَـدَّ مَقْتـا

A servant does not acquire complete *fiqh* [that is complete *baṣīrah* or deep insight], until for the sake of Allah he detests [those] people [who are not on His path], until he sees that the Qurʾān has many meanings [many applications]. Then he turns his attention to himself and is extremely outraged at his own self [because of its shortcomings and laxity in performing good deeds]. (ii)

Imam al-Riḍā (peace be upon him) has also said:

مِنْ عَلَامَاتِ الْفِقْهِ الْحِلْمُ وَ الْعِلْمُ وَ الصَّمْت

From the signs of *fiqh* is forbearance, knowledge and silence [accompanied by reflection]. (iii)

---

mediate and advanced. Respectively the *muqaddamāt*, *suṭūḥ* and *khārij* levels.

i. Ṭabāṭabāʾī, Barrasīhā-yi Islāmī, 10

ii. Qummī, Safīnah al-Bihār, under the root faqiha

iii. al-Mufid, al-Ikhtiṣās, 232

Likewise, Imam al-Ṣādiq (peace be upon him) in a lengthy narration, divides seekers of knowledge into several groups and describes those who seek knowledge to understand and have deep insight in religion (that is *tafaqquh*), in the following manner:

صَاحِبُ الْفِقْهِ وَ الْعَقْلِ ذُو كَآبَةٍ وَ حَزَنٍ وَ سَهَرٍ قَدْ تَحَنَّكَ فِي بُرْنُسِهِ وَ قَامَ اللَّيْلَ فِي حِنْدِسِهِ يَعْمَلُ وَ يَخْشَى وَجِلًا دَاعِياً مُشْفِقاً مُقْبِلًا عَلَى شَأْنِهِ عَارِفاً بِأَهْلِ زَمَانِهِ مُسْتَوْحِشاً مِنْ أَوْثَقِ إِخْوَانِهِ فَشَدَّ اللَّهُ مِنْ هَذَا أَرْكَانَهُ وَ أَعْطَاهُ يَوْمَ الْقِيَامَةِ أَمَانَه

The man of deep understanding in religion and [the man of] intellect is [one who is] grief-stricken, heavyhearted and remains awake at night. He has tied his cap with the loose end of his turban, and remains standing in the dark of the night.[i] He works while he is scared and worried [that his actions will not be accepted]. He supplicates despite being afraid, is attentive to his work, acquainted with the people of his time, and apprehensive of his most trusted brother [because of the importance he gives to his own religion]. Therefore, God strengthens his pillars [of faith] and grants him amnesty on the Day of Resurrection.[ii]

Because the seeker of comprehension is after true realities, as Imam al-Ṣādiq (peace be upon him) says, he acts attentively:

اطْلُبُوا الْعِلْمَ وَ تَزَيَّنُوا مَعَهُ بِالْحِلْمِ وَ الْوَقَارِ وَ تَوَاضَعُوا لِمَنْ تُعَلِّمُونَهُ الْعِلْمَ وَ تَوَاضَعُوا لِمَنْ طَلَبْتُمْ مِنْهُ الْعِلْمَ وَ لَا تَكُونُوا عُلَمَاءَ جَبَّارِينَ فَيَذْهَبَ بَاطِلُكُمْ بِحَقِّكُمْ.

Seek knowledge and beautify it with forbearance and dignity. Show humility in front of those whom you teach and show humility in front of those from whom you seek knowledge. Do not be oppressive scholars [who trample upon the

---

i. A figure of speech meaning that he has devoted himself to worship.

ii. al-Kulaynī, al-Kāfī, 1:49, narration 5

> rights of others], such that the falsehood in you destroys the truth in you.[i]

In his social interactions, one who seeks comprehension observes this instruction of Amīr al-Mu'minīn (peace be upon him):

> أَ لَا أُخْبِرُكُمْ بِالْفَقِيهِ حَقِّ الْفَقِيهِ مَنْ لَمْ يُقَنِّطِ النَّاسَ مِنْ رَحْمَةِ اللَّهِ وَ لَمْ يُؤْمِنْهُمْ مِنْ عَذَابِ اللَّهِ وَ لَمْ يُرَخِّصْ لَهُمْ فِي مَعَاصِي اللَّهِ وَ لَمْ يَتْرُكِ الْقُرْآنَ رَغْبَةً عَنْهُ إِلَى غَيْرِه
>
> Should I not inform you who is a true *faqīh*? One who does not cause people to despair in Allah's mercy, nor does he make them feel secure from Allah's punishment. He does not give them permission to disobey Allah, and he does not abandon the Qur'ān due to his inclination toward other things.[ii]

This is because this state in a scholar shows that he is always on the path of learning and teaching the truth, from anyone, or to anyone—whoever it may be. He is after implementing the truth in a manner that is appropriate for the people.

3) Teaching Others

At times man may think that if he spends his lifetime learning from others and researching sciences and religious teachings, then he will reach the true realities. However, this is a naïve conception. Unless man offers his knowledge to others, he will not:

a) Discover the shortcomings in his knowledge, as Imam ʿAlī (peace be upon him) says:

> الْكَاتِمُ لِلْعِلْمِ غَيْرُ وَاثِقٍ بِالْإِصَابَةِ فِيه
>
> One who conceals his knowledge is not confidant that he has reached the reality [through his knowledge].[iii]

---

i. Ibid., 1:36, narration 1

ii. Ibid., narration 3

iii. al-Āmudī, Ghurar al-Ḥikam, 44

b) Realize that there are other sciences that he is deprived of. This understanding is acquired through the exchange of information. Thus, Imam ʿAlī (peace be upon him) says,

زَكَاةُ الْعِلْمِ نَشْرُه

The *zakāt* [purification] of knowledge is to spread it. (i)

مَنْ كَتَمَ عِلْماً فَكَأَنَّهُ جَاهِل

One who conceals knowledge is as if he is ignorant. (ii)

Also, because knowledge is a spiritual blessing for man from Allah, therefore to give thanks for it, it must be passed on to the one who seeks it. Imam ʿAlī (peace be upon him) says:

شُكْرُ الْعَالِمِ عَلَى عِلْمِهِ عَمَلُهُ بِهِ وَ بَذْلُهُ لِمُسْتَحِقِّه

The scholar's gratefulness for his knowledge is to act upon it and to teach it to the one who deserves it. (iii)

With this act of thanks, the grounds are prepared for his progress, just as Allah the Exalted has promised:

لَئِنْ شَكَرْتُمْ لَأَزِيدَنَّكُمْ

If you are grateful, I will surely enhance you [in blessing] (14:7)

Everything has a beauty that befits it and in the words of Imam ʿAlī (peace be upon him):

جَمَالُ الْعِلْمِ نَشْرُه

The beauty of knowledge is to spread [it]. (iv)

---

i. Ibid.

ii. Ibid.

iii. Ibid.

iv. Ibid.

Section Three
Qualities of True Scholars

After clarifying the ways of applying knowledge and making it beneficial—especially the religious and Divine types of knowledge, some of which have a spiritual dimension—one must note that the main factor that makes knowledge useful for the scholar himself and others, is possessing good and praiseworthy qualities. Man's excellence and in particular a believer's proximity to Allah the Exalted, is through possessing noble qualities. Because knowledge is an immaterial entity and has a direct effect on man's soul, a scholar—even more than others—must possess praiseworthy qualities for his knowledge to truly bear fruit. It is only by acquiring these qualities, that the command of seeking knowledge to put it into practice, is fulfilled. [i] In reality, manifesting praiseworthy traits is an indication of man's rank in knowledge, his awareness of realities, his existential level and his connection to the Origin and the Resurrection. For this reason, Amīr al-Mu'minīn (peace be upon him) in a radiant narration, likens knowledge to a person having different organs, limbs, as well as outward and inward faculties. In the same way that each of these plays a specific role in a person, similarly each of these praiseworthy traits also has a specific relationship with the different aspects of knowledge.

In this section, we will examine the virtues of knowledge in this statement of Imam ʿAlī (peace be upon him):

Abū Baṣīr says I heard Imam al-Ṣādiq (peace be upon him) say:

كَانَ أَمِيرُ الْمُؤْمِنِينَ ع يَقُولُ يَا طَالِبَ الْعِلْمِ إِنَّ الْعِلْمَ ذُو فَضَائِلَ كَثِيرَةٍ فَرَأْسُهُ التَّوَاضُعُ ...

Amīr al-Mu'minīn (peace be upon him) used to [recurrently] say, "O seeker of knowledge! Certainly, knowledge

---

i. This is referring to Imam al- Sādiq's (peace be upon him) command to 'Unwān al-Basrī when he said

وَ اطْلُبِ الْعِلْمَ بِاسْتِعْمَالِهِ

Seek knowledge by applying it in actions

has many merits: Its head is humility . . ." (i)

1) Humility and Modesty

Man is a needy being, rather his entire existence is sheer need. In addition, Allah the Exalted has willed that people should fulfil their needs openly, through other beings that they are in connection with. Therefore, showing humility and humbling oneself in front of others is one of the necessities of man's existence. If someone does not possess this state and instead imagines himself to be greater and free of need from others, then he is heedless of his own existential rank and has transgressed his limit. Hence, Imam ʿAlī (peace be upon him) says:

التَّوَاضُعُ ثَمَرَةُ الْعِلْم

Humility is the fruit of knowledge. (ii)

As man's awareness of his existential rank increases, his humility and humbleness in front of his Creator also increases. Therefore, Imam ʿAlī (peace be upon him) says:

عَلَيْكَ بِالتَّوَاضُعِ فَإِنَّهُ مِنْ أَعْظَمِ الْعِبَادَة

I exhort you to acquire humility, for it is one of the greatest acts of worship. (iii)

Because it is humility before Allah the Exalted that causes man to succeed in performing acts of obedience and refraining from His disobedience. Therefore, by declaring his lowliness in front of Allah and His servants, not only does he not become small and abased, but in the words of the Messenger of Allah (peace and blessings be upon him and his family):

إِنَّ التَّوَاضُعَ يَزِيدُ صَاحِبَهُ رِفْعَة

Indeed, humility increases the station of the humble

---

i. al-Kulaynī, al-Kāfī, 1:48, narration 2

ii. al-Āmudī, Fihrist-i Mawdūʿī-yi Ghurar al-Hikam, 121, narration 1

iii. Majlisī, Bihār al-Anwār, 75:119, narration 5

person. (i)

Also, as said by Imam Ḥasan al-ʿAskarī (peace be upon him):

التَّوَاضُعُ نِعْمَةٌ لَا يُحْسَدُ عَلَيْهَا

Humility is a blessing which is not envied. (ii)

The reason being that humility is accompanied by a type of self-struggle, such that man controls the rebellion of the self-love within and does not allow his selfish nature to incorrectly manifest itself. Imam al-Riḍā (peace be upon him) describes one of its signs in the following manner:

التَّوَاضُعُ أَنْ تُعْطِيَ النَّاسَ مَا تُحِبُّ أَنْ تُعْطَاه

Humility is that you give people that [right] which you would like people to give you. (iii)

Thus, Imam ʿAlī (peace be upon him) says:

حَاصِلُ التَّوَاضُعِ الشَّرَف

The outcome of humility is nobility [and self-respect]. (iv)

He also says:

مَا تَوَاضَعَ إِلَّا رَفِيع

None acquires humility except a noble person. (v)

Given the excellence of this trait, one who wants to acquire noble traits by gaining knowledge—especially religious knowledge—must strive to acquire this trait. As Imam al-Kāẓim (peace be upon him) says:

---

i. al-Kulaynī, al-Kāfī, 2:121, narration 1

ii. al-Harrānī, Tuhaf al-ʿUqūl, 489

iii. al-Kulaynī, al-Kāfī, 2:124, narration 13

iv. al-Āmudī, Fihrist-i Mawḍūʿī-yi Ghurar al-Ḥikam, the chapter on *tawāḍuʿ* (humility)

v. Ibid.

إِنَّ الزَّرْعَ يَنْبُتُ فِي السَّهْلِ وَ لَا يَنْبُتُ فِي الصَّفَا فَكَذَلِكَ الْحِكْمَةُ تَعْمَرُ فِي قَلْبِ الْمُتَوَاضِعِ وَ لَا تَعْمَرُ فِي قَلْبِ الْمُتَكَبِّرِ الْجَبَّارِ لِأَنَّ اللَّهَ جَعَلَ التَّوَاضُعَ آلَةَ الْعَقْلِ وَ جَعَلَ التَّكَبُّرَ مِنْ آلَةِ الْجَهْلِ

Certainly, crops grow in soft earth and do not grow in hard earth. Similarly, wisdom prospers in a humble heart and does not flourish in an arrogant and haughty heart. That is because Allah has made humility to be the instrument of the intellect and has made pride to be the instrument of ignorance. (i)

Imam al-Ṣādiq (peace be upon him) also says:

تَوَاضَعُوا لِمَنْ تُعَلِّمُونَهُ الْعِلْمَ وَ تَوَاضَعُوا لِمَنْ طَلَبْتُمْ مِنْهُ الْعِلْمَ وَ لَا تَكُونُوا عُلَمَاءَ جَبَّارِينَ فَيَذْهَبَ بَاطِلُكُمْ بِحَقِّكُمْ.

Show humility to those whom you teach and those you seek knowledge from. Do not be amongst the arrogant and haughty scholars [those who do not submit to the truth] such that the falsehood in you destroys the truth in you. (ii)

When an arrogant person does not humble himself in front of the truth, he gradually does not understand the truth of matters, or he barely understands it. Inevitably, the falsehood in him overcomes the truth, and as a result, others pay no attention to his truthful statements.

Imam al-Ṣādiq (peace be upon him) describes the signs of humility in this manner:

مِنَ التَّوَاضُعِ أَنْ تَرْضَى بِالْمَجْلِسِ دُونَ الْمَجْلِسِ وَ أَنْ تُسَلِّمَ عَلَى مَنْ تَلْقَى وَ أَنْ تَتْرُكَ الْمِرَاءَ وَ إِنْ كُنْتَ مُحِقّاً وَ أَنْ لَا تُحِبَّ أَنْ تُحْمَدَ عَلَى التَّقْوَى.

It is of humility that you be content with sitting in a place lower than your status [you should not consider it your

---

i. Majlisī, Bihār al-Anwār, 78:312, narration 1

ii. al-Kulaynī, al-Kāfī, 1:36, narration 1

> right to sit in a special place in a gathering], you greet the person that you meet, you give up quarrelling with others even if you are correct, and you dislike others praising your *taqwā*.(i)

Due to the importance of this trait, Imam ʿAlī (peace be upon him) has likened it to the head of a body. The head is the place of the intellect, thought and other faculties of perception. If the head is missing or is unhealthy then man's being is non-existent or deficient. If the seeker of knowledge does not show humility in front of his teacher or his students or other people, inevitably he will disregard their rights, which in turn will result in a lack of humility before Allah the Exalted. In this state, neither his intellect can manifest itself or develop, nor can his other faculties of perception yield their desired effects, and he cannot earn other spiritual virtues and traits.

2) Being Aloof from Hasad (Envy)

Ḥasad refers to the state or attribute in which a person wishes that a blessing is taken away from another person who deserves that blessing.(ii)

Initially this appears in one's soul in the form of passing thoughts or insinuations that occur when he sees a blessing in another person. In this stage it is still not a blameworthy attribute. But if he pays heed to it and dwells upon the thought (which Satan also reinforces), then it becomes a blameworthy attribute. Therefore, Imam ʿAlī (peace be upon him) describing the qualities of knowledge and scholars, says:

وَ عَيْنُهُ الْبَرَاءَةُ مِنَ الْحَسَدِ

. . . and the eye of knowledge is being aloof from *ḥasad*.

These insinuations occur because man is heedlessness of his existential rank. He is unaware that he can also possess that blessing. These thoughts also stem from his weak faith or the lack of faith altogether in Allah and an ignorance that all blessings emanate from Him. It is God that has granted each person the ability to attain His blessings.

i. Ibid., 2:132, narration 6

ii. al-Iṣfahānī, al-Mufradāt, the root word *ḥasad*.

Moreover, He has permitted man to attain these blessings through logical and religiously permissible ways. Therefore, Imam al-Bāqir (peace be upon him) says:

إِنَّ الْحَسَدَ لَيَأْكُلُ الْإِيمَانَ كَمَا تَأْكُلُ النَّارُ الْحَطَبَ

Verily, *ḥasad* eats faith just as fire eats wood.(i)

Similarly, Imam al-Ṣādiq (peace be upon him) says:

إِيَّاكُمْ أَنْ يَحْسُدَ بَعْضُكُمْ بَعْضاً فَإِنَّ الْكُفْرَ أَصْلُهُ الْحَسَد

Refrain from harbouring *ḥasad* about one another, for the root of disbelief is *ḥasad*.(ii)

Perhaps ideological disbelief is not intended in this narration, rather what is meant is practical disbelief. For this reason, the Messenger of Allah (peace and blessings be upon him and his family) says:

قَالَ اللَّهُ عَزَّ وَ جَلَّ لِمُوسَى بْنِ عِمْرَانَ ع ... فَإِنَّ الْحَاسِدَ سَاخِطٌ لِنِعَمِي صَادٌّ لِقَسْمِيَ الَّذِي قَسَمْتُ بَيْنَ عِبَادِي

Allah said to Moses son of Amram (peace be upon him), "...Verily the envious person is angry about My blessings, hindering and preventing the portions [of blessings] that I have divided amongst My servants."(iii)

Therefore, if a person does not pay attention to the aforementioned points that curtail the growth of these insinuations, and *ḥasad* acquires the form of a state or an attribute of his soul, then as Imam ʿAlī (peace be upon him) says:

رَأْسُ الرَّذَائِلِ الْحَسَد

Ḥasad is the root [and the cause] of other moral vices.(iv)

---

i. al-Kulaynī, al-Kāfī, 2:306, narration 1

ii. Ibid., 8:8, narration 1

iii. Ibid., 2:307, narration 6

iv. al-Āmudī, Fihrist-i Mawdūʿī-yi Ghurar al-Hikam, the chapter on hasad (jealousy)

Imam ʿAlī (peace be upon him) also says:

الْحَسُودُ كَثِيرُ الْحَسَرَاتِ مُتَضَاعِفُ السَّيِّئَاتِ

The envious person's regret is great, and his sins increase.(i)

For this reason, *ḥasad* is the worst of diseases(ii) and causes physical, psychological as well as spiritual ailments. It has been proven that some bodily diseases originate as a result of psychological disorders or from moral vices. *Ḥasad* can lead to pride and sins of the tongue such as backbiting, accusation, slander, etc., just as it did in the case of Satan. Bearing this in mind, harbouring *ḥasad* with regards to spiritual blessings in another person, is even more reproachable.

Because the effect of knowledge is visible in society and a scholar is naturally the object of people's attention and respect, therefore when a person sees this in a scholar and is heedless of the fact that it is a Divine blessing, it leads him to be afflicted with *ḥasad* and its undesirable consequences. Such a person must remember that these Divine blessing have been bestowed upon the scholar due to his efforts. Anyone else, through their own efforts, can acquire the blessing of knowledge. Moreover, the motivation behind acquiring knowledge (which is a spiritual matter) and conveying its fruits to the people, should not be to gain the attention and respect of others. Therefore, Imam ʿAlī (peace be upon him) says:

لَا يَكُونُ الْعَالِمُ عَالِماً حَتَّى لَا يَحْسُدَ مَنْ فَوْقَهُ وَ لَا يَحْتَقِرَ مَنْ دُونَه

One does not become a scholar unless he does not harbour *ḥasad* about the one above him and does not scorn the one lower than him.(iii)

If this state of *ḥasad* is not remedied and it manifests itself in actions, and if a person commits sins due to it and does not repent, then as the Messenger of Allah (peace and blessings be upon him and his family)

---

i. Ibid.

ii. Ibid.

iii. al-Āmudī, Ghurar al-Ḥikam, 48, narration 258

has said: such a person is from the people of the Hellfire.[i]

3) Comprehension and Understanding

Understanding and comprehension is a state due to which a person discovers the reality of the concept he learnt.[ii] At times this state is obtained because of special Divine favour on a person through the medium of revelation (*waḥy*) or inspiration (*ilḥām*). Other times it appears due to the purity of the person's heart and because he is seeking the truth. Sometimes however, it is achieved by contemplating precisely the concepts one has learned—with the condition that the aim is seeking the truth. This requires learning the knowledge diligently through its correct means[iii] and using the intellect to comprehend the relationship between the information and concepts on the one hand, and their desired and real result on the other. Therefore, Imam ʿAlī (peace be upon him) in continuing the previously mentioned narration about the qualities of knowledge and scholars says:

وَ أُذُنُهُ الْفَهْمُ

... and the ear of knowledge is understanding.

Imam al-Ṣādiq (peace be upon him) also narrates from his esteemed forefathers (peace be upon them):

جَاءَ رَجُلٌ إِلَى رَسُولِ اللَّهِ ص فَقَالَ يَا رَسُولَ اللَّهِ مَا الْعِلْمُ قَالَ الْإِنْصَاتُ قَالَ ثُمَّ مَهْ قَالَ الِاسْتِمَاعُ قَالَ ثُمَّ مَهْ قَالَ الْحِفْظُ قَالَ ثُمَّ مَهْ قَالَ الْعَمَلُ بِهِ قَالَ ثُمَّ مَهْ يَا رَسُولَ اللَّهِ قَالَ نَشْرُهُ

One day a man came to the Messenger of Allah (peace and blessings be upon him and his family) and asked, "O Messenger of Allah! What is knowledge?" He replied, "Silence." He asked, "Then?" He said, "To listen." He asked, "Then?" The Messenger of Allah answered, "To retain [and

---

i. al-Kulaynī, al-Kāfi, 8:163, narration 170

ii. al-Iṣfahānī, al-Mufradāt, the root *fahima* (to comprehend)

iii. There are correct means to pursuing every field knowledge. For example, appropriate books and teachers would be the correct means to study.

> to memorize]." He asked, "Then?" He responded, "To act upon it." Then he asked, "O Messenger of Allah! After that?" He replied, "To spread it." (i)

Each field of knowledge has its own prerequisites, methodology and outcomes. By listening and pondering over them it is possible to understand its relation to man's existential rank, and how by acquiring this knowledge, he can fulfil his specific need.

4) Truthfulness

The untainted *fiṭrah* (innate disposition) of every human being seeks truthfulness. Man has been created with such a *fiṭrah;* he seeks the truth and everything that makes him reach it. Imam ʿAlī (peace be upon him) says about definition of truthfulness:

الصِّدْقُ مُطَابَقَةُ الْمَنْطِقِ لِلْوَضْعِ الْإِلَهِي

> Truthfulness is when speech conforms with the Divine system that has been established [by Allah]. (ii)

Also, about the fundamental effect of truthfulness, he says:

الصِّدْقُ صَلَاحُ كُلِّ شَيْءٍ

> Truthfulness is to make everything reach soundness and well-being. (iii)

Apart from having very desirable effects on the soul and actions of an individual and a society, truthfulness is also indicative of the spiritual well-being of the speaker. Imam al-Ṣādiq (peace be upon him) says:

أَحْسَنُ مِنَ الصِّدْقِ قَائِلُه

> The truthful man is better than [his] truthfulness. (iv)

---

i. al-Kulaynī, al-Kāfī, 1:48, narration 4

ii. al-Āmudī, Fihrist-i Mawḍūʿī-yi Ghurar al-Ḥikam, the chapter on *ṣidq* (truthfulness)

iii. Ibid.

iv. al-Ṭūsī, al-Amālī, 223, narration 385

For this reason, Allah has described Himself as the truest in speech,[i] because He is truth itself,[ii] and nothing but truth emanates from Him.[iii] He also wants from His servants that they do not speak anything save the truth, that which conforms to reality.[iv] If man is on the path of truth, if he situates all the affairs of his life on this path of reaching the Absolute Truth, then he will attain the station of truthfulness.[v]

The primary goal of seeking knowledge is to acquire awareness of the realities and truths of this world, to the extent of one's capacity. As a result, the seeker of knowledge should traverse multiple stages.[vi] In the first stage he should learn matters conforming to reality (be it a material or a non-material reality). In the second stage, he should consider his own capacity and ability, that is which field of knowledge suits him more? In the third stage, he should strive to acquire knowledge of those realities that his existence will always need, even if this knowledge is limited and brief. For example: knowledge of the Origin, the Return (the Hereafter), and the way to reach the desired goal of creation. In the fourth stage, he should recount to others the teachings he knows. Here he must not present himself to know what he does not. For if he does, then he will deceive others, and due to putting their confidence in him they will be afflicted by falsehood and deviation. In turn, he will face the evil consequences of this matter.

Thus, Imam ʿAlī continuing the description of knowledge and scholars says:

لِسَانُهُ الصِّدْقُ

... and the tongue of knowledge is truthfulness [truth].

---

i. (4:87) and (4:122)

ii. (24:25)

iii. (39:2), (39:5) and (33:4)

iv. (33:70)

v. (10:2) and (54:55)

vi. These stages enumerated by the author (may his blessings remain) are not necessarily distinct from one another. Nor is it necessary that the seeker of knowledge traverses one of them after other. Rather they constitute certain responsibilities that behove him.

Also, when a narrator asked Imam al-Ṣādiq (peace be upon him):

مَا حَقُّ اللَّهِ عَلَى خَلْقِهِ فَقَالَ أَنْ يَقُولُوا مَا يَعْلَمُونَ وَ يَكُفُّوا عَمَّا لَا يَعْلَمُونَ فَإِذَا فَعَلُوا ذَلِكَ فَقَدْ أَدَّوْا إِلَى اللَّهِ حَقَّه

"What is Allah's right on the people?" He answered, "That they say what they know, and desist from what they do not know. So, if they do this then certainly they have fulfilled Allah's right.' (i)

Similarly, Imam al-Bāqir (peace be upon him) says:

الْوُقُوفُ عِنْدَ الشُّبْهَةِ خَيْرٌ مِنَ الاقْتِحَامِ فِي الْهَلَكَةِ وَ تَرْكُكَ حَدِيثاً لَمْ تُرْوَهُ خَيْرٌ مِنْ رِوَايَتِكَ حَدِيثاً لَمْ تُحْصِهِ

Stopping at a doubtful matter is better than falling into perdition, and abandoning a narration not transmitted to you [that is one that you do not know] is better than relating a narration that has not reached you. (ii)

Imam al-Ṣādiq (peace be upon him) says:

لَا يَسَعُكُمْ فِيمَا يَنْزِلُ بِكُمْ مِمَّا لَا تَعْلَمُونَ إِلَّا الْكَفُّ عَنْهُ وَ التَّثَبُّتُ وَ الرَّدُّ إِلَى أَئِمَّةِ الْهُدَى حَتَّى يَحْمِلُوكُمْ فِيهِ عَلَى الْقَصْدِ وَ يَجْلُوا عَنْكُمْ فِيهِ الْعَمَى وَ يُعَرِّفُوكُمْ فِيهِ الْحَقَّ قَالَ اللَّهُ تَعَالَى فَسْئَلُوا أَهْلَ الذِّكْرِ إِنْ كُنْتُمْ لا تَعْلَمُون

With regards to what occurs [in your life] from the matters that you do not know, you do not have any right except that you desist from it [you do not say anything about it], you ascertain it, and refer it to the Imams of guidance (peace be upon them) so that they lead you to the middle path, remove your blindness and show you the truth in it. Allah the Exalted says, "Ask the People of the Reminder if you do

---

i. al-Kulaynī, al-Kāfī, 1:50, narration 12

ii. Ibid., narration 9

not know." (i) (ii)

5) Research and Investigation

To succeed in any work and attain its desired goal, man must continuously persist until he achieves the result. Hence, after understanding the merits of knowledge and importance of seeking it, one should put unremitting, continuous and serious efforts in acquiring knowledge. Just as Imam al-Ṣādiq (peace be upon him) said to ʿUnwān al-Baṣrī: "And seek knowledge." Undoubtedly man will encounter obstacles during these efforts. He must accurately recognize these obstacles and with a lofty determination, strive to eliminate them. In the words of Imam ʿAlī (peace be upon him):

مَنْ لَمْ يَصْبِرْ عَلَى مَضَضِ التَّعْلِيمِ بَقِيَ فِي ذُلِّ الْجَهْلِ

One who is impatient over the hardships of acquiring knowledge, remains in the abasement of ignorance. (iii)

Because man naturally seeks ease, in this path of seeking knowledge he must combat this. In this light Imam ʿAlī (peace be upon him) says:

لَا يُدْرَكُ الْعِلْمُ بِرَاحَةِ الْجِسْمِ

Knowledge cannot be acquired with comfort of the body. (iv)

Similarly, in this path one cannot refuse to learn things that he does not know. As Imam ʿAlī (peace be upon him) also says:

أَلَا لَا يَسْتَحْيِيَنَّ مَنْ لَا يَعْلَمُ أَنْ يَتَعَلَّمَ فَإِنَّ قِيمَةَ كُلِّ امْرِئٍ مَا يَعْلَم

Indeed! One who does not know should not feel shy to learn, for every man's worth is by what he knows. (v)

One of the obstacles occasionally faced by seekers of knowledge is

---

i. (16:43)

ii. al-Kulaynī, al-Kāfī, 1:50, narration 10

iii. al-Āmudī, Ghurar al-Hikam, 43

iv. Ibid., 44

v. Ibid., 43

laziness and a lack of motivation. However, man must pay attention to the goals of each science—in particular the religious sciences—and reflect on how there exist truths and realities that give indescribable pleasure when attained. Moreover, this knowledge is a very good, and a necessary preliminary to reach true perfection and Allah's servitude. If he does so then his laziness will disappear, and he will not become exhausted. As Imam ʿAlī (peace be upon him) says:

> عَلَى الْمُتَعَلِّمِ أَنْ يَدْأَبَ نَفْسَهُ فِي طَلَبِ الْعِلْمِ وَ لَا يَمَلَّ مِنْ تَعَلُّمِهِ وَ لَا يَسْتَكْثِرَ مَا عَلِم
>
> It is necessary for a student to subject his soul to hardship for the sake of seeking knowledge. He should not become tired of learning, and he should not consider what he knows as plenty.(i)

As mentioned in the Noble Qurʾān, human beings enter this world devoid of any knowledge.(ii) Therefore, without studying and learning from the scholars of every field, it is not possible to acquire knowledge. Imam ʿAlī (peace be upon him) says:

بِالتَّعَلُّمِ يُنَالُ الْعِلْم

Through learning, knowledge is acquired.

تَعَلَّمْ تَعْلَمْ...

Learn! You will gain knowledge...

مَنْ لَمْ يَتَعَلَّمْ لَمْ يَعْلَم

One who does not learn does not gain knowledge.(iii)

Therefore, to reach true perfection man must first know what perfection is, then know the way to reach it and the obstacles along its path. Thereafter he should constantly strive to acquire a deeper understanding of this knowledge. Also, he should not be heedless of this

---

i. Ibid.

ii. (16:78)

iii. al-Āmudī, Ghurar al-Hikam, 43

statement of the Messenger of Allah (peace and blessings be upon him and his family):

أُفٍّ لِرَجُلٍ لَا يُفَرِّغُ نَفْسَهُ فِي كُلِّ جُمُعَةٍ لِأَمْرِ دِينِهِ فَيَتَعَاهَدُهُ وَ يَسْأَلُ عَنْ دِينِه

> Woe unto a man who does not spare time every Friday for the affair of his religion, so that he makes a pact to abide by it and asks questions about his religion.(i)

Similarly, Imam al-Ṣādiq (peace be upon him) says:

لَوَدِدْتُ أَنَّ أَصْحَابِي ضُرِبَتْ رُءُوسُهُمْ بِالسِّيَاطِ حَتَّى يَتَفَقَّهُوا

> I wish that my companions were hit on the head with whips until they become learned [in the religion].(ii)

With incessant efforts, academic investigation and research, it is possible to keep the heart enlivened and always pay attention to the realities and various relationships in the world. As Imam ʿAlī (peace be upon him) in the next part of the tradition describing the qualities of knowledge and scholars says:

وَ حِفْظُهُ الْفَحْصُ

> ... and [from amongst the causes of] preserving knowledge is research and investigation.

One of the ways to achieve success in any work is to benefit from the experience of others or even one's own experience thereby making use of its positive aspects and avoiding its negative ones. For this reason, the Qur'ān and the Sunnah have laid great emphasis on consulting an experienced expert who is intelligent and compassionate in every affair. While also advising the Noblest Messenger (peace and blessings be upon him and his family)—who is the complete intellect(iii)—to

---

i. al-Kulaynī, al-Kāfī, 2:40, narration 5

ii. Ibid., 2:31, narration 8

iii. An indication to a concept discussed in the Islamic intellectual sciences. For this reason, some of the blessed narrations say that the first creation of Allah the Exalted

put his trust in Him, Allah says:

وَ شَاوِرْهُمْ فِي الْأَمْرِ

And consult them in the affairs. (3:159)

Also, He describes the conduct of the believers in this manner:

وَ أَمْرُهُمْ شُورَى بَيْنَهُمْ

And [they conduct] their affairs by counsel among themselves. (42:38)

Therefore, Amīr al-Mu'minīn ʿAlī (peace be upon him) says:

لَا ظَهِيرَ كَالْمُشَاوَرَة

There is not supporter like consultation. (i)

And about benefitting from past experiences he says:

التَّجَارِبُ عِلْمٌ مُسْتَفَاد

Experience is knowledge that was used and applied. (ii)

مَنْ أَحْكَمَ التَّجَارِبَ سَلِمَ مِنَ الْمَعَاطِبِ ... مَنْ غَنِيَ عَنِ التَّجَارِبِ عَمِيَ عَنِ الْعَوَاقِبِ

One who proficiently utilizes experiences, remains secure from destruction ... One who dispenses with experiences, is blinded from the consequences. (iii)

Similarly, he says:

رَأْيُ الرَّجُلِ عَلَى قَدْرِ تَجْرِبَتِه

A man's opinion is to the extent of his experience. (iv)

He also says:

---

was the intellect, while others say that it was the pure light of Muḥammad (peace and blessings be upon him and his family).

i. al-Raḍī, Nahj al-Balāghah, saying 54

ii. al-Āmudī, Ghurar al-Ḥikam, narration 1036

iii. Ibid., narration 8040

iv. Ibid., narration 7016

كَفَى بِالتَّجَارِبِ مُؤَدِّبا

Experience is sufficient for correcting [man].[i]

The Messenger of Allah (peace and blessings be upon him and his family) also says about the strengthening of knowledge and its growth:

أَعْلَمُ النَّاسِ مَنْ جَمَعَ عِلْمَ النَّاسِ إِلَى عِلْمِه

The most knowledgeable of people is one who combines the people's knowledge to his own knowledge.[ii]

This means he benefits from the paths others tread and from what they comprehended of the realities, either by learning directly from them, or reading their books, or benefitting from their wise conduct.

6) Ikhlās (Sincerity) in Seeking Knowledge

Ikhlāṣ is a type of attention and spiritual state that accompanies all man's actions, making them more valuable and giving them a real effect. *Ikhlāṣ* is desirable in all affairs and matters. Imam ʿAlī (peace be upon him) says:

الْإِخْلَاصُ خَيْرُ الْعَمَل

Ikhlāṣ is the best deed.[iii]

وَ أَخْلِصْ لِلَّهِ عَمَلَكَ وَ عِلْمَكَ وَ حُبَّكَ وَ بُغْضَكَ وَ أَخْذَكَ وَ تَرْكَكَ وَ كَلَامَكَ وَ صَمْتَك

Sincerely dedicate for Allah your actions, knowledge, love, hatred, that which you take, that which you abandon, your speech and silence.[iv]

Knowledge is an esoteric and spiritual entity and plays an important role in man's spiritual development. Therefore, *ikhlāṣ* in seeking

---

i. Ibid., narration 5426

ii. al-Ṣadūq, al-Amālī, 220, narration 13

iii. al-Āmudī, Ghurar al-Hikam, narration 305

iv. Ibid., narration 5964

knowledge has been specifically recommended. Imam ʿAlī (peace be upon him) says:

أَفْضَلُ الْعِلْمِ مَا أُخْلِصَ فِيه

The most meritorious knowledge is that which is accompanied by *ikhlāṣ*.[i]

That is because *ikhlāṣ* in the seeking of knowledge, in addition to itself being worship and the best of the actions, impels man to put his knowledge into practice. *Ikhlāṣ* in knowledge means that he should pursue it only because it is desirable in the eyes of Allah, it is the cause of illuminating the path, it shows the realities and the truth to man, it leads him to Allah, and it is the best foundation for performing actions. Therefore, Imam ʿAlī (peace be upon him), continuing the description of the qualities of knowledge and scholars says:

وَ قَلْبُهُ حُسْنُ النِّيَّةِ

... and the heart of knowledge is having a good intention.

On the other hand, if acquiring knowledge is not accompanied by *ikhlāṣ*, then its goal turns into that which is described by Imam al-Bāqir (peace be upon him):

مَنْ طَلَبَ الْعِلْمَ لِيُبَاهِيَ بِهِ الْعُلَمَاءَ أَوْ يُمَارِيَ بِهِ السُّفَهَاءَ أَوْ يَصْرِفَ بِهِ وُجُوهَ النَّاسِ إِلَيْهِ فَلْيَتَبَوَّأْ مَقْعَدَهُ مِنَ النَّارِ إِنَّ الرِّئَاسَةَ لَا تَصْلُحُ إِلَّا لِأَهْلِهَا.

One who seeks knowledge to exult over the scholars, to dispute with the ignorant, or to attract people's attention towards himself, then his dwelling place is in the Fire. That is because, leadership does not suit anyone except those qualified for it.[ii]

A person seeking knowledge naturally becomes the object of attention, be it the attention of the people, other scholars, the rulers, or the

---

i. Ibid., narration 2934

ii. al-Kulaynī, al-Kāfī, 1:47, narration 6

rich. Therefore, seekers of knowledge—especially religious knowledge—must be vigilant of their motivations. They should not pay heed to selfish and worldly motivations which always appear in the soul in the form of insinuations. Also, they should always be mindful lest the effects of these unworthy and ungodly motivations manifest in their actions.

7) Endeavouring to Know

The seeker of knowledge through research, investigation and *ikhlāṣ* in the pursuit of knowledge, must always endeavour to comprehend the realities of the world and its corollaries. He must accept these realities—and accept what they entail—from anyone who expresses them, even if they are not apparently famous or if they are a student or colleague.

The Messenger of Allah (peace and blessings be upon him and his family) says in this regard:

> اِقْبَلِ الحَقَّ مِمَّنْ أَتَاكَ بِهِ مِنْ صَغِيْرٍ أَوْ كَبِيْرٍ وَ إِنْ كَانَ بَغِيْضاً بَعِيْداً وَ ارْدُدِ البَاطِلَ عَلَى مَنْ جَاءَكَ بِهِ مِنْ صَغِيْرٍ أَوْ كَبِيْرٍ وَ إِنْ كَانَ حَبِيْباً قَرِيْباً
>
> Accept the truth from whoever brings it to you, whether he is young or old, even if he is detested and ignored [by others]. And reject falsehood from whoever brings it to you, whether he is young or old, even if he is loved and renowned [amongst the people]. (i)

Imam al-Kāẓim (peace be upon him) also says:

> قُلِ الْحَقَّ وَ إِنْ كَانَ فِيهِ هَلَاكُكَ فَإِنَّ فِيهِ نَجَاتَكَ أَيْ فُلَانُ اتَّقِ اللَّهَ وَ دَعِ الْبَاطِلَ وَ إِنْ كَانَ فِيهِ نَجَاتُكَ فَإِنَّ فِيهِ هَلَاكَكَ.
>
> Speak the truth even if there is destruction in it, for in it [speaking and accepting the truth] is your deliverance. And shun falsehood, even if there is deliverance in it, for in it

i. al-Hindī, Kanz al-ʿUmmāl, narration 43152

[speaking and accepting falsehood] is your destruction.[i]

Therefore, Imam ʿAlī (peace be upon him) continuing the description of the qualities of knowledge and scholars, says:

وَ عَقْلُهُ مَعْرِفَةُ الْأَشْيَاءِ وَ الْأُمُورِ

... and the intellect of knowledge is the knowledge of things and matters.

This means that just as how the role of the intellect is to precisely and genuinely know things, knowledge also must lead man to this objective. If one does not want to know the truth in the manner that it truly is, then certainly he will not act according to it. This knowledge of his is nothing save ignorance and deviation; it draws the one who knows it towards utter loss. Therefore, the Messenger of Allah (peace and blessings be upon him and his family) says:

أَتْقَى النَّاسِ مَنْ قَالَ الْحَقَ فِيمَا لَهُ وَ عَلَيْه

The most pious of the people is one who speaks the truth, be it in his favour or be it against him.[ii]

Also, Imam ʿAlī (peace be upon him) says:

إِنَّ الحَقَّ لَا يُعْرَفُ بِالرِّجَالِ اعْرِفِ الْحَقَ تَعْرِفْ أَهْلَه

Truth is not recognized through men [personalities]. Recognize the truth and you will recognize its adherents.[iii]

Therefore, what is paramount is to recognize the truth, the reality, and to act upon it. One must recognize all other things through this, and in light of this one must act upon them. Imam ʿAlī (peace be upon him) says:

إِنَّ أَفْضَلَ النَّاسِ عِنْدَ اللَّهِ مَنْ كَانَ الْعَمَلُ بِالْحَقِ أَحَبَّ إِلَيْهِ وَ إِنْ نَقَصَهُ وَ كَرَثَهُ مِنَ الْبَاطِلِ وَ إِنْ جَرَّ إِلَيْهِ فَائِدَةً وَ زَادَه

Verily the best person near Allah is one for whom acting on

---

i. al-Harrānī, Tuhaf al-ʿUqūl, 408

ii. al-Ṣadūq, al-Amālī, 27, narration 4

iii. al-Tabrasī, Majmaʿ al-Bayān, 1:211

the truth, even if it causes loss [apparently] and degrades him [in the opinion of others], is more beloved than acting on falsehood, even if it attracts some benefit to him and increases him. (i)

Also, he says in the description of the *muttaqīn*:

وَ وَقَفُوا أَسْمَاعَهُمْ عَلَى الْعِلْمِ النَّافِعِ لَهُم

They have dedicated their ears to [hearing and perceiving] the knowledge that is beneficial for them. (ii)

8) Compassion for Others

If a scholar wants his knowledge to benefit others and wants to himself derive benefit from its blessings, he must interact with people with compassion and concern. This is so that after being attracted towards him, they benefit from his guidance. Therefore, Imam ʿAlī (peace be upon him) continuing the description of the virtues of knowledge and scholars says:

وَ يَدُهُ الرَّحْمَةُ

... and the hand of knowledge is compassion.

This means that just as how man uses his hands to achieve goodness and pass it on to others, similar is the case of knowledge. In order that knowledge is not just stored within the scholar, and so that others benefit from it to reach its desired goal, the scholar must meet people with open arms. He should not refrain from putting his knowledge at the disposal of deserving people. Such conduct results in forbearance. It is for this reason that Allah the Exalted introduces the Heavenly Books—which are intended for man's guidance—as a mercy for man. (iii) Also, He says to His Noble Messenger (peace and blessings be upon him and his family):

---

i. al-Radī, Nahj al-Balāghah, sermon 125

ii. Ibid., sermon 193

iii. (7:154) and (7:203)

فَبِمَا رَحْمَةٍ مِنَ اللَّهِ لِنْتَ لَهُمْ وَ لَوْ كُنْتَ فَظّاً غَلِيظَ الْقَلْبِ لاَنْفَضُّوا مِنْ حَوْلِكَ

It is by Allah's mercy that you are gentle to them; had you been harsh and hard-hearted, they would have surely scattered from around you. (3:159)

Out of His mercy Allah has created human beings and other creatures, and arranged the means of his exoteric, esoteric and spiritual progress. By paying attention to these matters and by putting Allah's religion—which is a special mercy for man—into practice, man can attain a higher mercy from Allah.[i] Allah the Exalted says in the Noble Qurʾān, "and were it not for Allah's grace on you and His mercy, you would have surely been among the losers"[ii] or "there would have befallen you a great punishment"[iii] or "you would have surely followed Satan, except a few [of you]."[iv]

The same holds true for knowledge. Imam ʿAlī (peace be upon him) says:

بِبَذْلِ الرَّحْمَةِ تُسْتَنْزَلُ الرَّحْمَةُ

By granting mercy to others, mercy descends [from the heavens].[v]

9) Visiting the Scholars

To progress in any work of his, man must seek out the means and suitable conditions required for it. One of the ways to increase knowledge and to rectify its deficiencies is to be in contact with and visit the learned. Through such contact man can engage in academic discussion, benefit from their knowledge and scholarly method, find out his deficiencies and the obscure points in his own knowledge, and remain

---

i. (57:28)

ii. (2:24)

iii. (24:14)

iv. (4:83)

v. al-Āmudī, Ghurar al-Hikam, narration 4343

secure from deviation, self-seeking and self-centeredness in adhering to his own opinions and understanding. Therefore, Imam ʿAlī (peace be upon him), continuing the description of the virtues of knowledge and scholars, says:

وَ رِجْلُهُ زِيَارَةُ الْعُلَمَاءِ

... and the foot of knowledge is visiting the learned.

Man uses his foot to move around, fulfilling his needs from the material world and from other people, and providing for other people's needs if he can. This narration means that in the same way, for knowledge to grow and develop, and in order that its deficiencies are discovered, and it is imparted to other people, it needs visiting and academic contact with scholars. Through this, the purpose of knowledge is attained. For this reason, Imam al-Bāqir (peace be upon him) says:

تَزَاوَرُوا فِي بُيُوتِكُمْ فَإِنَّ ذَلِكَ حَيَاةٌ لِأَمْرِنَا رَحِمَ اللَّهُ عَبْداً أَحْيَا أَمْرَنَا

Visit each other in your houses, for in it is revival of our affair. May Allah have mercy on a servant who revives our affair. (i)

Imam al-Ṣādiq (peace be upon him) also says:

تَزَاوَرُوا فَإِنَّ فِي زِيَارَتِكُمْ إِحْيَاءً لِقُلُوبِكُمْ وَ ذِكْراً لِأَحَادِيثِنَا وَ أَحَادِيثُنَا تُعَطِّفُ بَعْضَكُمْ عَلَى بَعْضٍ فَإِنْ أَخَذْتُمْ بِهَا رَشَدْتُمْ وَ نَجَوْتُمْ وَ إِنْ تَرَكْتُمُوهَا ضَلَلْتُمْ وَ هَلَكْتُمْ فَخُذُوا بِهَا وَ أَنَا بِنَجَاتِكُمْ زَعِيمٌ.

Visit each other, for your visiting each other is a source of enlivening your hearts and a remembrance of our words. And our words will make you compassionate towards each other. Thus, if you hold on to our narrations [and abide by them and act according to them], you will grow and attain salvation. But if you forsake them, you will go astray and be destroyed. So, hold on to them and I guarantee your

i. Majlisī, Bihār al-Anwār, 2144, narration 6

deliverance.[i]

Imam al-Kāẓim (peace be upon him) also says:

لَيْسَ شَيْءٌ أَنْكَى لِإِبْلِيسَ وَ جُنُودِهِ مِنْ زِيَارَةِ الْإِخْوَانِ فِي اللَّهِ بَعْضِهِمْ لِبَعْض

Nothing is more reproachable for Satan and his troops than brothers in faith meeting each other for the sake of Allah.[ii]

When there are such merits in believers visiting one other, then certainly the merits of visiting scholars cannot be compared to this! The Messenger of Allah (peace and blessings be upon him and his family) says:

لَا تَجْلِسُوا إِلَّا عِنْدَ كُلِّ عَالِمٍ يَدْعُوكُمْ مِنْ خَمْسٍ إِلَى خَمْسٍ مِنَ الشَّكِّ إِلَى الْيَقِينِ وَ مِنَ الرِّيَاءِ إِلَى الْإِخْلَاصِ وَ مِنَ الرَّغْبَةِ إِلَى الرَّهْبَةِ وَ مِنَ الْكِبْرِ إِلَى التَّوَاضُعِ وَ مِنَ الْغِشِّ إِلَى النَّصِيحَةِ.

Do not sit in the company of a scholar except if he invites you [away] from five things, towards five things: from doubt towards certainty, from ostentation towards sincerity, from inclination [towards the world and Allah's disobedience] towards fear [of Allah and the Day of Resurrection], from pride towards humility, and from deceit and deception towards counsel and concern.[iii]

Similarly, Imam ʿAlī (peace be upon him) says:

جَالِسِ الْعُلَمَاءَ يَزْدَدْ عِلْمُكَ وَ يَحْسُنْ أَدَبُكَ وَ تَزْكُ نَفْسُك

Associate with the scholars so that your knowledge increases, your manners become good and your soul is purified.[iv]

---

i. al-Kulaynī, al-Kāfī, 2:186, narration 2

ii. Ibid., 2:188, narration 7

iii. Majlisī, Biḥār al-Anwār, 74:188, narration 18

iv. al-Āmudī, Ghurar al-Hikam, narration 4786

10) Soundness and Piety

The perfection of every being lies in possessing all that is required for its existence and for reaching the goal of this existence. Similarly, this perfection lies in being aloof from that which is incompatible with its existence or is an obstacle in reaching perfection and the goal of its existence. This is termed as the 'existential soundness' of that entity. For knowledge as well, soundness can be conceived in a manner that is in accordance to its position. Continuing his description of the virtues of knowledge and scholars, Imam ʿAlī (peace be upon him) says:

وَ هِمَّتُهُ السَّلَامَةُ

... and the endeavour of knowledge is soundness.

This means that just as how the endeavour of man is always to keep his body and spirit in a sound state, similarly knowledge endeavours to keep itself secure from defects. It endeavours to gain true and beneficial knowledge from its correct channel. One of the main defects pertaining to knowledge, is when a scholar unabashedly becomes afflicted with ideological, moral and practical deviation. Therefore, Imam ʿAlī (peace be upon him) says, continuing the description of virtues of knowledge and scholars:

وَ حِكْمَتُهُ الْوَرَعُ

... and the wisdom of knowledge is piety.

This means that if man seeks wisdom and comprehension of the realities of this world the way they really are, he must keep away from ideological, moral and spiritual impurities. Hence, Imam al-Ṣādiq (peace be upon him) says regarding the virtue and effect of piety:

لَا يَنْفَعُ اجْتِهَادٌ لَا وَرَعَ فِيهِ

An effort that is not accompanied by piety, brings no benefit. (i)

That is because when man takes efforts in a certain task but does not keep away from the obstacles, or he does not carry out the task in a

---

i. al-Kulaynī, al-Kāfī, 2:77, narration 4

complete manner, this effort will not yield results. Therefore, the Messenger of Allah (peace and blessings be upon him and his family) says:

أَفْضَلُ دِينِكُمُ الْوَرَعُ

The best of your religion is piety. (i)

He also says:

الْوَرَعُ سَيِّدُ الْعَمَلِ ، وَمَنْ لَمْ يَكُنْ لَهُ وَرَعٌ يَرُدُّهُ عَنْ مَعْصِيَةِ اللَّهِ تَعَالَى إِذَا خَلا بِهَا ، لَمْ يَعْبَأِ اللَّهُ بِسَائِرِ أَعْمَالِهِ، فَذَلِكَ مَخَافَةُ اللَّهِ فِي السِّرِّ وَ العَلانِيَةِ، وَ الإِقْتِصَادُ فِي الفَقْرِ وَ الغِنَى، وَ العَدْلُ عِنْدَ الرِّضَا وَ السَّخَطِ

Piety is the best of deeds. One who does not possess piety that stops him from Allah's disobedience when he encounters it, then Allah does not pay attention to his other deeds. So, piety is to fear Allah in secret and in open, to have moderation in poverty and in riches, and to be fair in happiness and in anger. (ii)

Imam ʿAlī (peace be upon him) also says:

الْوَرَعُ الْوُقُوفُ عِنْدَ الشُّبْهَة

Piety is to halt when encountering doubtful affairs. (iii)

Imam al-Ṣādiq (peace be upon him) also says:

لَيْسَ مِنَّا ... مَنْ كَانَ فِي مِصْرٍ فِيهِ مِائَةُ أَلْفٍ أَوْ يَزِيدُونَ وَ كَانَ فِي ذَلِكَ الْمِصْرِ أَحَدٌ أَوْرَعَ مِنْه

He is not from us ... one who lives in a city of a hundred thousand people or more and there is someone more pious than him in that city. (iv)

i. Majlisī, Biḥār al-Anwār, 70:304, narration 18

ii. al-Hindī, Kanz al-ʿUmmāl, narration 7299

iii. al-Āmudī, Ghurar al-Hikam, narration 2161

iv. al-Kulaynī, al-Kāfī, 2:78, narration 10

Therefore, when man's actions and his religion are rendered ineffective or their effect is diminished due to the absence or lack of piety, similarly knowledge without piety will not serve its purpose. Such knowledge will not pave the way to the desired goal. Instead, it will lead him to destruction. ʿAlī (peace be upon him) says:

لَا يَزْكُو الْعِلْمُ بِغَيْرِ وَرَعٍ

Knowledge is not purified without piety.[i]

This means that if knowledge of the Origin, the Return (the Hereafter), the soul, and the intricate laws governing the system of creation—all of which are a light and guidance—are accompanied by piety, then such knowledge will have certain characteristics. It will be aloof from doubts (that destroy knowledge and certainty in the realities) and it will cause man to act sincerely in his life and in all his activities, in a manner that is in accordance with this knowledge, until he is able to reach a higher level of purity.

11) Salvation and Well-being

Every being, either naturally or due to its instincts or its *fiṭrah*, is moving towards its existential goal. It is striving to reach the summit of its perfection by removing the obstacles in its path. Similarly, knowledge in its movement must also take man to the summit of his perfection: knowing Allah, His Divine Names, His Attributes, His existential perfections and the way to reach this knowledge. As Imam ʿAlī (peace be upon him), continuing the description of the virtues of knowledge and scholars, says:

وَ مُسْتَقَرُّهُ النَّجَاةُ

> ... and the abode of knowledge is the salvation and success [of man].

For knowledge to take man to salvation,[ii] he must—after know-

---

i. al-Āmudī, Ghurar al-Ḥikam, narration 10689

ii. The Arabic word '*najāh*' means a high place which due to its elevation is separated from other places around it. See the book al-Mufradāt of Rāghib al-Iṣfahānī, under

ing and paying attention to the lofty goal of knowledge and its true nature [i]—pursue the correct path to obtain this type of knowledge. He must always stay away from deviant paths and false manifestations of knowledge, which only lead man towards the world and worldly matters and imprison him in it. Therefore, Imam ʿAlī (peace be upon him), in the continuation of the description of the virtues of knowledge and scholars, says:

وَ قَائِدُهُ الْعَافِيَةُ

... and the leader of knowledge is well-being.

This means that man must make well-being to be his leader when seeking knowledge and acquiring it. This entails correct and careful deliberation about the different states and aspects of the beings, especially his own existence. The Noble Qurʾān has also expounded Allah's ontological and legislative signs so that man reflects on them and perceives their reality. [ii] It addresses man, saying:

وَ فِي أَنْفُسِكُمْ أَ فَلاَ تُبْصِرُونَ

And in your souls [as well]. Will you not then perceive? (51:21)

If man pays careful attention in this regard and observes the other requirements, then Allah will surely grant him deliverance and success. Imam al-Bāqir (peace be upon him) in the exegesis of this noble verse, "Let man consider his food," [iii] says:

عِلْمُهُ الَّذِي يَأْخُذُهُ عَمَّنْ يَأْخُذُهُ.

[Let him consider] his knowledge that he learns, from whom

---

the root نجد. (From the author)

i. The Noble Qurʾān describes the goal of creating the seven heavens, the similar number of earths, and the gradual descending of the command through them, as being that man should come to know the Omnipotence of Allah, and that His knowledge encompasses the world. Refer to 65:12. (From the author)

ii. (30,8), (30:21), (16:11), (16:44), (16:69) and (59:21)

iii. (80:24)

he acquires it.[i]

Imam al-Ṣādiq (peace be upon him) also says:

اعْرِفُوا مَنَازِلَ النَّاسِ عَلَى قَدْرِ رِوَايَتِهِمْ عَنَّا

Know the rank and the standing of the people through the extent of their transmitting [narrations] from us.[ii]

12) Fulfilling Promises

One of the characteristics that indicate a lofty spiritual personality, is to fulfil one's promises and agreements. This encompasses those agreements necessitated by man's existential rank, that is his existential relationship with the Sacred Divine Essence, his receiving of Divine Grace, and other affairs. Likewise, it encompasses his relationship with other entities and human beings with whom he engages in social interactions, giving rise to specific agreements.

If the knowledge of realities is to yield results, then a scholar must observe the covenants that come along with this type of knowledge. Fulfilling these covenants means to act according to the knowledge, as Imam ʿAlī (peace be upon him) says, continuing the description of the virtues of knowledge and scholars:

وَ مَرْكَبُهُ الْوَفَاءُ

... and the mount of knowledge is faithfulness.

In the same manner that a rider who ascends a swift mount reaches his destination, by riding the mount of fulfilling promises a scholar also reaches the purpose of acquiring knowledge. Therefore, the Noble Qurʾān mentions the fulfilling of Allah's covenants to be the first characteristics of those who possess intellect (*ulū al-albāb*):

الَّذِينَ يُوفُونَ بِعَهْدِ اللَّهِ

... those who fulfil Allah's covenant. (13:20)

The same covenant which was taken from all the human beings at

---

i. al-Kulaynī, al-Kāfī, 1:49, narration 8

ii. Ibid., 1:50, narration 13

the time of their creation:

> أَ لَمْ أَعْهَدْ إِلَيْكُمْ يَا بَنِي آدَمَ أَنْ لاَ تَعْبُدُوا الشَّيْطَانَ إِنَّهُ لَكُمْ عَدُوٌّ مُبِينٌ
>
> Did I not take covenant from you, O children of Adam, saying, "Do not worship Satan. He is indeed your manifest enemy, and Worship Me. That is a straight path"? (36:60)

Similarly, the Noble Qur'ān mentions that fulfilling a covenant made with any person, whoever he may be, is the sign of *taqwā* and truthfulness in one who is on the path towards true spirituality and faith:

> وَ الْمُوفُونَ بِعَهْدِهِمْ إِذَا عَاهَدُوا وَ الصَّابِرِينَ فِي الْبَأْسَاءِ وَ الضَّرَّاءِ وَ حِينَ الْبَأْسِ أُولَئِكَ الَّذِينَ صَدَقُوا وَ أُولَئِكَ هُمُ الْمُتَّقُونَ
>
> And those who fulfil their covenants, when they pledge themselves, and those who are patient in stress and distress, and in the heat of battle. They are the ones who are true [to their covenant], and it is they who are the pious. (2:77)

Similarly, it describes one of the qualities of a true believer in this manner:

> وَ الَّذِينَ هُمْ لِأَمَانَاتِهِمْ وَ عَهْدِهِمْ رَاعُونَ
>
> And those who keep their trusts and covenants. (23:8)

13) Softness of Speech

Speech is one of the Divine blessings bestowed on man. With it he can express that which is inside him and inform others about the realities of the world. With its help he can fulfil his needs and needs of others, as Allah the Immaculate says:

> خَلَقَ الْإِنْسَانَ عَلَّمَهُ الْبَيَانَ
>
> He created man, [and] taught him articulate speech. (55:3-4)

أَ لَمْ نَجْعَلْ لَهُ عَيْنَيْنِ وَ لِسَاناً وَ شَفَتَيْنِ

Have We not made for him two eyes, a tongue, and two lips? (90:8-9)

Amīr al-Mu'minīn (peace be upon him), describing the important role played by the tongue in showing a man's inside and his personality, says:

اللِّسَانُ مِيزَانُ الْإِنْسَان

The tongue is the scale [for examining] man. (i)

لِسَانُكَ تَرْجُمَانُ عَقْلِك

Your tongue is the translator of your intellect. (ii)

تَكَلَّمُوا تُعْرَفُوا فَإِنَّ الْمَرْءَ مَخْبُوءٌ تَحْتَ لِسَانِه

Speak and you will be known. For indeed a man is hidden behind his tongue. (iii)

Similarly, about the undesirable effects of speech on others he says:

ضَرْبُ اللِّسَانِ أَشَدُّ مِنْ ضَرْبِ السِّنَانِ

A blow caused by the tongue is more severe than the strike of a spear. (iv)

This undesirable effect is caused by accusation, indecent words, backbiting, rebuking, or by being harsh in one's speech. Therefore, Allah says to Prophet Moses and Aaron (peace be upon them) about how they should deal with the Pharaoh:

فَقُولاَ لَهُ قَوْلاً لَيِّناً لَعَلَّهُ يَتَذَكَّرُ أَوْ يَخْشَى

Speak to him in a soft manner; maybe he will take admonition or fear. (20:44)

---

i. al-Āmudī, Ghurar al-Hikam, narration 1282

ii. Majlisī, Bihār al-Anwār, 77:231, narration 2

iii. al-Radī, Nahj al-Balāghah, saying 392

iv. Majlisī, Bihār al-Anwār, 71:286, narration 42

Thus, if a scholar wants to convey his knowledge to others in the correct manner and wants them to benefit from it in their practical and intellectual life, then he must encounter them with soft speech and kindness. Not only while conveying his knowledge must he use soft, beautiful and pleasant words and expressions, but also in his normal conversations with others. This will cause him to have a marked effect, socially and religiously.

Therefore, Imam ʿAlī (peace be upon him) in continuing the description of the virtues of knowledge and scholars, says:

وَ سِلَاحُهُ لِينُ الْكَلِمَةِ

... and the weapon of knowledge is softness of speech.

Because through the instrument of soft speech, a person's logic and correct viewpoint is conveyed to others and no room is left for argument. On the contrary, if a scholar encounters them with harsh speech then even his logic and correct viewpoint will be disregarded and ignored.

14) Being Content

The nature of this world is that it is the place of competition and vying interests. Because of the contradiction between his selfish desires and the Divine *fiṭrah*, man cannot attain all his ambitions. On the other hand, by reflecting upon and paying careful attention to conclusive intellectual proofs, we come to know that all these affairs are endowed by Allah, the Wise and the Powerful, for man to reach a lofty goal. Therefore, to live a life of spiritual tranquillity and comfort, it is necessary that man has a state of satisfaction and contentment. Even when he is faced with unpleasant events and calamities—that he did not cause by his own wrong choices—such a state must be maintained. In this manner, with calmness, he can start to resolve these problems. Imam al-Ṣādiq (peace be upon him) says:

الرَّوحُ وَ الرَّاحَةُ فِي الرِّضَا وَ الْيَقِينِ وَ الْهَمُّ وَ الْحَزَنُ فِي الشَّكِّ وَ السَّخَطِ.

> Peace and comfort are in satisfaction and certainty, and distress and grief are in doubt and anger.[i]

Imam ʿAlī (peace be upon him) also says:

> إِنَّ أَهْنَأَ النَّاسِ عَيْشاً مَنْ كَانَ بِمَا قَسَمَ اللَّهُ لَهُ رَاضِيا
>
> Verily the most agreeable person with regards to his life, is one who is satisfied with what Allah has apportioned for him.[ii]

Undoubtedly, every event creates a particular responsibility for man. Satisfaction in the face of unpleasant events does not mean that a person does not strive to remedy the situation. Accordingly, in the Qurʾān and the Sunnah great stress is laid on acquiring this trait and it is considered as one of the lofty human characteristics.

Imam al-Ṣādiq (peace be upon him) says:

> رَأْسُ طَاعَةِ اللَّهِ الرِّضَا بِمَا صَنَعَ اللَّهُ فِيمَا أَحَبَّ الْعَبْدُ وَ فِيمَا كَرِه
>
> The foundation of Allah's obedience is satisfaction with respect to the acts of Allah, those which the servant likes and those which he dislikes.[iii]

By paying heed to the above-mentioned outlook, a believer is satisfied with everything that Allah, the Wise and Compassionate, has commanded him to perform. He carries out these commands with inward satisfaction and willingness. In the initial stages this is difficult because his soul is not accustomed to acts of obedience. However, if he continues to perform them keeping in mind the desirable effect of these acts of obedience, then because Allah's pleasure lies in them they are the cause of man's guidance to higher stations. As Allah says:

> يَهْدِي بِهِ اللَّهُ مَنِ اتَّبَعَ رِضْوَانَهُ سُبُلَ السَّلاَمِ وَ يُخْرِجُهُمْ مِنَ الظُّلُمَاتِ إِلَى النُّورِ بِإِذْنِهِ وَ يَهْدِيهِمْ إِلَى صِرَاطٍ مُسْتَقِي
>
> With it [the Qurʾān] Allah guides those who follow [the

i. Ibid., 71:159, narration 75

ii. al-Āmudī, Ghurar al-Hikam, narration 3397

iii. Majlisī, Biḥār al-Anwār, 71:139, narration 28

course of] His satisfaction to the ways of peace and brings them out from darkness into light by His will and guides them to a straight path. (5:16)

Through such guidance from Allah, a person slowly acquires the state of satisfaction and contentment with respect to the unpleasant events that happen in this world. One of the signs of this is that he is satisfied with those who harboured animosity towards him and oppressed him but then asked for forgiveness. Sometimes he reaches a higher station and is even satisfied with those who have not asked for forgiveness, hoping that Allah becomes pleased with him.

Possessing this state is a perfection for everyone, especially for the seekers of knowledge whose job is to understand the truths, realities and enlightening teachings of the Qurʾān and the Sunnah. To prevail over the failures and stagnation in their affairs when faced with the difficulties and discomforts of the physical world, such individuals must encounter these difficulties with the sword of satisfaction. As Imam ʿAlī (peace be upon him) says, continuing the description of the virtues of knowledge and scholars:

وَ سَيْفُهُ الرِّضَا

... and the sword of knowledge is satisfaction (*riḍā*)

Because, if he is not satisfied then he will be overpowered by the selfish desires and unpleasant events of this world, and the effect of knowledge will disappear from his being. As a result, he will not be able to guide others to the knowledge he has learnt and make them optimistic and hopeful regarding the realities of the world. In the words of Imam al-Ṣādiq (peace be upon him):

مَنْ لَمْ يَرْضَ بِمَا قَسَمَ اللَّهُ عَزَّ وَ جَلَّ اتَّهَمَ اللَّهَ تَعَالَى فِي قَضَائِه

One who is not satisfied with what Allah, the Mighty and the Exalted, has apportioned for him, has accused Allah [of unfairness] in His decree and command. (i)

i. Ibid., 75:202, narration 33 (This source was not included in the original Persian copy of the book)

That is because, the consequence of knowing that everything in this world is in a certain sense reliant on Allah, is being satisfied with the things one faces, just as Imam al-Ṣādiq (peace be upon him) says:

إِنَّ أَعْلَمَ النَّاسِ بِاللَّهِ أَرْضَاهُمْ بِقَضَاءِ اللَّه

> Verily, the most knowledgeable person about Allah is the one who is the most satisfied with Allah's decree. (i)

Similarly, Imam al-Sajjād (peace be upon him) asks Allah, the Exalted:

فَاجْعَلْ نَفْسِي ... رَاضِيَةً بِقَضَائِك

Make my soul ... satisfied with Your decree. (ii)

The Messenger of Allah (peace and blessings be upon him and his family) also describes the outcome of possessing this state in the following manner:

وَ ارْضَ بِقِسْمِ اللَّهِ تَكُنْ أَغْنَى النَّاس

> Be satisfied with Allah's division [of bounties and favours] and you will be the richest of people. (iii)

This state of needlessness from the people, when it is accompanied with maintaining various social, economic, family and cultural interactions with them, brings about esteem and respect for an individual. It also creates in him the zeal to perform his duty with regards to his activities. Especially if by struggling against his self, he becomes satisfied with those who have oppressed him, acted out of jealousy, or deprived him of some social and worldly matters. In this case he will live with comfort in this world and the next and will attain honour in the eyes of others and affect them in a beneficial manner.

---

i. Ibid., 71:158, narration 75

ii. Ibid., 100:264, narration 2

iii. Ibid., 69:368, narration 4

15) Tolerance with People

To fulfil his worldly needs, it is necessary that man seeks help from his fellow human beings and benefits from their thoughts, capabilities, actions and guidance. But to establish this relationship with them, he must also help them fulfil their own needs. Despite this, some people due to being selfish, lazy, feeble or irresponsible, breach this social agreement.

Naturally, for the strength, continuity and soundness of this mutual relationship, it is necessary to show leniency and behave kindly with those who unintentionally breach this social agreement, as long as its foundation remains intact.[i] Such conduct prevents the issue of coexistence with fellow human beings from being undermined, has a positive effect on other, and causes the one who possess this noble trait to increase in his tolerance, forbearance and perfection.

Without a doubt, tolerance with violators does not mean approving of their violations. Nor should it make people lax in observing the laws and norms that are in place for the reform of the society. Rather, this must be observed so that man lives a life of peace and tranquillity. Thus, one should recognize the various mentalities and capacities of people, and act with them in a manner that is lenient and courteous. As Imam ʿAlī (peace be upon him) says:

سَلَامَةُ الْعَيْشِ فِي الْمُدَارَاة

The soundness of life is in tolerance [with the people].[ii]

If man wants to act realistically, and if he uses his intellect to consider the level of understanding of the people and their different mentalities, then he will see that to derive results from his activities he must make leniency and tolerance to be the utmost priority in his life. As Imam ʿAlī (peace be upon him) says:

رَأْسُ الْحِكْمَةِ مُدَارَاةُ النَّاس ... ثَمَرَةُ الْعَقْلِ مُدَارَاةُ النَّاس

---

i. For example, in the face of social injustice and tyranny, there is no room for tolerance.

ii. al-Āmudī, Fihrist-i Mawdūʿī-yi Ghurar al-Hikam, the chapter on mudārāt (tolerance).

- The foundation of wisdom [having a realistic outlook] is tolerance with the people ... The fruit of the intellect is tolerance with the people.[i]

A life led with such an approach is the cause of strengthening social and family relationships, as well as solving several psychological afflictions.

Amīr al-Muʾminīn (peace be upon him) says:

دَارِ النَّاسَ تَسْتَمْتِعْ بِإِخَائِهِمْ وَ الْقَهُمْ بِالْبِشْرِ تُمِتْ أَضْغَانَهُم

Be tolerant with the people so that you benefit from their brotherly relationship. Meet them with cheerfulness so that the animosity [in your heart] towards them is destroyed.[ii]

Due to the importance of this approach in improving social relations and attracting people towards the path and creed of truth, the Messenger of Allah (peace and blessings be upon him and his family) says:

أَمَرَنِي رَبِّي بِمُدَارَاةِ النَّاسِ كَمَا أَمَرَنِي بِأَدَاءِ الْفَرَائِضِ

My Lord has enjoined me to be tolerant with the people in the same manner that he has ordered me to perform the obligatory actions.[iii]

Through this approach the Messenger of Allah (peace and blessings be upon him and his family) was able to spread his religion and due to this, everyone benefitted from his noble moral character. So much so that some people took advantage of him and called him an "ear."[iv] As Allah says:

وَ مِنْهُمُ الَّذِينَ يُؤْذُونَ النَّبِيَّ وَ يَقُولُونَ هُوَ أُذُنٌ قُلْ أُذُنُ خَيْرٍ لَكُمْ يُؤْمِنُ بِاللَّهِ وَ يُؤْمِنُ لِلْمُؤْمِنِينَ وَ رَحْمَةٌ لِلَّذِينَ آمَنُوا مِنْكُمْ

Among them are those who torment the Prophet, and say, "He is an ear." Say, "An ear that is good for you. He has faith

---

i. Ibid.

ii. Ibid.

iii. al-Kulaynī, al-Kāfī, 2:117, narration 4

iv. By this, the hypocrites meant that he listens to everything and everyone.

in Allah, trusts the faithful, and is a mercy for those of you who have faith." (9:61)

For this reason, Islamic teachings were communicated gradually, so that people acquire the ability to bear them. In order that people's religion and faith is safeguarded, these teachings command us to be tolerant with people. Imam ʿAlī (peace be upon him) says:

سَلاَمَةُ الدِّينِ وَ الدُّنْيَا فِي مُدَارَاةِ النَّاس

The safety of the religion and the world lies in being tolerant with people.[i]

Therefore, in addition to being a virtue of the human soul and one of the Divine attributes of perfection, anyone who possesses this trait will also earn benefits in this world and the Hereafter. Possessing this trait is even more necessary for a religious scholar, one whose duty is to fulfil the goals of the Noblest Messenger (peace and blessings be upon him and his family) and the Divine religion. Because a scholar is aware of the various capacities of the people in understanding religious teachings, and how these teachings must be imparted to each person to the extent of their intellectual ability, with gentleness and mercy. Such was the conduct of the Messenger of Allah (peace and blessings be upon him and his family) and the Imams (peace be upon them) in their role as a teacher and trainer. They would not forsake their duty due to the harsh behaviour of ignorant or spiteful individuals. Rather, they would react in a soft manner and with kindness, to the extent possible, and to the extent that the conditions of guidance allowed. Allah says to Prophet Moses and Aaron (peace be upon them):

اذْهَبْ أَنْتَ وَ أَخُوكَ بِآيَاتِي وَ لاَ تَنِيَا فِي ذِكْرِي اذْهَبَا إِلَى فِرْعَوْنَ إِنَّهُ طَغَى فَقُولاَ لَهُ قَوْلاً لَيِّناً لَعَلَّهُ يَتَذَكَّرُ أَوْ يَخْشَى

Go ahead, you and your brother, with My signs and do not flag in My remembrance. Both of you go to Pharaoh, for he has indeed rebelled. Speak to him in a soft manner; maybe

i. al-Āmudī, Fihrist-i Mawdu'i-yi Ghurar al-Hikm, the chapter on *mudārāt* (tolerance) he will take admonition or fear.)20:42-44)

Therefore, Imam ʿAlī (peace be upon him), continuing the description of the virtues of knowledge and scholars, says:

وَ قَوْسُهُ الْمُدَارَاةُ

... and the bow of knowledge is tolerance.

This means that in the same manner that a bow is flexible and by placing an arrow in it, it hits the target, similarly a scholar must have a state of flexibility and softness. For a scholar to succeed in his work when interacting with students, common people, adversaries, and people of the same level and rank, he must be lenient with them. In this way he can understand the appropriate manner of working with them so that he reaches the goal that he had in seeking knowledge.

16) Speaking with Scholars

Allah has made speech to be one of the important channels of communicating a person's outward and inward needs. For speech to be strong and unshakable, one must first deliberate and reflect on it, so that it does not lead to remorse. As Imam ʿAlī (peace be upon him) says:

لِسَانُ الْعَاقِلِ وَرَاءَ قَلْبِهِ وَ قَلْبُ الْأَحْمَقِ وَرَاءَ لِسَانِه

The tongue of a wise person is behind his heart and the heart of a fool is behind his tongue. (i)

تَكَلَّمُوا تُعْرَفُوا فَإِنَّ الْمَرْءَ مَخْبُوءٌ تَحْتَ لِسَانِه

Speak and you will be known. For indeed a man is concealed behind his tongue. (ii)

Therefore, a scholar who wishes to convey his knowledge to others in order that they benefit from it, should first pay careful attention to the type of knowledge he is acquiring. It should be knowledge that will profit him in this world and the Hereafter; it should be beneficial for others. Secondly, he should consider which source he is acquiring

---

i. al-Radī, Nahj al-Balāghah, saying 40

ii. Ibid., saying 392

it from. Imam al-Bāqir (peace be upon him) when he was asked about the noble verse, "let man consider his food," (i) as to what is meant by the word "food", he replied:

عِلْمُهُ الَّذِي يَأْخُذُهُ عَمَّنْ يَأْخُذُهُ.

> [He should consider] the knowledge which he acquires, from whom he acquires it. (ii)

Thirdly, both while he is studying and afterwards, a scholar must present his knowledge to experts in that field and engage in discussion with them so that:

- Firstly, the positive aspects of his knowledge become clear for him and he reaches certainty that the means and methods that he has used are correct. Consequently, he can pass on this knowledge to others.
- Secondly, he becomes aware of the deficient aspects of his knowledge and the incorrect methods he used to reach it. As a result, he does not remain in the state of compound ignorance and instead corrects this knowledge.
- Thirdly, he can inform others of the wrong and unsuccessful methods, as well as the incorrect knowledge (the compound ignorance) that he had.

In this situation, he has traversed the path of ascent, the path of the growth of knowledge and training true scholars. Therefore, Imam ʿAlī (peace be upon him) says, continuing the description of the virtues of knowledge and scholars:

وَ جَيْشُهُ مُحَاوَرَةُ الْعُلَمَاءِ

> ... and the army of knowledge is discussion with the learned.

A nation requires an army that is experienced and acquainted with warfare tactics so that it can achieve victory over its enemy and attain peace, tranquillity, and a standard of life that is comfortable and that

---

i. (80:24)

ii. al-Kulaynī, al-Kāfī, 1:49, narration 8

pleases Allah. In the same manner, a scholar must discuss and exchange views with experienced scholars in that field to achieve victory over the enemy of ignorance—be it his own ignorance or the ignorance of others. In this manner, by constantly strengthening his knowledge and resolutely utilizing definitive methods, he pushes away the army of ignorance and conquers its strongholds. For this reason, Imam ʿAlī (peace be upon him) says:

رُبَّ قَوْلٍ أَنْفَذُ مِنْ صَوْل

How often is a word more effective than an armed assault.[i]

رُبَّ كَلَامٍ أَنْفَذُ مِنْ سِهَام

How often is a speech more penetrating than an arrow![ii]

For this reason, the prophets, Imams (peace be upon them), and scholars possessing insight and awareness of their opponents—as described in the Qurʾān and the Sunnah—prevail in the debates that they engage in. Similarly, the correct sciences that are prevalent amongst the people and scholars today—whether it is sciences related to religion and man's felicity in the world and the Hereafter or knowledge of laws governing the material realm—have reached us through such scholars.

17) Having Refined Etiquettes (Adab)

Different definitions have been provided for the term '*adab*'. Ustād ʿAllāmah Ṭabāṭabāʾī says:

> *Adab* is a beautiful and desirable form that human nature and people's tendencies consider befitting, such that every lawful action should be performed in conformity with that form. In other words, *adab* means elegance and beauty of action. An action is beautiful when firstly it is lawful and secondly it is voluntary.[iii]

---

i. al-Raḍī, Nahj al-Balāghah, saying 394

ii. al-Āmudī, Ghurar al-Ḥikm, narration 5322

iii. Ṭabāṭabāʾī, Tafsīr al-Mīzān, 6:255-256

By paying attention to this passage it becomes clear that *akhlāq* pertains to the deeply-rooted qualities and temporary states of the soul, whereas *ādāb*[i] pertains to the beautiful forms that describe man's actions.[ii]

Therefore, *ādāb* are generally the same *mustaḥabb* actions taught by the *awliyā'* of the religion (peace be upon them) in relation to different ritual, individual and social actions. These *mustaḥabb* actions cause man's actions to become more luminous and meritorious, after one has performed the obligatory actions. It has been highly recommended that man beautifies his actions with different *ādāb*. In one such narration Imam ʿAlī (peace be upon him) says:

> إِنَّ رَسُولَ اللَّهِ ص أَدَّبَهُ اللَّهُ عَزَّ وَ جَلَّ وَ هُوَ أَدَّبَنِي وَ أَنَا أُؤَدِّبُ الْمُؤْمِنِينَ
>
> Indeed, Allah taught *adab* to the Messenger of Allah (peace and blessings be upon him and his family) and he taught it to me, and I teach these *adab* to the believers.[iii]

There are numerous Islamic narrations about the *ādāb* and the conduct of the Messenger of Allah (peace and blessings be upon him and his family) and the Imams (peace be upon them). Each of these is an excellent way to beautify oneself with Divine *ādāb*. Sometimes the term '*adab*' is used in the Islamic narrations in a broader sense, encompassing more than the *mustaḥabbāt*. As Imam ʿAlī (peace be upon him) says:

> أَفْضَلُ الْأَدَبِ أَنْ يَقِفَ الْإِنْسَانُ عِنْدَ حَدِّهِ وَ لَا يَتَعَدَّى قَدْرَه
>
> The best *adab* is that a man stops at his limit and does not transgress his capacity.[iv]

He also says:

> ضَبْطُ النَّفْسِ عِنْدَ الرَّغَبِ وَ الرَّهَبِ مِنْ أَفْضَلِ الْأَدَب

---

i. Plural of *adab*.

ii. Ṭabāṭabā'ī, Tafsīr al-Mīzān, 6:257

iii. Majlisī, Bihār al-Anwār, 77:267, narration 1

iv. al-Āmudī, Ghurar al-Hikam, narration 3241

> Restraining the soul at the time of desire and fear is the best *adab*.[i]

However, our aim in talking about *adab* here, is to explain its specific meaning that was first mentioned. While describing the virtues of this type of *adab*, Imam ʿAlī (peace be upon him) says:

> الْأَدَبُ كَمَالُ الرَّجُلِ ... حُسْنُ الْأَدَبِ أَفْضَلُ نَسَبٍ وَ أَشْرَفُ سَبَبٍ ... إِنَّ النَّاسَ إِلَى صَالِحِ الْأَدَبِ أَحْوَجُ مِنْهُمْ إِلَى الْفِضَّةِ وَ الذَّهَبِ
>
> *Adab* is the perfection of man ... Having good *adab* is the best lineage and the noblest means [to create relations] ... Indeed, people are more in need of befitting *adab* than silver and gold.[ii]

Similarly, in the words of Imam ʿAlī (peace be upon him):

لَا زِينَةَ كَالْآدَابِ

There is no ornament like *ādāb*.[iii]

Therefore, acquiring *ādāb* is an adornment for all, especially for seekers of religious knowledge. For this reason, continuing the description of the virtues of knowledge and scholars, the Imam (peace be upon him) says:

وَ مَالُهُ الْأَدَبُ

... and the wealth of knowledge is *adab*.

A person, with his wealth and monetary capital, engages in trade, earns profit, provides benefit to others and fulfils their material needs. Similarly, by beautifying his actions with different *ādāb*, a scholar himself benefits from his knowledge, and others also take an example from it, as well as from his conduct and manner. Therefore, the scholar should be the forerunner in acquiring *ādāb*. In this regard Imam ʿAlī (peace

---

i. Ibid., narration 5932

ii. Ibid., narrations 997, 4853, and 3590

iii. Ibid., narration 10466

be upon him) says:

مَنْ نَصَبَ نَفْسَهُ لِلنَّاسِ إِمَاماً فَلْيَبْدَأْ بِتَعْلِيمِ نَفْسِهِ قَبْلَ تَعْلِيمِ غَيْرِهِ وَ لْيَكُنْ تَأْدِيبُهُ بِسِيرَتِهِ قَبْلَ تَأْدِيبِهِ بِلِسَانِهِ وَ مُعَلِّمُ نَفْسِهِ وَ مُؤَدِّبُهَا أَحَقُّ بِالْإِجْلَالِ مِنْ مُعَلِّمِ النَّاسِ وَ مُؤَدِّبِهِم

> One who appoints himself as a leader of the people, then let him start with teaching his own self before teaching others. And let his conduct be adorned with *adab* before he enjoins others towards *adab* by his tongue. One who teaches his soul and beautifies it with *adab* is more deserving of praise than the one who teaches others and beautifies them with *adab*.(i)

Because of the great significance of acquiring religious *ādāb*, Imam al-Ṣādiq (peace be upon him) says:

إِنْ أُجِّلْتَ فِي عُمُرِكَ يَوْمَيْنِ فَاجْعَلْ أَحَدَهُمَا
لِأَدَبِكَ لِتَسْتَعِينَ بِهِ عَلَى يَوْمِ مَوْتِك

> If you were given two more days in your life, then use one day for acquiring *adab* so that you can seek help by means of it, for the day of your death.(ii)

Therefore, to actualize this matter, it is necessary to pay attention to and procure the following preliminaries.

Firstly, man should pay attention to the ugliness of some affairs and how his soul detests them and considers them repulsive. Imam ʿAlī (peace be upon him) says about this:

كَفَاكَ أَدَباً لِنَفْسِكَ اجْتِنَابُ مَا تَكْرَهُهُ مِنْ غَيْرِك

> It is sufficient for your *adab* that you avoid doing that which you dislike in others.(iii)

Also, in another narration he says:

إِذَا رَأَيْتَ فِي غَيْرِكَ خُلُقاً ذَمِيماً فَتَجَنَّبْ مِنْ نَفْسِكَ أَمْثَالَه

i. al-Radī, Nahj al-Balāghah, saying 73

ii. al-Kulaynī, al-Kāfī, 8:150, narration 132

iii. Majlisī, Bihār al-Anwār, 70:73, narration 27

> If you see a blameworthy trait in another person, then drive the likes of it from your own self. (i)

Secondly, he should adopt the company of good people and scholars. Imam ʿAlī (peace be upon him) says in this regard:

> جَالِسِ الْعُلَمَاءَ يَزْدَدْ عِلْمُكَ وَ يَحْسُنْ أَدَبُكَ وَ تَزْكُ نَفْسُكَ
>
> Associate with the scholars and your knowledge will increase, your *adab* will become good and your soul will be purified. (ii)

Also, Imam al-Sajjād (peace be upon him) says:

> مَجَالِسُ الصَّالِحِينَ دَاعِيَةٌ إِلَى الصَّلَاحِ
>
> Association with the righteous people invites [a person] towards well-being and deliverance. (iii)

Thirdly, he should increase his awareness of the realities and *ādāb*. Imam ʿAlī (peace be upon him) says in this regard:

> إِذَا زَادَ عِلْمُ الرَّجُلِ زَادَ أَدَبُه
>
> When a man's knowledge increases his *adab* increases. (iv)

Due to the importance of this topic, different dimensions and types of *adab* will be discussed here.

Dimensions of Adab

Man has an existential connection with different beings. Therefore, it is necessary that he observes the appropriate *adab* for each of them.

1) *Adab* in front of Allah the Exalted

Even though observing Allah's commands in different spheres of life is itself implementing *adab* in front of Him, in addition to that, Allah's majesty demands that while mentioning Him and His sacred names, man must mention them with reverence. As much as possible

---

i. al-Āmudī, Ghurar al-Hikam, narration 4098

ii. Ibid., narration 4786

iii. Majlisī, Bihār al-Anwār, 78:141, narration 35

iv. al-Āmudī, Ghurar al-Hikam, narration 4174

he should not mention the Divine Names without the suffixes: *jalla jalālahu* (exalted is His majesty), *ʿazza wa jalla* (the Invincible and Majestic), *subḥānahu* (Immaculate is He), or *tabāraka wa taʿāla* (the Provider of abundance and the Sublime). The Imams (peace be upon them) and the Divine scholars (may Allah be pleased with them) would act in this manner.

In summary, he should maintain a special demeanour regarding Allah, loving Him and showing humility in front of Him, and he should observe these matters. It is mentioned in a narration:

> A young man greeted the Revered Messenger (peace and blessings be upon him and his family) and expressed his joy at meeting him. The Prophet said to him, "Do you love me?" He said, "Yes, by Allah, O Messenger of Allah!" The Prophet asked him, "To the extent of your love for your mother?" The young man replied, "More than that." The Messenger of Allah asked again, "To the extent of your love for yourself?" He replied, "By Allah I love you more, O Messenger of Allah." The Prophet asked, "To the extent of your love for Allah?" Here this young man replied, "Allah, Allah, Allah. O Messenger of Allah! This position is not for you nor for anyone else, because I love you out of my love for Allah."
>
> The Messenger of Allah (peace and blessings be upon him and his family) then turned to his companions and said, "Love Allah because of His goodness to you and because He grants blessing to you and love me because of the love of Allah." [i]

Therefore, the *adab* of servitude in front of Allah the Exalted requires that man should never forget his existential rank and stature in front of Allah. He must bear in mind his state of abjectness when addressing, supplicating and beseeching Him, and to the extent possible he should not express his needs in the form of a command or a prohibition. The Noble Qurʾān narrates some of the requests made by the Divine messengers (peace be upon them) from Allah, in this manner. For example,

---

i. Ibn Abī al-Ḥadīd, Sharḥ-i Nahj al-Balāghah, 10:171

Prophet Abraham (peace be upon him), requesting forgiveness for the sinners, says:

وَ مَنْ عَصَانِي فَإِنَّكَ غَفُورٌ رَحِي

> And as for those who disobey me, You are indeed Forgiving, Merciful. (14:36)

Similarly, Prophet Jesus (peace be upon him) says:

إِنْ تُعَذِّبْهُمْ فَإِنَّهُمْ عِبَادُكَ وَ إِنْ تَغْفِرْ لَهُمْ فَإِنَّكَ أَنْتَ الْعَزِيزُ الْحَكِيمُ

> If You punish them, they are indeed Your creatures; but if You forgive them, You are indeed the Mighty, the Wise. (5:118)

In the same manner it quotes from Prophet Job (peace be upon him) when he made request to be cured:

أَنِّي مَسَّنِيَ الضُّرُّ وَ أَنْتَ أَرْحَمُ الرَّاحِمِي

> Indeed, distress has befallen me, and You are the most merciful of the merciful. (21:83)

2) *Adab* in front of the Messenger of Allah (peace and blessings be upon him and his family)

After beautifying himself with *adab* in front of Allah, a Muslim must also exhibit *adab* with respect to His Messenger (peace and blessings be upon him and his family). He should not mention his blessed name disrespectfully and without reciting *ṣalawāt,* and whenever possible he should not utter it unless in the state of *wuḍūʾ*. He should know that the Messenger of Allah (peace and blessings be upon him and his family) is present and sees his actions; he should consider him to be the foremost of all the prophets (peace be upon them), the *awliyāʾ*, and the righteous servants. He should try to follow his Sunnah and his conduct completely and should not disregard the *ādāb* which must be observed with regards to him, in the same manner that the Imams (peace be upon them) would do. For example, whenever Imam al-Ṣādiq (peace be upon him) wanted to say, "The Messenger of Allah (peace and blessings be upon him and his family) said ...", his colour would change. Sometimes it would turn pale green and sometimes it would turn yellow, such that those who knew him, would not recognize him![i]

Abū Hārūn says:

كُنْتُ جَلِيساً لِأَبِي عَبْدِ اللَّهِ ع بِالْمَدِينَةِ فَفَقَدَنِي أَيَّاماً- ثُمَّ إِنِّي جِئْتُ إِلَيْهِ فَقَالَ لَمْ أَرَكَ مُنْذُ أَيَّامٍ يَا أَبَا هَارُونَ- فَقُلْتُ وُلِدَ لِي غُلَامٌ فَقَالَ بَارَكَ اللَّهُ لَكَ- فَمَا سَمَّيْتَهُ قُلْتُ سَمَّيْتُهُ مُحَمَّداً- فَأَقْبَلَ بِخَدِّهِ نَحْوَ الْأَرْضِ وَ هُوَ يَقُولُ مُحَمَّدٌ مُحَمَّدٌ مُحَمَّدٌ- حَتَّى كَادَ يَلْصَقُ خَدُّهُ بِالْأَرْضِ- ثُمَّ قَالَ بِنَفْسِي وَ بِوُلْدِي وَ بِأَهْلِي وَ بِأَبَوَيَّ- وَ بِأَهْلِ الْأَرْضِ كُلِّهِمْ جَمِيعاً الْفِدَاءُ لِرَسُولِ اللَّهِ ص- لَا تَسُبَّهُ وَ لَا تَضْرِبْهُ وَ لَا تُسِئْ إِلَيْهِ- وَ اعْلَمْ أَنَّهُ لَيْسَ فِي الْأَرْضِ دَارٌ فِيهَا اسْمُ مُحَمَّدٍ- إِلَّا وَ هِيَ تُقَدَّسُ كُلَّ يَوْمٍ

> I would regularly visit Imam al-Ṣādiq (peace be upon him). A few days passed, and I was unable to visit him. Then, when I went to meet him, he said, "I did not see you for a few days." I said, "A son was born to me." The Imam asked, "May Allah bless you. What did you name him?" I replied, "I named him Muḥammad". The Imam put his cheek [his head] down and said, "Muḥammad, Muḥammad, Muḥammad." He repeated this so much that his cheek was about to touch the ground. Then he said, "May my soul, my children, my parents and all the dwellers of the Earth, be sacrificed for the Messenger of Allah (peace and blessings be upon him and his family). Do not insult him, do not hit him, do not wrong him, and know that there is no house on the face of this Earth that has the name Muḥammad, except that every day it is sanctified."[ii]

It is thus desirable that a person, due to his love for the Messenger of Allah (peace and blessings be upon him and his family), loves, honours and respects those who are related to him, whether it is outward

i. al-ʿĀmilī, Wasāʾil al-Shīʿah, 21:393, narration 27387

ii. Ibid.

relation like the *sādāt*[i] or a spiritual relation like the believers and religious scholars.

3) *Adab* in front of the Imams (peace be upon them)

One of the important duties of a believer after recognizing and loving the Imams (peace be upon them), is to observe *adab* with regards to mentioning their names, respecting their words and paying attention to the fact that they are aware of our deeds and actions. Similarly, being honoured to go for their *ziyārah* (visiting their graves) must be accompanied by observing humbleness, submissiveness, with the intention of seeking Allah's proximity, and in obedience to Him. Just as how Hishām ibn Ḥakam entered the presence of Imam al-Ṣādiq (peace be upon him), and the Imam asked him regarding his debate with ʿUmar ibn ʿUbayd (one of the Sunni scholars) on the issue of *imāmah* (leadership):

فَقَالَ هِشَامٌ يَا ابْنَ رَسُولِ اللَّهِ إِنِّي أُجِلُّكَ وَ أَسْتَحْيِيكَ وَ لَا يَعْمَلُ لِسَانِي بَيْنَ يَدَيْكَ فَقَالَ أَبُو عَبْدِ اللَّهِ إِذَا أَمَرْتُكُمْ بِشَيْءٍ فَافْعَلُوا

Hishām replied, "O the son of Messenger of Allah (peace and blessings be upon him and his family)! I feel shy and my tongue is incapable of speaking in your presence." So, the Imam replied, "When I command you to perform a certain action, then do it."[ii]

Similarly, one of the narrators says:

كُنْتُ عِنْدَ عَلِيِّ بْنِ جَعْفَرِ بْنِ مُحَمَّدٍ ع جَالِساً ... إِذْ دَخَلَ عَلَيْهِ أَبُو جَعْفَرٍ مُحَمَّدُ بْنُ عَلِيٍّ الرِّضَا ع الْمَسْجِدَ مَسْجِدَ رَسُولِ اللَّهِ فَوَثَبَ عَلِيُّ بْنُ جَعْفَرٍ بِلَا حِذَاءٍ وَ لَا رِدَاءٍ فَقَبَّلَ يَدَهُ وَ عَظَّمَهُ

i. *Sādāt* is the plural of *sayyid*. It refers to an individual whose lineage traces back to the Messenger of Allah (peace and blessings be upon him and his family). At times it is used in a broader sense, to refer to anyone from the progeny of Hāshim (the great-grandfather of the Messenger of Allah).

ii. al-Kulaynī, al-Kāfī, 1:169, narration 3

فَقَالَ لَهُ أَبُو جَعْفَرٍ ع يَا عَمِ اجْلِسْ رَحِمَكَ اللَّهُ فَقَالَ يَا سَيِّدِي كَيْفَ أَجْلِسُ وَ أَنْتَ قَائِمٌ فَلَمَّا رَجَعَ عَلِيُّ بْنُ جَعْفَرٍ إِلَى مَجْلِسِهِ جَعَلَ أَصْحَابُهُ يُوَبِّخُونَهُ وَ يَقُولُونَ أَنْتَ عَمُّ أَبِيهِ وَ أَنْتَ تَفْعَلُ بِهِ هَذَا الْفِعْلَ فَقَالَ اسْكُتُوا إِذَا كَانَ اللَّهُ عَزَّ وَ جَلَّ وَ قَبَضَ عَلَى لِحْيَتِهِ لَمْ يُؤَهِّلْ هَذِهِ الشَّيْبَةَ وَ أَهَّلَ هَذَا الْفَتَى وَ وَضَعَهُ حَيْثُ وَضَعَهُ أُنْكِرُ فَضْلَهُ نَعُوذُ بِاللَّهِ مِمَّا تَقُولُونَ بَلْ أَنَا لَهُ عَبْدٌ

[One day] I was sitting in the presence of ʿAlī Ibn Jaʿfar ibn Muḥammad [the brother of Imam al-Kāẓim (peace be upon him)] ... when Abū Jaʿfar Muḥammad ibn ʿAlī al-Riḍā [Imam al-Jawād] (peace be upon him) entered the mosque of the Messenger of Allah (peace and blessings be upon him and his family). ʿAlī Ibn Jaʿfar jumped up from his place without wearing his robe or shoes, kissed the hands of the Imam and honoured him. Abū Jaʿfar (peace be upon him) said to him, "O uncle! Please sit down. May Allah have mercy on you." He replied, "O my master, how can I sit while you are standing?!" When ʿAlī ibn Jaʿfar (peace be upon him) returned to his seat, those around him rebuked him saying, "You are the uncle of his father, why did you show him respect in this manner?" ʿAlī ibn Jaʿfar (peace be upon him) replied, "Keep quiet!" Then he held his beard in his hands and said, "When Allah despite my white beard, did not consider me worthy of this station (the station of *imāmah*) and placed this young man in this lofty position, should I still deny his merit and lofty station?! We seek refuge in Allah from what you say. In fact, I am a slave of his."[(i)]

Indeed, such is the case. In order to observe *adab* in the presence of the Imam when being honoured with the opportunity to visit him, instructions have been mentioned in the books of *ziyārah*.[(ii)] For this

---

i. Majlisī, Bihār al-Anwār, 47:266, narration 35

ii. Qummī, Mafātīh al-Jinān, chapter 3, etiquettes of ziyārah reason, when a group of companions of Imam al-Ṣādiq (peace be upon him) visited him and Abū Baṣīr, who was in the state of *janābah* (ritual impurity) was also with them, the Imam (peace be upon him) said to him at the time of leaving:

أَ مَا عَلِمْتَ أَنَّ بُيُوتَ الْأَنْبِيَاءِ- وَ أَوْلَادِ الْأَنْبِيَاءِ لَا يَدْخُلُهَا الْجُنُبُ

> Do you not know that the houses of the prophets and the children of the prophets are such that, one who is in the state of ritual impurity (*janābah*) does not enter them? (i)

4) *Adab* in front of Scholars

One of the means of man's success—especially the students of religious sciences and the scholars—is to respect and to venerate the teachers and pioneers of knowledge and spirituality. To the degree that a person's knowledge increases, his *adab* in relation to them should also increase. If he allows even the least amount of disrespect and rudeness in relation to them, his *tawfiqāt* will be taken away, he will be deprived of continuing the seeking of religious sciences, or he will not derive any spiritual benefit from his knowledge. Therefore, Imam al-Kāẓim (peace be upon him) has said:

عَظِّمِ الْعَالِمَ لِعِلْمِهِ وَ دَعْ مُنَازَعَتَه

> Venerate a scholar because of his knowledge and relinquish disputing him. (ii)

Imam ʿAlī (peace be upon him) says:

مَنْ وَقَّرَ عَالِماً فَقَدْ وَقَّرَ رَبَّه

One who revers a scholar has shown reverence to his Lord. (iii)

Similarly, Imam al-Ṣādiq (peace be upon him) narrates from Imam ʿAlī (peace be upon him):

---

i. al-ʿĀmilī, Wasā'il al-Shīʿah, 2:211

ii. Majlisī, Bihār al-Anwār, 75:309, narration 1

iii. al-Āmudī, Ghurar al-Hikam, narration 8704

إِنَّ مِنْ حَقِ الْعَالِمِ أَنْ لَا تُكْثِرَ عَلَيْهِ السُّؤَالَ وَ لَا تَأْخُذَ بِثَوْبِهِ وَ إِذَا دَخَلْتَ عَلَيْهِ وَ عِنْدَهُ قَوْمٌ فَسَلِّمْ عَلَيْهِمْ جَمِيعاً وَ خُصَّهُ بِالتَّحِيَّةِ دُونَهُمْ وَ اجْلِسْ بَيْنَ يَدَيْهِ وَ لَا تَجْلِسْ خَلْفَهُ وَ لَا تَغْمِزْ بِعَيْنِكَ وَ لَا تُشِرْ بِيَدِكَ وَ لَا تُكْثِرْ مِنَ الْقَوْلِ قَالَ فُلَانٌ وَ قَالَ فُلَانٌ خِلَافاً لِقَوْلِهِ وَ لَا تَضْجَرْ بِطُولِ صُحْبَتِهِ

It is from the right of a scholar that you do not ask him excessively [such that you make him weary], you do not grab at his clothes,(i) when you enter his presence and a group of people are present near him you greet them all and also greet the scholar specifically, you sit in front of him and do not sit behind his back, do not point to him with your eyes and fingers, do not say [to him] repeatedly that this person said this and this person said that, contrary to what he has said, and do not show weariness when his speech becomes lengthy.(ii)

Similarly, he has said:

إِذَا رَأَيْتَ عَالِماً فَكُنْ لَهُ خَادِما

When you meet a scholar, be his servant.(iii)

Also, the Messenger of Allah (peace and blessings be upon him and his family) has said:

مَنْ زَارَ عَالِماً فَكَأَنَّمَا زَارَنِي وَ مَنْ صَافَحَ عَالِماً فَكَأَنَّمَا صَافَحَنِي وَ مَنْ جَالَسَ عَالِماً فَكَأَنَّمَا جَالَسَنِي

One who visits a scholar, it is as if he has visited me; one who shakes the hands of a scholar, it is as if he has shaken hands with me; and one who sits with a scholar, it is as if

---

i. For example, when the scholar stands up to walk away one must not grab at his clothes to pull him back.

ii. al-Kulaynī, al-Kāfī, 1:37, narration 1

iii. al-Āmudī, Ghurar al-Hikam, narration 4044

he has sat with me. [i]

5) *Adab* with people and family

Society is truly human and moves in the direction of securing material and spiritual needs, when people knows their limits and capacities, abiding by them during their interactions with one another. One of the important *ādāb* of social interaction is that believers are soft and kind amongst themselves, encountering each other with happiness and good character, overlooking their mistakes, and attending to the needy and misfortunate.

These same things must also be observed within a family. Moreover, the relationship between members of a family should be even more intimate. This relationship should be accomplished by protecting each other's personality, mutual respect, appreciating each other's endeavours and efforts, and protecting the sanctuary of the home. Through this, the family bond becomes firmer.

Different Types of Adab

With a deep and a comprehensive outlook towards man's life, there are *ādāb* mentioned in the sacred *sharīʿah*, comprising of:

1) Individual *Ādāb*

Considering that the sacred religion of Islam—by virtue of the *wilāyah* and *imāmah* of the Infallible Imams (peace be upon them)—is a complete religion, Allah the Exalted has bestowed man with luminous laws and instructions so that in abiding by them, even the smallest of his individual actions acquire a Divine flavour. Such actions acquire a Divine character and are a sign of following instructions received from the unseen world. They are no longer mere material, physical and animalistic actions. Therefore, He has mentioned *ādāb* for all man's individual and physical actions, and the religious scholars have recorded these in their books. [ii] Some of these include: the *ādāb* of eating, drinking, sleeping, having marital relations, dressing, sitting,

---

i. Nūrī, Mustadrak al-Wasāʾil, 17:200, narration 21406

ii. Refer to the book *Makārim al-Akhlāq* of Marḥūm al-Ṭabarasī and *Ḥilyah al-Muttaqīn* of Marḥūm Majlisī (may Allah be pleased with them). (From the author)

beautifying oneself (general cleanliness, taking care of one's hair, beard, moustache, skin, cutting one's nails, applying perfume, and brushing one's teeth), exiting the house, going to the mosque, reciting the Noble Qur'ān, performing *istikhārā*, traveling, *ziyārah*, supplicating, giving charity, and entering the graveyard.

2) Social *Ādāb*

In addition to specifying the necessary duties and rights that govern man's various social relationships, Islam has also prescribed certain *mustaḥabb* instructions in the form of social *ādāb* for believers. These instructions cause social relationships to become firmer, more refined, and more luminous. In addition, they take man closer to Allah. Some of these include: the *ādāb* of greeting, meeting others (saying *salām*, shaking hands, having a cheerful disposition, using beautiful speech, possessing a neat appearance, observing the manners of sitting, humility and love, refraining from inappropriate behaviour like picking one's nose and spitting, being tolerant with brothers in faith), speaking, listening, criticizing, commanding to good and forbidding from evil, propagating religion, writing letters, friendship, joking, holding gatherings, enjoyment, encountering one's elders, hosting guests, being a guest, engaging in business, the rights of neighbours, being sick and visiting the sick, and teaching and learning. These *ādāb* are numerous and encompass a wide range of topics, some of which are mentioned in this book.[i]

18) Abstinence from Sins

Sins destroy the soul and the inclinations of man's *fiṭrah*. Therefore, the foundation of the invitation of the prophets and *awliyā'* (peace be upon them)—after inviting people towards monotheism and worship of the one God—was distancing oneself from disobeying religious instructions. Such disobedience has unpleasant worldly effects and is the cause of man's wretchedness. Due to its intense ugliness, Imam

i. For more information about these ādāb, refer to the book 'Akhlāq 1', published in the year 1382 by Markaz-i Tadwīn va Nashr-i Mutūn-i Darsī-yi Ḥawzah, written by Muḥammad Akbarī. (From the author)

ʿAlī (peace be upon him) says:

اجْتِنَابُ السَّيِّئَاتِ أَوْلَى مِنِ اكْتِسَابِ الْحَسَنَاتِ

> Refraining from misdeeds is worthier than earning good deeds. (i)

The intention of this narration is not that a person should avoid performing good deeds and religious obligations. Bear in mind that leaving Divine obligations is itself a disobedience to Allah. What is intended here is that a believer should not have the intention to rebel against Allah and oppose Him. If a person is not afraid of committing sins and at the same time he performs good deeds, he will not see a special effect from performing good deeds. He has merely relieved himself from his duty.

Therefore, as said by the Messenger of Allah (peace and blessings be upon him and his family):

إِنَّ الْمُؤْمِنَ لَيَرَى ذَنْبَهُ كَأَنَّهُ تَحْتَ صَخْرَةٍ يَخَافُ أَنْ تَقَعَ عَلَيْه

> A believer sees his sin as if he is under a rock which he fears would fall on him. (ii)

Now a scholar who strives to seek religious knowledge and is an example for others in his action, his attention towards staying away from sins must be more than others. Just as how Imam al-Ṣādiq (peace be upon him), addressing one of his close companions named Shaqrānī would had committed a sin, said:

إِنَّ الْحَسَنَ مِنْ كُلِّ أَحَدٍ حَسَنٌ وَ إِنَّهُ مِنْكَ أَحْسَنُ لِمَكَانِكَ مِنَّا

وَ إِنَّ الْقَبِيحَ مِنْ كُلِّ أَحَدٍ قَبِيحٌ وَ إِنَّهُ مِنْكَ أَقْبَح

> Verily, a good deed is good from everyone but because of your relation to us, it is better from you. And an ugly action is ugly from everyone, but it is uglier from you. (iii)

---

i. al-Āmudī, Ghurar al-Hikam, narration 1522

ii. al-Ṭūsī, al-Amālī, 537, narration 1162

iii. Majlisī, Bihār al-Anwār, 47:349, narration 5

Therefore, Imam ʿAlī (peace be upon him), continuing the description of the virtues of knowledge and scholars says:

ذَخِيرَتُهُ اجْتِنَابُ الذُّنُوبِ

... and the reserves of knowledge, are abstinence from sins.

Man keeps aside some money and necessities of life for a rainy day, so that he and his family can use them in the times of need, and if he does not do so then at the time of need he is forced to extend his hands and ask for help from anyone. This naturally tarnishes his reputation as a human being and a believer and may lead people to ignore him or even destroy his personality, status and reputation. In the same manner, if a scholar wants to benefit from his knowledge, if he wants it to remain with him, keep his path enlightened, and if he wants to have a fondness and attachment to his knowledge and continue to benefit from it on the day when people abandon him and forget about him, then he should stay away from sins and spiritual impurities. Therefore, Imam ʿAlī (peace be upon him) says:

الْعِلْمُ مَقْرُونٌ بِالْعَمَلِ فَمَنْ عَلِمَ عَمِلَ وَ الْعِلْمُ يَهْتِفُ بِالْعَمَلِ فَإِنْ أَجَابَهُ وَ إِلَّا ارْتَحَلَ عَنْه

Knowledge is coupled with action, so if a person knows he acts. And knowledge calls out towards action. So, if its call is answered [it stays], otherwise it departs.(i)

Imam al-Ṣādiq (peace be upon him) says:

إِنَّهُ يُغْفَرُ لِلْجَاهِلِ سَبْعُونَ ذَنْباً- قَبْلَ أَنْ يُغْفَرَ لِلْعَالِمِ ذَنْبٌ وَاحِد

Indeed, seventy sins of an ignorant person will be forgiven before a single sin of a scholar is forgiven.(ii)

---

i. Al-Radī, Nahj al-Balāghah, saying 366

ii. ʿAlī ibn Ibrāhīm, Tasfīr al-Qummī, 2:146

19) Performing Good Deeds

In his *fiṭrah*, man has a general perception of goodness. An inclination towards performing good deeds is ingrained in his being, as Allah the Exalted says:

وَ نَفْسٍ وَ مَا سَوَّاهَا فَأَلْهَمَهَا فُجُورَهَا وَ تَقْوَاهَا

By the soul and Him who fashioned it and inspired it with [discernment between] its virtues and vices. (91:7-8)

Although depending on his worldly inclinations, man sometimes acts against this *fiṭrah* and is thus rebuked. However, his perfection lies in the following: through free will and struggle he must overcome his natural inclinations towards bad actions and self-seeking, make the awareness and inclination of his *fiṭrah* dominant over them, establish himself as the manifestation of his Creator, and always remain on the path of conveying goodness to others. Conveying goodness to others is in reality a means of himself benefitting from good deeds.

As Imam al-Jawād (peace be upon him) says:

أَهْلُ الْمَعْرُوفِ إِلَى اصْطِنَاعِهِ أَحْوَجُ مِنْ أَهْلِ الْحَاجَةِ إِلَيْهِ لِأَنَّ لَهُمْ أَجْرَهُ وَ فَخْرَهُ وَ ذِكْرَهُ فَمَهْمَا اصْطَنَعَ الرَّجُلُ مِنْ مَعْرُوفٍ فَإِنَّمَا يَبْدَأُ فِيهِ بِنَفْسِهِ فَلَا يَطْلُبَنَّ شُكْرَ مَا صَنَعَ إِلَى نَفْسِهِ مِنْ غَيْرِهِ.

The people of virtuous actions are more in need of performing them than the needy. This is because the reward, honour and the memory of this action will remain for them. Therefore, whenever a person performs a virtuous deed he has started with himself. Hence, he should never seek thanks from others, for something which he has done for himself.[i]

Imam al-Ḥusayn (peace be upon him) also says the following about the merit of a virtuous deed:

---

i. Irbalī, Kashf al-Ghummah, 3:137

وَ اعْلَمُوا أَنَّ الْمَعْرُوفَ مُكْسِبٌ حَمْداً وَ مُعَقِّبٌ أَجْراً فَلَوْ رَأَيْتُمُ الْمَعْرُوفَ رَجُلًا لَرَأَيْتُمُوهُ حَسَناً جَمِيلًا يَسُرُّ النَّاظِرِينَ وَ يَفُوقُ الْعَالَمِينَ

Know that a virtuous deed earns praise and is followed by rewards. So, if you were to see a virtuous deed in the form of a man, then certainly you will see him beautiful and handsome such that he pleases those who look at him and is superior to all the worlds. (i)

This merit is such that the Messenger of Allah (peace and blessings be upon him and his family) says:

مَنْ تَصَدَّقَ بِصَدَقَةٍ عَلَى رَجُلٍ مِسْكِينٍ كَانَ لَهُ مِثْلُ أَجْرِهِ وَ لَوْ تَدَاوَلَهَا أَرْبَعُونَ أَلْفَ إِنْسَانٍ ثُمَّ وَصَلَتْ إِلَى مِسْكِينٍ كَانَ لَهُ أَجْراً كَامِلًا

One who gives charity to a needy man earns its reward even if this charity passes through the hands of forty thousand people and then reaches the needy, for him [each of them] will be a complete reward. (ii)

Because of such a reward and such merit of a virtuous deed, Imam ʿAlī (peace be upon him) says:

لَا تَسْتَصْغِرْ شَيْئاً مِنَ الْمَعْرُوفِ قَدَرْتَ عَلَى اصْطِنَاعِهِ إِيثَاراً لِمَا هُوَ أَكْثَرُ مِنْهُ فَإِنَّ الْيَسِيرَ فِي حَالِ الْحَاجَةِ إِلَيْهِ أَنْفَعُ لِأَهْلِهِ مِنْ ذَلِكَ الْكَثِيرِ فِي حَالِ الْغَنَاءِ عَنْهُ وَ اعْمَلْ لِكُلِّ يَوْمٍ بِمَا فِيهِ تَرْشُدْ.

Do not consider an action from the virtuous deeds that you are able to perform as being little, because you seek that [action] which is greater than it. Verily, a lesser deed for

i. Nūrī, Mustadrak al-Wasāʾil, 12:343, narration 14242

ii. al-Sadūq, Thawāb al-Aʿmāl, 342, narration 1

which there is a need, is more beneficial for its performer than a greater deed for which there is no need. Perform [a good deed] each day that which will cause you to progress. (i)

Therefore, a person who is on the path of perfection must always be seeking to perform virtuous deeds. As said by the Messenger of Allah (peace and blessings be upon him and his family):

اصْطَنِعِ الْخَيْرَ إِلَى مَنْ هُوَ أَهْلُهُ وَ إِلَى مَنْ هُوَ غَيْرُ أَهْلِهِ فَإِنْ لَمْ تُصِبْ مَنْ هُوَ أَهْلُهُ فَأَنْتَ أَهْلُهُ

Perform virtuous deeds, to a deserving person and to an undeserving person. Because if you do not reach a deserving person, then [nonetheless] you will be one of the deserving people [you will be one of the people of virtuous deeds]. (ii)

Such a person will be amongst the virtuous in the Hereafter as well. As said by Imam al-Ṣādiq (peace be upon him):

أَهْلُ الْمَعْرُوفِ فِي الدُّنْيَا هُمْ أَهْلُ الْمَعْرُوفِ فِي الْآخِرَة

The people of virtuous deeds in this world, they will be the people of virtuous deeds in the Hereafter. (iii)

Although, in the words of Imam ʿAlī (peace be upon him):

خَيْرُ الْمَعْرُوفِ مَا أُصِيبَ بِهِ الْأَبْرَار

The best virtuous deed is that which reaches righteous people. (iv)

Undoubtedly, one should first try to reach deserving people. As Imam al-Ṣādiq (peace be upon him) says:

عَلَامَةُ قَبُولِ الْعَبْدِ عِنْدَ اللّٰهِ أَنْ يُصِيبَ بِمَعْرُوفِهِ مَوَاضِعَهُ

The sign of a servant's acceptance with Allah is that his

---

i. Ibn al-Ashʿath, al-Jaʿfariyyāt, 233

ii. al-Ṣadūq, ʿUyūn Akhbār al-Riḍā (peace be upon him), 2:35, narration 76

iii. al-Ṭūsī, al-Amālī, 304, narration 619

iv. al-Āmudī, Ghurar al-Hikam, narration 4983

virtuous action reaches its deserving place.[i]

Therefore, when a good and virtuous deed possesses such merit, the one who knows these affairs and knows the good deeds—all of which have been instructed in the sacred *sharīʿah*—is more befitting to perform them. If he does not move in this direction then he has not gathered any provisions to ensure the protection, continuity and effectiveness of his knowledge. As Imam ʿAlī (peace be upon him) says, continuing the description of the virtues of knowledge and scholars:

وَ زَادُهُ الْمَعْرُوفُ

... and the provisions of knowledge are [performing] virtue.

In the end if a person wants his good deed to acquire the title of being 'virtuous', then he must act according to the saying of Imam ʿAlī (peace be upon him):

مِلَاكُ الْمَعْرُوفِ تَرْكُ الْمَنِّ بِه

The criterion for an action to be virtuous is to abstain from making the receiver feel under an obligation and reproaching him[ii]

Similarly, he has said:

إِذَا صُنِعَ إِلَيْكَ مَعْرُوفٌ فَاذْكُرْ

If someone does good to you remember it.

إِذَا صَنَعْتَ مَعْرُوفاً فَانْسَهُ

If you do good to someone then forget it.[iii]

Through this method the Imams (peace be upon them) want to train man's soul towards performing good deeds, making haste in performing them, and overtaking others in doing them. For this reason, Imam al-Kāẓim (peace be upon him) says:

---

i. Majlisī, Biḥār al-Anwār, 75:15, narration 8

ii. al-Āmudī, Ghurar al-Ḥikam, narration 9724

iii. Ibid., narration 4000

وَالصَّنِيعَةُ لَا تَتِمُّ صَنِيعَةً عِنْدَ الْمُؤْمِنِ لِصَاحِبِهَا إِلَّا بِثَلَاثَةِ أَشْيَاءَ تَصْغِيرِهَا وَ سَتْرِهَا وَ تَعْجِيلِهَا فَمَنْ صَغَّرَ الصَّنِيعَةَ عِنْدَ الْمُؤْمِنِ فَقَدْ عَظَّمَ أَخَاهُ وَ مَنْ عَظَّمَ الصَّنِيعَةَ عِنْدَهُ فَقَدْ صَغَّرَ أَخَاهُ وَ مَنْ كَتَمَ مَا أَوْلَاهُ مِنْ صَنِيعَةٍ فَقَدْ كَرُمَ فَعَالُهُ وَ مَنْ عَجَّلَ مَا وَعَدَ فَقَدْ هَنِئَ الْعَطِيَّةَ.

A good deed performed to a believer is not complete except through three things: considering it insignificant, concealing it and making haste in [performing] it. Therefore, whoever considers the good deed done to a believer to be insignificant has surely magnified his brother. And whoever considers the good deed done to a believer to be significant has surely belittled his brother. And whoever conceals the good deed that he chose [to perform] then surely, he has honoured it. And if a person makes haste in that which he has promised, then he has made his bestowal to be agreeable. [i]

Therefore, if someone intends to perform good deeds, then he should pay attention that there are plenty of such good actions in his day-to-day life, and that he can also benefit from small actions. Hence, the Messenger of Allah (peace and blessings be upon him and his family) says:

دَخَلَ عَبْدٌ الْجَنَّةَ بِغُصْنٍ مِنْ شَوْكٍ كَانَ عَلَى طَرِيقِ الْمُسْلِمِينَ فَأَمَاطَهُ عَنْه

A servant will enter Heaven because of removing a branch of thorns from the pathway of the Muslims. [ii]

He (peace and blessings be upon him and his family) has also said:

مَنْ رَدَّ عَنْ قَوْمٍ مِنَ الْمُسْلِمِينَ عَادِيَةَ مَاءٍ أَوْ نَارٍ وَجَبَتْ لَهُ الْجَنَّةُ

One who dispels harmful water or fire from a group of

---

i. al-Harrānī, Tuhaf al-ʿUqūl, 403

ii. al-Ṣadūq, al-Khiṣāl, 32, narration 111

Muslims, Paradise becomes obligatory on him.(i)

20) Forsaking Enmity (Engaging in Discussion and Debate)

Imam ʿAlī (peace be upon him), continuing the description of the virtues of knowledge and scholars, says:

وَ مَاوُهُ الْمُوَادَعَةُ

> ... and the refuge of knowledge is forsaking enmity with others [or engaging in discussion and debate].

The lexical meaning of the word '*muwādaʿah*' includes both enmity as well as debate. Hence, we will mention each of the two meanings in a manner that, in its usage here, both meanings go back to one other. With regards to enmity, knowledge forsaking its enmity with others is in the following manner. Firstly, a scholar should present his knowledge to others so that it is critiqued, and that he himself as well as others reach confidence about the knowledge being real. Therefore, the place of refuge and the abode of knowledge where it is safe from the harm of alteration and diminishing, is that it is put up for discussion and debated with the experts of every field. This is so that the knowledge is consolidated in man's mind and soul, it becomes complete, and it revolves around following the truth (regardless of whether this truth matches man's opinion or not). Therefore, Imam ʿAlī (peace be upon him) says:

أَنَّهُ وَجَدَ فِي قَائِمَةِ سَيْفٍ مِنْ سُيُوفِهِ ... قُلِ الْحَقَ وَ لَوْ عَلَى نَفْسِك

> He found on the sheath of one of the swords of the Messenger of Allah (peace and blessings be upon him and his family) ... "Speak the truth even if it is against you [it is to your harm]."(ii)

He also says:

---

i. al-Kulaynī, al-Kāfī, 5:55, narration 3

ii. Majlisī, Biḥār al-Anwār, 74:157, narration 4

مَنْ يَطْلُبِ الْعِزَّ بِغَيْرِ حَقٍّ يَذِلَّ وَ مَنْ عَانَدَ الْحَقَّ لَزِمَهُ الْوَهْن

One who desires honour without the truth will be abased; and one who is hostile to the truth, frailty accompanies him.(i)

Imam al-Ṣādiq (peace be upon him) also says:

الْعِزُّ أَنْ تَذِلَ لِلْحَقِّ إِذَا لَزِمَك

Honour and dignity is that you lower yourself in front of the truth [and accept it] when it comes to you.(ii)

Similarly, he says:

لَيْسَ مِنْ بَاطِلٍ يَقُومُ بِإِزَاءِ الْحَقِّ إِلَّا غَلَبَ الْحَقُّ الْبَاطِلَ وَ ذَلِكَ قَوْلُهُ بَلْ نَقْذِفُ بِالْحَقِ عَلَى الْباطِلِ فَيَدْمَغُهُ فَإِذا هُوَ زاهِقٌ

No falsehood resists against the truth, except that the truth prevails over it. And that is the speech of Allah: "Indeed, We hurl the truth against falsehood, and it crushes its head."(iii)(iv)

Therefore, the basis of questioning, replying and discussion should be in the manner mentioned by Imam ʿAlī (peace be upon him):

سَلْ تَفَقُّهاً وَ لَا تَسْأَلْ تَعَنُّتاً فَإِنَّ الْجَاهِلَ الْمُتَعَلِّمَ شَبِيهٌ بِالْعَالِمِ وَ إِنَّ الْعَالِمَ الْمُتَعَسِّفَ شَبِيهٌ بِالْجَاهِلِ الْمُتَعَنِّت

Ask to understand and do not ask to confound and torment, for an ignorant learner is like a scholar and an unjust scholar is like a stubborn, ignorant person seeking to pick a quarrel.(v)

---

i. al-Harrānī, Tuhaf al-ʿUqūl, 95

ii. Majlisī, Bihār al-Anwār, 78:228, narration 105

iii. (21:18)

iv. Majlisī, Bihār al-Anwār, 5:305, narration 24

v. al-Radī, Nahj al-Balāghah, saying 320

Likewise, the question asked should be about useful matters. Imam ʿAlī (peace be upon him) says:

سَلْ عَمَّا لَا بُدَّ لَكَ مِنْ عِلْمِهِ وَ لَا تُعْذَرُ فِي جَهْلِهِ

> Ask about that which it is necessary for you to know and that which you have no excuse in not knowing.(i)

Similarly, he should strive to ask in a good manner, even if in some instances the question is appropriate and in some it is not. Thus, it is narrated from the Lady Zahrāʾ (peace be upon her):

حُسْنُ الْمَسْأَلَةِ نِصْفُ الْعِلْم

Asking questions in a good manner is half of knowledge.(ii)

That is because it shows a person's perception and understanding of the issue and which question is related to which topic, and it does not waste one's time and one's life. In this regard, the basis of answering a question must be implementing the instruction of the Messenger of Allah (peace and blessings be upon him and his family) to Abū Dharr where he says:

إِذَا سُئِلْتَ عَنْ عِلْمٍ لَا تَعْلَمُهُ فَقُلْ لَا أَعْلَمُهُ تَنْجُ مِنْ تَبِعَتِهِ وَ لَا تُفْتِ بِمَا لَا عِلْمَ لَكَ بِهِ تَنْجُ مِنْ عَذَابِ اللَّهِ يَوْمَ الْقِيَامَة

> If you are asked about knowledge that you do not know, then say, "I do not know" so that you are saved from its repercussions. Do not give *fatwā* (pass a decree) regarding that which you do not know, so that you are saved from Allah's punishment on the Day of Resurrection.(iii)

When the basis of man's teaching, learning, academic discussions and debates, is following the luminous sayings of the Infallible Ahl al-Bayt (peace be upon them), certainly he will derive academic, practical and

---

i. al-Āmudī, Ghurar al-Hikam, narration 5595

ii. Majlisī, Bihār al-Anwār, 77:160, narration 159

iii. al-Ṭabrasī, Makārim al-Akhlāq, 2:364, narration 2661

spiritual benefit from these academic exchanges. Moreover, his teaching and learning will never result in enmity and vain arguments.

21) Arriving at Guidance

Whenever man's goal in seeking knowledge and imparting it is to reach the truths and realities of the world, and to then tread the path illuminated by them, in this case if he observes the aforementioned things he will certainly reach his goal. Because Allah the Exalted, who is Essential Knowledge (*'ilm bi al-dhāt*), will surely guide him to His knowledge and will unveil for him some of the realities of the world, existence, and His perfections. Just as how Allah the Exalted did so for a group of His messengers;[i] He says:

وَ كُلاًّ آتَيْنَا حُكْماً وَ عِلْماً

And to each We gave judgment and knowledge. (21:79)

Because His will necessitates that they reach His knowledge:

وَ لاَ يُحِيطُونَ بِشَيْءٍ مِنْ عِلْمِهِ إِلاَّ بِمَا شَاءَ

And they do not comprehend anything of His knowledge except what He wishes. (2:255)

For this reason, He says to the Noblest Messenger (peace and blessings be upon him and his family):

وَقُل رَّبِّ زِدْنِي عِلْمًا

And say, "My Lord! Increase me in knowledge." (20:14)

In relation to those other than the Messengers (peace and blessings be upon him and his family) and the *awliyā'* (peace be upon them) who possess special distinctions, Allah has used the expression 'giving knowledge,'[ii] and has caused certain effects to follow it:

يَرْفَعِ اللَّهُ الَّذِينَ آمَنُوا مِنْكُمْ وَ الَّذِينَ أُوتُوا الْعِلْمَ دَرَجَاتٍ

Allah will raise in rank those of you who have faith and

i. (12:22), (18:65), 27:15) ,(21:74() and (28:14)

ii. (16:27), (17:107), (56:03) ,(80:82) and (6:43)

those who have been given knowledge (58:11)

Therefore, the seeker of knowledge is always in need of Divine guidance that can lead him towards reality, as stated by Imam ʿAlī (peace be upon him) in the continuation of the description of the virtues of knowledge and scholars:

دَلِيلُهُ الْهُدَى

... and the guide of knowledge is Divine guidance.

If a scholar wishes to be guided by Divine guidance, he must always seek the truth and pursue it from any channel that is desirable in the eyes of the *sharīʿah* and the intellect. However, if he follows his selfish desires then he will be afflicted with deviation, and his knowledge will only increase him in confusion and perplexity about the relationship with the realities of existence. [i] Just as how Balʿam ibn Bāʿūrāʾ went astray as a result of following his base desires, despite being from the followers of Prophet Moses (peace be upon him) and one to whom Allah the Exalted had granted His signs and favours. The Noble Qurʾān says about him:

وَ اتْلُ عَلَيْهِمْ نَبَأَ الَّذِي آتَيْنَاهُ آيَاتِنَا فَانْسَلَخَ مِنْهَا فَأَتْبَعَهُ الشَّيْطَانُ فَكَانَ مِنَ الْغَاوِينَ

And relate to them the account of him to whom We gave Our signs, but he cast them off. Thereupon Satan pursued him, and he became one of the perverse. (7:175)

On the other hand, if a person's endeavour in acquiring knowledge is that which was mentioned, then he can benefit from any knowledge for his own guidance and for the guidance of others, even if that knowledge is non-religious knowledge. Therefore, the seeker of knowledge should first make his goal to be correct and lofty, and then by procuring the other conditions he should pursue knowledge.

---

i. (28:50)

22) Love of the Virtuous

One of the things that places man on the path of guidance and felicity is establishing a relationship of love and friendship with virtuous and pious individuals. A scholar is no exception to this matter, as Imam ʿAlī (peace be upon him) says while describing the last of the virtues of knowledge and scholars:

وَ رَفِيقُهُ مَحَبَّةُ الْأَخْيَارِ.

... and the companion of knowledge is love of the virtuous.

That is because everyone needs a companion to carry out any action in this worldly life. They can seek assistance from this companion and friend, as they traverse their path. Hence, Imam ʿAlī (peace be upon him) says:

سَلِ الرَّفِيقَ قَبْلَ الطَّرِيق

Ask about the companion before [you tread upon] the path.[i]

However, he describes a companion in the following manner:

إِنَّمَا سُمِّيَ الرَّفِيقُ رَفِيقاً لِأَنَّهُ يَرْفَقُكَ عَلَى صَلَاحِ دِينِكَ فَمَنْ أَعَانَكَ عَلَى صَلَاحِ دِينِكَ فَهُوَ الرَّفِيقُ الشَّفِيق

A companion is only called a companion because he accompanies you towards reforming your religion. So, if someone helps you in reforming your religion then he is a sympathetic companion.[ii]

For this reason, the Messenger of Allah (peace and blessings be upon him and his family) says:

إن اللهَ عزَّ و جلَّ رفيقٌ يحبُّ الرفقَ في الأمرِ كلِّه

Indeed, Allah the Invincible and the Majestic is a companion

---

i. al-Āmudī, Ghurar al-Ḥikam, narration 5596

ii. Ibid., narration 3878

Who loves to be tolerant in all the affairs. [i]

The Noble Qur'ān also introduces the prophets, the *ṣiddiqūn* (those who are truthful in their conduct), the *shuhadā* (witnesses) over the actions of others, and the righteous to be the best companions of man. [ii] Similarly it mentions some of the Divine messengers such as prophets Abraham, Isaac, Jacob, Prophet Ishmael, Elisha and Dhū al-Kifl, [iii] as definitely being amongst the virtuous and pious, such that harbouring their love results in a person being attracted towards them. Moreover, this companionship causes a person to acquire their character and himself become one of the virtuous. For this reason, Imam ʿAlī (peace be upon him) says:

> جُمِعَ خَيْرُ الدُّنْيَا وَ الْآخِرَةِ فِي كِتْمَانِ السِّرِّ وَ مُصَادَقَةِ الْأَخْيَار
>
> The good of the world and the Hereafter has been gathered together in concealing secrets and the friendship of the virtuous. [iv]

If this companionship is true and if it persists, then it results in a companionship after death—of which man is direly in need—and the virtuous assist him in the realm of *barzakh* (purgatory) and on the Day of Resurrection, giving him eternal deliverance. Therefore, if knowledge is to be effective in man's being, it should propel him to be the companion of the virtuous and the pious such that he benefits from their true knowledge and teachings.

Section Four
The Banes of Knowledge

Knowledge is an immaterial and noble reality, an effusion from the *qudsī* realm to man's soul. [v] Because man possesses natural and material

---

i. al-Hindī, Kanz al-ʿUmmāl, narration 5370

ii. (4:69)

iii. (38:47, 48)

iv. Majlisī, Bihār al-Anwār, 74:178, narration 17

v. The word *quds* means purity and being far from defect or fault. In the radiant Supplication of Kumayl, Amīr al-Mu'minīn (peace be upon him) asks Allah saying,

inclinations that can subjugate his *fiṭrī* and *malakūtī*(i) inclinations and give them an undesirable direction, therefore there are some specific pitfalls and banes that continuously threaten his knowledge and result in its corruption and waning. Naturally, some of these banes threaten the outward and the acquired knowledge itself, which in turn spreads to the real knowledge.(ii) On the other hand there are some banes that beset the possessors of knowledge, effacing the effects, blessings, and luminance of knowledge from their being. In this section we will point to some of them.

1) Deterioration of Knowledge

Knowledge has a distinct pleasure for its seekers, such that intellectually a person becomes infatuated with it. For this reason, a certain heedlessness overtakes him and as a result, the person becomes engrossed in his knowledge and fails to act according to it. However, as mentioned before, knowledge and action are intermingled with each other—each one influences the other. Therefore, it is evident that not acting in accordance to knowledge results in its deterioration, in the same manner that acting according to it causes its growth and perfection. Imam ʿAlī (peace be upon him) says in this regard:

الْعِلْمُ كُلُّهُ حُجَّةٌ إِلَّا مَا عُمِلَ بِهِ

> All of knowledge is a proof [against its possessor] except that which is accompanied by action.(iii)

الْعِلْمُ بِلَا عَمَلٍ وَبَال

"*bi haqqika wa bi qudsika*" (by the station of Your right, and Your *quds*). In the same sense, the *qudsī* realm here is a term referring to an immaterial realm where the purity of Allah is witnessed.

i. *Fiṭrī* inclinations are those inclinations present in the *fiṭrah* (the innate disposition of man). *Malakūtī* refers to the higher realms wherein the reality of Allah's true dominance over the creation is witnessed.

ii. Refer to Section One in this chapter for a detailed discussion of outward knowledge versus real knowledge.

iii. Majlisī, Biḥār al-Anwār, 2:29, narration 9

Knowledge without actions is a curse.[i]

Also, the Messenger of Allah (peace and blessings be upon him and his family) says:

يَطَّلِع قَوْمٌ مِنْ أَهْلِ الْجَنَّةِ عَلَى قَوْمٍ مِنْ أَهْلِ النَّارِ فَيَقُولُونَ مَا أَدْخَلَكُمُ النَّارَ وَ قَدْ دَخَلْنَا الْجَنَّةَ بِتَأْدِيبِكُمْ وَ تَعْلِيمِكُمْ فَيَقُولُونَ إِنَّا كُنَّا نَأْمُرُ بِالْخَيْرِ وَ لَا نَفْعَلُه

A group of the inhabitants of Paradise will turn to a group of the inhabitants of Hell and say to them, "What caused you to be thrown into the fire while we entered Paradise due to your training and education?" They will reply, "We commanded [others] to good deeds but did not ourselves perform them."[ii]

The evil effects of not acting according to knowledge—in addition to first reaching the scholar himself—is as the Messenger of Allah (peace and blessings be upon him and his family) said:

مَنِ ازْدَادَ عِلْماً وَ لَمْ يَزْدَدْ هُدًى لَمْ يَزْدَدْ مِنَ اللَّهِ إِلَّا بُعْداً

One who increases in knowledge but does not increase in guidance, only increases in remoteness from Allah.[iii]

They also spread to others, as Imam 'Alī (peace be upon him) has said:

إِنَّمَا زَهَّدَ النَّاسَ فِي طَلَبِ الْعِلْمِ كَثْرَةُ مَا يَرَوْنَ مِنْ قِلَّةِ مَنْ عَمِلَ بِمَا عَلِم

The people have only become disinterested in seeking knowledge because of how they consistently see a paucity of those who act according to their knowledge.[iv]

It is for this reason that the Islamic sources instruct people to strictly

---

i. al-Āmudī, Ghurar al-Ḥikam, narration 1587

ii. al-Ṭabrasī, Makārim al-Akhlāq, 2:364, narration 2661.

iii. Ibn Abī Firās, Tanbīh al-Khawātir, 2:21

iv. al-Āmudī, Ghurar al-Hikam, narration 3895

avoid contact with corrupt scholars and mention the criteria of genuine scholars that people should be in contact with. For instance, it is narrated from Prophet Jesus (peace be upon him):

> الدِّينَارُ دَاءُ الدِّينِ وَ الْعَالِمُ طَبِيبُ الدِّينِ فَإِذَا رَأَيْتُمُ الطَّبِيبَ يَجُرُّ الدَّاءَ إِلَى نَفْسِهِ فَاتَّهِمُوهُ وَ اعْلَمُوا أَنَّهُ غَيْرُ نَاصِحٍ لِغَيْرِهِ
> The world is the religion's ailment while the scholar is its doctor. Hence if you see the doctor pulling the ailment towards himself [that is he is himself afflicted with this ailment], then bring disrepute to him and know that he is not a well-wisher of others. (i)

Also, the Messenger of Allah (peace and blessings be upon him and his family) says:

> إِنَّ أَهْلَ النَّارِ لَيَتَأَذَّوْنَ مِنْ نَتْنِ رِيحِ الْعَالِمِ التَّارِكِ لِعِلْمِه
> Verily the people of Hell will suffer from the stench of a scholar who abandoned his knowledge. (ii)

Further, Imam al-Ṣādiq (peace be upon him) says:

> أَشَدُّ النَّاسِ عَذَاباً عَالِمٌ لَا يَنْتَفِعُ مِنْ عِلْمِهِ بِشَيْء
> The severest of people in terms of their punishment is a scholar who did not benefit in the least bit from his knowledge. (iii)

2) Following Base Desires

All human beings—due to their worldly dimension—have certain inclinations and are susceptible to having these inclinations prevail over their true inclinations. Naturally, those who enjoy a notable social position and status are more susceptible to this prevalence and domination. Therefore, one of the banes of knowledge and gnosis is indulgence in

---

i. al-Ṣadūq, al-Khiṣāl, 113, narration 91.

ii. Majlisī, Biḥār al-Anwār, 1:34, narration 30

iii. Ibid., 1:37, narration 53

sensuality and following one's base desires.

The Noble Qur'ān says regarding this:

وَاتْلُ عَلَيْهِمْ نَبَأَ الَّذِي آتَيْنَاهُ آيَاتِنَا فَانسَلَخَ مِنْهَا فَأَتْبَعَهُ الشَّيْطَانُ فَكَانَ مِنَ الْغَاوِينَ وَلَوْ شِئْنَا لَرَفَعْنَاهُ بِهَا وَلَٰكِنَّهُ أَخْلَدَ إِلَى الْأَرْضِ وَاتَّبَعَ هَوَاهُ ۚ فَمَثَلُهُ كَمَثَلِ الْكَلْبِ إِن تَحْمِلْ عَلَيْهِ يَلْهَثْ أَوْ تَتْرُكْهُ يَلْهَث ۚ ذَّٰلِكَ مَثَلُ الْقَوْمِ الَّذِينَ كَذَّبُوا بِآيَاتِنَا ۚ فَاقْصُصِ الْقَصَصَ لَعَلَّهُمْ يَتَفَكَّرُونَ

> Relate to them an account of him to whom We gave Our signs, but [in the end] he cast them off. Thereupon Satan pursued him, and he became one of the perverse. Had We wished, We would have surely raised him [raised his status] by their means [by means of the signs and knowledge he had been given], but he [out of his own choice] clung to the Earth and followed his [worldly] desires. So, his parable is that of a [rabid] dog: if you make for it, it lolls out its tongue, and if you let it alone, it [still] lolls out its tongue. Such is the parable of the people who deny Our signs. So, recount these narratives, perchance that they may reflect [thereupon they may wake up and comprehend the reality]. (7:175-176)

Different Dimensions of Following Base Desires

Following one's base desires has different dimensions, each of which is harmful for seekers of knowledge and prevents them from reaching their goal. These dimensions are particularly harmful for the seekers of religious knowledge. Some of them are:

A) Sins and Disobedience

Disobedience gradually causes man to turn away from the realities and knowledge he possesses. In the words of the Noble Qur'ān:

كَلَّا ۖ بَلْ ۜ رَانَ عَلَىٰ قُلُوبِهِم مَّا كَانُوا يَكْسِبُونَ

> No, that is not the case! Rather, their hearts have been

> sullied by what they have been earning. (83:14)

He even reaches a stage where he denies them, as the Noble Qurʾān has said:

> ثُمَّ كَانَ عَاقِبَةَ الَّذِينَ أَسَاءُوا السُّوأَىٰ أَن كَذَّبُوا بِآيَاتِ اللَّهِ وَكَانُوا بِهَا يَسْتَهْزِئُونَ
>
> Then the fate of those who committed misdeeds was [even more] evil, such that they denied the signs of Allah and they used to deride them. (30:10)

Imam ʿAlī (peace be upon him) also says:

> زَلَّةُ الْعَالِمِ كَبِيرَةُ الْجِنَايَةِ ... زَلَّةُ الْعَالِمِ تُفْسِدُ عَوَالِم
>
> The slip of a scholar is a grave crime ... the slip of a scholar corrupts all the worlds. [i]

B) Overindulging

Another dimension of following one's base desires is overeating and overindulging. This means that a person's sole concern is attending to his stomach and physical pleasures—albeit through *ḥalāl* (permissible) means. Such a state—in a particular and marked way—causes the light of wisdom and gnosis to be extinguished from man's heart. The pure and the immaculate Ahl al-Bayt (peace be upon them) have pointed to this matter in many narrations. The Messenger of Allah (peace and blessings be upon him and his family) says:

> نُورُ الْحِكْمَةِ الْجُوعُ وَ التَّبَاعُدُ مِنَ اللَّهِ الشِّبَعُ وَ الْقُرْبَةُ إِلَى اللَّهِ حُبُّ الْمَسَاكِينِ وَ الدُّنُوُّ مِنْهُمْ لَا تَشْبَعُوا فَيُطْفَأَ نُورُ الْمَعْرِفَةِ مِنْ قُلُوبِكُم
>
> Hunger is the light of wisdom, being satiated is remoteness from Allah, and loving the needy and drawing near

i. al-Āmudī, Fihrist-i Mawdūʿī-yi Ghurar al-Hikam, the chapter on ʿilm (knowledge)

to them is proximity to Allah. Do not fill your stomachs for [if you do so] the light of wisdom will be put out from your hearts. (i)

C) Seeking Power

Knowledge is man's guide towards reaching the realities. However, if knowledge is accompanied by an ambition for power, it not only deprives man from reaching the realities but eventually becomes a barrier in knowing and understanding them. Due to his love and power-hungry nature, such a person only seeks to attract others' attention towards himself and to promote himself in their eyes. As a result, he becomes heedless of reaching real perfection—both his own perfection and that of others—by means of following the truth and is not after understanding these perfections and procuring the things required to reach them. For this reason, Imam ʿAlī (peace be upon him) says:

آفَةُ الْعُلَمَاءِ حُبُّ الرِّئَاسَة

The bane of the scholars is the love of power. (ii)

Undoubtedly, seeking power is harmful for all. As Imam al-Ṣādiq (peace be upon him) says to Abū Ḥamzah al-Thumālī:

إِيَّاكَ وَ الرِّئَاسَةَ وَ إِيَّاكَ أَنْ تَطَأَ أَعْقَابَ الرِّجَالِ قَالَ قُلْتُ جُعِلْتُ فِدَاكَ أَمَّا الرِّئَاسَةُ فَقَدْ عَرَفْتُهَا وَ أَمَّا أَنْ أَطَأَ أَعْقَابَ الرِّجَالِ فَمَا ثُلُثَا مَا فِي يَدِي إِلَّا مِمَّا وَطِئْتُ أَعْقَابَ الرِّجَالِ فَقَالَ لِي لَيْسَ حَيْثُ تَذْهَبُ إِيَّاكَ أَنْ تَنْصِبَ رَجُلًا دُونَ الْحُجَّةِ فَتُصَدِّقَهُ فِي كُلِّ مَا قَالَ.

"Avoid power and walking in the footsteps of men." Abū Hamzah said, "I understood [the meaning of] power, but what is meant by walking in the footsteps of men? Two-thirds of what [knowledge] I possess I have acquired by

i. Majlisī, Bihār al-Anwār, 70:71, narration 20

ii. al-Āmudī, Ghurar al-Hikam, narration 3930

> walking in the footsteps of men [scholars]." The Imam replied, "The meaning is not what crossed your mind. [Rather, what is meant is that] you should refrain from appointing a person [to a position] without justifiable reason and confirming him in everything he says.'[(i)]

This issue holds true both for others and for an individual himself. If someone has really comprehended the true path and acted according to it, it then becomes incumbent upon him to make others reach it as well. This is incumbent upon him even if it entails taking a position of power—since usually making others reach the path cannot be accomplished otherwise. However, his goal in this process should not be reaching this position and becoming famous. Instead, the position and fame should be a tool for him to realize the lofty and the desired goal. As a result, such a person does not refrain from stating and confirming the truth, even if no one follows him or they ignore him as a result. And if another person performs this duty then he will support and strengthen him. In fact, if this other person performs this duty better than him, then he will abdicate and relinquish his position! Therefore, one of the narrators says:

> سَمِعْتُ أَبَا عَبْدِ اللَّهِ ع يَقُولُ أَ تَرَى لَا أَعْرِفُ خِيَارَكُمْ مِنْ شِرَارِكُمْ بَلَى وَ اللَّهِ وَ إِنَّ شِرَارَكُمْ مَنْ أَحَبَّ أَنْ يُوطَأَ عَقِبُهُ إِنَّهُ لَا بُدَّ مِنْ كَذَّابٍ أَوْ عَاجِزِ الرَّأْيِ
>
> I heard Imam al-Ṣādiq (peace be upon him) say, "Do you suppose that I do not recognize the good ones amongst you from the bad ones? But of course, I do by Allah! Verily the bad ones from amongst you is the one who desires that others walk behind him and follow him; [because] he is either a liar or his belief and opinion is weak.'[(ii)]

This means a person in such a state uses every possible means to safeguard his position. If he is not aware of the laws of the *sharīʿah*

---

i. al-Kulaynī, al-Kāfī, 2:298, narration 5

ii. Ibid., 2:299, narration 8

then either he responds by lying or he expresses his weak beliefs. In both cases he has destroyed himself as well as others. For this reason, Imam al-Ṣādiq (peace be upon him) says:

إِيَّاكُمْ وَ هَؤُلَاءِ الرُّؤَسَاءَ الَّذِينَ يَتَرَأَّسُونَ فَوَ اللَّهِ مَا خَفَقَتِ النِّعَالُ خَلْفَ رَجُلٍ إِلَّا هَلَكَ وَ أَهْلَكَ

> Stay away from those leaders [referring to the incompetent scholars in the Imam's time who were against his school of thought] who are leading. By Allah, the sandals [of those who are following them,] do not touch the ground except that they are destroyed, and they destroy [others]. (i)

D) Pride

Pride and haughtiness with respect to others is one of the offshoots of selfishness which comes about when man pays attention to his own possessions—be it those possessions that he has earned or those which Allah has favoured him with. (ii) This state has unpleasant effects in this world, in the Hereafter, and on the soul. It is a blameworthy trait for all, especially the scholars for whom it brings about stagnation with regards to seeking and increasing knowledge. Imam ʿAlī (peace be upon him) says:

لَا يَتَعَلَّمُ مَنْ يَتَكَبَّرُ

One who is proud does not gain knowledge. (iii)

This state does not allow a person to realize his own ignorance and to reach the realities and the truths. Imam Mūsā ibn Jaʿfar (peace be upon him) says:

---

i. Ibid., 2:297, narration 3

ii. Undoubtedly, even those possessions that man earned himself are due to the blessings of Allah, for man's existence is utter poverty. However, a conventional understanding is intended here.

iii. al-Āmudī, Ghurar al-Hikam, 65

إِنَّ الزَّرْعَ يَنْبُتُ فِي السَّهْلِ وَ لَا يَنْبُتُ فِي الصَّفَا فَكَذَلِكَ الْحِكْمَةُ تَعْمُرُ فِي قَلْبِ الْمُتَوَاضِعِ وَ لَا تَعْمُرُ فِي قَلْبِ الْمُتَكَبِّرِ الْجَبَّارِ لِأَنَّ اللَّهَ جَعَلَ التَّوَاضُعَ آلَةَ الْعَقْلِ وَ جَعَلَ التَّكَبُّرَ مِنْ آلَةِ الْجَهْلِ

Certainly, crops grow in soft earth and do not grow in hard earth. Similarly, wisdom prospers in a humble heart and does not flourish in an arrogant and haughty heart. That is because Allah has made humility to be the instrument of the intellect and has made pride to be the instrument of ignorance. (i)

An arrogant person always expects others to show humility in front of him and to undisputedly accept his words. This state necessitates that he considers others to be inferior and insignificant, and that he does not work for their progress. Naturally, others cannot tolerate such a demeanour being shown to them, thus a proud person is driven away by the people. Moreover, he does not discover his intellectual and spiritual shortcomings and is held back from progressing and moving towards perfection. Such a person gradually reaches a stage where he denies the truth! Imam al-Ṣādiq (peace be upon him) describes the consequences of this trait for the scholars in the following way:

وَ لَا تَكُونُوا عُلَمَاءَ جَبَّارِينَ فَيَذْهَبَ بَاطِلُكُمْ بِحَقِّكُمْ

Do not be amongst the arrogant scholars such that the falsehood in you destroys the truth in you. (ii)

Similarly, Amīr al-Mu'minīn 'Alī (peace be upon him) says:

مَنْ تَكَبَّرَ عَلَى النَّاسِ ذَل

One who is arrogant with the people is humiliated. (iii)

---

i. al-Harrānī, Tuhaf al-'Uqūl, 396

ii. al-Kulaynī, al-Kāfī, 1:36

iii. al-Āmudī, Ghurar al-Hikam, 310

E) Envy

To harbour envy and jealousy of others due to a blessing they enjoy, and to privately wish for the destruction of this blessing and that one should have it for himself, all this is a sign of someone who has not contemplated on the realities of the world.

That is because:

- Firstly, Allah has accorded in man the ability to acquire blessings
- Secondly, others have put this ability to use and have achieved results
- Thirdly, Allah has prepared and readied the blessings for those who strive on the path of obtaining them

However, the initial form of this state—the form of insinuations and thoughts—naturally occurs in man's soul. These insinuations and thoughts arise from laziness and seeking comfort, which in turn arises from selfishness. It is necessary therefore that by paying attention to the aforementioned points, one should prevent these thoughts from influencing him, lest they turn into a temporary state and eventually into the blameworthy trait of envy. This state can appear in anyone with regards to any blessing they see in another person, but there is a stronger possibility of it appearing in the people of knowledge. For this reason, Imam al-Bāqir (peace be upon him) says:

لَا يَكُونُ الْعَبْدُ عَالِماً حَتَّى لَا يَكُونَ حَاسِداً لِمَنْ فَوْقَهُ وَ لَا مُحَقِّراً لِمَنْ دُونَهُ.

> A servant does not become a scholar unless he does not envy those above him and does not belittle those lower than him.[i]

If this state appears in a person and leads him to act upon it—in a manner that he strives to remove the Divine gift of knowledge or its effects from another person—and if he does not repent for this action, then he will be one of the people of Hell. As the Messenger of Allah (peace and blessings be upon him and his family) has said:

---

i. al-Harrānī, Tuhaf al-ʿUqūl, 294

إِنَّ اللَّهَ يُعَذِّبُ السِّتَّةَ بِالسِّتَّةِ ... وَ الْفُقَهَاءَ بِالْحَسَدِ ...

Verily Allah will punish six [groups of people] due to six [traits] . . . and the *fuqahā'* due to envy . . .[(i)]

In conclusion, the trait of envy not only stops a person from reaping additional luminous benefits of knowledge, but it also becomes an obstacle for this person to reach felicity by their knowledge, thereby achieving its desired effect.

F) Being Infatuated with One's Knowledge

One of the dimensions of man's selfishness is being infatuated with his self and his possessions. This state can also afflict people of knowledge thus removing their name from the list of scholars. This is because knowledge is a light which brings about enlightenment so that man acquires gnosis about himself, his Origin, the world, the Resurrection, and so that he expresses humility and servitude before the Almighty Lord. Therefore, one must look at knowledge from this perspective. Just like how a mirror reflects things and a person sees things through it, however if he looks at the mirror itself it loses the quality of being a mirror and reflecting, and the observer is then deprived of observing things.

Therefore, paying attention to one's knowledge, being fascinated by it and boasting about it, all of these render the knowledge ineffective and take away its quality of illumination. Moreover, this hinders man from observing his own shortcomings, instead he imagines that he has knowledge of all disciplines and sciences. It is for this reason that the Noblest Messenger (peace and blessings be upon him and his family) says:

مَنْ قَالَ أَنَا عَالِمٌ فَهُوَ جَاهِلٌ

One who says, "I am a scholar", is an ignorant person.[(ii)]

That is because such a person is neither ready to consider others

i. al-Kulaynī, al-Kāfī, 8:163, narration 170

ii. Shahīd al-Thānī, Muniyah al-Murīd, 137

as scholars such that he benefits from them, nor does he declare his ignorance in Allah's presence so that knowledge is imparted to him. This is while Allah has commanded even His messenger:

وَقُل رَّبِّ زِدْنِي عِلْمًا

And say, "O my Lord! Increase me in knowledge." (20:114)

In addition, this state leads to other moral vices, one of which is the trait of humiliating, belittling and scorning others, especially those who are lower than oneself. Therefore, Imam al-Bāqir (peace be upon him) states:

لَا يَكُونُ الْعَبْدُ عَالِماً حَتَّى لَا يَكُونَ ... مُحَقِّراً لِمَنْ دُونَهُ.

A servant does not become a scholar unless he does not . . . belittle those lower than him. (i)

Amīr al-Mu'minīn 'Alī (peace be upon him) also states regarding such people:

رُبَّ عَالِمٍ قَتَلَهُ عِلْمُه

How many scholars are there whom their knowledge has killed! (ii)

Similarly, this great personality writes to his son Imam al-Ḥasan (peace be upon him):

قَرَعْتُكَ بِأَنْوَاعِ الْجَهَالاتِ لِئَلَّا تَعُدَّ نَفْسَكَ عَالِماً فَإِنْ وَرَدَ عَلَيْكَ شَيْءٌ تَعْرِفُهُ أَكْبَرْتَ ذَلِكَ فَإِنَّ الْعَالِمَ مَنْ عَرَفَ أَنَّ مَا يَعْلَمُ فِيمَا لَا يَعْلَمُ قَلِيلٌ فَعَدَّ نَفْسَهُ بِذَلِكَ جَاهِلًا فَازْدَادَ بِمَا عَرَفَ مِنْ ذَلِكَ فِي طَلَبِ الْعِلْمِ اجْتِهَاداً فَمَا يَزَالُ لِلْعِلْمِ طَالِباً وَ فِيهِ رَاغِباً وَ لَهُ مُسْتَفِيداً وَ لِأَهْلِهِ خَاشِعاً مُهْتَمّاً وَ لِلصَّمْتِ لَازِماً وَ لِلْخَطَإِ حَاذِراً

---

i. al-Harrānī, Tuhaf al-'Uqūl, 294

ii. al-Āmudī, Fihrist-i Mawdū'ī-yi Ghurar al-Hikam, the chapter on 'ilm (knowledge).

وَ مِنْهُ مُسْتَحْيِياً وَ إِنْ وَرَدَ عَلَيْهِ مَا لَا يَعْرِفُ لَمْ يُنْكِرْ ذَلِكَ لِمَا قَرَّرَ بِهِ نَفْسَهُ مِنَ الْجَهَالَة

I have reminded you of different types of ignorance, so that you do not consider yourself a scholar such that if you encounter a matter which you already know, you consider it [something] great. Because a scholar is someone who comprehends that the amount of knowledge he possesses is little compared to the knowledge which he does not possess. So, he considers himself ignorant, and due to realizing that he increases his efforts to acquire knowledge. Such a person is constantly seeking knowledge, passionate about it, deriving benefit from it, respecting those who possess it, observing silence, keeping aloof from mistakes and being shy of [committing] them, and when he encounters a matter which he does not understand he does not deny it. This is because he has established [this fact] that he does not have knowledge [of all things]. [i]

3) Obsession with the World and its Various Aspects

Allah the Exalted created man in this world with different inclinations, so that He can try him. In this trial, man is to manifest his true inclination to the Almighty and colour all other inclinations of his with a Divine colour. However, if his outward desires dominate, then his true and esoteric inclination towards the Almighty Truth will become weak and slowly be eliminated.

Know that everyone is susceptible to this test and calamity, especially those who have more potential for facing calamities in their activities and efforts, such as scholars. For scholars are usually the object of people's attention and care, and they themselves have an influence over the people. The love of the world causes man's efforts and movements to be directed towards destruction, especially scholarly endeavours and efforts that by their nature are illuminating and provide a way-out. This nature loses its effect because of the love of the world. Imam al-Ṣādiq

---

i. al-Harrānī, Tuhaf al-'Uqūl, 73

(peace be upon him) says in this regard:

إِذَا رَأَيْتُمُ الْعَالِمَ مُحِبّاً لِدُنْيَاهُ فَاتَّهِمُوهُ عَلَى دِينِكُمْ فَإِنَّ كُلَّ مُحِبٍّ لِشَيْءٍ يَحُوطُ مَا أَحَبَّ وَ قَالَ ص أَوْحَى اللَّهُ إِلَى دَاوُدَ ع لَا تَجْعَلْ بَيْنِي وَ بَيْنَكَ عَالِماً مَفْتُوناً بِالدُّنْيَا فَيَصُدَّكَ عَنْ طَرِيقِ مَحَبَّتِي فَإِنَّ أُولَئِكَ قُطَّاعُ طَرِيقِ عِبَادِيَ الْمُرِيدِينَ إِنَّ أَدْنَى مَا أَنَا صَانِعٌ بِهِمْ أَنْ أَنْزِعَ حَلَاوَةَ مُنَاجَاتِي عَنْ قُلُوبِهِمْ

If you see a scholar who loves the world then accuse him regarding your religion [do not take your religion from him], for one who loves a thing revolves around that which he loves. And Allah revealed unto Prophet David (peace be upon him), "Do not place a scholar who is seduced by the world [as an intermediary] between you and Me, lest he hinders you from the path of My love. Verily they are the ones that cut off the path of my servants who desire Me. Indeed, the least thing that I will do to them is that I will withdraw the sweetness of performing *munājāt* (whispered prayers) with Me, from their hearts.' [i]

Knowledge has different dimensions, aspects and banes which were explained up to now. These banes are essentially due to the effects of the love of the world. However, there are other banes of knowledge that have a stronger connection with the love of the world. In this section, we point to some of them:

A) Following Oppressive Rulers

When the love of the world settles in the heart of a person—especially a scholar—and he is infatuated with acquiring it, he automatically develops a relationship with worldly people and follows their ideas and actions. This results in the destruction and distortion of religion. The Messenger of Allah (peace and blessings be upon him and his family) states:

---

i. al-Kulaynī, al-Kāfī, 1:46, narration 4

الْفُقَهَاءُ أُمَنَاءُ الرُّسُلِ مَا لَمْ يَدْخُلُوا فِي الدُّنْيَا قِيلَ يَا رَسُولَ اللَّهِ وَ مَا دُخُولُهُمْ فِي الدُّنْيَا قَالَ اتِّبَاعُ السُّلْطَانِ فَإِذَا فَعَلُوا ذَلِكَ فَاحْذَرُوهُمْ عَلَى دِينِكُمْ.

> *Fuqahā'* (jurists) are the trustees of the messengers as long as they do not enter the world. He was asked, "What is [the meaning of] them entering the world?" He said, 'Following the sultan. Therefore, when they do so beware of them regarding your religion.' (i)

That is because their ambition in following an oppressive ruler is to acquire the world and its pleasures, and they pay no heed to the religion and the problems of religious people. Due to this, they weaken their own religion and make others pessimistic about religion and the true scholars, thus encouraging people to shun religion.

B) Greed

Having greed for the world and its affairs is a state which causes man to fall into hardship, takes away his honour, and destroys his religion as well as the religion of others. That is because the sole aim of a greedy person is acquiring the world, by any means possible. As a result, he does not care for human dignity and following Allah's religion, and thus naturally distances himself from the religion and Allah the Exalted. (ii) Especially if such a person is a religious scholar, then it leads to the weakening and destruction of his own religion as well as the religion of others. Thus, Imam al-Husayn (peace be upon him) describes greed in a scholar as one of the most abominable things. (iii)

Likewise, Imam ʿAlī (peace be upon him) states:

خَمْسٌ يُسْتَقْبَحْنَ مِنْ خَمْس ... الْحِرْصُ فِي الْحُكَمَاء

> Five things are abominable from five [types of people] . . .

---

i. Ibid., 5:121, narration 1

ii. al-Āmudī, Fihrist-i Mawdūʿī-yi Ghurar al-Hikam, the chapter on hirs (greed)

iii. al-Qummī, Kifāyah al-Athar, 233

greed from the wise.[i]

One of the clear instances of greed is to ask for a wage in return for teaching and guiding others.[ii] A narrator states:[iii]

قَالَ سَمِعْتُ أَبَا عَبْدِ اللَّهِ ع يَقُولُ مَنِ اسْتَأْكَلَ بِعِلْمِهِ افْتَقَرَ فَقُلْتُ لَهُ جُعِلْتُ فِدَاكَ إِنَّ فِي شِيعَتِكَ وَ مَوَالِيكَ قَوْماً يَتَحَمَّلُونَ عُلُومَكُمْ وَ يَبُثُّونَهَا فِي شِيعَتِكُمْ فَلَا يَعْدَمُونَ عَلَى ذَلِكَ مِنْهُمُ الْبِرَّ وَ الصِّلَةَ وَ الْإِكْرَامَ فَقَالَ ع لَيْسَ أُولَئِكَ بِمُسْتَأْكِلِينَ إِنَّمَا الْمُسْتَأْكِلُ بِعِلْمِهِ الَّذِي يُفْتِي بِغَيْرِ عِلْمٍ وَ لَا هُدًى مِنَ اللَّهِ عَزَّ وَ جَلَّ لِيُبْطِلَ بِهِ الْحُقُوقَ طَمَعاً فِي حُطَامِ الدُّنْيَا

I heard Imam al-Ṣādiq (peace be upon him) say, "One who seeks his livelihood using his knowledge becomes needy." I asked him, "May I be your ransom! There is a group amongst your Shīʿah and friends who carry your knowledge and propagate it amongst your Shīʿah. The Shīʿah [in return], do not refrain from acting with beneficence and giving them gifts and respect." The Imam (peace be upon him) said, "They are not those who obtain their living using knowledge. A person who earns his living using his knowledge is one who issues religious verdicts (*fatāwā*) without any knowledge or guidance from Allah, thereby nullifying the rights [of the people] to satisfy his greed for the lowly world."[iv]

This clarifies the limit of worldly greed in relation to seeking knowledge.

---

i. al-Āmudī, Ghurar al-Ḥikam, narration 5080

ii. al-Kulaynī, al-Kāfī, 5:121, narration 1.

iii. The narration that was referenced in the above footnote (not present in the text) addresses the issue of seeking wages. This following narration is intended to dispel a question that may arise in the minds of the respected readers, that what about if the believers provide a monetary gift to the scholars? Is this also reprimanded?

iv. al-Sadūq, Maʿānī al-Akhbār, 181, narration 1

C) *Riyāʾ* (Ostentation)

Having a good motivation in one's actions is a sign of having a strong drive and a pure soul. If this is the case, such an intention has a positive and desired effect on the soul, even after having completed the action. However, the opposite is true as well. Any action that requires having an intention of seeking Allah's proximity (*qurbah*) to be valid, if it is performed for other than Allah or if a partner is ascribed to Him in performing it, then such an action is invalid. This is the case in ritual acts of worship (*ʿibādāt*). Those who do not repeat such actions or perform its *qaḍāʾ* with the intention of Allah's proximity, will be reprimanded for it. [i]

Ikhlāṣ has different levels, and for every level there is a distinct effect which cleanses the action from insincerities. Gaining knowledge or teaching it to others is a sanctified act in the view of the people of intellect, the religion of Islam and the Imams (peace be upon them). That is because it is a noble and necessary preliminary to reaching the ultimate goal of creation.

Because a scholar is the object of people's attention and occupies a distinguished position amongst them, he is prone to the vice of *riyāʾ*. *Riyāʾ* has certain signs which have been specified in the Islamic narrations. It is necessary for seekers of knowledge, especially those seeking religious knowledge, to pay attention to these signs. By doing so they would be able to profit—both in this world and the Hereafter—from the efforts they have made on the path of spirituality, the hardships which they have endured, and the occasional unkindness of the ignorant people and those who follow their base desires. The Messenger of Allah (peace and blessings be upon him and his family) says about *riyāʾ* with regards to knowledge:

مَنْ تَعَلَّمَ عِلْماً لِغَيْرِ اللَّهِ وَ أَرَادَ بِهِ غَيْرَ اللَّهِ فَلْيَتَبَوَّأْ مَقْعَدَهُ مِنَ النَّارِ

> One who learns for other than Allah, or seeks other than Allah through his learning, then indeed his dwelling places

---

i. Repeating it refers to performing the act of worship once again before its allocated time has passed. Performing the *qaḍāʾ* means to perform it after this time has passed.

is in the Fire. (i)

Similarly, he says in another narration:

مَـنْ طَلَـبَ الْعِلْـمَ لِيُبَاهِـيَ بِـهِ الْعُلَمَـاءَ أَوْ يُمَـارِيَ بِـهِ السُّـفَهَاءَ أَوْ يَصْـرِفَ بِـهِ وُجُـوهَ النَّـاسِ إِلَيْـهِ فَلْيَتَبَـوَّأْ مَقْعَـدَهُ مِـنَ النَّـارِ

One who seeks knowledge to boast in front of the learned, to argue with the ignorant, or to attract people's attention in order that they respect him, then indeed his dwelling place is in the Fire. (ii)

In another statement he says:

مَـنْ تَعَلَّـمَ الْعِلْـمَ رِئَـاءً وَ سُـمْعَةً يُرِيـدُ بِـهِ الدُّنْيَـا نَـزَعَ اللَّـهُ بَرَكَتَـهُ وَ ضَيَّـقَ عَلَيْـهِ مَعِيشَـتَهُ وَ وَكَلَـهُ اللَّـهُ إِلَـى نَفْسِـهِ وَ مَـنْ وَكَلَـهُ اللَّـهُ إِلَـى نَفْسِـهِ فَقَـدْ هَلَـكَ

One who seeks knowledge to show off to others or to make them hear [so that they hear that he is seeking knowledge], and through this he desires the world, then Allah takes away his blessings, makes his life constricted and abandons him to himself. And one whom Allah abandons him to himself is certainly destroyed. (iii)

In conclusion, since man's understanding is a mere tool and a path for him to reach true perfection, he must obtain the necessary conditions and remain aloof from the banes of seeking knowledge.

---

i. al-Tirmidhī, Sunan al-Tirmidhī, 5:33, narration 2655

ii. al-Kulaynī, Usūl al-Kāfī, 1:46, narration 1

iii. al-Ṭabrasī, Makārim al-Akhlāq, 2:348, narration 2660

Chapter Three

The Fundamental Goal of Creation and Its Different Aspects

Introduction

Paying attention to the fundamental goal of man's creation and the way this attention affects man's academic, practical and moral endeavours, gives a special depth to his activities. Such attention ensures that he constantly remain on the path towards realizing this goal, contrary to activities that are performed without attention to this reality. The effect of activities devoid of this attention—even if they are good actions or traits—will be limited and outward. Movement towards man's goal, when coupled with such an attention, connects man with Allah the Exalted. Moreover, this movement has various stages and a well-defined beginning. By paying attention to the different dimensions of this matter, the levels of servitude can be traversed, until one reaches the ultimate goal which is Divine proximity. In this chapter we will examine this journey.

Section One
Servitude to Allah the Exalted

By paying attention to the previous discussions and deliberating on the teachings of the Qur'ān and the Sunnah [i], it is understood that the issue of servitude was the cornerstone of the prophets' (peace be

---

i. The word *sunnah* refers to the speech and conduct of the Prophet (peace and blessings be upon him and his family) as well as the Imams (peace be upon them).

upon them) invitation to religion and that of the *awliyāʾ* (peace be upon them). The Noble Qurʾān has explained this reality in different verses.[i] In a comprehensive manner, it says:

> وَلَقَدْ بَعَثْنَا فِي كُلِّ أُمَّةٍ رَّسُولًا أَنِ اعْبُدُوا اللَّهَ وَاجْتَنِبُوا الطَّاغُوتَ
>
> Certainly, We raised an apostle in every nation [to preach], "Worship Allah, and shun fake deities." (16:36)

Moreover, it describes servitude as being the goal of the creation of man and jinn,

> وَمَا خَلَقْتُ الْجِنَّ وَالْإِنسَ إِلَّا لِيَعْبُدُونِ
>
> I did not create the jinn and the humans except that they may worship Me. (51:56)

Also, the servants are not commanded to do anything in this world, save this:

> وَمَا أُمِرُوا إِلَّا لِيَعْبُدُوا اللَّهَ مُخْلِصِينَ لَهُ الدِّينَ
>
> Though they were not commanded except to worship Allah, dedicating their faith to Him. (98:5)

Of course, it should also be known that servitude is not achieved except by obeying Allah, His messenger (peace and blessings be upon him and his family) and the *Ūlū al-Amr* (the possessors of authority) in the different aspects of life.[ii] And if there are innumerable recommendations about seeking knowledge, creating the conditions for it and removing its obstacles, then all that is for reaching this fundamental goal.

The Definition and Types of Servitude

The Arabic word *ʿubūdiyyah* (servitude) literally means to express humility and insignificance.[iii] By considering this meaning, it becomes

---

i. (7:59), (7:65), (7:73) and (7:85)

ii. (4:59), (26:108), (26:110), (26:129), (26:131), (26:144), (26:150), (26:163) and (26:179)

iii. al-Iṣfahānī, al-Mufradāt, under root word "abd'

clear that this reality is only appropriate for the Sacred Divine Essence, because the control of the existence of all beings as well as the different aspects of their existence is always in His hands.[i] In addition, there are two types of servitude that can be conceived.

1) Ontological (Takwīnī) Servitude

The Noble Qur'ān confirms this type of servitude—which is accompanied by obedience—for all beings:

إِن كُلُّ مَن فِي السَّمَاوَاتِ وَالْأَرْضِ إِلَّا آتِي الرَّحْمَٰنِ عَبْدًا

There is none in the heavens and the Earth but that he comes to the Beneficent as a servant. (19:93)

In addition, the Qur'ān has affirmed the consequences of this humility and servitude for all beings, seen in how they glorify and prostrate in front of Allah the Exalted:

وَإِن مِّن شَيْءٍ إِلَّا يُسَبِّحُ بِحَمْدِهِ

There is not a thing but that celebrates His praise (17:44)

وَلِلَّهِ يَسْجُدُ مَن فِي السَّمَاوَاتِ وَالْأَرْضِ

To Allah prostrates whoever there is in the heavens and the Earth (13:15)

While it affirms that all beings have a certain cognition of this action of theirs:

كُلٌّ قَدْ عَلِمَ صَلَاتَهُ وَتَسْبِيحَهُ

Each knows his prayer and glorification (24:41)

At the same time, it addresses man and says:

وَلَٰكِن لَّا تَفْقَهُونَ تَسْبِيحَهُمْ

But you do not understand their glorification (17:44)

This means that human beings do not have an awareness or a specific attention to this glorification. It is not possible to perceive this

i. Aspects of their existence refers to their perfections and their actions.

humility shown by other beings in front of Allah the Immaculate, by using conventional methods.[i]

2) Volitional Servitude

This means to express humility and insignificance in front of the Sacred Divine Essence, out of understanding and volition. Some verses of the Qur'ān mention servitude to be the highest title and honour for the great Divine messengers and only after this do they list other titles and stations. It is as if this title is seen as the foremost amongst all their titles.

Comparing these two groups of verses of the Noble Qur'ān, it can be seen that servitude is a far-reaching reality, encompassing all created and contingent beings. However, in addition to possessing the ontological aspect of servitude, man can also possess a loftier station of servitude. Reaching this rank entails lofty spiritual perfections and stations; this station is known as, "conscious and voluntary humility in front of Allah the Exalted."

Even though the servitude of the Divine angels is also conscious and voluntary:

بَلْ عِبَادٌ مُّكْرَمُونَ لَا يَسْبِقُونَهُ بِالْقَوْلِ وَهُم بِأَمْرِهِ يَعْمَلُونَ

> Indeed, they are [His] honoured servants. They do not venture to speak ahead of Him, and they act by His command. (21:26, 27)

However, the station of man's servitude is incomparable to their servitude, such that the loftiest of stations such as prophethood and *imāmah* (leadership) are a consequence of man's station of servitude.[ii] Thus, Allah commands the angels to show humility in front of man, saying:

اسْجُدُوا لِآدَمَ

Prostrate before Adam. (2:34)

---

i. However, through spiritual wayfaring and purification, it is possible that one may develop the means within himself to be able to perceive this glorification.

ii. (38:45), (53:10), and (32:24)

وَلَقَدْ خَلَقْنَاكُمْ ثُمَّ صَوَّرْنَاكُمْ ثُمَّ قُلْنَا لِلْمَلَائِكَةِ اسْجُدُوا لِآ

Certainly, We created you, then We formed you, then We said to the angels, "Prostrate before Adam." (7:11)

Similarly, Allah has made the angels to be the intermediaries of His grace towards man so that he reaches certain special perfections.

The Relationship between Worship and Servitude

Servitude is the soul and spirit that must manifest in the shell of man's actions for these actions to acquire value. When void of servitude, man's deeds are an empty and worthless shell which would not be bought for anything in the Divine realm [i], nor do they have any effect on the perfection of their performer.

The individual, social, political, domestic, economic, ritual, artistic and emotional spheres are amongst the different spheres of life where Allah the Exalted's servitude can manifest itself and breathe life. This is only achieved through obeying the Divine commands in these different spheres, even if the person does not always have the intention of seeking Divine proximity. However, if he wants this obedience to have a greater effect in getting closer to Allah the Exalted, then he must perform the actions with such an intention, without *riyā'* (ostentation) and other worldly motives—in this case all these actions will be considered a type of worship.

Accordingly, acts of worship form one part of man's actions; the manner of performing them has been explained by Allah the Exalted. It is necessary that they are performed with the intention of seeking proximity to Allah; these are termed as *'ibādāt*. Examples include prayer, fasting, *Ḥajj*, *zakāt*, *khums*, charity, and supplications. These *'ibādāt* are as opposed to the *mu'āmalāt* (transactions) and other obligations and laws of *sharī'ah*. *'Ibādāt* have their complete effect and are valuable when they are placed on the path of Allah's servitude, sincere attention to Him, and expressing conscious humility and submission to Him and His *awliyā'* (peace be upon them).

---

i. When its reality is exposed it will be seen to be worthless.

When worship is performed with the backing of servitude to Allah the Exalted it is not repetitive, rather it brings about depth, progress and perfection.

Such worship—accompanied with correct obedience and an inward humility in front of Allah in the different spheres of life—removes the curtains and veils that exist between the Creator and the creation, until the wayfarer witnesses the beauty of the Beloved. Then this same worship, which until now was a means of spiritual progress and perfection, in this stage becomes a window to witnessing the Divine attributes of beauty and majesty. By means of this worship the wayfarer traverses through the realm of the *malakūt.* (i)

It is for this reason that Imam ʿAlī (peace be upon him) would at times go unconsciousness during prayer. (ii) Similarly Imam al-Sajjad (peace be upon him) would become inattentive of everything during prayer. (iii) Or once, Imam al-Ṣādiq (peace be upon him) fell unconscious while praying, and when the people asked about its reason he said:

> مَا زِلْتُ أُكَرِّرُ آيَاتِ الْقُرْآنِ حَتَّى بَلَغْتُ إِلَى حَالٍ كَأَنَّنِي سَمِعْتُهَا مُشَافَهَةً مِمَّنْ أَنْزَلَهَا
>
> I continued repeating the verses of the Qurʾān until I reached a state where it was as if I heard them being spoken from the One who revealed them. (iv)

Therefore, the claims made by some pseudo-*ʿurafā* who separate the exoteric aspect of *sharīʿah* from its esoteric aspect and make a distinction between the *sharīʿah* and the *ṭarīqah* (the spiritual path), are foolish and incorrect. They consider worship to only be necessary up until one reaches the station of certainty, thereafter it is not necessary

---

i. The word *malakūt*, is a noun derived from the word *mulk* meaning kingdom, dominance, or authority. The former however contains a higher level of intensity not present in the latter. The meaning in this context is a realm that the wayfarer enters after the reality of Allah's true dominance over the creation is witnessed.

ii. Majlisī, Bihār al-Anwār, 41:11, narration 1

iii. Ibid., 46:61, narration 19 and 46:66, narration 30

iv. Ibid., 47:58, narration 108

to perform acts of worship. However, the truth is that when a person reaches the station of certainty, this is the beginning of the reality of worship! This is beginning of a deep yearning for the Beloved and benefitting from the Divine attributes of beauty and majesty. Prior to this stage the reality of servitude had not manifested itself. Thus, the true *wāṣilūn* (i) and those who have found their way to the Alley of the Beloved worship their Lord with ardour and never feel tired or bored of it.

Levels of Servitude

As mentioned above, servitude means humility in front of the Sacred Divine Essence accompanied by a certain awareness, and it is of two types: ontological and volitional. Volitional servitude is specific to beings endowed with consciousness and free will, and its highest level can be traversed by man. This is because man possesses a vast potential for perfection, even the Divine angels cannot reach the extent of perfection that he can. Also, this servitude penetrates every sphere of man's life and existence. After these points have been clarified, it can be seen that depending on the different levels of perception people have, man's servitude of Allah the Sustainer can be divided into two overall levels. Each of these levels in turn, contain two ranks within them.

1) Outward Servitude

Outward servitude is obeying the commands of Allah the Exalted and His *awliyā'* in all aspects of life. Undoubtedly this is after having faith in Allah, belief in His essential perfections and different dimensions of *tawḥīd* (monotheism: in creation, in ontological and legislative authority, in worship, in actions, in attributes and in essence). Also, belief in the Divine angels, the messengers of Allah, and the truth of their religions and the books they brought in their own times is required. Lastly, belief in the prophethood of the Noblest Prophet (peace and blessings be upon him and his family), the *imāmah* of the

---

i. *Wāṣilūn* literally means those who are connected and here refers to those have reached the station of Divine Proximity and united with their Lord.

twelve Imams (peace be upon them), and the truth of everything they have said when explaining the true Islam.

This type of obedience is always incumbent on all believers. In the first stage, this takes the form of abiding by the mandatory commands (performing the obligatory actions and leaving the prohibited actions). In higher stages, this manifests itself through obedience in performing *mustaḥabb* (supererogatory) actions, leaving *makrūh* (disapproved) actions, rectifying one's motivation for performing acts of obedience, reforming one's moral traits, acquiring moral virtues and shunning moral vices. Everyone can traverse these ranks to the extent of their efforts.

2) True Servitude

The previous level was named 'outward servitude' because at that level, the servant's *tawḥīdī* (monotheistic) outlook is weak and he worships Allah as an entity separate and hidden from him.

Of course, the servitude of most men is of this type, even if some of them have a correct and deep intellectual understanding of Allah the Exalted. Because this is only an intellectual understanding of Allah, their level is still considered as 'outward servitude'. This level has desirable effects in causing man to reach a particular level of felicity. However, when someone carries out this level completely and accepts that it is possible to establish a closer connection with Allah the Exalted, a higher level can be attained. If he does not deny that by purification of the heart and deepening of faith it is possible to witness Allah, and simultaneously he pays attention to what is required from him and traverses the path towards perfection, a transformation will occur in him. He eventually reaches a level where he can witness his existential humility in front of Allah the Exalted through his heart. Such an individual inevitably witnesses the different dimensions of *tawḥīd* (*tawḥīd* in actions, attributes and in essence) through his heart. This station is called 'true servitude'. Undoubtedly, the servitude of the Noblest Messenger (peace and blessings be upon him and his family) and the Imams (peace be upon him) was true servitude. For this reason, when 'Unwān al-Baṣrī requests that Imam al-Ṣādiq (peace be upon him) allow him to benefit from his personality, the Imam says in reply:

فَإِنْ أَرَدْتَ الْعِلْمَ فَاطْلُبْ أَوَّلًا فِي نَفْسِكَ حَقِيقَةَ الْعُبُودِيَّة

> If you want this knowledge, then first seek the reality of servitude ['true servitude'] in yourself.

The Imam (peace be upon him) then proceeds to expound on true servitude, and that it means to not see ownership for oneself in anything and to not plan one's affairs. Naturally, this is only achieved when a person sees Allah the Exalted's ownership and planning in every aspect of existence. This is a matter pertaining to the heart and requires an extraordinary transformation in the servant whereby he acquires the Ahl al-Bayt's (peace be upon them) true knowledge. Witnessing the realities and establishing a direct and presential connection with Allah the Exalted are examples of the Ahl al-Bayt's (peace be upon them) true knowledge and are achieved by reaching true servitude.

For example, when a person asked Imam ʿAlī (peace be upon him), "Have you seen the God you worship?" He replied:

وَيْلَكَ ... لَمْ أَكُنْ بِالَّذِي أَعْبُدُ رَبّاً لَمْ أَرَهُ قَالَ فَكَيْفَ رَأَيْتَهُ صِفْهُ لَنَا قَالَ وَيْلَكَ لَمْ تَرَهُ الْعُيُونُ بِمُشَاهَدَةِ الْأَبْصَارِ وَ لَكِنْ رَأَتْهُ الْقُلُوبُ بِحَقَائِقِ الْإِيمَان

> "Woe unto you! ... I am not a person who would worship a God he has not seen." That person asked, "And how did you see him? Describe Him for us" The Imam (peace be upon him) said, "Woe unto you! Eyes do not see Him with outward sight, but hearts witness Him through the realities of faith." [i]

It is not just the case that the realization of this matter is possible for everyone, rather the Messenger of Allah (peace and blessings be upon him and his family) even exhorted Abu Dharr to reach this station, saying:

اعْبُدِ اللَّهَ كَأَنَّكَ تَرَاهُ فَإِنْ كُنْتَ لَا تَرَاهُ فَإِنَّهُ يَرَاك

---

i. al-Ṣadūq, al-Tawḥīd, 304, narration 1; 308, narration 2; 109, narration 6

> Worship Allah as if you see Him. For if you do not see Him then indeed He sees you. [i]

In this saying, the Messenger of Allah (peace and blessings be upon him and his family) has recommended two lofty stages of servitude: the first is Allah's servitude in a manner that the servant sees Allah, which inevitably has certain effects. The second stage has even greater effects, it is Allah's servitude in a manner that Allah sees His servant. In the first stage—despite being a kind of witnessing of the heart—the witnesser still assumes that it is he who witnesses Allah. Here the veils between the servant and the Master have not been completely lifted. However, the second stage is in reality an unveiling of how Allah sees His servant; this requires that the veils of light be cast aside. In this stage, Allah is witnessed in a manner such that He encompasses the existence of the servant and the different dimensions of his existence. This second stage is accompanied by witnessing His existential encompassment and this entails that the servant no longer sees any aspect of existence and its different dimensions as being for himself. Undoubtedly, this type of witnessing also has different levels and ranks, based on the levels of *tawḥīd* in actions, Divine names, attributes and essence.

This witnessing is in a manner that is worthy of the Absolute Unparalleled Divine Essence and requires a special purity. In this stage the veils of darkness and light are lifted from the visage of the servant's heart, and according to his existential capacity he witnesses Allah with himself and other beings in all their different dimensions (their actions, attributes and essence). This comes about because of a correct understanding of Allah, His Absolute Oneness, [ii] precise action in accordance with the commands of the sacred *sharīʿah*, observing the stages of *ikhlāṣ* (sincerity), constant vigilance on these matters, as well as strict accounting of his actions, his motivations and the states of his soul.

For this reason, after recommending these two stations of servitude

---

i. Majlisī, Biḥār al-Anwār, 77:78

ii. That is, how while being the First, He is also the Last, and while being the Last, He is also the First. And while being Apparent, He is also Hidden, and while being Hidden, He is also Apparent. He is with every being, encompassing them (from the author).

and presenting a correct monotheistic viewpoint—explaining how Allah wishes to be worshipped—the Messenger of Allah (peace and blessings be upon him and his family) gives numerous practical and moral counsels to Abū Dharr. He says:

احْفَظِ اللَّهَ يَحْفَظْكَ احْفَظِ اللَّهَ تَجِدْهُ أَمَامَكَ

> Preserve Allah and Allah will preserve you. Preserve Allah and you will find Him in front of you. [i]

By emphasizing the need to be vigilant about one's actions and behaviour and explaining that by means of this vigilance Allah protects his servant from impurities, the Prophet (peace and blessings be upon him and his family) explains that the ultimate result of this is to find Allah in front of him. This means to see Allah the Exalted as being apparent and encompassing over all existence and over the dimensions of himself as well as all beings. This state also has distinct consequences which appear with specific signs—these have been mentioned in the words of Imam al-Ṣādiq (peace be upon him) to ʿUnwān al-Baṣrī.

In the Noble Qurʾān Allah has mentioned some of His special servants, and has introduced some distinctive traits of theirs:

وَاذْكُرْ عِبَادَنَا إِبْرَاهِيمَ وَإِسْحَاقَ وَيَعْقُوبَ أُولِي الْأَيْدِي وَالْأَبْصَارِ

> And remember Our servants, Abraham, Isaac and Jacob, men of strength and insight. (38:45)

This means that they had reached certain realities and become connected to them, unlike other servants of Allah. In the successive verses Allah explains the reason that they were like this, saying:

إِنَّا أَخْلَصْنَاهُم بِخَالِصَةٍ ذِكْرَى الدَّارِ وَإِنَّهُمْ عِندَنَا لَمِنَ الْمُصْطَفَيْنَ الْأَخْيَارِ

> Indeed, We purified them with an exclusive remembrance of the abode [of the Hereafter]. Indeed, they are surely with Us among the elect of the best. (38: 46-47)

---

i. Majlisī, Biḥār al-Anwār, 77:87

This means that through true remembrance of the Hereafter and moving towards it by performing good deeds, they acquired a certain readiness within themselves. As a result, Allah brought about a special change in them, a change that fundamentally altered their outlook towards existence and its different dimensions.[i] This change resulted in certain effects for them, all of which illustrate a fundamental change in their outlook and relationship with Allah the Exalted. The highest station that they reached is indicated in what Allah says about them:

سُبْحَانَ اللَّهِ عَمَّا يَصِفُونَ إِلَّا عِبَادَ اللَّهِ الْمُخْلَصِينَ

> Clear is Allah of whatever they allege [about Him], [all] except Allah's exclusive servants. (37: 159, 160)

This verse approves these servants' description of the Sacred Divine Essence, considering it to be like Allah's description of Himself. This demonstrates that Allah, through His special favour upon them, has shown Himself to them the way He really is, without causing an existential limitation for Him or limiting His perfection in any way. Just as how when Allah describes Himself, it is a true description without any limitations. For example, the highest description of Allah the Exalted in His revealed words is in the blessed Sūrah al-Tawḥīd.[ii] There:

Firstly, He has been introduced with absolute oneness such that He can only be mentioned by hinting and allusion. At the same time, He is *al-ṣamad* and absolutely self-sufficient. Never does He descend from the station of absolute oneness.

The consequence of such a being is that while being the First, He is also the Last, and while being the Last, He is also the First. Also, while being Apparent, He is also Hidden, and while being Hidden, He is also Apparent.

Secondly, His creation of beings is not in the form of reproduction and separating of the beings from His Essence:

لَمْ يَلِدْ

---

i. Due to the change that Allah the Exalted caused in them, this group is known as the *mukhlaṣīn* (those whom Allah made to be sincere).

ii. The 112th chapter of the Noble Qur'ān

He neither begat (112:3)

Thirdly, such a Being does not originate from somewhere, rather He is without beginning and eternal:

وَلَمْ يُولَدْ

Nor was [He] begotten (112:3)

Fourthly, as a result He has no partner or parallel in terms of His existential rank, creation and existential perfections:

وَلَمْ يَكُن لَّهُ كُفُوًا أَحَدٌ

Nor has He any equal. (112:4)

Rather, all the beings in their existence and perfections are a complete manifestation and sign of Him; they only show Him, and He is never separate from them.

Paying careful attention to the teachings that have reached us from the Noblest Messenger (peace and blessings be upon him and his family) and the Imams (peace be upon them)—in particular the monotheistic sermons of Imam ʿAlī (peace be upon him) and Imam al-Riḍā (peace be upon him)—reveal that the exact same description of Allah has appeared in them.

The second characteristic of the *mukhlasīn* is that Allah quotes Satan saying:

قَالَ فَبِعِزَّتِكَ لَأُغْوِيَنَّهُمْ أَجْمَعِينَ إِلاَّ عِبَادَكَ مِنْهُمُ الْمُخْلَصِينَ

By Your might, I will surely pervert them, except Your exclusive servants among them. (38: 82-83)

This means that the *mukhlaṣīn* have reached a degree of existential perfection that not only do Satan's temptations not have any effect on them, but also when faced with Satan, they see him to be a manifestation of Allah. They see that he does not have any independent effect on man.

The third characteristic of the *mukhlaṣīn* is that Allah says:

فَإِنَّهُمْ لَمُحْضَرُونَ إِلاَّ عِبَادَ اللَّهِ الْمُخْلَصِينَ

So, they will indeed be mustered [in hell], [all] except Allah's exclusive servants. (37: 127-128)

This means that unlike other people they will not be summoned for accounting in the court of Divine Justice. That is because:

Firstly, they have settled their accounts in this world and therefore they will enter the Garden without reckoning and will only be present on the Day of Resurrection.

Secondly, through manifesting and witnessing the *tawḥīdī* realms, they have been saved from perdition. According to the verse:

كُلُّ شَيْءٍ هَالِكٌ إِلاَّ وَجْهَهُ

Everything is to perish except His Face. (28:88)

Those who have witnessed 'Allah's Face' (*wajh Allah*) shall never perish and thus there is no need to resurrect them in the Hereafter. Rather they are present in all the realms of *barzakh* (purgatory) and the Hereafter.

The fourth characteristic of the *mukhlaṣīn* is that Allah says regarding them:

وَ مَا تُجْزَوْنَ إِلاَّ مَا كُنتُمْ تَعْمَلُونَ إِلاَّ عِبَادَ اللَّهِ الْمُخْلَصِي

And you will be requited only for what you used to do, [all] except Allah's exclusive servants. (27: 39, 40)

This means that they have reached a station of *tawḥīdī* witnessing that they do not see any action for themselves such that they be rewarded for it. In other words, usually a reward is granted in return for a specific action. When a person does not see any action for himself, his reward will not be in return for his actions, rather it will be the appearance of existential perfection in him.

In the Noble Qur'ān examples of this *tawḥīdī* understanding of these servants are mentioned, but this is not the place to mention them and in the forthcoming discussion an indication will be made to one such example. Undoubtedly, the appearance of *tawḥīdī* states has certain signs which are known by those worthy of it—one must refer in this area to a proficient teacher who himself has traversed this reality.

In any case, it must be known that man is never absolved of the duties of servitude and the true servants of Allah never transgress the path of outward servitude in any sphere of their life. This issue is mentioned in the words of Imam al-Ṣādiq (peace be upon him) to ʿUnwān al-Baṣrī.

Of course, paying attention to the signs of true servitude—which are mentioned in the upcoming words of Imam al-Ṣādiq (peace be upon him) to ʿUnwān al-Baṣrī—has a marked effect in encouraging man to move towards true servitude. This is the case even though such attention is merely a conceptual perception. Because generally, in the beginning of his spiritual journey, man moves with the help of a correct conceptual understanding, be it regarding the Origin and perfections of Allah the Exalted or regarding the goal of man and the lofty stations he can attain. Even after witnessing the realms of *tawḥīd* through the heart, or after attaining spiritual states like contentment (*riḍā*) and submission (*taslīm*), a person continues to rely on the correct intellectual perception. In his normal day-to-day affairs, he relies on this perception—which is in accordance with what he has witnessed—and ensures that his actions and internal reactions conform to it. Therefore, having a correct and deep belief and understanding is one of the requirements of the spiritual and *tawḥīdī* journey. Similarly, paying attention to the signs of true servitude which will be discussed in the forthcoming section, is desirable.

The Methods of Attaining True Servitude

There are two overall methods for reaching the lofty stations, spiritual perfections, and for witnessing the Divine attributes of beauty and majesty through Allah's servitude.

The first is by traversing a journey and undergoing training (*tarbiyah*) based on adhering to the instructions of the Qurʾān and the Sunnah, in a step-by-step and stage-by-stage process. The first step in this journey is abiding by Allah's commands and staying away from His prohibitions (performing the obligatory actions and abandoning the forbidden actions). In the subsequent steps, the wayfarer's existence becomes more refined and elegant. Through correct, precise and persistent action according to special instructions, programs and by implementing the stages of *ikhlāṣ*, the veils of darkness and light are lifted from his monotheistic human disposition (*fiṭrat-i tawḥīdī*) and he takes the first step in witnessing the *tawḥīdī* realms.

Indeed, in all but the first steps of this journey the wayfarer needs a special teacher who has these qualities:

1. Firstly, he is aware of the fundamental teachings of the Qur'ān and the Sunnah.
2. Secondly, he has traversed this path and a portion of the *tawḥīdī* realms have been unveiled for him.
3. Thirdly, he can help and train those who are deserving.

The second method is the method of captivation (*jadhbah*). In this method a person, without traversing the different stages and by solely possessing a suitable spiritual background—because of Allah's special grace—reaches spiritual perfections. In this method, first the heart is attracted and drawn towards the *qudsī* realm and thereafter a level, or multiple levels, of the *tawḥīdī* realms are manifested to the heart. Subsequently, these states must be preserved and made firm through performing virtuous actions and being in connection with the Qur'ān, the Sunnah and pious scholars.

Distinctions of the Two Methods of Attaining True Servitude

Each of these two methods has their own characteristics and distinct effects:

1) The journey of spiritual training is voluntary and available for every wayfarer who intends to reach spiritual perfection, as long as he readies its prerequisites. Although in the first stage, taking heed and kindling the desire to undertake the journey towards Allah is not in his control, rather it is from Allah. On the contrary, in attaining the journey through captivation, man's free will does not play a role. It occurs due to creating the suitable ground within himself, possessing a special purity and an untainted *fiṭrah* (innate disposition), or due to his devout obedience to the instructions of the *sharīʿah* and not denying the realities. Suddenly, the spark of Allah the Exalted's love—out of His grace and wisdom—seizes one amongst thousands of seekers of reality and takes him to a level of perfection.

2) The process of spiritual training must be performed under the

guidance of and accompanied by a complete teacher or one who has traversed this path. In this manner, the teacher can systematically acquaint the wayfarer with the way, the method and the difficulties of the path—all in light of the luminous instructions of the Qur'ān and the Ahl al-Bayt (peace be upon them). He can take him through the difficult stages and stations and free him from the traps of the world, the nature, the selfish desires and satanic insinuations.

In previous discussions, intellectual and traditional proofs were provided regarding the need that wayfarers towards Allah have for a proficient teacher.[i] In addition to that, the folk of gnosis (*ahl al-maʿrifah*) and those who for years were in search of a suitable guide—until after relentless efforts Allah granted them success in achieving this—have greatly emphasized the need of having a teacher who himself has traversed the path.

Ḥāfiẓ-i Shīrāzī, considers the teacher to be like Noah (peace be upon him), guiding the ark of the wayfarer's existence amidst the hurricane of the path's calamities, to the shores of salvation and felicity:

یار مردان خدا باش که در کشتی نوح

هست خاکی که به آبی نخرد طوفان را

Be the friend of the men of God, for in the Ark of Noah,
There is dust that not a drop of the flood has touched.[ii]

And in another place, he says:

حافظ از دست مده صحبت این کشتی نوح

ور نه طوفان حوادث ببرد بنیادت

*Ḥ*āfiz! Don't let the companionship of Noah's Ark slip your hand,
Or else the deluge of life's calamities will ravage your foundation.[iii]

However, in the journey of captivation, without the guidance of a

---

i. Refer to the end of Chapter One.

ii. Shirāzī, Divān-i Ḥāfiẓ (Taṣḥīḥ-i Qudsī), ghazal 10, couplet 5

iii. Ibid., ghazal 72, couplet 7

teacher, the wayfarer reaches the intended destination to some extent. The folk of gnosis also call this method '*uwaysī*', because of Uways-i Qaranī, who attained *tawḥīdī* perfections by means of Divine captivation. He was not under the guidance of a specific teacher, but due to his untainted monotheistic disposition and by following the luminous instructions of the Noblest Messenger (peace and blessings be upon him and his family) and Amīr al-Mu'minīn (peace be upon him), he attained such perfections.

Similarly, based on evidence it can be concluded that Khwājah Ḥāfiẓ-i Shīrāzī began his spiritual wayfaring in the '*uwaysī*' manner. Like Uways-i Qaranī, he wanted to find the way to his Desired Jewel by himself. Despite extensive spiritual struggle (*mujāhadāt*) and self-mortifications (*riyāḍāt*), without a spiritual teacher he was not able to attain the Divine gnosis (*ma'ārif*) by means of unveiling and witnessing. He says in this regard:

گداخت جان که شود کار دل تمام و نشد

بسوختیم در این آرزوی خام و نشد

My soul burnt in pursuit of my heart's calling, but it was not to be,
We burnt away in this naive wish, yet it was not to be.

فغان که در طلب گنج گوهر مقصود

شدم خراب جهانی ز غم تمام و نشد

Alas! For in the search of the desired Treasured Jewel,
I became disgraced in the eyes of the people and full of sorrow, yet it was not to be.

دریغ و درد که در جست و جوی گنج حضور

بسی شدم به گدایی بر کرام و نشد

Alas for my sorrow and pain! While searching for the treasure of

Presence,[i]

Many a time did I beg from the generous, yet it was not to be.[ii]

For this reason, he guides other wayfarers and says that they must not enter this path without a teacher, because for years he tried this method unto no avail.[iii]

به کوی عشق منه بی دلیل راه قدم

که من به خویش نمودم صد اهتمام و نشد

Don't place your foot down in the Alley of Love without a guide,

For by myself I toiled a hundred toils, but it was of no avail.[iv]

He also says:

به کوی عشق منه بی دلیل راه قدم

که گم شد آن که درین ره به رهبری نرسید

Do not place your foot down in the Alley of Love without a guide,

For lost is the one who did not find a leader on this path.[v]

In another place he advises:

قطع این مرحله بی همرهی خضر مکن

ظلمات است بترس از خطر گمراهی

Unless you have Khiḍr[vi] as a companion, don't travel down this road,

For it is darkness, fear the danger of losing your way.[vii]

---

i. As explained by the author, presence here refers to attaining Divine gnosis by means of unveiling and witnessing with the heart.

ii. Shirāzī, Divān-i Ḥāfiẓ (Taṣḥīḥ-i Qudsī), ghazal 233, couplets 1-3

iii. Saʿādatparwar, Jamāl-i Āftāb, volume 3, preface.

iv. Shirāzī, Divān-i Ḥāfiẓ (Taṣḥīḥ-i Qudsī), ghazal 233, couplet 7

v. Ibid., ghazal 201, couplet 6

vi. In Sufi terminology, the name Khiḍr (peace be upon him) is used as an allusion, referring to a spiritual guide.

vii. Ibid., ghazal 572, couplet 7

3) In the method of spiritual training, after reaching spiritual perfections, the wayfarer can aid and help other wayfarers. That is because he himself has traversed the path of spiritual wayfaring with a teacher and has become acquainted with the means through which Satan and the selfish desires infiltrate. Furthermore, he has resisted against the obstacles along the path, become familiar with its difficulties and deviations, and knows the ways to avoid them. It is for this reason that—to the extent that he himself has traversed the path—he can be a guide for the seekers of the Alley of the Beloved. However, one who has reached the goal through Divine captivation has not traversed the path, nor has he become acquainted with the stages and stations of the spiritual journey. As a result, he can himself benefit from the enlivening Divine breeze, but others can only benefit from his pleasant spiritual state. He cannot transfer what he possesses to others; he cannot help and guide them on the path in a step-by-step manner.

The *wāṣil* teacher Marḥūm Āyatullāh Ḥājj Shaykh Saʿādatparwar (may Allah be pleased with him) says in this regard:

> ... If someone through captivation has reached the Object of his desire and the Unique Jewel of existence, even if he is complete, still he cannot be a guide for others because he has neither seen the path nor its pitfalls. (i)

4) Those who reach the goal of existence through captivation—because their existential capacity was not prepared to witness Allah the Exalted's beauty and majesty and suddenly they attained those lofty perfections—usually after a while, their souls resign from their bodies and they die due to the immensity and the greatness of what they have witnessed. Such people in the terminology of the folk of gnosis are called '*sūkhtih*' (burnt). (ii)

For others however, Allah's grace and mercy encompasses them after the first captivation and they are saved from death. (iii)

---

i. Saʿādatparwar, Jamāl-i Āftāb, volume 3, preface

ii. Amongst such *ʿurafā* are Marḥūm Waḥdat Kirmānshāhī and Ghubār Hamadānī who passed away in their youth because of Divine captivation. (From the author)

iii. The great *ʿārif*, Marḥūm Ayatullah Mīrzā Jawād Anṣārī, was one of the captivated

This method is not a general method, benefiting from it is dependent on the wise will of Allah the Exalted. On the other hand, Allah has created everyone so that they reach their true perfection and real servitude. Moreover, He has prepared the path for reaching this (by sending the prophets and the *awliyā'*, peace be upon them) and has granted man the necessary tools (the *fiṭrah* and its inclinations, the intellect, ability, and free will). He has also instructed that—after the prophets (peace be upon them) and the *awliyā'* (peace be upon them)—people should refer to and follow the experts in every field and those who have tread the path. This must be done after acquiring confidence about these experts, in terms of their knowledge and their having traversed the path. For this reason, the method of 'spiritual training' is the primary method, the established and reliable method which can be conveyed to others. Thus, it must be sought.

Considering what was said so far, it becomes clear that Imam al-Ṣādiq (peace be upon him) in his encounter with 'Unwān al-Baṣrī, employed the step-by-step method of spiritual training. After creating a spiritual readiness and true urge in him, the Imam corrected his outlook towards the path of gnosis and the goal of spiritual wayfaring. Then, after instructing him to seek the knowledge of the Ahl al-Bayt (peace be upon them) in order to apply it, and after asking him to seek its comprehension from Allah, he advised him to abide by Allah's commands and prohibitions. This is the first step in wayfaring. Thereafter, he advised him about some *mustaḥabb* and moral matters, at the same time alluding to the levels of servitude and explaining their reality—which has been explained to some extent in this section.

---

ones who was saved from death when Allah's mercy encompassed him. It is narrated from him that he said, "If a second captivation did not occur for me, I would have become *sūkhtih* and died like Ghubār Hamadānī." (From the author)

Section Two
Signs of True Servitude and its Manifestations

Introduction

True servitude of Allah is an elixir that turns the copper of man's existence into gold and brings about profound and noticeable transformations in man's perception, ideology, morals and actions. So much so that the Noble Qur'ān terms this marvellous transformation as '*ḥayātun ṭayyibatun*' (a pleasant life):

> مَنْ عَمِلَ صَالِحاً مِنْ ذَكَرٍ أَوْ أُنْثَى وَ هُوَ مُؤْمِنٌ فَلَنُحْيِيَنَّهُ حَيَاةً طَيِّبَةً
>
> Whoever acts righteously, [whether] male or female, should he be faithful, We shall revive him with a pleasant life (16:97)

The effects and blessings of this 'pleasant life' encompass man's personal and social life in its entirety. They connect him to the limitless perfection and infinite knowledge and power of Allah the Immaculate, and he witnesses his essential neediness, nonexistence and perishability in different affairs (in his actions, attributes and essence).

Such a magnificent transformation in man's outlook, morals and actions has certain effects, signs and manifestations. Initially, through conceptual awareness of the correct beliefs and inculcating them to himself, man must abide by these beliefs in his actions and in his soul's reactions. Eventually they are established in his heart and soul, and finally with specific conditions he can witness them through his heart.

Imam al-Ṣādiq (peace be upon him) in reply to 'Unwān al-Baṣrī's question when he asked, "What is the reality of servitude?" pointed to some of the most important effects and manifestations of true servitude.

The First Manifestation of Servitude – A Transformation in Man's Outlook (Perceiving Allah's Ownership)

A careful study of the system of creation reveals that there are certain prevailing conditions that are present, each with its own effects. One of these conditions is ownership (*mālikiyyah*), which is a special existential relationship between the owner (*mālik*) and the owned object (*mamlūk*). Ownership results in a type of control, and the right of the owner to utilize the object and profit from it. It is of different types, some of which are specific to man while others are exclusive to Allah.

A) Conventional Ownership

Man's relationship with his wealth and possessions is a kind of conventional ownership, considered and validated by social contracts. It is transferable to others and is limited in terms of place and time. This type of ownership has laws and conditions that are either derived from the *fiqh* (Islamic jurisprudence), or the intellectuals have enacted their own laws regarding it.

B) Real Ownership

Real ownership means that in addition to an existential connection between the two, there exists a kind of existential encompassment of the owner over the owned being. Man's ownership of the faculties of his being is a type of real ownership which cannot be transferred to others. For example, man's ownership of his faculty of vision or the faculty of perception and understanding, these exist without any contract or agreement and cannot be transferred to others. Real ownership itself is of two types:

1) Real Dependent Ownership

This type of ownership, despite being real ownership, has limitations. For example, man is a dependent being and as a result this entails restrictions and limitations on the things he owns. Man is the owner of all his faculties. However, he has not acquired them by himself, rather they have been bestowed upon him by Allah the Exalted. Therefore, from the point of view of the *sharīʿah*, he does not have complete freedom in employing his faculties and is only allowed to use them according to specific rules. Moreover, despite man's inward inclination, these faculties are exposed to strength and weakness, ups and downs, to the extent that it is possible that they are complete taken away from him. This last point is the strongest proof of man's being dependent in his control and ownership of his possessions:

اللَّهُ الَّذِي خَلَقَكُمْ مِنْ ضَعْفٍ ثُمَّ جَعَلَ مِنْ بَعْدِ ضَعْفٍ قُوَّةً ثُمَّ جَعَلَ مِنْ بَعْدِ قُوَّةٍ ضَعْفاً وَ شَيْبَةً يَخْلُقُ مَا يَشَاءُ وَ هُوَ الْعَلِيمُ الْقَدِيرُ

> It is Allah who created you from [a state of] weakness, then He gave you power after weakness. Then, after power, He ordained weakness and old age: He creates whatever He wishes, and He is the Knowing, the Powerful. (30:54)

2) Real Independent Ownership

This type of ownership is exclusive to Allah the Exalted; no created being possesses this type of ownership. Intellectual proofs and verses of the Qur'ān which attribute ownership of all beings to Allah,(i) prove this reality. Even the prophets (peace be upon them) and the Divine *awliyā'* (peace be upon them) whom Allah the Exalted has given abundant knowledge and power, consider themselves to be in need.(ii) While beseeching and crying, they call out to him:

إِلَهِي أَنَا الْفَقِيرُ فِي غِنَايَ فَكَيْفَ لَا أَكُونُ فَقِيراً فِي فَقْرِي

> O Allah! I am needy when I am rich. So how I would not be needy in my poverty?!(iii)

Noticing, knowing, believing in and witnessing Allah's true ownership and not considering oneself independent in one's wealth and belongings, is a very worthy and lofty perfection. One should be attentive of the fact that we are not independent in any of the faculties of our being and whatever we possess is not from ourselves. Rather, they are favours and benefits which Allah the Exalted has granted to man. The true owner of man's inward and outward faculties, and all his internal and external organs, is Allah the Exalted. He has made man the owner of all these real and conventional possessions for a specific and limited period of time. Imam al-Riḍā (peace be upon him) says in this regard:

---

i. (3:26), (3:189), and (5:17-18)

ii. (7:188) and (72:21)

iii. Ibn Ṭāwūs, Iqbāl al-A'māl, 348

هُوَ الْمَالِكُ لِمَا مَلَّكَهُمْ وَ الْقَادِرُ عَلَى مَا أَقْدَرَهُمْ عَلَيْه

> He [Allah] is the owner of that which He has made them owner of, and He has power over that which He has granted them power over.[(i)]

It is for this reason that sometimes man falls sick, while other times he is in good health. For a time, he is young and energetic, then later he becomes old and feeble. All these changes show that he is not independent in his belongings, because he lacks the ability to preserve, protect and maintain them. He only enjoys these blessings for a specific period.

Paying attention to these realities increases man's knowledge and gnosis (*maʿrifah*) about Allah's real ownership and man's dependent ownership. The more a person pays careful attention to this reality, the more he comprehends this matter in a deeper sense, and the more its effects manifest in a better and easier manner.

This lofty reality—that Allah is the absolute owner and the servants are the owned objects—is revealed for those virtuous individuals who have reached the truth, those who have crossed the level of *ʿilm al-yaqīn* have reached the stage of *ʿayn al-yaqīn* and *ḥaqq al-yaqīn.*[(ii)] In the same manner that the *malakūt* of the heavens and the Earth were shown to the Prophet Abraham (peace be upon him):

وَ كَذٰلِكَ نُرِي إِبْرَاهِيمَ مَلَكُوتَ السَّمَاوَاتِ وَ الْأَرْضِ وَ لِيَكُونَ مِنَ الْمُوقِنِي

> Thus, did We show Abraham the *malakūt* of the heavens

---

i. al-Sadūq, al-Tawhīd, 361

ii. These three terms are mentioned in the Noble Qur'ān and roughly translate to 'having knowledge of certainty', 'witnessing the certainty' and 'experiencing the certainty'. The late Martyr Murtaḍā Muṭahharī (may Allah be pleased with him) explains these concepts using the parable of fire. In the first level one cannot see the fire but due to its effects (such as its smoke) one becomes aware of its existence. In the second level one witnesses the fire firsthand. In the final level one is himself so close to the fire that he feels its heat and is burnt by it. Similarly, the servant's knowledge of Allah the Exalted may be divided into these three stages. Refer to Murtaḍā Muṭahharī, *Bīst Guftār*, the end of the article on *duʿā* (article #18).

> and the Earth, that he might be of those who possess certitude. (6:75)

Malakūt refers to that perspective of seeing the real link between the beings and Allah the Exalted, and His real ownership. Man's ownership of himself and other dimensions of his being is nothing but a manifestation of that real ownership, it is the manifestation of that in the realm of the *mulk*. (i) The realm of the *mulk* and its different dimensions are always established by the realm of the *malakūt*. This reality was shown to the Prophet Abraham (peace be upon him) and thereafter he declared this truth:

إِنِّي وَجَّهْتُ وَجْهِيَ لِلَّذِي فَطَرَ السَّمَاوَاتِ وَ الْأَرْضَ حَنِيفاً وَ مَا أَنَا مِنَ الْمُشْرِكِي

> Indeed, I have turned my face toward Him who originated the heavens and the Earth, as a *ḥanīf*, (ii) and I am not one of the polytheists. (6:79)

This means that I am not from those who believe that a being has any rank and reality in front of Allah the Exalted. Rather, I see all beings to be merely a sign of His essence and His existential perfections. For this reason, he requested Allah the Exalted that he be shown the reality of how living beings are given life, saying to the Almighty:

أَرِنِي كَيْفَ تُحْيِي الْمَوْتَى

My Lord! Show me how You revive the dead (2:260)

After specific instructions, Allah gave him a role to play in the process of giving life to the dead. He gave him permission to revive the dead so that from close range he could witness the execution of this *malakūtī* affair in the realm of the *mulk*:

---

i. The word '*mulk*' refers to the apparent world.

ii. The Arabic noun *al-ḥanaf* means to return from being astray to the straight path. Derived from this, the noun *ḥanīf* describes an individual who inclines towards the truth and the straight path. Refer to Rāghib al-Iṣfahānī, *al-Mufradāt*, under the root *ḥanafa*.

ثُمَّ ادْعُهُنَّ يَأْتِينَكَ سَعْياً

Then call them [the birds that were cut to pieces, mixed, and placed on the top of different mountains]; they will come to you hastening. (2:260)

Reviving the dead was also carried out at the hand of Prophet Jesus (peace be upon him):

وَ أُحْيِي الْمَوْتَى بِإِذْنِ اللَّهِ

I revive the dead by Allah's leave (3:49)

That is because he too had gained access to the *malakūt*, and attributed the *malakūt* of the heavens, the entire creation and the different aspects of his own existence to Allah the Exalted; he did not see anything from himself. In every station where Allah's true ownership is unveiled for such individuals, they witness Allah's existential encompassment. As Allah says to His Messenger (peace and blessings be upon him and his family):

قُلْ لاَ أَمْلِكُ لِنَفْسِي نَفْعاً وَ لاَ ضَرّاً إِلاَّ مَا شَاءَ اللَّ

Say, "I have no ownership over any benefit for myself, nor [over] any harm except what Allah may wish." (7:188)

This expression encompasses all dimensions of his being. Of course, this reality is not exclusive to the Messenger of Allah (peace and blessings be upon him and his family) and all the existents and men are like this, but he (peace and blessings be upon him and his family) witnesses these realities in their true sense.

It is for this reason that Allah attributes the perception of tawhīdī realities to His Messenger (peace and blessings be upon him and his family) in some of the verses of the Qurʾān and says:

فَلَمْ تَقْتُلُوهُمْ وَ لَكِنَّ اللَّهَ قَتَلَهُمْ وَ مَا رَمَيْتَ إِذْ رَمَيْتَ وَ لَكِنَّ اللَّهَ رَمَى

You did not kill them; rather, it was Allah who killed them; and you did not throw when you threw, rather, it was Allah who threw. (8:17(

This stage is the manifestation of *tawḥīd* in Divine acts which the Prophet (peace and blessings be upon him and his family) has reached through witnessing of the heart while others believe in this reality through intellectual and conceptual understanding.

Similarly, in another verse the perception of Allah's true ownership by witnessing the dimensions of *tawḥīd* in a comprehensive manner is attributed to the Messenger of Allah (peace and blessings be upon him and his family):

> قُلْ إِنَّ صَلاَتِي وَ نُسُكِي وَ مَحْيَايَ وَ مَمَاتِي لِلَّهِ رَبِّ الْعَالَمِينَ لاَ شَرِيكَ لَهُ وَ بِذٰلِكَ أُمِرْتُ وَ أَنَا أَوَّلُ الْمُسْلِمِينَ
>
> Say, "Indeed my prayer and my worship, my life and my death are for the sake of Allah, the Lord of all the worlds. He has no partner, and I have been commanded [to follow] this [creed], and I am the first of those who submit [to Allah]." (6:162-163)

Even though all the Messengers (peace be upon them) are undoubtedly amongst those whom Allah has made sincere (*mukhlaṣīn*) and amongst the righteous (*ṣāliḥīn*), but there are differences in their ranks:

> تِلْكَ الرُّسُلُ فَضَّلْنَا بَعْضَهُمْ عَلَى بَعْضٍ
>
> These are the apostles, some of whom We gave an advantage over others. (2:253)

Based on this, the Noblest Messenger (peace and blessings be upon him and his family) has the highest degree of submission before Allah. Thus, in the aforementioned verse he is introduced as the first of those who submit. Being first is not in terms of time, rather it means being first in terms of rank. This comprises of the highest level of submission in front of Allah. It means absolute submission of one's actions, traits and essence before Allah the Exalted. The true ownership of Allah is manifested in these three affairs (actions, traits and essence). Moreover, in this station man's existential humbleness before Allah is not only manifested, but the heart witnesses this reality. This occurs for the Noblest Messenger (peace and blessings be upon him and his family) in the highest possible manner. Thus, despite that fact that all the prophets (peace be upon them) are amongst the righteous,[i] Allah quotes Prophet Abraham (peace be upon him), Prophet Joseph (peace be upon him) and Prophet Solomon (peace be upon him) requesting Allah to unite them with the righteous.[ii] And only Prophet Abraham (peace be upon him) was promised that he would be united with the righteous in the Hereafter.[iii] From these verses, it becomes evident that there is a loftier rank of the righteous which Prophet Abraham (peace be upon him) will reach in the Hereafter. That is the rank of the complete servitude of the Messenger of Allah (peace and blessings be upon him and his family) as indicated in this verse:

إِنَّ وَلِيِّيَ اللَّهُ الَّذِي نَزَّلَ الْكِتَابَ ۖ وَهُوَ يَتَوَلَّى الصَّالِحِينَ

My guardian is indeed Allah who sent down the Book, and He takes care of the righteous. (7:196)

Therefore, witnessing Allah's true ownership has different ranks, the highest of which is possessed by the Noblest Messenger (peace and blessings be upon him and his family) and his family. These same ranks can be conceived in relation to planning one's affairs.

It is for this reason that Imam al-Ṣādiq (peace be upon him) explained the reality of servitude to be not *seeing* ownership for oneself; he did say that one should not *consider* ownership for oneself. This is because even the common people know this reality that they do not have anything from themselves. Such awareness is necessary, and the more a person understands this, the more he also recognizes its different dimensions. However, this reality must move from the mind to the heart. By acting in accordance to this understanding and by transforming it into belief, it is perceived by the heart in a deeper and deeper manner, until it is witnessed. At this point the true ownership of Allah is manifested for the wayfarer.

---

i. (21:72), (21:75), (21:86)

ii. (12:101), (26:83), (91:72)

iii. (2:130), (16:122), (29:27)

The Noble Quran in many verses—using subtle and beautiful expressions—has reminded man of the way different matters relate to him, and it has said:

آمِنُوا بِاللَّهِ وَرَسُولِهِ وَأَنفِقُوا مِمَّا جَعَلَكُم مُّسْتَخْلَفِينَ فِيهِ ۖ فَالَّذِينَ آمَنُوا مِنكُمْ وَأَنفَقُوا لَهُمْ أَجْرٌ كَبِيرٌ

> Have faith in Allah and His Apostle and spend out of that of which He has made you heirs. There is a great reward for those of you who have faith and spend [in Allah's way]. (57:7)

In this verse, man's ownership of his possessions and wealth is attributed to Allah's allocation (jaʿalakum). Therefore, man is not independent in his ownership of things. On the other hand, like his predecessors, man holds the position of ownership of wealth for a few days. He is the heir of the past owners, and this inheritance has been bestowed on him by Allah the Exalted. This being the state, spending wealth for achieving Allah's pleasure acquires a beautiful and attractive meaning. Hence, Allah says:

وَآتُوهُم مِّن مَّالِ اللَّهِ الَّذِي آتَاكُمْ

> And give them out of the wealth of Allah which He has given you. (24:33)

Seeing One's Affairs as Being Owned by Allah

By carefully studying Qurʾānic verses it can be understood that the repetition of this point (that all beings are owned by Allah) is intended to instil this viewpoint in man, so that applying its consequences and spending wealth in His path becomes easy. This is because—even though most people intellectually understand this viewpoint and believe in it—due to their selfishness in practice they do not act in accordance with it. Rather, they are neglectful of it. However, in addition to paying attention to this viewpoint, if a person struggles against his self and spends that which he possesses in the way of Allah, then his vision becomes stronger. As a result, he perceives the different aspects of Allah's ownership in a more extensive manner. That is because man initially deems this ownership to be confined to conventional matters and outward wealth. However, after careful deliberation about his existential rank—how he is not independent in preserving or utilizing any of his existential faculties, be they cognitive or physical faculties—his viewpoint regarding Allah's ownership of his different dimensions becomes more conscious and profound.

Therefore, man must struggle against his self in order to adhere to Divine commands in the various aspects of life and abide by different routines of worship. In addition, he must traverse certain stages of the spiritual path with his heart, set foot into the valley of *ikhlāṣ* and *tawḥīd*, and to some extent perceive his neediness and Allah's absolute needlessness. If he does so, then he can sever his heart's attachment to his possessions and spend that which the Beloved Lord has bestowed upon him; he can spend it on the path of His pleasure. In this stage, not only is spending, altruism, and munificence no longer difficult, rather it is pleasurable and enlivening for him. The Noble Qurʾān has praised this group of His liberated servants in many verses and has said:

> وَالَّذِينَ تَبَوَّءُوا الدَّارَ وَالْإِيمَانَ مِن قَبْلِهِمْ يُحِبُّونَ مَنْ هَاجَرَ إِلَيْهِمْ وَلَا يَجِدُونَ فِي صُدُورِهِمْ حَاجَةً مِّمَّا أُوتُوا وَيُؤْثِرُونَ عَلَىٰ أَنفُسِهِمْ وَلَوْ كَانَ بِهِمْ خَصَاصَةٌ ۚ وَمَن يُوقَ شُحَّ نَفْسِهِ فَأُولَٰئِكَ هُمُ الْمُفْلِحُونَ
>
> And [also] for those who were settled in the land [Madinah] and [abided] in faith before them [the muhājirūn], who love those who migrate toward them, and do not find in their breasts any jealousy for that which is given to them, but prefer others [the Immigrants] to themselves, though poverty be their own lot. And those who are saved from their own greed—it is they who are the felicitous. (59:9)

It is mentioned in a narration that:

جَاءَ رَجُلٌ إِلَى النَّبِيِّ صَلَّى اللّهُ عَلَيْهِ وَ آلِهِ فَشَكَا إِلَيْهِ الجَوْعَ فَبَعَثَ رَسُوْلُ اللّهِ صَلَّى اللّهُ عَلَيْهِ وَ آلِهِ إِلَى بُيُوْتِ أَزْوَاجِهِ فَقُلْنَ: مَا عِنْدَنَا إِلَّا المَاءُ ... فَقَالَ عَلِيُّ بْنُ أَبِيْ طَالِبٍ عَلَيْهِ السَّلَامُ: أَنَا لَهُ ... وَ أَتَى فَاطِمَةَ عَلَيْهَا السَّلَامُ، فَقَالَ لَهَا: مَا عِنْدَكِ يَا ابْنَةَ رَسُوْلِ اللّهِ؟ فَقَالَتْ: مَا عِنْدَنَا إِلَّا قُوْتُ العَشِيَّةِ لَكِنَّا نُؤَثِّرُ ضَيْفَنَا ... فَلَمَّا أَصْبَحَ عَلِيٌّ عَلَيْهِ السَّلَامُ غَدَا عَلَى رَسُوْلِ اللّهِ صَلَّى اللّهُ عَلَيْهِ وَ آلِهِ فَأَخْبَرَهُ الخَبَرَ فَلَمْ يَبْرَحْ حَتَّى أَنْزَلَ اللّهُ عَزَّ وَ جَلَّ «وَ يُؤْثِرُونَ عَلى أَنْفُسِهِمْ وَ لَوْ كانَ بِهِمْ خَصاصَةٌ وَ مَنْ يُوقَ شُحَّ نَفْسِهِ فَأُولئِكَ هُمُ الْمُفْلِحُونَ»

A man came to the Messenger of Allah (peace and blessings be upon him and his family) and complained of hunger. The Prophet (peace and blessings be upon him and his family) sent him to the house of his wives. They said, "We do not have anything except water." ... ʿAlī ibn Abī Ṭālib (peace be upon him) said, "I will bring food for him..." Then he went to Lady Fāṭimah (peace be upon her) and said, "O daughter of the Messenger of Allah! What do you have?" She replied, "We do not have anything except the food for dinner, but we will give preference to the guest [over ourselves]." ... The next morning, Imam ʿAlī (peace be upon him) went to the Messenger of Allah (peace and blessings be upon him and his family) and informed him about the incident. Immediately Allah (the Invincible and Majestic) revealed the verse, "They prefer others to themselves, though poverty be their own lot. And those who are saved from their own greed—it is they who are the felicitous".(i)

Imam al-Ṣādiq (peace be upon him) also says:

---

i. al-ʿArūsī, Tafsīr Nūr al-Thaqalayn, 5:285, narration 53

كَانَ عِنْـدَ فَاطِمَـةَ ع شَـعِيرٌ ... فَلَمَّـا أَنْضَجُوهَـا وَ وَضَعُوهَـا بَيْـنَ أَيْدِيهِـمْ جَـاءَ مِسْكِينٌ، فَقَـالَ الْمِسْـكِينُ رَحِمَكُـمُ اللَّـهُ، فَقَـامَ عَلِـيٌّ ع فَأَعْطَـاهُ ثُلُثـاً، فَلَـمْ يَلْبَـثْ أَنْ جَـاءَ يَتِيـمٌ فَقَـالَ الْيَتِيـمُ رَحِمَكُـمُ اللَّـهُ ، فَقَـامَ عَلِـيٌّ ع فَأَعْطَـاهُ الثُّلُـثَ، ثُـمَّ جَـاءَ أَسِيرٌ فَقَـالَ الْأَسِـيرُ رَحِمَكُـمُ اللَّـهُ فَأَعْطَـاهُ عَلِـيٌّ ع الثُّلُـثَ، وَ مَـا ذَاقُوهَـا- فَأَنْـزَلَ اللَّـهُ سُـبْحَانَهُ الآيَـاتِ فِيهِـمْ، وَ هِـيَ جَارِيَـةٌ فِـي كُلِّ مُؤْمِـنٍ فَعَـلَ ذَلِـكَ لِلَّـهِ عَـزَّ وَ جَـلَّ

[Once] Lady Fāṭimah (peace be upon her) had some barley ... when they had cooked it and placed it in front of themselves [in order to eat], a needy person came and said, "May Allah have mercy on you!" ʿAlī (peace be upon him) stood up and gave one-third of it to him. After a short while an orphan came and said, "May Allah have mercy on you!" So ʿAlī (peace be upon him) stood up and gave [another] one-third of it to him. Thereafter, a prisoner came and said, "May Allah have mercy on you!" So ʿAlī (peace be upon him) gave [the remaining] one-third to him while they had not [even] tasted it. Here, Allah the Immaculate revealed the verses of the Qurʾān about them,(i) and these [verses] are applicable to every believer who performs these actions for the sake of Allah (the Invincible and Majestic).(ii)

With regards to the merit of sacrifice (*īthār*), it is enough to know that Imam ʿAlī (peace be upon him) says:

الْإِيثَارُ أَعْلَى الْمَكَارِمِ

Sacrifice is the loftiest of noble traits.(iii)

الْإِيثَارُ أَحْسَنُ الْإِحْسَانِ وَ أَعْلَى مَرَاتِبِ الْإِيمَان

---

i. The verses being referred to are in Sūrah al-Insān, the 76th chapter of the Noble Qurʿān.

ii. al-ʿArūsī, Tafsīr Nūr al-Thaqalayn, 5:470, narration 20

iii. al-Āmudī, Ghurar al-Hikam, narration 986

Sacrifice is the best goodness and the loftiest degree of faith.[i]

الْإِيثَارُ أَفْضَلُ عِبَادَةٍ وَ أَجَلُّ سِيَادَةٍ

Sacrifice is the best worship and the greatest eminence.[ii]

Likewise, he says:

عَامِلْ سَائِرَ النَّاسِ بِالْإِنْصَافِ وَ عَامِلِ الْمُؤْمِنِينَ بِالْإِيثَار

Treat all the people with fairness, but act towards the believers with sacrifice.[iii]

The great *'ārif* Sayyid 'Alī Qāḍī (may Allah be pleased with him) at the height of poverty and destitution, would purchase goods from a poor merchant. He would buy old spoiling lettuce from him at the end of the day. In this manner, in addition to helping him without gaining anything in return, he would not aid him directly and offend his dignity.[iv]

The spirit of sacrifice and a life accompanied with a magnanimous nature, can only be possible with such a mindset and an outlook based on faith. This has desirable effects in this world, on the soul and also in the Hereafter.

The Scope of Infāq (Spending)

All of existence and all the affairs of man are dependent on Allah the Exalted (glorified be His remembrance); man is utterly needy before the One Lord. As a result, the scope of infāq extends to the extent of man's being and includes everything that Allah has bestowed upon him, such as his wealth, respect, social status, position, life, etc. To whatever extent the wayfarer has comprehended his servitude before Allah the Exalted, to that extent his infāq increases. Therefore, the Noble Qur'ān says in description of those who truly are on the path of

i. Ibid., narration 1705

ii. Ibid., narration 1148

iii. Ibid., narration 6342

iv. Hāshamiyān, Daryā-yi 'Irfān, 37

purity and faith in Allah and those who want to express their inward humility in front of Him:

وَمِمَّا رَزَقْنَاهُمْ يُنفِقُونَ

And they spend out of what We have provided for them. (2:3)

This matter encompasses all their affairs and possessions, both real and conventional possessions. That is because they truly attribute all of these to the Sacred Divine Essence. To the extent that like Abū ʿAbd Allah al-Ḥusayn (peace be upon him), with complete sincerity they offer their entire existence, and whisper the following to their Beloved:

تَرَكْتُ الخَلْقَ طُرّاً فِيْ هَوَاكَا

وَ أَيْتَمْتُ العِيَالَ لِكَيْ أَرَاكَا

I forsook all creation, yearning for Thee. And orphaned my family, that You I may see

This is as opposed to those who are not on the path of Allah's servitude. Such individuals not only do not spend, rather they act with stinginess and instruct others to be stingy as well. Even if they spend, it is either to show off and reach worldly motives, (i) to bar others from going towards the path of truth and reality, (ii) or they spend reluctantly. (iii)

The Noble Qurʾān likens the spending of the first group to a cold wind that destroys the tillage of a people who have wronged themselves and cultivated in an unsuitable place and time. (iv)

Likewise, it considers the spending of the second group as a cause of regret for them. Certainly, they will not reach their goal and will be defeated. (v) Also, it describes the spending of the third group as being

---

i. (4:37, 38)

ii. (8:36)

iii. (9:54)

iv. (3:117)

v. (8:36)

the cause of their punishment in this world. That is because they are transgressors who are not humble in the presence of Allah the Exalted. As a result, even if they spend willingly it shall not be accepted from them.[i]

For this reason, whilst seeking to explain a part of the manifestation of true servitude, Imam al-Ṣādiq (peace be upon him) in the narration of ʿUnwān al-Baṣrī brings up the issue of financial *infāq*. Although, servitude is not limited to this financial aspect. Rather it is a reality whose expanse encompasses man's entire existence and thus *infāq* is applicable to all the blessings that Allah has bestowed upon him. Based on this fact, Imam ʿAlī (peace be upon him) has regarded every good deed as charity and said:

كُلُ مَعْرُوفٍ صَدَقَة

Every good deed is a charity.[ii]

To encourage man to perform good deeds, the *awliyāʾ* of religion (peace be upon them) have used meaningful and lofty expressions while describing the merits of charity and good deeds. They have also mentioned its instances and examples. For example, the Messenger of Allah (peace and blessings be upon him and his family) says:

إِنَّ عَلَى كُلِ مُسْلِمٍ فِي كُلِ يَوْمٍ صَدَقَةً قِيلَ مَنْ يُطِيقُ ذَلِكَ قَالَ ص إِمَاطَتُكَ الْأَذَى عَنِ الطَّرِيقِ صَدَقَةٌ وَ إِرْشَادُكَ الرَّجُلَ إِلَى الطَّرِيقِ صَدَقَةٌ وَ عِيَادَتُكَ الْمَرِيضَ صَدَقَةٌ وَ أَمْرُكَ بِالْمَعْرُوفِ صَدَقَةٌ وَ نَهْيُكَ عَنِ الْمُنْكَرِ صَدَقَةٌ وَ رَدُّكَ السَّلَامَ صَدَقَةٌ.

"Indeed, it is incumbent upon every Muslim to give charity every day." A person asked, "And who has the ability to do that?" The Messenger of Allah (peace and blessings be upon him and his family) replied, "Clearing the road of things that may harm the people is charity. Giving directions to a person is charity. Visiting the sick is charity. Enjoining

i. (9:53–55)

ii. al-Sadūq, al-Khisāl, 134

what is right is charity. Forbidding what is wrong is charity. Replying someone's *salām* (greeting) is charity." (i)

Similarly, he says:

تَرْكُ الشَّرِّ صَدَقَةٌ

Abandoning evil is charity. (ii)

أَمْسِكْ لِسَانَكَ فَإِنَّهَا صَدَقَةٌ تَصَدَّقُ بِهَا عَلَى نَفْسِك

Withhold your tongue [from bad speech], for it is a charity which you give to yourself. (iii)

Likewise, Imam al-Ṣādiq (peace be upon him) says:

صَدَقَةٌ يُحِبُّهَا اللَّهُ إِصْلَاحٌ بَيْنَ النَّاسِ إِذَا تَفَاسَدُوا وَ تَقْرِيبٌ بَيْنَهُمْ إِذَا تَبَاعَدُوا

Settling differences between people when dispute occurs between them and [similarly] bringing them close when they become far from each other is a charity that Allah loves. (iv)

إِسْمَاعُ الْأَصَمِّ مِنْ غَيْرِ تَضَجُّرٍ صَدَقَةٌ هَنِيئَةٌ

Making a deaf person understand [something] without upsetting him is a pleasant charity. (v)

The Levels of Infāq

Infāq has various levels, according to the different levels of the wayfarer's faith.

1) Those who have comprehended and accepted Allah's ownership at the level of intellectual perception (*'ilm al-yaqīn*). For them, *infāq* is to the extent of financial obligations and supererogatory financial deeds. Performing this is usually accompanied with difficulty for them,

---

i. Majlisī, Biḥār al-Anwār, 75:50, narration 4.

ii. Ibid., 77:160, narration 168

iii. al-Kulaynī, al-Kāfī, 2:114, narration 7

iv. Majlisī, Biḥār al-Anwār, 74:388, narration 10

v. Ibid., 74:209, narration 1

because at this level man is attached to his wealth and possessions. That is because he sees himself as the owner of these objects, even if at the conceptual and verbal level he attributes them to Allah the Exalted. As a result, parting with them is difficult for him.

For this group of people, the verses of the Noble Qur'ān contain statements that are both encouraging and reprimanding. Some verses have drawn the attention of such people towards effects and blessings of *infāq* in this world and the Hereafter:

> مَّثَلُ الَّذِينَ يُنفِقُونَ أَمْوَالَهُمْ فِي سَبِيلِ اللَّهِ كَمَثَلِ حَبَّةٍ أَنبَتَتْ سَبْعَ سَنَابِلَ فِي كُلِّ سُنبُلَةٍ مِّائَةُ حَبَّةٍ ۗ وَاللَّهُ يُضَاعِفُ لِمَن يَشَاءُ ۗ وَاللَّهُ وَاسِعٌ عَلِيمٌ
>
> The parable of those who spend their wealth in the way of Allah is that of a grain which grows seven ears, in every ear a hundred grains. Allah enhances severalfold whomever He wishes, and Allah is Bounteous, Knowing. (2:261)

While in other verses, with a reprimanding tone, it invites the believers towards *infāq* and says:

> وَمَا لَكُمْ أَلَّا تُنفِقُوا فِي سَبِيلِ اللَّهِ وَلِلَّهِ مِيرَاثُ السَّمَاوَاتِ وَالْأَرْضِ
>
> Why should you not spend in the way of Allah, when to Allah belongs the heritage of the heavens and the Earth? (57:10)

2) After engaging in self-struggle, self-discipline, and paying attention to the positive effects of infāq in this world and the Hereafter, and thereafter performing the infāq itself, man's heart becomes enlightened. His attachment to his possessions takes on a Divine nature. Gradually, he begins to believe (at the level of ʿayn al-yaqīn) that he is an owned object (mamlūk) and Allah the Exalted is the owner (mālik). Such a person now does infāq to seek Allah's pleasure, although at the same time he enjoys the blessings of infāq in this world and the Hereafter.

For this group, doing infāq is not difficult and burdensome. With ease they give up their wealth and possessions on the path of Allah's pleasure. The Noble Qur'ān has described them in this manner:

وَمَثَلُ الَّذِينَ يُنفِقُونَ أَمْوَالَهُمُ ابْتِغَاءَ مَرْضَاتِ اللَّهِ وَتَثْبِيتًا مِّنْ أَنفُسِهِمْ كَمَثَلِ جَنَّةٍ بِرَبْوَةٍ أَصَابَهَا وَابِلٌ فَآتَتْ أُكُلَهَا ضِعْفَيْنِ فَإِن لَّمْ يُصِبْهَا وَابِلٌ فَطَلٌّ ۗ وَاللَّهُ بِمَا تَعْمَلُونَ بَصِيرٌ

The parable of [the charity of] those who spend their wealth seeking Allah's pleasure and to confirm themselves [in their faith], is that of a garden on a hillside: the downpour strikes it, whereupon it brings forth its fruit twofold; and if it is not a downpour that strikes it, then a light shower [is enough for it], and Allah watches what you do. (2:265)

3) After the wayfarer employs all his existential faculties (both cognitive and physical)—while believing that their true owner is Allah—on His path and to attain His pleasure and happiness and is not content with merely doing *infāq* of his outward wealth on the path of seeking Divine pleasure, but rather does *infāq* in a comprehensive manner, Allah removes more veils from the visage of his heart and makes him reach more profound levels of enlightenment. This reaches an extent where he sees his own actions to be owned by Allah and subservient to Him. He deems himself and all that is at his disposal to belong to his Master and Controller. For this reason, he spends Allah's wealth where He has commanded that it should be spent. In the words of Imam al-Ṣādiq (peace be upon him):

لَا يَرَى الْعَبْدُ لِنَفْسِهِ فِيمَا خَوَّلَهُ اللَّهُ مِلْكاً لِأَنَّ الْعَبِيدَ لَا يَكُونُ لَهُمْ مِلْكٌ يَرَوْنَ الْمَالَ مَالَ اللَّهِ يَضَعُونَهُ حَيْثُ أَمَرَهُمُ اللَّهُ بِهِ

The servant of Allah does not see for himself ownership over that which Allah has bestowed upon him. That is because the slaves do not own anything. In their eyes, their wealth is Allah's wealth, they place it [and spend it] wherever Allah has commanded them.

Likewise, he witnesses the reality of this noble verse through the illumination of his heart:

أَلَمْ يَعْلَمُوا أَنَّ اللَّهَ ... وَيَأْخُذُ الصَّدَقَاتِ

> Do they not know that it is Allah who ... receives the charities?! (9:104)

For this reason, with such insight he is not after earning the reward of the *infāq* he has performed. That is because he does not see himself independent in his *infāq*, rather he sees that even this action is dependent on Allah. As a result, not only is *infāq* not difficult for him, rather he precedes others in performing this action. The Noble Qur'ān praises such people in this manner:

> إِنَّ الَّذِينَ هُم مِّنْ خَشْيَةِ رَبِّهِم مُّشْفِقُونَ وَالَّذِينَ هُم بِآيَاتِ رَبِّهِمْ يُؤْمِنُونَ وَالَّذِينَ هُم بِرَبِّهِمْ لَا يُشْرِكُونَ وَالَّذِينَ يُؤْتُونَ مَا آتَوا وَّقُلُوبُهُمْ وَجِلَةٌ أَنَّهُمْ إِلَىٰ رَبِّهِمْ رَاجِعُونَ أُولَٰئِكَ يُسَارِعُونَ فِي الْخَيْرَاتِ وَهُمْ لَهَا سَابِقُونَ
>
> Indeed, those who are apprehensive for the fear of their Lord, and believe in the signs of their Lord, and do not ascribe partners to their Lord; who give [in the way of Allah] whatever they give while their hearts tremble with awe [and they know] that they are going to return to their Lord, it is they who are zealous in [performing] good works and take the lead in them. (23: 57-61)

It is based on this that Imam al-Ṣādiq (peace be upon him) in the next segment of his words to 'Unwān al-Baṣrī says:

> فَإِذَا لَمْ يَرَ الْعَبْدُ لِنَفْسِهِ فِيمَا خَوَّلَهُ اللَّهُ تَعَالَى مِلْكاً هَانَ عَلَيْهِ الْإِنْفَاقُ فِيمَا أَمَرَهُ اللَّهُ تَعَالَى أَنْ يُنْفِقَ فِيهِ
>
> Therefore, when a servant does not see for himself ownership over that which Allah has bestowed him, then *infāq* in that which Allah has commanded him to spend becomes easy for him.

The Merits of Infāq

Man has set foot into this world with material, psychological and spiritual needs. In addition to this, he has a variety of attractions and motivations regarding entities of this world and other people. Each of his activities is aimed towards securing these needs and fulfilling these motivations. One of the innate and psychological states of his is that he is moved at the sight of someone destitute, and this makes him inclined towards relieving the need of the destitute and assisting them. It is due to this that a person whose *fiṭrah* has not been destroyed or weakened, strives to give to the poor from the material commodities he has obtained. Moreover, considering the inevitable nature of this world and the changes that occur in it, he knows that it is possible that one day he become afflicted with this same difficulty and require the assistance of others.

Therefore, the Noble Qur'ān describes this as one of the qualities of the pious and those who seek to be on the path of purity of thought, action and social relationships. After having faith in the unseen, humility in front of the truth and establishing prayers this quality is mentioned: that they do *infāq* of the sustenance provided to them.[i] Likewise, the Noble Qur'ān has considered this to be one of the signs of those who possess intellect and deep understanding (of the system of creation and sound relationships between people).[ii] As a result, due to the great merit of this action, it has been introduced as a sign of faith in Allah,[iii] putting trust in Him,[iv] having humility in front of Him,[v] not having arrogance regarding Him,[vi] being a servant of Allah the Merciful,[vii] and being from those who take heed of the Divine signs.[viii]

In other words, it is befitting that these people possess the attribute of doing *infāq* to others, for by this they manifest their correct beliefs and

---

i. (2:3)

ii. (13:22)

iii. (8:3)

iv. (42:38)

v. (22:35)

vi. (32:16)

vii. (32:16)

viii. (25:67)

praiseworthy traits. Also, this action has a mutual effect in developing these true beliefs and commendable traits. Allah the Exalted has created man with a monotheistic disposition. As a result, even if a person does not have faith and does not possess all these praiseworthy traits, but if he is a person of intellect, aware of his existential rank, believes in sound relationships between humans, and then performs this action, then it will positively affect other existential aspects in him and place him on the path of truth.

Conditions for the Effectiveness of Infāq

By carefully observing the actions that man performs, it is understood that these actions stem from a certain background, thoughts and man's internal personality. Undoubtedly, external conditions and factors also affect these actions being performed. In addition, after an action is performed, it leaves its effects on that person and others.

Infāq is one of the desirable actions which has many such effects. The more the intellectual and spiritual conditions of it are fulfilled, the more effective the *infāq* will be, on that person as well as on others. These conditions are:

1) Faith and Sincerity

When these two elements accompany an action or a trait, they bring about very important effects in this world, the Hereafter and on the soul. Special emphasis has been laid on these elements in making matters such as *infāq* effective. Hence, the Noble Qur'ān describes the *infāq* performed by the faithless in the world and the Hereafter, in this manner:

مَثَلُ مَا يُنفِقُونَ فِي هَٰذِهِ الْحَيَاةِ الدُّنْيَا كَمَثَلِ رِيحٍ فِيهَا صِرٌّ
أَصَابَتْ حَرْثَ قَوْمٍ ظَلَمُوا أَنفُسَهُمْ فَأَهْلَكَتْهُ

> The parable of what they spend in the life of this world is that of a cold wind that strikes the tillage of a people who wronged themselves, destroying it. (3:117)

إِنَّ الَّذِينَ كَفَرُوا يُنفِقُونَ أَمْوَالَهُمْ لِيَصُدُّوا عَن سَبِيلِ اللَّهِ ۚ فَسَيُنفِقُونَهَا ثُمَّ تَكُونُ عَلَيْهِمْ حَسْرَةً ثُمَّ يُغْلَبُونَ

Indeed, the faithless spend their wealth to bar [people] from the way of Allah. Soon they will have spent it, then it will be a cause of regret to them, then they will be overcome. (8:36)

Similarly, it says about the hypocrites:

وَلَا يُنفِقُونَ إِلَّا وَهُمْ كَارِهُونَ فَلَا تُعْجِبْكَ أَمْوَالُهُمْ وَلَا أَوْلَادُهُمْ ۚ إِنَّمَا يُرِيدُ اللَّهُ لِيُعَذِّبَهُم بِهَا فِي الْحَيَاةِ الدُّنْيَا وَتَزْهَقَ أَنفُسُهُمْ وَهُمْ كَافِرُونَ

And [they] do not spend but reluctantly. So, let not their wealth and children impress you. Allah only desires to punish them with these in the life of this world, and that their souls may depart while they are faithless. (9:54-55)

Also, it says about those who do not maintain sincerity in *infāq*, those who spend their wealth to be seen by the people, to gain importance in their eyes, as well as those who make the needy feel obliged or trouble them:

يَا أَيُّهَا الَّذِينَ آمَنُوا لَا تُبْطِلُوا صَدَقَاتِكُم بِالْمَنِّ وَالْأَذَىٰ كَالَّذِي يُنفِقُ مَالَهُ رِئَاءَ النَّاسِ وَلَا يُؤْمِنُ بِاللَّهِ وَالْيَوْمِ الْآخِرِ ۖ فَمَثَلُهُ كَمَثَلِ صَفْوَانٍ عَلَيْهِ تُرَابٌ فَأَصَابَهُ وَابِلٌ فَتَرَكَهُ صَلْدًا ۖ لَّا يَقْدِرُونَ عَلَىٰ شَيْءٍ مِّمَّا كَسَبُوا

O you who have faith! Do not render your charities void by making [the needy] feel obliged and troubling [them], like those who spend their wealth to be seen by people and have no faith in Allah and the Last Day. Their parable is that of a rock covered with [a thin layer of] soil [on which they have planted seeds]: a downpour strikes it, leaving it bare. They have no power over anything of what they have earned. (2:264)

Of course, satanic insinuations normally appear and show themselves in man; Satan desires to blemish a person's actions. Therefore, Imam al-Ṣādiq (peace be upon him) says:

الصَّدَقَةُ وَ اللَّهِ فِي السِّرِّ أَفْضَلُ مِنَ الصَّدَقَةِ فِي الْعَلَانِيَة

By Allah! Giving charity secretly is superior to giving charity openly.(i)

Likewise, he says:

إِنَّ صَدَقَةَ اللَّيْلِ تُطْفِئُ غَضَبَ الرَّبِّ وَ تَمْحُو الذَّنْبَ الْعَظِيمَ وَ تُهَوِّنُ الْحِسَاب

Indeed, giving charity at night puts out the anger of the Lord, erases great sins and causes the reckoning to be easy.(ii)

He also says:

لَا تَتَصَدَّقْ عَلَى أَعْيُنِ النَّاسِ لِيُزَكُّوكَ فَإِنَّكَ إِنْ فَعَلْتَ ذَلِكَ فَقَدِ اسْتَوْفَيْتَ أَجْرَكَ وَ لَكِنْ إِذَا أَعْطَيْتَ بِيَمِينِكَ فَلَا تُطْلِعْ عَلَيْهَا شِمَالَكَ فَإِنَّ الَّذِي تَتَصَدَّقُ لَهُ سِرّاً يُجْزِيكَ عَلَانِيَة

Do not give charity before people's eyes so that they praise you. For if you do so [and the people praise you], then indeed you have obtained your full reward. Rather when you are giving with your right hand then do not let your left hand know about it! [Do it secretly.] For indeed the One for whom you secretly give charity, will reward you openly.(iii)

The conduct of the Imams (peace be upon them) was also this; they would give charity hiddenly and secretly. Imam al-Bāqir (peace be upon him) says about his father:

---

i. al-Kulaynī, al-Kāfī, 4:80, narration 2

ii. Majlisī, Bihār al-Anwār, 96:125, narration 39

iii. Ibid., 78:284, narration 1

أَنَّـهُ كَانَ يَخْـرُجُ فِـي اللَّيْلَـةِ الظَّلْمَـاءِ فَيَحْمِـلُ الْجِـرَابَ عَلَـى ظَهْـرِهِ حَتَّـى يَأْتِـيَ بَابـاً بَابـاً فَيَقْرَعُـهُ ثُـمَّ يُنَـاوِلُ مَـنْ كَانَ يَخْـرُجُ إِلَيْـهِ وَ كَانَ يُغَطِّـي وَجْهَـهُ إِذَا نَـاوَلَ فَقِيـراً لِئَـلَّا يَعْرِفَـه

He would leave his house in the darkness of the night carrying a sack of bread on his back until he would arrive at one door after the other. He would knock on the door and give [the bread] to whoever came out. He would cover his face while giving to the needy person, so that he would not recognize him.[i]

2) *Infāq through Permissible Means and for a Permissible Purpose*

Infāq and giving charity is primarily for purifying the soul of material attachments. Its secondary purpose is to purify the wealth and cause it to grow, just as the Noble Qur'ān says:

خُذْ مِنْ أَمْوَالِهِمْ صَدَقَةً تُطَهِّرُهُمْ وَتُزَكِّيهِم بِهَا

Take charity from their possessions to cleanse them and purify them thereby. (9:103)

Therefore, this wealth must have been acquired through pure means so that it can have that effect. Imam al-Ṣādiq (peace be upon him) says:

لَـوْ أَنَّ النَّـاسَ أَخَـذُوا مَـا أَمَرَهُـمُ اللَّهُ بِـهِ فَأَنْفَقُـوهُ فِيمَـا نَهَاهُـمْ عَنْـهُ مَـا قَبِلَـهُ مِنْهُـمْ وَ لَـوْ أَخَـذُوا مَـا نَهَاهُـمُ اللَّهُ عَنْـهُ فَأَنْفَقُـوهُ فِيمَـا أَمَرَهُـمُ اللَّهُ بِـهِ مَـا قَبِلَـهُ مِنْهُـمْ حَتَّـى يَأْخُـذُوهُ مِـنْ حَـقٍّ وَ يُنْفِقُـوهُ فِـي حَـقٍّ

Had people followed that which Allah has commanded them [had they acquired wealth through permissible means] and then done *infāq* of it in a place that Allah has prohibited, then it would not be accepted from them. And had they gone after that which Allah has prohibited them from [acquired wealth from impermissible means] and then done *infāq* in a place which Allah has commanded them, then it

i. Ibid., 46:89, narration 77

> would not be accepted from them. [This is the case] until they acquire through right [means] and spend it in the right [place].(i)

Similarly, Imam al-Bāqir (peace be upon him) says:

> كَانَ النَّاسُ حِينَ أَسْلَمُوا عِنْدَهُمْ مَكَاسِبُ مِنَ الرِّبَا وَ مِنْ أَمْوَالٍ خَبِيثَةٍ فَكَانَ الرَّجُلُ يَتَعَمَّدُهَا مِنْ بَيْنِ مَالِهِ فَيَتَصَدَّقُ بِهَا فَنَهَاهُمُ اللَّهُ عَنْ ذَلِكَ وَ إِنَّ الصَّدَقَةَ لَا تَصْلُحُ إِلَّا مِنْ كَسْبٍ طَيِّبٍ
>
> During the period when people were becoming Muslims they would possess with them earnings from usury and impure wealth. One of them would deliberately choose this part from his wealth and give it in charity. So, Allah prohibited them from this action [by revealing verse 267 of Sūrah al-Baqarah]. Charity is not suitable except from pure earnings.(ii)

3) Infāq of That Which is Dear

One of man's *fiṭrī* inclinations is his love for himself and things that are related to him. Through *infāq*, he tries to detach himself from these relationships. Therefore, to the extent that man pays attention to the benefits of *infāq*, enjoys a greater share of human dignity and character, or has a higher level of faith, to that same extent he will always try and ensure that his *infāq* possesses some special prominence. As a result, in addition to observing *ikhlāṣ* and the aforementioned matters, he will also spend from the best of his wealth. Just as how Allah the Exalted, after drawing man's attention towards this reality, addresses him and says:

> لَن تَنَالُوا الْبِرَّ حَتَّىٰ تُنفِقُوا مِمَّا تُحِبُّونَ ۚ وَمَا تُنفِقُوا مِن شَيْءٍ فَإِنَّ اللَّهَ بِهِ عَلِيمٌ
>
> You will never attain piety until you spend out of what you

---

i. al-Ṣadūq, Man Lā Yaḥḍuruhu al-Faqih, 2:57, narration 1694

ii. al-ʿAyyāshi, Tafsīr al-ʿAyyāshi, 1:149, narration 492

hold dear, and whatever you may spend of anything, Allah indeed knows it. (3:92)

This kind of outlook makes *infāq* easier for man. In addition to this, in another verse Allah says:

لَّيْسَ عَلَيْكَ هُدَاهُمْ وَلَٰكِنَّ اللَّهَ يَهْدِي مَن يَشَاءُ ۗ وَمَا تُنفِقُوا مِنْ خَيْرٍ فَلِأَنفُسِكُمْ ۚ وَمَا تُنفِقُونَ إِلَّا ابْتِغَاءَ وَجْهِ اللَّهِ ۚ وَمَا تُنفِقُوا مِنْ خَيْرٍ يُوَفَّ إِلَيْكُمْ وَأَنتُمْ لَا تُظْلَمُونَ

It is not up to you to guide them; rather, it is Allah who guides whomever He wishes. Whatever wealth you spend, it is for your own benefit, as you do not spend but to seek Allah's pleasure, and whatever wealth you spend will be repaid to you [its reward] in full and you will not be wronged. (2:272)

This means that the person himself obtains true benefit from infāq; he is recompensed with something better. It has come in a narration about Imam ʿAlī (peace be upon him) that:

اشْتَرَى ع ثَوْباً فَأَعْجَبَهُ فَتَصَدَّقَ بِهِ

He bought a garment and it impressed him, therefore he gave it in charity.(i)

Likewise, it is narrated that:

أَنَّهُ كَانَ يَتَصَدَّقُ بِالسُّكَّرِ فَقِيلَ لَهُ أَ تَتَصَدَّقُ بِالسُّكَّرِ فَقَالَ نَعَمْ إِنَّهُ لَيْسَ شَيْءٌ أَحَبَّ إِلَيَّ مِنْهُ فَأَنَا أُحِبُّ أَنْ أَتَصَدَّقَ بِأَحَبِّ الْأَشْيَاءِ إِلَيَّ.

[One day] he was giving sugar [which was a valuable commodity] in charity. It was said to him, "Are you giving sugar in charity?!" He said, "Yes! There is nothing which I like more than sugar. Therefore, I would like to give in charity

i. Majlisī, Bihār al-Anwār, 40:323

what I like the most." (i)

Also, it is sufficient for proving the merit of such *infāq* that when the Immaculate Ahl al-Bayt (peace be upon them) did *infāq* of their food, an important portion or all of Sūrah al-Insān was revealed in their praise (ii):

وَيُطْعِمُونَ الطَّعَامَ عَلَىٰ حُبِّهِ مِسْكِينًا وَيَتِيمًا وَأَسِيرًا

For the love of Him, they feed the needy, the orphan and the prisoner. (76:8)

4) Moderation in Infāq

The wisdom behind *infāq* is that it answers the innate call that enjoins man to relieve the need of the needy person. In addition to that, it also satisfies the sentiment within man that seeks to promote and help humanity. Therefore, in order that this action becomes widespread and perpetual amongst people, the mindset of an ordinary human being has been taken into consideration. Thus, exercising moderation while performing *infāq* has been advised. As Allah in describing the "servants of the Beneficent" says:

وَالَّذِينَ إِذَا أَنفَقُوا لَمْ يُسْرِفُوا وَلَمْ يَقْتُرُوا وَكَانَ بَيْنَ ذَٰلِكَ قَوَامًا

Those who are neither wasteful nor tightfisted when spending but balanced between these [two extremes]. (25:63)

Likewise, Imam al-Kāẓim (peace be upon him) says:

لَا تَبْذُلْ لِإِخْوَانِكَ مِنْ نَفْسِكَ مَا ضَرُّهُ عَلَيْكَ أَكْثَرُ مِنْ مَنْفَعَتِهِ لَهُمْ

Do not give from yourself to your brethren that whose harm to you is more than its benefit to them. (iii)

---

i. al-Kulaynī, al-Kāfī, 4:61, narration 3

ii. al-Rāzī, Tafsīr al-Kabīr, 30:243; al-Ṭabrasī, Majmaʿ al-Bayān 10:407; al-Zamakhsharī, al-Kashshāf, 4:197

iii. al-Kulaynī, al-Kāfī, 4:33, narration 2

The Effects of Infāq and Charity

The previous discussion was regarding the conditions and prerequisites required for *infāq*. The more these conditions are realized and the better they are, the better the effects of *infāq* will be—both in this world and the Hereafter. *Infāq* occurs in a variety of forms such as lending money, gifting it and so on. However, one of the important examples of it is to give charity. Due to this, the effects of charity will be explained.

1) Replacing What is Spent

By carefully studying the existential relationships between entities of this world, it can be understood that at times, interactions between entities leads to the destruction of one another. For instance, when man uses natural bounties to fulfil his needs, he causes them to diminish or even depletes them altogether. At the same time, Allah the Exalted is always bestowing existence. Even though some actions are apparently indicative of the depletion of something—for example giving one's wealth to another person in charity—it is not really so. Because charity is an immaterial matter, Allah the Exalted has promised that, in addition to recompensing man in the Hereafter, in this world that wealth will also be replaced:

قُلْ إِنَّ رَبِّي يَبْسُطُ الرِّزْقَ لِمَن يَشَاءُ مِنْ عِبَادِهِ وَيَقْدِرُ لَهُ ۚ وَمَا أَنفَقْتُم مِّن شَيْءٍ فَهُوَ يُخْلِفُهُ ۖ وَهُوَ خَيْرُ الرَّازِقِينَ

> Say, "Indeed my Lord expands the provision for whomever of His servants that He wishes and tightens it, and He will repay whatever you may spend, and He is the best of providers." (34:39)

By paying attention to the first part of this verse it can be understood that one of the ways to increase sustenance is to do *infāq* in the way of Allah. Naturally, this matter is within man's free will. Moreover, this is in addition to the sustenance that Allah has guaranteed upon Himself for all entities, especially man.

The Messenger of Allah (peace and blessings be upon him and his family) also says:

مَا نَقَصَ مَالٌ مِنْ صَدَقَةٍ قَطُّ فَأَعْطُوا وَ لَا تَجْبُنُو

> Never has wealth diminished because of [giving] charity. Therefore, give charity and do not be afraid.[i]

It is for this reason that when one of the family members of the Messenger of Allah (peace and blessings be upon him and his family) slaughtered a sheep (and gave a portion of it in charity), the Messenger of Allah (peace and blessings be upon him and his family) asked:

مَا بَقِيَ؟ فَقَالَتْ: مَا بَقِيَ إِلّا كَتِفُهَا، قَالَ: بَقِيَ كُلُّهَا غَيْرَ كَتِفِهَا

> "How much of it is left?" Ā'ishah replied, "Only its shoulder is remaining." He (peace and blessings be upon him and his family) said, "Everything [that was given away in charity] is remaining except its shoulder."[ii]

2) Repaying Debts and Blessings in Wealth

One of the examples of the immaterial effects that *infāq* and charity have, is the effect that they have on repaying debt and causing blessings in man's wealth.[iii] Imam al-Ṣādiq (peace be upon him) says:

الصَّدَقَةُ تَقْضِي الدَّيْنَ وَ تَخْلُفُ بِالْبَرَكَةِ

> Charity causes debts to be repaid and replaces them with blessings.[iv]

إِنِّي لَأُمْلِقُ أَحْيَاناً فَأُتَاجِرُ اللَّهَ بِالصَّدَقَةِ

> Sometimes I become empty-handed and poor, so I trade with Allah by giving charity.[v]

Likewise, Imam 'Alī (peace be upon him) says:

---

i. Majlisī, Bihār al-Anwār, 93:131, narration 62

ii. al-Hindī, Kanz al-'Ummāl, narration 16150

iii. That is, the blessings of the charity will allow the debtor to pay back his debt.

iv. Majlisī, Bihār al-Anwār, 96:134, narration 68

v. Ibid., 78:206, narration 54

إِذَا أَمْلَقْتُمْ فَتَاجِرُوا اللَّهَ بِالصَّدَقَة

When you are afflicted with poverty, trade with Allah by giving charity.(i)

This means that the other party involved in charity is Allah. He is the true receiver of it and He makes the charity profitable, causing it to send down provision.(ii) Just as how in one of the verses, after commanding the Noble Messenger (peace and blessings be upon him and his family) to take charity from the people, Allah says:

خُذْ مِنْ أَمْوَالِهِمْ صَدَقَةً تُطَهِّرُهُمْ وَتُزَكِّيهِم بِهَا وَصَلِّ عَلَيْهِمْ ۖ إِنَّ صَلَاتَكَ سَكَنٌ لَّهُمْ ۗ وَاللَّهُ سَمِيعٌ عَلِيمٌ أَلَمْ يَعْلَمُوا أَنَّ اللَّهَ هُوَ يَقْبَلُ التَّوْبَةَ عَنْ عِبَادِهِ وَيَأْخُذُ الصَّدَقَاتِ

Take charity from their possessions to cleanse them and purify them thereby and bless them. Indeed, your blessing is a comfort to them, and Allah is Hearing, Knowing. Do they not know that it is only Allah who accepts the repentance of His servants and receives the charities? (9:103-104)

The stronger a person's faith in the veracity of this statement and He who said it is, the more the effects of this action will manifest in his life. That is because, blessings (*barakah)* means the growth and increase of a thing, albeit a small thing.

3) Repelling Calamities

One of the immaterial effects of *infāq* and charity is that it prevents a person from being afflicted with unpleasant calamities. The Messenger of Allah (peace and blessings be upon him and his family) says:

الصَّدَقَةُ تَمْنَعُ سَبْعِينَ نَوْعاً مِنْ أَنْوَاعِ البَلَاءِ أَهْوَنُهَا الجُذَامُ و البَرَصُ

Charity holds back seventy types of calamities the least of

i. al-Radī, Nahj al-Balāghah, saying 258

ii. Majlisī, Biḥār al-Anwār, 78:68, narration 13

which are leprosy and vitiligo.[i]

Likewise, Imam ʿAlī (peace be upon him) says:

الصَّدَقَةُ تَدْفَعُ مِيتَةَ السَّوْءِ

Charity wards off an unpleasant death.[ii]

And if the descending of a calamity has been decreed, then in the words of Imam ʿAlī (peace be upon him):

وَ الصَّدَقَةُ دَوَاءٌ مُنْجِح

[iii].And charity is an effective cure

This means that charity creates a spiritual state in the person, enabling him to endure the calamity and causing his spiritual advancement.

4) Effects on the Day of Resurrection

The effects of *infāq* and charity are not limited to procuring the means of receiving sustenance, attaining blessings in it, and repelling worldly calamities. Rather, if they are performed with its requirements and if a person possesses some problems and mistakes in his actions, then they will ward off calamities in the Hereafter as well. As the Messenger of Allah (peace and blessings be upon him and his family) says:

أَرْضُ الْقِيَامَةِ نَارٌ مَا خَلَا ظِلَّ الْمُؤْمِنِ فَإِنَّ صَدَقَتَهُ تُظِلُّهُ

The ground on the Day of Resurrection is fire, except for the shade of the believer. That is because his charity provides a shade for him.[iv]

Likewise, Imam ʿAlī (peace be upon him) says:

الصَّدَقَةُ جُنَّةٌ

---

i. al-Hindī, Kanz al-ʿUmmāl, narration 15982

ii. al-Kulaynī, al-Kāfī, 4:2, narration 1

iii. al-Radī, Nahj al-Balāghah, saying 7

iv. al-Kulaynī, al-Kāfī, 4:3, narration 6

Charity is a shield [from the fire of Hell].[i]

The Best Infāq and Charity

Man's actions play a fundamental role in his felicity and wretchedness; he faces the consequences of his actions in this world as well as in the Hereafter:

وَأَن لَّيْسَ لِلْإِنسَانِ إِلَّا مَا سَعَىٰ وَأَنَّ سَعْيَهُ سَوْفَ يُرَىٰ ثُمَّ يُجْزَاهُ الْجَزَاءَ الْأَوْفَىٰ

That nothing belongs to man except what he strives for, and that he will soon be shown his endeavour, then he will be rewarded for it with the fullest reward. (53:39-41)

From this viewpoint, in the words of the Messenger of Allah (peace and blessings be upon him and his family):

أَفْضَلُ الْأَعْمَالِ أَحْمَزُهَا

The best of actions is those which are the most difficult.[ii]

Therefore, if a person does *infāq* whilst in the state of poverty, it will have profound effects. The Noble Messenger (peace and blessings be upon him and his family) says:

ثَلَاثٌ مِنْ حَقَائِقِ الْإِيمَانِ الْإِنْفَاقُ مِنَ الْإِقْتَارِ . . .

Three things are from the realities of the faith: Doing *infāq* in the face of poverty ...[iii]

Likewise, that noble personality (peace and blessings be upon him and his family) says:

أَفْضَلُ النَّاسِ رَجُلٌ يُعْطِي جُهْدَهُ

The best of people is one who gives to others what he has

---

i. al-ʿĀmilī, Wasāʾil al-Shīʿah, 6:258, narration 17

ii. Majlisī, Bihār al-Anwār, 70:191

iii. Ibid., 77:53, narration 3

acquired through his efforts and hard work.[i]

Similarly, when he was asked as to which charity is the best, he said in reply:

عَلَى ذِي الرَّحِمِ الْكَاشِحِ

> [Giving charity] to a blood-relative who conceals his enmity towards you.[ii]

This means that even though you know he is an enemy, yet you overlook this enmity and give charity to him. Such charity requires an exceptional amount of self-struggle. To conclude, the merit of every *infāq* that is accompanied with any type of hardship and self-struggle, is greater than other types of *infāq*. As the Noble Qur'ān says:

لَا يَسْتَوِي مِنكُم مَّنْ أَنفَقَ مِن قَبْلِ الْفَتْحِ وَقَاتَلَ ۚ أُولَٰئِكَ أَعْظَمُ دَرَجَةً مِّنَ الَّذِينَ أَنفَقُوا مِن بَعْدُ وَقَاتَلُوا

> Those of you who spent [their means] and fought before the victory [of Makkah] are not equal [to others]. They are greater in rank than those who have spent and fought afterwards. (57:10)

The Second Manifestation of Servitude – A Transformation in Man's Planning

The Manifestation of Divine Planning

By paying careful attention to the entities of this world, we discover the close relationship between the world's components and the appearance of wonderful effects from each entity. All these affairs run according to the planning and will of the Powerful, Knowing and Wise Lord. He directs this robust system that is free from any disorder, towards its lofty goal. At the same time, each of its entities also progresses towards their own specific goal, the goal that is close to their being. In this process of entities moving towards their respective

---

i. al-Hindī, Kanz al-ʿUmmāl, narration 16084

ii. al-Ṣadūq, Thawāb al-Aʿmāl, 171, narration 18

goals, man derives special benefit. The Noble Qur'ān explicitly mentions this reality, saying:

> اللَّهُ الَّذِي رَفَعَ السَّمَاوَاتِ بِغَيْرِ عَمَدٍ تَرَوْنَهَا ۖ ثُمَّ اسْتَوَىٰ عَلَى الْعَرْشِ ۖ وَسَخَّرَ الشَّمْسَ وَالْقَمَرَ ۖ كُلٌّ يَجْرِي لِأَجَلٍ مُسَمًّى ۚ يُدَبِّرُ الْأَمْرَ يُفَصِّلُ الْآيَاتِ لَعَلَّكُم بِلِقَاءِ رَبِّكُمْ تُوقِنُونَ
>
> It is Allah who raised the heavens without any pillars that you see, and then presided over the Throne. He disposed the sun and the moon, each moving for a specified term. He directs the command [of the creation], [and] elaborates the signs [of His], perchance you may be certain of encountering your Lord. (13:2)

The things explained in this verse and other verses—such as the raising of the heavens without pillars, presiding over the Throne, the creation of the sun and the moon—are all manifestations of Divine planning. They illustrate this reality that the creation of the world's entities along with the relationship between them (that constitute a marvellous order, one that cannot be completely fathomed), all originates from the station of Absolute Sovereignty. This station encompasses and dominates everything. This reality is not incompatible with how Allah the Exalted may have created intermediaries for carrying out His planning. As Allah says:

> وَالنَّازِعَاتِ غَرْقًا وَالنَّاشِطَاتِ نَشْطًا وَالسَّابِحَاتِ سَبْحًا فَالسَّابِقَاتِ سَبْقًا فَالْمُدَبِّرَاتِ أَمْرًا
>
> By those [angels] who wrest [the soul] violently [from the disbelievers], and by those [angels] who draw [it] out gently [from the believers], and by those who swim smoothly [in the unparalleled sea], then in preceding others [in obeying Allah] they take the lead, and they direct the affairs [of the servants] (79:1-5)

That is because the intermediaries of Divine grace are ontologically subservient to Allah the Exalted; their relationship to Him is vertical in nature. They have been created due to the existential limitations of the material world, for this world cannot directly receive grace from the Sacred Divine Essence. Thus, their actions and influence on different affairs in the world is in fact the influence of Allah. Moreover, they are never free of needing Allah's bestowal of existence and existential perfections, not even for a moment. In the same way, entities of the world need Allah's bestowal to influence each other.

Therefore, after establishing His Throne and creating a station to manifest His command and authority, Allah also created intermediaries of grace. By means of these intermediaries He can direct the different affairs of this world with knowledge and planning. It is for this reason that in some of the verses of the Noble Qur'ān, after mentioning how He presided over the Throne, Allah negates the effectiveness of any intercessor or *walī* without His leave. [i] This is so that the ability to act independently is not imagined for any entity. Thus, keeping in view this precise and coherent system—wherein every being is moving toward its specific goal, and this movement necessitates interaction with other beings—one must recognize that all of these subsist by means of Allah's command and bestowal. Man's planning of his various actions is also similar. Even though he has been created as a being possessing awareness, choice and volition, yet he is not independent in any of the aspects of his being. This is the case regardless of whether he accepts it or not, and regardless of whether he perceives it clearly or not.

The Extent of Divine Planning

The more one carefully considers the characteristics of entities, the clearer Allah's planning with regards to them becomes. Corporeal, vegetative, animal and human beings, with all their different species and types that man has discovered, all interact with each other in this world. They affect and are affected by one another, leading to the emergence of astonishing qualities and effects. Despite persistent efforts and devising new tools, scientists have only been able to uncover a small portion of these qualities and effects.

---

i. (10:3), (32:4)

The Noble Qur'ān constantly encourages man to carefully observe the characteristics of the created beings so that he is led to Allah's knowledge, power and wisdom. It says:

أَفَلَا يَنظُرُونَ إِلَى الْإِبِلِ كَيْفَ خُلِقَتْ وَإِلَى السَّمَاءِ كَيْفَ رُفِعَتْ
وَإِلَى الْجِبَالِ كَيْفَ نُصِبَتْ وَإِلَى الْأَرْضِ كَيْفَ سُطِحَتْ

> Do they not observe the camel, [to see] how it has been created? And the sky, how it has been raised? And the mountains, how they have been set? And the Earth, how it has been spread? (88:17-20)

In particular, Allah the Exalted instructs man to observe his own self and its intricate characteristics so that he obtains insights. He says:

وَفِي أَنفُسِكُمْ ۚ أَفَلَا تُبْصِرُونَ

> And in your souls [there are signs]. Will you not then perceive? (51:21)

That is because, in addition to possessing corporeal, vegetative, and animal qualities, man possesses complex psychological and spiritual characteristics, each of which has distinctive features and effects. To the extent that man reflects on the different dimensions of his existence and carefully investigates them—by means of experimental sciences and witnessing of the heart—he will discover many marvels in Allah's robust system. Eventually he will reach the conclusion that man in all his dimensions—be it material dimensions, psychological actions and reactions, or spiritual and immaterial dimensions—is subject to the planning of God's Divine Wisdom. The Noble Qur'ān refers to a few of the signs of Allah's planning with respect to man:

وَمِنْ آيَاتِهِ أَنْ خَلَقَ لَكُم مِّنْ أَنفُسِكُمْ أَزْوَاجًا لِّتَسْكُنُوا إِلَيْهَا
وَجَعَلَ بَيْنَكُم مَّوَدَّةً وَرَحْمَةً ۚ إِنَّ فِي ذَٰلِكَ لَآيَاتٍ لِّقَوْمٍ يَتَفَكَّرُونَ
وَمِنْ آيَاتِهِ خَلْقُ السَّمَاوَاتِ وَالْأَرْضِ وَاخْتِلَافُ أَلْسِنَتِكُمْ وَأَلْوَانِكُمْ ۚ

إِنَّ فِي ذَٰلِكَ لَآيَاتٍ لِّلْعَالِمِينَ وَمِنْ آيَاتِهِ مَنَامُكُم بِاللَّيْلِ وَالنَّهَارِ وَابْتِغَاؤُكُم مِّن فَضْلِهِ ۚ إِنَّ فِي ذَٰلِكَ لَآيَاتٍ لِّقَوْمٍ يَسْمَعُونَ

And of His signs is that He created for you mates from your own selves [your species] that you may take comfort in them, and He ordained affection and mercy between you. There are indeed signs in that [blessing] for a people who reflect. Among His signs [of His power] is the creation of the heavens and the Earth, and the difference of your languages and colors. There are indeed signs in that [as well] for those who know. And of His signs [of His wisdom] is your sleep by night and [mid] day, and your pursuit of His bounty [sustenance]. There are indeed signs in that [as well] for a people who listen. (30:21-23)

Therefore, the extent of Allah the Wise's planning encompasses all actions and reactions—both psychological and spiritual—as well as the different transformations that occur in man until he reaches the highest degree of perfection. This is so, regardless of whether they occur in this realm or other realms. As Allah the Exalted says:

يُدَبِّرُ الْأَمْرَ يُفَصِّلُ الْآيَاتِ لَعَلَّكُم بِلِقَاءِ رَبِّكُمْ تُوقِنُونَ

He directs the command [the creation], [and] elaborates the signs [of His] that you may be certain of encountering your Lord. (13:2)

The Manner of Allah's Planning with Regards to Man

Allah the Exalted has created all entities with a specific goal and has placed the tools required for reaching this goal in the constitution of every one of them. Aside for man and jinn, these beings do not have the free will and ability to choose the path of reaching their creation's goal. Rather, subject to the Divine ontological will, they are moving towards the destination which He has destined and specified for them:

الَّذِي خَلَقَ فَسَوَّىٰ وَالَّذِي قَدَّرَ فَهَدَىٰ

Who created and proportioned, who determined and

guided, (87:2-3)

However, man is equipped with a set of cognitive abilities so that by understanding his own self and the goal that he can reach, he consciously advances toward his felicity:

> إِنَّا هَدَيْنَاهُ السَّبِيلَ إِمَّا شَاكِرًا وَإِمَّا كَفُورًا
>
> Indeed, We have guided him to the way, be he grateful or ungrateful. (76:3)

Therefore, any type of reflection and thinking in this regard is worthy of praise and every systematic action accompanied with farsightedness and planning is affirmed by the Islamic viewpoint. The Noble Qur'ān says:

> وَمَنْ أَرَادَ الْآخِرَةَ وَسَعَىٰ لَهَا سَعْيَهَا وَهُوَ مُؤْمِنٌ فَأُولَٰئِكَ كَانَ سَعْيُهُم مَّشْكُورًا
>
> Whoever desires the Hereafter and strives for it with an endeavour worthy of it, should he be faithful, the endeavour of such will be well-appreciated [by God]. (17:19)

Based on this, in the first step of the journey, the wayfarer must recognize the goal of his creation. Through deliberating on his own being, he should ascertain his origin and place of return in the world of existence. He must deliberate about where he stands with respect to the goal and examine the set of ordinary and spiritual abilities and potentials that he possesses which can help him to reach the goal. Then he must begin to actualize these. At this point, he must consider the obstacles, banes and risks that lie on his path of perfection and engage in relieving and repelling them using the methods stated by sacred Islamic *sharīʿah*.

Recognizing the path and its guides is one of the other matters which the wayfarer needs, during his movement toward perfection.

In the view of the sacred Islamic *sharīʿah,* paying attention to this process and observing it is called '*tadbīr*'. *Tadbīr* is an outcome of learning, thinking, prudence, farsightedness, consultation, etc. All these keywords occupy an important and valuable place in the discussion on

Islamic training. Carelessness with respect each one of them disrupts the wayfarer's movement towards perfection. Imam ʿAlī (peace be upon him) has said:

> التَّدْبِيرُ قَبْلَ الْفِعْلِ يُؤْمِنُ الْعِثَار
>
> *Tadbīr* before performing an action, makes a person secure against errors. (i)
>
> مَنْ سَاءَ تَدْبِيرُهُ بَطَلَ تَقْدِيرُه
>
> One whose *tadbīr* is poor, that which has been apportioned for him [in his affairs] is rendered void. (ii)
>
> مَنْ تَأَخَّرَ تَدْبِيرُهُ تَقَدَّمَ تَدْمِيرُه
>
> One whose *tadbīr* is delayed, his destruction advances. (iii)

Of course, a person's *tadbīr* along with observing its conditions, is only instrumental when it is accompanied by *tawakkul* (trust) in Allah and *tawassul* to His noble *awliyāʾ* (peace be upon them):

> فَإِذَا عَزَمْتَ فَتَوَكَّلْ عَلَى اللَّهِ ۚ إِنَّ اللَّهَ يُحِبُّ الْمُتَوَكِّلِينَ
>
> And once you are resolved, put your trust in Allah. Indeed, Allah loves those who trust in Him. (3:159)

That is because, when man's *tadbīr* is accompanied with *tawakkul* in Allah, then even if he does not achieve apparent results, it still leads to the true result and opens his eyes towards the realities of the world. He understands that there are benefits in the world that he will obtain at an appropriate time, and only God is aware of them. Thus, He says:

> وَمَن يَتَوَكَّلْ عَلَى اللَّهِ فَهُوَ حَسْبُهُ ۚ إِنَّ اللَّهَ بَالِغُ أَمْرِهِ ۚ قَدْ جَعَلَ اللَّهُ لِكُلِّ شَيْءٍ قَدْرًا
>
> And whoever puts his trust in Allah, He will suffice him. Indeed, Allah carries through His commands. Certainly, Allah has ordained a measure [and extent] for everything.

---

i. al-Āmudī, Fihrist-i Mawḍūʿī-yi Ghurar al-Ḥikam, chapter on *tadbīr*

ii. Ibid.

iii. Ibid.

(65:3)

By carefully observing this existential journey, it can be understood that in reality, all entities are ontologically subject to the wise *tadbīr* of the Powerful and the Absolute Truth, Allah the Immaculate:

> يُدَبِّرُ الْأَمْرَ مِنَ السَّمَاءِ إِلَى الْأَرْضِ
> He directs the command [of all the worlds] from the heaven [including the heavens] to the Earth; (32:5)

Certainly, the *tadbīr* of man and jinn are special; Allah has designated a responsibility and religion for them so that they willingly place themselves under this Divine *tadbīr* and achieve its lofty results:

> وَمَا خَلَقْتُ الْجِنَّ وَالْإِنسَ إِلَّا لِيَعْبُدُونِ
> I did not create the jinn and the humans except that they may worship Me. (51:56)

> يَا مَعْشَرَ الْجِنِّ وَالْإِنسِ أَلَمْ يَأْتِكُمْ رُسُلٌ مِّنكُمْ يَقُصُّونَ عَلَيْكُمْ آيَاتِي
> O company of jinn and humans! Did there not come to you apostles from yourselves, recounting to you My signs. (6:130)

If man's *tadbīr* is done whilst keeping in mind the aforementioned points as well as those which will be explained in detail, then this *tadbīr* is in the direction of servitude and Allah's *tadbīr* for him. In this manner, Imam al-Ṣādiq's (peace be upon him) statement about the second pillar of servitude will be realized:

وَ لَا يُدَبِّرُ الْعَبْدُ لِنَفْسِهِ تَدْبِيراً

And that the servant does not direct his own affairs.

On the contrary, if he does not do *tadbīr* in this manner, then he has certainly not placed himself under Allah's *tadbīr*. Rather, he has independently done *tadbīr* for himself, the examples of which will be explained in the next discussion.

The Banes of Tadbīr

By carefully looking at the nature of the world, it becomes clear that attaining any goal in it is accompanied with obstacles that must be considered and removed from the path. Man's *tadbīr* is no exception to this rule. As Imam ʿAlī (peace be upon him) has said, bad *tadbīr* draws man towards destruction and failing in reaching his goals.[i]

Thus, it is necessary to be attentive of the banes that impair man's *tadbīr* and remain aloof from them, so that through correct *tadbīr* one can obtain the desired result.

1) Ignoring the Effective Factors in Tadbīr

Tadbīr is the end result of a collection of factors such as studying and learning, thinking and prudence, farsightedness, consultation and trust in Allah. It is evident that negligence in bringing about any of these elements, will lead to shakiness in man's *tadbīr* and will spoil his management.

Learning concepts and subjects that are effective in man's spiritual and personal development, and which play a key role in training (*tarbiyah*)—be they ideological, ethical or practical concepts—are indispensable and necessary. That is because, thinking and reasoning cause these concepts to be digested and understood in man's soul, moving them from the confines of the mind to his soul. Moreover, in the process of employing these realities and moving towards the goal, farsightedness and consultation complete the process of *tadbīr* and assist man in his movement towards felicity.

Imam ʿAlī (peace be upon him) has considered negligence in acquiring knowledge as being equal to remaining behind the caravan of perfection. He says:

مَنْ لَمْ يُدْئِبْ نَفْسَهُ فِي اكْتِسَابِ الْعِلْمِ لَمْ يُحْرِزْ قَصَبَاتِ السَّبْقِ

i. Ibid. This reference has apparently been derived from multiple narrations found in this source, such as the following two:

سُوءُ التَّدْبِيرِ سَبَبُ التَّدْمِيرِ

Bad *tadbīr* is the cause of destruction.

مَنْ سَاءَ تَدْبِيرُهُ بَطَلَ تَقْدِيرُهُ

One whose *tadbīr* is poor, that which is ordained for him is nullified.

> One who does not make his soul bear hardship on the path of gaining knowledge, does not reach the peaks of prominence.(i)

Likewise, in another narration he alludes to the constructive role of the intellect in man's spiritual development and says:

> نَاظِرُ قَلْبِ اللَّبِيبِ بِهِ يُبْصِرُ رُشْدَهُ وَ يَعْرِفُ غَوْرَهُ وَ نَجْدَه
>
> The one who sees with an understanding heart, through it [this heart] he sees his own development and knows its depths and heights.(ii)

Similarly, the Imam (peace be upon him) explains the importance of consultation in this manner:

> الِاسْتِشَارَةُ عَيْنُ الْهِدَايَة
>
> Consultation is guidance itself.(iii)
>
> شَاوِرْ ذَوِي الْعُقُولِ تَأْمَنِ الزَّلَلَ وَ النَّدَم
>
> Consult with people of intellect, you will be protected from mistakes and remorse.(iv)

Therefore, a lack of farsightedness in *tadbīr* will lead to destruction and weakness such that:

> مَنْ خَالَفَ الْحَزْمَ هَلَكَ ... مَنْ لَمْ يُقَدِّمْهُ الْحَزْمُ أَخَّرَهُ الْعَجْزُ
>
> One who opposes farsightedness is destroyed ... One whom farsightedness does not advance, weakness keeps him behind.(v)

---

i. Ibid., chapter on *ʿilm*

ii. Ibid., chapter on *ʿaql*

iii. Ibid., chapter on *mashwirah*

iv. Ibid.

v. Ibid., chapter on *ḥazm*

2) Fantasizing Instead of Being Realistic

Paying attention to one's intellectual and physical potentials and abilities, careful consideration of time and space conditions, and keeping in mind the average lifespan and man's survival in the world when doing *tadbīr*, brings a person closer to the realities. As a result, he is not afflicted with poor *tadbīr*. As opposed to one who bases his decisions and arranges his affairs on unfounded imaginations and vain hopes. Such an individual charts out an unnatural life for himself without sound and logical accounting.

It is for this reason that Imam al-Ṣādiq (peace be upon him) has said:

تَجَنَّبُوا الْمُنَى فَإِنَّهَا تُذْهِبُ بَهْجَةَ مَا خُوِّلْتُمْ وَ تَسْتَصْغِرُونَ بِهَا مَوَاهِبَ اللَّهِ تَعَالَى عِنْدَكُمْ و تُعْقِبُكُمُ الْحَسَرَاتِ فِيمَا وَهَّمْتُمْ بِهِ أَنْفُسَكُمْ

> Avoid vain hopes. For indeed they remove the splendour and delight of that which has been bestowed upon you, cause you to belittle the gifts of Allah the Exalted that you possess, and cause great regret to follow you because of the vain hopes and illusions you had about yourself. (i)

Likewise, Imam ʿAlī (peace be upon him) likens far-fetched hopes to a mirage which deceives a thirsty person and draws him towards itself, but in the end this person returns disappointed from it whilst still thirsty and longing for his thirst to be quenched. In a short but very meaningful narration he says:

أَيْنَ يَغُرُّكُمْ سَرَابُ الْآمَالِ

> Till when [where] will the mirage of hopes mislead you. (ii)

3) Having a Polytheistic Outlook in Tadbīr

Very often, people who do *tadbīr* of their material and spiritual affairs are practically afflicted with self-conceit and are fascinated with

---

i. al-Kulaynī, al-Kāfī, 5:85, narration 7

ii. al-Āmudī, Fihrist-i Mawḍūʿī-yi Ghurar al-Ḥikam, chapter on *amal*

themselves. This is the case even though in theory they possess a firm monotheistic belief that their entire being—from the ontological and legislative perspective—is subject to Divine *tadbīr*. Despite this, they practically see themselves to be independent in their *tadbīr,* and they consider the coordination of their affairs to be in their own hands. They attribute their knowledge, thoughts and decisions to themselves! This is the biggest calamity that afflicts those who do *tadbīr* and prevents them from material and spiritual progress. As Imam ʿAlī (peace be upon him) says:

الْعُجْبُ يَمْنَعُ الازْدِيَاد

Self-conceit prevents progress. (i)

الْإِعْجَابُ ضِدُّ الصَّوَابِ وَ آفَةُ الْأَلْبَاب

Being self-conceited is contrary to that which is right and is the bane of the intellects. (ii)

Such an outlook that is tainted with polytheism is a great impediment to man's felicity, for it distances him from the realities of the world. That is because in reality, it is Allah the Immaculate who has willed that man should traverse the path of salvation by means of his own tadbīr. Therefore, man's resolve is subservient and vertical in nature to Allah's resolve, not independent of it and horizontal in nature. Furthermore, all the cognitive faculties and other factors required by man for tadbīr and management are from Allah. They are from Him and they also subsist due to Him. Man does not have any kind of independence in any of the stages of decision-making. Of course, this does not mean predestination, for man can still make decisions and exert his own will and choice. However, he is not independent in tadbīr and in his resolve. This understanding is one of the stages of Tawhīd of Divine Acts.

To save a person from being fascinated with himself and to show him that he lacks independence in *tadbīr*, sometimes Allah the Exalted causes certain circumstances to occur. He causes man's planning to fall

---

i. Ibid., chapter on *ʿujb*

ii. Ibid.

apart; man's plans are not implemented in the manner foreseen by him! Imam ʿAlī (peace be upon him) says in this regard:

تَذِلُّ الْأُمُورُ لِلْمَقَادِيرِ حَتَّى يَكُونَ الْحَتْفُ فِي التَّدْبِيرِ

The affairs are subservient to [Divine] ordainments to the extent that one's death can lie in their *tadbīr*.(i) (ii)

إِذَا حَلَّتِ الْمَقَادِيرُ بَطَلَتِ التَّدَابِير

When [Divine] ordainments descend, the *tadābīr* [plural of *tadbīr*] are nullified.(iii)

Imam al-Ḥusayn (peace be upon him) in the supplication of ʿArafah—which is replete with gnosis—describes the wisdom behind such changes in this manner:

إِلَهِي عَلِمْتُ بِاخْتِلَافِ الْآثَارِ وَ تَنَقُّلَاتِ الْأَطْوَارِ أَنَّ مُرَادَكَ مِنِّي أَنْ تَتَعَرَّفَ إِلَيَّ فِي كُلِّ شَيْءٍ

O my God! From the [incessant] changing of effects and shifting of states, I came to know that Your wish from me is that in everything, You present Yourself to me.(iv)

Imam ʿAlī (peace be upon him) has also mentioned that these transformations and changes are the cause of recognizing Allah the Exalted. He says:

عَرَفْتُ اللَّهَ سُبْحَانَهُ بِفَسْخِ الْعَزَائِمِ وَ حَلِّ الْعُقُودِ وَ نَقْضِ الْهِمَمِ

I recognized Allah the Immaculate through the failure of resolutions, the resolving of entanglements and the destruction of ambitions.(v)

---

i. Perhaps this blessed narration is saying although man does *tadbīr* for a period of time hoping and assuming that he will remain alive, the Divine ordainment is that he will pass away.

ii. al-Āmudī, Fihrist-i Mawḍūʿī-yi Ghurar al-Ḥikam, chapter on *taqdīr*

iii. Ibid.

iv. Ibn Ṭāwūs, Iqbāl al-Aʿmāl, 348

v. al-Radī, Nahj al-Balāghah, saying 250; Majlisī, Bihār al-Anwār, 5:197 and 58:40

In conclusion, Islam's monotheistic outlook dictates that man utilize all the abilities that Allah has granted him for the *tadbīr* of his affairs in this world and the Hereafter. Also, he should do *tadbīr* of his affairs based on realities and not imaginations and fantasy. However: Firstly, he should not rely on his *tadbīr* and have confidence in it, rather he should put his trust and confidence in Allah. As the Noble Qur'ān has said:

فَإِذَا عَزَمْتَ فَتَوَكَّلْ عَلَى اللَّهِ

And once you are resolved, put your trust in Allah.
(3:159)

Secondly, he should consider all his *tadbīr* to be from Allah and subsisting due to Him. He should not imagine that he is independent in *tadbīr*.

The Levels of Man's Tadbīr

Considering what was mentioned so far, it should be clear that the manner of man's *tadbīr* of himself, differs in accordance with his level of servitude. The most important of these levels are:

1) Tadbīr Tainted with Polytheism

There are some who have the correct foundations of faith, they recognize that they themselves and the world are subject to Allah's ontological *tadbīr.* Despite this, due to weak perception or feeble resolve, they are afflicted with a type of practical polytheism. In a general sense, this has two types:

A) *Tadbīr* That Neglects Allah's Commands

Allah the Exalted has done *tadbīr* for man prior to his creation; He has arranged a complete path and method for man to reach the lofty goal of his creation and placed it at his disposal. Sometimes however, due to the rebellion of his selfish desires, man exits the domain of being subject to Divine *tadbīr* and laws. During his own decision-making and *tadbīr*, he enters the abyss of the *tadbīr* of selfish desires and Satan, which is a type of practical polytheism. Imam al-Bāqir (peace be upon

---

and 83:189 and...

him) explains the noble verse, "And most of them do not believe in Allah without ascribing partners to Him" (i) in the following manner:

> شِرْكُ طَاعَةٍ لَيْسَ بِشِرْكِ عِبَادَةٍ وَ الْمَعَاصِي الَّتِي يَرْتَكِبُونَ فَهِيَ شِرْكُ طَاعَةٍ أَطَاعُوا فِيهَا الشَّيْطَانَ فَأَشْرَكُوا بِاللَّهِ فِي الطَّاعَةِ لِغَيْرِهِ
>
> [The verse is about] polytheism in obedience and not polytheism in worship. The sins which people commit is polytheism in obedience, whereby they obey Satan and hence ascribe partners to Allah by obeying other than Him. (ii)

The same holds true for man's *tadbīr* with respect to the attributes of his soul. If he does not follow the praiseworthy traits that Allah and His *awliyā'* (peace be upon them) have outlined for him—in his psychological and moral responses—then he is headed towards the weakening of his faith or even losing it altogether. This again is a type of practical polytheism, for example, harbouring the trait of jealousy. (iii)

B) Tadbīr That is Heedless of Allah's Influence

Despite observing the previous level, it is possible man is still afflicted with a type of practical polytheism. This is because polytheism has different levels (just as faith has different levels). This occurs when a person, in the *tadbīr* of his affairs, only pays attention to the causes and effects of this world. He is heedless of having trust in Allah during his affairs, nor does he pay attention to His influence over the affairs of this world. Unfortunately, most of the believers are entangled in this type of polytheism. Thus, the Noble Qur'ān in numerous places—through admonition as well as intellectual proofs—has warned man of such an outlook that is tainted with polytheism. It reminds man of the instances where his planning fails, so that he awakens and pushes aside this heedlessness. For example, Imam al-Bāqir (peace be upon

---

i. (12:106)

ii. Majlisī, Bihār al-Anwār, 72:99, narration 26

iii. al-Kulaynī, al-Kāfī, 8:8, narration 1

him) explained the aforementioned verse [i] as also referring to a person who takes an oath in the name of other than Allah, [ii] while imagining that this oath is going to improve his situation. Likewise, Imam al-Ṣādiq (peace be upon him) considered the belief that the movement of celestial spheres independently cause the coming of rain to be an instance of this verse. [iii] Also, another instance is the statement of a person who says, "were it not for such and such a person I would have been destroyed", or "were it not for that person I would not have obtained a certain benefit", or "if it were not for that person my family would have been destroyed." [iv] In these situations, such a person has considered something other than Allah to be effective in directing the affairs of the world and his life.

2) Tadbīr with Attention to Belief in Tawḥīd

After acquiring the correct *tawḥīdī* (monotheistic) belief, if man wants to reach the desired result and derive existential and spiritual benefits from this belief, then he must ensure the *tadbīr* of his practical life is based on this *tawḥīdī* outlook. This means that he first ensures his actions and spiritual reactions are in accordance to the various Divine commands, and secondly that he is attentive of Allah's influence in directing the material and spiritual affairs of himself and others. In this manner his life becomes a life of faith.

Of course, this attentiveness is normally a mental and intellectual awareness—there is no escaping this state—but gradually this belief penetrates the heart and man's attention turns into a spiritual state and an attention of the heart. Imam al-Ṣādiq (peace be upon him) says in this regard:

لَا تَدَعْ طَلَبَ الرِّزْقِ مِنْ حِلِّهِ، فَإِنَّهُ أَعْوَنُ لَكَ عَلَى دِينِكَ، وَ
اعْقِلْ رَاحِلَتَكَ وَ تَوَكَّلْ

---

i. (12:106)

ii. Majlisī, Biḥār al-Anwār, 72:98, narration 21

iii. al-Kulaynī, al-Kāfī, 8:99, narration 23

iv. Ibid., 8:99, narration 37

> Do not forsake seeking sustenance through permissible ways. For indeed it will help you more in [protecting] your religion. Tie the straps of your steed [horse] and put your trust in Allah. (i)

This means that the process of *tadbīr* must be based on following the religion, and it must be accompanied by trust in Allah so that it protects and strengthens one's religion. Likewise, such *tadbīr* when void of reliance and confidence in Allah the Exalted, is itself remoteness from Him and entanglement in the trap of Satan. As the Messenger of Allah (peace and blessings be upon him and his family) says:

لَا تَتَّكِلْ إِلَى غَيْرِ اللَّهِ فَيَكِلَكَ اللَّه

> Do not rely on other than Allah, for Allah will entrust you to him. (ii)

Similarly, Imam ʿAlī (peace be upon him) says:

إِيَّاكَ وَ الثِّقَةَ بِنَفْسِكَ فَإِنَّ ذَلِكَ مِنْ أَكْبَرِ مَصَايِدِ الشَّيْطَان

> Refrain from relying on your own self. For certainly that is one of the biggest traps of Satan. (iii)

It can be understood from the collection of these statements, that the believer's *tadbīr* must be based on implementing the commands of the sacred *sharīʿah* along with attention to Allah's influence in the management of his affairs. If either of these elements are missing, his activities—in terms of faith—are flawed and afflicted with practical polytheism.

Missing the second element is to have confidence in oneself. This means to consider oneself independent in actions, activities and achieving results. On the contrary, being attentive of Allah's *tadbīr* means that man does not consider himself an independent agent in achieving the results of his activities. He sees himself and all the dimensions of his existence as merely preparing the ground for obtaining results. It is due

---

i. al-Ṭūsī, al-Amālī, 193, narration 326

ii. Nūrī, Mustadrak al-Wasāʾil, 11:217, narration 12790

iii. al-Āmudī, Ghurar al-Hikam, narration 2678

to this that we have been commanded to start all work by saying and paying attention to the meaning of "*bismillāh al-raḥmān al-raḥīm.*" Similarly, and at the end of the work, when the result is achieved, one should say "*al-ḥamdu lillāh rabb al-ʿālamīn,*" and pay attention to and believe in its meaning, praising Allah for the accomplishment of this matter and considering Him worthy of absolute perfection.

Therefore, this stage is the first step towards reaching true servitude and utilizing Divine *tadbīr* for oneself. This is when man, in the words Imam al-Ṣādiq (peace be upon him), does not have any *tadbīr* for himself:

وَ لَا يُدَبِّرُ الْعَبْدُ لِنَفْسِهِ تَدْبِيراً

And the servant does not direct (do *tadbīr* of) his own affairs.

3) Tadbīr While Witnessing Tawḥīd in Divine Acts

Through the following means the veils of darkness are removed from the visage of the wayfarer's heart and his heart becomes enlightened with the light of faith. These means are: continuously obeying the commands of Allah and His *awliyāʾ* (peace be upon them) in the different dimensions of life, adopting virtuous traits in social interactions, having trust in Allah and seeking assistance from His *awliyāʾ* (peace be upon them). When this is done, gradually the realities of faith are manifested to the wayfarer, and with the reality of his existence he perceives that he is not independent in any of his activities, faculties and abilities. As a result, he sees the effects of the entities of this world and all its events to be subsisting due to Allah the Exalted, including his own *tadbīr* of his affairs. In reality, he sees Allah the Immaculate to be the one performing the *tadbīr* of his affairs, for he has only undertaken this *tadbīr* by means of the resolve and abilities that Allah granted him. Just as how Allah says to the Noblest Messenger (peace and blessings be upon him and his family) on the night of *miʿrāj*, in praise of the people of *zuhd* (abstinence):

قَدْ أُعْطُوا الْمَجْهُودَ مِنْ أَنْفُسِهِمْ لَا مِنْ خَوْفِ نَارٍ، وَ لَا مِنْ شَوْقٍ إِلَى الجَنَّةِ [شَوْقِ جَنَّةٍ] وَ لَكِنْ يَنْظُرُونَ فِي مَلَكُوتِ السَّمَاوَاتِ وَ الْأَرْضِ، كَأَنَّمَا يَنْظُرُونَ إِلَى مَنْ فَوْقَهَا، فَيَعْلَمُونَ أَنَّ اللَّهَ سُبْحَانَهُ أَهْلٌ لِلْعِبَادَةِ

> They take much efforts and struggle to the extent of their ability [performing acts of obedience in different spheres of their lives], not out of fear of the Hellfire or eagerness for the Garden, but because they have looked at the *malakūt* of the Heavens and the Earth, just as how they look at the One who is much loftier than the Heavens and the Earth, and they have recognized that Allah the Immaculate is worthy of worship. [i]

The vision mentioned in this narration is the same witnessing of the *malakūt* through the heart, whereby man witnesses Allah's *tadbīr* of his affairs.

Allah the Exalted says to His Messenger (peace and blessings be upon him and his family):

إِنَّهُ لَيَتَقَرَّبُ إِلَيَّ بِالنَّافِلَةِ حَتَّى أُحِبَّهُ فَإِذَا أَحْبَبْتُهُ كُنْتُ سَمْعَهُ الَّذِي يَسْمَعُ بِهِ وَ بَصَرَهُ الَّذِي يُبْصِرُ بِهِ وَ لِسَانَهُ الَّذِي يَنْطِقُ بِهِ وَ يَدَهُ الَّتِي يَبْطِشُ بِهَا

> Indeed, a servant [continuously] seeks my proximity through [performing] *nāfilah* (supererogatory) deeds until I love him. Then when I love him, I become his ears through which he hears, his eyes through which he sees, his tongue through which he speaks and his hand through which he grasps [perform actions]. [ii]

The state of such a wayfarer cries out, saying:

---

i. Kāshānī, al-Wāfī, 3:40, (part 2 of volume 3)

ii. al-Kulaynī, al-Kāfī, 2:352, narrations 7 and 8

> إِلَهِي حُكْمُكَ النَّافِذُ وَ مَشِيَّتُكَ الْقَاهِرَةُ لَمْ يَتْرُكَا لِذِي مَقَالٍ مَقَالًا وَ لَا لِذِي حَالٍ حَالًا إِلَهِي كَمْ مِنْ طَاعَةٍ بَنَيْتُهَا وَ حَالَةٍ شَيَّدْتُهَا هَدَمَ اعْتِمَادِي عَلَيْهَا عَدْلُكَ بَلْ أَقَالَنِي مِنْهَا فَضْلُكَ ... إِلَهِي كَيْفَ أَعْزِمُ وَ أَنْتَ الْقَاهِرُ وَ كَيْفَ لَا أَعْزِمُ وَ أَنْتَ الْآمِر
>
> O my God! Your binding command and overpowering wish has not left anything to say for one who speaks and has not left any state for one who possesses states. O my God! How many acts of obedience did I produce and how many states did I firmly establish, but Your justice demolished my reliance upon them. Rather Your favour delivered me from them ... O my God! How can I resolve while You are Dominant [over me] and how can I not resolve while You have commanded [to do so]? [i]

This means that such a person is attentive to all the outward affairs according to which Allah has created the world, and he acts according to His legislative commands. In addition to that—by readying the required preliminaries and conditions—he witnesses that all his actions are subject to the *tadbīr* of Allah the Exalted. He sees Allah's *tadbīr* to be dominant over the *tadbīr* of all created entities. This level is the second stage wherein the servant does not perform *tadbīr* of his own affairs; in other words, he does not see any *tadbīr* from himself.

4) Tadbīr Accompanied with Witnessing the Tawhīd of Divine Names and Attributes

In the previous level, the *tawḥīd* of Divine Acts was manifested for the wayfarer. He saw all general and specific *tadbīr* to be completely dependent on Allah the Exalted, and he arranged his practical life on this basis. After this stage, the wayfarer acquires the spiritual readiness for Allah to reveal a higher and deeper level of His Oneness for him. At this new level, He is manifested with His Names and Attributes—that constitute the basis of His actions. That is because, *tadbīr* of affairs is

i. Ibn Tāwūs, Iqbāl al-Aʿmāl, 348

dependent on knowledge and power. As Allah the Exalted says:

> اللَّهُ الَّذِي خَلَقَ سَبْعَ سَمَاوَاتٍ وَمِنَ الْأَرْضِ مِثْلَهُنَّ يَتَنَزَّلُ الْأَمْرُ بَيْنَهُنَّ لِتَعْلَمُوا أَنَّ اللَّهَ عَلَىٰ كُلِّ شَيْءٍ قَدِيرٌ وَأَنَّ اللَّهَ قَدْ أَحَاطَ بِكُلِّ شَيْءٍ عِلْمًا
>
> It is Allah who has created seven heavens, and of the Earth [a number] like them. The command [of Allah] gradually descends through them, that you may know that Allah has power over all things, and that Allah comprehends all things in knowledge. (65:12)

This verse indicates the tremendous importance of knowing the absolute power and Encompassing knowledge of Allah (Majestic is His Greatness). To the extent that acquiring such knowledge has been considered the final goal of creating and directing the affairs of the Heavens, the Earth and all beings. However, this knowledge is of two types: conceptual knowledge which comprises of mental concepts (*taṣawwur*) and judgments (*taṣdīq*), and presential knowledge whereby that reality is witnessed and perceived with the heart and one's entire being. For example, everybody witnesses and presentially knows about their own existence, with their entire being.

Of course, the level of presential knowledge cannot be compared to that of conceptual knowledge and therefore it has arduous conditions before the veils of darkness and some of the veils of light (paying attention to and seeing one's actions and *tadbīr*) can be lifted and the visage of the wayfarer's heart can acquire a special illumination. After this point, to the extent of his capacity, the wayfarer first witnesses the attributes of Divine Knowledge and Power themselves, and then he witnesses them while also paying attention to the Sacred Divine Essence. This essence—when payed attention to while witnessing the specific attribute at hand—is known as a 'name' (*ism*). However, the words 'Knowledgeable' and 'Powerful' themselves are the names of this reality.[i] Also—because Divine Knowledge is in fact the very realities

i. This precise and deep discussion illustrates certain states of the wayfarer towards

of this world—the realities of matters and the relationship between things are now manifested for the wayfarer whilst doing *tadbīr*. He understands or presentially knows that he does not possess knowledge and *maʿrifah* from himself and everything that he witnesses is a manifestation of the infinite knowledge of Allah. That is because, in this state a transformation occurs in his cognitive faculties and he is linked to the source of Divine grace. Just as how Allah the Exalted, after granting numerous favours to His lovers and those who act to achieve His pleasure, says regarding them:

لَأَسْتَغْرِقَنَّ عَقْلَهُ بِمَعْرِفَتِي وَ لَأَقُومَنَّ لَهُ مَقَامَ عَقْلِهِ

> Indeed, I will submerge his intellect in my *maʿrifah* and certainly I will put myself in the place of his intellect.(i)

نکهت جانبخش دارد خاک کوی گلرخان

عارفان، ز آنجا مشام عقل مشکین کرده اند

> The dust of the Beloved's alleyway has an invigorating fragrance, The ʿurafā have inhaled that musk with the nose of their intellect.(ii) (iii)

Consequently, this type of *tadbīr* is the highest level of Divine *tadbīr* for the servant that he can possibly reach whereat this reality is unveiled for him, just as Imam al-Ṣādiq (peace be upon him) explained

---

Allah. Initially he witnesses the Divine attributes without witnessing their relationship to Allah. This is known as *tawḥīd-i ṣifāt*. Of course, with his intellect he recognizes that these attributes belong to Allah, but he has not yet witnessed this with his being. Later he reaches a stage wherein he witnesses this connection of the attribute to the Divine Essence, and this is known as *tawḥīd-i asmāʾ*. The word 'name' (*ism*) is used in two manners in this text. For more information about these two usages, refer to *Tafsīr al-Mīzān*, under the first verse (the *basmalah*) of the first chapter of the Noble Qurʾān.

i. Kāshānī, al-Wāfī, 3:40, Bāb Mawāʿiz Allāh Subhānahu

ii. That is, they have satisfied their intellect and made it content with that pure musk.

iii. Shirāzī, Divān-i Hāfiz (Tashīh-i Qudsī), ghazal 261

to ʿUnwān al-Baṣrī.[i] This is that same 'true knowledge' which he was seeking, that knowledge of the Ahl al-Bayt (peace be upon him) which manifests itself through this lofty level of servitude and which Imam al-Ḥusayn (peace be upon him) requests from Allah the Exalted in the supplication of ʿArafah:

> إِلَهِي أَقِمْنِي [أَغْنِنِي] بِتَدْبِيرِكَ لِي عَنْ تَدْبِيرِي وَ اخْتِيَارِكَ [بِاخْتِيَارِكَ] لِي عَنِ اخْتِيَارِي
>
> O my God! Make me free of want [or establish me] by means of your *tadbīr* instead of my *tadbīr*, and by your choosing instead of my choosing.[ii]

Undoubtedly, this statement does not mean abandoning *tadbīr* of one's affairs and ceasing to use the cognitive and physical faculties in different affairs of his life. Rather what is meant is making these affairs subservient to the Divine *tadbīr* with attention and while witnessing this reality that Allah through His encompassing knowledge and infinite power is directing and doing *tadbīr* of him by means of man and other entities. Of course, the witnessing in this level and the previous level is through the heart and one's entire existence, and it is an instantaneous matter. However, even under normal circumstances, its effects are manifested in man's perception and conduct; this perception and conduct takes on a *tawḥīdī* nature. In this manner, the servant becomes content with everything that occurs for him from the affairs of this world, the Hereafter and his soul.

The Link between Tadbīr and Calamities

Man cannot escape being afflicted by calamities, deficiencies, pain and suffering in this world. That is because, conflict and limitations are inherent characteristics of this world, and they result in the occurrence of such events. It is this very fact that is the cause of Divine tests and

---

i. When the Noble Imam (peace be upon him) said, "And the servant does not direct (do *tadbīr* of) his own affairs."

ii. Ibn Ṭāwūs, Iqbāl al-Aʿmāl, 349

tribulations for the servants. As the Noble Qur'ān says:

وَلَنَبْلُوَنَّكُم بِشَيْءٍ مِّنَ الْخَوْفِ وَالْجُوعِ وَنَقْصٍ مِّنَ الْأَمْوَالِ وَالْأَنفُسِ وَالثَّمَرَاتِ ۗ وَبَشِّرِ الصَّابِرِينَ الَّذِينَ إِذَا أَصَابَتْهُم مُّصِيبَةٌ قَالُوا إِنَّا لِلَّهِ وَإِنَّا إِلَيْهِ رَاجِعُونَ

> Be sure we shall test you with something of [for example] fear and hunger, some loss in goods or lives or the fruits [of your toil] but give glad tidings to those who patiently persevere. [Those are the ones] who say, when afflicted with calamity, "To Allah We belong, and to Him is our return." (2:155-156)

According to an overall division, the calamities that befall man are of two types:

1) Calamities Resulting from Man's Actions

Man's good and evil deeds have a significant effect on his being, on those around him and even on the entire world of existence. Much of the evil, problems and calamities that afflict man are the outcome of his unbecoming actions. The Noble Qur'ān has said in this regard:

ظَهَرَ الْفَسَادُ فِي الْبَرِّ وَالْبَحْرِ بِمَا كَسَبَتْ أَيْدِي النَّاسِ لِيُذِيقَهُم بَعْضَ الَّذِي عَمِلُوا لَعَلَّهُمْ يَرْجِعُونَ

> Corruption has appeared in the land and sea because of the doings of the people's hands, that He may make them taste [the recompense of] something of what they have done, so that they may come back. (30:41)

وَمَا أَصَابَكُم مِّن مُّصِيبَةٍ فَبِمَا كَسَبَتْ أَيْدِيكُمْ وَيَعْفُو عَن كَثِيرٍ

> Whatever [type of] affliction that may visit you is because of what your hands have earned, and He excuses many [an offense of yours]. (42:30)

In view of these two verses, firstly, calamities such as illnesses, bankruptcy, disputes with other people, are sometimes the result of a person's evil deeds.

Secondly, the appearance of these calamities is a favour from Allah for man so that he takes admonition, repents, returns towards the Truth, and follows the religion. It is in this that his salvation lies.

Thirdly, Allah's kindness entails that He does not cause the effects of all sins to materialize. If this were not the case, as is said in another verse:

وَلَوْ يُؤَاخِذُ اللَّهُ النَّاسَ بِظُلْمِهِم مَّا تَرَكَ عَلَيْهَا مِن دَابَّةٍ

Were Allah to take mankind to task [and punish them] for their wrongdoing, He would not leave any living being upon it [the Earth]. (16:61)

Paying attention to these verses and implementing the solutions that were mentioned, makes enduring difficulties easy when a person is beset by them. That is because man realizes that he is subject to Allah the Exalted's *tadbīr*. Even though initially he had not placed himself under Allah's specific *tadbīr* by following His commands, but now to deliver himself from affliction in this world—as well as possible affliction in the Hereafter—he must take the following course of action. He should repent and be sorry for his evil deeds and abominable traits, and firmly resolve to follow the Divine commands and then act according to this resolution. In this manner, at the very least he will be spared from calamities and entanglements in the Hereafter.

2) Calamities that are the Divine Precedent in the World

Based on His knowledge and wisdom, Allah (the Provider of abundance and the Sublime) causes calamities to occur in this world that may not have any relation to man's outward conduct. These types of calamities also have numerous constructive dimensions; reference to this has been made in some verses:

مَا أَصَابَ مِن مُّصِيبَةٍ فِي الْأَرْضِ وَلَا فِي أَنفُسِكُمْ إِلَّا فِي كِتَابٍ مِّن قَبْلِ أَن نَّبْرَأَهَا ۚ إِنَّ ذَٰلِكَ عَلَى اللَّهِ يَسِيرٌ لِّكَيْلَا تَأْسَوْا عَلَىٰ مَا فَاتَكُمْ وَلَا تَفْرَحُوا بِمَا آتَاكُمْ ۗ وَاللَّهُ لَا يُحِبُّ كُلَّ مُخْتَالٍ فَخُورٍ

No affliction visits the land or yourselves, but it is in a Book before We bring it about – that is indeed easy for Allah – so

> that you may not grieve for what escapes you, nor boast for what comes your way, and Allah does not like any swaggering braggart. (57:23-24)
>
> مَا أَصَابَ مِن مُّصِيبَةٍ إِلَّا بِإِذْنِ اللَّهِ ۗ وَمَن يُؤْمِن بِاللَّهِ يَهْدِ قَلْبَهُ ۚ وَاللَّهُ بِكُلِّ شَيْءٍ عَلِيمٌ
>
> No affliction visits [anyone] except by Allah's leave. Whoever has faith in Allah, He guides his heart, and Allah has knowledge of all things. (64:11)

It can also be extracted from these two verses that man's attention to the causes and effects of this world has the following effect: it creates heedlessness of the unseen world as well as the connection between affairs of this world and that world. This in turn leads to moral vices like boasting and self-conceit, even if a person is not involved in performing evil actions. Thus, the appearance of calamities is intended to awaken man to the unseen world, so that he no longer considers what he has obtained to be independent of Allah's bestowal. Moreover, calamities are intended to rectify vices such as boasting and relying on one's self. If man is deprived of acquiring a certain blessing, he should understand that there is some wisdom at play and that it is not in his interest. In this manner the servant comprehends that these calamities are subject to Divine *tadbīr* and hence enduring them becomes easy for him, since they exist to take him to lofty understandings and train him.

Ordinary people are afflicted with both types of these calamities. But those who have entered the domain of *tawḥīd* and have been delivered from the calamities caused by evil actions, are only afflicted with the second type of calamities. In their encounter with these calamities, such individuals derive benefit to train themselves; they witness the connection of these calamities to Allah. As a result, they are never affected or pained by them.

Imam ʿAlī (peace be upon him) describes the difficult period of *jihād* and battle against the enemies in this manner:

فَلَقَدْ كُنَّا مَعَ رَسُولِ اللَّهِ ص وَ إِنَ الْقَتْلَ لَيَدُورُ عَلَى الْآبَاءِ وَ الْأَبْنَاءِ وَ الْإِخْوَانِ وَ الْقَرَابَاتِ فَمَا نَزْدَادُ عَلَى كُلِّ مُصِيبَةٍ وَ شِدَّةٍ إِلَّا إِيمَاناً وَ مُضِيّاً عَلَى الْحَقِّ وَ تَسْلِيماً لِلْأَمْرِ وَ صَبْراً عَلَى مَضَضِ الْجِرَاحِ

> Indeed, we would be alongside the Messenger of Allah (peace and blessings be upon him and his family) while death would envelop our fathers, children, brothers and kinsmen [in the battlefield]. Yet, with the coming of every calamity and hardship we would only increase in faith, and in our determination to traverse the path of truth, to submit to Divine commands and to remain patient over the burning pain of the wounds. (i)

Men who take steps on the path of *tawḥīd* and have been liberated from the attachments of their self and the world, and who have understood the nature of the relationship between events in this world and the Divine Will, such people are not just free from agony as a result of calamities, rather they will have a smile of contentment with the Beloved on their faces. Just as the face of Imam al-Ḥusayn (peace be upon him) shined with more and more intensity at the peak of difficulties during the last moments of his life, and his fondness and faith in Allah the Exalted increased. (ii) In the words of Shaykh Bahāʾī (may Allah be pleased with him):

بی وفا نگار من، می کند به کار من

خنده های زیر لب، عشوه های پنهانی

My disloyal Beloved responds to my acts [my expressions of love],
With a silent giggle and hidden flirting.

ما سیه گلیمان را جز بلا نمی شاید

i. al-Radī, Nahj al-Balāghah, sermon 122

ii. Majlisī, Biḥār al-Anwār, 44:297

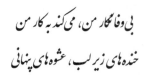

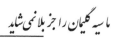

بر دل بهائی نه هر بلاکه بتوانی

Us who are clothed in black robes [of unworthiness] deserve naught but affliction,
Place every affliction that You can on the heart of Bahāʾī! (i)

It is on this basis that Imam al-Ṣādiq (peace be upon him), while describing true servitude, says:

وَ إِذَا فَوَّضَ الْعَبْدُ تَدْبِيرَ نَفْسِهِ عَلَى مُدَبِّرِهِ هَانَ عَلَيْهِ مَصَائِبُ الدُّنْيَا

And when the servant entrusts direction of his affairs to its [true] director, the afflictions of this world become easy for him.

The important point to note is that Imam al-Ṣādiq (peace be upon him) only mentioned worldly afflictions. That is because, afflictions of the Hereafter shall never reach Allah's faithful servants who enter the Day of Resurrection with purity of spirit and action. Rather, in their supplications they beseech Allah like this:

اللَّهُم ... وَ لَا تَجْعَلْ مُصِيبَتَنَا فِي دِينِنَا وَ لَا تَجْعَلِ الدُّنْيَا أَكْبَرَ هَمِّنَا وَ لَا مَبْلَغَ عِلْمِنَا

O Allah! ... Do not place our calamity to be in our religion, and do not make the world our greatest preoccupation [of our heart] nor the ultimate reach of our knowledge. (ii)

The actions of such individuals are not moving on a course that would lead to calamities in the Hereafter. Moreover, Allah has promised them that these will not reach them. However, they are still uncertain of themselves, will the calamities afflict them or not? Therefore, they constantly implore Allah, with humility and lamenting, to keep them aloof from the afflictions of the Hereafter.

The Third Manifestation of Servitude – A

---

i. Shaykh Bahāʾī.

ii. Ibn Ṭāwūs, Iqbāl al-Aʿmāl, 700

Transformation in Man's Conduct

Giving Importance to Obedience

The first thing that results from man's thoughts and beliefs and occurs so that he may fulfil his needs, are the activities carried out by his external faculties. These are termed as man's *ʿamal*. During a period of man's life in this world, (i) these activities were mostly performed instinctively, intended to satisfy his material needs. However, when a person reaches a clear perception and comprehension regarding his existential rank, he acquires certain thoughts and insights about his existential relationship—or the lack thereof—with the Unseen World. As a result, he naturally organizes his actions based on these. The more carefully man pays attention to this relationship, the more accurate insights he develops and the more his faith in the Unseen World takes shape. Therefore, after believing that he is a servant of Allah the Exalted, man tries to make all his affairs be subject to the *tadbīr* of his Master. It is for this reason that the first and foremost level of a believing servant's *tadbīr*, is obedience to Allah the Exalted to the extent of performing the Divine obligations and forsaking the prohibited actions. Just as how Imam al-Ṣādiq (peace be upon him) explains the third manifestation of servitude to ʿUnwān al-Baṣrī in this manner:

وَ جُمْلَةُ اشْتِغَالِهِ فِيمَا أَمَرَهُ تَعَالَى بِهِ وَ نَهَاهُ عَنْهُ

> And his complete occupation is in what Allah the Exalted has commanded him to do and what He has prohibited him from.
>
> It is also for this reason that the Messenger of Allah (peace and blessings be upon him and his family) says:

اعْمَلْ بِفَرَائِضِ اللَّهِ تَكُنْ أَتْقَى النَّاسِ

> Perform the things Allah has ordained and you will be the most pious of the people. (ii)

Likewise, Imam ʿAlī (peace be upon him) says:

---

i. When he was a child.

ii. al-Kulaynī, al-Kāfī, 2:82, narration 4

> إِنَّ اللَّهَ [سُبْحَانَهُ قَدْ] فَرَضَ عَلَى جَوَارِحِكَ كُلِّهَا فَرَائِضَ يَحْتَجُّ بِهَا عَلَيْكَ يَوْمَ الْقِيَامَةِ
>
> Indeed, Allah [the Immaculate] has ordained obligations for all your limbs and He will contend against you through them on the Day of Resurrection.(i)

Imam al-Ḥasan (peace be upon him) also says:

> أَنَّ اللَّهَ عَزَّ وَ جَلَّ بِمَنِّهِ وَ رَحْمَتِهِ لَمَّا فَرَضَ عَلَيْكُمُ الْفَرَائِضَ لَمْ يَفْرِضْ عَلَيْكُمْ لِحَاجَةٍ مِنْهُ إِلَيْهِ بَلْ رَحْمَةً مِنْه إِلَيْكُمْ لَا إِلَهَ إِلَّا هُوَ لِيَمِيزَ الْخَبِيثَ مِنَ الطَّيِّبِ وَ لِيَبْتَلِيَ ما فِي صُدُورِكُمْ وَ لِيُمَحِّصَ ما فِي قُلُوبِكُم
>
> Indeed, Allah the Invincible and Majestic out of His favour and mercy, when He ordained obligations for you, He did not do so because He needs it. Rather, it is a mercy from Him towards you—there is no god except Him—so that He may separate the bad ones from the good and so that He may test what is in your breasts, and that He may purge what is in your hearts.(ii)

Therefore, as said by Imam al-Ṣādiq (peace be upon him), one of the most difficult things that Allah has made obligatory upon people is that they remember Him frequently. Thereafter, he said:

> لَا أَعْنِي سُبْحَانَ اللَّهِ وَ الْحَمْدُ لِلَّهِ وَ لَا إِلَهَ إِلَّا اللَّهُ وَ اللَّهُ أَكْبَرُ وَ إِنْ كَانَ مِنْهُ وَ لَكِنْ ذِكْرَ اللَّهِ عِنْدَ مَا أَحَلَّ وَ حَرَّمَ فَإِنْ كَانَ طَاعَةً عَمِلَ بِهَا وَ إِنْ كَانَ مَعْصِيَةً تَرَكَهَا
>
> I do not mean [saying] *subḥānallāh, al-ḥamdulillāh, lā ilāha illallāh* and *Allāhu akbar*—although they are a part of it [Allah's remembrance], rather to remember Allah in

---

i. al-Radī, Nahj al-Balāghah, saying 382

ii. Majlisī, Biḥār al-Anwār, 23:99, narration 3

that which He has made lawful and prohibited. Hence, if it is an act of obedience he performs it and if it is an act of disobedience then he abandons it.[(i)]

However, obligations are of two types:

1) Worship (*ʿibādāt*): Here having the intention of seeking Allah's proximity is a condition; these constitute a limited number of the servant's actions.

2) Matters that are not worship: These obligations are known as '*wājibāt-i tawaṣṣulī*'. For example, the obligation of enjoining what is right and forbidding what is wrong, rules of financial transactions and family matters. Abandoning forbidden actions is also obligatory and does not require one to have an intention of seeking proximity. However, if a servant abandons forbidden actions or performs the *tawaṣṣulī* obligations with such an intention, then this will have rewards and spiritual effects. Moreover, it prepares the ground for increasing his spiritual inclination towards persevering in obedience and extending the sphere of his obedience by performing *mustaḥabb* actions and abandoning disliked (*makrūh*) actions. When a servant busies himself with this to the extent of his bodily ability and spiritual inclination, all his movements take on a character of servitude and humility in front of Allah the Exalted. He reaches the level that he desires that no *mubāḥ* (permissible) action be performed by him. Rather, he gives the *mubāḥ* action (which is neither *mustaḥabb* nor *makrūh*) a character of servitude and obedience by having a Divine intention, in the same manner that the Commander of Eloquence Imam ʿAlī (peace be upon him) requests Allah—while taking multiple oaths by His name—that He grant him this type of conduct in all his actions:

أَسْأَلُكَ بِحَقِّكَ وَ قُدْسِكَ وَ أَعْظَمِ صِفَاتِكَ وَ أَسْمَائِكَ أَنْ تَجْعَلَ أَوْقَاتِي مِنَ [فِي] اللَّيْلِ وَ النَّهَارِ بِذِكْرِكَ مَعْمُورَةً وَ بِخِدْمَتِكَ مَوْصُولَةً وَ أَعْمَالِي عِنْدَكَ مَقْبُولَةً حَتَّى يَكُونَ أَعْمَالِي و إرادتي [وَ أَوْرَادِي] كُلُّهَا وِرْداً وَاحِداً وَ حَالِي فِي خِدْمَتِكَ سَرْمَدا

---

i. al-Kulaynī, al-Kāfī, 2:80, narration 4

> I ask you by Your right, Your Holiness and the greatest of Your Attributes and Names, that you make my day and night to be filled with Your remembrance and attached to Your service. And [I ask you that] my actions to be acceptable in Your presence, until all my actions, recitals [wishes] become a single litany and my state becomes perpetually in Your service.[(i)]

Specific Effects of Giving Importance to Obedience

One of the effects and blessings of undertaking the path of true servitude of Allah and giving importance to His obedience, is that one's social relationships are rectified. That is because true servants are only after earning the pleasure and satisfaction of their Beloved and the Object of their worship; they position their selfish desires and that of others towards a single direction: seeking Allah's pleasure. Therefore, in their worldly activities and when afflicted with vices such disputing with others and boasting to them, they pay attention to this existential inclination present in them. As a result, they are not tainted by these filthy traits, just as Imam al-Ṣādiq (peace be upon him) said to ʿUnwān al-Baṣrī:

> وَ إِذَا اشْتَغَلَ الْعَبْدُ بِمَا أَمَرَهُ اللَّهُ تَعَالَى وَ نَهَاهُ لَا يَتَفَرَّغُ مِنْهُمَا إِلَى الْمِرَاءِ وَ الْمُبَاهَاةِ مَعَ النَّاسِ
>
> And when the servant busies himself with [observing] Allah's commands and His prohibitions, he does not get free time for disputes with the people and boasting.

Abstaining from Dispute (Mirāʾ) and Boasting (Mubāhāt)

The lexical meaning of the word *mirāʾ* is to argue about a matter that is ambiguous,[(ii)] while *mubāhāt* means to boast and flaunt one's possessions in front of others.[(iii)] The quality of disputing normally

---

i. Ibn Ṭāwūs, Iqbāl al-Aʿmāl, 709

ii. al-Isfahānī, al-Mufradāt, the root word mariya (مري).

iii. Ibid., the root word *fakhara* (فخر).

appears in man's encounter with ignorant people. In such situations, he wants to prevail over them—by any means possible—in discussions and when expressing opinions, and he only considers himself. Boasting on the other hand, comes about in one's encounter with scholars. In a narration, Imam al-Bāqir (peace be upon him) says:

مَـنْ طَلَـبَ الْعِلْـمَ لِيُبَاهِـيَ بِـهِ الْعُلَمَـاءَ أَوْ يُمَـارِيَ بِـهِ السُّـفَهَاءَ أَوْ يَصْـرِفَ بِـهِ وُجُـوهَ النَّـاسِ إِلَيْـهِ فَلْيَتَبَـوَّأْ مَقْعَـدَهُ مِـنَ النَّـارِ

> One who seeks knowledge to boast to the scholars, to dispute with the ignorant, or to attract peoples' attention towards himself, his dwelling place shall be filled by the Fire.[i]

These two traits (disputing and boasting) are amongst the moral vices that man becomes entangled with during the various affairs of life. They have been strongly condemned and cause numerous evil effects on a person's spirit and soul. Because if man's goal and intention in a worldly matter—even an academic matter—is to cause the truth to prevail and to convey it to others, then he must pursue the matter through its specific means and only to a specific extent, thereafter he should leave it aside. For if he continues, then this indicates his ill-intention that has an ill effect on his own soul as well as others'. As the Messenger of Allah (peace and blessings be upon him and his family) says:

أَوْرَعُ النَّاسِ مَنْ تَرَكَ الْمِرَاءَ وَ إِنْ كَانَ مُحِقّا

> The most pious of people is one who abandons disputing even if he is right.[ii]

Imam 'Alī (peace be upon him) also says:

مَنْ ضَنَّ بِعِرْضِهِ فَلْيَدَعِ الْمِرَاء

> Whoever is stingy about his dignity, then let him forsake

i. al-Kulaynī, al-Kāfī, 1:47, narration 6

ii. al-Ṣadūq, al-Amālī, 28, narration 4

disputing. (i)

This means that, disputing causes man to exit the state of piety (*wara'*) and loose dignity. In the words of that same Imam (peace be upon him):

مَنْ صَحَّ يَقِينُهُ زَهِدَ فِي الْمِرَاء

One whose certainty is in order, renounces disputing. (ii)

This means that engaging in dispute destroys man's certainty, especially in matters pertaining to religion. Fayḍ Kashānī (may Allah be pleased with him) also says in this regard:

> One should know that to engage in debate to seek prominence, silence the other party, show off one's merit and honour to the people, and similarly a debate which is performed with the intention of boasting, disputing and drawing people's attention, [such a debate] is the source of all good things that are ugly and detestable near Allah, but are good and praiseworthy near His enemy Satan. The relationship of these traits with internal sins like self-conceit, self-love, ostentation, jealousy, rivalry, self-praise, power-seeking and other such qualities, is like the relationship of drinking alcohol with external sins like adultery, slander, murder and theft. If a person must choose between drinking alcohol and committing other sins, he considers drinking alcohol to be insignificant compare to all the others and commits it. But then in the state of intoxication, this very sin draws him to commit other sins. In this same manner, a person whose temperament is dominated by love of condemning others, overpowering them in debate, seeking power and boasting, these same repulsive habits impel him to gather all the filth in his heart, and all the blameworthy traits are aroused in him. (iii)

In addition to having ominous personal effects, engaging in dispute

---

i. al-Radī, Nahj al-Balāghah, saying 362

ii. al-Āmudī, Ghurar al-Ḥikam, narration 8709

iii. Kāshānī, al-Maḥajjah al-Bayḍā', 1:198

also disrupts man's social relationships. Imam ʿAlī (peace be upon him) says:

إِيَّاكُمْ وَ الْمِرَاءَ وَ الْخُصُومَةَ فَإِنَّهُمَا يُمْرِضَانِ الْقُلُوبَ عَلَى الْإِخْوَانِ وَ يَنْبُتُ عَلَيْهِمَا النِّفَاقُ

Abstain from dispute and hostility. For these two make the hearts sick [with rancour] with respect to the brethren, and cause hypocrisy to grow.(i)

Likewise, Imam al-Hādī (peace be upon him) says:

الْمِرَاءُ يُفْسِدُ الصَّدَاقَةَ الْقَدِيمَةَ وَ يُحَلِّلُ الْعُقْدَةَ الْوَثِيقَةَ وَ أَقَلُّ مَا فِيهِ أَنْ تَكُونَ فِيهِ الْمُغَالَبَةُ وَ الْمُغَالَبَةُ أُسُّ أَسْبَابِ الْقَطِيعَةِ

Disputing causes long-lasting friendships to be undermined, and binding pacts to be violated. The least that is in it is to prevail [over the other party], and prevailing is the chief cause of severing [friendly and family] relationships.(ii)

The Extent and Scope of Disputing

In the Islamic culture, disputing is divided into two types: one performed in the best manner (*al-aḥsan*) and one that is not performed in the best manner (*ghayr al-aḥsan*). Disputing or debating about religious matters in the best manner is a praiseworthy and laudable act such that Allah the Exalted has commanded the Noblest Messenger (peace and blessings be upon him and his family) to academically confront the polytheists using this method:

وَجَادِلْهُم بِالَّتِي هِيَ أَحْسَنُ

And dispute with them in a manner that is best. (16:125)

Similarly, in another verse it advises all Muslims to engage in this type of disputing (*al-jidāl al-aḥsan*) with the People of the Book:

وَلَا تُجَادِلُوا أَهْلَ الْكِتَابِ إِلَّا بِالَّتِي هِيَ أَحْسَنُ

i. al-Kulaynī, al-Kāfī, 2:300, narration 1

ii. al-Daylamī, Aʿlām al-Dīn, 311

> Do not argue with the People of the Book except in a manner which is best. (29:46)

Disputing that is not performed in the best manner means to discuss and argue in an illogical and unacademic manner. This has been reproached by Allah (the Provider of abundance and the Sublime) in numerous verses:

> وَمِنَ النَّاسِ مَن يُجَادِلُ فِي اللَّهِ بِغَيْرِ عِلْمٍ وَيَتَّبِعُ كُلَّ شَيْطَانٍ مَّرِيدٍ
> Among the people are those who dispute about Allah without any knowledge and follow every obstinate Satan. (22:3)

> أَلَمْ تَرَ إِلَى الَّذِينَ يُجَادِلُونَ فِي آيَاتِ اللَّهِ أَنَّىٰ يُصْرَفُونَ
> Have you not regarded those who dispute the signs of Allah, where they are being led away [from the Truth]? (40:69)

In these two verses, Allah has reproached those who dispute about Allah without any intellectual proof, who want to follow the rationale of the obstinate Satan, and those who cast doubts upon and dispute about Allah's signs. That said, the Imams (peace be upon them) would engage in debate—in the best manner—with the enemies and deniers of Allah, the prophets and their heirs. They would also train their companions for this and would encourage those who were strong and knew the techniques of debating against falsehood.

It is narrated that one of the scholars from Damascus came to Imam al-Ṣādiq (peace be upon him) to debate with him about the Shīʿah faith. The Imam said to one of his companions whose name was Yūnus:

> وَدِدْتُ أَنَّكَ يَا يُونُسُ لَوْ كُنْتَ تُحْسِنُ الْكَلَام
> O Yūnus! I wish that you speak a nicely [debate in the best manner].

Yūnus said in astonishment:

> جُعِلْتُ فِدَاكَ إِنِّي سَمِعْتُكَ تَنْهَى عَنِ الْكَلَامِ وَ تَقُولُ وَيْلٌ لِأَصْحَابِ الْكَلَامِ يَقُولُونَ هَذَا يَنْقَادُ وَ هَذَا لَا يَنْقَادُ وَ هَذَا يَنْسَاقُ وَ هَذَا لَا يَنْسَاقُ وَ هَذَا نَعْقِلُهُ وَ هَذَا لَا نَعْقِلُه

May I be your ransom! Indeed, I have heard that you forbid polemical debates and that you have said, "Woe unto the people of debate and dispute! They say this matter can be critiqued and that matter cannot be critiqued. [They say to the opposite party] this is acceptable and that is not acceptable, this matter our intellect accepts and that matter our intellect does not accept."

The Imam (peace be upon him) said in reply:

إِنَّمَا قُلْتُ فَوَيْلٌ لَهُمْ إِنْ تَرَكُوا مَا أَقُولُ وَ ذَهَبُوا إِلَى مَا يُرِيدُونَ

I only said, "Woe unto them" if they forsake what I say [the method of debating that I have taught] and they act in a manner that they themselves wish.

Thereafter, Imam summoned Ḥumrān ibn Aʿyan, Muḥammad ibn al-Ṭayyār, Hishām ibn Sālim and Qays al-Māṣir and they debated with the man from Damascus in the Imam's presence. The last of them was Hishām ibn Ḥakam whose style of debating was particularly encouraged by the Imam. (i)

About al-Ṭayyār the Imam (peace be upon him) said:

رَحِمَهُ اللَّهُ وَ لَقَّاهُ نَضْرَةً وَ سُرُوراً فَقَدْ كَانَ
شَدِيدَ الْخُصُومَةِ عَنَّا أَهْلَ الْبَيْت

May Allah have mercy on him and encounter him with happiness and joy! For indeed he would severely dispute to defend us the Ahl al-Bayt. (ii)

Similarly, Imam Mūsā al-Kāẓim (peace be upon him) advised Muḥammad ibn Ḥakam:

كلم الناس و بين لهم الحق الذي أنت عليه و بين لهم
الضلالة التي هم عليها

Speak to the people, show them the [creed of] truth on which you stand, and make clear to them the error in which

---

i. al-Kulaynī, al-Kāfī, 1:171, narration 4

ii. Majlisī, Bihār al-Anwār, 73:404

they are.[i]

Therefore, engaging in logical debate to establish the truth of the religion and the creed is a desirable thing. However, a dispute that is not in the best manner is absolutely forbidden and blameworthy.

A person came to Imam al-Ḥusayn (peace be upon him) and said:

> اجْلِسْ حَتَّى نَتَنَاظَرَ فِي الدِّينِ فَقَالَ يَا هَذَا أَنَا بَصِيرٌ بِدِينِي مَكْشُوفٌ عَلَيَّ هُدَايَ فَإِنْ كُنْتَ جَاهِلًا بِدِينِكَ فَاذْهَبْ فَاطْلُبْهُ مَا لِي وَ لِلْمُمَارَاةِ وَ إِنَّ الشَّيْطَانَ لَيُوَسْوِسُ لِلرَّجُلِ وَ يُنَاجِيهِ وَ يَقُولُ نَاظِرِ النَّاسَ لِئَلَّا يَظُنُّوا بِكَ الْعَجْزَ وَ الْجَهْلَ ثُمَّ الْمِرَاءُ لَا يَخْلُو مِنْ أَرْبَعَةِ أَوْجُهٍ إِمَّا أَنْ تَتَمَارَى أَنْتَ وَ صَاحِبُكَ فِيمَا تَعْلَمَانِ فَقَدْ تَرَكْتُمَا بِذَلِكَ النَّصِيحَةَ وَ طَلَبْتُمَا الْفَضِيحَةَ وَ أَضَعْتُمَا ذَلِكَ الْعِلْمَ أَوْ تَجْهَلَانِهِ فَأَظْهَرْتُمَا جَهْلًا وَ خَاصَمْتُمَا جَهْلًا وَ إِمَّا تَعْلَمُهُ أَنْتَ فَظَلَمْتَ صَاحِبَكَ بِطَلَبِ عَثْرَتِهِ أَوْ يَعْلَمُهُ صَاحِبُكَ فَتَرَكْتَ حُرْمَتَهُ وَ لَمْ تُنَزِّلْهُ مَنْزِلَتَهُ وَ هَذَا كُلُّهُ مُحَالٌ فَمَنْ أَنْصَفَ وَ قَبِلَ الْحَقَّ وَ تَرَكَ الْمُمَارَاةَ فَقَدْ أَوْثَقَ إِيمَانَهُ
>
> "Sit [with me] so that we debate with each other regarding the religion." The Imam (peace be upon him) said to him in reply, "O person! I am informed of my religion and the guidance is unveiled for me. If you are ignorant about the religion, then go and seek it. What have I to do with disputing?! Indeed, Satan suggests and whispers to man, saying, 'Debate and dispute with people so that they do not imagine you are incapable and ignorant.' So then, disputing is confined to one of these four forms: Either you and your companion dispute over a matter whose reality is known to both of you, then certainly through this action you have forsaken sympathy and concern, sought disgrace and wasted the knowledge; or you both are ignorant of it, then in this

---

i. al-Mufīd, Taṣḥīḥ-i I'tiqādāt al-Imāmiyyah, 68

> case you have disclosed your ignorance and you quarrel with each other out of ignorance; or you know the reality of the matter [and he is ignorant], then in this case you have oppressed your companion by looking for his mistake; or your companion knows the reality of the matter [and you do not], then you have not accorded him respect and you have not preserved his esteem. All of these are impossible [for me]. Therefore, one who is impartial, accepts the truth and abandons dispute, then [such a person] has truly made his faith firm. [i]

In view of these statements, it becomes clear that engaging in debate and discussion about things which are beneficial for someone themself as well as others—be it in matters pertaining to this world or the Hereafter, academic matters or practical—is only truly beneficial if it is conducted in the correct manner with the honest aim of reaching the truth. In this case it is praiseworthy, commendable, and yields desirable results. However, if it is not conducted in the correct manner, or not done honestly to reach the truth, then it is reproachable, it distances man from the truth and reality and has other undesirable effects which were alluded to.

The Disapproval of Boasting to Others

One of the blameworthy traits which usually afflicts man in his worldly relationships is boasting to others about one's possessions. This state leads to a feeling of superiority over others and is normally accompanied with stinginess with respect to one's possessions. It is for this reason that the Noble Qur'ān mentions this reality in several places:

وَاللَّهُ لَا يُحِبُّ كُلَّ مُخْتَالٍ فَخُورٍ الَّذِينَ يَبْخَلُونَ وَيَأْمُرُونَ النَّاسَ بِالْبُخْلِ

> And Allah does not like any swaggering braggart. Those who are [themselves] stingy and bid [other] people to be stingy. (57:23-24)

i. al-Thānī, Muniyah al-Murīd, 171

It introduces this state as one of the characteristics of this worldly life:

اعْلَمُوا أَنَّمَا الْحَيَاةُ الدُّنْيَا لَعِبٌ وَلَهْوٌ وَزِينَةٌ وَتَفَاخُرٌ بَيْنَكُمْ وَتَكَاثُرٌ فِي الْأَمْوَالِ وَالْأَوْلَادِ

> Know that the life of this world is mere diversion and play, glamour and mutual vainglory among you and rivalry for wealth and children. (57:20)

If man is not awake, vigilant, undeceived by these conditions, and if he does not set off towards the desired goal of creation, it is possible that heedlessness will bring about the vice of boasting to others, even boasting over performing spiritual and virtuous acts. However, moving towards the desired goal of creation (attained by establishing correct, logical and lawful relationships with the world and worldly matters) causes a conscious and humble relationship with Allah the Exalted, and prevents such vices from appearing in man. For this reason, as said by Imam ʿAlī (peace be upon him), vainglory and boasting destroys a person.[i] Thus, Imam al-Riḍā (peace be upon him) also says:

إِنَّ أَمِيرَ الْمُؤْمِنِينَ ع عَادَ صَعْصَعَةَ بْنَ صُوحَانَ فِي مَرَضِهِ فَلَمَّا قَامَ مِنْ عِنْدِهِ قَالَ يَا صَعْصَعَةُ لَا تَفْتَخِرَنَّ عَلَى إِخْوَانِكَ بِعِيَادَتِي إِيَّاكَ وَ اتَّقِ اللَّهَ

> Amīr al-Mu'minīn (peace be upon him) visited Ṣaʿṣaʿah ibn Ṣūḥān [who was one of his select companions] during his sickness. When he stood up from near him [to leave], he said, "O Ṣaʿṣaʿah! Do not boast to your brethren about my coming to visit you and be wary of Allah."[ii]

Likewise, Imam ʿAlī (peace be upon him) in another narration says:

مَنْ صَنَعَ شَيْئاً لِلْمُفَاخَرَةِ حَشَرَهُ اللَّهُ يَوْمَ الْقِيَامَةِ أَسْوَد

> One who performs an action to boast to others, Allah will

---

i. al-Sadūq, al-Khisāl, 69, narration 102

ii. Nūrī, Mustadrak al-Wasā'il, 12:90, narration 13599

raise him dark on the Day of Resurrection.[i]

That is because, an action in this manner is devoid of light and reality, and there exists a specific type of unity between the action and the doer. It is due to this that Imam ʿAlī (peace be upon him) says:

لَقَدْ كَانَ رَسُولُ اللَّهِ ص إِذَا ذَكَرَ لِنَفْسِهِ فَضِيلَةً قَالَ وَ لَا فَخْر

Whenever the Messenger of Allah (peace and blessings be upon him and his family) would mention a virtue that he possessed, he would say, "It is nothing to boast about."[ii]

In fact, this noble personality in another narration has said:

الْفَقْرُ فَخْرِي

Neediness and indigence is my pride.[iii]

The Cure for Quarrelling and Boasting

These two traits are amongst the vices that also show themselves in speech; they are examples of banes of the tongue. The best way to cure these vices—as well as other moral vices—is to pay attention to the lofty goal of creation and one's existential rank. This means that:

Firstly, regardless of what man acquires, he is needy and a slave in Allah's presence.

Secondly, he will be separated from that which he acquires and is incapable of preserving it.

Thirdly, that which is associated with Allah will remain for us.

Thus, Imam al-Ṣādiq (peace be upon him) draws our attention to this fundamental matter that someone whose entire preoccupation is obedience of the Sustainer is not distracted by disputing and boasting with others. Therefore, to reach the truth or lead others to it—be it the truth in terms of thoughts or worldly rights—such a person only moves to the extent allowed by the *sharīʿah* and within its bounds. He shuns any movement other than that, regardless of where it may take

i. Majlisī, Bihār al-Anwār, 73:292, narration 20

ii. Ibid., 16:341, narration 33

iii. Ibid., 72:30, narration 26

them. Similarly, when he acquires something, he does not boast about it. Imam ʿAlī (peace be upon him) says:

ضَعْ فَخْرَكَ وَ احْطُطْ كِبْرَكَ وَ اذْكُرْ قَبْرَك

> Put aside your pride, abandon your arrogance and self-conceit, and remember your grave. (i)

In another description he says:

مَا لِابْنِ آدَمَ وَ الْفَخْرِ أَوَّلُهُ نُطْفَةٌ وَ آخِرُهُ جِيفَةٌ وَ لَا يَرْزُقُ نَفْسَهُ وَ لَا يَدْفَعُ حَتْفَه

> What has son of Adam to do with boasting?! His beginning is a drop of sperm and his end is a carcass. He cannot provide for himself [independently] and he cannot repel his death. (ii)

By implementing these solutions that are to do with thoughts, man's faith in the Beginning and the Resurrection becomes stronger, and the potential of being afflicted by moral and practical vices is removed. This is as opposed to other solutions that do not address the root problem; after one is afflicted with spiritual and practical diseases, they suggest a cure which may not fix the problem from its root. (iii) On the other hand, paying attention to one's servitude and Allah the Exalted's Absolute Lordship in all aspects of life causes man's pride to lie in expressing this servitude. All his efforts are in order to obey the Divine commands, just as Imam ʿAlī (peace be upon him) addressing Allah humbly says:

كَفَى بِي فَخْراً أَنْ تَكُونَ لِي رَبّاً أَنْتَ كَمَا أُحِبُّ فَاجْعَلْنِي كَمَا تُحِب

> It is enough of an honour for me that You are my Sustainer.

---

i. al-Radī, Nahj al-Balāghah, saying 398

ii. Ibid., sermon 216

iii. As an example, a prescription given by a psychologist to go on a vacation and forget about the woes of life. This would temporarily help but does not rectify the root issue at hand.

You are as I like, therefore make me to be as You like. (i)

Similarly, Imam al-Ṣādiq (peace be upon him) says:

ثَلَاثٌ هُنَّ فَخْرُ الْمُؤْمِنِ وَ زَيْنُهُ فِي الدُّنْيَا وَ الْآخِرَةِ الصَّلَاةُ فِي آخِرِ اللَّيْلِ وَ يَأْسُهُ مِمَّا فِي أَيْدِي النَّاسِ وَ وَلَايَتُهُ الْإِمَامَ مِنْ آلِ مُحَمَّدٍ

Three things are the source of pride and beauty for the believer in the world and the Hereafter: Prayer in the concluding part of the night, his despair from that which is in people's hands and his *wilāyah* (ii) towards the Imam from the progeny of Muḥammad (peace and blessings be upon him and his family). (iii)

---

i. Majlisī, Bihār al-Anwār, 74:402

ii. *Wilāyah* here refers to a relationship of love and obedience that a servant establishes with a divinely appoint leader.

iii. al-Kulaynī, al-Kāfī, 8:234, narration 311

Chapter Four

Effects of Attaining the Different Dimensions of Servitude

Reaching Taqwā, its Different Levels, and Staying Aloof from the Obstacles on the Path to Perfection

Paying attention to each of the different dimensions of servitude and implementing them yields its own specific result, as was explained in the previous sections. In addition to that, there are effects which arise from all the dimensions of servitude collectively, which Imam al-Ṣādiq (peace be upon him) has mentioned to ʿUnwān al-Baṣrī. Also, there are obstacles on the path to true perfection which the wayfarer must accurately recognize, and with lofty determination, trust in Allah the Exalted, and tawassul to His *awliyā*ʾ (peace be upon them), he must remove them from his path. He should learn the way to remove these obstacles from the teachings of these *awliyā*ʾ (peace be upon them), for there is no path to perfection without obstacles. Man's true progress is achieved after recognizing the necessary conditions and obstacles along the path of perfection, and then relentlessly striving to procure the conditions and remove the obstacles from the path. The more man's perception of the goal of creation and his determination to reach it is, the more obstacles appear and manifest themselves. As a result, his efforts in removing them must be greater and more profound. Undoubtedly, the results which he obtains in this process are unimaginable for others. In short, in each stage of man's perfection certain obstacles appear on his path, and it is only after these obstacles are removed that the trait of *taqwā* comes about in his soul, allowing him to traverse its different levels.

The greatest obstacles for wayfarers in reaching the lofty spiritual perfections are the self, Satan and the world. The commanding self in its role as an internal force, continuously draws man towards the transient worldly desires. Through insinuations and deceit, Satan beautifies unlawful desires and presents worldly matters as being perfect, thereby preventing man from the path of truth. Just as how the Noble Qur'ān narrates from the words of Prophet Joseph (peace be upon him):

وَمَا أُبَرِّئُ نَفْسِي إِنَّ النَّفْسَ لَأَمَّارَةٌ بِالسُّوءِ إِلَّا مَا رَحِمَ رَبِّي إِنَّ رَبِّي غَفُورٌ رَّحِيمٌ

> Yet I do not absolve my [own] soul, for the soul indeed prompts [men] to evil, except he upon whom my Lord has mercy. For indeed, my Lord is Forgiving, Merciful. (12:53)

Undoubtedly, those who are drowned in heedlessness also make the circumstances required for progress unfavourable and prepare the ground for the self and Satan's activity. Therefore, a deep understanding of each of these matters is necessary and essential for wayfarers of the path of spirituality. This will be explained in the forthcoming sections.

Section One
Keeping Away from Worldly Attachments

In Allah the Exalted's system of creation, the creation furthest away from the source of Divine Grace is the world and the material realm. Due to its remoteness from the Origin of Light, it has acquired unique characteristics. Paying attention to and carefully studying the realities and truths related to the world guides man as to how he should interact with this world, stay immune from its pitfalls, and the dos and don'ts related to it. That is because every being that has come into existence in this world was soundly and wisely created by Allah. Due to man's relationship with these beings and the different types of attachments his soul forms with them, this world is called '*dunyā*'.[i] The *dunyā* has certain characteristics.

Characteristics of the World

1) The Last Creation of Allah

By paying attention to and carefully studying the teachings of the Qur'ān and Sunnah,[ii] it can be seen that Allah the Immaculate has created a great number of realms, each of which has its own characteristics. From these realms, the *dunyā* is the lowest of rank and has certain specific limitations. As a result, it is remote from the special infinite Divine mercy and is not the object of His special attention except in that it is a manifestation of His perfections. In fact, the *dunyā* has been created so that man takes heed of these perfections and acquires them.

Imam ʿAlī (peace be upon him) describing this characteristic of the world says:

---

i. The word *dunyā* literally refers to something that is low or close by. Thus, because of the attachments man forms with the items of this world—items that are close to him and he is connected to—this world is called the *dunyā*.

ii. The word *sunnah* refers to the speech and conduct of the Prophet (peace and blessings be upon him and his family) as well as the Imams (peace be upon them).

فَمَا لَهَا عِنْدَ اللَّهِ عَزَّ وَ جَلَّ قَدْرٌ وَ لَا وَزْنٌ وَ لَا خَلْقٌ فِيمَا بَلَغَنَا خَلْقاً أَبْغَضَ إِلَيْهِ مِنْهَا وَ لَا نَظَرَ إِلَيْهَا مُذْ خَلَقَهَا وَ لَقَدْ عَرَضَتْ عَلَى نَبِيِّنَا ص بِمَفَاتِيحِهَا وَ خَزَائِنِهَا لَا يَنْقُصُهُ ذَلِكَ مِنْ حَظِّهِ مِنَ الْآخِرَةِ فَأَبَى أَنْ يَقْبَلَهَا لِعِلْمِهِ أَنَّ اللَّهَ عَزَّ وَ جَلَّ أَبْغَضَ شَيْئاً فَأَبْغَضَهُ وَ صَغَّرَ شَيْئاً فَصَغَّرَه

> It neither has any worth nor any value near Allah. He has not created any creation—of which we are informed—that is more hateful to Him than it. He has not gazed upon it [with His special mercy] since He created it. It was offered to our Prophet (peace and blessings be upon him and his family) with its keys and its treasures, in a manner that would not diminish from his share in the Hereafter. However, he refused to accept it because of his knowledge that if Allah hates something he should also hate it, and if Allah considers something insignificant he should also consider it insignificant.[i]

Therefore, those who have bound their hearts to Allah's affection can never give their hearts to a thing that is the object of their Beloved's inattentiveness and anger. Allah says in one of the *aḥādīth al-qudsiyyah*[ii]:

يَا ابْنَ آدَمَ، أَخْرِجْ حُبَّ الدُّنْيَا مِنْ قَلْبِكَ، فَإِنَّهُ لاَ يَجْتَمِعُ حُبَّ الدُّنْيَا وَ حُبِّي فِي قَلْبٍ وَاحِدٍ أَبَداً.

> O son of Adam! Remove love of the world from your heart. For surely love of the world and my love cannot ever come together in one heart.[iii]

i. Rayshahrī, Mīzān al-Hikmah, 2:910

ii. The *aḥādīth al-qudsiyyah* are narrations in which the content is from Allah the Exalted, but the words are from the Prophet or the Imam (peace be upon them). For example, Allah inspired this message to them and they narrated it to the people in their own words.

iii. al-ʿĀmilī, al-Jawāhir al-Saniyyah fī al-Ahādīth al-Qudsiyyah, 79

2) Stench and Darkness

The material realm due to its remoteness from the Origin of Light, is always dark and full of stench. However, for those who have grown fond of it—like a bat being fond of the dark—it is not possible to perceive this reality. Allah has advised His Prophet Jesus (peace be upon him) that:

> يَا عِيسَى إِنَّ الدُّنْيَا سِجْنٌ مُنْتِنُ الرِّيحِ وَحْشٌ فِيهَا مَا قَدْ تَذَابَحَ عَلَيْهِ الْجَبَّارُونَ
>
> O Jesus! Indeed, this world is a foul smelling and frightening prison. The cruel oppressors slaughter each other for its sake.[i]

Imam ʿAlī (peace be upon him) also says in this regard:

> هَؤُلَاءِ أَنْبِيَاءُ اللَّهِ وَ أَصْفِيَاؤُهُ تَنَزَّهُوا عَنِ الدُّنْيَا ... ثُمَّ اقْتَصَ الصَّالِحُونَ آثَارَهُم ... وَ أَنْزَلُوا الدُّنْيَا مِنْ أَنْفُسِهِمْ كَالْمَيْتَةِ الَّتِي لَا يَحِلُّ لِأَحَدٍ أَنْ يَشْبَعَ مِنْهَا إِلَّا فِي حَالِ الضَّرُورَةِ إِلَيْهَا وَ أَكَلُوا مِنْهَا بِقَدْرِ مَا أَبْقَى لَهُمُ النَّفَسَ وَ أَمْسَكَ الرُّوحَ وَ جَعَلُوهَا بِمَنْزِلَةِ الْجِيفَةِ الَّتِي اشْتَدَّ نَتْنُهَا فَكُلُّ مَنْ مَرَّ بِهَا أَمْسَكَ عَلَى فِيه ... إِخْوَانِي وَ اللَّهُ لَهِيَ فِي الْعَاجِلَةِ وَ الْآجِلَةِ لِمَنْ نَاصَحَ نَفْسَهُ فِي النَّظَرِ وَ أَخْلَصَ لَهَا الْفِكَرَ أَنْتَنُ مِنَ الْجِيفَةِ وَ أَكْرَهُ مِنَ الْمَيْتَةِ غَيْرَ أَنَّ الَّذِي نَشَأَ فِي دِبَاغِ الْإِهَابِ لَا يَجِدُ نَتْنَهُ وَ لَا تُؤْذِيهِ رَائِحَتُهُ مَا تُؤْذِي الْمَارَّ بِهِ وَ الْجَالِسَ عِنْدَه
>
> These are Allah's prophets and chosen servants that have been purified from this world ... Thereafter, the virtuous men followed in their footsteps ... The world for them is like a carcass, which it is not permissible to fill one's stomach with except out of necessity. They eat from it to the extent that

---

i. Ibid., 105

they remain alive and their soul is protected. They consider it a foul-smelling corpse such that if any one passes by it he covers his mouth with his hands ... O my brothers! By Allah, the *dunyā* in the current life and the next—for the one who looks at it sympathetically and ponders over it sincerely—is more foul-smelling than a corpse and more detestable than a carcass. But [alas], the one who has spent his life in a tannery [where animal skins are made into leather] does not sense the foul odour and is not troubled by it, unlike the one passing by or sitting next to it. (i)

3) Its Transient Nature

One of the other characteristics of this *dunyā* is its limitations; it can never satisfy man's soul that is constantly seeking perfection. Allah (the Provider of abundance and the Sublime) advises Prophet Jesus (peace be upon him):

إِيَّاكَ وَ الدُّنْيَا فَكُلُّ نَعِيمِهَا يَزُولُ وَ مَا نَعِيمُهَا إِلَّا قَلِيل

Beware of this world! For all its blessing shall fade away and its blessings are only little. (ii)

The limitations of the *dunyā* cause many imperfections, deficiencies, sufferings and hardships. These always leave a bitter taste in the mouth of those enamoured by it, and unpleasant memories fill their minds. Imam ʿAlī (peace be upon him) says:

الدُّنْيَا مَلِيئَةٌ بِالْمَصَائِبِ طَارِقَةٌ بِالْفَجَائِعِ وَ النَّوَائِب

The world is replete with difficulties and afflictions. It constantly knocks [at the door] with unpleasant happenings and calamities. (iii)

Also, in another narration he says:

---

i. Rayshahrī, Mīzān al-Ḥikmah, 2:892

ii. al-ʿĀmilī, al-Jawāhir al-Saniyyah fī al-Ahādīth al-Qudsiyyah, 105

iii. al-Āmudī, Fihrist-i Mawdūʿī-yi Ghurar al-Hikam, chapter on the dunyā, 106

دَارٌ هَانَـتْ عَلَـى رَبِّهَـا فَخُلِـطَ حَلاَلُهَـا بِحَرَامِهَـا وَ خَيْرُهَـا بِشَـرِّهَا وَ حَيَاتُهَـا بِمَوْتِهَـا وَ حُلْوُهَـا بِمُرِّهَـا لَـمْ يَصْفُهَـا اللّٰـهُ لِأَوْلِيَائِـهِ وَ لَـمْ يَضُـنَّ بِهَـا عَلَـى أَعْدَائِـه

[The world] is a despicable abode in the view of its Lord. Therefore, its permissible things are mixed with its impermissible things, its good is mixed with its evil, its life is mixed with its death and its sweetness is mixed with bitterness. He has not described it for His *awliyā'* and has not restrained it from His enemies. (i)

One of the characteristics of the *dunyā* is the transient and impermanent nature of it and its blessings. In the words of the Noble Qur'ān:

كُلُّ مَنْ عَلَيْهَا فَانٍ

Everyone on it [the Earth] must pass away (55:26)

It is for this reason that men of intellect do not attach their hearts to something perishable and like Prophet Abraham (peace be upon him) they call out saying

لَا أُحِبُّ الْآفِلِينَ

I do not like those who set. (6:76)

These people never place their trust in the perishable *dunyā*. In the words of Imam al-Ṣādiq (peace be upon him):

إِنْ كَانَتِ الدُّنْيَا فَانِيَةً فَالطُّمَأْنِينَةُ إِلَيْهَا لِمَا ذَا

If the *dunyā* is perishable, then why place trust in it?! (ii)

The *dunyā* enjoys only a very small share of existence, in the words of Allah the Exalted:

قُلْ مَتَاعُ الدُّنْيَا قَلِيلٌ

Say, "The enjoyments of [this] world are trifle." (4:77)

Imam 'Alī (peace be upon him) says in this regard:

---

i. Rayshahrī, Mīzān al-Ḥikmah, 2:910

ii. Rayshahrī, Mīzān al-Hikmah, 2:904

إِنَّمَا سُمِّيَتِ الدُّنْيَا دُنْيَا لِأَنَّهَا أَدْنَى مِنْ كُلِّ شَيْءٍ وَ سُمِّيَتِ الْآخِرَةُ آخِرَةً لِأَنَّ فِيهَا الْجَزَاءَ وَ الثَّوَابَ

The *dunyā* has only been named *dunyā* [the lowly and base] because it is lower and more wretched than everything, and the Hereafter has been named *ākhirah* [the conclusion and consequence] because in it there is recompense and reward.[i]

This is one of the important reasons to not attach the heart to this *dunyā*, as Luqman the Wise advised his son:

يَا بُنَيَّ لَا تَرْكَنْ إِلَى الدُّنْيَا وَ لَا تَشْغَلْ قَلْبَكَ بِهَا فَمَا خَلَقَ اللَّهُ خَلْقاً هُوَ أَهْوَنُ عَلَيْهِ مِنْهَا

O my dear son! Do not rely on the *dunyā* and do not preoccupy your heart with it. For Allah has not created a creation that is more despicable, in His view, than it.[ii]

4) Its Attractiveness and Seductive Nature

Allah the Immaculate based on His wisdom and for man to benefit from the worldly blessings, has placed a natural attraction in them. In the words of the Noble Qur'ān:

إِنَّا جَعَلْنَا مَا عَلَى الْأَرْضِ زِينَةً لَّهَا لِنَبْلُوَهُمْ أَيُّهُمْ أَحْسَنُ عَمَلًا

Indeed, We have made whatever is on the Earth an adornment for it that We may test them [to see] which of them is best in conduct. (18:7)

In another verse it says:

الْمَالُ وَالْبَنُونَ زِينَةُ الْحَيَاةِ الدُّنْيَا

Wealth and children are the adornment of the life of the *dunyā*. (18:46)

---

i. Ibid., 2:890

ii. Ibid., 4:3126

Therefore, with the aim of utilizing the *dunyā* in the optimal manner, it is necessary to benefit from these attractive blessings to gain proximity to Allah. Just as Allah advised Prophet Jesus (peace be upon him):

> يَا عِيسَى إِنَّ الدُّنْيَا حُلْوَةٌ وَ إِنَّمَا اسْتَعْمَلْتُكَ فِيهَا فَجَانِبْ مِنْهَا مَا حَذَّرْتُكَ وَ خُذْ مِنْهَا مَا أَعْطَيْتُكَ عَفْوا
>
> O Jesus! Indeed, the *dunyā* is sweet, and I have engaged you in it [placed you in it] so that you obey me. Therefore, shun from it what I have warned you about and take from it [and enjoy] what I have granted you while overlooking its faults.[i]

Therefore, attaching one's heart to worldly attractions is illogical and blameworthy. Imam ʿAlī (peace be upon him) says in this regard:

> احْذَرُوا هَذِهِ الدُّنْيَا الْخَدَّاعَةِ الْغَدَّارَةِ الَّتِي قَدْ تَزَيَّنَتْ بِحُلِيِّهَا وَ فَتَنَتْ بِغُرُورِهَا ... فَأَصْبَحَتْ كَالْعَرُوسِ الْمَجْلُوَّةِ وَ الْعُيُونُ إِلَيْهَا نَاظِرَة
>
> Beware of this deceitful and treacherous *dunyā*, which has adorned itself with its ornaments and tested [people] with its deception ... It is like a beautified bride such that the eyes are gazing upon her.[ii]

The Dunyā in the Eyes of the Divine Awliyāʾ

Those who have given their hearts to the Almighty Lord and drunk from the spring of gnosis, have closed the eyes of their heart to anything other than the Beloved. They have made their beliefs, morals and actions to be Divine in nature. Therefore, the reality of the *dunyā* has been manifested for them and they perceive its wretchedness and insignificance with their entire existence. In many of his sermons Amīr al-Muʾminīn (peace be upon him), the champion of the arena of *tawḥīd* (monotheism), explains the abjectness and despicability of this word

i. al-ʿĀmilī, al-Jawāhir al-Saniyyah fī al-Ahādīth al-Qudsiyyah, 109

ii. Rayshahrī, Mīzān al-Hikmah, 2:902

in his eyes, using words such as these:

> وَ اللَّهِ لَدُنْيَاكُمْ هَذِهِ أَهْوَنُ فِي عَيْنِي مِنْ عِرَاقِ خِنْزِيرٍ فِي يَدِ مَجْذُوم
>
> By Allah! This *dunyā* of yours is more insignificant in my eyes than the bone of a pig in the hand of a leper.[i]

In another statement he says:

> دُنْيَاكُمْ هَذِهِ أَزْهَدَ عِنْدِي مِنْ عَفْطَةِ عَنْز
>
> This *dunyā* of yours is more abject near me than the sneezing of a goat.[ii]

Similarly, he has said:

> إِنَّ دُنْيَاكُمْ عِنْدِي لَأَهْوَنُ مِنْ وَرَقَةٍ فِي فَمِ جَرَادَةٍ تَقْضَمُهَا مَا لِعَلِيٍّ وَ لِنَعِيمٍ يَفْنَى
>
> Indeed, this *dunyā* of yours is more insignificant to me than a leaf in the mouth of a grasshopper that has picked it up [is biting it]. What has ʿAlī to do with transient pleasures?![iii]

These statements exemplify the repeated warning of the Divine *awliyāʾ* to men, regarding what type of outlook and relationship they should have with the *dunyā* and its different affairs. That is because man's soul is very quickly influenced by the deceitful attractions of the *dunyā*, and as a result his intellect and real perception of this world becomes heedless.

Therefore, throughout history there have always been great and liberated individuals who, by reaching the station of certainty, attained true servitude. They have become free from the trap of worldly attachments; the world has become abject and insignificant in their eyes, and they have made complete use of it to reach their desired goal and meet their Beloved.

It is for this reason that Amīr al-Muʾminīn ʿAlī (peace be upon

---

i. al-Radī, Nahj al-Balāghah, saying 236

ii. Ibid., sermon 3

iii. Ibn Abī al-Ḥadīd, Sharḥ-i Nahj al-Balāghah, 11:246

him)—himself at the peak of liberation from the world—has described its positive characteristics as such, saying:

إِنَّ الدُّنْيَا دَارُ صِدْقٍ لِمَنْ صَدَقَهَا وَ دَارُ عَافِيَةٍ لِمَنْ فَهِمَ عَنْهَا وَ دَارُ غِنًى لِمَنْ تَزَوَّدَ مِنْهَا وَ دَارُ مَوْعِظَةٍ لِمَنِ اتَّعَظَ بِهَا مَسْجِدُ أَحِبَّاءِ اللَّهِ وَ مُصَلَّى مَلَائِكَةِ اللَّهِ وَ مَهْبِطُ وَحْيِ اللَّهِ وَ مَتْجَرُ أَوْلِيَاءِ اللَّهِ اكْتَسَبُوا فِيهَا الرَّحْمَةَ وَ رَبِحُوا فِيهَا الْجَنَّةَ فَمَنْ ذَا يَذُمُّهَا وَ قَدْ آذَنَتْ بِبَيْنِهَا وَ نَادَتْ بِفِرَاقِهَا وَ نَعَتْ نَفْسَهَا وَ أَهْلَهَا فَمَثَّلَتْ لَهُمْ بِبَلَائِهَا الْبَلَاءَ وَ شَوَّقَتْهُمْ بِسُرُورِهَا إِلَى السُّرُورِ رَاحَتْ بِعَافِيَةٍ وَ ابْتَكَرَتْ بِفَجِيعَةٍ تَرْغِيباً وَ تَرْهِيباً وَ تَخْوِيفاً وَ تَحْذِيراً فَذَمَّهَا رِجَالٌ غَدَاةَ النَّدَامَةِ وَ حَمِدَهَا آخَرُونَ يَوْمَ الْقِيَامَةِ ذَكَّرَتْهُمُ الدُّنْيَا [فَذَكَّرُوا] فَتَذَكَّرُوا وَ حَدَّثَتْهُمْ فَصَدَّقُوا وَ وَعَظَتْهُمْ فَاتَّعَظُوا

Indeed, this world is an abode of truth for the truthful ones [those whose actions are truthful], it is an abode of well-being for those who understand it, it is an abode of riches for those who take provisions from it, and it is an abode of advice for those who take admonition from it. The world is the place of prostration for the lovers of Allah, the place of prayers for the angels of Allah, and the place where Allah's revelation descends. It is the place [the means] of trading for the *awliyā'* of Allah, wherein they earn mercy and they gain the Paradise. So, who then can reproach the world, while it has announced its separation, and called out that it is transient and informed of its destruction and the destruction of its dwellers. Through its tribulations it has given an example of tribulation and through its rejoicing it encourages people to be happy. It passes with safety at the beginning of the night and returns in the morning with destructive afflictions. [It does so] to make [people] eager, to threaten, frighten and warn [them]. Then, a group of people reproach the world in the mornings with regret, while others will praise it on the Day of Resurrection. [That is because] the world reminded them [of the realities] and they were reminded. It spoke to them [through different events] and they affirmed it. It admonished them, and they took heed.(i)

One of these individuals is a person about whom Imam al-Ṣādiq (peace be upon him) says:

اسْتَقْبَلَ رَسُولُ اللَّهِ ص حَارِثَةَ بْنَ مَالِكِ بْنِ النُّعْمَانِ الْأَنْصَارِيَّ فَقَالَ لَهُ كَيْفَ أَنْتَ يَا حَارِثَةَ بْنَ مَالِكٍ النُّعْمَانِيَ فَقَالَ يَا رَسُولَ اللَّهِ مُؤْمِنٌ حَقّاً فَقَالَ لَهُ رَسُولُ اللَّهِ ص لِكُلِّ شَيْءٍ حَقِيقَةٌ فَمَا حَقِيقَةُ قَوْلِكَ فَقَالَ يَا رَسُولَ اللَّهِ عَزَفَتْ نَفْسِي عَنِ الدُّنْيَا فَأَسْهَرَتْ لَيْلِي وَ أَظْمَأَتْ هَوَاجِرِي وَ كَأَنِّي أَنْظُرُ إِلَى عَرْشِ رَبِّي وَ قَدْ وُضِعَ لِلْحِسَابِ وَ كَأَنِّي أَنْظُرُ إِلَى أَهْلِ الْجَنَّةِ يَتَزَاوَرُونَ فِي الْجَنَّةِ وَ كَأَنِّي أَسْمَعُ عُوَاءَ أَهْلِ النَّارِ فِي النَّارِ فَقَالَ رَسُولُ اللَّهِ ص عَبْدٌ نَوَّرَ اللَّهُ قَلْبَهُ أَبْصَرْتَ فَاثْبُتْ فَقَالَ يَا رَسُولَ اللَّهِ ادْعُ اللَّهَ لِي أَنْ يَرْزُقَنِي الشَّهَادَةَ مَعَكَ فَقَالَ اللَّهُمَّ ارْزُقْ حَارِثَةَ الشَّهَادَةَ فَلَمْ يَلْبَثْ إِلَّا أَيَّاماً حَتَّى بَعَثَ رَسُولُ اللَّهِ ص سَرِيَّةً فَبَعَثَهُ فِيهَا فَقَاتَلَ فَقَتَلَ تِسْعَةً أَوْ ثَمَانِيَةً ثُمَّ قُتِلَ

[One day] the Messenger of Allah (peace and blessings be upon him and his family) saw Ḥāritah ibn Mālik ibn al-Nuʿmān al-Anṣārī and asked him, "In what state are you, O Ḥāritah ibn Mālik al-Nuʿmān?" He replied, "O Messenger of Allah! I am in the state of true belief." Then, the Messenger of Allah said to him, "Everything has a reality. So, what is the reality of your words?" He said, "O Messenger of Allah! My soul has turned away from the *dunyā*, therefore I spend my night awake and my day hungry. It is as if I can see the Throne of my Lord while it has been placed for the accounting. I can see the inhabitants of Paradise visiting each other in Paradise; I can hear the cries of the inhabitants of Hell in

i. al-Raḍī, Nahj al-Balāghah, saying 31

> the Hellfire." The Messenger of Allah (peace and blessings be upon him and his family) said, "[This is] a servant whose heart Allah has enlightened. You have acquired foresight so preserve it." He said, "O Messenger of Allah! Pray to Allah that He provides me with martyrdom by your side." The Messenger of Allah said, "O Allah! Provide Ḥāritah with martyrdom." Hardly a few days had passed after this incident that the Messenger of Allah (peace and blessings be upon him and his family) sent forth a contingent of soldiers [for a battle] and he was one of them. He fought, killed nine or eight people, and was then martyred.[(i)]

Indeed, such is the case. Imam al-Ṣādiq (peace be upon him) expresses his ardent love for such free men and says:

> آهِ آهِ عَلَى قُلُوبٍ حُشِيَتْ نُوراً وَ إِنَّمَا كَانَتِ الدُّنْيَا عِنْدَهُمْ بِمَنْزِلَةِ الشُّجَاعِ الْأَرْقَمِ وَ الْعَدُوِّ الْأَعْجَمِ أَنِسُوا بِاللَّهِ وَ اسْتَوْحَشُوا مِمَّا بِهِ اسْتَأْنَسَ الْمُتْرَفُونَ أُولَئِكَ أَوْلِيَائِي حَقّاً وَ بِهِمْ تُكْشَفُ كُلُّ فِتْنَةٍ وَ تُرْفَعُ كُلُّ بَلِيَّةٍ
>
> Alas! Those people whose hearts are filled with light, the *dunyā* in their eyes is merely a colourful snake and a speechless barbaric enemy, they are intimately fond of Allah and are disgusted by that which the lavish and opulent people are fond of. They are truly my friends (*awliyā'*), through them every discomfort is eased, and every difficulty is solved.[(ii)]

Therefore, only the following group of people are secure from the dangers and entanglements of this *dunyā*. Those who are on the path of true servitude of Allah, have entrusted their affairs to Him, and consider Him to be the true owner of themselves and the *dunyā*. Those whose only ambition in the affairs of this *dunyā* is Allah the Exalted's obedience, and their sole concern is implementing Allah's commands. If such people acquire worldly leadership and extensive sovereignty

---

i. Majlisī, Bihār al-Anwār, 64:287

ii. al-Harrānī, Tuhaf al-ʿUqūl, 301

like Prophet Solomon (peace be upon him), their intention will be to implement Allah's *wilāyah* and sovereignty. For example, during the period of Amīr al-Mu'minīn's (peace be upon him) apparent rule, he was once patching his shoes during the Battle of Jamal. Ibn ʿAbbas said to him, "You are doing this work in such a situation?!" The Imam (peace be upon him) said, "By Allah, it [these shoes] should have been dearer to me than ruling over you but for the fact that I may establish right and ward off wrong." (i)

Even if such a person abdicates his Divine position, he never refrains from servitude of Allah the Exalted. Thus, after Amīr al-Mu'minīn (peace be upon him) presented himself to the people and came forward to acquire Divine leadership but did not achieve it, this did not worry him. In the same way, whether people welcome the servants of Allah or they turn their backs on them, this does not affect their morale and course of action; rather the focus of their efforts is solely to perform the duties of servitude. They are secure from the outward and psychological discomforts faced by those who are attached to this world. It is for this reason that Imam al-Ṣādiq (peace be upon him) says:

مَنْ أَصْبَحَ وَ أَمْسَى وَ الدُّنْيَا أَكْبَرُ هَمِّهِ جَعَلَ اللَّهُ تَعَالَى الْفَقْرَ بَيْنَ عَيْنَيْهِ وَ شَتَّتَ أَمْرَهُ وَ لَمْ يَنَلْ مِنَ الدُّنْيَا إِلَّا مَا قَسَمَ اللَّهُ لَهُ وَ مَنْ أَصْبَحَ وَ أَمْسَى وَ الْآخِرَةُ أَكْبَرُ هَمِّهِ جَعَلَ اللَّهُ الْغِنَى فِي قَلْبِهِ وَ جَمَعَ لَهُ أَمْرَهُ

> One who begins his morning and evening while the *dunyā* is his biggest concern, God places poverty in front of him and causes his affairs to become disjointed and dissipated, while he does not attain anything except what has been apportioned for him. And as for one who begins his morning and evening while his biggest concern is the Hereafter, God puts contentment in his heart and gives a wholeness and unity to his affairs. (ii)

---

i. al-Radī, Nahj al-Balāghah, sermon 33

ii. al-Kulaynī, al-Kāfi, 2:319, narration 15

This means that the first group of people always remain in a state of anxiety and apprehension with respect to the *dunyā* and its affairs. They never become satisfied and content by attaining the *dunyā*, and their affairs are also not accomplished. On the other hand, the second group live with tranquillity and satisfaction regarding their affairs, and Allah also secures these affairs for them.

Section Two
Staying Aloof from Satan

The Characteristics of Satan

The lexical meaning of the Arabic word '*Shayṭān*' (Satan), is a wicked and evil entity. Due to its repeated usage, it is now used to signify Iblīs.[i]

Satan is one of the creations of Allah belonging to the species of jinn. For years he was busy worshipping Allah amongst the angels. After the creation of Prophet Adam (peace be upon him), Allah the Immaculate commanded all those who dwelled in the Station of Allah's proximity to prostrate before the reality of Adam. But Satan acted with haughtiness, refused Allah's command, and was driven away from the Divine proximity. That is because the Station of Allah's proximity is exclusively for worship and magnification of Allah the Exalted.[ii] Hence, Allah said to Satan:

قَالَ فَاهْبِطْ مِنْهَا فَمَا يَكُونُ لَكَ أَن تَتَكَبَّرَ فِيهَا فَاخْرُجْ إِنَّكَ مِنَ الصَّاغِرِينَ

> He said, "Get down from it [that station]! It is not for you to be arrogant therein." (7:13)

Imam 'Alī (peace be upon him) says in this regard:

فَاعْتَبِرُوا بِمَا كَانَ مِنْ فِعْلِ اللَّهِ بِإِبْلِيسَ إِذْ أَحْبَطَ عَمَلَهُ الطَّوِيلَ وَ جَهْدَهُ الْجَهِيدَ وَ كَانَ قَدْ عَبَدَ اللَّهَ سِتَّةَ آلَافِ سَنَةٍ لَا يُدْرَى أَ مِنْ سِنِي الدُّنْيَا أَمْ مِنْ سِنِي الْآخِرَةِ عَنْ كِبْرِ سَاعَةٍ وَاحِدَةٍ فَمَنْ ذَا بَعْدَ إِبْلِيسَ يَسْلَمُ عَلَى اللَّهِ بِمِثْلِ مَعْصِيَتِهِ

> Take heed from that which Allah did with Iblīs when He nullified his many actions and relentless efforts. He had worshipped Allah for six thousand years, and it is not known if these were years of this world or years of the Hereafter,

---

i. Ṭabāṭabā'ī, Tafsīr al-Mīzān, 7321:

ii. Ibid., 8:23

> [but] because of one moment of pride and haughtiness [He nullified it all]. So, who is there after Iblīs that can commit the same sin and still be guaranteed security from Allah?![i]

It is here that Iblīs was separated from the angels, as the Noble Qur᾿ān says:

> كَانَ مِنَ الْجِنِّ فَفَسَقَ عَنْ أَمْرِ رَبِّهِ
>
> He was one of the jinn, so he transgressed against his Lord's command. (18:50)

It can be concluded from the verses of the Qur᾿ān and Islamic traditions, that Satan believed in the Origin and the Hereafter and was completely aware of the exalted station of the Infallible Imams' (peace be upon them) sacred light near Allah. He had knowledge of the Divine attributes of beauty and majesty and was aware of the different stations and ranks of perfection. On the practical side also, he had worshipped Allah for many long years, such that he had the privilege of worshipping Him amongst the ranks of the angels. However, the cause of his deviation was the moral vices in his character, such as pride and envy. He said to Allah:

> أَنَا خَيْرٌ مِّنْهُ خَلَقْتَنِي مِن نَّارٍ وَخَلَقْتَهُ مِن طِينٍ
>
> I am better than him, You created me from fire and You created him from clay. (7:12)

> شیطان که رانده شد به جز یک خطا نکرد
>
> خود را برای سجده ی آدم رضا نکرد
>
> Satan was thrown out for but a single mistake, He did not agree to prostrate himself before Adam.[ii]

After Iblīs was deprived of being in the Divine presence, his heart was filled with animosity towards Adam and his children:

---

i. al-Radī, Nahj al-Balāghah, sermon 192

ii.

قَالَ رَبِّ بِمَا أَغْوَيْتَنِي لَأُزَيِّنَنَّ لَهُمْ فِي الْأَرْضِ وَلَأُغْوِيَنَّهُمْ أَجْمَعِينَ

He said, "My Lord! As You have consigned me to being astray, I will surely glamorize [sin] for them on the Earth, and I will surely cause them all to deviate." (15:39)

Allah (the Provider of abundance and the Sublime) has introduced Satan in the Qurʾān, as being the enemy of man and has said:

إِنَّ الشَّيْطَانَ لِلْإِنسَانِ عَدُوٌّ مُّبِينٌ

Satan is indeed man's manifest enemy. (12:5)

Satan, who was expelled from the Divine presence and cursed, cannot bear to see any good for man:

وَإِن يَدْعُونَ إِلَّا شَيْطَانًا مَّرِيدًا لَّعَنَهُ اللَّهُ

And they invoke none but a rebellious Satan, whom Allah has cursed (4:117-118)

This animosity of Satan has prepared the ground in this *dunyā* for distinguishing the righteous individuals from the corrupt. In the words of the Noble Qurʾān:

لِّيَجْعَلَ مَا يُلْقِي الشَّيْطَانُ فِتْنَةً لِّلَّذِينَ فِي قُلُوبِهِم مَّرَضٌ وَالْقَاسِيَةِ قُلُوبُهُمْ

That He may make what Satan casts a test for those in whose hearts is a sickness and [also] those whose hearts have hardened. (22:53)

In this verse Allah has mentioned a benefit of the satanic insinuations: they are a means through which most people are tested. This is one of the consistent laws of this world, the reaching of perfection by the virtuous individuals and the damnation of the corrupt is dependent on these tests. Satanic insinuations take those in whose hearts there is disease and the people of evil conduct and cast them into the pit of wretchedness. This is a necessary consequence of Allah's system of spiritual training. The Qurʾān says:

كُلًّا نُّمِدُّ هَٰؤُلَاءِ وَهَٰؤُلَاءِ مِنْ عَطَاءِ رَبِّكَ ۚ وَمَا كَانَ عَطَاءُ رَبِّكَ مَحْظُورًا

To these and to those—to all We extend the bounty of your Lord, and the bounty of your Lord is not confined. (17:20)

Therefore, it is necessary for wayfarers to pay attention to and know the methods which Satan uses to infiltrate and deceive, and the extent of his activity.

The Extent of Satan's Activities

It becomes clear from the verses of the Qurʾān and the Islamic traditions, that the extent of Satan's activity is man's perceptions. His tool for influencing man is man's emotions and feelings. Satan introduces deceptive imaginations and false thoughts in man's soul, which are called satanic insinuations or temptations (*waswās*):

الْوَسْوَاسِ الْخَنَّاسِ الَّذِي يُوَسْوِسُ فِي صُدُورِ النَّاسِ

The sneaky tempter who puts temptations into the breasts of humans, (114:4-5) [i]

Even in the instances where Satan has manifested himself in front of some people, performed an action for them, or taught them something, it has been through affecting their mind and thoughts. He was only personified for them in their minds. [ii] In this manner, Iblīs personified himself to many of the prophets and discussed different issues with them.

As a result, Satan does not have any power to compel man or deprive him of his free will. As the Noble Qurʾān has said:

وَمَا كَانَ لَهُ عَلَيْهِم مِّن سُلْطَانٍ إِلَّا لِنَعْلَمَ مَن يُؤْمِنُ بِالْآخِرَةِ مِمَّنْ هُوَ مِنْهَا فِي شَكٍّ

He [Satan] had no authority over them, but that We may ascertain those who believe in the Hereafter from those who

---

i. Ṭabāṭabāʾī, Tafsīr al-Mīzān, 8:40

ii. Ibid., 6:212

are in doubt about it, (34:21)

By carefully examining this verse, it is seen that Satan does not even have authority over those who disbelieve in the Hereafter. It is not the case that he takes away their free will and they are compelled to follow him. Rather, it is due to their own wrong decision that they choose to follow Satan, and because of this he then dominates them. This is contrary to what some people suppose, that first Satan prevails over them and then they are compelled to follow him. As a result, those deceived by Satan will have no excuse for their deviation, as Allah says quoting the words of Iblīs on the Day of Resurrection:

وَمَا كَانَ لِيَ عَلَيْكُم مِّن سُلْطَانٍ إِلَّا أَن دَعَوْتُكُمْ فَاسْتَجَبْتُمْ لِي ۖ فَلَا تَلُومُونِي وَلُومُوا أَنفُسَكُم

I had no authority over you, except that I called you and you responded to me. So, do not blame me, but blame yourselves. (14:22)

Of course, the root cause behind these people following Satan is the doubt and uncertainty that exists in their heart about the Hereafter.[i]

The Noble Qur'ān has summarized the efforts made by Satan to deceive man in three parts:[ii]

1) Satanic Wasāwis and their Different Aspects

The Arabic word '*waswasah*' (plural *wasāwis*) means to invite towards something in a secret and concealed manner.[iii]

Waswasah is one of the most important tools of Iblīs for leading man astray and it manifests itself in different forms. Promising man that Allah is forgiving and merciful is one of the deceiving *wasāwis* of Satan, about which Allah has warned man:

وَلَا يَغُرَّنَّكُم بِاللَّهِ الْغَرُورُ

---

i. Ibid., 16:366

ii. Ibid., 6:120

iii. Ibid., 8:34

> ... nor let the Deceiver deceive you concerning [the generosity of] Allah. (31:33)

Being deceived concerning Allah means that Satan afflicts man with heedlessness and injustice in terms of his conduct, by disobeying Allah.

Satan manifests Allah's forbearance, patience, forgiveness and pardon in man's eyes and sometimes he also assures him that he is safe from Allah's punishment, *istidrāj*, (i) and plotting. As a result, because of becoming engrossed in the world, forgetting the Hereafter, and turning away from the truth, man does not perceive any punishment or reprimand. In his view he sees that the more the worldly individuals seek this world, pass their days in heedlessness, and submerge themselves in the sea of sin and transgression, the more their life become better and easier and they acquire a higher status and esteem amongst people. It is here that Satan suggests to them that the sole cause of advancement and honour is by taking more benefit from this world, and there is nothing beyond this. All the things said by the prophets regarding accounting of deeds, the books of deeds, Allah's promise of Paradise and threats of Hell, all of these are either superstitions or figurative statements.

Because of these *wasāwis*, man loses the correct understanding of Allah's forgiveness and mercy; he feels a false sense of security from death, Allah's punishment and His compensation. Thus, he commits sins, transgressions and amasses this world without any barrier, using any possible way that he fancies. (ii)

Intimidating and instilling fear in man's heart is also one of Satan's weapons. As the Noble Qur'ān says:

الشَّيْطَانُ يَعِدُكُمُ الْفَقْرَ وَيَأْمُرُكُم بِالْفَحْشَاءِ ۖ وَاللَّهُ يَعِدُكُم مَّغْفِرَةً مِّنْهُ وَفَضْلًا

> Satan frightens you about poverty and prompts you to

---

i. *Istidrāj* is a type of Allah's punishment where He increases the worldly blessings of a sinner, allowing them to increase in sin and rebellion. The Noble Qur'ān says, "As for those who deny Our signs, We will perform *istidrāj* to them, whence they do not know." (7:182)

ii. Ṭabāṭabā'ī, Tafsīr al-Mīzān, 17:17

> [commit] indecent acts. But Allah promises you His forgiveness and bounty. (2:268)

> إِنَّمَا ذَٰلِكُمُ الشَّيْطَانُ يُخَوِّفُ أَوْلِيَاءَهُ
>
> That is Satan who frightens his friends. (3:175)

When a person wants to perform good and virtuous actions like charity or helping others, Satan turns his attention towards the possibility of his own poverty and need in the future and dissuades him from such virtuous deeds.

On the Day of Resurrection, Satan will reproach those who were deceived by his *waswasah* and false tricks:

> وَقَالَ الشَّيْطَانُ لَمَّا قُضِيَ الْأَمْرُ إِنَّ اللَّهَ وَعَدَكُمْ وَعْدَ الْحَقِّ وَوَعَدتُّكُمْ فَأَخْلَفْتُكُمْ ۖ وَمَا كَانَ لِيَ عَلَيْكُم مِّن سُلْطَانٍ إِلَّا أَن دَعَوْتُكُمْ فَاسْتَجَبْتُمْ لِي ۖ فَلَا تَلُومُونِي وَلُومُوا أَنفُسَكُم ۖ مَّا أَنَا بِمُصْرِخِكُمْ وَمَا أَنتُم بِمُصْرِخِيَّ ۖ إِنِّي كَفَرْتُ بِمَا أَشْرَكْتُمُونِ مِن قَبْلُ ۗ إِنَّ الظَّالِمِينَ لَهُمْ عَذَابٌ أَلِيمٌ
>
> When the matter is all over [and the court of judgement has been established], Satan will say, "Indeed Allah made you a promise that was true and I [too] made you a promise, but I failed you. I had no authority over you, except that I called you and you responded to me. So, do not blame me, but blame yourselves. I cannot respond to your distress calls, neither can you respond to my distress calls. Indeed, I disavow your taking me for [Allah's] partner aforetime. There is indeed a painful punishment for the wrongdoers." (14:22)

Types of Satanic *Waswasah*

1) *Waswasah* in Beliefs

From the beginning of man's intellectual maturity—in order that the correct beliefs do not become firm in man and to misguide him—Satan attacks his beliefs and, in this manner, afflicts him with doubt.

إِنَّ رَجُلًا أَتَى رَسُولَ اللَّهِ ص فَقَالَ يَا رَسُولَ اللَّهِ إِنَّنِي نَافَقْتُ فَقَالَ وَ اللَّهِ مَا نَافَقْتَ وَ لَوْ نَافَقْتَ مَا أَتَيْتَنِي تُعْلِمُنِي مَا الَّذِي رَابَكَ أَظُنُّ الْعَدُو الْحَاضِرَ أَتَاكَ فَقَالَ لَكَ مَنْ خَلَقَكَ فَقُلْتَ اللَّهُ خَلَقَنِي فَقَالَ لَكَ مَنْ خَلَقَ اللَّهَ قَالَ إِي وَ الَّذِي بَعَثَكَ بِالْحَقِّ لَكَانَ كَذَا فَقَالَ إِنَّ الشَّيْطَانَ أَتَاكُمْ مِنْ قِبَلِ الْأَعْمَالِ فَلَمْ يَقْوَ عَلَيْكُمْ فَأَتَاكُمْ مِنْ هَذَا الْوَجْهِ لِكَيْ يَسْتَزِلَّكُمْ فَإِذَا كَانَ كَذَلِكَ فَلْيَذْكُرْ أَحَدُكُمُ اللَّهَ وَحْدَهُ.

It is narrated that a man came to the Messenger of Allah (peace and blessings be upon him and his family) and said, "[Rescue me! Because] verily I have become a hypocrite." The Messenger of Allah (peace and blessings be upon him and his family) said to him, "By Allah! You have not become a hypocrite. If you had become a hypocrite, you would not have come to me and informed me about that which has put you in this doubt and uncertainty. It seems the manifest enemy [Satan] came to you and said, 'Who created you?' and you answered, 'Allah has created me.' So, he asked, 'Who created Allah?'" That man replied, "Yes, I swear by He who sent you with the truth, this is the case." The Messenger of Allah (peace and blessings be upon him and his family) said, "Indeed, Satan [first] approaches you through your actions. When he is unable to dominate you through them, he approaches through this channel to misguide you. Therefore, whenever you are afflicted with such a state, remember Allah alone." (i)

Waswasah in matters pertaining to beliefs should be controlled through various intellectual and practical solutions. For if they continue, they lead man to doubt and even rejection.

The primary intellectual solution is to pay attention to the undeniable intellectual arguments in every matter related to beliefs and ignore

i. al-Kulaynī, al-Kāfī, 2:425

these satanic insinuations. Similarly, the best practical solution is to seek refuge in Allah the Exalted. This has also been recommended in several verses of the Qur'ān.[i] In this regard, reciting the noble invocations "*lā ilāha illā Allah*" (there is no god except for Allah) and "*lā ḥawla wa lā quwwata illā billāh*" (there is no power and no strength save in Allah) are also very effective.[ii]

2) *Waswasah* in Practical Matters

Some human beings who have weak souls, are influenced by thoughts and *wasāwis*. As a result, using insinuations related to actions, Satan afflicts them with uncertainty. If he cannot stop them altogether from performing an action, then he creates doubt in them regarding the manner of performing that action:

> عَنْ زُرَارَةَ وَ أَبِي بَصِيرٍ قَالا قُلْنَا لَهُ الرَّجُلُ يَشُكُّ كَثِيراً فِي صَلَاتِهِ ... قَالَ يَمْضِي فِي شَكِّهِ ثُمَّ قَالَ لَا تُعَوِّدُوا الْخَبِيثَ مِنْ أَنْفُسِكُمْ بِنَقْضِ الصَّلَاةِ فَتُطْمِعُوهُ فَإِنَّ الشَّيْطَانَ خَبِيثٌ يَعْتَادُ لِمَا عُوِّدَ فَلْيَمْضِ أَحَدُكُمْ فِي الْوَهْمِ ... إِنَّمَا يُرِيدُ الْخَبِيثُ أَنْ يُطَاعَ فَإِذَا عُصِيَ لَمْ يَعُدْ إِلَى أَحَدِكُمْ.
>
> Zurārah and Abu Baṣīr asked Imam al-Ṣādiq (peace be upon him) about a person who doubts a lot during prayers ... The Imam (peace be upon him) replied, "He should ignore his doubt." And then he continued and said, "Do not make Satan accustomed to you by breaking and repeating your prayers, such that he desires you. This is because Satan is wicked, he becomes addicted to that which he is used to. Therefore, each one of you must ignore these thoughts ... The wicked Satan only desires to be obeyed. Hence, if he is disobeyed then he does not return to you."[iii]

Paying careful attention to the Imam's statement keeps man away

i. (7:200), (41:36), (16:98)

ii. al-Kulaynī, al-Kāfī, 2:424

iii. Ibid., 3:358

from the danger of satanic insinuations in practical matters. In other words, when the merit of a certain action is proven through the sacred *sharīʿah* or the intellect, then one should perform that action without delay. Similarly, when the ruling of a certain actions is conclusively known, then one should not doubt about the manner of performing it. There is no room to doubt about it should be performed.[i] If such doubts are entertained, man will either be deprived of performing that action altogether, or he will be preoccupied with repeating and invalidating it. In either situation, he will be deprived of benefitting from its reality and merits, both of which are the wish of Satan.

3) Insinuations in Ethical Matters

The danger of satanic insinuations in matters pertaining to ethics and character is not less than other types of insinuations. That is because, if they become firmly rooted in the soul then it will require great difficulty to free oneself from them.

Satanic insinuations in these matters normally manifest themselves in the form of evil thoughts and misgivings about others, envy, rancour, pride, self-conceit, being pleased with oneself and one's own actions, or having a bad opinion about the happenings of this world and Allah's actions. It is necessary to think about the appropriate ethical measures that must be taken for each of these, based on religious teachings. By being in contact with scholars of ethics, the appropriate solution can be determined, both in terms of thought and action. If such steps are not carried out, man will be afflicted by moral vices.

2) Taswīl (To Glamorize and Beautify)

Taswīl means to glamorize and beautify a thing which man's soul is inclined and attracted towards. It means to beautify a filthy matter, for the soul.[ii]

Sometimes, by beautifying actions, Satan draws man into deviation.

---

i. For example, when the Divine *sharīʿah* has explained that washing an impure (*najis*) item in a large body of water causes it to become pure (*ṭāhir*), there is no need to doubt about its purity after washing it.

ii. Ṭabāṭabāʾī, Tafsīr al-Mīzān, 18:241

In the words of the Noble Qur'ān:

وَزَيَّنَ لَهُمُ الشَّيْطَانُ مَا كَانُوا يَعْمَلُونَ

... and Satan had made what they had been doing seem decorous to them. (6:43)

زُيِّنَ لَهُمْ سُوءُ أَعْمَالِهِمْ

Their evil deeds appear to them as decorous (9:37)

Satan's beautifying actions is in the following manner. He causes an action to appear very beautiful and good in the eyes of man. He provokes and incites all man's inner faculties and feelings of the heart that are related to that action, such that man derives pleasure from it, his heart becomes inclined towards it and he does not get a chance to think about its ominous consequences and filthy effects. In this manner he proceeds to commit that deed.

Also, sometimes Satan presents false and vain matters in front of man:

كَمَثَلِ الشَّيْطَانِ إِذْ قَالَ لِلْإِنسَانِ اكْفُرْ

... like Satan when he tells man, "Disbelieve!" (59:16)

Or he makes the transient life of this world appear attractive. As he himself says:

قَالَ رَبِّ بِمَا أَغْوَيْتَنِي لَأُزَيِّنَنَّ لَهُمْ فِي الْأَرْضِ وَلَأُغْوِيَنَّهُمْ أَجْمَعِينَ

He said, "My Lord! As You have consigned me to perversity, I will surely glamorize [sin] for them on the Earth, and I will surely pervert all of them" (15:39)

3) Leading Man Astray (Ighwā)

Ighwā means to lead man astray from the straight path (*ṣirāt al-mustaqīm*). Therefore, *ighwā* occurs after man pays attention to satanic *wasāwis* and *taswīl* and himself chooses to act according to them. However, under no circumstances is man's will under Satan's control such that he is compelled to perform an action. His free will is never taken away. Rather, the way that Satan affects man's cognitive faculties changes. For example, *wasāwis* are like short messages that affect man's mind and thoughts in a variety of different ways. When man pays attention to these messages, his desire to carry out the message of the *waswasah* is aroused. On the contrary, if he does not pay attention to them, then these *wasāwis* are rendered ineffective. Such insinuations exist in all human beings, even the Divine *awliyā'*. The only difference between them and others is that *waswasah* do not have any effect on them.

Also, in the stage of *ighwā*, the final level of Satan's influence on man is his faculty of imagination. The difference at this stage is that paying heed to satanic *wasāwis* and *taswīl* in the past, causes man's intellectual cognition to now be veiled.[i] There remains no possibility for positive thinking, no escape from the negative satanic suggestions.

It is for this reason that the will of such people is always under the influence of these suggestions. Satan's inability to directly affect man's will leaves no excuse for man as to why he followed Satan. Thus, on the Day of Resurrection Satan will disown his followers, using a strong argument and saying to them:

> وَقَالَ الشَّيْطَانُ لَمَّا قُضِيَ الْأَمْرُ إِنَّ اللَّهَ وَعَدَكُمْ وَعْدَ الْحَقِّ
> وَوَعَدتُّكُمْ فَأَخْلَفْتُكُمْ ۖ وَمَا كَانَ لِيَ عَلَيْكُم مِّن سُلْطَانٍ إِلَّا أَن
> دَعَوْتُكُمْ فَاسْتَجَبْتُمْ لِي ۖ فَلَا تَلُومُونِي وَلُومُوا أَنفُسَكُم ۖ مَّا أَنَا
> بِمُصْرِخِكُمْ وَمَا أَنتُم بِمُصْرِخِيَّ ۖ إِنِّي كَفَرْتُ بِمَا أَشْرَكْتُمُونِ مِن
> قَبْلُ ۗ إِنَّ الظَّالِمِينَ لَهُمْ عَذَابٌ أَلِيمٌ
>
> When the matter is all over [and the judgement takes place], Satan will say, "Indeed Allah made you a promise that was true and I [too] made you a promise, but I failed you. I

i. This discussion is alluding to the faculties of man's perception, as explained in Islamic philosophy. Man has various faculties that encompass one another and contribute to his perception. In order, the intellect encompasses the imagination which in turn encompasses man's anger and desires. These last two faculties encompass the five senses. By overpowering and influencing man's faculty of imagination, Satan has effectively veiled the intellect.

> had no authority over you, except that I called you and you responded to me. So, do not blame me, but blame yourselves. I cannot respond to your distress calls, neither can you respond to my distress calls. Indeed, I disavow your taking me for [Allah's] partner aforetime. There is indeed a painful punishment for the wrongdoers." (14:22)

Therefore, Satan's influence over man does not mean that he is deprived of free will. Rather, it means that Satan's influence penetrates man's beliefs and other areas that affect his decision making.

It is for this reason that when Satan pledged to deceive man and said:

لَأُغْوِيَنَّهُمْ أَجْمَعِينَ

I will surely pervert them (15:39; 38:82)

Allah in reply said to him that you will not have any power over My servants except those deceived individuals who themselves have chosen to follow you:

إِنَّ عِبَادِي لَيْسَ لَكَ عَلَيْهِمْ سُلْطَانٌ إِلَّا مَنِ اتَّبَعَكَ مِنَ الْغَاوِينَ

> Indeed, as for My servants you do not have any authority over them, except the perverse who follow you (15:42)

It is only after a person is lead astray by Satan, that Allah's punishment befalls this deceived person:

كُتِبَ عَلَيْهِ أَنَّهُ مَن تَوَلَّاهُ فَأَنَّهُ يُضِلُّهُ وَيَهْدِيهِ إِلَىٰ عَذَابِ السَّعِيرِ

> About whom [Satan] it has been decreed that he will mislead those who take him for an ally and conduct them toward the punishment of the Blaze. (22:4)

The Close Friends of Satan

Satan exercises his influence the most on those who have chosen him as their *walī* (guardian). These are people who either do not believe in Allah and the various dimensions of His *tawḥīd*, or like Satan, they arrogantly declare their opposition to Allah's legislative authority by their disobedience. In the words of the Noble Qur'ān:

إِنَّا جَعَلْنَا الشَّيَاطِينَ أَوْلِيَاءَ لِلَّذِينَ لَا يُؤْمِنُونَ

We have indeed made the devils to be the close friends of those who have no faith. (7:27)

أَفَتَتَّخِذُونَهُ وَذُرِّيَّتَهُ أَوْلِيَاءَ

Will you then take him [Satan] and his offspring as close friends? (18:50)

Satan's becoming the guardian of man has various dimensions and levels. For those who have been deceived by him, his guardianship means that they obey and follow him:

أَلَمْ أَعْهَدْ إِلَيْكُمْ يَا بَنِي آدَمَ أَن لَّا تَعْبُدُوا الشَّيْطَانَ إِنَّهُ لَكُمْ عَدُوٌّ مُّبِينٌ

Did I not exhort you, O children of Adam, saying, "Do not worship Satan, he is indeed your manifest enemy?" (36:60)

However, for Satan-worshippers who believe that he is effective in the administration of the world, the meaning of Satan's guardianship over them is that they worship and magnify him. This is like the *wathaniyyah* sect (a group of pagans), who worshipped the angels hoping to benefit from their goodness and worshipped the jinn to be saved from their evil.[i]

The Noble Qur'ān states that ominous fate lies in wait for the close friends of Satan. It says:

كُتِبَ عَلَيْهِ أَنَّهُ مَن تَوَلَّاهُ فَأَنَّهُ يُضِلُّهُ

It has been decreed that he [Satan] will mislead those who take him as a close friend. (22:4)

The Companions of Satan

Some people, due to turning away from Allah's remembrance and the intensity of their obedience of Iblīs, have a constant and evil companion with them. This companion is from the same species as Satan,

---

i. Ibid., 13:325

and he always harms and deceives them Unfortunately, at times this companionship is so strong that it continues in the realm of *barzakh* (purgatory) and on the Day of Judgement as well:

وَمَن يَعْشُ عَن ذِكْرِ الرَّحْمَٰنِ نُقَيِّضْ لَهُ شَيْطَانًا فَهُوَ لَهُ قَرِينٌ وَإِنَّهُمْ لَيَصُدُّونَهُمْ عَنِ السَّبِيلِ وَيَحْسَبُونَ أَنَّهُم مُّهْتَدُونَ حَتَّىٰ إِذَا جَاءَنَا قَالَ يَا لَيْتَ بَيْنِي وَبَيْنَكَ بُعْدَ الْمَشْرِقَيْنِ فَبِئْسَ الْقَرِينُ وَلَن يَنفَعَكُمُ الْيَوْمَ إِذ ظَّلَمْتُمْ أَنَّكُمْ فِي الْعَذَابِ مُشْتَرِكُونَ

And We assign a devil to be the companion of him who turns his heart away from the remembrance of the Beneficent. Indeed, they bar them from the way [of Allah], while they suppose that they are [rightly] guided. Until he comes to Us [with his companion], he will say [to his companion], "I wish there had been between me and you the distance between the east and the west! What an evil companion [you are]!" Today that [sorrow] will be of no avail to you. As you did wrong, so will you share in the punishment. (43:36-39)

The companions of Satan are constantly tormented and hurt due to this permanent companionship:

أَلَمْ تَرَ أَنَّا أَرْسَلْنَا الشَّيَاطِينَ عَلَى الْكَافِرِينَ تَؤُزُّهُمْ أَزًّا

Have you not regarded that We unleash the *shayāṭīn* (devils) upon the faithless to urge them vigorously [towards sins]? (19:83)

One of the signs of the presence of such a companion is being constantly insinuated towards sins, disobeying Allah and being aloof from good matters. When a person who is a companion of Satan visits sacred places, associates with Divine scholars, or enters a blessed period like the month of Ramaḍān, he experiences tranquillity and freedom from the commands and insinuations of Satan. That is because the devils are forbidden from carrying out their activities in these areas.

To ensure that he does not have such a companion, man must examine his heart by paying careful attention to his condition before and after his presence in such enlightening places and times. If he sees a change in his state and the emancipation from satanic insinuations when in these areas, he must think of a remedy. It is incumbent that he free himself from the companionship of Satan and separate himself from this companion before the advent of death.

The Directions of Satan's Influence

Satan deceives man from several directions, as the Qurʾān quotes him saying:

> ثُمَّ لَآتِيَنَّهُم مِّن بَيْنِ أَيْدِيهِمْ وَمِنْ خَلْفِهِمْ وَعَنْ أَيْمَانِهِمْ وَعَن شَمَائِلِهِمْ
>
> Then I will come at them from their front and from their rear, and from their right and their left ... (7:17)

Sometimes he deceives man by placing aspirations and wishes in front of him. He makes him preoccupied with affairs that please the self and from which it derives pleasure, like future possessions or a promise of position and status. Or at times he approaches him using things that are feared and dreaded by man (like poverty). He may scare man, that if he does *infāq* of his wealth then he will be afflicted with destitution and poverty. Or similarly, he may blame and reproach those who embarked upon a virtuous act and did *infāq*.

That which is intended by Satan misguiding man from the rear is his deception by means of children and offspring. That is because Satan suggests to man that, through his children, he will live forever. In this manner he makes him heedless of death which detaches people from one another. Due to this false notion, man is anguished at the distress of his children and rejoices in their happiness. To this end he busies himself in amassing wealth for them—by any means possible, permissible (*ḥalāl*) or impermissible (*ḥarām*). He procures all the facilities that he can for them, to the extent that he even endangers and destroys himself to secure a better life for them.

The right side means the aspect of man's strength and blessings in religious and *fiṭrī*[i] matters that are linked to man's felicity. Man's being deceived from this side is by going to the extreme in religious affairs and burdening himself with things that Allah has not commanded. Examples include obsession (*waswās*) in matters of ritual purity (*ṭahārah* and *najāsah*) or in the recitations and actions of prayers. The Qur'ān names these types of satanic insinuations as a '*khuṭwah*' (step) and says:

يَا أَيُّهَا النَّاسُ كُلُوا مِمَّا فِي الْأَرْضِ حَلَالًا طَيِّبًا وَلَا تَتَّبِعُوا خُطُوَاتِ الشَّيْطَانِ ۚ إِنَّهُ لَكُمْ عَدُوٌّ مُّبِينٌ

> O mankind! Eat of what is lawful and pure in the Earth, and do not follow in Satan's steps. Indeed, he is your manifest enemy. (2:168)

Satan deceiving man from the left side means his insinuations in non-*fiṭrī* matters and desires. Through this channel, Satan glamorizes desires and evil in man's eyes and invites him to commit sin and follow the selfish desires.

Therefore, everyone has their own weak point and it is possible Satan only insinuates him from this one angle. It is also possible that Satan allures him from all sides. Thus, man must be vigilant and avoid every thought, action, or trait that causes heedlessness from Allah the Exalted and the path of His servitude. Anything that eventually leads to heedlessness and remoteness from Allah is a step of Satan. The Noble Qur'ān has described examples of these steps, such as promising man poverty when he wants to help others, indecent acts (*faḥshā*),[ii] as well as drinking alcohol, gambling, and idol worship.[iii]

Categories of People against Satan's Deceit

Satan at the beginning of his deviation from the path of Divine servitude, swore that he would misguide all human beings except a few:

---

i. *Fiṭrī* matters are those present in the *fiṭrah* (the innate disposition of man).

ii. (2:268), (24:21)

iii. (5:90)

قَالَ أَرَأَيْتَكَ هَٰذَا الَّذِي كَرَّمْتَ عَلَيَّ لَئِنْ أَخَّرْتَنِ إِلَىٰ يَوْمِ الْقِيَامَةِ لَأَحْتَنِكَنَّ ذُرِّيَّتَهُ إِلَّا قَلِيلًا

> He [Satan] said, "Do You see this one whom You have honoured above me? If You give me respite until the Day of Resurrection, I will surely cause his progeny to perish, [all of them] save a few.'" (17:62)

This small group are the ones whose existence is purified and freed from every attachment and attention to other than Allah. The Noble Qur'ān calls these individuals '*mukhlaṣ*' and quotes Satan saying about them:

وَلَأُغْوِيَنَّهُمْ أَجْمَعِينَ إِلَّا عِبَادَكَ مِنْهُمُ الْمُخْلَصِينَ

> I will surely pervert them, all except Your *mukhlaṣ* servants among them. (15: 39,40)

In another verse, this group has been introduced as the grateful ones:

وَلَا تَجِدُ أَكْثَرَهُمْ شَاكِرِينَ

> And You will not find most of them to be grateful. (7:17)

To deviate man, Satan needs a point of weakness and something he can cling onto such as love of the world, love of the self, etc. By means of these he causes man to exit from the path of the *fiṭrah* and afflicts him with Allah's disobedience. The root of these weak points in man's existence that Satan can cling to, are the impurities and attachments that have subjugated and conquered his existence.

However, there are always men with lofty ambition who free their heart from such foreign occupation through their efforts and self-struggle (*mujāhidah*), turning it into the safe sanctuary of the Divine. As a result, Satan is incapable of ensnaring them because there is no excuse for him, no weak point that he can cling to and thereby enter the domain of their being. These are the *mukhlaṣūn*, the purified one who according to the above-mentioned verse, Satan himself has admitted that he is unable to ensnare them.

Allah (the Provider of abundance and the Sublime) has attributed the purifying of these servants to Himself and has described it in the following manner:

> إِنَّا أَخْلَصْنَاهُم بِخَالِصَةٍ ذِكْرَى الدَّارِ
>
> Indeed, We purified them with a special purification, that is the exclusive remembrance of the abode [of the Hereafter]. (38:46)

This group of people have reached a station of *tawḥīd* whereby they do not see any independence for a being other than Allah the Exalted. They see Satan to be a wretched and weak creature who is surrounded by Allah's existence, subject to His infinite power, and who manifests some of the attributes of Allah's majesty such as '*al-muḍill*' (the One who leads astray). Therefore, even in their encounter with Satan they derive *tawḥīdī* benefits.

These are the same people who through Allah's grace and by means of struggle, have found their way to the reality of servitude. While describing them to ʿUnwān al-Baṣrī, Imam al-Ṣādiq (peace be upon him) says, "Satan becomes abject and insignificant in their eyes."

Marḥūm ʿAllāmah Ṭabāṭabāʾī describing the state of the *mukhlaṣīn*, says:

> The *mukhlaṣīn* are the ones who have become purified and exclusive for Allah. Therefore, in their worship and servitude they do not ascribe a partner to Him, they do not allocate a portion for other than Allah, they do not remember anything save their Lord and they have forgotten everything other than Allah, even their own selves. As a result, in their heart there is none except Allah the Immaculate and there is no place in their being for Satan or his beautifying.
>
> The *shākirīn* [the grateful ones] are those in whose existence the trait of gratefulness has become established in its absolute sense. As a result, they do not encounter a blessing except that they are grateful. This means that they utilize the blessings—through their words and actions—such that it becomes evident these blessings are from their Lord who has favoured them with this. They do not come across anything (be it themselves or others), except that they are in the state of remembering their Lord before they encounter it, while

they are with it and after it. They remember that it is Allah the Exalted's property in the absolute sense; they do not own anything of it themselves. Thus, their remembrance of Allah in this manner makes them forget the remembrance of others, except by means of Allah. Thus, [Allah says in the Noble Qur'ān], "Allah has not put two hearts within any man." (i)

Therefore, if the words are given their true meaning, then definitely the *shākirīn* are the *mukhlaṣīn*. Satan's statement in which he excludes the *shākirīn* or the *mukhlaṣīn* from being encompassed by his *ighwā* and misguidance, is a true statement expressing the reality of the situation. He has not uttered it vainly, nor is it to oblige the children of Adam with a favour, or out of pity on them or other such reasons. Thus, these are the very words that he uttered to the Source of Honour and Exaltedness [Allah]. I mean his statement, "As You have consigned me to perversity, I will surely lie in wait for them on Your straight path." Till he said, "and You will not find most of them to be grateful." So, he informed that he will seek them from every possible way and he will corrupt the affair of most of them by removing them from the straight path (*al-ṣirāt al-mustaqīm*). (ii)

The second group with regards to Satan's deceit, consists of individuals who have placed the bonds of Allah's servitude on their necks, but their hearts have not entirely become free from attachment to other than Allah. Sometimes they fall prey to satanic insinuations. Nonetheless, Allah has removed them from the domination of Satan:

إِنَّ عِبَادِي لَيْسَ لَكَ عَلَيْهِمْ سُلْطَانٌ

Indeed, as for My servants you do not have any authority over them, (15:42)

The third group are those who always follow the *ighwā* of Satan, are persistent in their opposition to Allah the Exalted and do not humble

i. (33:4)

ii. Ṭabāṭabā'ī, Tafsīr al-Mīzān, 8:32

themselves before Him. These are the same perverse and astray people who have removed themselves from Allah's servitude and have placed themselves under the authority of Satan. Therefore, Allah says:

إِنَّا جَعَلْنَا الشَّيَاطِينَ أَوْلِيَاءَ لِلَّذِينَ لَا يُؤْمِنُونَ

We have indeed made the devils friends of those who have no faith. (7:27)

إِنَّهُمُ اتَّخَذُوا الشَّيَاطِينَ أَوْلِيَاءَ مِن دُونِ اللَّهِ

They took devils for guardians instead of Allah. (7:30)

The Ways of Freeing Oneself from Satan's Evil

In the same manner that there are different grades and levels of being caught in the trap of Satan, likewise escaping from Iblīs' trap also has various degrees.

1) Freedom from Satan's evil of for those who are astray

For those who are astray—those whom Satan has penetrated their entire existence and is their constant companion—it is necessary that they seek deliverance from the evil of Satan by following the truth in the matters related to ideology and belief, by fulfilling the rights of people, and by humbling beseeching Allah and His *awliyā'*. Also, they must repent from all the sins and deviations that came about due to following Satan.

2) Freedom from Satan's evil for the believers

Most of the believers are afflicted by the *waswasah* of Satan and succumb to acting upon this *waswasah*. Only those who have made their existence to be exclusively for Allah (the Provider of abundance and the Sublime), are freed from this trap:

وَلَأُغْوِيَنَّهُمْ أَجْمَعِينَ إِلَّا عِبَادَكَ مِنْهُمُ الْمُخْلَصِينَ

And I will surely pervert them, all except Your dedicated servants among them. (15:39-40)

وَلَا تَجِدُ أَكْثَرَهُمْ شَاكِرِينَ

And You will not find most of them to be grateful. (7:17)

Therefore, it is necessary that those who have set out on the path of union with the Beloved should pay attention to the ways of deliverance from Satan's evil. These will be mentioned shortly.

3) Freedom from Satan's evil for the *mukhlaṣīn*

Even those who have made their existence to be exclusively for the Divine—despite having reached a level of *tawḥīd* such that their lofty gnosis keeps them safe from Satan's *ighwā*—are not free from the *waswasah* of that accursed creature. However, the difference is that his *waswasah* affects others, but does not affect the heart of such a person. By reaching a certain level of Allah's remembrance, these individuals are secure from Satan's evil.

In this section, we point out some of the methods of staying secure from Satan.

1) Allah's Remembrance

Satan's goal is to lie in wait for man on the straight path, so that he can bring man into confrontation with Allah and cause him to claim independence from Him. Therefore, every action that is contrary to this prevents Satan from working towards this goal. The most important of these actions is Allah's remembrance which comprises of three levels, each of which has their own effect: the heart, actions and the tongue. Placing trust (*tawakkul*) in Allah the Exalted, which is considered remembrance of the heart, brings about tranquillity in the heart and releases man from Satan's authority. As Allah says:

إِنَّهُ لَيْسَ لَهُ سُلْطَانٌ عَلَى الَّذِينَ آمَنُوا وَعَلَى رَبِّهِمْ يَتَوَكَّلُونَ

> Indeed, he does not have any authority over those who have faith and put their trust in their Lord. (16:99)

The folk of gnosis (*ahl-i maʿrifah*) consider Satan to be the guard dog of the Master's court. He attacks strangers and intruders who approach that sacred precinct, and only a small number of elite (the *mukhlaṣīn*) are completely secure from his evil. Therefore, those who seek the alley of the Beloved and desire to humble themselves in servitude before His needless presence, it is necessary that they think of a plan to deliver themselves from Satan's evil. That is because he has laid his trap for the wayfarers to the Alley of the Beloved. Imam al-Ṣādiq (peace be upon him) says to ʿAbd Allah ibn Jundab:

يَا عَبْدَ اللَّهِ لَقَدْ نَصَبَ إِبْلِيسُ حَبَائِلَهُ فِي دَارِ الْغُرُورِ فَمَا يَقْصِدُ فِيهَا إِلَّا أَوْلِيَاءَنَا

> O ʿAbd Allah! Indeed, Iblīs has installed his ropes in the abode of delusion [the world], and [through them] he only aims at those who are our friends.[i]

The best method for escaping from Satan when confronted by him, is to be engaged in one of the levels of remembrance (*dhikr*). Undoubtedly, this means remembrance at the level of one's actions accompanied by remembrance of the heart and the tongue. Thus, this kind of remembrance has been highly recommended. One of the levels of remembrance of the heart and the tongue is to seek refuge in Allah. That is because the control of all the beings, including Satan, are in Allah's hands. This is the recommendation of the Qur'ān, that says:

وَإِمَّا يَنزَغَنَّكَ مِنَ الشَّيْطَانِ نَزْغٌ فَاسْتَعِذْ بِاللَّهِ ۚ إِنَّهُ سَمِيعٌ عَلِيمٌ

> Should a temptation from Satan disturb you, seek refuge in Allah; indeed, He is Hearing, Knowing. (7:200)

إِنَّ الَّذِينَ اتَّقَوْا إِذَا مَسَّهُمْ طَائِفٌ مِّنَ الشَّيْطَانِ تَذَكَّرُوا فَإِذَا هُم مُّبْصِرُونَ

> When those who are pious are touched by a visitation of Satan, they remember [Allah] and, behold, they perceive. (7:201)

This verse elucidates the conduct of the *muttaqīn* (the pious) in their encounter with Satan. When they are faced with the deceitful *waswasah* of Satan, they remember that Allah is their administrator and sustainer, and that all their affairs are in His powerful hands. Hence, they delegate this matter to Him as well, so that Allah does away with Satan's plot and trap and removes the veil of heedlessness from the

---

i. al-Ḥarrānī, Tuḥaf al-ʿUqūl, 301

eye of their heart. Consequent to this remembrance, Divine Light enlightens their souls, the veil of heedlessness is removed from their interior (*bāṭin*), and Satan's hands are severed from their hearts.

Therefore, *isti'ādhah* means to seek refuge in Allah the Exalted and is reckoned to be a type of remembrance as well as one of the stations of *tawakkul* (reliance on Allah).

Based on this very same point, the Ahl al-Bayt (peace be upon them) in their supplications, would request Allah that they remain secure from Satan's evil and that his authority be repelled from them:

> وَ أَعِذْنِي وَ ذُرِّيَّتِي مِنَ الشَّيْطَانِ الرَّجِيمِ، فَإِنَّكَ خَلَقْتَنَا وَ أَمَرْتَنَا وَ نَهَيْتَنَا وَ رَغَّبْتَنَا فِي ثَوَابِ مَا أَمَرْتَنَا وَ رَهَّبْتَنَا عِقَابَهُ، وَ جَعَلْتَ لَنَا عَدُوّاً يَكِيدُنَا، سَلَّطْتَهُ مِنَّا عَلَى مَا لَمْ تُسَلِّطْنَا عَلَيْهِ مِنْهُ، أَسْكَنْتَهُ صُدُورَنَا، وَ أَجْرَيْتَهُ مَجَارِيَ دِمَائِنَا، لَا يَغْفُلُ إِنْ غَفَلْنَا، وَ لَا يَنْسَى إِنْ نَسِينَا، يُؤْمِنُنَا عِقَابَكَ، وَ يُخَوِّفُنَا بِغَيْرِكَ. إِنْ هَمَمْنَا بِفَاحِشَةٍ شَجَّعَنَا عَلَيْهَا، وَ إِنْ هَمَمْنَا بِعَمَلٍ صَالِحٍ ثَبَّطَنَا عَنْهُ، يَتَعَرَّضُ لَنَا بِالشَّهَوَاتِ، وَ يَنْصِبُ لَنَا بِالشُّبُهَاتِ، إِنْ وَعَدَنَا كَذَبَنَا، وَ إِنْ مَنَّانَا أَخْلَفَنَا، وَ إِلَّا تَصْرِفْ عَنَّا كَيْدَهُ يُضِلَّنَا، وَ إِلَّا تَقِنَا خَبَالَهُ يَسْتَزِلَّنَا. اللَّهُمَّ فَاقْهَرْ سُلْطَانَهُ عَنَّا بِسُلْطَانِكَ حَتَّى تَحْبِسَهُ عَنَّا بِكَثْرَةِ الدُّعَاءِ لَكَ فَنُصْبِحَ مِنْ كَيْدِهِ فِي الْمَعْصُومِينَ بِكَ.
>
> Give me and my progeny refuge from the accursed Satan, for You have created us, commanded us, and prohibited us, and made us desire the reward of what You have commanded, and fear its punishment! You assigned to us an enemy who schemes against us, gave him an authority over us in a way that You did not give us authority over him, allowed him to dwell in our breasts and let him run in our blood vessels; he is not heedless, though we be heedless, he does not forget, though we forget; he makes us feel secure from Your punishment and fills us with fear toward other than You. If we are about to commit an indecency, he gives us courage to do

> so, and if we are about to perform a righteous work, he holds us back from it. He opposes us through passions and sets up for us doubts. If he promises us, he lies, and if he raises our hopes, he fails to fulfil them. If You do not turn his trickery away from us, he will misguide us, and if You do not protect us from his corruption, he will cause us to slip. O God, so defeat his authority over us through Your authority, such that You hold him back from us through the frequency of our supplication to You and we leave his trickery and rise up among those preserved by You from sin! (i)

Many of the *wājib* (obligatory) and *mustaḥabb* (supererogatory) actions that have been prescribed throughout the day and night, are also intended to help ward off Satan's evil by seeking refuge in Allah. Therefore, one should not be heedless of them, even if it is only possible to perform a few of them. As has been narrated in the supplication recited after morning prayers:

أَعُوذُ بِاللَّهِ السَّمِيعِ الْعَلِيمِ مِنْ هَمَزَاتِ الشَّيَاطِينِ وَ أَعُوذُ بِاللَّهِ أَنْ يَحْضُرُونِ إِنَّ اللَّهَ هُوَ السَّمِيعُ الْعَلِيم

> I seek refuge in Allah the Hearing, the Knowing, from the insinuations of the devils. And I seek refuge in Allah from their presence near me. Indeed, He is the Hearing, the Knowing. (ii)

Therefore, the grace and mercy of Allah the Immaculate are the sole factor for deliverance from Satan's evil. Hence, we must seek assistance from Him, for:

وَلَوْلَا فَضْلُ اللَّهِ عَلَيْكُمْ وَرَحْمَتُهُ لَاتَّبَعْتُمُ الشَّيْطَانَ إِلَّا قَلِيلًا

> And were it not for Allah's grace upon you and His mercy, you would have surely followed Satan, [all] except a few. (4:83)

> Entreating and pleading before Allah is also one of the ways of taking refuge in the Sustainer from the devils' evil.

---

i. Imam Zayn al-ʿĀbidīn (ʿa), al-Ṣaḥīfah Al-Sajjādiyyah, supplication 25

ii. Qummī, Mafātīḥ al-Jinān, the section regarding the *taʿqībāt* of the morning prayer

Likewise, doing *tawassul* to the Divine *awliyā'* also causes them to give us refuge from *wasāwis* of Satan and the self. As we say describing the *awliyā'* (peace be upon them):

وَ كَهْفِ الْوَرَى ... وَ الذَّادَةِ الْحُمَاة

And [you are] the refuge of the people [other than yourselves] ... and those who drive away [that which is evil] and support.[i]

2) Remembrance of the Hereafter

One of Satan's tactics is that he presents man's existence and that of the world as being infinite in man's view. Remembering the Hereafter prevents this type of *waswasah* from being effective.

For this reason, Allah (the Provider of abundance and the Sublime) has considered remembrance of the Hereafter and paying attention to it as being the factor that caused the *mukhlaṣīn* to reach their lofty station. It was this factor that purified them from paying attention to anything else (other than God). As He says:

إِنَّا أَخْلَصْنَاهُم بِخَالِصَةٍ ذِكْرَى الدَّارِ

Indeed, We purified them with exclusive remembrance of the abode [of the Hereafter]. (38:46)

Similarly, it is this matter that prevents Satan from being able to influence them. As is mentioned in another verse, the only group from amongst the believers that is free from being subjugated by the *wasāwis* of Iblīs, are those that have conviction in the Hereafter and remember it. As for those who view the Hereafter with doubt and uncertainty, they believe in the empty promises of Satan:

وَلَقَدْ صَدَّقَ عَلَيْهِمْ إِبْلِيسُ ظَنَّهُ فَاتَّبَعُوهُ إِلَّا فَرِيقًا مِّنَ الْمُؤْمِنِينَ وَمَا كَانَ لَهُ عَلَيْهِم مِّن سُلْطَانٍ إِلَّا لِنَعْلَمَ مَن يُؤْمِنُ بِالْآخِرَةِ مِمَّنْ هُوَ مِنْهَا فِي شَكٍّ ۗ وَرَبُّكَ عَلَىٰ كُلِّ شَيْءٍ حَفِيظٌ

i. Majlisī, Biḥār al-Anwār, 102:103

Certainly, Iblīs had his conjecture come true about them. So, they followed him, all except a part of the faithful. He had no authority over them, but that We may ascertain those who believe in the Hereafter from those who are in doubt about it, and your Lord is watchful over all things. (34:20)

In addition to this, forgetting the Hereafter leads to straying away from the path of Allah:

إِنَّ الَّذِينَ يَضِلُّونَ عَن سَبِيلِ اللَّهِ لَهُمْ عَذَابٌ
شَدِيدٌ بِمَا نَسُوا يَوْمَ الْحِسَابِ

Indeed, there is a severe punishment for those who stray from the way of Allah, because of their forgetting the Day of Reckoning. (38:26)

That is because Satan's job is to distract man with his own self, the world and its different affairs thus making him heedless of man's reality and his connection to the Unseen Realm. As a result (of being occupied with the world), man becomes afflicted with the diseases of worldliness. In the words of Amīr al-Mu'minīn (peace be upon him):

ذِكْرُ الدُّنْيَا أَدْوَأُ الْأَدْوَاءِ ... وَ ذِكْرُ الْآخِرَةِ دَوَاءٌ وَ شِفَاء

Remembrance of the world is the worst of diseases ... and remembrance of the Hereafter is a remedy and cure. [i]

He also says:

كُلُّ شَيْءٍ مِنَ الدُّنْيَا سَمَاعُهُ أَعْظَمُ مِنْ عِيَانِهِ وَ كُلُّ شَيْءٍ مِنَ الْآخِرَةِ عِيَانُهُ أَعْظَمُ مِنْ سَمَاعِهِ فَلْيَكْفِكُمْ مِنَ الْعِيَانِ السَّمَاعُ وَ مِنَ الْغَيْبِ الْخَبَر

Everything in this world, hearing about it is grander than seeing it and everything in the Hereafter, seeing it is grander than hearing about it. Therefore, hearing should suffice you with regards to that which is visible [in this world] and being

i. al-Āmudī, Ghurar al-Hikam, narration 5175

informed should suffice you with regards to the unseen.[i]

---

i. al-Radī, Nahj al-Balāghah, sermon 114

Section Three
Not Being Affected by People's Judgement on the Path of Truth

Allah the Exalted has provided everybody with the tools required for reaching the true goal. Also, everyone perceives this goal and the meaningful nature of their creation and the system of the world. In view of this, the true value of a person lies in having correctly understood the goal and the path required to reach it, and then applied it in the different aspects of life. While it is true that people affect one another in their thoughts, ideas, and actions, however no one can prevent others from choosing the correct thoughts, beliefs, and a course of action that gravitates around the truth. In their social interactions, everyone is tested by one another, and choosing to act in accordance with the truth entails discomfort, hardship, and requires that a person combat the fleeting and at times vain desires of the self. Thus, those individuals who act in this manner form the smallest group of people amongst mankind; most people spend their lives heedless and ignorant about the reality of their existence. The Noble Qur'ān also considers proximity to Allah and *taqwā* to be the criteria for determining the value of human beings:

إِنَّ أَكْرَمَكُمْ عِندَ اللَّهِ أَتْقَاكُمْ

> Indeed, the noblest of you in the sight of Allah is the one amongst you with the most *taqwā*. (49:13)

It has reproached most of the people, those who have strayed away from this goal and the path, saying:

(أَكْثَرُهُمْ لَا يَعْقِلُونَ)، (أَكْثَرَهُمْ لَا يَعْلَمُونَ)، (أَكْثَرَهُمْ لَا يَشْكُرُونَ)، (وَأَكْثَرُهُمْ فَاسِقُونَ)، (أَكْثَرَهُمْ يَجْهَلُونَ)، (أَكْثَرُهُمْ لَا يُؤْمِنُونَ)، (أَكْثَرُهُم مُّشْرِكِينَ)

> Most of them do not use their reason. (5:103) Most of them do not know. (6:37) Most of them do not give thanks. (10:60) Most of them are transgressors. (9:8) Most of them are ignorant. (6:111) Most of them do not believe. (2:100)

Most of them are polytheists. (30:42)

Necessary Matters for Realizing the Path of Truth

Based on the point just mentioned, the Noble Qur'ān and the Imams (peace be upon them) have provided certain advice to the wayfarers of the path of servitude. By virtue of acting upon these teachings, they can be saved from the difficulties of the surrounding environment and society. Some of them are:

1) Distinguishing Truth from Falsehood

An inclination towards the truth is one of the things ingrained in man's *fiṭrah* (innate disposition); no human being desires falsehood. That is because the tool for perceiving truth has been placed in him. However, due to other inclinations that have also been placed in man—especially love of the self and selfishness—recognizing the truth from falsehood in all matters is normally difficult for him. Therefore, to reach the true goal of man's existence and the world—the flourishing of one's potential—one must carefully utilize their different cognitive faculties so that the truth can correctly be distinguished from falsehood. This is because recognizing the truth allows a person to recognize the people of truth, those who adhere to the truth in society, and to keep aloof from the people of falsehood. Amīr al-Mu'minīn (peace be upon him) says in this regard:

إِنَّ الْحَقَّ وَ الْبَاطِلَ لَا يُعْرَفَانِ بِالنَّاس

Truth and falsehood are not recognized through people. (i)

لَا يُعرَفُ الْحَقُ بِالرِّجَالِ اعْرِفِ الْحَقَّ تَعْرِفْ أَهْلَه

Truth is not recognized through men. Recognize the truth [first], and you will come to know its adherents. (ii)

Throughout the course of history, there have been many people

i. Majlisī, Bihār al-Anwār, 22:105

ii. Ibid., 40:126

who inclined towards deviated groups and individuals due to not distinguishing between the truth and falsehood in society. This led to the corruption and destruction of their spiritual fate, all because they lacked the criterion for distinguishing between truth and falsehood.

Al-Ḥasan al-Baṣrī[14] is one such person, who due to this very reason, kept aloof from Amīr al-Mu'minīn (peace be upon him) and was deprived of perceiving the truth. It is narrated that:

مَرَّ أَمِيرُ الْمُؤْمِنِينَ ع بِالْحَسَنِ الْبَصْرِيِّ وَ هُوَ يَتَوَضَّأُ فَقَالَ يَا حَسَنُ أَسْبِغِ الْوُضُوءَ فَقَالَ يَا أَمِيرَ الْمُؤْمِنِينَ لَقَدْ قَتَلْتَ بِالْأَمْسِ أُنَاساً يَشْهَدُونَ أَنْ لَا إِلَهَ إِلَّا اللَّهُ وَحْدَهُ لَا شَرِيكَ لَهُ وَ أَنَّ مُحَمَّداً عَبْدُهُ وَ رَسُولُهُ يُصَلُّونَ الْخَمْسَ وَ يُسْبِغُونَ الْوُضُوءَ فَقَالَ لَهُ أَمِيرُ الْمُؤْمِنِينَ ع قَدْ كَانَ مَا رَأَيْتَ فَمَا مَنَعَكَ أَنْ تُعِينَ عَلَيْنَا عَدُوَّنَا فَقَالَ وَ اللَّهِ لَأَصْدُقَنَّكَ يَا أَمِيرَ الْمُؤْمِنِينَ- لَقَدْ خَرَجْتُ فِي أَوَّلِ يَوْمٍ فَاغْتَسَلْتُ وَ تَحَنَّطْتُ وَ صَبَبْتُ عَلَيَّ سِلَاحِي وَ أَنَا لَا أَشُكُّ فِي أَنَّ التَّخَلُّفَ عَنْ أُمِّ الْمُؤْمِنِينَ عَائِشَةَ هُوَ الْكُفْرُ فَلَمَّا انْتَهَيْتُ إِلَى مَوْضِعٍ مِنَ الْخُرَيْبَةِنَادَى مُنَادٍ يَا حَسَنُ إِلَى أَيْنَ ارْجِعْ فَإِنَّ الْقَاتِلَ وَ الْمَقْتُولَ فِي النَّارِ فَرَجَعْتُ ذُعْراً وَ جَلَسْتُ فِي بَيْتِي فَلَمَّا كَانَ الْيَوْمُ الثَّانِي لَمْ أَشُكَّ أَنَّ التَّخَلُّفَ عَنْ أُمِّ الْمُؤْمِنِينَ عَائِشَةَ هُوَ الْكُفْرُ فَتَحَنَّطْتُ وَ صَبَبْتُ عَلَيَّ سِلَاحِي وَ خَرَجْتُ إِلَى الْقِتَالِ-حَتَّى انْتَهَيْتُ إِلَى مَوْضِعٍ مِنَ الْخُرَيْبَةِ فَنَادَانِي مُنَادٍ مِنْ خَلْفِي يَا حَسَنُ إِلَى أَيْنَ مَرَّةً بَعْدَ أُخْرَى فَإِنَّ الْقَاتِلَ وَ الْمَقْتُولَ فِي النَّارِ قَالَ عَلِيٌّ ع صَدَقْتَ أَ فَتَدْرِي مَنْ ذَلِكَ الْمُنَادِي قَالَ لَا قَالَ ع ذَاكَ أَخُوكَ إِبْلِيسُ وَ صَدَقَكَ أَنَّ الْقَاتِلَ مِنْهُمْ وَ الْمَقْتُولَ فِي النَّارِ فَقَالَ الْحَسَنُ الْبَصْرِيُّ الْآنَ عَرَفْتُ يَا أَمِيرَ الْمُؤْمِنِينَ أَنَّ الْقَوْمَ هَلْكَى

Once Amīr al-Mu'minīn (peace be upon him) passed by al-Ḥasan al-Baṣrī while he was making *wuḍū'*. He said to him, "O Ḥasan! Perform the *wuḍū'* correctly." He replied, "O Amīr al-Mu'minīn! Yesterday you killed men who testified to Allah's oneness and that Muḥammad (peace and blessings be upon him and his family) is His servant and messenger, who prayed and who performed the *wuḍū'* correctly." Amīr al-Mu'minīn (peace be upon him) said to him, "What you saw, did [indeed] transpire. So, what prevented you from helping us against our enemy?" He said, "By Allah! I acknowledge what you have said. O Amīr al-Mu'minīn! Indeed, on the first day, I came out, performed *ghusl*, applied *ḥunūṭ*[i] and picked up my weapon. This was while I had no doubt that going against the Mother of Believers 'Ā'ishā is disbelief. Thereafter, when I reached a part of [an area named] *Kharībah*, a voice called out and said, 'O Ḥasan! Where are you going? Turn back, for both the killer and the killed are in the Hellfire.' So, I returned in the state of fear and confined myself to my home. On the second day [as well] I did not have any doubt that going against the Mother of Believers 'Ā'ishā is disbelief, therefore I applied *hunūṭ*, took my weapon and came out towards the battlefield, until I reached a part of [an area named] *Kharībah*, a voice called me from behind, 'O Ḥasan! Where are you going?' It repeated this a few times [then said], 'Turn back, for both the killer and the killed are in the Hellfire.'" 'Alī (peace be upon him) said, "You have spoken the truth. Do you know who was the one who called you?" He replied, "No." He (peace be upon him) said, "That was your brother Satan and he said the truth; those who killed and those who were killed from amongst them [the army of "Ā'ishā] are in the Hellfire.' Al-Ḥasan al-Baṣrī said, "O Amīr al-Mu'minīn! Now I understand that all of that group have been destroyed."[ii]

---

i. *Ḥunūṭ* is a substance placed on a corpse after the ghusl has been performed. Here it indicates how al-Ḥasan al- Baṣrī was ready to die.

ii. Majlisī, Bihār al-Anwār, 42:141

It is for this reason that the Imams (peace be upon them) would beseech Allah in their supplications with the following words:

اللّهُمَّ صَلِّ عَلَى مُحَمَّدٍ وَ آلِ مُحَمَّدٍ وَ أَرِنِي الْحَقَ حَقّاً فَأَتَّبِعَهُ وَ الْبَاطِلَ بَاطِلًا فَأَجْتَنِبَهُ وَ لَا تَجْعَلْهُ عَلَيَّ مُتَشَابِهاً فَأَتَّبِعَ هَوَايَ بِغَيْرِ هُدًى مِنْكَ وَ اجْعَلْ هَوَايَ تَبَعاً لِطَاعَتِكَ وَ خُذْ رِضَا نَفْسِكَ مِنْ نَفْسِي وَ اهْدِنِي لِمَا اخْتُلِفَ فِيهِ مِنَ الْحَقِّ بِإِذْنِكَ إِنَّكَ تَهْدِي مَنْ تَشَاءُ إِلَى صِرَاطٍ مُسْتَقِيم

O Allah! Send your salutations on Muḥammad and the progeny of Muḥammad. Show me the truth as [being the] truth, so that I follow it and show me the falsehood as [truly being] falsehood so that I avoid it. Do not make it obscure for me such that I follow my desires without [any] guidance from You. Make my desires follow Your obedience and be pleased with me. By Your permission, guide me to the truth in that which there is a difference [of opinion]. Indeed, You guide whomever You wish to a straight path. (i)

2) The Companionship of Pure Individuals

After a person has distinguished truth from falsehood and has recognized the true adherents of truth who have put the truth into practice, associating with them is one of the requirements of spiritual wayfaring towards true perfection. Therefore, the Noble Qur'ān does not consider belief in Allah the Exalted, belief in other realities, and being on the path of purity as being sufficient. Rather, it says:

يَا أَيُّهَا الَّذِينَ آمَنُوا اتَّقُوا اللَّهَ وَكُونُوا مَعَ الصَّادِقِينَ

O you who have faith! Be wary of Allah and be with the Truthful. (9:119)

Truthful here means those people who—both inwardly and outwardly—are truthful in their beliefs, morals and actions, in all aspects

i. Ibid., 99:22

of their life. To be truthful in these matters means that their beliefs, morals and actions conform with the truth. However, to be able to accompany the truthful requires that one turns his back on the transient worldly desires, does not pay attention to the seekers of the world, and undertakes a spiritual struggle against the self. The Messenger of Allah (peace and blessings be upon him and his family) says:

> قَالُوا يَا رُوحَ اللَّهِ فَمَنْ نُجَالِسُ إِذاً قَالَ مَنْ يُذَكِّرُكُمُ اللَّهَ رُؤْيَتُهُ وَ يَزِيدُ فِي عِلْمِكُمْ مَنْطِقُهُ وَ يُرَغِّبُكُمْ فِي الْآخِرَةِ عَمَلُهُ.
>
> [The disciples of Prophet Jesus (peace be upon him)] said, "O *Rūḥullah*! (i) Who should we keep company with?" He replied, "With one who seeing him reminds you of Allah, his words increase your knowledge, and his actions motivate you towards the Hereafter." (ii)

Imam ʿAlī (peace be upon him) also says:

> جَالِسِ الْعُلَمَاءَ يَزْدَدْ عِلْمُكَ وَ يَحْسُنْ أَدَبُكَ وَ تَزْكُ نَفْسُك
>
> Keep company with the scholars, [for if you do] your knowledge will increase, your manners become good and your soul will be purified. (iii)

Likewise, Imam al-Sajjād (peace be upon him) says:

> مَجَالِسُ الصَّالِحِينَ دَاعِيَةٌ إِلَى الصَّلَاحِ
>
> Keeping the company of the righteous invites [a person] towards righteousness. (iv)

For this reason, associating with such liberated individuals—who on the one hand are very few and on the other hand are scorned and troubled by the people—requires steadfastness and perseverance. The

---

i. *Rūḥullah* means the spirit of Allah and is a title of the Prophet Jesus (peace be upon him). Refer to the Noble Qurʾān (4:171)

ii. al-Harrānī, Tuhaf al-ʿUqūl, 44

iii. al-Āmudī, Ghurar al-Hikam, narration 4786

iv. Majlisī, Bihār al-Anwār, 78:141, narration 35

Divine prophets and their followers were always ridiculed and rebuked by the disbelievers and polytheists. Despite this, they never abandoned the path of truth and in fact, invited others towards it. The Noble Qur'ān has pointed to this in numerous verses. Allah describes the words of Prophet Noah (peace be upon him) when he enjoined his people to have *taqwā* and was faced with their harsh response, in the following words:

> فَاتَّقُوا اللَّهَ وَأَطِيعُونِ قَالُوا أَنُؤْمِنُ لَكَ وَاتَّبَعَكَ الْأَرْذَلُونَ قَالَ وَمَا عِلْمِي بِمَا كَانُوا يَعْمَلُونَ إِنْ حِسَابُهُمْ إِلَّا عَلَىٰ رَبِّي ۖ لَوْ تَشْعُرُونَ وَمَا أَنَا بِطَارِدِ الْمُؤْمِنِينَ إِنْ أَنَا إِلَّا نَذِيرٌ مُّبِينٌ قَالُوا لَئِن لَّمْ تَنتَهِ يَا نُوحُ لَتَكُونَنَّ مِنَ الْمَرْجُومِينَ
>
> "So be wary of Allah and obey me." They said, "Shall we believe in you, when it is the riffraff who follow you?" He [Noah] said, "What do I know as to [the details of] what they used to do? Their reckoning is only with my Lord, should you be aware. I will not drive away the faithful. I am just a manifest warner." They said, 'Noah, if you do not desist, you will certainly be stoned [to death].' (26: 110-116)

Thus, Allah addresses the Noblest Messenger (peace and blessings be upon him and his family) and says:

> وَلَا تَطْرُدِ الَّذِينَ يَدْعُونَ رَبَّهُم بِالْغَدَاةِ وَالْعَشِيِّ يُرِيدُونَ وَجْهَهُ ۖ مَا عَلَيْكَ مِنْ حِسَابِهِم مِّن شَيْءٍ وَمَا مِنْ حِسَابِكَ عَلَيْهِم مِّن شَيْءٍ فَتَطْرُدَهُمْ فَتَكُونَ مِنَ الظَّالِمِينَ
>
> Do not drive away those who supplicate their Lord morning and evening desiring His face. Neither are you accountable for them in any way, nor are they accountable for you in any way, so that you may drive them away and thus become one of the wrongdoers. (6:52)

Likewise, on different occasions Imam ʿAlī (peace be upon him) has advised that the scarcity or abundance of supporters should not affect the believers' truth-centred spirit [i]:

إِنَّ هَذَا الْأَمْرَ لَمْ يَكُنْ نَصْرُهُ وَ لَا خِذْلَانُهُ بِكَثْرَةٍ وَ لَا بِقِلَّةٍ وَ هُوَ دِينُ اللَّهِ الَّذِي أَظْهَرَهُ وَ جُنْدُهُ الَّذِي أَعَدَّهُ وَ أَمَدَّهُ حَتَّى بَلَغَ مَا بَلَغَ وَ طَلَعَ حَيْثُ طَلَعَ وَ نَحْنُ عَلَى مَوْعُودٍ مِنَ اللَّه

Neither is the success of this affair due to an abundance [of supporters] nor is its failure due to a scarcity. It is Allah's religion that He has manifested and His army that He has prepared and aided, so that it shall reach wherever it reaches, and shine wherever it shines—and we have hope in Allah's promise. [ii]

لَا تَسْتَوْحِشُوا فِي طَرِيقِ الْهُدَى لِقِلَّةِ أَهْلِه

Do not be afraid of the scarcity of supporters, on the path of guidance. [iii]

3) Staying Away from the Heedless and Its Different Manners

One of the vulnerable points that affects man's spirituality, is associating with heedless and worldly individuals. Due to its initial inclination towards the *dunyā* and its distractions, man's self is quickly influenced from this angle. Therefore, associating with heedless and sinful people prevents man from paying attention to Allah and the Hereafter.

This importance of this issue is such that Allah has commanded the Noblest Messenger (peace and blessings be upon him and his family) in a special manner, saying:

---

i. A truth-centred spirit means that man makes the truth to be the focus of his activities, always revolving around the truth and reality.

ii. al-Radī, Nahj al-Balāghah, sermon 146

iii. Ibid., sermon 201

فَأَعْرِضْ عَن مَّن تَوَلَّىٰ عَن ذِكْرِنَا وَلَمْ يُرِدْ إِلَّا الْحَيَاةَ الدُّنْيَا ذَٰلِكَ مَبْلَغُهُم مِّنَ الْعِلْمِ ۚ إِنَّ رَبَّكَ هُوَ أَعْلَمُ بِمَن ضَلَّ عَن سَبِيلِهِ وَهُوَ أَعْلَمُ بِمَنِ اهْتَدَىٰ

So, avoid those who turn away from Our remembrance and desire nothing but the life of the world. That is the ultimate reach of their knowledge. Indeed, your Lord knows best [the state of] those who stray from His way, and He [also] knows best those who are [rightly] guided. (53:29-30)

Avoiding heedless and sinful people is achieved in two ways:

1) Outward Avoidance

This is necessary for those who are at the beginning of their spiritual journey. Imam al-Ṣādiq (peace be upon him) has said:

لَا تَصْحَبُوا أَهْلَ الْبِدَعِ وَ لَا تُجَالِسُوهُمْ فَتَصِيرُوا عِنْدَ النَّاسِ كَوَاحِدٍ مِنْهُم

Do not associate with those who innovate (*ahl al-bidaʿ*) [in the religion] and do not sit in their company, for [if you do so] you will become one of them in the eyes of the people.[i]

Likewise, he says:

إِيَّاكُمْ وَ مُجَالَسَةَ الْمُلُوكِ وَ أَبْنَاءِ الدُّنْيَا فَفِي ذَلِكَ ذَهَابُ دِينِكُمْ وَ يُعَقِّبُكُمْ نِفَاقاً وَ ذَلِكَ دَاءٌ دَوِيٌّ لَا شِفَاءَ لَهُ وَ يُورِثُ قَسَاوَةَ الْقَلْبِ وَ يَسْلُبُكُمُ الْخُشُوعَ

Avoid associating with the kings and worldly people. For in that is the destruction of your religion, it causes hypocrisy to ensue, it is a chronic illness which has no cure, it causes hardness of the heart, and takes away humility [in front of Allah and the truth].[ii]

---

i. al-Kulaynī, al-Kāfī, 2:375, narration 3

ii. Nūrī, Mustadrak al-Wasā'il, 8:337, narration 9595

And Amīr al-Mu'minīn 'Alī (peace be upon him) says:

مُجَالَسَةَ أَهْلِ الْهَوَى مَنْسَاةٌ لِلْإِيمَانِ وَ مَحْضَرَةٌ لِلشَّيْطَانِ

Keeping the company of those who follow their selfish desires causes faith to be forgotten and Satan to appear.[i]

Undoubtedly, staying away from these people has social repercussions. However, the person who is on the path towards reaching the lofty stages of faith and true perfection endures these repercussions. As Imam al-Ṣādiq (peace be upon him) says:

إِنْ قَدَرْتُمْ أَنْ لَا تُعْرَفُوا فَافْعَلُوا وَ مَا عَلَيْكَ إِنْ لَمْ يُثْنِ عَلَيْكَ النَّاسُ وَ مَا عَلَيْكَ أَنْ تَكُونَ مَذْمُوماً عِنْدَ النَّاسِ إِذَا كُنْتَ عِنْدَ اللَّهِ مَحْمُوداً.

If you can [act in such a manner that you do] not become known, then do so; there is no harm for you if people do not praise you. And if you are praiseworthy near Allah then it does not matter if you are condemned by the people.[ii]

خوشا آنان که ترک کام کردند

به کام عار ننگ از نام کردند

Fortunate are those who left aside their passions,
The passion of seeking disdain led them to disgrace their name,

به خلوت انس با جانان گرفتند

به عزلت خویش را گمنام کردند

In isolation they sought the affection of their Beloved,
Resigned to solitude, they made themselves unknown,

به حق پرداختند از خلق رستند

---

i. al-Raḍī, Nahj al-Balāghah, sermon 86

ii. Majlisī, Bihār al-Anwār, 67:110

به شغل خاص ترک عام کردند

They immersed themselves with the Truth, emancipated from the creation,
Engaged with the Select, they abandoned the public. [i]

Imam Mūsā ibn Jaʿfar (peace be upon him) in a narration says the following to Hishām:

يَا هِشَامُ الصَّبْرُ عَلَى الْوَحْدَةِ عَلَامَةُ قُوَّةِ الْعَقْلِ فَمَنْ عَقَلَ عَنِ اللَّهِ اعْتَزَلَ أَهْلَ الدُّنْيَا وَ الرَّاغِبِينَ فِيهَا وَ رَغِبَ فِيمَا عِنْدَ اللَّهِ وَ كَانَ اللَّهُ أُنْسَهُ فِي الْوَحْشَةِ وَ صَاحِبَهُ فِي الْوَحْدَةِ وَ غِنَاهُ فِي الْعَيْلَةِ وَ مُعِزَّهُ مِنْ غَيْرِ عَشِيرَةٍ.

O Hishām! Patience in the face of loneliness is a sign of the intellect's strength. Therefore, one who has [some] recognition of Allah, dissociates from the people of the *dunyā* and those inclined towards it. He desires that which is with Allah. Allah is his companion in loneliness, his companion in solitude, his needlessness in the difficulties [of the world], and his source of honour without needing a family. [ii]

Undoubtedly, Islam does not approve of completely secluding oneself from the people and refraining from individual and social duties. That is because Allah has prescribed certain programs and duties for everyone and performing them requires a presence in society. Examples of this include earning *ḥalāl* income, learning one's religious obligations, attending religious ceremonies, and attending to the believers' affairs to the extent possible. It is narrated that:

قَالَ لَهُ رَجُلٌ جُعِلْتُ فِدَاكَ رَجُلٌ عَرَفَ هَذَا الْأَمْرَ لَزِمَ بَيْتَهُ وَ لَمْ يَتَعَرَّفْ إِلَى أَحَدٍ مِنْ إِخْوَانِهِ قَالَ كَيْفَ يَتَفَقَّهُ هَذَا فِي دِينِهِ.

A person said to Imam al-Ṣādiq (peace be upon him), "May

---

i. Fayḍ Kāshānī.

ii. al-ʿĀmilī, Wasā'il al-Shīʿah, 11:284

I be your ransom! A man who knows this matter [he is from amongst the Shīʿah], has confined himself at home and has no contact with any of his brothers [in faith]." Imam asked [with surprise], "Then how does he acquire knowledge about the religious obligations?!" (i)

2) Avoiding Heedless People at the Level of the Heart

This type of avoidance is considered a positive value in Islamic ethical teachings. That is because under no circumstances should a believer harbour the love of sin and sinners in his heart. As his belief becomes stronger and reaches higher levels, to that same extent he will not love those who are heedless of the Sacred Divine Essence. Although, it is possible that sometimes he himself commits a mistake and heedlessness overtakes his heart. Thus, the believer's heart is always humbly present in front of the Divine. The highest example of this can be seen in the Messenger (peace and blessings be upon him and his family), to whom Allah the Exalted says:

وَلَا تُطِعْ مَنْ أَغْفَلْنَا قَلْبَهُ عَن ذِكْرِنَا وَاتَّبَعَ هَوَاهُ وَكَانَ أَمْرُهُ فُرُطًا

> And do not obey him whose heart We have made oblivious to Our remembrance, and who follows his own desires, and whose conduct [the foundation of it] is extravagance. (18:28)

Being heedless of Allah has various degrees; any attachment to other than Allah is considered heedlessness of the Station of the *Rabb*. Therefore, higher levels of Allah's servitude are obtained by severing the heart's attachments to other than Him. Imam al-Bāqir (peace be upon him) says in this regard:

لَا يَكُونُ الْعَبْدُ عَابِداً لِلَّهِ حَقَّ عِبَادَتِهِ حَتَّى يَنْقَطِعَ عَنِ الْخَلْقِ كُلِّهِمْ إِلَيْهِ فَحِينَئِذٍ يَقُولُ هَذَا خَالِصٌ لِي فَيَقْبَلُهُ بِكَرَمِهِ.

> The servant does not become a true servant of Allah until he is cut off from all the creation [and turns] towards Him. At that moment Allah says, "This is [a servant who

i. Ibid.

> is] exclusively for me." Then He accepts him with His generosity.[i]

Undoubtedly, to reach this level it is necessary to avoid people outwardly. Thus, when Imam al-Ṣādiq (peace be upon him) was asked about the reason behind his withdrawal and detachment from the people, he said:

فَسَدَ الزَّمَانُ وَ تَغَيَّرَ الْإِخْوَانُ فَرَأَيْتُ الِانْفِرَادَ أَسْكَنَ لِلْفُؤَادِ

> The time has become corrupt and the brothers have changed. Therefore, I saw seclusion and loneliness more comforting for the heart.[ii]

Such individuals prefer loneliness over associating with people without sound reason, as long as such association is not required due to religious or ethical demands. For example, enjoining what is right and forbidding what is wrong, executing Divine laws or guiding people would require that they associate with the people. For this reason, Imam ʿAlī (peace be upon him) says:

الِانْفِرَادُ رَاحَةُ الْمُتَعَبِّدِينَ

Loneliness is the comfort of the worshippers.[iii]

مَنِ اسْتَوْحَشَ عَنِ النَّاسِ أَنِسَ بِاللَّهِ سُبْحَانَه

> One who secludes himself from the people becomes familiar with Allah the Immaculate.[iv]

Hence, the encouragement of being alone or sometimes secluding oneself from the people, is for special people and intended for them to attain such a state. It is not the primary rule, intended for everyone, in religious teachings.

---

i. Majlisī, Bihār al-Anwār, 67:111

ii. Ibid., 47:60, narration 116

iii. al-Āmudī, Ghurar al-Ḥikam, narration 661

iv. Ibid., narration 8644

4) Not Being Affected by Society

Man is naturally affected by the environment around him. In many instances, being affected in this manner results in him deviating from the truth. That is because the general public spend their lives heedless and oblivious of Allah and the Hereafter; their activities are also performed in a heedless way. To prevent this, the noble religion of Islam has encouraged the attention of Allah and remembrance of the Hereafter in society. That is because, being attentive to these realities prevents a person from excessively striving to please other people and satisfy their wishes. For this reason, Imam ʿAlī (peace be upon him) says:

مَنْ أَصْلَحَ مَا بَيْنَهُ وَ بَيْنَ اللَّهِ أَصْلَحَ اللَّهُ مَا بَيْنَهُ وَ بَيْنَ النَّاسِ

> One who rectifies that which is between him and Allah [by following His commands], then Allah rectifies that which is between him and the people.[i]

Likewise, in a letter addressed to one of his companions, he writes about observing Allah's right irrespective of people's views:

وَ اعْلَمْ أَنَّ حِسَابَ اللَّهِ أَعْظَمُ مِنْ حِسَابِ النَّاسِ

> And know that Allah's reckoning is greater that the reckoning of the people.[ii]

Therefore, Allah's remembrance causes other people and their wrong wishes to become low and insignificant in man's eyes, other than those wishes and expectations that bring about Allah's pleasure. Even in this case, it is gaining Allah's pleasure that is of primary importance. According to the statement of Amīr al-Mu'minīn (peace be upon him):

عَظُمَ الْخَالِقُ فِي أَنْفُسِهِمْ فَصَغُرَ مَا دُونَهُ فِي أَعْيُنِهِمْ

> In their [the *muttaqīn's*] souls the Creator has become great and everything other than Him has become insignificant in their eyes.[iii]

---

i. al-Radī, Nahj al-Balāghah, saying 89

ii. Ibid., letter 40

iii. Ibid., sermon 193

For this same reason, one of the effects of reaching the station of servitude—as mentioned by Imam al-Ṣādiq (peace be upon him)—is that the opinions and judgments of others becomes insignificant and minor.

In the concluding part of this section, it is necessary to pay attention to the advice of the Noble Messenger of Islam (peace and blessings be upon him and his family) to Abū Dharr. This will cause man to be at ease on the path of Allah the Exalted's servitude and be undeterred by the words and reactions of people with regards to his correct decisions:

> يَا أَبَا ذَرٍّ لَا يَفْقَهُ الرَّجُلُ كُلَّ الْفِقْهِ حَتَّى يَرَى النَّاسَ فِي جَنْبِ اللَّهِ تَبَارَكَ وَ تَعَالَى أَمْثَالَ الْأَبَاعِرِ ثُمَّ يَرْجِعُ إِلَى نَفْسِهِ فَيَكُونَ هُوَ أَحْقَرَ حَاقِرٍ لَهَايَا أَبَا ذَرٍّ لَا تُصِيبُ حَقِيقَةَ الْإِيمَانِ حَتَّى تَرَى النَّاسَ كُلَّهُمْ حَمْقَاءَ فِي دِينِهِمْ عُقَلَاءَ فِي دُنْيَاهُم
>
> O Abū Dharr! Man has not reached the pinnacle of *fiqh* (deep understanding and comprehension) unless, from the side [out of the pleasure] of Allah, he sees the people as if they are camels! Then he returns to himself and sees himself to be the lowest of all people. O Abū Dharr! You will not reach the true faith until you see all the people as fools with regards to their religion and intellectuals with regards to their *dunyā*. (i)

i. Majlisī, Bihār al-Anwār, 74:83

Section Four
The Need to Manage the Spiritual Affairs of the Soul

Allah the Exalted has equipped man with different abilities to reach perfection and lofty spiritual ranks. It is by the aid of these abilities that man can optimally make use of his worldly life so that his Hereafter is prosperous.

Each of these faculties and abilities create attractions and inclinations in man's being. It is necessary to appropriately respond to each of these demands. Not responding to these inclinations and internal conflicts, suppressing them, or satisfying them unconditionally and without any bounds, all these deprive man from reaching spiritual and eternal life. As Allah the Exalted says:

> وَابْتَغِ فِيمَا آتَاكَ اللَّهُ الدَّارَ الْآخِرَةَ ۖ وَلَا تَنسَ نَصِيبَكَ مِنَ الدُّنْيَا ۖ وَأَحْسِن كَمَا أَحْسَنَ اللَّهُ إِلَيْكَ ۖ وَلَا تَبْغِ الْفَسَادَ فِي الْأَرْضِ ۖ إِنَّ اللَّهَ لَا يُحِبُّ الْمُفْسِدِينَ
>
> Seek the abode of the Hereafter by means of what Allah has given you, while not forgetting your share of this world. Be good just as Allah has been good to you, and do not try to cause corruption in the land. Indeed, Allah does not like the agents of corruption. (28:77)

In view of this, man direly needs correct management of his spiritual affairs. By virtue of such management, he can organize the collection of his soul's inclinations and desires, and not be afflicted from going to the destructive and deadly extremes (excessiveness or laxity).

Amīr al-Mu'minīn (peace be upon him) says about the inward conflicts that occur in man:

> أَعْجَبُ مَا فِي الْإِنْسَانِ قَلْبُهُ وَ لَهُ مَوَادٌّ مِنَ الْحِكْمَةِ وَ أَضْدَادٌ مِنْ خِلَافِهَا فَإِنْ سَنَحَ لَهُ الرَّجَاءُ أَذَلَّهُ الطَّمَعُ وَ إِنْ هَاجَ بِهِ الطَّمَعُ أَهْلَكَهُ الْحِرْصُ وَ إِنْ مَلَكَهُ الْيَأْسُ قَتَلَهُ الْأَسَفُ وَ إِنْ عَرَضَ لَهُ الْغَضَبُ اشْتَدَّ بِهِ الْغَيْظُ وَ إِنْ سُعِدَ بِالرِّضَا نَسِيَ التَّحَفُّظَ وَ إِنْ

> نَالَهُ الْخَوْفُ شَغَلَهُ الْحَذَرُ وَ إِنِ اتَّسَعَ لَهُ الْأَمْنُ اسْتَلَبَتْهُ الْغِرَّةُ وَ إِنْ جُدِّدَتْ لَهُ النِّعْمَةُ أَخَذَتْهُ الْعِزَّةُ وَ إِنْ أَصَابَتْهُ مُصِيبَةٌ فَضَحَهُ الْجَزَعُ وَ إِنِ اسْتَفَادَ مَالًا أَطْغَاهُ الْغِنَى وَ إِنْ عَضَّتْهُ فَاقَةٌ شَغَلَهُ الْبَلَاءُ وَ إِنْ جَهَدَهُ الْجُوعُ قَعَدَ بِهِ الضَّعْفُ وَ إِنْ أَفْرَطَ فِي الشِّبَعِ كَظَّتْهُ الْبِطْنَةُ فَكُلُّ تَقْصِيرٍ بِهِ مُضِرٌّ وَ كُلُّ إِفْرَاطٍ بِهِ مُفْسِد
>
> The most astonishing thing in man is his heart. It has a store of wisdom and [also] also things contrary to it. So, if hope presents itself to it, aspiration makes him abject; if aspiration overtakes him, greed destroys him; if despair dominates him, grief kills him; if anger appears in him, his rancour intensifies; if he benefits from *riḍā* (contentment and pleasure), he forgets self-control; if fear envelops him, he resorts to avoiding and shunning things; if security and peace reaches him, he becomes heedless; if blessing reaches him, conceit seizes him; if a calamity afflicts him, impatience disgraces him; if he acquires wealth, his needlessness makes him rebellious; if he is tormented with poverty, afflictions preoccupy him; if hunger exhausts him, weakness paralyzes him; if he overeats, gluttony harms him. Therefore, every inadequacy in him is harmful and every extravagance in him causes corruption. (i)

Some Islamic factions—those that have distanced themselves from the conduct (*sīrah*) of the Ahl al-Bayt (peace be upon them)—through self-mortification, attempt to suppress and destroy their selfish inclinations instead of giving them a Divine direction. These actions are contrary to man's ontological and innate constitution; and if the mortifications are against the *sharīʿah*, then they also prevent man from reaching spiritual perfections. Although it is possible that such a person acquires the ability to perform extraordinary feats, but these are not proof that they are on the true path or have achieved perfection. Marḥūm ʿAllāmah Ṭabāṭabāʾī (may Allah be pleased with him) says

---

i. Majlisī, Bihār al-Anwār, 67:52

in this regard:

> Swallowing fire or glass pieces of a lantern, piercing one's body with a sword and removing it from behind, none of these are a sign of being on the true path ... One of the dervishes came to me on a dusty street near the *Gunbad-i Sabz* in Mashhad. He said many things [to me], for instance he said, "It has been thirty years that water has not come in contact with my body." I asked him, "But don't you do *wuḍū'*?!" He replied, "We are beyond these things." Is this *taqwā*?! Sinning is never and cannot possibly be *fanā fillāh* [to reach the station of annihilation oneself in Allah]. Extraordinary actions can be performed either through magic, the strange sciences (i) and self-mortifications, or through worship; the prophets (peace be upon them) were also capable of manifesting such things. (ii)

Having the Correct Outlook and Relationship with the World (Dunyā)

The world (*dunyā*) is one of the creations of Allah; whether it is good or bad depends on the manner that man looks at it and how he benefits from it. If man considers this world to be a passageway towards the Hereafter and the place for him to sow what he will reap in that world, then this world is the best opportunity for attaining proximity to Allah the Exalted and intimacy with Him. From this perspective, not only is it not an object of reproach, rather it is the object of attention of the Divine *awliyā'*. Thus, when Imam ʿAlī (peace be upon him)—himself the greatest critic of this world—heard someone once condemning the world despite himself being mesmerized and intoxicated by it, the Imam addressed him and said:

---

i. *ʿUlum-i Gharībah* (the strange sciences) refers to a set of sciences that were not publicly taught but existed in the Islamic civilization as well as other civilizations. By researching the properties of letters, numbers and shapes these sciences can determine matters that are close to reality.

ii. Dar Maḥḍar-i ʿAllāmah Ṭabāṭabā'ī, 250

أَيُّهَا الذَّامُّ لِلدُّنْيَا الْمُغْتَرُّ بِغُرُورِهَا الْمَخْدُوعُ بِأَبَاطِيلِهَا ... ثُمَّ تَذُمُّهَا ...إِنَّ الدُّنْيَا دَارُ صِدْقٍ لِمَنْ صَدَقَهَا وَ دَارُ عَافِيَةٍ لِمَنْ فَهِمَ عَنْهَا وَ دَارُ غِنًى لِمَنْ تَزَوَّدَ مِنْهَا وَ دَارُ مَوْعِظَةٍ لِمَنِ اتَّعَظَ بِهَا مَسْجِدُ أَحِبَّاءِ اللَّهِ وَ مُصَلَّى مَلَائِكَةِ اللَّهِ وَ مَهْبِطُ وَحْيِ اللَّهِ وَ مَتْجَرُ أَوْلِيَاءِ اللَّهِ اكْتَسَبُوا فِيهَا الرَّحْمَةَ وَ رَبِحُوا فِيهَا الْجَنَّةَ فَمَنْ ذَا يَذُمُّهَا وَ قَدْ آذَنَتْ بِبَيْنِهَا وَ نَادَتْ بِفِرَاقِهَا وَ نَعَتْ نَفْسَهَا وَ أَهْلَهَا فَمَثَّلَتْ لَهُمْ بِبَلَائِهَا الْبَلَاءَ وَ شَوَّقَتْهُمْ بِسُرُورِهَا إِلَى السُّرُورِ رَاحَتْ بِعَافِيَةٍ وَ ابْتَكَرَتْ بِفَجِيعَةٍ تَرْغِيباً وَ تَرْهِيباً وَ تَخْوِيفاً وَ تَحْذِيراً- فَذَمَّهَا رِجَالٌ غَدَاةَ النَّدَامَةِ وَ حَمِدَهَا آخَرُونَ يَوْمَ الْقِيَامَةِ ذَكَّرَتْهُمُ الدُّنْيَا [فَذَكَّرُوا] فَتَذَكَّرُوا وَ حَدَّثَتْهُمْ فَصَدَّقُوا وَ وَعَظَتْهُمْ فَاتَّعَظُوا

O you who condemns the world while he is deceived by its deceit and tricked by its falsehood ... [despite this] then you condemn it ... Indeed, this world is an abode of truth for the truthful ones [those whose actions are truthful], it is an abode of well-being for those who understand it, it is an abode of riches for those who take provisions from it, it is an abode of advice for those who take admonition from it. The world is the place of prostration of the lovers of Allah, the place of prayers of the angels of Allah, the place where Allah's revelation descends. It is the place [the means] of trading for the *awliyā'* of Allah, wherein they earn mercy and they gain the Paradise. So, who then can reproach the world, while it has announced its separation, and called out that it is transient and informed of its destruction and the destruction of its dwellers. Through its tribulations it has given example of tribulation and through its rejoicing it encourages people to be happy. It passes with safety at the beginning of the night and returns in the morning with destructive afflictions. [It does so] to make [people] eager, threaten, frighten and warn [them]. Then, a group of people reproach the world in the mornings with regret, while others

> will praise it on the Day of Resurrection. [That is because] the world reminded them [of the realities] and they were reminded. It spoke to them [through different events] and they affirmed it. It admonished them, and they took heed.[i]

However, if man looks independently at the world, gradually he makes it the goal of his activities and his relationship with the world becomes one of love and ardent attachment! At this point, seeking more and more from this world and its bounties becomes his sole concern. He brags about his worldly possessions to others and his entire life is limited to these matters. The Noble Qur'ān expresses this in these words:

> اعْلَمُوا أَنَّمَا الْحَيَاةُ الدُّنْيَا لَعِبٌ وَلَهْوٌ وَزِينَةٌ وَتَفَاخُرٌ بَيْنَكُمْ وَتَكَاثُرٌ فِي الْأَمْوَالِ وَالْأَوْلَادِ ۖ كَمَثَلِ غَيْثٍ أَعْجَبَ الْكُفَّارَ نَبَاتُهُ ثُمَّ يَهِيجُ فَتَرَاهُ مُصْفَرًّا ثُمَّ يَكُونُ حُطَامًا ۖ وَفِي الْآخِرَةِ عَذَابٌ شَدِيدٌ وَمَغْفِرَةٌ مِّنَ اللَّهِ وَرِضْوَانٌ ۚ وَمَا الْحَيَاةُ الدُّنْيَا إِلَّا مَتَاعُ الْغُرُورِ
>
> Know that the life of this world is mere diversion and play, glamour and mutual vainglory among you and rivalry for wealth and children. [Its example is] like rain, whose growth [of the crops due to the rain] impresses the farmer. Then it [the crops] withers and you see it turn yellow, then it becomes chaff. Whereas in the Hereafter there is forgiveness from Allah and His approval [for the believers] and a severe punishment [for those who worshipped this world]. And the life of this world is nothing but the wares of delusion. (57:20)

When this state appears in man's being, it is called 'obsession with the world'. The sole concern of people obsessed with the world is seeking more and more. Such people are never content with what they have from the world's wealth and power; when they attain a desire of their's, their thirst for amassing this world only increases. This is because the world is like seawater, the more a person drinks from it, the thirstier

i. al-Radī, Nahj al-Balāghah, saying 131

he becomes. As a result, a state of poverty and emptiness perpetually exists in those who are obsessed with the world. As Imam al-Ṣādiq (peace be upon him) said:

> مَنْ أَصْبَحَ وَ أَمْسَى وَ الدُّنْيَا أَكْبَرُ هَمِّهِ جَعَلَ اللَّهُ تَعَالَى الْفَقْرَ بَيْنَ عَيْنَيْهِ وَ شَتَّتَ أَمْرَهُ وَ لَمْ يَنَلْ مِنَ الدُّنْيَا إِلَّا مَا قَسَمَ اللَّهُ لَه
>
> One who begins his morning and evening while the *dunyā* is his biggest concern, God places poverty in front of him and causes his affairs to become disjointed and dissipated, while he does not attain anything except what has been apportioned for him. (i)

The great *ʿārif* Imam Khumaynī (may Allah be pleased with him), explaining this narration, says:

> The more you look at this world with wonder and love, and the more your heart is attached to it, proportionally to this love your needs will also increase, a sense of poverty will manifest in you both internally and externally, and your affairs will become scattered and unorganized. Your heart will become anxious, sorrowful, and fearful; your affairs will not be carried out according to your heart's desire. Your longings and greed will increase day-by-day. Grief and regret will seize you; despair and bewilderment will occupy your heart. Imam al-Ṣādiq (peace be upon him) alluded to some of these points in the following noble traditions:
>
> عَنْ أَبِي عَبْدِ اللَّهِ ع قَالَ: مَنْ كَثُرَ اشْتِبَاكُهُ بِالدُّنْيَا كَانَ أَشَدَّ لِحَسْرَتِهِ عِنْدَ فِرَاقِهَا
>
> Imam al-Ṣādiq (peace be upon him) is reported to have said, "One who is extremely embroiled and entangled with the world, his regret at the time of parting from it will be immense." (ii)

---

i. al-Kulaynī, al-Kāfī, 2:320, narration 16 and 17

ii. Ibid.

عَنِ ابْنِ أَبِي يَعْفُورٍ قَالَ سَمِعْتُ أَبَا عَبْدِ اللَّهِ ع يَقُول
مَنْ تَعَلَّقَ قَلْبُهُ بِالدُّنْيَا تَعَلَّقَ قَلْبُهُ بِثَلَاثِ خِصَالٍ هَمٍّ
لَا يَفْنَى- وَ أَمَلٍ لَا يُدْرَكُ وَ رَجَاءٍ لَا يُنَالُ

Ibn Abī Yaʿfūr says, "I heard Imam al-Ṣādiq (peace be upon him) saying, 'Whoever's heart is attached to the world, his heart is attached to three qualities: unceasing distress, unattainable hopes, and unachievable expectations.'" (i)

But those who are people of the Hereafter, the nearer they come to God's Generous Abode, the more joyful and tranquil their hearts become. They turn away from the world, nay, they flee from the world and are disgusted by it and whatever is in it. If the Almighty had not appointed the time of their death, they would not have tarried for a single moment in this world ... So, my dear, you have been reminded about the evils of this attachment and love. You have learnt that this love destroys man, deprives him of faith, and causes his life in this world and the Hereafter to be scattered and distraught. Therefore, make every effort! Try to curtail your heart's attachments to this world, as far as possible. Consider this short life as insignificant and its blessings as wretched—mixed as they are with punishment, suffering, and pain. Seek *tawfīq* (success) from God the Exalted, so that He may free you from its suffering and pain and make your heart fond of His Generous Abode. For whatever lies with Allah is better and more lasting. (ii)

The Cure for Obsession with the World

1) Remembering Death

Remembering death and paying attention to the Hereafter has numerous effects and blessings on man's soul and psyche. It controls and balances man's inward inclinations. It releases him from the trap of worldly attachments and develops an attachment to the *Qudsī* realm.

---

i. Ibid.

ii. Khumaynī, Sharḥ-i Chihil Ḥadīth, 128

Imam ʿAlī (peace be upon him) says in this regard:

> فَأَكْثِرُوا ذِكْرَ الْمَوْتِ عِنْدَ مَا تُنَازِعُكُمْ إِلَيْهِ أَنْفُسُكُمْ مِنَ الشَّهَوَاتِ، وَ كَفَى بِالْمَوْتِ وَاعِظاً، وَ كَانَ رَسُولُ اللَّهِ (صَلَّى اللَّهُ عَلَيْهِ وَ آلِهِ) كَثِيراً مَا يُوصِي أَصْحَابَهُ بِذِكْرِ الْمَوْتِ، فَيَقُولُ: أَكْثِرُوا ذِكْرَ الْمَوْتِ، فَإِنَّهُ هَادِمُ اللَّذَّاتِ، حَائِلٌ بَيْنَكُمْ وَ بَيْنَ الشَّهَوَاتِ.
>
> When your self is inclined towards [*ḥarām*] desires, then remember death a great deal. For death is sufficient as an admonisher. The Messenger of Allah (peace and blessings be upon him and his family) would repeatedly advise his companions to remember death and would say, "Remember death a great deal, for it is the destroyer of pleasures. It is a separation between you and your desires.' (i)

Remembering death dissuades man from seeking excess, amassing and boasting in this world.

ای خواجه ز فکر گور غم می باید
اندر دل و دیده سوز و نم می باید

O Khwājah! (ii) Upon reflecting over the grave indeed you must,
Endure a burning sadness in the heart and moisture in the eye.

صد وقت برای کار دنیا داری
یک وقت به فکر گور هم می باید

When a hundred periods of time you allocate for the work of this world,
Set aside but a single moment to reflect over the grave! (iii)

---

i. al-Ṭūsī, al-Amālī, p. 28.

ii. The word *khwājah* was used in old Persian to respectfully address a man of status and honour.

iii. Abū Saʿīd Abū al-Khayr

Therefore, to control and direct one's inclinations, it is necessary and essential to be attentive of death both in the state of poverty and riches. As the Noblest Messenger (peace and blessings be upon him and his family) has said:

> أَكْثِرُوْا ذِكْرَ المَوْتِ فَإِنَّهُ يُمَحِّصُ الذُّنُوْبَ وَ يُزَهِّدُ فِي الدُّنْيَا فَإِنْ ذَكَرْتُمُوْهُ عِنْدَ الغِنَى هَدَمَهُ وَ إِنْ ذَكَرْتُمُوْهُ عِنْدَ الفَقْرِ أَرْضَاكُمْ بِعَيْشِكُمْ.
>
> Remember death often, for indeed it purges sins and makes man disinterested in the world. So, if you remember it during riches, it destroys it [the rebellious attitude], and if you remember it during poverty it makes you content and satisfied with your life. (i)

2) Humility Despite Being at the Peak of Affluence

One of the methods of controlling inward inclinations is to express humility and lowliness in front of Allah and His servants. As the Noblest Messenger (peace and blessings be upon him and his family) has said:

> إِنَّ اللَّهَ أَوْحَى إِلَيَّ أَنْ تَوَاضَعُوْا حَتَّى لَا يَفْخَرُ أَحَدٌ عَلَى أَحَدٍ
>
> Indeed, Allah revealed to me that you all should be humble with each other until [a stage comes such that] no one boasts to another. (ii)

The Revered Messenger of Islam (peace and blessings be upon him and his family), despite being at the peak of supremacy and possessing lofty spiritual perfection, was the humblest of people. When he enumerated Allah's favours upon him not only was he humble in his heart, but he was also expressed this humility in his speech. In a marvellous statement, while enumerating a small portion of his exclusive

i. Pāyandih, Nahj al-Fasāhah, narration 444. Note: A reference for the above narration was not provided in the original Persian copy of the book.

ii. Mandharī, al-Targhīb wa al-Tarhīb, 3:558, narration 1

ranks, he says:

أَنَا سَيِّدُ وُلْدِ آدَمَ وَ لَا فَخْر

I am the eminent chief of the children of Adam—and I say this without boasting.[i]

In another narration he says:

لَمَّا عُرِجَ بِي إِلَى السَّمَاءِ ... قَالَ لِي تَقَدَّمْ يَا مُحَمَّدُ ... فَتَقَدَّمْتُ وَ صَلَّيْتُ بِهِمْ وَ لَا فَخْرَ

When I was taken to the heavens ... He [Gabriel] said to me, "Step forward O Muhammad!" ... So, I stepped forward and lead them in prayers, and I say this without boasting.[ii]

3) Attention to One's Weaknesses and Shortcomings

Taking notice of one's weaknesses and shortcomings stops man from boasting and presenting himself as being superior to others. In the words of Imam ʿAlī (peace be upon him):

مَا لِابْنِ آدَمَ وَ الْفَخْرِ أَوَّلُهُ نُطْفَةٌ وَ آخِرُهُ جِيفَةٌ وَ لَا يَرْزُقُ نَفْسَهُ وَ لَا يَدْفَعُ حَتْفَه

What has the son of Adam to do with boasting?! His beginning is a drop of semen and his end is a carcass. He cannot provide for himself and cannot ward off his death.[iii]

Paying Attention to the States of those Detached from the World

The great people who have acquired Allah's gnosis due to worship and servitude, can never view the world in an independent light. They can never see it as being greater in value than what it really is. Therefore,

i. Majlisī, Bihār al-Anwār, 8:48

ii. Ibid., 84:139

iii. al-Radī, Nahj al-Balāghah, saying 454

neither do they attach their hearts to it, nor do they seek excess from this world more than their need, nor are they afflicted with pride and boasting to others.

Nawf al-Bakkālī, one of the companions and aids of Imam ʿAlī (peace be upon him), says:

رَأَيْتُ أَمِيرَ الْمُؤْمِنِينَ ع ذَاتَ لَيْلَةٍ وَ قَدْ خَرَجَ مِنْ فِرَاشِهِ فَنَظَرَ إِلَى النُّجُومِ فَقَالَ يَا نَوْفُ أَ رَاقِدٌ أَنْتَ أَمْ رَامِقٌ فَقُلْتُ بَلْ رَامِقٌ يَا أَمِيرَ الْمُؤْمِنِينَ فَقَالَ يَا نَوْفُ طُوبَى لِلزَّاهِدِينَ فِي الدُّنْيَا الرَّاغِبِينَ فِي الْآخِرَةِ أُولَئِكَ قَوْمٌ اتَّخَذُوا الْأَرْضَ بِسَاطاً وَ تُرَابَهَا فِرَاشاً وَ مَاءَهَا طِيباً وَ الْقُرْآنَ شِعَاراً وَ الدُّعَاءَ دِثَاراً ثُمَّ قَرَضُوا الدُّنْيَا قَرْضاً عَلَى مِنْهَاجِ الْمَسِيحِ ع

> One night I saw Amīr al-Muʾminīn (peace be upon him) while he had left his bed and was looking at the stars. He said, "O Nawf! Are you awake or are you asleep?" I said, "I am awake, O Amīr al-Muʾminīn!" So, he said, "O Nawf! Blessed are those who are detached from the world and are eager for the Hereafter. They are a people who have taken the Earth as their carpet, its dust as a cushion, its water as being delicious, the Qurʾān as an inside garment, and supplication as their outer garment. They have passed through the world in the manner of the Messiah (peace be upon him)." (i)

It is reported that one of the great ʿ*urafā* said, "We are in this world [only] to the extent that is necessary."

عاشقی در بندگی ها سر به راهم کرده است

بی نیاز از بندگان لطف الاهم کرده است

From being enslaved [by other than Him], the love [of Him] has made me firmly on the path,

i. Majlisī, Bihār al-Anwār, 66:276

God's grace has rendered me needless of the servants. [i]

The true servants of Allah never go after the world for seeking excess and for boasting, as Imam al-Ṣādiq (peace be upon him) says to ʿUnwān al-Baṣrī:

وَ لَا يَطْلُبُ الدُّنْيَا تَكَاثُراً وَ تَفَاخُراً

And he does not desire the world for rivalry and vainglory.

Such people have faith in this statement of the Messenger of Allah (peace and blessings be upon him and his family) where he says:

الدُّنْيَا دُوَلٌ فَمَا كَانَ لَكَ مِنْهَا أَتَاكَ عَلَى ضَعْفِكَ وَ مَا كَانَ عَلَيْكَ لَمْ تَدْفَعْهُ بِقُوَّتِكَ وَ مَنِ انْقَطَعَ رَجَاهُ مِمَّا فَاتَ اسْتَرَاحَ بَدَنُهُ وَ مَنْ رَضِيَ بِمَا رَزَقَهُ اللَّهُ قَرَّتْ عَيْنُه

The fortunes of this world alternate. So that which is for you from it, will reach you despite your weakness; and that which is harmful for you from it, you cannot repel despite your strength. One who does not place his hope in that which he missed, his body finds rest and comfort. And one who is content with what Allah has provided him, is in a state of comfort and delight. [ii]

Therefore, when they pursue their worldly needs it is based on the criterion which Imam al-Ṣādiq (peace be upon him) has presented:

لِيَكُنْ طَلَبُكَ لِلْمَعِيشَةِ فَوْقَ كَسْبِ الْمُضَيِّعِ وَ دُونَ طَلَبِ الْحَرِيصِ الرَّاضِي بِدُنْيَاهُ الْمُطْمَئِنِّ إِلَيْهَا وَ أَنْزِلْ نَفْسَكَ مِنْ ذَلِكَ بِمَنْزِلَةِ الْمُنْصِفِ الْمُتَعَفِّفِ تَرْفَعْ نَفْسَكَ عَنْ مَنْزِلَةِ الْوَاهِنِ الضَّعِيفِ وَ تَكْتَسِبْ مَا لَا بُدَّ لِلْمُؤْمِنِ مِنْه

Let your seeking of livelihood be more than the earning of a futile person but less than the seeking of someone who

---

i. Fayḍ Kāshānī

ii. Majlisī, Biḥār al-Anwār, 100:36

is greedy, content with his world and confidant about it. Place yourself in relation to this affair, in the position of a just and chaste person. Raise yourself above the level of a lazy and weak person and earn that much which is necessary for a believer.[i]

Being Aloof from Seeking Superiority

Allah the Exalted, out of His wise power, created human beings different from one other. To each He has given a share from the world, in order that they need each other. As a result, they strive to meet their needs and organize a social life. In the process they manifest the perfections of their being and reach true perfection, which is the Divine proximity that everyone can equally achieve. Allah the Exalted says:

نَحْنُ قَسَمْنَا بَيْنَهُم مَّعِيشَتَهُمْ فِي الْحَيَاةِ الدُّنْيَا ۚ وَرَفَعْنَا بَعْضَهُمْ فَوْقَ بَعْضٍ دَرَجَاتٍ لِّيَتَّخِذَ بَعْضُهُم بَعْضًا سُخْرِيًّا ۗ وَرَحْمَتُ رَبِّكَ خَيْرٌ مِّمَّا يَجْمَعُونَ

It is We who have dispensed among them [the means of] their livelihood in the present life, and raised some of them above others in rank, so that some may take others into service, and your Lord's mercy is better than what they amass. (43:32)

This matter is a test from Allah the Exalted for human beings, as Allah says:

وَهُوَ الَّذِي جَعَلَكُمْ خَلَائِفَ الْأَرْضِ وَرَفَعَ بَعْضَكُمْ فَوْقَ بَعْضٍ دَرَجَاتٍ لِّيَبْلُوَكُمْ فِي مَا آتَاكُمْ

It is He who has made you successors [of each other] on the Earth and raised some of you in rank above others so that He may test you in respect to what He has given you. (6:165)

In view of these statements, it becomes clear that if all human beings

---

i. Ibid.

were the same in terms of their existential faculties and the blessings that they enjoy, then this path would not be tread and that true goal would not be attained. As Imam ʿAlī (peace be upon him) says:

لَا يَزَالُ النَّاسُ بِخَيْرٍ مَا تَفَاوَتُوا فَإِذَا اسْتَوَوْا هَلَكُوا

People are always in the state of well-being and goodness as long as they are different from each other. Therefore, if they were all to be the same, they would have perished.[i]

However, due to his worldly inclinations, man always desires that everything be placed at his disposal, for him to reach his aim. He should derive benefit and acquire domination over everything in front of him, including animals, plants, inanimate objects and even other human beings. In the view of Marḥūm ʿAllāmah Ṭabāṭabāʾī, this verse of the Qurʾān necessitates that such a state exists in every single human being:

إِنَّ الْإِنسَانَ لَظَلُومٌ كَفَّارٌ

Indeed, man is most unfair and ungrateful! (14:34)

To control and organize man's life and to prevent anarchy, Allah the Immaculate has enacted laws in the form of the *sharīʿah* and the *fiqhī* commands. These allow man's social life to be administered in a correct and logical manner, with a Divine colour, and such that his inclinations and greed are controlled. However, it should be noted that the *fiqhī* commands and Islam's social laws only regulate the outward aspect of human interactions. To reform and manage the inclination of seeking superiority that is present inside man, one must also refer to Islam's *akhlāqī* instructions. Paying attention to this point is necessary for those who travel upon the path of perfection. Stopping at Islam's initial program does not rectify the roots of seeking superiority, domineering and greed in man's being, it merely regulates his outward relationships. On the other hand, reaching perfections and lofty ranks in the Hereafter is dependent upon man giving direction to all his inclinations, both outward and inward. For this reason, the Noble Qurʾān introduces both the inward aspect of domineering as well as

i. Ibid., 74:383

the outward aspect of causing corruption as being a hindrance for man to reach perfection, saying:

تِلْكَ الدَّارُ الْآخِرَةُ نَجْعَلُهَا لِلَّذِينَ لَا يُرِيدُونَ عُلُوًّا فِي الْأَرْضِ وَلَا فَسَادًا ۚ وَالْعَاقِبَةُ لِلْمُتَّقِينَ

> That is the abode of the Hereafter, which We shall grant to those who do not desire to domineer in the Earth nor to cause corruption, and the outcome will be in favour of the *muttaqīn*. (28:83)

This verse mentions the Hereafter with greatness and magnificence, saying: We have made the abode of the Hereafter to be for those who are not only completely free from the inclination to domineer and cause corruption on the Earth, but they do not even have a desire to do so. In other words, these people have uprooted the roots of such inclinations from their being. This is only realized through attention to the Divine Supremacy and one's existential neediness. The true effect of such realization is absolute humility in front of His Sacred Essence, complete obedience to His commands and humility in front of His creation.

Islam's moral advice that is intended to balance this tendency of man, is as follows.

Being Needless of People

Allah the Exalted has created people in a manner that they need one other; He has made each person a cause to fulfil the needs and wants of others. This reality is a Divine law that governs human society. Imam al-Ṣādiq (peace be upon him) says in this regard:

أَبَى اللَّهُ أَنْ يُجْرِيَ الْأَشْيَاءَ إِلَّا بِأَسْبَابٍ فَجَعَلَ لِكُلِّ شَيْءٍ سَبَبا

> Allah has refused to carry out affairs except through their causes. So, he has assigned a cause for everything.[i]

In order that this necessary connection, be formed based on a *tawḥīdī*

i. al-Kulaynī, al-Kāfī, 1:183, narration 7

outlook and bring about the desired spiritual and psychological effects, the following points must be considered:

1) Man should not view the people who are the cause and the medium by which his needs are fulfilled, in an independent manner.

In an exegesis of Allah's (the Invincible and Majestic) words:

وَمَا يُؤْمِنُ أَكْثَرُهُم بِاللَّهِ إِلَّا وَهُم مُّشْرِكُونَ

> And most of them do not believe in Allah without ascribing partners to Him. (12:106)

Imam al-Ṣādiq (peace be upon him) says:

هُوَ قَوْلُ الرَّجُلِ لَوْ لَا فُلَانٌ لَهَلَكْتُ وَ لَوْ لَا فُلَانٌ مَا أَصَبْتُ كَذَا وَ كَذَا وَ لَوْ لَا فُلَانٌ لَضَاعَ عِيَالِي أَ لَا تَرَى أَنَّهُ قَدْ جَعَلَ لِلَّهِ شَرِيكاً فِي مُلْكِهِ يَرْزُقُهُ وَ يَدْفَعُ عَنْهُ قُلْتُ فَيَقُولُ مَا ذَا يَقُولُ لَوْ لَا أَنْ مَنَّ اللَّهُ عَلَيَّ بِفُلَانٍ لَهَلَكْتُ قَالَ نَعَمْ لَا بَأْسَ بِهَذَا أَوْ نَحْوِهِ.

> "This is [referring to the] words of a person, 'Were it not for such and such a person, I would have perished', 'Were it not for that person, such and such an affliction would not have happened to me', and 'Were it not for that person, my family would have been ruined.' Do you not see that he has ascribed a partner to Allah in His authority, such that this partner provides for him and wards off [evil]?" [The reporter of the tradition says:] I asked, "Should a person say, 'Were it not that Allah favoured me through such and such person, I would have certainly perished?'" The Imam replied, "Yes, there is no problem in this and other such similar expressions." (i)

2) He should only put his trust in Allah (the Invincible and Majestic) with regards to fulfilling his needs. This will ensure that there is always ease and relief in the affairs of his life. However, if this is not the case, then he will be afflicted with difficulty and constriction. As Imam al-Ṣādiq (peace be upon him) says:

---

i. al-ʿĀmilī, Waṣāʾil al-Shīʿah, 11:16

أَوْحَى اللَّهُ عَزَّ وَ جَلَّ إِلَى دَاوُدَ ع مَا اعْتَصَمَ بِي عَبْدٌ مِنْ عِبَادِي دُونَ أَحَدٍ مِنْ خَلْقِي عَرَفْتُ ذَلِكَ مِنْ نِيَّتِهِ ثُمَّ تَكِيدُهُ السَّمَاوَاتُ وَ الْأَرْضُ وَ مَنْ فِيهِنَّ إِلَّا جَعَلْتُ لَهُ الْمَخْرَجَ مِنْ بَيْنِهِنَّ وَ مَا اعْتَصَمَ عَبْدٌ مِنْ عِبَادِي بِأَحَدٍ مِنْ خَلْقِي عَرَفْتُ ذَلِكَ مِنْ نِيَّتِهِ إِلَّا قَطَعْتُ أَسْبَابَ السَّمَاوَاتِ وَ الْأَرْضِ مِنْ يَدَيْهِ وَ أَسَخْتُ الْأَرْضَ مِنْ تَحْتِهِ وَ لَمْ أُبَالِ بِأَيِّ وَادٍ هَلَكَ

Allah (the Invincible and Majestic) revealed to Prophet David (peace be upon him), "If a servant from amongst My servants clings onto Me and forsakes everyone else from My creation—and I know this from his intention—then even if the heavens, the Earth and whoever there is in them plot against him, I will make a way out for him from amongst them. [On the contrary], if a servant from amongst My servants clings onto the people—and I know this from his intention—I will cut off the means of the heavens and the Earth in front of him, I will pull away the Earth from under him, and I do not care in which valley he is destroyed.[i]

As is clear from this narration, placing trust in Allah and not being needy of the people is an inward state pertaining to the heart. It is not inconsistent with having an outward relationship with others and fulfilling one's needs through them. In other Islamic narrations as well, this matter has been clearly mentioned. Imam al-Ṣādiq (peace be upon him) says:

إِذَا أَرَادَ أَحَدُكُمْ أَنْ لَا يَسْأَلَ رَبَّهُ شَيْئاً إِلَّا أَعْطَاهُ فَلْيَيْأَسْ مِنَ النَّاسِ كُلِّهِمْ وَ لَا يَكُونُ لَهُ رَجَاءٌ إِلَّا عِنْدَ اللَّهِ فَإِذَا عَلِمَ اللَّهُ عَزَّ وَ جَلَّ ذَلِكَ مِنْ قَلْبِهِ لَمْ يَسْأَلِ اللَّهَ شَيْئاً إِلَّا أَعْطَاهُ.

If anyone amongst you desires [a station whereby] he does not ask his Lord for anything except that He grants it to

i. al-Kulaynī, al-Kāfī, 2:63, narration 1

> him, then let him despair from all the people, and let him not have any hope except in Allah. If Allah (the Invincible and Majestic) knows this from [the state of] his heart, then he will not ask Allah for anything except that He grants it to him.[i]

3) Observing Islamic Ethics when Interacting with People

Seeing Allah as independent and relying on Him to fulfil one's needs does not mean ignoring those who are the intermediaries of Divine grace. These individuals have been placed as a cause of the management of man's affairs. Thus, it is possible to combine these two matters, because one pertains to the heart while the other pertains to man's outward interactions. It is for this reason that Imam ʿAlī (peace be upon him) would always advise this:

> لِيَجْتَمِعْ فِي قَلْبِكَ الافْتِقَارُ إِلَى النَّاسِ وَ الاِسْتِغْنَاءُ عَنْهُمْ فَيَكُونَ افْتِقَارُكَ إِلَيْهِمْ فِي لِينِ كَلَامِكَ وَ حُسْنِ بِشْرِكَ وَ يَكُونَ اسْتِغْنَاؤُكَ عَنْهُمْ فِي نَزَاهَةِ عِرْضِكَ وَ بَقَاءِ عِزِّكَ
>
> You must combine in your heart, both neediness towards the people and needlessness from them. Let your neediness towards them be [expressed] in soft speech and having a cheerful face and let your needlessness from them be [expressed] through protecting your reputation and retaining your honour.[ii]

Expressing gratitude and appreciation to those whom Allah has made the means of carrying out man's affairs, is one of the duties in social interactions—attention must be paid to this. The Imams (peace be upon them) have also emphasized this. Imam al-Ṣādiq (peace be upon him) says:

> مَكْتُوبٌ فِي التَّوْرَاةِ اشْكُرْ مَنْ أَنْعَمَ عَلَيْكَ وَ أَنْعِمْ عَلَى مَنْ شَكَرَكَ فَإِنَّهُ لَا زَوَالَ لِلنَّعْمَاءِ إِذَا شُكِرَتْ وَ لَا بَقَاءَ لَهَا إِذَا كُفِرَتْ

---

i. Ibid., 2:148, narration 2

ii. Ibid., 2:149, narration 7

> It is written in the Torah: Thank the person who bestows a blessing upon you and bestow a blessing upon the person who thanks you. For verily, the blessings shall never cease when there is gratitude towards them and they shall never remain if there is ingratitude." (i)

The Noble Messenger of Islam (peace and blessings be upon him and his family) has also said:

لَا يَشْكُرُ اللَّهَ مَنْ لَا يَشْكُرُ النَّاس

> One who does not thank the people has not thanked Allah. (ii)

4) Refraining from Commanding Others

One of the etiquettes of interacting with people, improving relationships with them, and allowing these relationships to continue, is to refrain from commanding them. Even when asking for one's needs, imperative commands should not be used. That is because, change in man's internal characteristics happens gradually and in an unnoticeable manner. For this reason, constantly commanding and prohibiting others and considering them to be base and inferior, slowly causes the trait of pride to become deeply-rooted in man's being. As a result, one's relationship with them becomes agitated. In many Islamic narrations, commanding others has been prohibited.

Imam al-Ṣādiq (peace be upon him) says:

جَاءَتْ فَخِذٌ مِنَ الْأَنْصَارِ إِلَى رَسُولِ اللَّهِ ص- فَسَلَّمُوا عَلَيْهِ فَرَدَّ عَلَيْهِمُ السَّلَامَ فَقَالُوا يَا رَسُولَ اللَّهِ لَنَا إِلَيْكَ حَاجَةٌ فَقَالَ هَاتُوا حَاجَتَكُمْ قَالُوا إِنَّهَا حَاجَةٌ عَظِيمَةٌ فَقَالَ هَاتُوهَا مَا هِيَ قَالُوا تَضْمَنُ لَنَا عَلَى رَبِّكَ الْجَنَّةَ قَالَ فَنَكَسَ رَسُولُ اللَّهِ ص رَأْسَهُ ثُمَّ نَكَتَ فِي الْأَرْضِ ثُمَّ رَفَعَ رَأْسَهُ فَقَالَ أَفْعَلُ ذَلِكَ بِكُمْ عَلَى أَنْ لَا تَسْأَلُوا أَحَداً شَيْئاً قَالَ فَكَانَ الرَّجُلُ مِنْهُمْ يَكُونُ فِي السَّفَرِ

i. Ibid., 2:94, narration 3

ii. al-Ṭūsī, al-Amālī, 383

فَيَسْقُطُ سَوْطُهُ فَيَكْرَهُ أَنْ يَقُولَ لِإِنْسَانٍ نَاوِلْنِيهِ فِرَاراً مِنَ الْمَسْأَلَةِ وَ يَنْزِلُ فَيَأْخُذُهُ وَ يَكُونُ عَلَى الْمَائِدَةِ- فَيَكُونُ بَعْضُ الْجُلَسَاءِ أَقْرَبَ إِلَى الْمَاءِ مِنْهُ فَلَا يَقُولُ نَاوِلْنِي حَتَّى يَقُومَ فَيَشْرَبَ.

> Some of the Anṣār visited the Messenger of Allah (peace and blessings be upon him and his family) and greeted him. He replied their greeting. They said, "O Messenger of Allah, we have a request for you." He said, "Present your request." They said, "Verily, it is a great request!" So, he said, "Present it. What is it?" They said, "That you guarantee for us, from your Lord, the Garden of Paradise." The Messenger of Allah (peace and blessings be upon him and his family) put his head down. Then he paused for a moment and then raised his head and said, "I will do that, but on the condition that you never ask others for anything." Then [after this incident], if the whip of one of them would fall on the ground while travelling, he would be unwilling to ask another person to pick it up for him, lest he ask someone [to do something for him]. Rather, he would descend from his mount and pick it up himself. [Similarly] while having food if another person was closer to the water, he would not ask that person to give it to him, rather he would rise from his place and drink. [i]

Many of the great personalities and Divine scholars who had eradicated the roots of pride and self-conceit from their being, would not even command the closest of their family members for the most basic of their needs. Āyatullāh Bahjat quotes someone saying:

> [One day] we went to visit Marḥūm Mīrzā Muḥammad Taqī Shīrāzī, two or three hours after *ẓuhr*. We saw meat broth placed in front of him, but he had not eaten any of it. He was asked, "Why have you not eaten it?" He replied, "No one brought bread!" To this extent, he was not ready

i. al-ʿĀmilī, Wasāʾil al-Shīʿah, 6:307

to command anyone.[i]

Allah's sincere servants are those who have reached the station of true servitude and have found true honour in Allah's worship and servitude. By managing their inner inclinations, these individuals have liberated themselves from seeking domination and considering themselves superior to others. Their interaction with other people in all the spheres of life (in physical matters, educational matters, etc.) takes place based on a *tawḥīdī* outlook, and even if there is a command or a prohibition in their words, it is not accompanied with pride. This is because their commands and prohibitions are within the bounds of the instructions of the *sharīʿah* and *akhlāq*. At times they are solely expressing the direct command of Allah and the Imams (peace be upon them). At other times they issue social and governmental commands that are similarly based on Allah's obedience, because He has commanded that the interactions of society and government be in that manner. Or at times they may pertain to personal matters. In this case, such individuals always strive to not issue a command or prohibition, rather they communicate in the form of a request or a conditional statement. For example, they would say, "It would be very good if I had that thing."

Imam al-Ṣādiq (peace be upon him) also alludes to this matter and says to ʿUnwān al-Baṣrī:

لَا يَطْلُبُ مَا عِنْدَ النَّاسِ عِزّاً وَ عُلُوّاً

He does not seek what is with the people out of might and arrogance

Utilizing Opportunities

One of greatest assets that man possesses to allow him to reach lofty perfections and ultimately witness the Beauty of the Beloved, are the days of his life. By making the optimal and correct use of these days, he can reach eternal felicity. In words of Amīr al-Muʾminīn ʿAlī (peace be upon him):

إِنَّ عُمُرَكَ مَهْرُ سَعَادَتِكَ إِنْ أَنْفَذْتَهُ فِي طَاعَةِ رَبِّك

i. Rukhshād, Dar Mahdar-i Ayatullah Bahjat, 1:268

Indeed, your lifetime is the dowry of your felicity if you spend it in the obedience of your Lord. (i)

إِنَ أَنْفَاسَكَ أَجْزَاءُ عُمُرِكَ فَلَا تُفْنِهَا إِلَّا فِي طَاعَةٍ تُزْلِفُكَ

Indeed, your breaths are portions of your lifespan. So, do not exhaust them except in obedience that will take you to [the station of] proximity. (ii)

Thus, time management plays a decisive and important role in spiritual wayfaring, allowing one to benefit from every single moment of his life in the path of seeking Allah's pleasure. Even a single moment can be instrumental in securing man's felicity, it can cause him to attain union with the Beloved and be the fruit of all the joys and moments of this perishable worldly life. As the Noble Qur'ān says, "the Night of *Qadr* is better than a thousand months." (iii)

وقت را غنیمت دان، آن قدر که بتوانی

حاصل از حیات ای جان! یک دم است تا دانی

Value your time, to the extent possible,
O soul! Know that the product of your life are these very moments.

پندِ عاشقان بشنو، و از در طرب باز آ

کاین همه نمی ارزد، شُغلِ عالَمِ فانی

Pay heed to the advice of the lovers and enter through the doorway of ecstasy,
For all of this is worthless, it is merely the occupation of the passing world. *(iv)*

In view of these remarks, it becomes clear that a person's remaining

---

i. al-Āmudī, Fihrist-i Mawḍū'ī-yi Ghurar al-Hikam, the chapter on 'umr (lifespan)

ii. Ibid.

iii. (97:3)

iv. Shirāzī, Divān-i Hāfiz (Tashīh-i Qudsī), ghazal 593, couplet 1, 7

life is a very precious and important elixir. Using this elixir, the copper of man's existence can be turned into gold. In the words of Amīr al-Mu'minīn (peace be upon him):

> لَيْسَ شَيْءٌ أَعَزَّ مِنَ الْكِبْرِيتِ الْأَحْمَرِ إِلَّا مَا بَقِيَ مِنْ عُمُرِ الْمُؤْمِنِ
> There is nothing more valuable than *al-kibrīt al-aḥmar* [a precious metal] except the remainder of a believer's lifetime. (i)

گل عزیز است، غنیمت شمریدش صحبت

که به باغ آمد از این راه و از آن خواهد شد

Precious is the rose, value the worth of its company!
For it came to the garden down this path, and along that same path shall it go.

ای دل! ار عشرت امروز به فردا فکنی

مایه نقد بقا را، که ضمان خواهد شد؟

O heart! If you delay the pleasure of today till tomorrow,
Who then shall guarantee that the capital [of life] shall remain? *(ii)*

Unfortunately, it is only a few people who are aware of the real importance of the days of their lives. They are the true servants of Allah who are disgusted with vanity and idleness. As Amīr al-Mu'minīn (peace be upon him) says:

> لَا يَعْرِفُ قَدْرَ مَا بَقِيَ مِنْ عُمُرِهِ إِلَّا نَبِيٌّ أَوْ صِدِّيق
> No one knows the value of the remainder of his life except a prophet or a *ṣiddīq* [one whose belief, character, and actions are in line with the truth]. (iii)

---

i. al-Āmudī, Fihrist-i Mawdū'ī-yi Ghurar al-Hikam, the chapter on 'umr (lifespan)

ii. Shirāzī, Divān-i Ḥāfiẓ (Taṣḥīḥ-i Qudsī), ghazal 259, couplet 3, 5

iii. al-Āmudī, Ghurar al-Hikam, narration 10801

Imam al-Ṣādiq (peace be upon him) as well, while introducing these people to ʿUnwān al-Baṣrī, says:

وَ لَا يَدَعُ أَيَّامَهُ بَاطِلًا

They do not waste the days of their life in vanity and idleness.

این یک دو دم که مهلت دیدار ممکن است

دریاب کام دل که نه پیداست کار عمر

In these few moments during which meeting the Beloved is possible,
Rush to reach your heart's desire! For the fate of life is unclear. (i)

Making efficient use of the moments and days of one's life is not restricted to performing great and important tasks and refraining from doing trivial tasks. Rather, such efficient use is realized when both the trivial and great actions of man takes place with a Divine intention and on the path of Allah's servitude. The primary difference between the Divine *awliyā'* and others lies in this very point: the most important and significant actions of most men are devoid of the light of *ikhlāṣ* (sincerity), while the most trivial actions of the Divine *awliyā'* (like sleeping, going to the toilet, etc.) are illuminated with the light of worship and servitude.

The enraptured *ʿārif*, Marḥūm Ḥājj Shaykh Maḥmūd Taḥrīrī (may Allah be pleased with him) narrates:

> Marḥūm Ḥājj Shaykh Muḥammad Murtaḍā Zāhid would always stay awake at night in the state of worship; he was someone who had achieved fantastic spiritual states. On his wedding night he initially decided to busy himself with prayers and prostration, to benefit from this worship, as was his normal routine. However, he realized that tonight Allah's servitude entails reducing his worship and attending to his wife. At dawn, his wife saw a dream that the Divine Angels were busy giving *ghusl* to the Shaykh.

How many free and liberated men reached lofty spiritual ranks by

---

i. Shirāzī, Divān-i Ḥāfiẓ (Taṣḥīḥ-i Qudsī), ghazal 291, couplet 6

means of a small but sincere deed! This same matter is the secret behind how one strike of Amīr al-Mu'minīn's (peace be upon him) sword in the battle of Khandaq, acquired such value that:

> لَضَرْبَةُ عَلِيٍّ يَوْمَ الْخَنْدَقِ أَفْضَلُ مِنْ عِبَادَةِ الثَّقَلَيْنِ.
>
> 'Alī's strike of sword on the day of Khandaq is better than the worship of the *thaqalayn*.[i]

---

i. Majlisī, Bihār al-Anwār, 41:96; Ibn Tāwūs, Iqbāl al-A'māl, 467

Section Five
Reaching the State of Taqwā

Taqwā and its Levels

Taqwā means to maintain the bounds of Allah's *rubūbiyyah* and one's servitude. Because Allah's servitude encompasses a wide spectrum, *taqwā* also has different levels and a wide-ranging scope.

Some spiritual states and stations are exclusive to a specific stage of spiritual wayfaring; others, like faith (*īmān*) and *taqwā*, envelop all the stages and levels of a person's spiritual life and must be the object of the wayfarer's attention from the beginning till the end.

Imam al-Ṣādiq's (peace be upon him) statement addressed to ʿUnwān al-Baṣrī wherein he says, "This is the first level of piety", also indicates that *taqwā* has stages. Some of these levels which occur in man's progressive spiritual movement, will be mentioned here.

1) Taqwā at the Level of Actions

The first level of *taqwā* is to arrange one's actions in accordance with Divine laws. Performing the obligatory actions (*wājibāt*) and refraining from the prohibited actions (*muḥarramāt*) is one of the first requirements of this level. In the words of the Messenger of Allah (peace and blessings be upon him and his family):

اعْمَلْ بِفَرَائِضِ اللَّهِ تَكُنْ أَتْقَى النَّاسِ.

> Perform Allah's ordinances and you will be the most pious of the people [the one with the most *taqwā*].[i]

There are also other dimensions and perspectives to taqwā at the level of actions. For more information, refer to the books 'Sīmā-yi Mukhbitīn' and 'Jilwihā-yi Lahūtī' by this same author.

Imam al-Ṣādiq (peace be upon him) lists a number of qualities and then says, "This is the first stage of piety." The qualities comprise of: stepping onto the path of Allah's true servitude, seeking the world with a correct outlook, not establishing relations with other people with

---

i. al-Kulaynī, al-Kāfī, 2:82, narration 4

pride and haughtiness, and making the best use of one's life. Thereafter he recites this verse, "This is the abode of the Hereafter, which We shall grant to those who do not desire to domineer in the Earth nor cause corruption, and the outcome will be in favour of those who have *taqwā*." [i] It thus becomes clear that this verse applies to one who implements *taqwā* entirely in his actions. Such an individual will also succeed in shunning moral vices and traversing the higher levels of *taqwā*.

2) Taqwā at the Level of the Heart

At certain stages of the spiritual journey, man's heart must also acquire the trait of taqwā and maintain the limits of servitude in front of his Lord. This means that the wayfarer must pay attention to the attachments of his heart, to shun moral vices and unite with Allah the Exalted. This statement of Amīr al-Mu'minīn (peace be upon him) also points to this very level of taqwā:

حَرَامٌ عَلَى كُلِ قَلْبٍ مُتَوَلِّهٍ بِالدُّنْيَا أَنْ يَسْكُنَهُ التَّقْوَى

> It is forbidden upon a heart that is infatuated with the world, that *taqwā* reside in it. [ii]

That is because, being infatuated with the world prepares the ground for the appearance of other moral vices. It is also possible that the growth of this vice causes man's taqwā at the level of actions to weaken.

3) Taqwā at the Level of Gnosis

At this stage of the tawhīdī journey and the nurturing of man's secret, taqwā means to first protect one's esoteric dimension from ungodly motivations, and then become immune from paying attention to other than Allah. At this level the sole focus of the heart is Allah's remembrance. Perhaps this noble verse is an indication of this level of taqwā, when it says:

يَا أَيُّهَا الَّذِينَ آمَنُوا اتَّقُوا اللَّهَ حَقَّ تُقَاتِهِ وَلَا تَمُوتُنَّ إِلَّا وَأَنتُم مُّسْلِمُونَ

---

i. (28:83)

ii. al-Āmudī, Ghurar al-Hikam, narration 4904

> O you who have faith! Be wary of Allah with the wariness due to Him and do not die except as Muslims [those who have submitted in front of Allah]. (3:102)

This is the highest level of taqwā; it means complete humility and absolute submission to the Divine commands.

The Role of Divine Tawfīq in Spiritual Wayfaring

Even a cursory look at existence and beings in the realm of this world, and how they constantly change and progress, will lead us to understand that every phenomenon requires specific causes and conditions. Procuring some of these causes is within man's free will, while others are beyond the domain of his free will. For example, performing the ziyārah of the House of Allah (the Kaʿbah)—considering how it is a virtuous deed—requires knowledge and information, a will and resolution, as well as preparing the expenses and other necessities of the journey. But in addition to these things, there are numerous other conditions and causes without which the journey would not be possible, and man's resolve has no role in procuring them. It is due to this that often, even though all apparent required conditions are fulfilled, performing an act becomes impossible.

When Allah the Exalted brings about the causes and provides coherence to them, in order that a virtuous deed is performed, it is called Divine tawfīq. (i)

A person asked Imam al-Sādiq (peace be upon him) about the exegesis of the verse:

وَمَا تَوْفِيقِي إِلَّا بِاللَّهِ

And my *tawfīq* lies only with [the help of] Allah (11:88)

As well as the verse:

إِن يَنصُرْكُمُ اللَّهُ فَلَا غَالِبَ لَكُمْ ۖ وَإِن يَخْذُلْكُمْ
فَمَن ذَا الَّذِي يَنصُرُكُم مِّن بَعْدِهِ

If Allah helps you, no one can overcome you, but if He

---

i. al-Turayhī, Majmaʿ al-Bahrayn, 5:247

forsakes you, who will help you after Him? (3:160)

In response, this noble personality said:

إِذَا فَعَلَ الْعَبْدُ مَا أَمَرَهُ اللَّهُ عَزَّ وَ جَلَّ بِهِ مِنَ الطَّاعَةِ كَانَ فِعْلُهُ وِفْقاً لِأَمْرِ اللَّهِ عَزَّ وَ جَلَّ وَ سُمِّيَ الْعَبْدُ بِهِ مُوَفَّقاً وَ إِذَا أَرَادَ الْعَبْدُ أَنْ يَدْخُلَ فِي شَيْءٍ مِنْ مَعَاصِي اللَّهِ فَحَالَ اللَّهُ تَبَارَكَ وَ تَعَالَى بَيْنَهُ وَ بَيْنَ تِلْكَ الْمَعْصِيَةِ فَتَرَكَهَا كَانَ تَرْكُهُ لَهَا بِتَوْفِيقِ اللَّهِ تَعَالَى ذِكْرُهُ وَ مَتَى خَلَّى بَيْنَهُ وَ بَيْنَ تِلْكَ الْمَعْصِيَةِ فَلَمْ يَحُلْ بَيْنَهُ وَ بَيْنَهَا حَتَّى يَرْتَكِبَهَا فَقَدْ خَذَلَهُ وَ لَمْ يَنْصُرْهُ وَ لَمْ يُوَفِّقْهُ

When a servant performs what Allah (the Invincible and Majestic) has commanded him from [the acts of] obedience, then his actions are in conformity with the command of Allah (the Invincible and Majestic) and the servant is termed as someone given *tawfiq.* [(i)] [Similarly], when a servant desires to enter into an act of disobedience and Allah (the Provider of abundance and the Sublime) comes between him and the disobedience [preventing him from it], and he abandons it, then this abandoning of his is due to *tawfiq* from Allah. [However,] if He leaves him alone with that sins and does not come between him and the sin, such that he performs it, then He has forsaken him, has not helped him, and has not given him *tawfiq.* [(ii)]

ʿAllāmah Tabātabāʾī (may Allah be pleased with him) says about this narration:

The summary of the Imam's (peace be upon him) statement is that the *tawfiq* of Allah the Exalted and His forsaking are from the Attributes of His Actions (those attributes that manifest themselves in His action, because the existence

i. The Arabic root *wafiqa* means to fit or conform. Hence in this blessed narration, the Imam (peace be upon him) shows how the word *tawfiq* has been derived from this root, for the actions of the *muwaffaq* servant (one who has been given *tawfiq*) are in conformity (*wifq*) to Allah's command.

ii. al-Sadūq, al-Tawhīd, 242, narration 1

> of the servant and the causes required for the deed are all actions of Allah). (i) Hence, *tawfiq* means to arrange the causes for him in such a manner that it pulls the servant towards the virtuous deed, or [it means] to not bring about some of the causes that would help him perform acts of disobedience. However, the forsaking [of Allah] is the contrary to these matters and it is also from Him. (ii)

In the statements of the Amīr of Eloquence Imam ʿAlī (peace be upon him), Divine tawfīq is reckoned as a type of Providential captivation and attraction (jadhbah), a mercy and favour from Allah the Exalted, and an asset for securing salvation. (iii)

Signs of Tawfīq

Any virtuous action or instance of abandoning a sin can only be considered as Divine tawfīq if it is accompanied by certain signs and indicators of tawfīq. This is because, it is possible that a certain action be ostensibly performed, however in terms of its reality and value, there was no Divine tawfīq involved. Hence, it is not counted as an accepted deed. These signs are as follows:

1) Conformity with the Intellect (ʿAql)

One of the important signs that an idea, thought, action or manifestation of a trait in man are in line with the *ḥaqq* (truth) is its being in conformity with the self-evident and indisputable verdicts of the intellect. This is also a sign that the Divine causes have been procured and Allah is pleased with this action. As the most intelligent amongst all the world's intelligent people, Amīr al-Muʾminīn (peace be upon him), says:

التَّوْفِيقُ مُمِدُّ الْعَقْلِ

---

i. In a division discussed in Islamic theology, the names of Allah the Exalted are divided into Attributes of His Essence (*al-Ṣifāt al-Dhātiyyah*) and the Attributes of His Actions (*al-Ṣifāt al-Fiʿliyyah*).

ii. Ṭabāṭabāʾī, Tafsīr al-Mīzān, 10:376

iii. Rayshahrī, Mizān al-Ḥikmah, 4:3416

Tawfiq is the helper of the intellect.[i]

Likewise, its opposite—that is when man is forsaken and lost in the abyss of perplexity—is a helper of ignorance or in other words, not treading in accordance with the *ḥaqq*.[ii]

2) Effectiveness of the Action and Achieving It

If Divine *tawfiq* comes to the aid of man in performing an action, that action will produce results. It is possible that initially the results are not obtained, but by carefully considering the action and taking heed of its hindrances, after procuring some of the missing causes or removing these hindrances, the action will produce results. However, without Divine *tawfiq* the action will be ineffective and remain incomplete. In the words of Amīr al-Muʾminīn (peace be upon him):

مَنْ لَمْ يُمِدَّهُ التَّوْفِيقُ لَمْ يُنِبْ إِلَى الْحَق

> One whom *tawfiq* does not aid, does not turn back to the truth.[iii]

3) Being Free from Afflictions

Often man performs virtuous actions, but his actions are accompanied with numerous banes and afflictions such as self-conceit, pride, bragging, making the other party feel obliged, etc.

The existence of such afflictions is a sign of the lack of *tawfiq* in performing that action. That is because Amīr al-Muʾminīn (peace be upon him) has said:

لَمْ يُوَفَّقْ مَنِ اسْتَحْسَنَ الْقَبِيحَ وَ أَعْرَضَ عَنْ قَوْلِ النَّصِيح

> A person who considers abominable actions as good and turns away from the counsel of the admonisher, has not been given *tawfiq*.[iv]

---

i. al-Āmudī, Ghurar al-Hikam, narration 718

ii. al-Āmudī, Ghurar al-Hikam, narration 11

iii. Ibid.

iv. Ibid., narration 104

$$\text{مَنْ أَمَدَّهُ التَّوْفِيقُ أَحْسَنَ الْعَمَل}$$

One who is aided by *tawfīq*, performs action in a good manner. [i]

4) Spiritual Pleasure

Man's actions and worship become pleasurable and refreshing when performed by means of Divine *tawfīq*; in this case the person perceives that he has earned Allah's pleasure. However, if this is not so, his action will be nothing but a lifeless and withered form, just as Amīr al-Mu'minīn (peace be upon him) says:

$$\text{كَيْفَ يَتَمَتَّعُ بِالْعِبَادَةِ مَنْ لَمْ يُعِنْهُ التَّوْفِيق}$$

How can a person whom *tawfīq* has not aided benefit from worship?! [ii]

The secret of this matter is that *tawfīq* is a name from Allah's Names of Beauty [iii] and is a manifestation of His Special Mercy. Hence, an action or an act of worship that is performed with Divine *tawfīq* enjoys Allah's presence and intimacy.

Factors that Bring About Tawfīq

As explained, *tawfīq* means the coming together of the causes of any affair—in order for that affair to materialize—and some of these causes are placed within man's being and under his volition. Considering this, the factors that bring about *tawfīq* and are under man's volition are the following:

1) Supplication (Du'ā')

Man's indigence and neediness before the Divine is a level of his perfection and indicates his capacity to receive Divine Grace. Humility and expressing one's needs in His presence, is considered as laying the groundwork to attract Divine *tawfīq*. Imam 'Alī (peace be upon him)

---

i. Ibid., narration 300

ii. Ibid., narration 566

iii. (4:35)

says in this regard:

أَيُّهَا النَّاسُ إِنَّهُ مَنِ اسْتَنْصَحَ اللَّهَ وُفِّقَ وَ مَنِ اتَّخَذَ قَوْلَهُ دَلِيلاً هُدِيَ لِلَّتِي هِيَ أَقْوَمُ فَإِنَّ جَارَ اللَّهِ آمِنٌ وَ عَدُوَّهُ خَائِفٌ

O people! Indeed, one who seeks exhortation and admonition from Allah, receives *tawfiq*. One who takes His words as the guide of the path, is directed to what is most upright. That is because one who seeks refuge in Allah is secure and His enemy is in fear.[i]

Likewise, in another narration he says:

مَنِ اسْتَنْصَحَ اللَّهَ حَازَ التَّوْفِيق

One who seeks admonition from Allah, obtains *tawfiq*.[ii]

One of the recommendations of the Imams (peace be upon them) to the people is that they should request *tawfiq* from Allah in all the affairs of their life. Imam ʿAlī (peace be upon him) in his testament to Imam al-Ḥasan (peace be upon him) says:

وَ ابْدَأْ قَبْلَ نَظَرِكَ فِي ذَلِكَ بِالاسْتِعَانَةِ بِإِلَهِكَ وَ الرَّغْبَةِ إِلَيْهِ فِي تَوْفِيقِكَ

Before you probe into this [treading the path of the pure ones], you should begin by seeking aid from your God and desiring from Him [that He grants you] *tawfiq*.[iii]

In many of the supplications of the Infallibles (peace be upon them), they request for *tawfiq* from Allah the Exalted. Imam Zayn al-ʿĀbidīn and Imam al-Bāqir (peace be upon them) would recite this supplication every day during the blessed month of Ramaḍān:

i. Al-Radī, Nahj al-Balāghah, sermon 147

ii. al-Āmudī, Ghurar al-Ḥikam, narration 302

iii. Al-Radī, Nahj al-Balāghah, letter 31

$$اللّٰهُمَّ صَلِّ عَلَى مُحَمَّدٍ وَ آلِهِ وَ وَفِّقْنِي فِيهِ لِلَيْلَةِ الْقَدْرِ عَلَى$$

$$أَفْضَلِ حَالٍ تُحِبُّ أَنْ يَكُونَ عَلَيْهَا أَحَدٌ مِنْ أَوْلِيَائِكَ وَ أَرْضَاهَا$$

$$لَكَ$$

O Allah shower Your blessings upon Muḥammad and his family. Grant me *tawfīq* in it [the month of Ramadhan] to [perceive] the Night of Qadr, in the best state which You love for one of Your *awliyā'*, and the state which is most pleasing to You. [i]

2) Ambition and Determination

The measure of Divine *tawfīq* is proportional to the amount of ambition man has. That is because ambition and determination are the best provisions for the wayfarers of the Alley of the Beloved, just as Imam Zayn al-'Ābidīn addressing Allah says:

$$وَ قَدْ عَلِمْتُ أَنَّ زَادَ الرَّاحِلِ إِلَيْكَ عَزْمُ إِرَادَةٍ يَخْتَارُكَ بِهَا$$

Indeed, I have come to know that the best provision for the wayfarer towards You is firm will through which he chooses You. (ii)

Man's intention changes as per his ambition, and in turn he receives Divine *tawfīq* to the extent and quality of his intention. Imam 'Alī (peace be upon him) has indicated this reality in different narrations:

$$عَلَى قَدْرِ النِّيَّةِ تَكُونُ مِنَ اللَّهِ الْعَطِيَّة$$

Allah's bestowal is to the extent of [one's] intention. [iii]

$$مَنْ حَسُنَتْ نِيَّتُهُ أَمَدَّهُ التَّوْفِيق$$

One whose intention is good and virtuous, tawfīq comes to his aid. [iv]

---

i. Majlisī, Bihār al-Anwār, 98:102

ii. Ibid., 98:20

iii. al-Āmudī, Ghurar al-Hikam, narration 306

iv. Ibid.

As a result, people of low ambition who are incapable of reaching lofty spiritual stations, cannot expect to receive lofty Divine tawfīq. In the words of Imam al-Sādiq (peace be upon him):

إِنَّمَا قَدَّرَ اللَّهُ عَوْنَ الْعِبَادِ عَلَى قَدْرِ نِيَّاتِهِمْ فَمَنْ صَحَّتْ نِيَّتُهُ تَمَّ عَوْنُ اللَّهِ لَهُ وَ مَنْ قَصُرَتْ نِيَّتُهُ قَصُرَ عَنْهُ الْعَوْنُ بِقَدْرِ الَّذِي قَصَّرَ.

> Indeed, Allah has apportioned the servants' help to the extent of their intentions. Therefore, one whose intention is rectified, Allah's help becomes complete for him; and one whose intention is defective, Allah's help is diminished to the extent of the defect.[i]

3) Exerting Efforts and Struggling

To perform any volitional action, it is necessary that all the causes and conditions required for carrying it out, exist. The absence of one or a few factors renders the occurrence of this action impossible.

Being motivated, possessing knowledge, exerting efforts, actively working, and receiving Divine *tawfīq* are amongst the fundamental factors required for the performance of a virtuous deed. Therefore, if a person takes efforts and strives to perform a virtuous deed, but Divine *tawfīq* does not accompany him, then in Imam 'Alī's (peace be upon him) view his efforts will be of no benefit:

لَا يَنْفَعُ اجْتِهَادٌ بِغَيْرِ تَوْفِيق

Striving without *tawfīq* does not have benefit.[ii]

خَيْرُ الِاجْتِهَادِ مَا قَارَنَهُ التَّوْفِيق

The best striving is that which is accompanied by *tawfīq*.[iii]

---

i. Majlisī, Bihār al-Anwār, 70:211, narration 24

ii. al-Āmudī, Ghurar al-Ḥikam, narration 406

iii. Ibid., narration 431

In the view of this distinguished personality, knowledge without *tawfiq* is also futile:

لَا يَنْفَعُ عِلْمٌ بِغَيْرِ تَوْفِيق

Knowledge without *tawfiq* does not have benefit.(i)

In the same way, the mere ability to perform an action without practising and implementing this ability and putting efforts is also not beneficial. Imam al-Riḍā (peace be upon him) in response to a person who asked him about *tawfiq*, said:

لَوْ كُنْتَ مُوَفَّقاً كُنْتَ عَامِلًا وَ قَدْ يَكُونُ الْكَافِرُ أَقْوَى مِنْكَ وَ لَا يُعْطَى التَّوْفِيقَ فَلَا يَكُونُ عَامِلا

If you had *tawfiq*, you would be performing [virtuous] actions. At times a disbeliever is stronger than you, but he is not granted *tawfiq* and hence he cannot perform that action.(ii)

On the contrary, those who request Allah the Exalted for *tawfiq* and the attainment of spiritual and moral perfections without efforts and striving, are merely ridiculing themselves. Imam al-Riḍā (peace be upon him) says in this regard:

سَبْعَةُ أَشْيَاءَ بِغَيْرِ سَبْعَةِ أَشْيَاءَ مِنَ الِاسْتِهْزَاءِ مَنِ اسْتَغْفَرَ بِلِسَانِهِ وَ لَمْ يَنْدَمْ بِقَلْبِهِ فَقَدِ اسْتَهَزَأَ بِنَفْسِهِ وَ مَنْ سَأَلَ اللَّهَ التَّوْفِيقَ وَ لَمْ يَجْتَهِدْ فَقَدِ اسْتَهَزَأَ بِنَفْسِهِ وَ مَنِ اسْتَحْزَمَ وَ لَمْ يَحْذَرْ فَقَدِ اسْتَهَزَأَ بِنَفْسِهِ وَ مَنْ سَأَلَ اللَّهَ الْجَنَّةَ وَ لَمْ يَصْبِرْ عَلَى الشَّدَائِدِ فَقَدِ اسْتَهَزَأَ بِنَفْسِهِ وَ مَنْ تَعَوَّذَ بِاللَّهِ مِنَ النَّارِ وَ لَمْ يَتْرُكْ شَهَوَاتِ الدُّنْيَا فَقَدِ اسْتَهَزَأَ بِنَفْسِهِ وَ مَنْ ذَكَرَ الْمَوْتَ وَ لَمْ يَسْتَعِدَّ لَهُ

i. Ibid., narration 387

ii. Majlisī, Bihār al-Anwār, 5:142

فَقَدِ اسْتَهْزَأَ بِنَفْسِهِ وَ مَنْ ذَكَرَ اللَّهَ وَ لَمْ يَسْتَبِقْ إِلَى لِقَائِهِ فَقَدِ اسْتَهْزَأَ بِنَفْسِهِ

> Seven things without seven [other] things are [merely] a mockery. One who seeks forgiveness through his tongue, while his heart is not remorseful has indeed ridiculed himself. One who asks Allah for *tawfiq* but does not strive has indeed ridiculed himself. One who has foresight but is not cautious and prudent [about its vast scope and how it may lead to far-fetched ambitions] has indeed ridiculed himself. One who asks Allah for Paradise but is not patient in hardships has indeed ridiculed himself. One who seeks refuge in Allah from the Hellfire but does not shun selfish desires has indeed ridiculed himself. One who remembers death but does not prepare himself for it has indeed ridiculed himself. One who remembers Allah but does not seek the lead in moving towards [preparing for] meeting Him has indeed ridiculed himself.[i]

Therefore, no one should reckon that their laziness and negligence on the path of spirituality is a lack of tawfīq from Allah. On the other hand, if their efforts and struggling in performing an action does yield results, then they should be certain that their actions were performed with the help of Divine tawfīq; they were not independent in performing it. In any case, after considering and being aware of the action and one's own strength—even if is little strength—and while also seeking tawfīq from Allah, man should embark upon performing a virtuous action and should not be concerned with its end-result. Despite this, an end-result will undoubtedly be achieved. Because fundamentally, it is acting in accordance to one's duty as a servant that is the principle cause of man's perfection and produces positive effects in this world and the Hereafter.

Imam al-Bāqir (peace be upon him) was asked the meaning of "lā hawlā wa lā quwwata illā billāh." He replied saying:

---

i. Ibn Abī Firās, Majmūʿah Warrām, 2:111

مَعْنَاهُ لَا حَوْلَ لَنَا عَنْ مَعْصِيَةِ اللَّهِ إِلَّا بِعَوْنِ اللَّهِ وَ لَا قُوَّةَ لَنَا عَلَى طَاعَةِ اللَّهِ إِلَّا بِتَوْفِيقِ اللَّهِ عَزَّ وَ جَل

> It means that there is no hindrance stopping us from Allah's disobedience except the help of Allah, (i) and we do not have any strength over the obedience of Allah except through the *tawfiq* of Allah (the Invincible and Majestic). (ii)

Imam al-Sādiq (peace be upon him) also—after explaining the aforementioned matters and before elucidating some specific recommendations related to practical and moral matters—asks Allah the Exalted to grant 'Unwān al-Basrī tawfīq, so that he succeeds in acting upon these instructions. (iii)

---

i. The word *ḥawl* is often translated as power or might, but one of the linguistic meanings of it is a barrier or hindrance.

ii. al-Sadūq, al-Tawhīd, 242, narration 3

iii. A reference to the part of the noble narration of 'Unwān al-Baṣrī, when Imam (peace be upon him) says:

أُوصِيكَ بِتِسْعَةِ أَشْيَاءَ فَإِنَّهَا وَصِيَّتِي لِمُرِيدِي الطَّرِيقِ إِلَى اللَّهِ تَعَالَى وَ اللَّهَ أَسْأَلُ أَنْ يُوَفِّقَكَ لِاسْتِعْمَالِهِ

> I enjoin you towards nine things. For indeed, it is my admonition to [all] those who desire the path towards Allah and I ask Allah to grant you success (tawfiq) in acting upon them.

Chapter Five

Specific Instructions for Spiritual Development

Introduction

In addition to drawing ʿUnwān al-Basrī's attention to the essence of servitude—that is to perform Allah's commands and refrain from His prohibitions—in the concluding part of his conversation, Imam al-Sādiq (peace be upon him) gives some specific pieces of advice and instructions. These instructions and advice encompass three very important aspects of the wayfarer's life:

1) Physical health
2) The ethics of interacting with others
3) The pursuit of knowledge

This division presented by Imam al-Sādiq (peace be upon him) and the importance given by him to these three aspects, illustrate a set of principles in relation to planning one's personal life. These principles are extremely important and worthy of pondering upon.

The way the Imam has summarized the instructions into these three aspects illustrates that it is crucial and important to pay attention to the body, ethics (akhlāq) and one's educational routine to nurture the spirit of servitude. Any kind of excessiveness (ifrāt), laxity (tafrīt) or disruption in these three aspects causes a deficiency in an important part of man's existence. Thus, one who sets out upon the path of Allah's servitude must blend physical heath with spiritual vitality. That is because, physical health and soundness is not a perfection if it is not accompanied by spirituality; on the other hand, it is not possible to benefit from a life of spirituality without a healthy body.

Section One
Paying Attention to a Routine for the Body

The programs and instructions from the Ahl al-Bayt (peace be upon them) regarding medicine and hygiene prevent the onset of anomalies in the body. They do so by focusing on the principles that govern man's body. As Amīr al-Mu'minīn (peace be upon him) says to Imam al-Hasan (peace be upon him):

أَ لَا أُعَلِّمُكَ أَرْبَعَ خِصَالٍ تَسْتَغْنِي بِهَا عَنِ الطِّبِّ فَقَالَ بَلَى يَا أَمِيرَ الْمُؤْمِنِينَ قَالَ لَا تَجْلِسْ عَلَى الطَّعَامِ إِلَّا وَ أَنْتَ جَائِعٌ وَ لَا تَقُمْ عَنِ الطَّعَامِ إِلَّا وَ أَنْتَ تَشْتَهِيهِ وَ جَوِّدِ الْمَضْغَ وَ إِذَا نِمْتَ فَاعْرِضْ نَفْسَكَ عَلَى الْخَلَاءِ فَإِذَا اسْتَعْمَلْتَ هَذَا اسْتَغْنَيْتَ عَنِ الطِّبِّ.

> Should I not teach you four habits which will make you free from medicine? He replied, "Yes, surely O Amīr al-Mu'minīn." He said, "Do not sit to eat food except when you are hungry, do not stand up from the food [and stop eating] except that you [still] have a desire for it, chew [your food] properly and when you want to sleep [first] use the toilet. If you put these into practice, you will not need medicine [and you will not need to visit a doctor]." (i)

Imam al-Sādiq's (peace be upon him) instructions to 'Unwān al-Basrī about physical health are also of the same kind. Despite their simplicity, they can be applied by everyone and do not have any negative side-effects. He says:

أَمَّا اللَّوَاتِي فِي الرِّيَاضَةِ فَإِيَّاكَ أَنْ تَأْكُلَ مَا لَا تَشْتَهِيهِ فَإِنَّهُ يُورِثُ الْحَمَاقَةَ وَ الْبَلَهَ وَ لَا تَأْكُلْ إِلَّا عِنْدَ الْجُوعِ وَ إِذَا أَكَلْتَ فَكُلْ حَلَالًا وَ سَمِّ اللَّهَ وَ اذْكُرْ حَدِيثَ الرَّسُولِ ص مَا مَلَأَ آدَمِيٌّ وِعَاءً

i. al-Ṣadūq, al-Khiṣāl, 1:28, narration 67

شَـرّاً مِـنْ بَطْنِـهِ فَـإِنْ كَانَ وَ لَا بُـدَّ فَثُلُـثٌ لِطَعَامِـهِ وَ ثُلُـثٌ لِشَـرَابِهِ وَ ثُلُـثٌ لِنَفَسِـهِ

As for the affairs which pertain to controlling the soul: do not eat that for which you have no appetite, because it leads to stupidity and foolishness. Do not eat except when you are hungry. When you eat, eat that which is *ḥalāl* (permissible) and take Allah's name [over it]. Remember the words of the Messenger of Allah (peace and blessings be upon him and his family), "A human being has not filled any container worse than his stomach. When one must partake of food, he should allot one-third for food, one-third for water and one-third for breathing."

Elucidation and Explanation

These words have various dimensions to them, some of which are:

1) Eating Permissible (Halāl) Food

The Noble Qur'ān has made a distinction between permissible and impermissible sustenance:

قُل لَّا يَسْتَوِي الْخَبِيثُ وَالطَّيِّبُ وَلَوْ أَعْجَبَكَ كَثْرَةُ الْخَبِيثِ

Say, "The good and the bad are not equal, though the abundance of the bad should amaze you." (5:100)

The difference between permissible and impermissible food is not limited to their effects in the Hereafter. Rather, some things that Allah has made impermissible directly create disorder in man's body. Others also leave a lasting effect on his soul and psyche and consequently the body is negatively affected.

According to this verse, the abundance of impermissible sustenance does not have any effect on that which has been apportioned for man. It is reported that one day:

دَخَـلَ عَلِـيٌّ ع الْمَسْـجِدَ وَ قَـالَ لِرَجُـلٍ أَمْسِـكْ عَلَـى بَغْلَتِـي فَخَلَـعَ لِجَامَهَـا وَ ذَهَـبَ بِـهِ فَخَـرَجَ عَلِـيٌّ ع بَعْـدَ مَـا قَضَـى صَلَاتَـهُ وَ

بِيَدِهِ دِرْهَمَانِ لِيَدْفَعَهُمَا إِلَيْهِ مُكَافَأَةً لَهُ فَوَجَدَ البَغْلَةَ عَطَلًا فَدَفَعَ إِلَى أَحَدِ غِلْمَانِهِ الدِّرْهَمَيْنِ لِيَشْتَرِيَ بِهِمَا لِجَاماً فَصَادَفَ الغُلَامُ اللِّجَامَ المَسْرُوْقَ فِي السُّوْقِ قَدْ بَاعَهُ الرَّجُلُ بِدِرْهَمَيْنِ فَأَخَذَهُ بِالدِّرْهَمَيْنِ وَ عَادَ إِلَى مَوْلَاهُ فَقَالَ عَلِيٌّ ع إِنَّ العَبْدَ لَيَحْرُمُ نَفْسَهُ الرِّزْقَ الحَلَالَ بِتَرْكِ الصَّبْرِ وَ لَا يُزَادُ عَلَى مَا قُدِرَ لَهُ.

ʿAlī (peace be upon him) entered the mosque [first entrusting his mule to a man]. He said, "Take care of my mule [until I return]." That man removed the bridle [of the Imam's mule] and ran away with it. ʿAlī (peace be upon him) exited the mosque after he had completed his prayers, with two *dirhams* in his hands. He wanted to give these to the man in return [for his work]. However, he saw that the bridle of the mule had been stolen! So, he gave the two *dirhams* to one of his servants and asked him to purchase a bridle. The servant coincidentally came across the same stolen bridle in the market! The man had sold it for two *dirhams*, so the servant again purchased it for two *dirhams* and then returned to his master. [Upon seeing this event,] ʿAlī (peace be upon him) said, "Indeed a servant can deny himself permissible sustenance due to his impatience, while nothing is added to that which was apportioned for him." (i)

Eating that which is permissible and refraining from the impermissible is of such importance that the Messenger of Allah (peace and blessings be upon him and his family) says:

تَرْكُ لُقْمَةِ حَرَامٍ أَحَبُّ إِلَى اللَّهِ تَعَالَى مِنْ صَلَاةِ أَلْفَيْ رَكْعَةٍ تَطَوُّعا

Abandoning an impermissible morsel is more beloved to Allah than two thousand units of supererogatory prayers. (ii)

Likewise, in another narration he says:

الْعِبَادَةُ مَعَ أَكْلِ الْحَرَامِ كَالْبِنَاءِ عَلَى الرَّمْلِ وَ قِيلَ عَلَى الْمَاء

i. Ibn Abī al-Ḥadīd, Sharḥ-i Nahj al-Balāghah, 061:3

ii. Ibn Abī Firās, Tanbīh al-Khawātir, volume 3, narration 120

> Worship accompanied with partaking of that which is impermissible is like raising a building on sand [or it has also been said, on water].[i]

Similarly, Imam al-Bāqir (peace be upon him) says:

إِنَّ الرَّجُلَ إِذَا أَصَابَ مَالًا مِنْ حَرَامٍ لَمْ يُقْبَلْ مِنْهُ حَجٌّ، وَ لَا عُمْرَةٌ، وَ لَا صِلَةُ رَحِمٍ، حَتَّى إِنَّهُ يَفْسُدُ فِيهِ الْفَرْجُ.

> One who acquires impermissible wealth, his Ḥajj, ʿUmrah and *ṣilah al-raḥim*[ii] are not accepted. Even his children become corrupt [or his sperm becomes such that future children will become corrupt].[iii] [iv]

Overall, earning a permissible income is so valuable that the Messenger of Allah (peace and blessings be upon him and his family) says:

الْعِبَادَةُ عَشَرَةُ أَجْزَاءٍ تِسْعَةُ أَجْزَاءٍ فِي طَلَبِ الْحَلَالِ

> Worship is ten portions, nine of which are in seeking permissible [sustenance].[v]

Committing impermissible acts has an extremely undesirable effect on man's soul and prevents him from reaching perfections. One of these impermissible acts is to partake of impermissible food. Imam ʿAlī (peace be upon him) says:

إِذَا رَغِبْتَ فِي الْمَكَارِمِ فَاجْتَنِبِ الْمَحَارِمِ

> If you strongly desire to attain noble traits, then shun that which is impermissible.[vi]

---

i. al-Ḥillī, ʿUddah al-Dāʿī, 153

ii. *Ṣilah al-Raḥim* is one of the Islamic injunctions where every believer is required to establish a cordial relationship with his family.

iii. Needless to say, such narrations are informing us about one contributing factor amongst many factors that could result in a child becoming corrupt.

iv. al-Ṭūsī, al-Amālī, 680, narration 1447

v. Majlisī, Biḥār al-Anwār, 103:18, narration 81

vi. al-Āmudī, Ghurar al-Hikam, narration 4069

When explaining these words of Allah (the Invincible and Majestic):

وَقَدِمْنَا إِلَىٰ مَا عَمِلُوا مِنْ عَمَلٍ فَجَعَلْنَاهُ هَبَاءً مَّنثُورًا

> Then We shall attend to the works they (the disbelievers) have done and turn them into scattered dust.[i]

Imam al-Sādiq (peace be upon him) says:

أَمَا وَ اللَّهِ إِنْ كَانَتْ أَعْمَالُهُمْ أَشَدَّ بَيَاضاً مِنَ الْقَبَاطِي وَ لَكِنْ كَانُوا إِذَا عَرَضَ لَهُمُ الْحَرَامُ لَمْ يَدَعُوهُ

> By Allah! Know that even though these people had actions brighter than a thing [and shining] Egyptian garment, but when impermissible actions were presented to them they would not abandon it.[ii]

Therefore, keeping the stomach chaste and protecting it from impermissible food is considered worship. In the words of Imam al-Bāqir (peace be upon him):

مَا عُبِدَ اللَّهُ بِشَيْءٍ أَفْضَلَ مِنْ عِفَّةِ بَطْنٍ وَ فَرْجٍ

> Allah has not been worshipped with anything greater than chastity (*'iffah*) of the stomach and the private parts.[iii]

2) Staying Away from Doubtful (Mushtabah) Matters

The word 'mushtabah' refers to a matter whose being permissible or impermissible is not established with certainty. In terms of foods, it refers to food obtained from money whose owner does not care how he has obtained it. He is not bothered if it is obtained from usury, bribery, buying and selling impermissible things, or through permissible means. It is not important for him if khums or zakāt is applicable on this money. Abstaining from such morsels and such food protects a person from becoming polluted with impermissible acts. In the Islamic

---

i. (25:23)

ii. al-Kulaynī, al-Kāfī, 2:81, narration 5

iii. Ibid., 2:79, narration 10

narrations, such doubtful matters have been considered as being on the brink of prohibited actions. Wayfarers towards Allah's path and His servitude—for the purity of their soul and as a means of preparing themselves to traverse the stages of servitude—should earnestly stay away from doubtful ideological, moral, or practical matters, as well as doubtful food.

It for this reason that the Messenger of Allah (peace and blessings be upon him and his family) says:

> حَلَالٌ بَيِّنٌ وَ حَرَامٌ بَيِّنٌ وَ شُبُهَاتٌ بَيْنَ ذَلِكَ فَمَنْ تَرَكَ الشُّبُهَاتِ نَجَا مِنَ الْمُحَرَّمَاتِ وَ مَنْ أَخَذَ بِالشُّبُهَاتِ ارْتَكَبَ الْمُحَرَّمَاتِ وَ هَلَكَ مِنْ حَيْثُ لَا يَعْلَم
>
> [Affairs are]: clearly permissible, clearly impermissible and doubtful things that lie between these two. So, one who leaves aside the doubtful matters is saved from the prohibited ones. But one who performs the doubtful [eventually also] commits the prohibited and is destroyed from whence he does not know.[i]

Imam ʿAlī (peace be upon him) also says:

> إِيَّاكَ وَ الْوُقُوعَ فِي الشُّبُهَاتِ وَ الْوُلُوعَ بِالشَّهَوَاتِ فَإِنَّهُمَا يَقْتَادَانِكَ إِلَى الْوُقُوعِ فِي الْحَرَامِ وَ رُكُوبِ كَثِيرٍ مِنَ الْآثَام
>
> Abstain from falling into doubtful things and from greedily craving the desires, for these two draw you towards falling into impermissible [actions] and committing many sins.[ii]

3) Abstaining from Eating that for Which You Have No Appetite

Eating when one has no appetite for the food leads to stupidity. The Messenger of Allah (peace and blessings be upon him and his

---

i. Ibid., 1:68, narration 10

ii. al-Āmudī, Ghurar al-Hikam, narration 2723

family) says:

كُلْ وَ أَنْتَ تَشْتَهِي وَ أَمْسِكْ وَ أَنْتَ تَشْتَهِي

> Eat when you have appetite [for the food] and stop eating while you [still] have appetite [for it].[i]

4) Abstaining from Overeating and its Effects

Overeating and gluttony is one of the very disgusting habits which is the cause of many indecent actions and blameworthy traits (akhlāq). Furthermore, it is also very harmful for man's health.

Some of the effects of overeating are:

i) Effects in the Hereafter

Salmān al-Fārsī narrated from the Messenger of Allah (peace and blessings be upon him and his family) that he said:

إِنَّ أَكْثَرَ النَّاسِ شِبَعاً فِي الدُّنْيَا أَكْثَرُهُمْ جُوعاً فِي الْآخِرَةِ

> Indeed, one who is the most satiated of people in this world [one who overeats] will be the hungriest of people in the Hereafter.[ii]

Perhaps, hunger in the Hereafter means that a person perceives that he lacks spiritual perfections and is afflicted with the consequences of this.

ii) Spiritual Effects

Heedlessness, remoteness from Allah and a disinclination towards worship are some of the ill-effects of overeating. One day Prophet Jesus (peace be upon him) recited a sermon and said:

---

i. Majlisī, Bihār al-Anwār, 62:290

ii. al-Ṭūsī, al-Amālī, 221

يَا بَنِي إِسْرَائِيلَ لَا تَأْكُلُوا حَتَّى تَجُوعُوا وَ إِذَا جُعْتُمْ فَكُلُوا وَ لَا تَشْبَعُوا فَإِنَّكُمْ إِذَا شَبِعْتُم غَلُظَتْ رِقَابُكُمْ وَ سَمِنَتْ جُنُوبُكُمْ وَ نَسِيتُمْ رَبَّكُم

O Children of Israel! Do not eat until you are hungry. When you are hungry partake of food but do not fill your stomach. Because verily if you fill your stomach your neck thickens, the lower side of your body [your stomach] fattens and you forget your Lord.(i)

Imam al-Sādiq (peace be upon him) also said:

إِنَّ الْبَدَنَ لَيَطْغَى مِنْ أَكْلَةٍ ... وَ أَبْغَضُ مَا يَكُونُ الْعَبْدُ إِلَى اللَّهِ إِذَا امْتَلَأَ بَطْنُهُ.

Indeed, the body can rebel because of one morsel [of over-eating] ... And the most hateful state of the servant near Allah is when his stomach is full.(ii)

Likewise, in another narration he says to a companion named Hafs:

ظَهَرَ إِبْلِيسُ لِيَحْيَى بْنِ زَكَرِيَّا ع وَ إِذَا عَلَيْهِ مَعَالِيقُ مِنْ كُلِّ شَيْءٍ فَقَالَ لَهُ يَحْيَى مَا هَذِهِ الْمَعَالِيقُ يَا إِبْلِيسُ فَقَالَ هَذِهِالشَّهَوَاتُ الَّتِي أَصَبْتُهَا مِنِ ابْنِ آدَمَ قَالَ فَهَلْ لِي مِنْهَا شَيْءٌ قَالَ رُبَّمَا شَبِعْتَ فَثَقَّلَتْكَ عَنِ الصَّلَاةِ وَ الذِّكْرِ قَالَ يَحْيَى لِلَّهِ عَلَيَّ أَنْ لَا أَمْلَأَ بَطْنِي مِنْ طَعَامٍ أَبَداً فَقَالَ إِبْلِيسُ لِلَّهِ عَلَيَّ أَنْ لَا أَنْصَحَ مُسْلِماً أَبَداً ثُمَّ قَالَ أَبُو عَبْدِ اللَّهِ ع يَا حَفْصُ لِلَّهِ عَلَى جَعْفَرٍ وَ

---

i. al-ʿĀmilī, Wasāʾil al-Shīʿah, 16:409

ii. Majlisī, Bihār al-Anwār, 66:33, narration 25.
Note: referring to the original source of this blessed narration, the Arabic text that was found reads, «مِنْ أَكْلِهِ» and not «مِنْ أَكْلَةٍ». This would slightly change the meaning, making it, "...because of its [over]eating" as opposed to "...because of one morsel." It appears that both readings are acceptable.

آلِ جَعْفَرٍ أَنْ لَا يَمْلَئُوا بُطُونَهُمْ مِنْ طَعَامٍ أَبَداً وَ لِلَّهِ عَلَى جَعْفَرٍ وَ
آلِ جَعْفَرٍ أَنْ لَا يَعْمَلُوا لِلدُّنْيَا أَبَداً

"Iblīs appeared in front of John the son of Zechariah (peace be upon them) while there were different types of chains on him. John asked him, 'O Iblīs! What are these chains?' He said, 'These are the desires with which I afflict the son of Adam.' John asked, 'Is there something amongst them for me?' Iblīs replied, 'Sometimes you eat till your stomach is full and thus I make prayers and Allah's remembrance [seem] burdensome for you.' John (peace be upon him) said, 'By Allah, I make it incumbent upon myself to never fill my stomach.' Then Iblīs said, 'By Allah, I make in incumbent upon myself to never admonish a Muslim.'" Thereafter Imam al-Ṣādiq (peace be upon him) said, "O Ḥafṣ! By Allah, it is incumbent upon Jaʿfar and the family of Jaʿfar that they will never fill their stomach with food. And by Allah, it is incumbent upon Jaʿfar and the family of Jaʿfar that they will never act for the sake of the *dunyā*." (i)

iii) Bodily Effects

The Messenger of Allah (peace and blessings be upon him and his family) says:

إِيَّاكُمْ وَ الْبِطْنَةَ فَإِنَّهَا مَفْسَدَةٌ لِلْبَدَنِ وَ مَوْرَثَةٌ لِلسَّقَمِ وَ مَكْسَلَةٌ
عَنِ الْعِبَادَةِ

Abstain from gluttony. For it corrupts the body, causes disease, and makes [a person] indolent towards worship. (ii)

It has also been narrated:

مَنْ قَلَّ طَعَامُهُ صَحَّ بَدَنُهُ وَ صَفَا قَلْبُهُ وَ مَنْ كَثُرَ طَعْمُهُ سَقِمَ
بَدَنُهُ وَ قَسَا قَلْبُهُ

---

i. Ibid., 66:334, narration 18

ii. Ibid., 66:338, narration 35

> One who eats less his body becomes healthy and his heart becomes pure; and one who eats a lot his body becomes ill and his heart hardens.[(i)]

Similarly, Imam al-Sādiq (peace be upon him) says:

> كُلُّ دَاءٍ مِنَ التُّخَمَةِ مَا خَلاَ الْحُمَّى فَإِنَّهَا تَرِدُ وُرُودا
>
> Every disease is due to overeating except fever, for it enters [the body] in a [specific] different manner.[(ii)]

The Messenger of Allah (peace and blessings be upon him and his family) has considered eating while the stomach is full as the reason behind skin problems. He says:

> الْأَكْلُ عَلَى الشِّبَعِ يُورِثُ الْبَرَصَ.
>
> Eating while the stomach is full leads to leprosy.[(iii)]

Becoming old early and destruction of the features of the face are other harms of overeating. It is narrated from the Noble Messenger of Islam (peace and blessings be upon him and his family) that he said:

> مَرَّ أَخِي عِيسَى ع بِمَدِينَةٍ وَ فِيهَا رَجُلٌ وَ امْرَأَةٌ يَتَصَايَحَانِ فَقَالَ مَا شَأْنُكُمَا قَالَ يَا نَبِيَّ اللَّهِ هَذِهِ امْرَأَتِي وَ لَيْسَ بِهَا بَأْسٌ صَالِحَةٌ وَ لَكِنِّي أُحِبُّ فِرَاقَهَا قَالَ فَأَخْبِرْنِي عَلَى كُلِّ حَالٍ مَا شَأْنُهَا قَالَ هِيَ خَلَقَةُ الْوَجْهِ مِنْ غَيْرِ كِبَرٍ قَالَ لَهَا يَا امْرَأَةُ أَ تُحِبِّينَ أَنْ يَعُودَ مَاءُ وَجْهِكِ طَرِيّاً قَالَتْ نَعَمْ قَالَ لَهَا إِذَا أَكَلْتِ فَإِيَّاكِ أَنْ تَشْبَعِي لِأَنَّ الطَّعَامَ إِذَا تَكَاثَرَ عَلَى الصَّدْرِ فَزَادَ فِي الْقَدْرِ ذَهَبَ مَاءُ الْوَجْهِ فَفَعَلَتْ ذَلِكَ فَعَادَ وَجْهُهَا طَرِيّا
>
> My brother Jesus (peace be upon him) passed by a city while a man and a woman were shouting at each other. He [saw this and] asked, "What are you doing?" The man replied,

---

i. Ibid., 66:338, narration 35

ii. Ibid., 66:336, narration 29

iii. al-Ṣadūq, al-Amālī, 324

> "O prophet of Allah! This is my wife. There is no problem in her. She is virtuous, but I want to separate from her." Jesus (peace be upon him) said, "In any case, tell me what her problem is." That man replied, "Her face is ugly, despite being young." Jesus (peace be upon him) then turned to the woman and said, "Do you not want the freshness [and features] of your face to return?" She said, "Yes." So, he said to her, "When you partake of food, do not eat so much that your stomach becomes full. That is because when food increases in the chest [the stomach] and exceeds its measure, it takes away the freshness from the face." That lady did so, and her face became fresh [and young] again. (i)

Imam al-Sādiq (peace be upon him) mentions a narration from the Messenger of Allah (peace and blessings be upon him and his family) for controlling the amount of intake of food according to man's need. The Messenger of Allah (peace and blessings be upon him and his family) says:

> مَا مَلَأَ آدَمِيٌّ وِعَاءً شَرّاً مِنْ بَطْنِهِ فَإِنْ كَانَ وَ لَا بُدَّ فَثُلُثٌ لِطَعَامِهِ وَ ثُلُثٌ لِشَرَابِهِ وَ ثُلُثٌ لِنَفَسِهِ
>
> A human being has not filled any container worse than his stomach. When one must partake of food, he should allot one-third for food, one-third for water and one-third for breathing.

The Etiquette of Eating

It is desirable that a believer observes the aforementioned instructions regarding the quantity of food and other necessary matters. In addition, for his spiritual growth it is recommended that he pay attention to how he eats and the food itself. In Imam al-Sādiq's (peace be upon him) conversation with 'Unwān al-Basrī some of these have been mentioned. We will also mention other narrations as well to complete this discussion.

---

i. Majlisī, Bihār al-Anwār, 66:334, narration 15

1) Reciting Bismillāh When One Begins to Eat

Being far from Satan and forgiveness of sins are some of the blessings of reciting bismillāh when one begins to eat.

Imam al-Sādiq (peace be upon him) says:

قَالَ رَسُولُ اللَّهِ ص إِذَا وُضِعَتِ الْمَائِدَةُ حَفَّتْهَا أَرْبَعَةُ آلَافِ مَلَكٍ فَإِذَا قَالَ الْعَبْدُ بِسْمِ اللَّهِ- قَالَتِ الْمَلَائِكَةُ بَارَكَ اللَّهُ عَلَيْكُمْ فِي طَعَامِكُمْ ثُمَّ يَقُولُونَ لِلشَّيْطَانِ اخْرُجْ يَا فَاسِقُ لَا سُلْطَانَ لَكَ عَلَيْهِمْ فَإِذَا فَرَغُوا فَقَالُوا الْحَمْدُ لِلَّهِ قَالَتِ الْمَلَائِكَةُ قَوْمٌ أَنْعَمَ اللَّهُ عَلَيْهِمْ فَأَدَّوْا شُكْرَ رَبِّهِمْ وَ إِذَا لَمْ يُسَمُّوا قَالَتِ الْمَلَائِكَةُ لِلشَّيْطَانِ ادْنُ يَا فَاسِقُ فَكُلْ مَعَهُمْ فَإِذَا رُفِعَتِ الْمَائِدَةُ وَ لَمْ يَذْكُرُوا اسْمَ اللَّهِ عَلَيْهَا قَالَتِ الْمَلَائِكَةُ قَوْمٌ أَنْعَمَ اللَّهُ عَلَيْهِمْ فَنَسُوا رَبَّهُمْ.

The Messenger of Allah (peace and blessings be upon him and his family) said, "When the table is set, four thousand angels gather around it, and when the servant says *bismillāh*, the angels says, 'May Allah grant blessing [*barakah*] in your food.' Then they say to the Satan, 'Leave O transgressor! You have no authority over him.' And when he finishes eating and says *alḥamdulillāh*, the angels say, '[These are] a group whom Allah has granted blessings and they in turn show their gratitude to their Lord.' On the other hand, when the servant does not say *bismillāh*, the angels say to the Satan, 'O transgressor! Come near and eat with him.' And when he finishes eating and does not remember Allah, the angels say, '[These are] a group whom Allah has granted blessings, but they have forgotten their Lord.'" (i)

Similarly, Imam al-Sādiq (peace be upon him) has said in another narration:

---

i. al-ʿĀmilī, Wasāʾil al-Shīʿah, 16:482

إِذَا أَكَلْتَ الطَّعَامَ فَقُلْ بِسْمِ اللَّهِ فِي أَوَّلِهِ وَ آخِرِهِ فَإِنَّ الْعَبْدَ إِذَا سَمَّى فِي طَعَامِهِ قَبْلَ أَنْ يَأْكُلَ لَمْ يَأْكُلْ مَعَهُ الشَّيْطَانُ وَ إِذَا لَمْ يُسَمِّ أَكَلَ مَعَهُ الشَّيْطَانُ وَ إِذَا سَمَّى بَعْدَ مَا يَأْكُلُ وَ أَكَلَ الشَّيْطَانُ مَعَهُ تَقَيَّأَ مَا كَانَ أَكَلَ

> When you are eating food, say *bismillāh* in the beginning and at the end. For when a servant takes Allah's name before he starts partaking of food, Satan does not eat with him. However, when he does not take Allah's name then Satan eats with him. And when he takes Allah name at the end—and Satan had eaten with him—then Satan vomits that which he had eaten.[i]

Also, in another narration it says:

مَنْ ذَكَرَ اسْمَ اللَّهِ عَلَى الطَّعَامِ لَمْ يُسْأَلْ عَنْ نَعِيمِ ذَلِكَ الطَّعَامِ أَبَداً

> One who takes Allah's name while eating will never be questioned concerning the blessings of this food.[ii]

The Messenger of Allah (peace and blessings be upon him and his family) said to Imam ʿAlī (peace be upon him):

إِذَا أَكَلْتَ فَقُلْ بِسْمِ اللَّهِ وَ إِذَا فَرَغْتَ فَقُلِ الْحَمْدُ لِلَّهِ فَإِنَّ حَافِظَيْكَ لَا يَبْرَحَانِ يَكْتُبَانِ لَكَ الْحَسَنَاتِ حَتَّى تُبْعِدَهُ عَنْكَ

> When you partake of food, say *bismillāh* and when you finish eating say *alḥamdulillāh*. In this manner, the two angels who are recording your deeds continuously write good deeds for until you detach yourself from the food.[iii]

In the higher levels of servitude, saying bismillāh before every meal opens a door of maʿrifah (gnosis) for the servant. It causes him to traverse through the Divine names and reach the source of grace from

---

i. Majlisī, Bihār al-Anwār, 66:372, narration 13

ii. Ibid., 66:367, narration 1

iii. Ibid., 66:371, narration 12

which this blessing has originated. For example, when such servants drink water—which is a manifestation of Divine mercy—they reach the attribute of mercy, one of Allah's Names of Beauty. In this manner, they are spiritually quenched by this pure and sweet attribute.

As they start partaking of their food they begin their journey in the spiritual horizons; they behold the spectacle of the Benefactor's beauty in every blessing. It for this reason that supplications have been recommended to be recited at the end of the meal. These are but a means of drawing the servant's attention to these realities. Asbagh ibn Nubātah says:

> دَخَلْتُ عَلَى أَمِيرِ الْمُؤْمِنِينَ ع وَ بَيْنَ يَدَيْهِ شِوَاءٌ فَدَعَانِي وَ قَالَ هَلُمَّ إِلَى هَذَا الشِّوَاءِ فَقُلْتُ أَنَا إِذَا أَكَلْتُ ضَرَّنِي فَقَالَ أَ لَا أُعَلِّمُكَ كَلِمَاتٍ تَقُولُهُنَّ وَ أَنَا ضَامِنٌ لَكَ أَنْ لَا يُؤْذِيَكَ طَعَامٌ قُلِ اللَّهُمَّ إِنِّي أَسْأَلُكَ بِاسْمِكَ خَيْرِ الْأَسْمَاءِ مِلْءَ الْأَرْضِ وَ السَّمَاءِ الرَّحْمَنِ الرَّحِيمِ الَّذِي لَا يَضُرُّ مَعَهُ دَاءٌ فَلَا يَضُرُّكَ أَبَدا
>
> I entered the presence of Imam ʿAlī (peace be upon him) and there was cooked meat placed near him. He called me and said, "Come near [and have] this food." I said to him, "Whenever I eat, it harms me." The Imam said, "Should I not teach you something that if you recite, I guarantee you that no food will harm you. Recite: 'O Allah I ask You by Your name, the best of names, which has filled the Earth and the heaven, the Beneficent, the Merciful, with which no malady can cause harm,' and never will it harm you." (i)

According to such narrations, if one takes Allah's name before eating, is careful about eating healthy food, and believes in the effect of Allah's name in warding off difficulties and harms, then reciting Allah's name over foods that one imagines are harmful causes its harm to be repelled. Moreover, if someone has strong faith in the effectiveness of Allah's name then even if he is certain about the harmfulness of the food, its

---

i. Ibid., 66:37, narration 42

harm will still be repelled. This can be seen in the abovementioned narration. In another narration Imam ʿAlī (peace be upon him) also said:

ضَمِنْتُ لِمَنْ سَمَّى اللَّهَ تَعَالَى عَلَى طَعَامِهِ أَنْ لَا يَشْتَكِيَ مِنْهُ فَقَالَ ابْنُ الْكَوَّاءِ يَا أَمِيرَ الْمُؤْمِنِينَ لَقَدْ أَكَلْتُ الْبَارِحَةَ طَعَاماً فَسَمَّيْتُ عَلَيْهِ فَآذَانِي فَقَالَ أَمِيرُ الْمُؤْمِنِينَ ع أَكَلْتَ أَلْوَاناً فَسَمَّيْتَ عَلَى بَعْضِهَا وَ لَمْ تُسَمِّ عَلَى كُلِّ لَوْنٍ يَا لُكَع

> I guarantee that one who recites Allah the Exalted's name on his food will not suffer any harm from it. Ibn al-Kawwāʾ [one of the hypocrites] said, "O Amīr al-Muʾminīn! I ate a certain food in the morning and recited Allah's name on it but [still] it caused harm to me." Amīr al-Muʾminīn (peace be upon him) said, "You ate a number of different foods and you only recited Allah's name on some of them. You did not recite it on every single one item, wretched man!"(i)

It is for this reason that when he was asked what one should do if they forgot to mention Allah's name at the start of eating, Imam al-Sādiq (peace be upon him) responded to the narrator saying:

بِسْمِ اللَّهِ فِي أَوَّلِهِ وَ آخِرِهِ

> Recite, "*bismillāh fi awwalihi wa ākhirihi*" [*bismillāh* in its beginning and its end]."(ii)

2) Acting on the Recommendations of Imam al-Hasan (peace be upon him)

Imam al-Hasan (peace be upon him) says:

فِي الْمَائِدَةِ اثْنَتَا عَشْرَةَ خَصْلَةً يَجِبُ عَلَى كُلِ مُسْلِمٍ أَنْ يَعْرِفَهَا أَرْبَعٌ مِنْهَا فَرْضٌ وَ أَرْبَعٌ سُنَّةٌ وَ أَرْبَعٌ تَأْدِيبٌ فَأَمَّا الْفَرْض فَالْمَعْرِفَةُ وَ الرِّضَا وَ التَّسْمِيَةُ وَ الشُّكْرُ وَ أَمَّا السُّنَّةُ فَالْوُضُوءُ قَبْلَ الطَّعَامِ

i. Ibid., 66:369, narration 6

ii. Ibid., 66:379, narration 44

وَ الْجُلُوسُ عَلَى الْجَانِبِ الْأَيْسَرِ وَ الْأَكْلُ بِثَلَاثِ أَصَابِعَ وَ لَعْقُ الْأَصَابِعِ وَ أَمَّا التَّأْدِيبُ فَالْأَكْلُ مِمَّا يَلِيكَ وَ تَصْغِيرُ اللُّقْمَةِ وَ تَجْوِيدُ الْمَضْغِ وَ قِلَّةُ النَّظَرِ فِي وُجُوهِ النَّاسِ.

There are twelve qualities for the time of eating which are necessary for every Muslim to know. Four of them are obligatory, four others are supererogatory (*sunnah*) and the remaining four are etiquettes (*ādāb*). As for the obligatory ones, they are recognition [of the blessing and its benefactor that is Allah the Exalted], satisfaction [with it], taking Allah's name and gratefulness to Allah. As for the supererogatory ones, they are washing hands before food, sitting with the weight of the body on the left leg, eating with three fingers and licking the fingers [after eating the food with hands]. As for the etiquettes, they are eating that which is beside you, taking small morsels, chewing properly and not looking often at the face of [other] people. (i)

3) Washing Your Hands Before and After Food

Imam al-Sādiq (peace be upon him) says:

الْوُضُوءُ قَبْلَ الطَّعَامِ وَ بَعْدَهُ يَزِيدُ فِي الرِّزْقِ

Washing your hands before and after food, increases sustenance. (ii)

Also, it is narrated that the Messenger of Allah (peace and blessings be upon him and his family) says:

... أَوَّلُهُ يَنْفِي الْفَقْرَ وَ آخِرُهُ يَنْفِي الْهَم

[Washing your hands] at the start of eating removes poverty and washing them at the end takes away sorrow and grief. (iii)

Imam al-Bāqir (peace be upon him) says:

---

i. al-ʿĀmilī, Wasā'il al-Shīʿah, 16:539, narration 1

ii. Majlisī, Biḥār al-Anwār, 66:352, narration 2

iii. Ibid., 66:352, narration 3

صَاحِبُ الرَّحْلِ يَتَوَضَّأُ أَوَّلَ الْقَوْمِ قَبْلَ الطَّعَامِ وَ آخِرَ الْقَوْمِ بَعْدَ الطَّعَام

Before the food, the host should be the first one to wash his hands. And after the food, he should be the last one to wash his hands. (i)

Imam al-Sādiq (peace be upon him) says:

فَلْيَغْسِلْ أَوَّلًا رَبُّ الْبَيْتِ يَدَهُ ثُمَّ يَبْدَأُ بِمَنْ عَنْ يَمِينِهِ وَ إِذَا رُفِعَ الطَّعَامُ بَدَأَ بِمَنْ عَلَى يَسَارِ صَاحِبِ الْمَنْزِلِ وَ يَكُونُ آخِرَ مَنْ يَغْسِلُ يَدَهُ صَاحِبُ الْمَنْزِلِ

First the host should wash his hands and then starting with the one on his right side. After the food, the one on the left of the host should first wash his hands while the last one to wash his hands should be the host. (ii)

إِذَا غَسَلْتَ يَدَكَ لِلطَّعَامِ فَلَا تَمْسَحْ يَدَكَ بِالْمِنْدِيلِ فَإِنَّهُ لَا يَزَالُ الْبَرَكَةُ فِي الطَّعَامِ مَا دَامَتِ النَّدَاوَةُ فِي الْيَد

When you wash your hands for food, do not dry your hands with a towel. That is because as long as there is wetness in your hand the food will have blessings (*barakah*) in it. (iii)

Imam al-Bāqir (peace be upon him) says:

مَنْ غَسَلَ يَدَهُ قَبْلَ الطَّعَامِ وَ بَعْدَهُ عَاشَ فِي سَعَةٍ وَ عُوفِيَ مِنْ بَلْوَى جَسَدِه

One who washes his hands before and after food, his life will be prosperous, and the disease of his body will be cured. (iv)

Imam al-Sādiq (peace be upon him) in a narration says:

اغْسِلُوا أَيْدِيَكُمْ قَبْلَ الطَّعَامِ وَ بَعْدَهُ فَإِنَّهُ يَنْفِي الْفَقْرَ وَ يَزِيدُ فِي الْعُمُر

---

i. Ibid., 66:353, narration 8

ii. Ibid., 66:354, narration 10

iii. Ibid., 66:355, narration 13

iv. Ibid., 66:356, narration 16

Wash your hands before and after food, for verily that removes poverty and prolongs one's life. [i]

4) To Eat Salt at the Beginning and End of a Meal

Imam al-Sādiq (peace be upon him) says:

قَالَ رَسُولُ اللَّهِ ص لِعَلِيٍّ ع افْتَتِحْ طَعَامَكَ بِالْمِلْحِ وَ اخْتِمْ بِهِ فَإِنَّ مَنِ افْتَتَحَ طَعَامَهُ بِالْمِلْحِ وَ خَتَمَ بِهِ عُوفِيَ مِنِ اثْنَيْنِ وَ سَبْعِينَ نَوْعاً مِنْ أَنْوَاعِ الْبَلَاءِ مِنْهُ الْجُنُونُ وَ الْجُذَامُ وَ الْبَرَصُ.

The Messenger of Allah (peace and blessings be upon him and his family) said to Imam ʿAlī (peace be upon him), "Start and end your food with salt. For one who starts and ends his food with salt is cured from seventy-two types of diseases, from which are insanity, leprosy and vitiligo." [ii]

5) Avoiding Very Hot and Cold Food

Imam ʿAlī (peace be upon him) says:

أَقِرُّوا الْحَارَّ حَتَّى يَبْرُدَ فَإِنَّ رَسُولَ اللَّهِ ص قُرِّبَ إِلَيْهِ طَعَامٌ حَارٌّ فَقَالَ أَقِرُّوهُ حَتَّى يُمْكِنَ مَا كَانَ اللَّهُ لِيُطْعِمَنَا نَاراً وَ الْبَرَكَةُ فِي الْبَارِدِ

Keep aside hot [food and wait] until it cools down. For verily hot food was once brought before the Messenger of Allah (peace and blessings be upon him and his family) and he said, "Keep it aside until it is possible [to eat it]. Allah has not made us eat fire. *Barakah* (abundant blessings) is in the food which is cool." [iii]

Also, one of the narrators says:

---

i. Ibid., 66:356, narration 20

ii. al-ʿĀmilī, Wasā'il al-Shīʿah, 24:403, narration 1

iii. Ibid., 24:399, narration 4

بَعَثَ إِلَيْنَا أَبُو عَبْدِ اللَّهِ ع بِطَعَامٍ سَخِنٍ وَ
قَالَ كُلُوا قَبْلَ أَنْ يَبْرُدَ فَإِنَّهُ أَطْيَبُ

Imam al-Ṣādiq (peace be upon him) sent warm food for us and said, "Eat before it becomes cold. Indeed, that is more pleasing and delicious." (i)

6) Eating That Which Falls Off the Table

Imam al-Sādiq (peace be upon him) says:

قَالَ أَمِيرُ الْمُؤْمِنِينَ ع كُلُوا مَا يَسْقُطُ مِنَ الْخِوَانِ فَإِنَّهُ شِفَاءٌ مِنْ كُلِّ دَاءٍ بِإِذْنِ اللَّهِ لِمَنْ أَرَادَ أَنْ يَسْتَشْفِيَ بِهِ.

Amīr al-Mu'minīn (peace be upon him) said, "Eat that which falls off the table. It is a cure for every ailment—by Allah's leave—for the one who wishes [who believes] to be cured by it." (ii)

However, as said by Imam al-Ridā (peace be upon him):

مَنْ أَكَلَ فِي الصَّحْرَاءِ أَوْ خَارِجاً فَلْيَتْرُكْهُ لِلطَّيْرِ وَ السَّبُعِ

When a person eats food in the desert or outside [of his house], then he should leave it [that which falls] for the birds and predatory animals. (iii)

7) Not Blowing on Food and Drink

Imam al-Sādiq (peace be upon him) narrates from the Messenger of Allah (peace and blessings be upon him and his family), through his forefathers, that:

نَهَى أَنْ يُنْفَخَ فِي طَعَامٍ أَوْ شَرَابٍ وَ أَنْ يُنْفَخَ فِي مَوْضِعِ السُّجُودِ

The Messenger of Allah (peace and blessings be upon him

---

i. Ibid., 24:401, narration 1

ii. Ibid., 24:378, narration 3

iii. Ibid., 24:375, narration 1

and his family) forbade others from blowing on food, drinks and the place of prostration.[i]

8) Not Eating Food from the Marketplace

It is narrated from the Messenger of Allah (peace and blessings be upon him and his family) that:

الْأَكْلُ فِي السُّوقِ دَنَاءَةٌ

Eating in the marketplace is vileness [or causes vitiligo].[ii]

9) Using a Toothpick After Food[iii]

Imam al-Sādiq (peace be upon him) says:

نَاوَلَ النَّبِيُّ ص جَعْفَرَ بْنَ أَبِي طَالِبٍ خِلَالًا فَقَالَ يَا جَعْفَرُ تَخَلَّلْ فَإِنَّهُ مَصْلَحَةٌ لِلْفَمِ أَوْ قَالَ لِلِّثَةِ مَجْلَبَةٌ لِلرِّزْقِ.

The Messenger of Allah (peace and blessings be upon him and his family) gave a toothpick to Jaʿfar ibn Abī Ṭālib and said to him, "O Jaʿfar! Use a toothpick, for it makes the mouth healthy (or he said it strengthens the gums, the doubt is from the narrator) and attracts sustenance."[iv]

Using a toothpick has been given so much importance and recommended to the extent that the details about the type of toothpick have also been mentioned. For example, Imam Mūsā ibn Jaʿfar (peace be upon him) says:

لَا تَخَلَّلُوا بِعُودِ الرَّيْحَانِ وَ لَا بِقَضِيبِ الرُّمَّانِ
فَإِنَّهُمَا يُهَيِّجَانِ عِرْقَ الْجُذَامِ

---

i. Ibid., 24:401, narration 1

ii. Ibid., 24:395, narration 2

iii. The primary purpose of a toothpick (*khilāl* in Arabic) is as a tool of maintaining hygiene and removing food that is stuck between the teeth. This purpose may be accomplished today using modern tools such as dental floss.

iv. Ibid., 24:421, narration 7

> Do not use the wood of the basil plant or a branch of the pomegranate tree as a toothpick, for these two provoke the blood vessel of leprosy.[i]

Likewise, the Messenger of Allah (peace and blessings be upon him and his family) has prohibited using the wood from the myrtle (ās) and bamboo (qasab) plants as a toothpick.[ii]

10) Brushing the Teeth (Using Miswāk)[iii]

Brushing the teeth (or using miswāk) is of such importance in the view of the Imams (peace be upon them) that it is not limited to after eating. Thus, the Messenger of Allah (peace and blessings be upon him and his family) says:

لَوْ لَا أَنْ أَشُقَّ عَلَى أُمَّتِي لَأَمَرْتُهُمْ بِالسِّوَاكِ مَعَ كُلِّ صَلَاةٍ

> If it would not cause hardship to my nation (*ummah*), I would have commanded them to brush their teeth with every prayer.[iv]

Similarly, he says to Imam ʿAlī (peace be upon him):

عَلَيْكَ بِالسِّوَاكِ وَ إِنِ اسْتَطَعْتَ أَنْ لَا تُقِلَّ مِنْهُ فَافْعَلْ فَإِنَّ كُلَّ صَلَاةٍ تُصَلِّيهَا بِالسِّوَاكِ تَفْضُلُ عَلَى الَّتِي تُصَلِّيهَا بِغَيْرِ سِوَاكٍ أَرْبَعِينَ يَوْماً

> I enjoin you to brush your teeth and if it is possible for you to use it frequently, then do so. For verily every prayer that you pray after brushing your teeth is better than forty days'

---

i. Ibid., 24:423, narration 1

ii. Ibid., 24:424, narration 5

iii. The narrations mentioned in this section containing the Arabic word '*siwāk*' or '*miswāk*.' This refers to a twig from some specific trees which was used to brush the teeth in the olden days. However, similar to the previous discussion on a toothpick, the primary purpose and importance is for maintaining hygiene. Such hygiene may be maintained in modern ways such as using a toothbrush.

iv. al-Kulaynī, al-Kāfī, 3:22, narration 1

prayer that you pray without brushing your teeth. (i)

Imam al-Sādiq (peace be upon him) also says:

فِي السِّوَاكِ اثْنَتَا عَشْرَةَ خَصْلَةً هُوَ مِنَ السُّنَّةِ وَ مَطْهَرَةٌ لِلْفَمِ وَ مَجْلَاةٌ لِلْبَصَرِ وَ يُرْضِي الرَّحْمَنَ وَ يُبَيِّضُ الْأَسْنَانَ وَ يَذْهَبُ بِالْحَفَرِ وَ يَشُدُّ اللِّثَةَ وَ يُشَهِّي الطَّعَامَ وَ يَذْهَبُ بِالْبَلْغَمِ وَ يَزِيدُ فِي الْحِفْظِ وَ يُضَاعَفُ بِهِ الْحَسَنَاتُ وَ تَفْرَحُ بِهِ الْمَلَائِكَةُ.

There are twelve qualities in brushing teeth: it is part of the Sunnah (ii), it purifies the mouth, illuminates the eyesight, pleases the Merciful Lord, whitens the teeth, removes the yellowness on the teeth, strengthen the gums, increases the desire for food, does away with phlegm, sharpens the memory, multiplies the good acts, and is delightful to the angels. (iii)

The Messenger of Allah (peace and blessings be upon him and his family) has also said:

عَلَيْكُمْ بِالسِّوَاكِ فَإِنَّهُ يُذْهِبُ وَسْوَسَةَ الصَّدْرِ

I enjoin you to brush the teeth, for verily it takes away the *waswasah* (satanic insinuations) of the heart. (iv)

Imam al-Ridā (peace be upon him) says:

السِّوَاكُ ... يُنْبِتُ الشَّعْرَ وَ يَذْهَبُ بِالدَّمْعَةِ

Brushing the teeth ... causes the hair to grow and does away with watery eyes [for one who suffers from watery eyes and excessive tearing]. (v)

---

i. Majlisī, Bihār al-Anwār, 76:137, narration 48

ii. The word *sunnah* refers to the speech and conduct of the Prophet (peace and blessings be upon him and his family) as well as the Imams (peace be upon them).

iii. al-Sadūq, al-Khisāl, 481, narration 53

iv. Majlisī, Bihār al-Anwār, 76:126, narration 2

v. Ibid., 76:137, narration 48

It is mentioned in a narration that the Messenger of Allah (peace and blessings be upon him and his family) would brush his teeth horizontally, and that he would brush three times every night: first before sleeping, second when he would wake up to engage in dhikr (remembrance of Allah) and third before the morning prayers.[i]

i. Ibid., 76:137, narration 47

Section Two
Paying Attention to a Routine for One's Ethics (Forbearance)

Numerous practical and ethical instructions have been given to us for reforming and strengthening social relationships. These relationships are the object of Allah's attention as well as His awliyāʾ. Each one of these instructions has its own specific effect in this important domain. However, Imam al-Sādiq (peace be upon him)—in the continuation of his advice to ʿUnwān al-Basrī—considered forbearance (hilm) to be the pivot of this group of instructions. He said to him:

فَمَنْ قَالَ لَكَ إِنْ قُلْتَ وَاحِدَةً سَمِعْتَ عَشْراً فَقُلْ إِنْ قُلْتَ عَشْراً لَمْ تَسْمَعْ وَاحِدَةً

> When someone says to you, "If you say a word [against me,] you will hear ten [against you]," say to him, "If you say ten things [against me], you will not even hear one."

That is because, by paying attention to the meaning and reality of this trait, it becomes clear that it has a considerable effect on reforming, solidifying and strengthening social relationships, and in nurturing a person's outward and inward temperament.

Rāghib al-Isfahānī while defining forbearance says:

> Forbearance is to protect the soul from the kindling of anger. Some have said: forbearance means firmness and stability in one's affairs, which is the outcome of balancing the faculty of anger and which stops the soul from becoming affected when encountered with unpleasant and painful events.(i)

In addition to this, there are some other factors due to which forbearance occupies a pivotal role in Imam al-Sādiq's (peace be upon him) ethical advice. Firstly, because forbearance and knowledge are closely connected. To the extent that Imam al-Sādiq (peace be upon him) says in this regard:

عَلَيْكَ بِالْحِلْمِ فَإِنَّهُ رُكْنُ الْعِلْمِ

i. al-Isfahānī, Mufradāt Alfāz al-Qurʾān, the root word hilm

I enjoin you to [acquire] forbearance for it is the pillar of knowledge.(i)

Imam al-Bāqir (peace be upon him) also says in this regard:

الْحِلْمُ لِبَاسُ الْعَالِمِ فَلَا تَعْرَيَنَّ مِنْه

Forbearance is the garment of a scholar. Therefore, never remove it from yourself.(ii)

Imam ʿAlī (peace be upon him) says:

لَنْ يُثْمِرَ الْعِلْمُ حَتَّى يُقَارِنَهُ الْحِلْم

Knowledge does not bear fruit unless it is accompanied by forbearance.(iii)

الْعِلْمُ أَصْلُ الْحِلْم، و الْحِلْمُ زِينَةُ الْعِلْم

Knowledge is the root of forbearances and forbearance is the adornment of knowledge.(iv)

The secret behind this close link between knowledge and forbearances is that:

Firstly, one who wishes to display the state of forbearance to enjoy its privileges, needs knowledge about the manner of healthy relationships with other human beings. Such knowledge is needed so that he is not afflicted with excessiveness (ifrāt) or laxity (tafrīt).

Secondly, knowledge of the reality of the creation, the type of relationship between different beings, or the knowledge of the type of relationship between people, leads man to be influenced and change the manner of his interactions. If this change of style is not accompanied by forbearances, then man's knowledge and scholarship lose its value. For this reason, in some verses of the Qurʾān, Allah has been praised with these two traits:

وَاللَّهُ يَعْلَمُ مَا فِي قُلُوبِكُمْ ۚ وَكَانَ اللَّهُ عَلِيمًا حَلِيمًا

i. al-Ṣadūq, al-Amālī, p. 491, narration 9

ii. al-Kulaynī, al-Kāfī, 8:55, narration 16

iii. al-Āmudī, Ghurar al-Hikam, p. 44.

iv. Ibid., p. 286.

Allah knows what is in your hearts, and Allah is Knowing, Forbearing. (33:51)

In this verse, immediately after mentioning Allah's knowledge and awareness of man's actions and interactions, the trait of forbearance is also mentioned. This is so that one does not suppose that due to Allah's awareness of the minute details of man's actions, His punishment and displeasure would follow. The Messenger of Allah (peace and blessings be upon him and his family) has said in this regard:

وَ الَّذِي نَفْسِي بِيَدِهِ مَا جُمِعَ شَيْءٌ إِلَى شَيْءٍ أَفْضَلُ مِنْ حِلْمٍ إِلَى عِلْمٍ

By the One in whose hands is my soul! No two things have joined together that are loftier than knowledge joined with forbearance.(i)

The second factor which necessitates that one should possess the quality of forbearance in social interactions, is its role in completing the intellect. To establish correct social relations and strengthen them, man needs to apply his intellect and thought. The more people's relationships are based on comprehending the reality of man, the better man's needs will be fulfilled. However, to comprehend better and understand more, it is necessary to display forbearances and bear unpleasant events. As Imam ʿAlī (peace be upon him) says:

الْحِلْمُ تَمَامُ الْعَقْلِ

Forbearances is [the cause of] the completion of the intellect [*ʿaql*].(ii)

الْحِلْمُ نُورٌ جَوْهَرُهُ الْعَقْلِ

Forbearance is a light, whose essence is the intellect.(iii)

The third factor due to which forbearance has acquired an important

---

i. al-Ṣadūq, al-Khiṣāl, 5, narration 11

ii. al-Āmudī, Ghurar al-Hikam, narration 10055

iii. Ibid., narration 1185

position in Imam al-Sādiq's (peace be upon him) advice, is its role in bridling and controlling moral vices such as hastiness and anger. In the words of Imam ʿAlī (peace be upon him):

الْحِلْمُ حِجَابٌ مِنَ الْآفَات

Forbearance is a prevention from calamities. (i)

الْحِلْمُ يُطْفِئُ نَارَ الْغَضَبِ وَ الْحِدَّةُ تُؤَجِّجُ إِحْرَاقَه

Forbearances puts out the fire of anger whereas harshness ignites its flames. (ii)

Acquiring many of the praiseworthy moral traits is dependent on the presence of forbearance. In the words of the Messenger of Allah (peace and blessings be upon him and his family):

فَأَمَّا الْحِلْمُ فَمِنْهُ رُكُوبُ الْجَمِيلِ وَ صُحْبَةُ الْأَبْرَارِ وَ رَفْعٌ مِنَ الضِّعَةِ وَ رَفْعٌ مِنَ الخَسَاسَةِ وَ تَشَهِّي الْخَيْرِ وَ تَقَرُّبُ صَاحِبِهِ مِنْ مَعَالِي الدَّرَجَاتِ وَ الْعَفْوُ وَ الْمَهَلُ وَ الْمَعْرُوفُ وَ الصَّمْتُ فَهَذَا مَا يَتَشَعَّبُ لِلْعَاقِلِ بِحِلْمِه

As for forbearance, from it springs forth beautiful actions, companionship of the virtuous, remoteness from ignobility, remoteness from lowliness, and a desire for good. It brings its possessor close to lofty stations and [from it branches out] forgiveness, [giving] respite, goodness and thoughtful silence. So, these are the things that an intelligent person gets from forbearance. (iii)

---

i. Ibid., narration 775

ii. Ibid., narration 2063

iii. al-Harrānī, Tuhaf al-ʿUqūl, 16

Factors that Cause Forbearance

1) Feigning Forbearance

Some traits of the soul come into existence by repeatedly dictating them to oneself, as well as by practicing. Forbearance is one of those traits; it is possible to acquire this trait by feigning patience and superficially expressing it. Imam ʿAlī (peace be upon him) says:

إِنْ لَمْ تَكُنْ حَلِيماً فَتَحَلَّمْ فَإِنَّهُ قَلَّ مَنْ تَشَبَّهَ بِقَوْمٍ إِلَّا أَوْشَكَ أَنْ يَكُونَ مِنْهُم

> If you are not forbearing, then pretend to be forbearing. For indeed, seldom does it happen that a person makes himself resemble a [group of] people except that he comes close to becoming one of them.[i]

When first acquiring praiseworthy traits, it is usually difficult to possess them. One must impose them on his soul so that gradually it takes the form of a state and thereafter turns into a deep-rooted characteristic. Therefore, to develop the trait of forbearance a person must force himself to be forbearing. As Imam ʿAlī (peace be upon him) says:

مَنْ لَا يَتَحَلَّمْ لَا يَحْلُم

> One who does not pretend to be forbearing, will not develop forbearance.[ii]

مَنْ تَحَلَّمَ حَلُم

> One who makes a pretence of forbearance, becomes forbearing.[iii]

قَدْ يَتَزَيَّا بِالْحِلْمِ غَيْرُ الْحَلِيم

> Sometimes a person who is not forbearing acquires the appearance of a forbearing person.[iv]

---

i. al-Radī, Nahj al-Balāghah, 506

ii. Majlisī, Bihār al-Anwār, 74:283

iii. al-Āmudī, Ghurar al-Hikam, narration 7655

iv. Ibid., narration 6654

2) Being Calm and Composed

One of the principles of ethics is that man's exoteric actions affect his inward and hidden dimension. Based on this, if a person conducts himself with calmness and composure outwardly, then this develops the trait of forbearance inside him. In the words of Imam ʿAlī (peace be upon him):

لَا يَكُونُ حَلِيماً حَتَّى يَكُونَ وَقُورا

> A person does not become forbearing unless he possesses calmness and composure. [i]

3) Knowledge and Awareness

Having awareness of the reality of the world, the nature of appropriate human relationships, and different human temperaments—even if this awareness is weak—impels a person to act with forbearance when faced with the undesirable behaviour of others. Just as how Imam ʿAlī (peace be upon him) has considered forbearance to be the fruit of knowledge, saying:

عَلَيْكَ بِالْحِلْمِ فَإِنَّهُ ثَمَرَةُ الْعِلْم

> I enjoin you towards forbearance, for indeed it is the fruit of knowledge. [ii]

Each of these factors—collectively or individually—prepare the ground for developing the trait of forbearance.

The Effects of Forbearance

Forbearance is one of the beautiful names of Allah. Despite constantly encountering the undesirable behaviour of His servants with Him—when they violate the sanctity of His Station of Lordship by disobeying His commands or being heedless of His absolute presence—He displays forbearance with them. He does not immediately afflict them with the unpleasant consequences of their actions. Rather,

i. Majlisī, Biḥār al-Anwār, 78:157

ii. al-Āmudī, Ghurar al-Ḥikam, 6084

he gives them respite and allows them to return to Him. Similarly, anyone who possesses forbearance—to the extent they possess it—has attained one of Allah's attributes. In addition to this, forbearance and patience have other individual and social effects, some of which are:

1) Social Status

Displaying forbearance in social interactions leads people to be inclined and attracted towards the man. Imam ʿAlī (peace be upon him) says in this regard:

بِالْحِلْمِ تَكْثُرُ الْأَنْصَار

By means of forbearance, a person's helpers increase.(i)

Magnanimity and esteem is the result of displaying forbearance and patience with people. In the words of Imam ʿAlī (peace be upon him):

مَنْ حَلُمَ سَاد

One who displays forbearance achieves magnanimity.(ii)

الْحِلْمُ رَأْسُ الرِّئَاسَة

Forbearance is the foundation of leadership.(iii)

Interacting in this manner makes a forbearing person benefit from people's support. In the words of Imam ʿAlī (peace be upon him):

إِنَّ أَوَّلَ عِوَضِ الْحَلِيمِ مِنْ خَصْلَتِهِ أَنَّ النَّاسَ أَعْوَانُهُ عَلَى الْجَاهِل

Indeed, the first reward a forbearing person obtains from this trait, is that people help him against an ignorant person.(iv)

2) Predominance Over Enemies and Opponents

Forbearance confers a position upon a person in the eyes of the people, that safeguards him against his enemies. Imam al-Sādiq (peace

i. Ibid., narration 4185

ii. Majlisī, Bihār al-Anwār, 74:210

iii. al-Āmudī, Ghurar al-Ḥikam, narration 770

iv. al-Shaʿīrī, Jamiʿ al-Akhbār, 319, narration 896

be upon him) says:

كَفَى بِالْحِلْمِ نَاصِر

Forbearance is sufficient as a helper. (i)

Imam ʿAlī (peace be upon him) says:

مَنْ حَلُمَ مِنْ عَدُوِّهِ ظَفِرَ بِهِ

One who acts forbearingly with his enemies achieves victory over them. (ii)

Therefore, a person must pay attention that those who act forbearingly with him, will achieve a better outcome. In the words of Imam ʿAlī (peace be upon him):

مَنِ اسْتَعَانَ بِالْحِلْمِ عَلَيْكَ غَلَبَكَ وَ تَفَضَّلَ عَلَيْك

One who seeks the help of forbearance against you, has overpowered you and has achieved superiority over you. (iii)

3) Safety from Difficulties

Forbearance is a strong fortress. It protects the forbearing person from the difficulties and suffering caused by anger or a lack of patience in the face of others' unpleasant behaviour. Amīr al-Muʾminīn (peace be upon him) has pointed to this reality:

السِّلْمُ ثَمَرَةُ الْحِلْم

Safety [from faults and inappropriate actions] is the outcome of forbearance. (iv)

الْحِلْمُ حِلْيَةُ الْعِلْمِ وَ عِلَّةُ السِّلْم

Forbearance is the adornment of knowledge and the cause of safety. (v)

---

i. al-Kulaynī, al-Kāfī, 2:112, narration 6

ii. Kanz al-Fawāʾid, 1:319

iii. al-Āmudī, Ghurar al-Ḥikam, narration 9132

iv. Ibid., narration 901

v. Ibid., narration 1336

Due to the great number of effects and blessings that forbearance causes in the wayfarer's individual and social life, Imam al-Sādiq (peace be upon him)—in his ethical advice to ʿUnwān al-Basrī—instructed him to acquire forbearance and said:

فَمَنْ قَالَ لَكَ إِنْ قُلْتَ وَاحِدَةً سَمِعْتَ عَشْراً فَقُلْ إِنْ قُلْتَ عَشْراً لَمْ تَسْمَعْ وَاحِدَةً وَ مَنْ شَتَمَكَ فَقُلْ لَهُ إِنْ كُنْتَ صَادِقاً فِيمَا تَقُولُ فَأَسْأَلُ اللَّهَ أَنْ يَغْفِرَ لِي وَ إِنْ كُنْتَ كَاذِباً فِيمَا تَقُولُ فَاللَّهَ أَسْأَلُ أَنْ يَغْفِرَ لَكَ وَ مَنْ وَعَدَكَ بِالْخَنَا فَعِدْهُ بِالنَّصِيحَةِ وَ الرِّعَاءِ

> When someone says to you, "If you say a word [against me,] you will hear ten [against you]," say to him, "If you say ten things [against me], you will not even hear one." Also, if anyone slanders you, say to him, "If what you have said is true, then may Allah forgive me, but if you are lying, then I ask Allah to forgive you." Likewise, if anyone threatens you with something unpleasant, then [in return] promise him good-will and that you will observe [his rights].

This statement from the Imam is the same concept presented in the verse of the Qurʾān that describes Allah's special servants, saying:

وَعِبَادُ الرَّحْمَٰنِ الَّذِينَ يَمْشُونَ عَلَى الْأَرْضِ هَوْنًا وَإِذَا خَاطَبَهُمُ الْجَاهِلُونَ قَالُوا سَلَامًا

> The servants of the Beneficent are those who walk humbly on the Earth, and when the ignorant address them, say, "Peace!" (25:63)

The Noble Messenger of Islam (peace and blessings be upon him and his family) has also said in this regard:

أَحْلَمُ النَّاسِ مَنْ فَرَّ مِنْ جُهَّالِ النَّاس

> The most forbearing person is the one who flees [and distances himself] from the ignorant amongst the people.[i]

---

i. Majlisī, Biḥār al-Anwār, 77:112, narration 2

Imam al-Sādiq (peace be upon him) also says regarding the value of displaying forbearance with ignorant people:

إِذَا وَقَعَ بَيْنَ رَجُلَيْنِ مُنَازَعَةٌ نَزَلَ مَلَكَانِ فَيَقُولَانِ لِلسَّفِيهِ مِنْهُمَا قُلْتَ وَ قُلْتَ وَ أَنْتَ أَهْلٌ لِمَا قُلْتَ سَتُجْزَى بِمَا قُلْتَ وَ يَقُولَانِ لِلْحَلِيمِ مِنْهُمَا صَبَرْتَ وَ حَلُمْتَ سَيَغْفِرُ اللَّهُ لَكَ إِنْ أَتْمَمْتَ ذَلِكَ قَالَ فَإِنْ رَدَّ الْحَلِيمُ عَلَيْهِ ارْتَفَعَ الْمَلَكَانِ.

> When a dispute occurs between two people, two angels descend and say to the ignorant of the two, "You kept on saying things while those things [that you said] befitted you. Soon you will be reciprocated for what you said." And they say to the forbearing of the two, "You were patient and acted with forbearance. Soon Allah will forgive you, if you continue to act in this manner." Then the Imam said, "If the forbearing person rejects it, then both the angels ascend." (i)

In view of these statements, displaying forbearance is desirable for all and has spiritual, ethical and outward effects. Moreover, forbearance is even more necessary for one who seeks to traverse the journey of servitude and render his temperament and traits to be Divine. Thus, Imam al-Ridā (peace be upon him) says:

لَا يَكُونُ الرَّجُلُ عَابِداً حَتَّى يَكُونَ حَلِيما

> A person does not become a servant until he acquires forbearance. (ii)

That is because Allah's servitude and worship require that a person act suitably without making mistakes when faced with the ignorance of others. This is necessary for one who wishes to express humility in front of the Divine by means of his actions and character and wants to acquire His proximity. If this individual disputes with others and does not tolerate their undesirable behaviour, then he will be distanced from the Divine proximity and eventually commit actions that are against

i. al-Kulaynī, al-Kāfī, 2:112, narration 9

ii. Ibid., 2:112, narration 6

Divine commands and the ethics that God desires from him. In this case, his worship has not been carried out in a complete manner. For this reason, this trait has been introduced as one of the clear traits possessed by Allah's servants.

Section Three
Organizing an Educational Routine

In addition to the things mentioned in the second chapter regarding knowledge, its merits and the characteristics of scholars—points that are necessary to pay attention to on the path of servitude—Imam al-Sādiq (peace be upon him) in the concluding part of his remarks, gives advice about an educational routine:

> وَ أَمَّا اللَّوَاتِي فِي الْعِلْمِ فَاسْأَلِ الْعُلَمَاءَ مَا جَهِلْتَ وَ إِيَّاكَ أَنْ تَسْأَلَهُمْ تَعَنُّتاً وَ تَجْرِبَةً وَ إِيَّاكَ أَنْ تَعْمَلَ بِرَأْيِكَ شَيْئاً وَ خُذْ بِالاحْتِيَاطِ فِي جَمِيعِ مَا تَجِدُ إِلَيْهِ سَبِيلًا وَ اهْرُبْ مِنَ الْفُتْيَا هَرَبَكَ مِنَ الْأَسَدِ وَ لَا تَجْعَلْ رَقَبَتَكَ لِلنَّاسِ جِسْراً
>
> And as for the things [which must be observed] with regards to knowledge: Ask the scholars what you do not know, do not ask them to render them powerless or to test them. Abstain from acting according to your own opinion [without relying on any religious or intellectual justification], and act with *iḥtiyāṭ* (precaution) in all the affairs for which you find a way [to do so]. Flee from giving *fatwā* (legal opinion) like you flee from a lion, and do not make your neck a bridge for the people.

This section of the Imam's remarks can be summarized in three central themes:

1) Asking questions
2) Making use of knowledge
3) Formulating new opinions and advancing knowledge

These three themes comprise the three main phases of the academic life of any distinguished individual. These phases are: the phases of acquiring knowledge and studying, the phase of applying the available knowledge (by means of research and formulating opinions), and the phase of giving academic output and presenting academic services.

Each of these phases has certain characteristics and rules, and it is necessary to pay attention to them to develop and grow academically.

Asking Questions

Allah (the Provider of abundance and the Sublime) has created man in this world with a mind empty of knowledge, and given him the tools of learning, so that using it he can acquire knowledge.

> وَاللَّهُ أَخْرَجَكُم مِّن بُطُونِ أُمَّهَاتِكُمْ لَا تَعْلَمُونَ شَيْئًا وَجَعَلَ لَكُمُ السَّمْعَ وَالْأَبْصَارَ وَالْأَفْئِدَةَ ۙ لَعَلَّكُمْ تَشْكُرُونَ
>
> Allah has brought you forth from the bellies of your mothers while you did not know anything. And He made for you hearing, eyesight, and hearts so that you may give thanks. (16:78)

Expressing gratitude for each part of the body is by using it to achieve its true goal, that goal for which it has been created. This important task cannot be fulfilled except by gaining the knowledge that draws man's attention towards his existential connection with the Origin of Creation and the reality of his own existence. Such knowledge acquaints him with the correct and secure path which Allah has outlined for him. In addition to gaining this knowledge, he must put it into practice in the different spheres of his life.

Amīr al-Mu'minīn (peace be upon him) says in his will to Imam al-Hasan (peace be upon him):

> قَرَعْتُكَ بِأَنْوَاعِ الْجَهَالاتِ لِئَلَّا تَعُدَّ نَفْسَكَ عَالِما ... فَإِنَّ الْعَالِمَ مَنْ عَرَفَ أَنَّ مَا يَعْلَمُ فِيمَا لَا يَعْلَمُ قَلِيلٌ فَعَدَّ نَفْسَهُ بِذَلِكَ جَاهِلًا فَازْدَادَ بِمَا عَرَفَ مِنْ ذَلِكَ فِي طَلَبِ الْعِلْمِ اجْتِهَاداً فَمَا يَزَالُ لِلْعِلْمِ طَالِباً وَ فِيهِ رَاغِباً وَ لَهُ مُسْتَفِيداً وَ لِأَهْلِهِ خَاشِعا...
>
> I have reminded you of different types of ignorance, so that you do not consider yourself a scholar . . . Because a scholar is someone who comprehends that the amount of knowledge he possesses is little compared to the knowledge which he does not possess. So, he considers himself ignorant, and due to realizing that, he increases his efforts to acquire

> knowledge. Such a person is constantly seeking knowledge, passionate about it, deriving benefit from it, respecting those who possess it . . .[(i)]

Studying and asking questions are some of the most important causes of gaining knowledge. For this reason, they have been introduced as something of merit in Islam. The Honoured Messenger of Islam (peace and blessings be upon him and his family) says:

الْعِلْمُ خَزَائِنُ وَ مَفَاتِيحُهُ السُّؤَالُ فَاسْأَلُوا رَحِمَكُمُ اللَّهُ فَإِنَّهُ تُؤْجَرُ أَرْبَعَةٌ السَّائِلُ وَ الْمُتَكَلِّمُ وَ الْمُسْتَمِعُ وَ الْمُحِبُّ لَهُمْ.

> Knowledge is a treasure and its key is asking questions. Therefore, ask questions, may Allah have mercy on you. For indeed, four [groups] are rewarded [in relation to questioning]: the questioner, the speaker, the listener and one who loves them.[(ii)]

The Etiquette of Asking Questions

1) Asking Correctly

Posing the question precisely and correctly while refraining from superfluous and unnecessary things, all play an important role in getting the correct answer. So much so that Amīr al-Mu'minīn (peace be upon him) considered asking the question correctly to be half of knowledge, saying:

حُسْنُ الْمَسْأَلَةِ نِصْفُ الْعِلْم

Asking a question correctly is half of knowledge.[(iii)]

That is because, when a person wants to ask a question correctly, he must think properly and pay careful, albeit brief, attention to the matter about which he is asking. Moreover, he must comprehend the answer with attentiveness.

---

i. al-Raḍī, Nahj al-Balāghah, letter 31

ii. Rayshahrī, Mīzān al-Ḥikmah, 4:331

iii. al-Ḥarrānī, Tuḥaf al-ʿUqūl, 56

2) Refraining from Questions that Cause Difficulty

Knowing certain things causes disruption in life, increases man's duties and responsibilities, and leads to other problems. Therefore, it is necessary that man's questions are well-deliberated and beneficial. If not, he will become entangled in difficulties like the Children of Israel. By asking illogical questions about the cow that they were commanded to slaughter, they put themselves in hardships. The Noble Qur'ān reproaches this action of theirs, says:

أَمْ تُرِيدُونَ أَن تَسْأَلُوا رَسُولَكُمْ كَمَا سُئِلَ مُوسَىٰ مِن قَبْلُ

Would you question your Apostle as Moses was questioned formerly? (2:108)

The Messenger of Allah (peace and blessings be upon him and his family) has said:

ذَرُونِي مَا تَرَكْتُكُمْ ، فَإِنَّمَا هَلَكَ مَنْ كَانَ قَبْلَكُمْ بِكَثْرَةِ سُؤَالِهِمْ وَاخْتِلَافِهِمْ عَلَى أَنْبِيَائِهِمْ ، فَإِذَا أَمَرْتُكُمْ بِشَيْءٍ فَأْتُوا مِنْهُ مَا اسْتَطَعْتُمْ ، وَإِذَا نَهَيْتُكُمْ عَنْ شَيْءٍ فَدَعُوهُ

Leave me as long as I have left you [and have not commanded you], for verily those before you perished because of their excessive questioning and disputing about their prophets. So, when I command you regarding something, perform however much of it you can. And when I forbid you from something then refrain from it.[i]

Based on this, the Noble Qur'ān has presented a general rule, saying:

يَا أَيُّهَا الَّذِينَ آمَنُوا لَا تَسْأَلُوا عَنْ أَشْيَاءَ إِن تُبْدَ لَكُمْ تَسُؤْكُمْ

O you who have faith! Do not ask about things, which, if they are disclosed to you, will upset you. (5:101)

---

i. al-Hindī, Kanz al-ʿUmmāl, narration 916

3) Asking Scholars

The intellect dictates that every question be asked of the experts in that field. Asking those who are not experts and are unfamiliar with the matter, leads man to confusion and deviation. This is what happened to people after the demise of the Messenger of Islam (peace and blessings be upon him and his family). In the matter of their religion they turned to those who were incompetent and unaware of religion, and this led to their own destruction and the destruction of others. Thus, the Noble Qur᾽ān says:

فَاسْأَلُوا أَهْلَ الذِّكْرِ إِن كُنتُمْ لَا تَعْلَمُونَ

Ask the People of the Reminder if you do not know
(16:43)

4) Asking to Understand

One of the etiquettes of asking questions is that one should ask to gain knowledge and not to challenge the other person or to promote oneself. That is because, such behaviour distances a person from being amongst the seekers of knowledge and places him in the circle of the ignorant. Also, this behaviour indicates that the person is not after comprehending the reality the way it is, rather he wishes to disclose the weakness of others. As a result, the outcome of his action is ignorance.

In the words of Imam ʿAlī (peace be upon him) to someone who questioned him regarding a difficulty:

سَلْ تَفَقُّهاً وَ لَا تَسْأَلْ تَعَنُّتاً فَإِنَّ الْجَاهِلَ الْمُتَعَلِّمَ شَبِيهٌ بِالْعَالِمِ وَ إِنَّ الْعَالِمَ الْمُتَعَسِّفَ شَبِيهٌ بِالْجَاهِلِ الْمُتَعَنِّتِ

> Ask to understand and do not ask to confound and torment, for an ignorant learner is like a scholar and an unjust scholar is like a stubborn, ignorant person seeking to pick a quarrel.[i]

Imam al-Sādiq (peace be upon him) in his advice to ʿUnwān al-Basrī

---

i. al-Radī, Nahj al-Balāghah, saying 320

regarding knowledge, has also drawn his attention to this important matter.

5) Asking to the Extent of One's Ability

If a person does not take into consideration his mental, intellectual and spiritual capacity when asking academic questions, then he will undoubtedly be deprived of reaching the goal. That is because attaining perfection occurs gradually in this world and when the necessary conditions are fulfilled. One of these conditions is paying attention to one's intellectual capacity and that of the other person, so that the answer provided is comprehendible. For this reason, Imam ʿAlī (peace be upon him) says:

مَنْ سَأَلَ فَوْقَ قَدْرِهِ اسْتَحَقَّ الْحِرْمَان

One who asks beyond his capacity deserves to be deprived. (i)

مَنْ سَأَلَ مَا لَا يَسْتَحِقُّ قُوبِلَ بِالْحِرْمَان

One who asks for that which he does not deserve, will be met with deprivation. (ii)

Just as how Prophet Moses (peace be upon him)—after speaking with Allah—requested that he see Allah the Exalted. After mentioning certain things, Allah said to him:

قَالَ يَا مُوسَىٰ إِنِّي اصْطَفَيْتُكَ عَلَى النَّاسِ بِرِسَالَاتِي وَبِكَلَامِي فَخُذْ مَا آتَيْتُكَ وَكُن مِّنَ الشَّاكِرِينَ

He said, "O Moses, I have chosen you over the people with My messages and My speech. So, take what I give you, and be among the grateful." (7: 144)

---

i. al-Āmudī, Ghurar al-Hikam, narration 8579

ii. Ibid., narration 8939

6) Refraining from Too Many Questions

Reaching any goal in the realm of this world is dependent on certain conditions; at the same time there are also barriers to reach it. Acquiring knowledge is no exception to this rule. Insistence on a certain academic matter and asking too many questions, not only exhausts the questioner and makes him disinclined to pursue academic matters, but it also dissuades the answerer from continuing the discussion. Additionally, it stagnates the mind of the questioner and prevents him from thinking about unknown matters and uncovering them using his own knowledge. Therefore, Imam ʿAlī (peace be upon him) says:

كَثْرَةُ السُّؤَالِ تُورِثُ الْمَلَالَ

Asking too many questions brings about weariness.[i]

مَنْ أَكْثَرَ مَسْأَلَةَ النَّاسِ ذَل

One who asks much from the people will be abased.[ii]

Research and Developing Academic Views

After the learning phase, the period of absorbing the knowledge, applying it and doing academic research begins. In this period, it is also necessary that man abide by certain matters, so that in addition to deriving maximum benefit from this stage, he is secure from its dangers. Some of those points are:

1) Not Considering One's Opinion to be Absolute and Definitive

Knowledge is a limitless ocean such that claiming to have reached its end, is a sign of man's ignorance. In words of Amīr al-Muʾminīn (peace be upon him):

مَنِ ادَّعَى مِنَ الْعِلْمِ غَايَتَهُ فَقَدْ أَظْهَرَ مِنْ جَهْلِهِ نِهَايَتَه

One who claims that he has reached the limit of knowledge,

---

i. Ibid., narration 7094

ii. Ibid., narration 8154

> then indeed he has revealed the utmost degree of his ignorance.[(i)]

Likewise, if a person unconditionally says that "I am a scholar" then according to Imam ʿAlī (peace be upon him):

مَنْ قَالَ أَنَا عَالِمٌ فَهُوَ جَاهِل

He who says, "I am a scholar" is an ignorant person.[(ii)]

Therefore, unconditional reliance on one's knowledge, distances a person from the path of guidance and prevents him from reaching the pinnacles of scholarship. In the words of Khwājah Hāfiz-i Shīrāzī:

> As long as you see [your own] merit and knowledge, of Divine Wisdom you are bereft.[(iii)]

2) Refraining from One's Own Opinion

When making decisions, man's academic conclusions are subject to deviation and risk. This deviation and risk may arise because of his limited knowledge, the interferences of his selfish desires, cultural and environmental biases, or other such factors. For this reason, to reach a firm and conclusive opinion about an academic issue, in addition to utilizing strong and established means, one must refer to the opinion of other experts and carefully study their arguments. This is necessary so that a person's opinion is not developed in isolation. Thus, it is detestable to conceal one's knowledge because in this case one's opinion are not presented to the scholars. As a result, they are not scrutinized by them, and their flaws are not rectified. As Imam ʿAlī (peace be upon him) says:

الْكَاتِمُ لِلْعِلْمِ غَيْرُ وَاثِقٍ بِالْإِصَابَةِ فِيه

One who conceals his knowledge is not confidant that he

---

i. Ibid., narration 91193

ii. Shahīd al-Thānī, Munyah al-Murīd, 137
Note: Referring to this source, it appears that the blessed narration is in fact from the Messenger of Allah (peace and blessings be upon him and his family).

iii. Shirāzī, Divān-i Ḥāfiẓ (Taṣḥīḥ-i Qudsī), ghazal 538, first line from couplet 3.

has reached the reality.[i]

On the other hand, he says:

مُنَاقَشَةُ الْعُلَمَاءِ تُنْتِجُ فَوَائِدَهُمْ وَ تَكْسِبُ فَضَائِلَهُم

Debating with scholars and criticizing [their views] leads to benefitting from their strengths and earning their merits.[ii]

Likewise, the Messenger of Allah (peace and blessings be upon him and his family) says:

أَعْلَمُ النَّاسِ مَنْ جَمَعَ عِلْمَ النَّاسِ إِلَى عِلْمِه

The most knowledgeable person is one who gathers the knowledge of the people [and adds it] to his own knowledge.[iii]

This method keeps a person away from being self-centred in his academic opinions which would cause him to reject the scholarship of others.

Divine scholars paid due attention to these deviating factors when deducing and researching academic issues. It is narrated that when ʿAllāmah Hillī (may Allah be pleased with him) wanted to carry out research and give his opinion about water in wells becoming impure (najāsah), he first filled and blocked all the wells in his house. He did so to ensure that his personal inclination and benefit would not interfere with his research. Only then did he express his opinion, going against the prevalent opinion in his time that if the water of a well becomes najis, the well must be filled.

In this phase of a person's academic life, the best thing that protects him against the dangers of knowledge, is observing precaution (ihtiyāt) and refraining from one's own opinion. Thus, Imam al-Sādiq (peace be upon him) advised ʿUnwān al-Basrī:

---

i. al-Āmudī, Ghurar al-Hikam, narration 1544

ii. Ibid., narration 9804

iii. al-Ṣadūq, al-Amālī, 27, narration 4

إِيَّاكَ أَنْ تَعْمَلَ بِرَأْيِكَ شَيْئاً وَ خُذْ بِالاحْتِيَاطِ
فِي جَمِيعِ مَا تَجِدُ إِلَيْهِ سَبِيلاً

Refrain from acting according to your opinion and act with precaution in every matter you can.

In conclusion, observing precaution, refraining from acting and speaking recklessly, is necessary for all, especially those who are unaware of the academic standards and criteria.

Spreading Knowledge and Formulating New Options

Spreading and advancing knowledge is the duty of the scholars, fulfilled through different means—both written and unwritten. The Noble Qur'ān and the narrations have put a great deal of emphasis on this sensitive and crucial duty. Allah the Exalted says:

إِنَّ الَّذِينَ يَكْتُمُونَ مَا أَنزَلْنَا مِنَ الْبَيِّنَاتِ وَالْهُدَىٰ مِن بَعْدِ مَا بَيَّنَّاهُ
لِلنَّاسِ فِي الْكِتَابِ ۙ أُولَٰئِكَ يَلْعَنُهُمُ اللَّهُ وَيَلْعَنُهُمُ اللَّاعِنُونَ

Indeed, those who conceal what We have sent down of manifest proofs and guidance, after We have clarified it in the Book for mankind, they shall be cursed by Allah and cursed by the cursers. (2:159)

The Noble Messenger of Islam (peace and blessings be upon him and his family) has also said:

مَنْ سُئِلَ عَنْ عِلْمٍ يَعْلَمُهُ فَكَتَمَهُ أُلْجِمَ يَوْمَ الْقِيَامَةِ بِلِجَامٍ مِنْ نَارٍ

One who is asked about knowledge he knows, and he conceals that knowledge [from those are worthy of it], then he will be bridled with a bridle of fire on the Day of Resurrection.[i]

Imam ʿAlī (peace be upon him) also says:

زَكَاةُ الْعِلْمِ نَشْرُه

i. al-Ṭūsī, al-Tibyān, 2:45

The *zakāt* of knowledge is to spread it.[i]

Likewise, in Imam ʿAlī's (peace be upon him) view the obligation of teaching is prior to the obligation of learning. He says:

مَا أَخَذَ اللَّهُ عَلَى أَهْلِ الْجَهْلِ أَنْ يَتَعَلَّمُوا حَتَّى أَخَذَ عَلَى أَهْلِ الْعِلْمِ أَنْ يُعَلِّمُوا

> Allah did not take a pledge from the ignorant people that they should learn except that he took a pledge from the people possessing knowledge that they should teach.[ii]

What is important when offering academic services, is to advance new knowledge and present new theories and opinions based on the appropriate principles and fundamental laws of every discipline. Those who fulfil the conditions have the duty to guide the people and rescue them from ignorance, deviation and error, in matters pertaining to sharīʿah. Specifically, this is the case in topics and detailed issues where the people need an informed opinion. It is for this reason that the Imams (peace be upon them) gave general instructions to the scholars to spread their knowledge and forbade them from concealing it from those who are worthy. In addition, they encouraged the scholars to issue fatāwā (legal rulings) derived from the general rulings of the sharīʿah. Imam al-Sādiq (peace be upon him) says:

إِنَّمَا عَلَيْنَا أَنْ نُلْقِيَ إِلَيْكُمُ الْأُصُولَ وَ عَلَيْكُمْ أَنْ تُفَرِّعُوا

> Certainly, it is our duty to outline the principles [and the fundamental and general rules], and it is upon you to ramify and branch them [and apply them to individual situations].[iii]

That is because, on the one hand the sacred religion of Islam is a perfect religion, it will be alive until the Day of Resurrection, and it is

---

i. al-Āmudī, Ghurar al-Hikam, narration 5444

ii. al-Radī, Nahj al-Balāghah, saying 478

iii. Majlisī, Bihār al-Anwār, 2:245, narration 54; al-ʿĀmilī, Wasā'il al-Shīʿah, 27:61, narration 26

able to answer man's innumerable needs in the different spheres of life. On the other hand, the teachings of the Qur'ān and the Sunnah—the words of the Messenger of Allah (peace and blessings be upon him and his family) and the Imams (peace be upon them)—that have reached us, are complete and comprehensive statements that must be applied and observed in the particular situations of man's life. Naturally, not everyone can carry out this task. Rather, experts in the Islamic sciences who have a good command over Islamic teachings must undertake this task. The Imams' (peace be upon them) statements also indicate this point. Moreover, the Imams (peace be upon them) would specifically instruct only a few of their students to give fatāwā. For example, Imam al-Bāqir (peace be upon him) says to Abān Bin Taghlab—who was a distinguished companion of Imam al-Sajjād (peace be upon him), Imam al-Bāqir (peace be upon him) and Imam al-Sādiq (peace be upon him):

اجْلِسْ فِي مَسْجِدِ الْمَدِينَةِ وَ أَفْتِ النَّاسَ فَإِنِّي أُحِبُّ أَنْ يُرَى فِي شِيعَتِي مِثْلُكَ

> Sit in the mosque of Madinah and issue *fatāwā* for the people. For indeed I love to see likes of you in my Shīʿah.[i]

Or they referred the people to individuals such as Yūnis bin Abd al-Rahmān, ʿAlī bin Hadīd, Zakariyyā bin Ādam, Muhammad bin Muslim al-Thaqafī, Zurarah bin Aʿyan, Abū Basīr Layth al-Murādī, Burayd bin Muʿāwiyah al-ʿAjalī; and said regarding these people:

وَ لَوْ لَا هَؤُلَاءِ لَانْدَرَسَ الدِّيْنُ

> If it were not for these people, certainly the religion would have been wiped out.[ii]

Similarly, in the period of the ghaybah (the occultation of the current Imam), the religious scholars must shoulder this responsibility. In

---

i. al-Khū'ī, Muʿjam Rijāl al-Hadīth, 1:147

ii. al-Āmilī, Wasā'il al-Shīʿah, 27:144, chapter 11; Majlisī, Bihār al-Anwār, 2:249, narrations 60, 61, 66, 67 and 68
Note: the exact text quoted by the author (may Allah protect him) was not found during the translation, but similar narrations were found in the above sources.

addition to propagating the religious teachings through various means, those amongst them who can issue fatāwā and voice their opinion—if they meet the criteria of being just and safeguarding the religion—must assume this role. It is also necessary—both intellectually and in the sharʿīah—that the common people refer to them to learn the different aspects of religion, and that they follow them. As the Imam of the time (may Allah hasten his reappearance) writes in his noble letter (tawqīʿ):

أَمَّا الْحَوَادِثُ الْوَاقِعَةُ فَارْجِعُوا فِيهَا إِلَى رُوَاةِ حَدِيثِنَا

> And regarding the incidents [and issues] that occur, refer in them to the transmitters of our narrations. (i)

What is intended by "transmitters of narrations" is those scholars who can discern the sayings of the Imams (peace be upon them) that are related to different aspects of life. They can differentiate the view of the Imams (peace be upon them) from those mentioned by others. Such individuals are none other the qualified jurists (mujtahids).

Therefore, the following points can be concluded from the overall teachings of the Qurʾān and the Sunnah. Islam—along with the wilāyah of the Imams (peace be upon them)—is the most perfect Divine religion such that till the Day of Resurrection no other religion will be sent for mankind. Moreover, the teachings of Islam—in particular, the laws (ahkām) and commands—must be understood and implemented in all spheres of life. At first, this responsibility is on the shoulders of all those have accepted this religion as the most perfect and everlasting Divine religion. However, because all men—due to the nature of life in this world and the task of managing it—do not have the ability or possibility of learning Islamic teachings in an extensive manner. Because of these points, it is necessary that a group of people who see the potential and commitment in themselves, undertake the learning of religious knowledge. Such individuals are knowns as 'committed scholars'. Others must refer to them for acquiring their religious knowledge and they in turn must not refuse to impart this knowledge—to the extent of their ability and the aptitude of their addressees.

---

i. al-Ṭūsī, al-Ghaybah, 177

Undoubtedly, only those who have the competence to express opinion with regards to the Divine laws should assume this duty and lofty religious position. They must be able to derive the ruling of particular issues from the general teachings of the sharīʿah and thus issue fatāwā for the people, such that the people refer to them to know their particular religious laws and do taqlīd of them.

Refraining from One's Own Opinion

In view of the aforementioned points, it becomes clear that those who lack familiarity and awareness on a certain issue do not have the right to explain it, let alone express their opinion and belief about it. This act is censured and forbidden by the intellect, the customary norms (ʿurf) and the sharīʿah, especially in relation to religious matters. This is because, man's felicity in the world and the Hereafter depends upon understanding these religious matters correctly and acting upon them. Therefore, the people must refer to those who possess knowledge. On the contrary, wretchedness and misfortune in this world and the Hereafter lies in denying religious teachings, having a distorted understanding of them, or entirely forsaking them.

This action [of speaking and expressing opinion without knowledge] is referred in the Qurʾān as 'fabricating a lie against Allah':

وَإِنَّ مِنْهُمْ لَفَرِيقًا يَلْوُونَ أَلْسِنَتَهُم بِالْكِتَابِ لِتَحْسَبُوهُ مِنَ الْكِتَابِ
وَمَا هُوَ مِنَ الْكِتَابِ وَيَقُولُونَ هُوَ مِنْ عِندِ اللَّهِ وَمَا هُوَ مِنْ عِندِ
اللَّهِ وَيَقُولُونَ عَلَى اللَّهِ الْكَذِبَ وَهُمْ يَعْلَمُونَ

> And verily there is a group of them who alter their voice while reading out a text [that they have themselves authored], so that you may suppose it to be from the Book, though it is not from the Book, and they say, "It is from Allah," though it is not from Allah, and they attribute lies to Allah, and they know [it]. (3:78)

The following verses are also applicable to such people:

وَمَن لَّمْ يَحْكُم بِمَا أَنزَلَ اللَّهُ فَأُولَٰئِكَ هُمُ الْكَافِرُونَ

> Those who do not judge by what Allah has sent down, it is they who are the faithless. (5:44)
>
> وَمَن لَّمْ يَحْكُم بِمَا أَنزَلَ اللَّهُ فَأُولَٰئِكَ هُمُ الْفَاسِقُونَ
>
> Those who do not judge by what Allah has sent down, it is they who are the transgressors. (5:47)

The Imams (peace be upon them) have also strongly reproached the expressing of one's opinion in religious matters without a solid academic backing and without deducing it from principles of the Qur'ān, the Sunnah and the indisputable laws of the intellect and the intellectuals. That is because, it leads to innovation (bidʿah) in the religion, is the origin of most deviations and the cause behind the different Islamic sects. For this reason, Zurārah narrates:

> سَأَلْتُ أَبَا جَعْفَرٍ الْبَاقِرَ ع مَا حَقُّ اللَّهِ عَلَى الْعِبَادِ قَالَ أَنْ يَقُولُوا مَا يَعْلَمُونَ وَ يَقِفُوا عِنْدَ مَا لَا يَعْلَمُونَ
>
> I asked Abū Jaʿfar Imam al-Bāqir (peace be upon him), "What is Allah's right over the servants?" The Imam replied, "That they say what they know and desist from what they do not know [they do not say anything and do not express their own opinion]." (i)

Imam al-Sādiq (peace be upon him) also says:

> إِنَّ اللَّهَ تَبَارَكَ وَ تَعَالَى عَيَّرَ عِبَادَهُ بِآيَتَيْنِ مِنْ كِتَابِهِ أَنْ لَا يَقُولُوا حَتَّى يَعْلَمُوا وَ لَا يَرُدُّوا مَا لَمْ يَعْلَمُوا قَالَ اللَّهُ عَزَّ وَ جَلَ أَ لَمْ يُؤْخَذْ عَلَيْهِمْ مِيثَاقُ الْكِتَابِ أَنْ لا يَقُولُوا عَلَى اللَّهِ إِلَّا الْحَقَ وَ قَالَ بَلْ كَذَّبُوا بِما لَمْ يُحِيطُوا بِعِلْمِهِ وَ لَمَّا يَأْتِهِمْ تَأْوِيلُهُ.
>
> Indeed, Allah (the Provider of abundance and the Sublime) has reproached His servants in two verses of His Book. [The first is] that they should not say until they know and [the second is] that they should not reject what they do not

---

i. Majlisī, Bihār al-Anwār, 2:113, narration 2

know. Allah (the Invincible and Majestic) says, "Was not the covenant of the Book taken with them that they shall not attribute anything to Allah except the truth?" (i) and He says, "Indeed, they deny something whose knowledge they do not comprehend, and whose explanation has not yet come to them." (ii) (iii)

Also, he said to Fadl ibn Yazīd:

أَنْهَاكَ عَنْ خَصْلَتَيْنِ فِيهِمَا هَلْكُ الرِّجَالِ أَنْ تَدِينَ اللَّهَ بِالْبَاطِلِ وَ تُفْتِيَ النَّاسَ بِمَا لَا تَعْلَمُ

I forbid you from two traits that have destroyed people: that you worship Allah through falsehood [on the basis of falsehood you accept Allah's religion] and that you issue *fatāwā* in a matter you have no knowledge of. (iv)

Imam al-Ridā (peace be upon him) narrates through his noble forefathers (peace be upon them) from Amīr al-Mu'minīn (peace be upon him):

قَالَ رَسُوْلُ اللهِ ص مَنْ أَفْتَى النَّاسَ بِغَيْرِ عِلْمٍ لَعَنَهُ مَلَائِكَةُ السَّمَاوَاتِ وَ الْأَرْضِ

The Messenger of Allah (peace and blessings be upon him and his family) said, "One who issues *fatāwā* to the people without knowledge, the angels of the heavens and the Earth curse him." (v)

Imam al-Bāqir (peace be upon him) in another narrations says:

---

i. (7:169)

ii. (10:39)

iii. Majlisī, Biḥār al-Anwār, 2:113, narration 3

iv. Ibid., 2:114, narrations 5 and 6

v. Ibid., 2:115, narration 12

مَـنْ أَفْتَـى النَّـاسَ بِغَيْـرِ عِلْـمٍ وَ لَا هُـدًى مِـنَ اللَّـهِ لَعَنَتْـهُ مَلَائِكَـةُ الرَّحْمَـةِ وَ مَلَائِكَـةُ الْعَـذَابِ وَ لَحِقَـهُ وِزْرُ مَـنْ عَمِـلَ بِفُتْيَـاهُ.

The angels of mercy and the angels of punishment curse a person who issues *fatāwā* without knowledge or guidance from Allah, and the burden [of the sin] of the one who acts according to his *fatāwā* is upon him. (i)

One of the narrators says:

سَـمِعْتُ أَبَـا عَبْـدِ اللَّـهِ ع يَقُـولُ مَـنِ اسْـتَأْكَلَ بِعِلْمِـهِ افْتَقَـرَ فَقُلْـتُ لَـهُ جُعِلْـتُ فِـدَاكَ إِنَّ فِـي شِـيعَتِكَ وَ مَوَالِيـكَ قَوْمـاً يَتَحَمَّلُـونَ عُلُومَكُـمْ وَ يَبُثُّونَهَـا فِـي شِـيعَتِكُمْ فَـلَا يَعْدَمُـونَ عَلَـى ذَلِـكَ مِنْهُـمُ الْبِـرَّ وَ الصِّلَـةَ وَ الْإِكْـرَامَ فَقَـالَ ع لَيْـسَ أُولَئِـكَ بِمُسْـتَأْكِلِينَ إِنَّمَـا الْمُسْـتَأْكِلُ بِعِلْمِـهِ الَّـذِي يُفْتِـي بِغَيْـرِ عِلْـمٍ وَ لَا هُـدًى مِـنَ اللَّـهِ عَـزَّ وَ جَـلَّ لِيُبْطِـلَ بِـهِ الْحُقُـوقَ طَمَعـاً فِـي حُطَـامِ الدُّنْيَـا

I heard Imam al-Ṣādiq (peace be upon him) say, "One who seeks his livelihood using his knowledge becomes needy." I asked him, "May I be your ransom! There is a group amongst your Shīʿah and friends who carry your knowledge and propagate it amongst your Shīʿah. The Shīʿah [in return], do not refrain from acting with beneficence and giving them gifts and respect." The Imam (peace be upon him) said, "They are not those who obtain their living using knowledge. A person who earns his living using his knowledge is one who issues religious verdicts (*fatāwā*) without any knowledge or guidance from Allah, thereby nullifying the rights [of the people] to satisfy his greed for the lowly world." (ii)

Likewise, a narrator in another narration says that I heard Imam ʿAlī (peace be upon him) on the pulpit of Kūfah, saying:

---

i. Ibid., 2:117, narration 23

ii. Ibid., 2:116, narration 14

أَيُّهَا النَّاسُ ثَلَاثٌ لَا دِينَ لَهُمْ لَا دِينَ لِمَنْ دَانَ بِجُحُودِ آيَةٍ مِنْ كِتَابِ اللَّهِ وَ لَا دِينَ لِمَنْ دَانَ بِفِرْيَةِ بَاطِلٍ عَلَى اللَّهِ وَ لَا دِينَ لِمَنْ دَانَ بِطَاعَةِ مَنْ عَصَى اللَّهَ تَبَارَكَ وَ تَعَالَى ثُمَّ قَالَ أَيُّهَا النَّاسُ لَا خَيْرَ فِي دِينٍ لَا تَفَقُّهَ فِيهِ

"O people! Three [types of] people do not have any religion. There is no religion for one who believes while rejecting a verse from the Book of Allah, there is no religion for one who believes while attributing falsehood to Allah, and there is no religion for one who believes while obeying the one who disobeys Allah (the Provider of abundance and the Sublime)." Then he said, "O people! There is no good in a religion in which there is no *tafaqquh*." (i) (ii)

ʿAlī ibn Jaʿfar narrates from Mūsā ibn Jaʿfar (peace be upon him) who in turn narrates from his father that ʿAlī ibn al-Husayn (peace be upon him) said:

لَيْسَ لَكَ أَنْ تَقْعُدَ مَعَ مَنْ شِئْتَ لِأَنَّ اللَّهَ تَبَارَكَ وَ تَعَالَى يَقُولُ وَ إِذا رَأَيْتَ الَّذِينَ يَخُوضُونَ فِي آياتِنا فَأَعْرِضْ عَنْهُمْ حَتَّى يَخُوضُوا فِي حَدِيثٍ غَيْرِهِ وَ إِمَّا يُنْسِيَنَّكَ الشَّيْطانُ فَلا تَقْعُدْ بَعْدَ الذِّكْرى مَعَ الْقَوْمِ الظَّالِمِينَ وَ لَيْسَ لَكَ أَنْ تَتَكَلَّمَ بِمَا شِئْتَ لِأَنَّ اللَّهَ عَزَّ وَ جَلَّ قَالَ- وَ لا تَقْفُ ما لَيْسَ لَكَ بِهِ عِلْمٌ وَ لِأَنَّ رَسُولَ اللَّهِ ص قَالَ رَحِمَ اللَّهُ عَبْداً قَالَ خَيْراً فَغَنِمَ أَوْ صَمَتَ فَسَلِمَ وَ لَيْسَ لَكَ أَنْ تَسْمَعَ مَا شِئْتَ لِأَنَّ اللَّهَ عَزَّ وَ جَلَّ يَقُولُ إِنَّ السَّمْعَ وَ الْبَصَرَ وَ الْفُؤادَ كُلُّ أُولئِكَ كانَ عَنْهُ مَسْؤُلًا.

You are not allowed to sit with [and be in the company of] whomsoever you like. That is because Allah (the Provider

---

i. *Tafaqquh* is from the root word *fiqh* which means to acquire deep knowledge and understanding.

ii. Majlisī, Biḥār al-Anwār, 2:117, narration 19

> of abundance and the Sublime) says, "When you see those who gossip impiously about Our signs, avoid them until they engage in some other discourse; but if Satan makes you forget, then after remembering, do not sit with the wrongdoing lot."[i] [Also] you are not allowed to say whatever you like. That is because Allah (the Invincible and Majestic) says, "Do not pursue that of which you have no knowledge,"[ii] and also because the Messenger of Allah (peace and blessings be upon him and his family) has said, "May Allah have mercy on a person who speaks good [words] and benefits from it or remains silent and stays safe." [Also] you are not allowed to listen to whatever you like. That is because Allah says, "Indeed the hearing, eyesight, and the heart, all of these, are accountable."[iii] [iv]

Pertaining to this same topic, Imam al-Bāqir (peace be upon him) narrates from the Messenger of Allah (peace and blessings be upon him and his family) that he said:

> مَنْ عَمِلَ بِالْمَقَايِيسِ فَقَدْ هَلَكَ وَ أَهْلَكَ وَ مَنْ أَفْتَى النَّاسَ وَ هُوَ لَا يَعْلَمُ النَّاسِخَ مِنَ الْمَنْسُوخِ وَ الْمُحْكَمَ مِنَ الْمُتَشَابِهِ فَقَدْ هَلَكَ وَ أَهْلَكَ
>
> One who acts based on *qiyās*[v] is certainly destroyed and has destroyed others as well. [Also] one who issues *fatāwā* for the people, while he cannot differentiate the abrogating law (*nāsikh*) from the abrogated one (*mansūkh*), and the definitive (*muḥkam*) from the metaphorical (*mutashābih*), then certainly he has destroyed himself and has destroyed

---

i. (6:68)

ii. (17:36)

iii. (17:36)

iv. Majlisī, Biḥār al-Anwār, 2:116, narration 13

v. *Qiyās* is a method of deduction and inference based on analogy. One of the sources of deriving the laws of *sharīʿah* for the Ahl al-Sunnah, this method has been strongly forbidden by the Ahl al-Bayt (peace be upon them).

others as well.[i]

In view of these statements, Imam al-Ṣādiq (peace be upon him) in his last advice to ʿUnwān al-Baṣrī says:

> وَ اهْرُبْ مِنَ الْفُتْيَا هَرَبَكَ مِنَ الْأَسَدِ وَ لَا تَجْعَلْ رَقَبَتَكَ لِلنَّاسِ جِسْراً
> Flee from giving *fatāwā* (legal opinion) like you flee from a lion, and do not make your neck a bridge for the people.
> That is because, one who lacks the conditions required for giving *fatwā* but does so, has made his neck a bridge for others to reach Heaven, while he himself will be condemned to the Hellfire.
> As a result, one who wishes to traverse the path of Allah's true servitude, must have a precise understanding of the goal and the correct path. He must recognize the deviant paths, and only move on the Straight Path (*ṣirāṭ al-mustaqīm*) as exemplified by the immaculate Ahl al-Bayt (peace be upon them). In this manner, he can reach the intended destination with safety.

---

i. Majlisī, Biḥār al-Anwār, 2:118, narration 24

Section Four
Planning a Daily Schedule

Introduction

Keeping in mind the different discussions presented in this book—discussions that are beneficial for systematically traversing the path of servitude—in this section we will present some points to summarize the entire discussion. These points provide practical solutions for those who aspire to traverse the path of Allah the Exalted's servitude, in a manner that is far removed from the extremes of excessiveness and laxity (*ifrāṭ* and *tafrīṭ*) and does not need a specific spiritual teacher:

1) Any practical effort and undertaking that lacks the support of the Qur'ān and the Sunnah is in vain and futile. Keeping this in mind, the instructions mentioned in this section have been taken from the general recommendations and instructions of the Qur'ān, the Sunnah and the words of the infallible and the immaculate Ahl al-Bayt (peace be upon them).

2) The discussions mentioned in this section have been recommended by scholars of *akhlāq* and *tarbiyah*, who are well aware of the fundamental teachings of the Qur'ān and the Sunnah.

3) These discussions are an example of a correct and systematic practical journey during the initial stages. If someone strictly abides by this, then Allah will assist him and increase his capacity. As a result, his eagerness and desire for higher spiritual stations will increase and he can then request Allah to show him higher and more precise paths towards Him. Without a doubt, Allah—who is man's guide towards Himself—will help such a person and place him under the care of a suitable and virtuous servant so that he can then guide him to higher levels of servitude.

The fundamental goal of man's creation is Allah the Exalted's servitude, and this servitude means to consciously express humility before Allah the Self-Sufficient. Such an expression of humility requires that one possess correct *tawḥīdī* (monotheistic) beliefs. This in turn is realized—in the first stage—by continuous obedience to the commands of Allah and His *awliyā'* (peace be upon them). Keeping this in mind, it is necessary for the seeker—to reach Reality and perform servitude—that in the first stage he acquire knowledge of the matters in which he is required to obey Allah. The religion of Allah covers all dimensions of man's life (ritual, domestic, economic, social, political, etc.) and has issued instructions pertaining to them, all of which must be implemented. Hence, it is necessary for everybody to acquire the knowledge of these matters to the extent of their need, especially those matters that he encounters regularly. This must be done either by means of *taqlīd*[(i)] or *ijtihād*[(ii)]. It is for this reason that Imam al-Ṣādiq (peace be upon him) said to ʿUnwān al-Baṣrī, "Seek knowledge by applying it in actions."

Imam al-Ṣādiq (peace be upon him) explained the third pillar of servitude as being that the servant's sole preoccupation is in performing what Allah the Exalted has commanded him to do and abstaining from what He has prohibited him from. Also, he explained the second pillar as being that the servant does not plan his own affairs. Based on these statements as well as other statements of the Imams (peace be upon them) that provide practical solutions for the different dimensions of life, one's daily schedule and activities must be planned in a manner that is approved by Allah and His *awliyāʾ* (peace be upon them). That which is appropriate for the general masses—in the view of the author—shall now be presented.

Practical Instructions

The matters that must be observed by one who aspires to reach the Truth and servitude—to ascertain that he has reached the first level of Allah the Exalted's servitude—are as follows:

---

i. *Taqlīd* means to follow an expert (a *mujtahid*) in the field of Islamic jurisprudence.

ii. *Ijtihād* means the expertise required to derive Islamic laws from their sources.

1) Repentance from the Beginning of Taklīf [i]

Repentance is one of the important instructions of the Qur'ān [ii] and the Sunnah, which remedies the shortcomings in a person's actions and *akhlāq* and is a movement towards acquiring perfections. Therefore, one who wishes to undertake a fundamental journey to perfect his soul, should carefully ponder about his past actions, from the beginning of *taklīf* until this thought of self-reformation occurred to him. He should take account of his actions in these two areas:

1. The rights of Allah (*ḥaqqullāh*). This includes the obligatory (*wājib*) and prohibited *(ḥarām)* actions. That is, he should take account of himself and see, has he left aside any obligatory actions or performed any prohibited actions, or not? If he has not forsaken any obligatory actions and has not committed any mistakes, then he should thank Allah and determine to continue acting in this manner. However, if he has left aside any obligatory actions, then he must slowly perform their *qaḍā,* [iii] according to the verdict of his *marjaʿ*. If he has committed a mistake, he must seek forgiveness, feel remorseful about performing that action and make a firm decision to never perform it again.
2. The rights of people (*ḥaqq al-nās*). This includes matters such as having destroyed someone else's wealth without seeking forgiveness or compensating them. In such situations, firstly he should ask that person to forgive him or he should compensate him for the loss incurred by paying him its monetary value. If the property destroyed was public property, then then he should pay the compensation to the concerned institution or government body. However, if he does not know the person or it is not possible to reach him, then he should pay the amount

---

i. *Taklīf* here refers to the age when a person reaches *bulūgh* (an Islamic definition of puberty) and it becomes obligatory on him to abide by all the laws of the *sharīʿah*.

ii. (11:3), (11:52), (11:61), (11:90), (24:31), and (66:8)

iii. *Qaḍā* is a means of compensating for certain missed obligatory actions. When a person does not perform that action in its stipulated time, then he is required to perform it outside the time. This is known as *qaḍā*.

to a *mujtahid* under the title of *radd-i maẓālim.* [i] Likewise, if he has falsely accused someone, backbit him, used indecent words against him, or performed such undesirable interactions, then in each instance he must make amends according to what the *sharīʿah* has commanded him.

The more carefully and precisely this act of accounting is performed, the more effective it is in purifying the soul. Afterwards, if the person recites the prayer of *tawbah* as instructed by the Messenger of Allah (peace and blessings be upon him and his family), then it is even better. This prayer can be found in the book Mafātīḥ al-Jinān under the section pertaining to the actions of the month of Dhū al-Qaʿdah.

2) Vigilance (Murāqabah) in Performing the Obligatory Actions (Wājibāt) and Abandoning the Prohibited Actions (Muharramāt)

The first and the most fundamental deed required for Allah the Exalted's servitude and obedience, is to persistently adhere to performing the obligatory actions of the *sharīʿah* and forsaking the prohibited actions. This adherence is not achieved except through having vigilance (*murāqabah*) and attentiveness (*muwāẓabah*) over the soul. That is because, at times people perform obligatory actions and forsake prohibited actions, but they are not attentive of all their actions and movements. Therefore, because of not being vigilant and attentive it is possible that they miss an obligatory action or perform a prohibited action. In this case, this individual's struggle and efforts will not yield much results. Hence, great emphasis has been laid on practicing self-vigilance and self-attentiveness, just as Allah the Exalted says:

يَا أَيُّهَا الَّذِينَ آمَنُوا اتَّقُوا اللَّهَ وَلْتَنظُرْ نَفْسٌ مَّا قَدَّمَتْ لِغَدٍ ۖ وَاتَّقُوا اللَّهَ ۚ إِنَّ اللَّهَ خَبِيرٌ بِمَا تَعْمَلُونَ

i. *Radd-i maẓālim* refers to a ruling of the *sharīʿah* to do with financial rights. If a believer owes someone money but does not know who it is or is unable to reach them, he instead pays the amount to a qualified jurist (*mujtahid*) who in turn distributes it to the needy. Some *marājiʿ* allow the believers to directly distribute this amount amongst the needy.

O you who have faith! Be wary of Allah, and let every soul consider what it sends ahead for tomorrow and be wary of Allah. Allah is indeed well aware of what you do. (59:18)

In this verse, in addition to being instructed to be observe *taqwā*, the believers have been recommended to overlook and vigilantly observe the activities of the soul. Imam ʿAlī (peace be upon him) says regarding the way that this should be done:

اجْعَلْ مِنْ نَفْسِكَ عَلَى نَفْسِكَ رَقِيباً وَ اجْعَلْ لِآخِرَتِكَ مِنْ دُنْيَاكَ نَصِيبا

Appoint a watcher over yourself from within yourself and allot a portion for your hereafter from your world.[i]

Likewise, he says:

يَنْبَغِي أَنْ يَكُونَ الرَّجُلُ مُهَيْمِناً عَلَى نَفْسِهِ مُرَاقِباً قَلْبَهُ ...

It is befitting that a man has control over his soul, is vigilant and attentive of his heart...[ii]

Without doubt, this self-vigilance becomes complete through taking account of the soul (*muḥāsabah*). Imam ʿAlī (peace be upon him) explains the virtue of this, saying:

مَنْ حَاسَبَ نَفْسَهُ وَقَفَ عَلَى عُيُوبِهِ وَ أَحَاطَ بِذُنُوبِهِ وَ اسْتَقَالَ الذُّنُوبَ وَ أَصْلَحَ الْعُيُوب

One who takes account of his self, becomes aware of his defects and thoroughly grasps his sins, [and as a result] he seeks forgiveness for the sins and rectifies the defects.[iii]

Based on this, the outcome of self-accounting is that a person discovers his practical and ethical shortcomings. Until man does not find his shortcomings, he will not seek to rectify and remedy them; rather

---

i. al-Āmudī, Ghurar al-Hikam, narration 2429

ii. Ibid., narration 10947

iii. Ibid., narration 8927

he remains in the illusion that he is seeking perfection and is perfect. Therefore, Imam ʿAlī (peace be upon him) in another statement of his says:

> مَنْ حَاسَبَ نَفْسَهُ رَبِحَ وَ مَنْ غَفَلَ عَنْهَا خَسِر
>
> One who takes account of his soul has made profit and one who becomes heedless of it has suffered loss.[i]

In another statement of his, this profit has been explained as felicity.[ii] As for the manner of carrying out self-accounting, he explains it as follows:

> عَلَى الْعَاقِلِ أَنْ يُحْصِيَ عَلَى نَفْسِهِ مَسَاوِيَهَا فِي الدِّينِ وَ الرَّأْيِ وَ الْأَخْلَاقِ وَ الْأَدَبِ فَيَجْمَعَ ذَلِكَ فِي صَدْرِهِ أَوْ فِي كِتَابٍ وَ يَعْمَلَ فِي إِزَالَتِهَا
>
> It is incumbent upon an intelligent person that he lists his evil traits pertaining to religion, beliefs, ethics and etiquette and records them in his heart or in a book and then strives to eliminate them.[iii]

Similarly, Imam al-Kāẓim (peace be upon him) describes the outcome of self-accounting in the following words:

> لَيْسَ مِنَّا مَنْ لَمْ يُحَاسِبْ نَفْسَهُ فِي كُلِّ يَوْمٍ فَإِنْ عَمِلَ حَسَناً اسْتَزَادَ اللَّهَ وَ إِنْ عَمِلَ سَيِّئاً اسْتَغْفَرَ اللَّهَ مِنْهُ وَ تَابَ إِلَيْهِ.
>
> He is not from us, one who does not take account of his soul each day such that if he has performed a good deed, he seeks that Allah increase him and if he has performed an evil deed, then he seeks forgiveness from Allah and repents to Him.[iv]

---

i. Majlisī, Bihār al-Anwār, 70:73, narration 27

ii. Nūrī, Mustadrak al-Wasāʾil, 12:154, 13761

iii. al-Āmudī, Ghurar al-Ḥikam, narration 8927

iv. al-Kulaynī, al-Kāfī, 2:453, narration 2

Therefore, to manage the affairs of the soul, one must persistently follow this method until gradually it becomes a fixed trait (*malakah*) in him. Although if he commits a mistake, then he should not despair. Rather, he should renew and strengthen his determination to continue the path of obedience. This is one of the advantages of this method, that it strengthens a person's will power for performing actions. Additionally, this method ensures that man's activities are performed in a regular and organized manner. Having such regularity and organization in one's affairs--both affairs of this world and the Hereafter—is one of the highly emphasized instructions of the *awliyāʾ* of religion (peace be upon them).

It is true that initially *murāqabah* (self-vigilance) and *muḥāsabah* (self-accounting) will be performed in a sluggish and slow manner. This is only natural, because man's soul desires to be free and in most cases does not like to be under limitations and restraints. Therefore, it is necessary that one persistently continue—even in the least possible manner—such that slowly and gradually this vigilance increases and encompasses all the daily activities of that person's life. In particular, if someone has social responsibilities, then applying this instrumental method and making it a habit will take a longer time.

Certainly, one who has a lofty goal in his life and efforts, must have a strong motivation and earnest determination to move towards it and persevere, so that he can reach the desired outcomes. To achieve this, self-stipulation (*mushāraṭah*) is an essential element whereby the wayfarer at the beginning of the day, exhorts his own soul towards the duties of servitude and warns it that if it does not perform its duties then it will suffer loss. As Imam ʿAlī (peace be upon him) says:

كُنْ وَصِيَّ نَفْسِك

Be an admonisher for your soul.[i]

And:

مَنْ أَهْمَلَ نَفْسَهُ خَسِر

---

i. al-Āmudī, Ghurar al-Hikam, narration 7171

> One who neglects his soul [leaves it without supervision], suffers loss.[(i)]

When taking account of his soul, if the wayfarer realizes that he was not on the path of servitude and missed an obligatory action or performed a prohibited action, he should reproach himself. That is because, he did not abide by the stipulation and agreement made pertaining his soul and was not watchful over it. As the great Divine teacher, Amīr al-Mu'minīn 'Alī (peace be upon him) has advised:

كُنْ مُؤَاخِذاً نَفْسَكَ مُغَالِباً سُوءَ طَبْعِك

> Punish your soul and prevail over the evil in your temperament.[(ii)]

Of course, the reproaching of the soul should not be severe and continuous. Moreover, chastising it should be in accordance with the instructions of the Divine *sharī'ah* and man should not impose upon himself another heavy burden like making a vow (*nadhr*) or taking an oath (*qasam*) or a pledge (*'ahd*) to not perform a permissible action. That is because, a servant should act with leniency and moderateness with his soul. The Imams (peace be upon them) have said in this regard:

إِنَ نَفْسَكَ مَطِيَّتُكَ إِنْ أَجْهَدْتَهَا قَتَلْتَهَا وَ إِنْ رَفَقْتَ بِهَا أَبْقَيْتَهَا

> Indeed, your soul is your steed. If you exert it, you will kill it [it will throw you down from its back and flee all responsibility] but if you are gentle with it, you will preserve it.[(iii)]

Therefore, according to Imam 'Alī's (peace be upon him) statement, reprimanding should be based on renewing the determination to continue performing the obligatory actions and forsaking the prohibited actions. In this manner, self-vigilance and self-accounting can be carried out with increased strength. Although at the onset of the spiritual journey it is difficult to implement this, but this has a profound effect on one's spiritual development. Therefore, one should not become

---

i. Ibid., narration 4753

ii. Ibid., narration 4822

iii. Ibid., narration 3643

heedless of this and under this pretext, embark upon performing other easy acts like reciting *dhikr* or performing certain devotional acts for forty days, while not paying attention to *murāqabah* and *muḥāsabah*. That is because, even if these other actions are desirable in the *shar'īah*, they will not have a noticeable effect. At the same time, paying attention to *mustaḥabb* (supererogatory) actions on this path is also necessary.

3) Performing Mustahabb Actions and Leaving Makrūh (Disapproved) Actions

In order to strengthen and reinforce the first level of servitude—in addition to paying attention to performing obligatory actions and refraining from prohibited actions and being vigilant about this—one must also give importance to some of the *mustaḥabb* actions as well. As Imam al-Bāqir (peace be upon him) has said that the verse about those who pray that says, "those who persevere in their prayers" [(i)], refers to the *nāfilah*. [(ii)] Of course, the word '*nāfilah*' means any *mustaḥabb* action. That is because, the word '*nāfilah*' comes from the root word '*nafl*' which means 'an additional and surplus entity' [(iii)] and the *mustaḥabb* actions are in addition to the obligatory actions. Again, as said by Imam al-Bāqir (peace be upon him), these *mustaḥabb* actions compensate for shortcomings in the obligatory actions. [(iv)]

It is for this reason that in the Divine *sharī'ah*—in the different matters of life—many supererogatory instructions have been mentioned in addition to the obligatory actions. By observing them, man's actions become luminous and lead to the enlightenment of his heart. Therefore, in the famous narration of '*man balagh*' Imam al-Ṣādiq (peace be upon him) says:

مَنْ سَمِعَ شَيْئاً مِنَ الثَّوَابِ عَلَى شَيْءٍ فَصَنَعَهُ كَانَ لَهُ وَ إِنْ لَمْ يَكُنْ عَلَى مَا بَلَغَهُ

i. (70:23)

ii. al-Kulaynī, al-Kāfī, 3:269, narration 12

iii. al-Isfahānī, al-Mufradāt, the root nafala

iv. al-Kulaynī, al-Kāfī, 3:269, narration 11

> One who hears about a certain reward [*thawāb*] for a certain action that he then performs, will be granted it [that reward], even if [in reality] the matter was not as had reached him. [i]

Of course, one should pay attention to this statement of Imam ʿAlī (peace be upon him):

إِذَا أَضَرَّتِ النَّوَافِلُ بِالْفَرَائِضِ فَارْفُضُوهَا

> If the supererogatory actions harm the obligatory actions, then abandon them. [ii]

In other words, the foundation of servitude and obedience is to perform obligatory actions and to abandon prohibited actions. Performing *mustaḥabb* actions play a supporting role for this foundation. However, if they are destroying the foundation, then as said by Imam ʿAlī (peace be upon him), they do not lead a person to the proximity of Allah. [iii]

Therefore, even though there are etiquettes (*ādāb*) for the different matters of life (as we pointed out in the discussion about *ādāb*, and explained some of them [iv]), but that which is extremely recommended is to endure and persevere in performing virtuous actions, even if they are little. Imam al-Bāqir (peace be upon him) says in this regard:

مَا مِنْ شَيْءٍ أَحَبَّ إِلَى اللَّهِ عَزَّ وَ جَلَّ
مِنْ عَمَلٍ يُدَاوَمُ عَلَيْهِ وَ إِنْ قَلَّ

> There is nothing more beloved to Allah than an action which is performed persistently, even if it is a small action. [v]

Likewise, Imam al-Ṣādiq (peace be upon him) says:

---

i. Ibid., 2:87, narration 1 and 2

ii. al-Radī, Nahj al-Balāghah, saying 279

iii. Ibid., saying 39

iv. Refer to Chapter 2, Section 3, quality number 17

v. al-Kulaynī, al-Kāfī, 2:87, narration 3

إِذَا كَانَ الرَّجُلُ عَلَى عَمَلٍ فَلْيَدُمْ عَلَيْهِ سَنَةً ثُمَّ يَتَحَوَّلُ عَنْهُ إِنْ شَاءَ إِلَى غَيْرِهِ وَ ذَلِكَ أَنَّ لَيْلَةَ الْقَدْرِ يَكُونُ فِيهَا فِي عَامِهِ ذَلِكَ مَا شَاءَ اللَّهُ أَنْ يَكُونَ

When a person performs a certain [virtuous] action, then he should continue performing it for a year. Thereafter, if he wishes he can switch and engage himself in another action. That is because the Night of Ordainment (*Laylah al-Qadr*) will occur during that year such that Allah desires that this action takes place in it. (i)

Therefore, one who wants to traverse the path of Allah the Exalted's servitude, it is desirable that he preoccupy himself with a few actions that have a significant effect in supporting the *wājibāt* and illuminating the heart. Thereafter, slowly he can increase them such that his soul (*nafs*) becomes accustomed to it and can perceive its effects. For this reason, such *mustaḥabb* actions will now be discussed with attention to the instructions and recommendations of the Qur'ān, the Sunnah and the great personalities in the field of spiritual training (*tarbiyah*) and gnosis (*maʿrifah*).

A) Observing the Mustahabb actions related to the prayers

Prayers is one of the important branches of the religion; it has been enjoined greatly, and many outcomes and benefits have been mentioned for it. As said by Imam al-Bāqir (peace be upon him):

الصَّلَاةُ عَمُودُ الدِّينِ

Prayer is the foundational pillar of the religion. (ii)

And as said by Imam al-Ṣādiq (peace be upon him):

مَا أَعْلَمُ شَيْئاً بَعْدَ الْمَعْرِفَةِ أَفْضَلَ مِنْ هَذِهِ الصَّلَاةِ

I do not know of anything greater than prayers after Allah's

---

i. Ibid., al-Kāfī, 2:87, narration 1

ii. al-Barqī, al-Maḥāsin, 1:116, narration 117

ma'rifah (gnosis).(i)

It is also the last will of the prophets (peace be upon them).(ii) In view of this, prayer has many obligatory and *mustaḥabb* rules. As said by Imam al-Ṣādiq (peace be upon him), it has four thousand rules or chapters.(iii) The more these obligatory conditions and *mustaḥabb* etiquettes are observed, the greater the proximity to Allah that results will be. Therefore, we will explain some of important *mustaḥabb* actions related to it so that the wayfarer—at the very least—performs them. If someone wants to perform more *mustaḥabb* actions then he should refer to the book of practical laws of their *marja'* (*al-risālah al-'amaliyyah*), Mafātīḥ al-Jinān and other books that have been complied on this subject.

1) Praying at the Beginning of the Time

Imam al-Ṣādiq (peace be upon him) says in this regard:

إِنَّ فَضْلَ الْوَقْتِ الْأَوَّلِ عَلَى الْآخِرِ كَفَضْلِ الْآخِرَةِ عَلَى الدُّنْيَا

The merit of the initial time [of prayers] over the end time is like the merit of the Hereafter over the world.(iv)

2) Praying in Congregation

One of the narrators says:

قُلْتُ لِأَبِي عَبْدِ اللَّهِ ع مَا يَرْوِي النَّاسُ أَنَّ الصَّلَاةَ فِي جَمَاعَةٍ أَفْضَلُ مِنْ صَلَاةِ الرَّجُلِ وَحْدَهُ بِخَمْسٍ وَ عِشْرِينَ صَلَاةً فَقَالَ صَدَقُوا الْحَدِيثَ

I informed Imam al-Ṣādiq (peace be upon him) about what the people narrate, that the merit of praying in congregation is twenty-five times the merit of praying alone. He

---

i. al-Kulaynī, al-Kāfī, 3:264, narration 1

ii. al-Ṣadūq, Man La Yaḥḍurhū al-Faqih, 1:210, narration 638

iii. al-Kulaynī, al-Kāfī, 3:272, narration 6

iv. Ibid., 3:274, narration 6

responded, "They have said the truth." (i)

Likewise, Imam al-Bāqir (peace be upon him) in another narration says:

فَضْلُ صَلَاةِ الْجَمَاعَةِ عَلَى صَلَاةِ الرَّجُلِ فَرْداً خَمْسٌ وَ عِشْرُونَ دَرَجَةً فِي الْجَنَّةِ

The merit of congregational prayers over prayer prayed alone by a person is twenty-five stations in Paradise. (ii)

Similarly, Imam al-Ṣādiq (peace be upon him) narrates through his forefathers (peace be upon them) that the Messenger of Allah (peace and blessings be upon him and his family) said:

وَ مَنْ مَشَى إِلَى مَسْجِدٍ يَطْلُبُ فِيهِ الْجَمَاعَةَ كَانَ لَهُ بِكُلِّ خُطْوَةٍ سَبْعُونَ أَلْفَ حَسَنَةٍ وَ يُرْفَعُ لَهُ مِنَ الدَّرَجَاتِ مِثْلُ ذَلِكَ فَإِنْ مَاتَ وَ هُوَ عَلَى ذَلِكَ وَكَّلَ اللَّهُ بِهِ سَبْعِينَ أَلْفَ مَلَكٍ يَعُودُونَهُ فِي قَبْرِهِ وَ يُبَشِّرُونَهُ وَ يُؤْنِسُونَهُ فِي وَحْدَتِهِ وَ يَسْتَغْفِرُونَ لَهُ حَتَّى يُبْعَثَ.

One who walks towards a mosque intending [to pray in] congregation, seventy thousand good deeds are [written] for him for every step he takes, and he is raised a similar number of ranks. If he dies while being in this state, Allah appoints seventy thousand angels who visit him in his grave. They give him glad-tidings, they become his companions in his loneliness and they seek forgiveness for him until he is raised [from the grave]. (iii)

Also, the Messenger of Allah (peace and blessings be upon him and his family) says in a narration:

أَمَّا الْجَمَاعَةُ فَإِنَّ صُفُوفَ أُمَّتِي كَصُفُوفِ الْمَلَائِكَةِ وَ الرَّكْعَةَ فِي الْجَمَاعَةِ أَرْبَعٌ وَ عِشْرُونَ رَكْعَةً كُلُّ رَكْعَةٍ أَحَبُّ إِلَى اللَّهِ عَزَّ

---

i. Ḥurr al-Āmilī, Waṣā'il al-Shī'ah, 8:286, narration 3

ii. Ibid., 8:286, narration 5

iii. Ibid., 8:287, narration 7

وَ جَلَّ مِنْ عِبَادَةِ أَرْبَعِينَ سَنَةً ... فَمَا مِنْ مُؤْمِنٍ مَشَى إِلَى الْجَمَاعَةِ إِلَّا خَفَّفَ اللَّهُ عَلَيْهِ أَهْوَالَ يَوْمِ الْقِيَامَةِ- ثُمَّ يَأْمُرُ بِهِ إِلَى الْجَنَّةِ.

As for the congregational prayers, indeed the ranks of my Ummah [when they stand in congregation for prayers] are like the ranks of the angels. One unit of prayer in congregation is equal to twenty-four units of prayers [prayed alone] such that each unit is more beloved to Allah (the Invincible and Majestic) than forty years of worship ... Therefore, no believer walks towards the congregation except that Allah lightens the terrors of the Day of Resurrection for him and then commands that he enter the Paradise.[i]

In another narration he says:

مَنْ صَلَّى الْفَجْرَ فِي جَمَاعَةٍ ثُمَّ جَلَسَ يَذْكُرُ اللَّهَ عَزَّ وَ جَلَّ حَتَّى تَطْلُعَ الشَّمْسُ كَانَ لَهُ فِي الْفِرْدَوْسِ سَبْعُونَ دَرَجَةً بُعْدُ مَا بَيْنَ كُلِّ دَرَجَتَيْنِ كَحُضْرِ الْفَرَسِ الْجَوَادِ الْمُضَمَّرِ سَبْعِينَ سَنَةً وَ مَنْ صَلَّى الظُّهْرَ فِي جَمَاعَةٍ كَانَ لَهُ فِي جَنَّاتِ عَدْنٍ خَمْسُونَ دَرَجَةً بُعْدُ مَا بَيْنَ كُلِّ دَرَجَتَيْنِ كَحُضْرِ الْفَرَسِ الْجَوَادِ خَمْسِينَ سَنَةً وَ مَنْ صَلَّى الْعَصْرَ فِي جَمَاعَةٍ كَانَ لَهُ كَأَجْرِ ثَمَانِيَةٍ مِنْ وُلْدِ إِسْمَاعِيلَ- كُلُّهُمْ رَبُّ بَيْتٍ يُعْتِقُهُمْ وَ مَنْ صَلَّى الْمَغْرِبَ فِي جَمَاعَةٍ كَانَ لَهُ كَحَجَّةٍ مَبْرُورَةٍ وَ عُمْرَةٍ مَقْبُولَةٍ وَ مَنْ صَلَّى الْعِشَاءَ فِي جَمَاعَةٍ كَانَ لَهُ كَقِيَامِ لَيْلَةِ الْقَدْرِ.

One who prays the morning prayers (*fajr*) in congregation and thereafter sits and recites *dhikr* of Allah (the Invincible and Majestic) until sunrise, then for him are seventy stations in Paradise such that the distance between every two stations is the distance traversed by a fast horse in seventy

i. Ibid., 8:287, narration 10

> years. And one who recites the afternoon prayers (*ẓuhr*) in congregation, then for him are fifty stations in the Gardens of Eden such that the distance between every two stations is the distance traversed by a fast horse in fifty years. And one who recites the late afternoon prayers (*ʿaṣr*) in congregation, then his reward is like the reward of eight of the children of Ishmael (peace be upon him), all of whom own a house and were freed by him. And one who recites the evening prayer (*maghrib*) in congregation, for him is [the reward of] one who performed a Ḥajj an ʿUmrah that were accepted. And one who prays the late evening prayers (*ʿishāʾ*) in congregation, then his reward is like that of standing in worship in the Night of Ordainment (*Layat al-Qadr*).(i)

In view of these narrations, it becomes clear that if the congregational prayer is accompanied with *ikhlāṣ* (sincerity) and the other conditions required for the validity and acceptability of prayer, then it enjoys all these distinctions. Moreover, these recommendations are different from the emphasis given to the Friday prayer (*ṣalāt al-jumʿah*) which has its own merits.

3) Praying in the Mosque

Praying in the mosque has innumerable virtues. Imam al-Ṣādiq (peace be upon him) says:

مَنْ مَشَى إِلَى الْمَسْجِدِ لَمْ يَضَعْ رِجْلًا عَلَى رَطْبٍ وَ لَا يَابِسٍ إِلَّا سَبَّحَتْ لَهُ الْأَرْضُ إِلَى الْأَرَضِينَ السَّابِعَةِ.

> One who walks towards a mosque, he does not place his foot on anything fresh or withered except that the Earth up until the seventh Earth glorify him.(ii)

Likewise, the Messenger of Allah (peace and blessings be upon him and his family) in another narration says:

---

i. Ibid., 8:288., narration 11

ii. Ibid., 8:200, narration 1

مَنْ مَشَى إِلَى مَسْجِدٍ مِنْ مَسَاجِدِ اللَّهِ فَلَهُ بِكُلِّ خُطْوَةٍ خَطَاهَا حَتَّى يَرْجِعَ إِلَى مَنْزِلِهِ عَشْرُ حَسَنَاتٍ وَ مُحِيَ عَنْهُ عَشْرُ سَيِّئَاتٍ وَ رُفِعَ لَهُ عَشْرُ دَرَجَاتٍ.

One who walks towards a mosque from amongst Allah's mosques, then for every step he takes until he returns to his house, ten good deeds are [written] for him, ten misdeeds are erased, and he is raised ten stations.(i)

Similarly, Amīr al-Mu'minīn (peace be upon him) has said:

مَنِ اخْتَلَفَ إِلَى الْمَسْجِدِ أَصَابَ إِحْدَى الثَّمَانِ أَخاً مُسْتَفَاداً فِي اللَّهِ أَوْ عِلْماً مُسْتَطْرَفاً أَوْ آيَةً مُحْكَمَةً أَوْ يَسْمَعُ كَلِمَةً تَدُلُّهُ عَلَى هُدًى أَوْ رَحْمَةً مُنْتَظَرَةً أَوْ كَلِمَةً تَرُدُّهُ عَنْ رَدًى أَوْ يَتْرُكُ ذَنْباً خَشْيَةً أَوْ حَيَاءً.

One who regularly visits the mosque attains one of these eight: either a brother who benefits him with regards to Allah, or an interesting piece of knowledge, or a firm sign [perhaps this refers to a change in one's spiritual state]. Or he hears a word that leads him to guidance, or a mercy that he was awaiting, or a word that turns him away from perdition, or he abandons a sin due to fear or modesty.(ii)

These merits are separate from the merits mentioned for the Mosque of Kūfa, Masjid al-Ḥarām, and Masjid al-Nabī (peace and blessings be upon him and his family).(iii)

4) Reciting Adhān and Iqāmah

One other *mustaḥabb* actions of prayer that has been greatly emphasized is reciting the adhān and iqāmah. In addition to carrying a great

---

i. Ibid., 8:201, narration 3

ii. Ibid., 8:197, narration 1

iii. Ibid., 8:288

reward for the one who recites it (*mu'addhin*), Amīr al-Mu'minīn (peace be upon him) says:

مَنْ صَلَّى بِأَذَانٍ وَ إِقَامَةٍ صَلَّى خَلْفَهُ صَفَّانِ مِنَ الْمَلَائِكَةِ لَا يُرَى طَرَفَاهُمَا وَ مَنْ صَلَّى بِإِقَامَةٍ صَلَّى خَلْفَهُ مَلَكٌ.

One who prays [after reciting] adhān and iqāmah, two rows of angels pray behind him and each row is such that its end cannot been seen. And one who prays [after reciting] Iqāmah [only], an angel prays behind him.(i)

5) Reciting the *Ta'qībāt*(ii) of the Prayers

Reciting the *ta'qībāt* is also one of the *mustaḥabb* actions related to prayers which has effects in this world and the Hereafter.

Imam al-Ṣādiq (peace be upon him) says:

التَّعْقِيبُ أَبْلَغُ فِي طَلَبِ الرِّزْقِ مِنَ الضَّرْبِ فِي الْبِلَادِ.

Reciting *ta'qībāt* after prayers is more effective in seeking sustenance than journeying in the cities.(iii)

Likewise, Imam al-Bāqir (peace be upon him) says, narrating from the Messenger of Allah (peace and blessings be upon him and his family), who in turn narrates from Allah (the Invincible and Majestic), that He has said:

يَا ابْنَ آدَمَ اذْكُرْنِي بَعْدَ الْفَجْرِ سَاعَةً وَ اذْكُرْنِي بَعْدَ الْعَصْرِ سَاعَةً أَكْفِكَ مَا أَهَمَّكَ

O son of Adam! Remember me for a while after *fajr* and remember me for a while after *'aṣr* and I will suffice you in the important affairs.(iv)

---

i. Ibid., 8:382, narration 5

ii. *Ta'qībāt* literally means something which comes after another thing. Therefore, the *ta'qībāt* of prayer means those supplications and *dhikr* that have been recommended to recite after prayer.

iii. al-'Āmilī, Waṣā'il al-Shī'ah, 6:429, narration 1

iv. Ibid., narration 3

Imam al-Ṣādiq (peace be upon him) says in another narration:

إِنَّ اللّٰهَ فَرَضَ عَلَيْكُمُ الصَّلَوَاتِ الْخَمْسَ فِي أَفْضَلِ السَّاعَاتِ فَعَلَيْكُمْ بِالدُّعَاءِ فِي أَدْبَارِ الصَّلَوَاتِ.

Indeed, Allah has made the five daily prayers obligatory upon you in the best of the hours. Therefore, supplicate to Allah after the prayers.[i]

Similarly, it is quoted from this noble personality that:

يُسْتَجَابُ الدُّعَاءُ فِي أَرْبَعَةِ مَوَاطِنَ فِي الْوَتْرِ وَ بَعْدَ الْفَجْرِ وَ بَعْدَ الظُّهْرِ وَ بَعْدَ الْمَغْرِبِ

Supplications are answered in four places: In *watr,*[ii] after *fajr*, after *ẓuhr* and after *maghrib*.[iii]

The *taʿqībāt* of the prayers usually contain supplications related to the matters of the world and the Hereafter. They also contain *adhkār* that are the cause of spiritual, psychological and material relief. Therefore, it is not befitting that one remains heedless of them. At the least one should recite the *tasbīḥ* of Lady Fāṭimah (peace be upon her),[iv] as it has been emphasized greatly. Imam al-Ṣādiq (peace be upon him) says:

تَسْبِيحُ فَاطِمَةَ ع فِي كُلِّ يَوْمٍ فِي دُبُرِ كُلِّ صَلَاةٍ أَحَبُّ إِلَيَّ مِنْ صَلَاةِ أَلْفِ رَكْعَةٍ فِي كُلِّ يَوْمٍ

Reciting the *tasbīḥ* of Fāṭimah (peace be upon her) daily after every prayer is more beloved to me than reciting one thousand units of prayers every day.[v]

---

i. Ibid., 6:431, narration 8

ii. *Watr* is the one unit prayer to be recited as part of the Night Prayer (*Ṣalāt al-Layl*).

iii. Ibid., 6:430, narration 4

iv. The *tasbīḥ* of Lady Fāṭimah (peace be upon her) is a *dhikr* to be recited after every prayer. It comprises of '*Allāhu akbar*' thirty-four times, '*al-ḥamdulillāah*' thirty-three times and '*subḥānallah*' thirty-three times.

v. al-ʿĀmilī, Waṣāʾil al-Shīʿah, 6:443, narration 2

B) Reciting Mustahabb prayers

The Imams (peace be upon them) in their sayings, have laid more emphasis on reciting *mustaḥabb* prayers than performing other *mustaḥabb* actions, as can be understood from the narrations that were just mentioned. In addition to that, Imam al-Ṣādiq (peace be upon him) says:

إِنَّ طَاعَةَ اللَّهِ عَزَّ وَ جَلَّ خِدْمَتُهُ فِي الْأَرْضِ وَ لَيْسَ شَيْءٌ مِنْ خِدْمَتِهِ يَعْدِلُ الصَّلَاةَ فَمِنْ ثَمَّ نَادَتِ الْمَلَائِكَةُ زَكَرِيَّا وَ هُوَ قَائِمٌ يُصَلِّي فِي الْمِحْرَابِ

> Indeed, Allah's (the Invincible and Majestic) obedience is to serve Him in the Earth and there is no act through which He is served that equals prayers. It is for this reason that the angels called out to Zechariah while he stood praying in the prayer-niche.[i]

This means that a person can become someone whom the angels call out to, by reciting prayers. Likewise, this noble personality (peace be upon him) says about his Shīʿah:

شِيعَتُنَا أَهْلُ الْوَرَعِ وَ الِاجْتِهَادِ وَ أَهْلُ الْوَفَاءِ وَ الْأَمَانَةِ وَ أَهْلُ الزُّهْدِ وَ الْعِبَادَةِ أَصْحَابُ الْإِحْدَى وَ خَمْسِينَ رَكْعَةً فِي الْيَوْمِ وَ اللَّيْلَةِ الْقَائِمُونَ بِاللَّيْلِ الصَّائِمُونَ بِالنَّهَارِ يُزَكُّونَ أَمْوَالَهُمْ وَ يَحُجُّونَ الْبَيْتَ وَ يَجْتَنِبُونَ كُلَّ مُحَرَّمٍ.

> Our Shīʿah are people of piety and exerting efforts, people of loyalty and trustworthiness, people detached [from the world] and people of worship. They are those who abide by the fifty-one units of prayers during the day and the night.[ii] They stand in prayers during the night and fast during the day. They pay *zakāt* from their wealth, perform the Ḥajj

---

i. Ibid., 4:39, narration 5

ii. Fifty-one units of prayers during the day and the night includes the seventeen units of obligatory prayers and thirty-four units of daily *nāfilah* prayers.

and avoid every prohibited action. (i)

Therefore, the most emphasis is laid on reciting the daily *nawāfil* prayers. One should start with the most important amongst them and then if he wishes he should gradually complete it and recite all of them. Hence, here we mention the most important of them in sequence.

1) The Night Prayer (Salāt al-Layl)

One of the most important *mustaḥabb* prayers is the Night Prayer. Many virtues and merits have been stated for it, to the extent that Imam al-Ṣādiq (peace be upon him) says:

مَا مِنْ عَمَلٍ حَسَنٍ يَعْمَلُهُ الْعَبْدُ إِلَّا وَ لَهُ ثَوَابٌ فِي الْقُرْآنِ إِلَّا صَلَاةَ اللَّيْلِ فَإِنَّ اللَّهَ لَمْ يُبَيِّنْ ثَوَابَهَا لِعِظَمِ خَطَرِهَا عِنْدَه فَقَال تَتَجَافَىٰ جُنُوبُهُمْ عَنِ الْمَضَاجِعِ يَدْعُونَ رَبَّهُمْ خَوْفًا وَطَمَعًا وَمِمَّا رَزَقْنَاهُمْ يُنفِقُونَ فَلا تَعْلَمُ نَفْسٌ ما أُخْفِيَ لَهُمْ مِنْ قُرَّةِ أَعْيُنٍ جَزاءً بِما كانُوا يَعْمَلُون

> There is no good deed that the servant performs but that its reward is mentioned in the Qur'ān, except the Night Prayer. For indeed, Allah has not clarified its reward due to its greatness and immensity near Him. He says, "Their sides vacate their beds to supplicate their Lord in fear and hope, and they spend out of what We have provided them. So, no one knows what delights have been kept hidden for them as a reward for what they used to do." (ii) (iii)

Similarly, the Messenger of Allah (peace and blessings be upon him and his family) enjoined Imam ʿAlī (peace be upon him) three times about the Night Prayer. (iv)

Imam al-Ṣādiq (peace be upon him) also says:

---

i. al-ʿĀmilī, Waṣā'il al-Shīʿah, 4:57, narration 26

ii. (32:16-17)

iii. al-ʿĀmilī, Waṣā'il al-Shīʿah, 8:163, narration 13

iv. Ibid., 8:145, narration 1

شَرَفُ الْمُؤْمِنِ صَلَاتُهُ بِاللَّيْل

The honour of a believer is his prayer during the night.[(i)]

Likewise, in another narration under the verse of the Qur᾿ān, "Indeed good deeds do away with misdeeds"[(ii)], he elaborates:

صَلَاةُ الْمُؤْمِنِ بِاللَّيْلِ تَذْهَبُ بِمَا عَمِلَ مِنْ ذَنْبٍ بِالنَّهَارِ

A believer's prayer during the night does away with the misdeeds he performed during the daytime.[(iii)]

Similarly, Imam al-Bāqir (peace be upon him) while explaining Allah's (the Invincible and Majestic) words, "Their sides vacate their beds"[(iv)] says:

أُنْزِلَتْ فِي أَمِيرِ الْمُؤْمِنِينَ ع- وَ أَتْبَاعِهِ مِنْ شِيعَتِنَا يَنَامُونَ فِي أَوَّلِ اللَّيْلِ فَإِذَا ذَهَبَ ثُلُثَا اللَّيْلِ أَوْ مَا شَاءَ اللَّهُ فَزِعُوا إِلَى رَبِّهِمْ رَاغِبِينَ رَاهِبِينَ طَامِعِينَ فِيمَا عِنْدَهُ فَذَكَرَهُمُ اللَّهُ فِي كِتَابِهِ لِنَبِيِّهِ ص وَ أَخْبَرَهُ بِمَا أَعْطَاهُمْ وَ أَنَّهُ أَسْكَنَهُمْ فِي جِوَارِهِ أَدْخَلَهُمْ جَنَّتَهُ وَ آمَنَ خَوْفَهُمْ وَ آمَنَ رَوْعَتَهُم

This verse was revealed in [the merit] of Amīr al-Mu᾿minīn (peace be upon him) and his followers amongst our Shīʿah. They sleep in the beginning of the night and when two-thirds of the night—or that which Allah wishes—has passed, they seek refuge in Allah with eagerness and awe, and with desire for what is with Him. So, Allah has reminded His Prophet (peace and blessings be upon him and his family) about them in His Book and has informed him of that which He has bestowed upon them such that He has settled them in His vicinity, made them enter His paradise, and secured them from His fear and His awe [on the Day

i. Ibid.

ii. (11:114)

iii. al-ʿĀmilī, Waṣā᾿il al-Shīʿah, 8:146, narration 4

iv. (32:16)

of Resurrection].(i)

Imam al-Ṣādiq (peace be upon him) also in a narration says:

صَلَاةُ اللَّيْلِ تُحَسِّنُ الْوَجْهَ وَ تُحَسِّنُ الْخُلُقَ وَ تُطَيِّبُ الرِّيحَ وَ تُدِرُّ الرِّزْقَ وَ تَقْضِي الدَّيْنَ وَ تَذْهَبُ بِالْهَمِّ وَ تَجْلُو الْبَصَر

The Night Prayer makes the face beautiful, beautifies the *akhlāq*, makes a person pleasant-smelling, provides abundant sustenance, pays off loans, removes worry and makes the eyes radiant.(ii)

2) The Daily Nāfilah Prayers

After recommending the Night Prayer, the next to be recommended is the *nāfilah* of the morning prayer. As Imam al-Bāqir (peace be upon him) says to one of the narrators:

صَلِّ صَلَاةَ اللَّيْلِ وَ الْوَتْرَ وَ الرَّكْعَتَيْنِ فِي الْمَحْمِل

Recite the Night Prayer, the *watr* prayer and two units [of *nāfilah* of fajr] whilst in the litter [whilst you are on the journey].(iii) (iv)

It is reported in a narration that the Messenger of Allah (peace and blessings be upon him and his family) would recites these thirteen units of prayers (the eight units of Night Prayer, two units of *shaf* prayers, one unit of *watr* prayer and the *nāfilah* of the morning prayer), regardless of whether he was a on a journey or in his homeland.(v)

Next after the *nāfilah* of the morning prayer, the *nāfilah* of the *maghrib* prayer enjoys special importance such that it is not dropped

---

i. al-ʿĀmilī, Waṣā'il al-Shīʿah, 8:154, narration 26

ii. Ibid., 8:151, narration 17. For more information about the Night Prayer refer to the book Mafātīḥ al-Jinān or the *risāalah al-ʿamaliyyah* (th practical Islamic Laws book) of your *marjaʿ* (From the author).

iii. A litter is a covered box-like structure which was mounted on an animal such as a camel. It was used as a mode of transport in the olden days.

iv. al-ʿĀmilī, Waṣā'il al-Shīʿah, 4:90, narration 2

v. Ibid., 4:91, narration 6

while travelling or at home.[i]

Likewise, praying the *nāfilah* of the *ẓuhr* and *ʿaṣr* prayers has been greatly emphasized in numerous narrations. Imam al-Bāqir (peace be upon him) says:

كَانَ رَسُولُ اللَّهِ ص لَا يُصَلِّي بِالنَّهَارِ شَيْئاً حَتَّى تَزُولَ الشَّمْسُ وَ إِذَا زَالَتْ صَلَّى ثَمَانِيَ رَكَعَاتٍ وَ هِيَ صَلَاةُ الْأَوَّابِينَ تُفَتَّحُ فِي تِلْكَ السَّاعَةِ أَبْوَابُ السَّمَاءِ وَ يُسْتَجَابُ الدُّعَاءُ وَ تَهُبُّ الرِّيَاحُ وَ يَنْظُرُ اللَّهُ إِلَى خَلْقِه

> The Messenger of Allah (peace and blessings be upon him and his family) would not recite any prayer until the sun would start declining [at the midday] and when the sun would start declining he would recite eight units of prayers. And that is the prayer of the penitents. In that hour, the doors of the Heavens are opened, prayers are answered, the breeze [of Divine mercy] blows and Allah looks at His creation.[ii]

In several narrations, the *nāfilah* of *ʿishā* has also become recommended. Imam al-Bāqir (peace be upon him) says:

مَنْ كَانَ يُؤْمِنُ بِاللَّهِ وَ الْيَوْمِ الْآخِرِ فَلَا يَبِيتَنَّ إِلَّا بِوَتْرٍ

> One who has faith in Allah and the Last Day, then he should not sleep at night except after reciting the *watr*.[iii]

In this narration, the *nāfilah* of *ʿishā* is termed as '*watr*' but this is different from the *watr* prayer which is recited along with the Night Prayer. Rather, it has been named *watr* (literally meaning single or one) because it is reckoned as one unit of prayer.

In view of the recommendations of the Imams (peace be upon them), the wayfarers of the path towards Allah—those who wish to set out on this path and achieve its spiritual results—must act firstly with leniency

---

i. Ibid., 4:86, narration 1

ii. Ibid., 4:61, narration 6

iii. Ibid., 4:94, narration 1

and moderation, and secondly with a light but constant and lasting practical routine. Bearing this in mind, it is necessary that they engage in performing these *nāfilah* prayers prescribed during the day and the night, to the extent of their physical strength and the inclination of the soul. Also, they should gradually increase this amount so that soul becomes accustomed to performing them. They should start with the most important *nāfilah* prayers until they succeed in performing all of them. For this same reason (to slowly train the believer), it is recommended to perform their *qaḍā*. It is possible to perform the *qaḍā* of the *nāfilah* of the daytime during night and vice versa. (i)

In fact, it has been recommended in the narrations that if one desires to profit from the merits of the *nāfilah* prayers and is not able to perform their *qaḍā*, then for every two units of prayers he can give one *mudd* (750 grams) of food to the needy. (ii)

3) Other Mustahabb Prayers

In view of the points mentioned, it is suitable that the wayfarer—to remain on the path of servitude—engages in performing some other *mustaḥabb* prayers that have been recommended to be performed on specific days of the week or months of the lunar calendar. This is because each of these has its own radiance, especially during the noble months of Rajab, Shaʿbān and Ramaḍān.

In addition to this, there are prayers recommended by the Imams (peace be upon them) to the Shīʿah for the fulfilment of various needs. This shows that in face of difficulties, in addition to performing the outward duties and employing the overt means of every affair, man must also express his humility in front of the absolutely independent Divine presence. This is so that Allah directs the effects of these means towards the desired result. These prayers have been mentioned in the noble book Mafātīḥ al-Jinān and other books of Islamic narrations.

---

i. Ibid., 4:75-78

ii. Ibid., 4:75, narration 2

C) Reciting the Noble Qurʾān

In various verses and narrations, reciting the Noble Qurʾān, teaching and learning it, has all been greatly recommended; innumerable merits have been stated for these actions. (i) Even merely listening to and looking at it has been considered worship. (ii)

Imam al-Ṣādiq (peace be upon him) says:

> مَنِ اسْتَمَعَ حَرْفاً مِنْ كِتَابِ اللَّهِ مِنْ غَيْرِ قِرَاءَةٍ كَتَبَ اللَّهُ لَهُ حَسَنَةً وَ مَحَا عَنْهُ سَيِّئَةً وَ رَفَعَ لَهُ دَرَجَةً وَ مَنْ قَرَأَ نَظَراً مِنْ غَيْرِ صَلَاةٍ كَتَبَ اللَّهُ لَهُ بِكُلِّ حَرْفٍ حَسَنَةً وَ مَحَا عَنْهُ سَيِّئَةً وَ رَفَعَ لَهُ دَرَجَةً وَ مَنْ تَعَلَّمَ مِنْهُ حَرْفاً ظَاهِراً كَتَبَ اللَّهُ لَهُ عَشْرَ حَسَنَاتٍ وَ مَحَا عَنْهُ عَشْرَ سَيِّئَاتٍ وَ رَفَعَ لَهُ عَشْرَ دَرَجَاتٍ قَالَ لَا أَقُولُ: بِكُلِّ آيَةٍ وَ لَكِنْ بِكُلِّ حَرْفٍ بَاءٍ أَوْ تَاءٍ أَوْ شِبْهِهِمَا قَالَ وَ مَنْ قَرَأَ حَرْفاً وَ هُوَ جَالِسٌ فِي صَلَاةٍ كَتَبَ اللَّهُ لَهُ بِهِ خَمْسِينَ حَسَنَةً وَ مَحَا عَنْهُ خَمْسِينَ سَيِّئَةً وَ رَفَعَ لَهُ خَمْسِينَ دَرَجَةً وَ مَنْ قَرَأَ حَرْفاً وَ هُوَ قَائِمٌ فِي صَلَاتِهِ كَتَبَ اللَّهُ لَهُ مِائَةَ حَسَنَةٍ وَ مَحَا عَنْهُ مِائَةَ سَيِّئَةٍ وَ رَفَعَ لَهُ مِائَةَ دَرَجَةٍ وَ مَنْ خَتَمَهُ كَانَتْ لَهُ دَعْوَةٌ مُسْتَجَابَةٌ مُؤَخَّرَةً أَوْ مُعَجَّلَةً
>
> "One who listens to one letter from the Book of Allah without reciting it, Allah writes one good for him, erases one evil deed from him and raises him one rank. And one who recites it and looks at it while he is not in prayer, then [again] for every letter Allah writes one good deed for him, erases one evil deed from him, and raises him one rank. And one who learns one apparent letter from it [the Qurʾān], Allah writes ten good deeds for him, erases ten evil deeds

i. Ibid., 6:165-260

ii. Ibid., 6:205, narration 5-6

from him, and raises him ten ranks." Then he said, "I am not saying for every verse, rather for every letter--*bāʾ*, *tāʾ* or [any letter] like them." Then he said, "And one who recites a letter while sitting in prayer, Allah writes fifty good deeds for him, erases fifty evil deeds from him, and raises him fifty ranks. And one who recites a letter while standing in prayer, Allah writes a hundred good deeds for him, erases a hundred evil deeds from him and raises him a hundred ranks. And one who completes a recitation of the Qurʾān, his prayers are answered, either swiftly or with delay." (i)

Likewise, it is recommended to recite the Qurʾān in every state and merits have been mentioned for its specific *sūrahs* (chapters). However, it is suitable that the wayfarer acts upon this statement of Imam al-Ṣādiq (peace be upon him):

الْقُرْآنُ عَهْدُ اللَّهِ إِلَى خَلْقِهِ فَقَدْ يَنْبَغِي لِلْمَرْءِ الْمُسْلِمِ أَنْ يَنْظُرَ فِي عَهْدِهِ وَ أَنْ يَقْرَأَ مِنْهُ فِي كُلِّ يَوْمٍ خَمْسِينَ آيَةً

The Quran is Allah's covenant with His creation. Therefore, it is befitting for a Muslim that he looks at His covenant and recites fifty verses from it every day. (ii)

Similarly, Imam al-Ṣādiq (peace be upon him) narrates from Amīr al-Muʾminīn (peace be upon him):

الْبَيْتُ الَّذِي يُقْرَأُ فِيهِ الْقُرْآنُ- وَ يُذْكَرُ اللَّهُ عَزَّ وَ جَلَّ فِيهِ تَكْثُرُ بَرَكَتُهُ وَ تَحْضُرُهُ الْمَلَائِكَةُ وَ تَهْجُرُهُ الشَّيَاطِينُ وَ يُضِيءُ لِأَهْلِ السَّمَاءِ كَمَا تُضِيءُ الْكَوَاكِبُ لِأَهْلِ الْأَرْضِ وَ إِنَّ الْبَيْتَ الَّذِي لَا يُقْرَأُ فِيهِ الْقُرْآنُ- وَ لَا يُذْكَرُ اللَّهُ عَزَّ وَ جَلَّ فِيهِ تَقِلُّ بَرَكَتُهُ وَ تَهْجُرُهُ الْمَلَائِكَةُ وَ تَحْضُرُهُ الشَّيَاطِينُ

The house in which the Qurʾān is recited and Allah (the Invincible and Majestic) is remembered, its blessing

---

i. Ibid., 6:188, narration 6

ii. Ibid., 6:198, narration 1

increases, angels visit it, and the devils keep away from it. It shines for the inhabitants of the Heaven, just as the stars shine for the inhabitants of the Earth. And [as for] the house in which the Qur'ān is not recited and Allah (the Invincible and Majestic) is not remembered, its blessing decreases, angels keep away from it and the devils visit it.(i)

D) Reciting Supplications (Du'ā') and Dhikr(ii)

Reciting supplications and praying for the fulfilment of one's needs is one of the matters that is greatly recommended in the Qur'ān and the Sunnah. It is termed as worship (*'ibādah*),(iii) the foundation of worship,(iv) and in fact the best type of worship.(v) Imam al-Bāqir (peace be upon him) has introduced those who are disdainful of Allah's worship and do not ask Him for that which is with Him, as being the most hateful servants in the eyes of Allah.(vi) Therefore, when asked which worship is better and more meritorious, he replied:

مَا مِنْ شَيْءٍ أَفْضَلَ عِنْدَ اللّٰهِ عَزَّ وَ جَلَّ مِنْ أَنْ يُسْأَلَ وَ يُطْلَبَ مِمَّا عِنْدَه

There is nothing more meritorious in the eyes of Allah (the Invincible and Majestic) than asking for and seeking that which is with Him.(vii)

Likewise, one of the narrators says:

---

i. Ibid., 6:199, narration 2

ii. Lexically the word *dhikr* (plural is *adhkār*) means to remember or remind. As an Islamic term it is used to refer to the words and phrases by which Almighty Allah is mentioned, praised, thanked, glorified, or besought for help.

iii. Ibid., 7:24, narration 4

iv. Ibid., 7:28, narration 14

v. Ibid., 7:30, narration 1

vi. Ibid., 7:23, narration 3

vii. Ibid., 7:30, narration 2

سَمِعْتُ أَبَا عَبْدِ اللَّهِ ع يَقُولُ عَلَيْكُمْ بِالدُّعَاءِ فَإِنَّكُمْ لَا تَقَرَّبُونَ بِمِثْلِه

I heard Imam al-Ṣādiq (peace be upon him) say, "I enjoin you to supplicate. For there is nothing like it for achieving proximity [to Allah]." (i)

In any case, supplications have two facets to them. The first is invoking Allah the Immaculate with attributes of beauty and majesty, while the second is imploring Him to fulfil one's needs to do with this world and the Hereafter. Both have been recommended and etiquettes (*ādāb*) regarding them have been mentioned. Similarly, numerous supplications pertaining to both facets have been narrated from the Imams (peace be upon them). These supplications contain an ocean of *tawḥīdī*, moral, educative and practical teachings. Such supplications are one of the unique features of the Shīʿah creed. No other sect—be it Islamic or non-Islamic—possesses such inexhaustible teachings.

Supplications for different occasions, times, places and for various needs have been narrated from the Ahl al-Bayt (peace be upon them), such that there is no need for those who make a business out of writing supplications. One should simply recite these supplications and humbly implore the Sufficient Lord, after preparing their necessary conditions, the most important of which is having firm belief in their effectiveness. Therefore, supplicating frequently has been recommended in the narrations. Imam al-Ṣādiq (peace be upon him) says:

فَإِنَّ اللَّهَ يُحِبُّ مِنْ عِبَادِهِ الْمُؤْمِنِينَ أَنْ يَدْعُوه

Indeed, Allah loves that his believing servants invoke him. (ii)

Discussion about Dhikr

Based on previous discussions, *dhikr* is divided into three types: that of the heart, that of one's action (practical), and that of the tongue (verbal). Each has its own importance and effects. The fundamental

---

i. Ibid., narration 3

ii. Ibid., 7:26, narration 6

type of *dhikr* is the *dhikr* of the heart and one's action, which was discussed previously. [i] At the same time however, one should not be heedless of the verbal *dhikr* that have been mentioned and recommended by the Ahl al-Bayt (peace be upon them) for various actions and for different days and places. Imam al-Bāqir (peace be upon him) says:

> لَا يَزَالُ الْمُؤْمِنُ فِي صَلَاةٍ مَا كَانَ فِي ذِكْرِ اللَّهِ عَزَّ وَ جَلَّ قَائِماً كَانَ أَوْ جَالِساً أَوْ مُضْطَجِعاً إِنَّ اللَّهَ عَزَّ وَ جَلَّ يَقُولُ الَّذِينَ يَذْكُرُونَ اللَّهَ قِيَاماً وَ قُعُوداً وَ عَلَى جُنُوبِهِمْ
>
> A believer is perpetually in the state of prayer as long as he remembers [does *dhikr* of] Allah (the Invincible and Majestic), whether he is standing, sitting, or lying down. Verily Allah (the Invincible and Majestic) says, "[They] remember Allah standing, sitting, and lying on their sides [when they are asleep]." [ii]

Likewise, Imam al-Ṣādiq (peace be upon him) says:

> أَوْحَى اللَّهُ إِلَى مُوسَى يَا مُوسَى ... لَا تَدَعْ ذِكْرِي عَلَى كُلِّ حَالٍ ... وَ إِنَّ تَرْكَ ذِكْرِي يُقَسِّي الْقُلُوب
>
> Allah revealed to Moses, "O Moses ... do not disregard my remembrance in any situation ... For indeed, abandoning my remembrance hardens the hearts.' [iii]

The Noblest Prophet (peace and blessings be upon him and his family) also says:

> أَكْسَلُ النَّاسِ عَبْدٌ صَحِيحٌ فَارِغٌ لَا يَذْكُرُ اللَّهَ بِشَفَةٍ وَ لَا بِلِسَان
>
> The laziest of people is a servant who is healthy and unoccupied but does not remember Allah with his month or

---

i. Reference to these different types of *dhikr* was made towards the end of Chapter Four, Section Two. Refer to the title, 'Allah's Remembrance'.

ii. al-ʿĀmilī, Waṣā'il al-Shīʿah, 7:150, narration 5

iii. Ibid., 7:151, narration 1

his tongue.[i]

It is reported that:

عَنْ أَبِي عَبْدِ اللَّهِ ع قَال مَا مِنْ شَيْءٍ إِلَّا وَ لَهُ حَدٌّ يَنْتَهِي إِلَيْهِ إِلَّا الذِّكْرَ فَلَيْسَ لَهُ حَدٌّ يَنْتَهِي إِلَيْه ... ثُمَّ تَلَا يا أَيُّهَا الَّذِينَ آمَنُوا اذْكُرُوا اللَّهَ ذِكْراً كَثِيراً وَ سَبِّحُوهُ بُكْرَةً وَ أَصِيلًا ... قَالَ وَ كَانَ أَبِي كَثِيرَ الذِّكْرِ لَقَدْ كُنْتُ أَمْشِي مَعَهُ وَ إِنَّهُ لَيَذْكُرُ اللَّهَ وَ آكُلُ مَعَه الطَّعَامَ وَ إِنَّهُ لَيَذْكُرُ اللَّهَ وَ لَقَدْ كَانَ يُحَدِّثُ الْقَوْمَ وَ مَا يَشْغَلُهُ ذَلِكَ عَنْ ذِكْرِ اللَّهِ وَ كُنْتُ أَرَى لِسَانَهُ لَازِقاً بِحَنَكِهِ يَقُولُ لَا إِلَهَ إِلَّا اللَّه ... ثُمَّ قَالَ جَاءَ رَجُلٌ إِلَى النَّبِيِّ ص- فَقَالَ مَنْ خَيْرُ أَهْلِ الْمَسْجِدِ فَقَالَ أَكْثَرُهُمْ لِلَّهِ عَزَّ وَ جَلَّ ذِكْرا

Imam al-Sadiq (peace be upon him) said, "For everything there is a limit where it ends [that action is finished and then there is no more responsibility], except for *dhikr*. There is no limit for it where it ends." Thereafter he recited [the verses that command], "O you who have faith! Remember Allah with frequent remembrance and glorify Him morning and evening."[ii] ... [Then] he said, "My father would remember Allah frequently. I would walk alongside him, and he would be remembering Allah. I would eat with him, and he would be remembering Allah. And indeed, when he would be speaking with the people that still did not preoccupy him from Allah's remembrance. I would see his tongue stuck to his chin as he would be reciting, '*lā ilāhā illā Allah*'" ... then he said, "A man came to the Prophet (peace and blessings be upon him and his family) and asked, "Who is the best of the people of the mosque?" He replied, "The one who remembers Allah (the Invincible and Majestic) the most."[iii]

---

i. Ibid., narration 2

ii. (33:41-42)

iii. al-ʿĀmilī, Waṣā'il al-Shīʿah, 7:154, narration 2

In conclusion, innumerous merits have been mentioned for *dhikr*. Therefore, it necessary for a person who is on the path of reaching Allah and achieving His servitude that:

Firstly, he must not pay attention to every *dhikr* that comes to him from anyone. Rather, in the first stage, he should adhere devoutly to the *adhkār* that have come from the true people of *dhikr* (the Imams, peace be upon them). That is because, they spiritually encompass the realities of the world and the temperaments of man. They are fully aware of man's various needs, especially his spiritual needs, as well as the relationship between these needs and the appearance of Divine perfections in the world and in man's existence. The appearance of these perfections is known as the manifestation of Divine names and attributes. Also, it is through the Imams (peace be upon them) that these realities are invoked and requested. Therefore, the *dhikrs* should be learned from their speech and conduct.

Secondly, he must devoutly and sincerely adhere to their instructions. With such attention and belief, undoubtedly no harm will come to him. Rather, he will achieve its outcome and obtain its benefit.

Thirdly, if someone gives him a specific instruction about a certain *dhikr*, then he can rely on it specifically and benefit from it on one condition. The condition is that the one who gave him the *dhikr* must be a qualified individual who keeps in view and abides by the sayings of the Imams (peace be upon them) and is familiar with their *tawḥīdī*, ethical, educational and practical teachings. Such an individual must have benefitted from the methods of training (*tarbiyah*) taught by the Imams (peace be upon them) and thus be able to give such instructions. Naturally, this is not for everyone.

Fourthly, reciting the *adhkār* narrated from Ahl al-Bayt (peace be upon them) is extremely desirable and necessary for everyone, especially for those who want to traverse the path of Allah's servitude without being in contact with a spiritual teacher. From amongst them, special attention has been given to the following *adhkār*: the *taʿqībāt* of the prayers, *adhkār* for the morning and the evening, *adhkār* for the night of Friday and its daytime,[i] as well as *adhkār* of the noble months such as Rajab, Shaʿbān, Ramaḍān and Dhū al-Ḥijjah.

Generally speaking, these *adhkār* are a collection of recitations seeking forgiveness (*istighfār*), saying '*lā ilāhā illā Allah*', reciting *takbīr*,[ii] *alḥamdulillāh*, *subḥānallāh*, *ṣalawāt*, and *istiʿādhah*. *Istiʿādhah* means to seek refuge in Allah from the evil of the devils—both devils of the men and jinn—from spiritual, psychological and material calamities and afflictions. Each one of these *adhkār* is a real medicine for various ailments of the human being. The respectable book Mafātīḥ al-Jinān is sufficient for the general masses for carrying out these *adhkār*. However, those who want to refer to the primary sources are recommended to refer to the chapter on *dhikr* in the books Uṣūl al-Kāfī, Wasāʾil al-Shīʿah, Mustadrak al-Wasāʾil as well as the book Miftāḥ al-Falāḥ of Shaykh Bahāʾī.

Remembrance of Death

In numero1us narrations, remembering death and the resurrection has been highly recommended. That is because it has a considerable effect in purifying the soul and severing the non-Divine attachments from man's soul. It is due to this that the Messenger of Allah (peace and blessings be upon him and his family) says:

أَكْثِرُوا مِنْ ذِكْرِ هَادِمِ اللَّذَّاتِ فَقِيلَ يَا رَسُولَ اللَّهِ فَمَا هَادِمُ اللَّذَّاتِ قَالَ الْمَوْتُ فَإِنَّ أَكْيَسَ الْمُؤْمِنِينَ أَكْثَرُهُمْ ذِكْراً لِلْمَوْتِ و أَشَدُّهُمْ لَهُ اسْتِعْدَادا

> "Remember the destroyer of pleasures often." He was asked, "O Messenger of Allah! What is the destroyer of pleasures?" He said, "Death. For indeed the most astute of believers is

---

i. The night of Friday refers to Thursday night.

ii. *Takbīr* means to recite the phrase 'Allāhu Akbar' (Allah is greater). In a narration from the sixth Imam (peace be upon him) he explains the meaning of takbīr saying,

اللَّهُ أَكْبَرُ مِنْ أَنْ يُوصَفَ

Allah is greater than can be described

al-ʿĀmilī, Waṣāʾil al-Shīʿah, 7:191, narration 1

the one who remembers death the most and is the most prepared for it." (i)

Likewise, Imam al-Ṣādiq (peace be upon him) says in this regard:

ذِكْرُ الْمَوْتِ يُمِيتُ الشَّهَوَاتِ فِي النَّفْسِ وَ يَقْلَعُ مَنَابِتَ الْغَفْلَةِ وَ يُقَوِّي الْقَلْبَ بِمَوَاعِدِ اللَّهِ وَ يُرِقُّ الطَّبْعَ وَ يَكْسِرُ أَعْلَامَ الْهَوَى وَ يُطْفِئُ نَارَ الْحِرْصِ وَ يُحَقِّرُ الدُّنْيَا

The remembrance of death kills the selfish desires, extracts the roots of heedlessness, strengthens the heart with regards to Allah's promises, makes man's temperament tender, shatters the signs of passion, extinguishes the fire of greed and debases the world [in man's eyes]. (ii)

Therefore, visiting the graveyard and escorting a funeral has been highly recommended so that the memory of death is revived in man and the above-mentioned effects are achieved. Hence, it is necessary that the wayfarer of Allah has a weekly or monthly routine, albeit a short one, to visit the graveyard and ponder about death.

E) Tawassul to the Ahl al-Bayt (Peace be Upon Them)

Tawassul means to seek a means of recourse through something, to reach someone or some position. In the Qur'ān and Sunnah, believers have been greatly enjoined to take recourse to a precise and trustworthy path and leader to reach Allah the Exalted. There is no path except the straight path (*al-ṣirāṭ al-mustaqīm*) (iii) which is the path of those who have not incurred His wrath and who are not astray. Likewise, the true leaders are only those who have been given the blessing of Divine *wilāyah*, that is the prophets (peace be upon them), the truthful, the martyrs, and the righteous. (iv) Therefore Allah the Exalted says:

---

i. Majlisī, Bihār al-Anwār, 82:167, narration 3

ii. Ibid., 6:133, narration 32

iii. (1:6-7)

iv. (4:69)

> يَـا أَيُّهَـا الَّذِيـنَ آمَنُـوا اتَّقُـوا اللَّـهَ وَابْتَغُـوا إِلَيْـهِ الْوَسِـيلَةَ وَجَاهِـدُوا فِـي سَـبِيلِهِ لَعَلَّكُـمْ تُفْلِحُـونَ
>
> O you who have faith! Be wary of Allah, and seek the means of recourse to Him, and wage *jihād* in His way, so that you may be felicitous. (5:35)
>
> يَا أَيُّهَا الَّذِينَ آمَنُوا اتَّقُوا اللَّهَ وَكُونُوا مَعَ الصَّادِقِينَ
>
> O you who have faith! Be wary of Allah and be with the Truthful. (9:119)

A sound intellect also passes the same judgment in this matter. Therefore, after having belief in the necessity of such a path and such leaders, the first and the fundamental level of *tawassul* is to accompany them and truthfully follow them, to which we have alluded in previous discussions. The second level of *tawassul* is to follow them in their merits, words and conduct as well as to harbour enmity to their enemies. This is necessary for strengthening one's relationship with them, remaining far from their enemies and continuously expressing love for them.

Imam al-Ṣādiq (peace be upon him) says:

> مَـا اجْتَمَـعَ فِـي مَجْلِـسٍ قَـوْمٌ لَـمْ يَذْكُـرُوا اللَّـهَ عَـزَّ وَ جَـلَّ وَ لَـمْ يَذْكُرُونَـا إِلَّا كَانَ ذَلِـكَ الْمَجْلِسُ حَسْـرَةً عَلَيْهِـمْ يَـوْمَ الْقِيَامَـةِ ثُـمَّ قَـالَ قَـالَ أَبُـو جَعْفَـرٍ ع إِنَّ ذِكْرَنَـا مِـنْ ذِكْـرِ اللَّـهِ وَ ذِكْـرِ عَدُوِّنَـا مِـنْ ذِكْـرِ الشَّـيْطَانِ
>
> "A group of people do not assemble in a gathering where Allah (the Invincible and Majestic) is not remembered and we are [also] not remembered, except that it will be a source of remorse for them on the Day of Resurrection." Then he said, "Imam al-Bāqir (peace be upon him) has said, 'Our remembrance is from the remembrance of Allah and the remembrance of our enemies [in a way that approves of them] is from the remembrance of Satan.'"[i]

---

i. al-Kulaynī, al-Kāfī, 2:496, narration 2

Innumerable merits have been mentioned for this level of *tawassul*. The third level of *tawassul* is to perform their *ziyārah*. This is a way of expressing love and proclaiming loyalty to them; the etiquettes and merits of this have also been mentioned. Also, for each one of the Imams (peace be upon them) exclusive *ziyārāt* have reached us from them. In addition, they have given us general *ziyārāt* that can be recited for all of them. It has been recommended to perform their *ziyārah* during the year, especially on certain special occasions. The higher a person's *maʿrifah* (gnosis) of them, their path and their methodology are, the more he will benefit from their *ziyārah*.

It is necessary for everyone—especially those who are on the path of Allah the Exalted's servitude—to have a daily relationship with them through the means of *ziyārah*, even if it is recited from far. For example, specific *ziyārāt* have been narrated to us from them that are to be recited during the days of the week. Each day of the week has a *ziyārah* for one of the Imams or a few them (peace be upon them). This has been mentioned in Mafātīḥ al-Jinān.[i] Likewise, it is necessary that the wayfarer recites a *ziyārah* for the Imam of the time (peace be upon him) every day, even if it is a short one. Such *ziyārāt* are also mentioned in Mafātīḥ al-Jinān.[ii] In this manner, the wayfarer's relationship of *wilāyah* with the Imams becomes perpetual and he pays attention to his duty throughout the day. Undoubtedly, the key to reaching felicity in this world and the Hereafter is by following them in terms of one's actions. Such examples of *tawassul* are intended to help us reach that goal.

The fourth level of *tawassul*, is to organize and participate in gatherings with the aim of reviving their goals, path and conduct, stating

---

i. Refer to the fifth *faṣl* (section) of the first *bāb* (chapter) in the book Mafātīḥ al-Jinān.

ii. Refer for example to the tenth *faṣl* (section) of the third *bāb* (chapter) in the book Mafātīḥ al-Jinān. Also, the commonly recited supplication starting with the words "*Allāhumma kun li waliyyik*", is a means of establishing such a daily relationship with the Imam of the time (may Allah hasten his appearance). This is also found in Mafātīḥ al-Jinān under the third *faṣl* of the second *bāb*, amongst the recommended actions for the Night of Qadr.

their merits, the oppression meted out to them, and the afflictions that befell them. These gatherings are also for explaining the oppression of those who usurped the right of *wilāyah* and *imāmah* (leadership), their path and conduct, expressing disgust towards their deeds, and shedding tears over the tragedies that befell them. This is so that the wayfarer's emotions and feelings are aroused, and he is firmly placed on the practical path of following the Imams (peace be upon them) in his actions. This level of *tawassul* has also been highly recommended in the words of the Imams (peace be upon them); many merits and results have been mentioned for such *tawassul*. Obviously, to whatever extent the contents of these gathering are better and deeper, to that extent man's relationship with the Imams (peace be upon them) will become better and deeper. This relationship should be a relationship of culture, love, *wilāyah*, the intellect and gnosis (*maʿrifah*).

Imam al-Ṣādiq (peace be upon him) says:

نَفَسُ الْمَهْمُومِ لَنَا الْمُغْتَمِّ لِظُلْمِنَا تَسْبِيحٌ وَ هَمُّهُ لِأَمْرِنَا عِبَادَةٌ وَ كِتْمَانُهُ لِسِرِّنَا جِهَادٌ فِي سَبِيلِ اللَّه

> The breathing of a person aggrieved for us, anguished at the oppression done to us is Allah's glorification. And his concern for our affair is worship, and his concealing of our secret is *jihād* in Allah's way. (i)

For this same reason, organizing and participating in gatherings of celebration and joy on the occasion of their birth is also recommended—with the condition that they should not be accompanied by forbidden acts.

The fifth level of *tawassul* is to make them intermediaries for the fulfilment of one's needs in this word and the Hereafter, as well as spiritual perfections. One must ask them for these such that by Allah's leave they favour us with them—if it is in our interest. That is because, by paying attention to the Islamic narrations, they are intermediaries of Divine Grace; with His leave they take entities and men towards

---

i. al-Kulaynī, al-Kāfī, 2:226, narration 16

the perfection worthy of them. One of the means of preparing the grounds for this mediation in man is by beseeching and doing *tawassul* to them, accompanied by belief in their spiritual stations as well as other necessary conditions.

In the *ziyārāt* of the Imams (peace be upon them) and their admonitions, attention has also been drawn to this level of *tawassul*.

However, one should pay attention that the levels of *tawassul* are not limited to these five. Moreover, one should be mindful that these levels of *tawassul* are mutually exclusive such that by carrying out one of them man is not needless of the others.

F) Fasting

One of the important things that has a considerable effect on a person's physical and spiritual well-being and Imam al-Ṣādiq (peace be upon him) also recommended it to ʿUnwān al-Baṣrī, is to abstain from overeating and according to some narrations to be in state of hunger.

The best type of abstinence and staying hungry is to fast. In addition to fasting in the blessed month of Ramaḍān which is obligatory, keeping *mustaḥabb* fasts is also highly recommended and is the cause of many merits.

The Messenger of Allah (peace and blessings be upon him and his family) says:

مَنْ صَامَ يَوْماً تَطَوُّعاً فَلَوْ أُعْطِيَ مِلْءَ الْأَرْضِ ذَهَباً مَا وُفِّيَ أَجْرَهُ دُونَ يَوْمِ الْحِسَابِ

> One who fasts for a day voluntarily [keeps a *mustaḥabb* fast], even if he is given the amount of gold that would fill the entire world, he has not been paid his full reward other than on the Day of Reckoning.[i]

مَنْ صَامَ يَوْماً تَطَوُّعاً ابْتِغَاءَ ثَوَابِ اللَّهِ وَجَبَتْ لَهُ الْمَغْفِرَةُ

> One who fasts for a day voluntarily [keeps a *mustaḥabb* fast] seeking Allah's reward, for him forgiveness become

i. al-Sadūq, Maʿānī al-Akhbār, 409, narration 91

incumbent.[i]

Likewise, Lady Zahrā' (peace be upon her) says:

فَفَرَضَ اللّٰهُ الصِّيَامَ تَثْبِيتاً لِلْإِخْلاص

Allah ordained fasting to reinforce *ikhlāṣ*.[ii]

It is sufficient for the merit of fasting that Imam al-Ṣādiq (peace be upon him) says:

إِنَّ اللَّهَ تَبَارَكَ وَ تَعَالَى يَقُولُ الصَّوْمُ لِي وَ أَنَا أَجْزِي عَلَيْه

Indeed, Allah (the Provider of abundance and the Sublime) says, "Fasting is for me and I will give its reward [or I am its reward]."[iii]

نَوْمُ الصَّائِمِ عِبَادَةٌ وَ صَمْتُهُ تَسْبِيحٌ وَ عَمَلُهُ
مُتَقَبَّلٌ وَ دُعَاؤُهُ مُسْتَجَابٌ

The sleep of a person who is fasting is worship, his silence is glorification of Allah, his actions are accepted, and his prayers are answered.[iv]

That is because, fasting is an excellent means of preparing the conditions for controlling all the members and organs. The complete fast is that in which—according to the Imam—one's ears, eyes, hairs, skin and other parts of man are all in the state of fasting,[v] and do not perform any forbidden action. This is an excellent means of preparing the ground to control man's other inclinations such that he reaches the level of the fasting of thoughts, the soul and the heart. In this manner, man attains higher ranks in his spiritual movement.

Imam 'Alī (peace be upon him) says:

---

i. al-Ṣadūq, al-Amālī, 443, narration 2

ii. Majlisī, Bihār al-Anwār, 96:367, narration 4

iii. al-Kulaynī, al-Kāfi, 4:63, narration 6

iv. al-Ṣadūq, Man La Yaḥḍuruhū al-Faqih, 2:76, narration 1783

v. al-Kulaynī, al-Kāfi, 4:87, narration 1

صِيَامُ الْقَلْبِ عَنِ الْفِكْرِ فِي الْآثَامِ أَفْضَلُ
مِنْ صِيَامِ الْبَطْنِ عَنِ الطَّعَامِ

The fasting of the heart from thoughts about sins is better than the fasting of the stomach from food. (i)

صَوْمُ النَّفْسِ عَنْ لَذَّاتِ الدُّنْيَا أَنْفَعُ الصِّيَام

The fasting of the self from the worldly pleasures is the most beneficial type of fasting. (ii)

In view of these admonitions and other statements of the Imams (peace be upon them) in this regard, it is suitable that a person in his practical routine suffices himself with the least level of this action and acts according to this statement of the Messenger of Allah (peace and blessings be upon him and his family):

مَنْ صَامَ ثَلَاثَةَ أَيَّامٍ مِنْ كُلِّ شَهْرٍ كَانَ كَمَنْ صَامَ الدَّهْر

One who fasts for three days in every month is like one who has fasted for entire lifetime. (iii)

According to other narrations, these three days are, the first and the last Thursday of the lunar month, as well as the Wednesday after the middle of the month. In addition to this, fasting in the months of Rajab, Shaʿbān, Dhū al-Ḥijjah, and the first nine days of the month of Muḥarram have been specifically recommended. However, one should avoid going to extremes in this matter and should consider his bodily condition, family situation and other matters that have been instructed by the Divine *sharīʿah*, so that he can obtain the desired result.

Consequently, to whatever extent man practically adheres to these acts of *tawassul* and other advice mentioned in this section as well as the previous sections of this book, Allah will cause its spiritual effects to occur in his soul. In this manner, the wayfarer succeeds in attaining higher levels of Allah the Exalted's servitude and forms a deeper

---

i. al-Āmudī, Ghurar al-Hikam, narration 5873

ii. Ibid., narration 5874

iii. al-Maghribī, Daʿā'im al-Islām, 1:283

relationship with the Imams (peace be upon them). By realizing these higher levels of servitude (which is that same 'true servitude' mentioned in the book), access to the true knowledge of the Imams (peace be upon them) and contact with the reality of *wilāyah* and their station of light becomes feasible. Although, in this case the wayfarer needs a specific teacher who can guide him in the stages of *ikhlāṣ* and thereafter in the stages of *khulūṣ* until he takes him to the intended destination. This destination is witnessing the realms of *tawḥīd* and reaching the station of Allah's *maʿrifah* (gnosis).

When a person traverses the initial levels of Allah's servitude (which were discussed in this book) and the ground is prepared for traversing higher levels, if he takes refuge in Allah and in His *awliyā'* (peace be upon them) then Allah the Exalted will provide this personal teacher to him.

In the end, I ask Allah the Exalted and the Imams (peace be upon them) to bestow upon me the station of true servitude and joining with the Station of the Light of His *awliyā'* (peace be upon them). I gift the reward of this meagre work (if it carries any reward) to the great soul of my father who showed me the path and taught me the ways of servitude. Also, to the teachers, who after my father, trained me in this path, namely the great *mufassir* (exegete) of the Noble Qur'ān Āyatullāh al-ʿUẓmā ʿAllāmah Ṭabāṭabā'ī and Ḥaḍrat Āyatulḥaqq, the perfect *ʿĀrif*, Ḥājj Shaykh ʿAlī Saʿādatparwar (may Allah be pleased with them). I also dedicate its reward to the great soul of the man who succeeded in actualizing a portion of Allah's servitude and the *wilāyah* of the Imams (peace be upon them) by establishing an Islamic government, Āyatullāh al-ʿUẓmā Imam Khumaynī (may Allah be pleased with him).

This piece of writing was completed just before the anniversary of Imam Mūsā ibn Jaʿfar's (peace be upon him) martyrdom (in the year 1429 AH) in the proximity of his honourable daughter, the Generous Lady of the Ahl al-Bayt (peace be upon them), Ḥaḍrat Maʿṣūmah (peace be upon her).[i]

i. The English translation of this noble work was completed on Thursday, the 26th of Dhul-Qaʿdah, 1439. I say to the master of this age (may Allah the Exalted hasten his noble appearance),

Bibliography

Akbarī, Mahmūd. n.d. Kitāb-i Akhlāq-i 1. Markaz-i Tadwīn wa Nashr-i Mutūn-i Darsī-yi Hawzah.

al-ʿĀmilī, Hurr. n.d. al-Jawāhir al-Saniyyah fī al-Ahādīth al-Qudsiyyah. Mashhad: Intishārāt-i Tūs.

—. 1409. *Waṣāʾil al-Shīʿah.* Qom: Muʿassasah Āl al-Bayt.

al-Barqī, Aḥmad. 1371. *al-Maḥāsin.* Qom: Dār al-Kitāb al-Islāmiyyah.

al-Daylamī, Ibn Abī al-Ḥasan. 1408. *Aʿlām al-Dīn fī Ṣifāt al-Muʾminīn.* Muʿassasah Āl al-Bayt.

al-Ḥadīd, Ibn Abī. 1404. *Sharḥ-i Nahj al-Balāgah (Edited by Muḥammad Abū al-Faḍl Ibrāhīm).* Qom: Kitābkhānih-yi Āyatullāh Marʿashī Najafī.

al-Ḥarrānī, Ibn Shuʿbah. 1380. *Tuḥaf al-ʿUqūl.* Najaf: Manshūrāt al-Maktabah wa al-Matbaʿah al-Ḥaydariyyah.

al-Ḥillī, Ibn Fahd. 1407. *ʿUddah al-Dāʿī wa Najāḥ al-Sāʿī.* Intishārāt-i Dār al-Kitāb al-Islāmī.

al-Hindī, Muttaqī. n.d. *Kanz al-ʿUmmāl fī Sunan al-Aqwāl wa al-Afʿāl.* Beirut: Muʾassasah al-Risālah.

al-Ḥuwayzī, al-ʿArūsī. 1415. *Tafsīr Nūr al-Thaqalayn.* Qom: Intishārāt-i Ismāʿīliyān.

al-Iṣfahānī, Rāghib. 1404. *al-Mufradāt fī Gharīb al-Qurʾān.* Daftar-i Nashr-i Kitāb.

al-Khūʾī, Sayyid. n.d. *Muʿjam Rijāl al-Ḥadīth.*

al-Kūfī, Ibn al-Ashʿath. n.d. *al-Jaʿfariyyāt (al-Ashʿathiyyāt).*

al-Kulaynī, Thiqah al-Islām. 1365. *al-Kāfī.* Tehran: Dār al-Kitāb al-Islāmīyyah.

al-Maghribī, Qāḍī Nuʿmān. 1385. *Daʿāʾim al-Islām.* Egypt: Dār al-Maʿārif.

al-Mufīd, Shaykh. 1413. *al-Amālī.* Qom: The Shaykh Mufīd Congress.

Humbly do I kneel master beseeching thee,
Sacrificed for your cheek's birthmark may I be,
This weak attempt please accept out of your mercy,
Permit its light to shine forth upon those thirsty.

—. 1414. *al-Ikhtiṣās (Persian Translation by ʿAlī Akbar Ghaffārī).* Beirut: Dar al-Mufīd.
—. n.d. *Taṣḥīḥ-i Iʿtiqādāt al-Imāmiyyah (Researched by Ḥusaynī Dargāhī).* Beirut: Dār al-Mufīd.
al-Qummī, ʿAlī bin Ibrāhīm. 1411. *Tafsīr al-Qummī.* Beirut: Dār al-Surūr.
al-Qummī, Al-Khazzār. n.d. *Kifāyah al-Athar (Researched by ʿAbd al-Laṭīf al-Ḥusaynī al-Kūhkamaraʾī al-Khūʾī).* Intishārāt-i Bīdār.
al-Rāzī, Fakhr al-Dīn. 1420. *Tafsīr Mafātīḥ al-Ghayb (al-Tafsīr al-Kabīr).* Dār Iḥyāʾ al-Turāth al-ʿArabī.
al-Ṣadūq, Shaykh. n.d. *al-Amālī.* Intishārāt-i Kitābkhānih-yi Islāmiyyih.
—. 1403. *al-Khiṣāl.* Qom: Jāmiʿi-yi Mudarrisīn.
—. 1398. *al-Tawḥīd.* Qom: Intishārāt-i Jāmiʿi-yi Mudarrisīn.
—. 1361. *Maʿānī al-Akhbār.* Qom: Intishārāt-i Jāmiʿi-yi Mudarrisīn.
—. 1413. *Man Lā Yaḥḍurhū al-Faqīh.* Qom: Intishārāt-i Jāmiʿih-yi Mudarrisīn.
—. 1364. *Thawāb al-Aʿmāl.* Intishārāt-i Sharīf-i Raḍī.
—. 1378. *ʿUyūn Akhbār al-Riḍā (peace be upon him).* Intishārāt-i Jahān.
al-Shaʿīrī, Tāj al-Dīn. 1363. *Jāmiʿ al-Akhbār.* Intishārāt Raḍī .
al-Ṭabrasī, Amīn al-Islām. 1415. *Majmaʿ al-Bayān fī Tafsīr al-Qurʾān.* Beirut: Muʾassasah al-Aʿlamī lil-Maṭbūʿāt.
al-Ṭabrasī, Ḥasan. 1412. *Makārim al-Akhlāq.* Qom: Intishārāt-i Sharīf al-Raḍī.
al-Thānī, Shahīd. 1409. *Muniyah al-Murīd fī Ādāb al-Mufīd wa al-Mustafīd.* Qom: Intishārāt-i Daftar-i Tablīghāt.
al-Tirmidhī, Muḥammad. 1403. *Sunan al-Tirmidhī (Edited and Corrected by ʿAbd al-Raḥmān Muḥammad ʿUthmān).* Beirut: Dār al-Fikr.
al-Ṭurayḥī, Fakhr al-Dīn. 1985. *Majmaʿ al-Baḥrayn.* Beirut: Maktabah al-Hilāl.
al-Ṭūsī, Shaykh. 1414. *al-Amālī.* Qom: Dār al-Thaqāfah.
—. 1411. *al-Ghaybah li al-Ḥujjah.* Qom: Muʾassasah-yi Maʿārif-i Islāmī.
—. 1409. *al-Tibyān fī Tafsīr al-Qurʾān (Researched by Aḥmad Ḥabīb Qaṣīr al-ʿĀmilī).* Maktab al-Iʿlām al-Islāmī.
al-Zamakhsharī, Jārullāh. 1416. *al-Kashshāf ʿan Ḥaqāʾiq-i Ghawāmiḍ al-Tanzīl wa ʿUyūn al-Aqāwīl fī Wujūh al-Taʾwīl.* Qom: Daftar-i Tablīghāt-i Islāmī.
Āmulī, Ḥasanzādih-yi. n.d. *Duwwumīn Yādnāmih-yi ʿAllāmah Ṭabāṭabāʾī.*
ʿAṭṭār, Farīd al-Dīn. n.d. *Tadhkirah al-Awliyāʾ (Based on Nicholson's version).*

Nashr-i Bihzād.
ʿAyyāshi, Muḥammad. n.d. *Tafsīr al-ʿAyyāshi*. Chāpkhānih-yi ʿIlmiyyih-yi Tihrān.
1381. *Faryādgar-i Tawḥīd*. Qom: Intishārāt-i Anṣāriyān.
Hāshamiyān, Hādī. n.d. *Daryā-yi ʿIrfān (The Biography and Conditions of Āyatullāh Sayyid ʿAlī Qāḍī)*.
Ibn Abī Firās, Warrām. n.d. *Tanbīh al-Khawāṭir wa Nuzhah al-Nawāẓir (Commonly known as Majmūʿah Warrām)*. Qom: Maktabah al-Faqīh.
Ibn Ṭāwūs, Sayyid. 1367. *al-Iqbāl bi al-Aʿmāl al-Ḥasanah (Iqbāl al-Aʿmāl)*. Tehran: Dār al-Kitāb al-Islāmiyyah.
Imam ʿAlī (peace be upon him, compiled by ʿAbd al-Wāḥid al-Tamīmī al-Āmidī). n.d. *Fihrist-i Mawḍūʿī-yi Ghurar al-Ḥikam wa Durar al-Kalim*. University of Tehran.
—. 1366. *Ghurar al-Ḥikam wa Durar al-Kalim*. Daftar-i Tablīghāt-i Islāmī.
Imam ʿAlī (peace be upon him, compiled by Sayyid Al-Raḍī). n.d. *Nahj al-Balāgah*. Qom: Intishārāt-i Dār al-Ḥijrah.
Irbalī, ʿAlī. 1381. *Kashf al-Ghummah ʿan Maʿrifah Aḥwāl Al-Aʾimmah Wa Ahl Bayt al-ʿIṣmah*. Tabriz: Maktabah Banī Hashimī.
Karājakī, Abū al-Fatḥ. 1410. *Kanz al-Fawāʾid*. Dār al-Dhakhāʾir.
Kāshānī, Mullā Fayḍ. n.d. *al-Maḥajjah al-Bayḍāʾ fī Tahdhīb al-Iḥyāʾ*. Intishārāt-i Jāmiʿi-yi Mudarrisīn.
—. 1404. *al-Wāfī*. Qom: Manshūrāt-i Maktabah-yi Āyatullāh Al-ʿUẓmā Marʿashī Najafī.
Khumaynī, Imam. n.d. *Dīwān-i Imam Khumaynī, The Institute for Compilation and Publication of Imam Khomeini's Works*.
—. n.d. *Jihād-i Akbar*. Qom: Jāmiʿih-yi Mudarrisīn.
—. n.d. *Miṣbāḥ al-Hidāyah*.
—. n.d. *Nuqtah-yi ʿAṭf: ʿIrfāni Poems of Imām Khumaynī*. The Institute for Compilation and Publication of Imam Khomeini's Works.
—. n.d. *Ṣaḥīfah-yi Nūr*. The Institute for Compilation and Publication of Imam Khomeini's Works.
—. n.d. *Sharḥ-i Chihil Ḥadīth*. The Institute for Compilation and Publication of Imam Khomeini's Works.
—. n.d. *Sharḥ-i Junūd-i ʿAql wa Jahl*. The Institute for Compilation and Publication of Imam Khomeini's Works.

—. n.d. *Tibyān.*
Majlisī, ʿAllāmah. 1404. *Biḥār al-Anwār.* Beirut: Muʾassasah Al-Wafāʾ.
—. n.d. *Ḥilyah al-Muttaqīn.*
Mandharī, Ḥāfiz-i. n.d. *al-Targhīb wa al-Tarhīb.*
n.d. *Mukāshafāt-i Awliyā-yi Ilāhī.*
Nūrī, Mīrzā. 1408. *Mustadrak al-Wasāʾil wa Mustanbaṭ al-Masāʾil.* Qom: Muʾassasah Āl al-Bayt.
Nūrmuḥammadī, Muḥammad Jawād. n.d. *Du ʿĀrif-i Sālik (Memoirs of ʿĀrif bi-Allāh Āyatullāh Ḥājj Shaykh ʿAbbas Tihrānī and ʿĀrif-i Farzānih Mīrzā ʿAbdullāh Shālchī Tabrīzī).*
Qāsimlū, Yaʿqūb. 1379. *Ṭabīb-i ʿĀshiqān (Memories and Poetry of ʿAllāmah Ṭabāṭabāʾī may Allah be pleased with him).* Nasīm-i Ḥayāt.
Qummī, Shaykh ʿAbbās. n.d. *Mafātīḥ al-Jinān (Persian Translation by Qomshi-yī).* Daftar-i Nashr-i Farhang-i Islāmī.
—. 1371. *Muntahā al-Āmāl.* Intishārāt-i Ḥijrat.
—. 1416. *Safīnah al-Biḥār.* Āstān-i Quds-i Raḍawī.
Rayshahrī, Muḥammad. 1375. *Mizān al-Ḥikmah.* Dār al-Ḥadīth.
—. 1377. *Tandīs-i Ikhlāṣ.* Intishārāt-i Dār al-Ḥadīth.
Rukhshād, Muḥammad Ḥusayn. 1386. *Dar Maḥḍar-i ʿAllāmah Ṭabāṭabāʾī.* Qom: Intishārāt-i Samāʾ.
—. 1382. *Dar Maḥḍar-i Āyatullāh al-ʿUẓmā Bahjat.* Qom: Intishārāt-i Samāʾ.
Saʿādatparwar, ʿAlī. 1380. *Jamāl-i Āftāb wa Āftāb-i Har Naẓar (Sharḥ-i Ḥāfiẓ).* Shirkat-i Intishārat-i Iḥyā-yi Kitāb.
n.d. *Sabū-yi ʿIshq.*
Ṣadrā, Mullā. n.d. *al-Maẓāhir al-Ilāhiyyah.*
Sayfullāhī, Muḥammad Ḥasan. 1382. *Aqā Shaykh Murtaḍā-yi Zāhid.* Masjid-i Muqaddas-i Jamkarān.
Shīrāzī, Ḥāfiẓ-i. n.d. *Dīwān-i Ḥāfiẓ (Taṣḥīḥ-i Qudsī).* Intishārāt-i Ishrāqī.
Ṭabāṭabāʾī, ʿAllāmah. 1393. *al-Mīzān fī Tafsīr al-Qurʾān.* Beirut: Muʾassasah al-Aʿlamī li al-Maṭbūʿāt.
—. n.d. *Barrasīhā-yi Islāmī.*
—. n.d. *Risālah-yi Lubb al-Albāb dar Sayr wa Sulūk-i Ulū al-Albāb.* Intishārāt-i Ḥikmat.
—. 1362. *Shīʿah dar Islām.* Qom: Daftar-iIntishārāt-i Islāmī.
Tihrānī, ʿAllāmah. n.d. *Rūḥ-i Mujarrad.* Intishārāt-i Ḥikmat.

—. n.d. *Tawḥīd-i ʿAynī wa ʿAmalī.* 1369.
Yād-i Yār, Islamic Republic of Iran Newspaper, 13th Khordād 1369.
Zayn al-ʿĀbidīn (peace be upon him), Imam. 1376. *al-Ṣaḥīfah al-Sajjādiyyah.* Daftar-i Nashr-i Al-Hādī.

Endnotes

1 Abū ʿAbd Allah Muḥammad ibn Makkī al-ʿĀmilī (734-786 AH), famously known as al-Shahīd al-Awwal, was one of the great Shīʿah scholars and jurists of the eighth century. He was born in Lebanon and travelled to many cities in search of knowledge such as Hilla, Baghdad, Damascus, Makkah, Madinah, Jerusalem, Hebron, and Egypt. Completely aware of both Shīʿah and Sunnī fiqh, he even had permission to narrate *aḥādīth* from 40 Sunnī scholars.

2 Hishām Ibn Ḥakam (d. 179 AH) was a young scholar who was both astute and good-looking. At the onset he expressed incorrect opinions with regards to *tawḥīd* and was rejected by the Imams (peace be upon them). One day he came to Imam al-Ṣādiq (peace be upon him) and asked him about the names of Allah. The noble Imam (peace be upon him) expounded some of the treasures of the knowledge of *tawḥīd*, and then said to him, "Have you know understood these matters such that you can respond to our enemies, the disbelievers and the polytheists?" He replied, "Yes." From then onwards he became one of the exclusive students of Imam al-Ṣādiq (peace be upon him) and used to debate with renown scholars from amongst the Christians and the disbelievers, such that he would guide them to Islam. Imam al-Ṣādiq (peace be upon him) praised him immensely. For more information see *al-Tawḥīd* of Shaykh al-Ṣadūq, pages 220, 274, and 295. (From the author)

3 Ibn Abī al-ʿAwjāʾ (d. 155 AH) was initially from the students of al-Ḥasan al-Baṣrī but later apostatized. During the days of the Ḥajj he would go to Makkah and ridicule those performing the Ḥajj. One day he encountered Imam al-Ṣādiq (peace be upon him) and after engaging in a debate him, he was so mesmerized by the spirituality of the Imam that he described the noble Imam (peace be upon him) in the

following manner: "This is not a normal human! Rather, he is a spiritual being in this world that at times appears in the form of a body and at other times is hidden as a tender spirit . . ." However, despite this, he never ceased from his erroneous path and in the end during one of his debates with the Imam (peace be upon him), he felt a severe burning in his heart. After returning from the Imam's presence back to a group of his followers, he died in the state of disbelief and misguidance. For more information see *al-Tawḥīd* of Shaykh al-Ṣadūq, pages 126, 253, 293 and onwards. (From the author)

4 Shaykh Murtaḍā Zāhid (1285-1371 AH) was born in Tehran. After completing his studies under scholars such as his father Mullā Buzurg Majd Al-Dhākirīn Tehrānī and Shaykh Faḍlallāh Nūrī, he busied himself in propagating the religion and spreading the *sharīʿah*. He conducted sessions of admonition, *akhlāq*, and was the *imām-i jamāʿah* (leader of the congregational prayers) at the *jāmiʿ masjid* in the bazaar of Tehran. He was well known for his piety and *zuhd* (abstinence)—he dedicated his life towards guiding and teaching others.

5 Bahāʾ al-Dīn Muḥammad al-ʿĀmilī, famously known as Shaykh Bahāʾī (953-1031 AH) was one of the outstanding polymaths of history. He was an accomplished poet, philosopher, mathematician, astronomer, engineer, jurist, exegete of the Noble Qurʾān and doctor. Born in Baalbek, Lebanon, he was the son of a scholar named Shaykh Ḥusayn, himself a student of the great Shīʿah jurist, Al-Shahīd Al-Thāni. Along with his father, Shaykh Bahāʾī moved to Iran at a young age. Eminent scholars such as Mullā Ṣadrā, Fayḍ al-Kāshānī and ʿAllamah Muḥammad Taqī Majlisī were some of his students. He is buried near the pure grave of Imam al-Riḍā (peace be upon him) in Mashhad.

6 Shaykh Rajab ʿAlī Nikūgūyān (1262-1381 AH) worked for many years as a tailor and is thus famously known as *Khayyāṭ* (tailor). In in an incident during his youth, he controlled his selfish desires and managed to escape from a trap of Satan. After this incident, he received the special attention and spiritual blessings of Allah. Refer to the book *Kīmiyā-yi Muḥabbat*, which has been translated into English as 'The Elixir of Love'. (From the author)

7 Ayatullāh Maḥmūd Taḥrīrī (1338-1409 AH) was the late

father of the author (may his blessing persist). From a young age he associated with spiritual personalities such as Shaykh Rajab ʿAlī Khayyāt and Āyatullāh Shāh Ābādī, while studying in the Islamic seminaries of Tehran. He later studied in the Islamic seminaries of Qom under great scholars such as Ayatullāh Marʿashī Najafī, Ayatullāh Gulpaygāni, Imam Khumaynī and ʿAllāmah Tabātabāʾī. He passed away in the mosque just before leading prayers in the year 1990 and is buried in the blessed shrine of Shāh ʿAbd al-ʿAẓīm in the south of Tehran.

8 Khwājah Shams al-Dīn Muḥammad (727-792 AH), known as Ḥāfiz-i Shirāzī is one of the well-known scholars and *ʿurafāʾ* of the eighth century AH. His poetry is considered to be the pinnacle of *ʿirfān*, such that very few have the capacity to understand the subtle, *ʿirfānī* points therein.

9 Muḥammad bin Ibrāhīm Shīrāzī (d. 1050 AH), famously known as Mullā Ṣadrā, was born in Shiraz. He was the son of a wealthy businessman and Safavid vizier, who spared no cost in educating his only son. From a young age, Mullā Ṣadrā showed a unique aptitude and brilliance, and after completing his studies in Shiraz he moved to Isfahan. There he studied both the traditional and intellectual sciences, under great scholars such as Shaykh Bahāʾī, Mīr Dāmād, and Mīr Findiriskī. Mullā Ṣadrā transformed the science of Islamic Philosophy, founding a philosophical system named *al-Ḥikmat al-Mutaʿāliyah* (Transcendental Philosophy). This system merged the different currents in Islamic Philosophy, conclusively answering many of the points of conflicts between them.

10 Shaykh Murtaḍā Anṣārī (1214-1281 AH) was born in the city of Dezful, Iran. At a young age he moved to Iraq and studied under great scholars such as Sharīf al-ʿUlamā Māzandarānī and Shaykh Mūsā Kāshif al-Ghiṭā. On a trip to Mashhad in the year 1240 AH, he stopped in the city of Kashan where he remained for four years, benefitting from the presence of the *ʿārif*, Mullā Aḥmad Narāqī. He later became the *marjaʿ* of the entire Shīʿah community and trained many great scholars such as Mulla Ḥusaynqulī Hamadānī and Ākhūnd Khurāsānī. In addition, he authored many important textbooks and

brought about fundamental changes to the science of Uṣūl al-Fiqh (the principles of jurisprudence).

11 Āyatullāh Shaykh ʿAbbās Tehrānī (1309 -1385 AH) was an eminent teacher of *akhlāq*. Born in Tehran, he first began his studies there, then moved to Najaf where he studied under great scholars such as Mirzā Nāʾīnī and Āqā Ḍiyāʾ al-Dīn ʿIrāqī. He later returned to Iran and studied under Ayatullah Ḥāʾirī Yazdī—also benefitting from the presence of the great *ʿārif* Mirzā Jawād Malikī Tabrīzī. He is buried in the blessed shrine of Lady Maʿṣūmah (peace be upon her) in the holy city of Qom.

12 Āyatullāh Mullā Ḥusaynqulī Hamadānī (1239-1311 AH) was born in the Hamadan Province of Iran. After initially studying in Tehran and then Sabzwar, he moved to Najaf where he studied under great scholars such as Ṣāhib-i Jawāhir, Shaykh Anṣārī and Mirzā Shirāzī. Moreover, for many years he attended the classes of *akhlāq* and *ʿirfān* of Sayyid ʿAlī Shūshtarī and himself attained a lofty spiritual station. He left behind many great students, such as Mirzā Jawād Malikī Tabrizī, Mirzā Nāʾīnī and Ākhūnd-i Khurāsānī. He is buried in the blessed shrine of the Master of Martyrs in Karbala.

13 Ayatullah Shaykh ʿAbd al-Karīm Ḥāʿirī Yazdī (1267-1355 AH) was born in a village in the Yazd Province of Iran. At a young age he began his studies in Yazd, and later moved to Iraq. There, he studied in Karbala and Samarra, under great scholars such as Mirzā Shīrāzī. In the year 1340 AH the scholars of Qom requested him to move there and bring life to the thousand-year old *ḥawzah* (Islamic seminary) in that city. With him, other scholars and students also settled in Qom and new life was breathed into the *ḥawzah*. Some of his students include Imam Khumaynī, Ayatullah Gulpaygānī, Ayatullah Marʿāshī Najafī.

14 Al-Ḥasan al-Baṣrī (21-110 AH) was one of the famous personalities from amongst the *tābiʿīn* (those who did not meet the Prophet, peace and blessings be upon him and his family, but met his companions). Known as a theologian, an exegete of the Noble Qurʾān, a narrator of *aḥādīth*, and a jurist, al-Ḥasan is highly revered amongst the Ahl al-Sunnah. However, various narrations exist from the Immaculate Ahl al-Bayt (peace be upon them) condemning al-Ḥasan.

CPSIA information can be obtained
at www.ICGtesting.com
Printed in the USA
LVHW111818070720
660010LV00012B/308/J

9 781953 192004